The Moyne Report

REPORT OF
WEST INDIA ROYAL COMMISSION

THE MOYNE
REPORT

WITH AN INTRODUCTION
BY DENIS BENN

Published in Jamaica, 2011 by
Ian Randle Publishers
11 Cunningham Avenue
Box 686
Kingston 6
www.ianrandlepublishers.com

© Introduction, Denis Benn 2011

A catalogue record for this book is available from the National Library of Jamaica

ISBN 978-976-637-406-8 (pbk)

All rights reserved. No part of this publication may be reproduced, stored in a retrieval system, or transmitted in any form, or by any means electronic, photocopying, recording or otherwise without prior permission of the author or publisher.

Cover and book design by Ian Randle Publishers
Printed in United States of America

INTRODUCTION

The Moyne Commission Report, which is contained in this volume, is a seminal document in the economic, social and political development of the Caribbean. Appointed in the wake of a series of disturbances in the region between 1936 and 1938, the Commission was mandated to investigate and make recommendations on the social and economic conditions in the various territories and matters connected therewith.

The disturbances in the region during the 1930s, which took the form of sporadic strikes, rioting and looting of businesses were, in effect, the product of years of social neglect by the colonial administration in the period since emancipation. This was combined with the impact of economic recession which resulted in a decline in the price of the major agricultural exports of the region in the face of a rapid contraction in world demand for such exports. The situation was aggravated by the return to the region of large numbers of workers who had emigrated to other countries, notably Panama, Cuba and the USA, in search of employment. The disturbances also reflected the significant shortcomings of the Crown Colony system of governance which excluded the majority of the population from participation in the political process.

The Report, which is a comprehensive document detailing all facets of the social and economic situation, unequivocally confirmed the highly unsatisfactory conditions in which the bulk of the population of the region was forced to exist. It pointed to, for example, the significant shortcomings in health conditions which were characterised by chronic illness, as a result of an inadequate diet, and a high rate of infant mortality. It also highlighted the poor housing conditions and the urgent need for slum clearance. On the issue of education, the Commission pointed to the mismatch between the school curriculum and the needs of societies largely dependent on agricultural production, the small percentage of children with secondary education and inadequate teacher training.

In elaborating its position on education, in the face of the demand by some witnesses for the establishment of a university-level institution in the Caribbean, the Commission felt that this was a goal that should be pursued when sufficient funds were available. Still, it was somewhat sceptical that a sufficient demand existed at the time for this level of education. It felt that in structuring such an institution it would be necessary to allocate different faculties among the various territories instead of establishing a centralised university in a single territory. The

INTRODUCTION

University of the West Indies in 1948, in the wake of significant constitutional change in the region, proved to be a timely investment. It served, together with the trade union movement, as a major instrument for the preparation of a leadership cadre that was able to capitalise on the constitutional reforms recommended by the Moyne Commission and, on this basis, to manage the transition to political independence as well as the post-independence political process.

Not unexpectedly, given the presence on the Commission of Sir Walter Citrine, General Secretary of the British Trade Union Congress, unemployment, labour conditions and the role of trade unions featured prominently on its agenda. The Commission was genuinely concerned that increased employment opportunities should be provided, given the level of unemployment and under-employment. It expressed concern about the working conditions which existed in region, including, in particular, those endured by sugar workers. In an effort to reduce the number of work-related accidents, it proposed more frequent workplace inspections. Similarly, it called for an end to child labour and discrimination against women. Noting that wages were exclusively determined by the employer, it also asserted the right of workers to bargain for the terms of their remuneration. In addition, it called for the establishment of Labour Departments in the various territories, many of which instituted these departments in 1942. It also felt that trade unions should be encouraged in order to protect the interests of workers, but recommended that such unions should be subject to compulsory registration and periodic audits of their funds.

A central assumption of the Report is the notion that the prospect for the development of the region depended almost exclusively on agriculture, although it focused not only on plantation agriculture but also emphasised the importance of expanding peasant production. Indeed, it saw little prospect for the development of industry, except as small-scale industrial activities, ancillary to agriculture and forestry. This was of course a dominant assumption of British colonial policy in the Caribbean. The Commission therefore recommended an increase in local production of essential foodstuff. In respect of sugar, it proposed an increase in the quota assigned to the colonial empire and also an increase in the level of preferences granted in the UK market. However, as early as 1938, Arthur Lewis, in his famous pamphlet entitled 'Labour in the West Indies,' had challenged the prevailing thesis regarding an almost exclusive reliance on agriculture as the key to Caribbean prosperity and had advocated instead the industrialisation of the Caribbean based on the importation of foreign capital to be used in combination

INTRODUCTION

with local labour. The theoretical justification for this approach was more fully elaborated in his 1950 publication entitled *The Industrialisation of the British West Indies* which, contrary to the recommendations of the Moyne Report, was to serve as the blueprint for Caribbean development in the 1950s and 1960s.

The issue of federation also featured prominently in the analysis contained in the Report. Indeed, there is a fairly long history of attempts by the British government to rationalise the structure of colonial governance by attempting to promote common services and, more specifically, federation, among the Leeward and Windward Islands. There was also a growing sentiment among the local population during the early twentieth century for the establishment of a federal regime in the region. However, in addressing the issue, the 1922 Wood Report concluded that 'as long as public opinion stands as it is today, it is inappropriate, inopportune and impracticable to attempt to amalgamate existing governments into anything approaching a genuine federal system.' Subsequent to the publication of the Report, there was evidence of continuing local support for closer political integration, especially between Trinidad and Tobago and the Leeward Islands. More importantly, in its evidence before the Commission, the British Guiana and West Indies Labour Congress presented a specific proposal for the establishment of a West Indies Federation. However, the Commission, following the logic of the Wood Report, expressed scepticism regarding the desirability of introducing 'any large scheme of federation.'

Despite the reservation expressed by the Commission, some two decades later, the proposal by the British Guiana and West Indies Labour Congress was to find expression in the West Indies Federation (1958–62) which was vitiated by competing conceptions, notably between Jamaica and Trinidad and Tobago, regarding the distribution of power between the federal government and its constituent units. Against this background, the negative vote in the 1962 Jamaica referendum sounded the death-knell of the federal experiment. In this regard, the focus at the Moyne Commission was essentially on political integration. The subsequent movement towards economic integration, as is currently embodied in the Caribbean Community (CARICOM), was in effect a pragmatic response to the collapse of the Federation, based on the perceived advantage of such integration.

A major recommendation of the Moyne Commission was its proposal for the establishment of a West Indian Welfare Fund which it proposed should be financed for a period of 20 years, based on an annual grant of £1,000,000 from the British government. The Fund was to be headed by a Comptroller whose salary, together with that of the administrative support staff,

INTRODUCTION

was to be met from an additional allocation from the British Exchequer. The recommendation led to the adoption of the Colonial Welfare Development Act of 1940 which provided the legal basis for the establishment of the Fund. The Fund, which was established in 1942, operated for 18 years until 1959. During this period, it financed a large number of infrastructural and social development projects in health, education, housing and water supply and therefore played a significant role in effecting improvements in the social conditions in the colonies in the post-Second World War period.

As stated earlier, the terms of reference of the Moyne Commission called upon it to enquire into the social and economic conditions of the colonies and matters connected therewith. Based on its interpretation of its mandate, which was specifically endorsed by the Secretary of State for the Colonies, the Commission concluded that it was entitled to consider constitutional reform if it was satisfied that the issue was relevant to the improvement in the social and economic conditions of region. Based on the sentiments expressed by a large body of public opinion in the region that a programme of social reconstruction depended in large measure on improved arrangements for the more effective participation of the local population in the political process, the Commission concluded that it was satisfied that, based on the evidence presented to it, the demand for constitutional reform was,

> ...sufficiently widespread to make it doubtful whether any schemes of social reform, however wisely conceived or efficiently conducted, would be completely successful unless they are accompanied by the largest measure of constitutional development which is thought to be judicious in the circumstances.

Notwithstanding the importance of other elements of its mandate, this was in fact the fundamental issue bearing upon political advancement in the region.

In addressing the issue, the Commission focused on the possibilities for ensuring the increased participation of the population in the governance process. In this regard, it noted that two extreme propositions were presented by various witnesses, namely, a further expansion of the power of the Governor, on the one hand, and the grant of complete self-government, on the other. However the Commission rejected both of these options. Instead, it proposed the appointment to the Executive Council of elected members of the Legislative Council. It also proposed the establishment of a Committee System in the larger colonies in order to provide the unofficial members of the legislature

INTRODUCTION

with an insight into the functioning of the administration. Equally important, it underlined the importance of making the legislature more fully representative of all important sectors of the community by giving the people an increased share in their government, without compromising the essential financial control by the executive. Also, the Commission was unanimous in its view that universal adult suffrage should be the ultimate goal of electoral reform, even though it was split between those when felt it should be introduced immediately and those who felt it should be introduced later. The Commission therefore recommended that a fully representative committee should be appointed in each colony to determine the need for a reduction in voting qualifications with a view to enlarging the electorate 'to as great an extent as local conditions make possible.' This recommendation paved the way for the introduction of universal adult suffrage in Jamaica in 1944 followed by Barbados and Trinidad in 1946 and by St Lucia in 1949. It may be said, therefore, that by recommending the lowering of the qualifications for voting the Moyne Commission laid the basis for the emergence of mass-based parties which were to serve as the instrument for propelling the various territories towards political independence.

Viewed in the context of previous attempts at constitutional reform in the Caribbean, the Moyne Commission sought to build on the various initiatives introduced by the Colonial Office throughout the nineteenth century and early twentieth century dealing with the nature of the relationship between the executive and the legislature under the Crown Colony system and also the respective roles of the elected and the official members of both the executive and the legislature. However, in identifying the need to reduce the qualifications for voting with a view to the introduction of adult suffrage, it fundamentally changed the trajectory of constitutional development in the Caribbean, since previous policy had left virtually touched the issue of voter qualifications which in fact limited participation to the privileged strata of colonial society.

Compared to previous Royal Commissions appointed by the British government to investigate issues relevant to the economic, social and political development of the Caribbean, the Moyne Commission adopted a comparatively progressive stance on the issues it examined. This was due, in part, to the recognition that the scale of the problems facing the various territories required a proactive response on the part of the British government. In contrast, therefore, to the laissez-faire posture of the nineteenth and early twentieth century, the Commission embraced a more interventionist approach in dealing with economic, social and political issues, as was evident in the recommendations

INTRODUCTION

contained in its Report.

In conclusion, it may be said that the recommendations contained in the Moyne Commission Report laid the foundation, notably through the work of the West Indian Welfare Fund, for the development of a modern social infrastructure in the Caribbean during the post-Second World War period and also paved the way for the democratisation of the political process in the region. Its contribution is therefore equalled only by the work of the more recent West Indian Commission which, in an equally comprehensive report, advanced a number of prescriptions for dealing with the challenges facing the Caribbean region. As such, the Moyne Commission Report represents a historic document which deserves the attention of scholars, policymakers and members of the general public who are interested in learning about the historical antecedents that have shaped the modern Caribbean.

DENIS BENN
Michael Manley Professor of Public Policy
University of the West Indies, Mona
2011

WEST INDIA ROYAL COMMISSION REPORT

*Presented by the Secretary of State for the Colonies to Parliament
by Command of His Majesty
July 1945*

LONDON
HIS MAJESTY'S STATIONERY OFFICE
Price 7s. 6d. net

Crnd. 6607

Note.—Chapters IV, XVI and XVII are based on the relevant parts of Professor Engledow's Report on Agriculture in the West Indies which is published separately as Cmd. 6608.

TABLE OF CONTENTS   *Page*

The Royal Warrant xi

REPORT.

Preface xiii
Illustrations

PART I.—THE GENERAL BACKGROUND.

Chapter I.   Historical Survey 2
   1. General 2
   2. Economic Aspects 3
   3. Social Aspects 6

Chapter II.   The Economic Position and Outlook
   1. The Growth of Population 9
   2. Non-Agricultural Activities 13
   3. The Agricultural Export Outlook 17
   4. The Sugar Position 24
   5. The World Economic Background 27

Chapter III.   Social Structure and Conditions ... 29

Chapter IV.   The Agricultural System
   1. General Remarks 37
   2. Inherent Agricultural Circumstances 38
   3. Survey of West Indian Agriculture 40
   4. Land Ownership and Use 41
   5. Peasant Agriculture 43
   6. Estate Agriculture 45
   7. Soil Erosion 48
   8. Maintenance of Soil Fertility 49
   9. Export Crops 50
   10. Economic Organisation 51
   11. Agricultural Credit and Finance 53
   12. Agricultural Departments 54

Chapter V.   The Administrative Background ... 55
   1. Brief Description of Constitutions 55
   2. Relation of Executive and Legislature 56
   3. Public Opinion and the Civil Service 58
   4. Colour Prejudice and Colour Discrimination ... 59
   5. Other Criticisms of Administration 61
   6. Work of the Civil Services 66

Chapter VI.   The Public Finances
   1. Public Debt 67
   2. Revenue and Expenditure of Government ... 70
   3. Imperial Assistance and Treasury Control ... 73

	Page
4. Taxation	75
(a) Income Tax	76
(b) Estate and Legacy Duties	81
(c) Relative Burdens of Direct and Indirect Taxation	83
(d) Miscellaneous Taxation Questions	87
5. Finance of Local Authorities	88
(a) Indebtedness	88
(b) Revenue of Local Authorities	89
(c) New Sources of Revenue	90

PART II.—SOCIAL SERVICES—EXISTING POSITION AND NEEDS.

Chapter VII. Education

1. Descriptive	92
2. Previous Expert Reports	105
3. Assessment of the desirable Aims and Objects of Education in the West Indies	117
4. Deficiencies and Remedies	122
(a) Teaching Staff	122
(b) Accommodation	123
(c) Equipment	124
(d) Curricula	125
(e) Films	126
(f) Broadcasting	126
(g) Adult Education	127
(h) Organisation of Education Departments	128
(i) Grading of Schools	129
(j) Education for Girls	130
(k) Health, Nutrition and Clothing	131
(l) Denominational Control	132
(m) Educational Adviser for The West Indies	132
5. Finance	132

Chapter VIII. Public Health

1. Descriptive	134
(a) Vital Statistics	134
(b) Nature of Ill-health	139
(c) Expenditure on Medical Services	141
(d) Existing Medical Organisation	142
(e) Staff of Medical Departments	144
(f) Medical Institutions	145
(g) Dispensaries	147
(h) Special Clinics	148
(i) Availability of Medical Treatment	148
(j) Payment for Treatment	150
(k) Schemes for supplying Medical Care	151
(l) Private Practitioners	152
(m) Other Defects of West Indian Medical Systems	153
(n) Conclusions	154

	Page
2. Recommendations	155
(1) Appointment of Medical Adviser for the West Indies	156
(2) Unification of Medical Services	157
(3) Centralisation of Medical Institutions	158
(4) Creation of School of Hygiene	161
(5) Development of Long-term Health Policies	162
(6) Reorganisation of Medical Services	163
(a) Development of Preventive Outlook	164
(b) Increase of Auxiliary Staff	164
(c) Better facilities for Medical Treatment	164
(7) Increase in Preventive Measures	168
(a) Housing	168
(b) General Sanitation	168
(c) Anti-Malarial Measures	169
(d) Maternity and Child Welfare Work	170
(e) Venereal Diseases Clinic	170
(f) School Medical Services	170
(g) Employment of Women Doctors	171
(h) Education of the Public in Health Matters	171
3. Defective Diets and Malnutrition	171
Chapter IX. Housing	174
1. Existing Conditions	174
2. Nature of the Housing Problem	176
3. Siting and Types of Houses	178
4. Government Housing Schemes in Towns	181
5. Estate and Company Housing	183
6. Other Rural Housing	186
7. Finance and Supervision	188
Chapter X. Labour and Trade Unions	
1. General	190
2. Character of Employment	192
3. Unemployment Problems	195
4. Regulation of Wages and Conditions	196
5. Trade Unions	197
6. Labour Departments	202
7. Industrial and Protective Legislation	206
8. Local Welfare Levies	213
Chapter XI. Other Social Needs and Services	
1. Social Welfare	215
(a) Social Conditions	215
(b) The Status of Women	217
(c) Lack of Family Life	220
(d) Need for a well-defined Programme of Social Welfare	222
(e) Special Duties of Social Welfare Workers	226
(f) Conclusions	230

	Page
2. Prisons	232
(a) The Young Offender	232
(b) Industrial Schools for Boys	233
(c) The Delinquent Girl	234
(d) The Adult Prisoner	234
(e) Prison Treatment and Accommodation	235
(f) The Ticket-of-Leave System	236
(g) After-Care	236
(h) Recommendations	237
3. Remaining Social Problems	237
(a) Poor Law Relief	237
(b) Poor Law Homes and Asylums	238
(c) Outdoor and Casual Relief	238
(d) Prostitution	239
(e) Other Social Evils	239

PART III.—PROBLEMS OF POLICY.

Chapter XII.	The Problem of Population	242
Chapter XIII.	The Problem of Employment	247
1. Industrial Development and Local Protection		247
2. Public Works and the Tourist Trade		254
3. General		256
4. Marketing		257
5. Inter-Island Trade		259
Chapter XIV.	Preferential Assistance	261
Chapter XV.	Sugar Policy	
1. The International Sugar Agreement		267
2. The Disadvantages of Increased Colonial Sugar Production		271
3. Proposals regarding Increased Production		276
4. Prices and Preferences		279
5. Peace-time Proposals		280
6. Objects and Conditions of Proposals		286
Chapter XVI.	Agricultural Policy	
1. General Remarks		287
2. Food Supply		287
3. Soil and Land Surveys		289
4. Land Ownership and Use		289
5. Peasant Agriculture		291
6. Estate Agriculture		292
7. Soil Erosion		292
8. Maintenance of Soil Fertility		293
9. Export Crops		294
10. Economic Organisation		294
11. Agricultural Credit and Finance		295

		Page
12. Veterinary Matters...		296
13. Agricultural Departments		297
14. Agricultural Education		298
15. Need for Defined Agricultural Policy...		299
16. Imperial College of Tropical Agriculture		300
17. Special Agricultural Problems ...		303
(a) Banana Industry in Jamaica		303
(b) Agricultural Development in British Honduras		304
(c) Sugar Factory and Land Settlement in Nevis		305
(d) Agricultural Aspects of Population Problem in Barbados		306
(e) Drainage Problems in British Guiana		306
(f) Rice Industry in British Guiana		308
(g) Cocoa Industry in Trinidad and Grenada		309
18. Forestry		310
Further note on the Banana Industry in Jamaica		312

Chapter XVII. Land Settlement

1. The Nature of Land Settlement		313
2. General Considerations		313
3. Central Farm		314
4. Special Considerations		315
5. Credit Facilities and Other Assistance		315
6. Value of Land Settlement and its Financial Aspects		316
7. Existing and Projected Settlements ...		317
(a) Jamaica		317
(b) British Honduras		318
(c) Anguilla		319
(d) St. Kitts		319
(e) Nevis		319
(f) Antigua		319
(g) Montserrat		320
(h) Dominica		320
(i) St. Lucia		320
(j) St. Vincent		321
(k) Grenada		321
(l) Barbados		321
(m) British Guiana		322
(n) Trinidad		322
8. General Conclusions and Recommendations		323

Chapter XVIII. Closer Union and the Unification of Local Services

1. History of Question of Closer Union...		324
2. Evidence of Present Local Opinion		326
3. Advantages of Federation		327
4. Amalgamation of Leeward Islands and Windward Islands		328
5. Present Extent of Unification of Services		329
6. Unification of Local Services		331

Chapter XIX. Communications

1. Services by Sea ... 334
   - (a) External Services ... 334
   - (b) Inter-Island Services ... 339
2. Air Services ... 341
3. Railways and River Services ... 342
4. Communications by Road ... 345
5. Telephone Services ... 347
6. Wireless Communications ... 350
7. Broadcasting ... 351

Chapter XX. West Indian Welfare Fund ... 354

Chapter XXI. Problems of Administration ... 363

Chapter XXII. Constitutional Problems

1. Reasons for Considering these Problems ... 373
2. Composition of Executive and Legislative Councils ... 374
3. Extension of the Franchise ... 377
4. Qualifications for Membership of the Legislative Councils ... 381
5. Representation of West Indian Colonies in Parliament ... 382
6. Local Government ... 383

PART IV.—OTHER QUESTIONS.

Chapter XXIII. Miscellaneous General Questions ... 386

1. Reconstitution of the British West Indies Regiment ... 386
2. Grievances of Ex-Service Men ... 386
3. Tourist Trade ... 387
4. Praedial Larceny ... 388
5. Indebtedness ... 388
6. Census and Other Statistics ... 389
7. The Press ... 390
8. Fisheries ... 390

Chapter XXIV. Local and Sectional Questions ... 392

1. Barbados ... 392
2. British Guiana ... 394
   - (a) Public Debt ... 395
   - (b) Air Services ... 397
   - (c) Aboriginal Indians ... 398
   - (d) Local Government ... 398
3. British Honduras ... 399
   - (a) Labour Conditions for Forest Workers ... 400
   - (b) Education ... 401
   - (c) Communications ... 402

		Page
(d) Debt Remission	... ...	402
(e) The Non-Negro Population	... ...	403
4. Jamaica	... ...	404
5. Leeward Islands	... ...	405
(a) Anguilla	... ...	406
(b) Antigua	... ...	407
(c) Dominica	... ...	407
6. Trinidad	... ...	408
7. Windward Islands ...	... ...	409
(a) St. Lucia	... ...	409
(b) St. Vincent	... ...	411
(c) Grenada	... ...	412
8. The Smaller Islands	... ...	413
9. East Indian Problems	... ...	415

PART V.—CONCLUSIONS AND RECOMMENDATIONS.

Chapter XXV.   Conclusions and Recommendations   ...   422

1. The Problem   422
2. Conclusions   423
   (a) Social Conditions   423
   (b) Economic Position and Outlook   425
   (c) Agricultural Position and Outlook   426
3. Recommendations
   (a) West Indian Welfare Fund and Comptroller   427
   (b) Social Services
       (i) Education   432
       (ii) Public Health   434
       (iii) Housing   436
       (iv) Labour and Trades Unions   437
       (v) Other Social Needs and Services   ...   439
   (c) Economic Problems   440
   (d) Agriculture   444
   (e) Land Settlement   446
   (f) Communications   447
   (g) Constitutional and Closer Union   449
   (h) Local Unification of Services   450
   (i) Administration and Public Opinion   451
   (j) Miscellaneous Local and Sectional Questions   453

Acknowledgments...   455

APPENDICES

	Page
A. List of Witnesses who appeared before the Commission...	457
B. Individuals and Associations, other than those who gave oral evidence, from whom Memoranda were received ...	476
C. Average Annual Revenue and Expenditure of self-balancing Departments during the three years ending on the latest date up to which financial returns were available ...	481
D. Analysis of Average Annual Revenue (excluding grants received from H.M. Government and the Revenue of self-balancing Departments) during the three years ending on the latest date up to which financial returns were available ; the amount received under each head is also shown as a percentage of the Total Revenue ...	482
E. Analysis of Average Annual Expenditure (excluding that of self-balancing Departments) during the three years ending on the latest date up to which financial returns were available ; the amount expended under each head is also shown as a percentage of the Total Expenditure...	483

MAP.

The Caribbean Area, British Guiana and British Honduras.

ROYAL WARRANT.
Dated 5th August, 1938.

GEORGE R.I.

GEORGE THE SIXTH, By the Grace of God of Great Britain, Ireland and the British Dominions beyond the Seas King, Defender of the Faith, Emperor of India: To Our Right Trusty and Well-beloved Counsellor Walter Edward, Baron Moyne, Companion of Our Distinguished Service Order; Our Trusty and Well-beloved: Sir Reginald Edward Stubbs, Knight Grand Cross of Our Most Distinguished Order of Saint Michael and Saint George; Dame Rachel Eleanor Crowdy, Dame Commander of Our Most Excellent Order of the British Empire, upon whom has been conferred the Decoration of the First Class of the Royal Red Cross; Sir Walter McLennan Citrine, Knight Commander of Our Most Excellent Order of the British Empire; Sir Percy Graham Mackinnon, Knight; Ralph Assheton, Esquire; Mary Georgina Blacklock; Frank Leonard Engledow, Esquire, Commander of Our Most Distinguished Order of Saint Michael and Saint George; Hubert Douglas Henderson, Esquire; and Morgan Jones, Esquire, Greeting.

Whereas We have deemed it expedient that a Commission should forthwith issue to investigate social and economic conditions in Barbados, British Guiana, British Honduras, Jamaica, the Leeward Islands, Trinidad and Tobago, and the Windward Islands, and matters connected therewith, and to make recommendations:

Now know ye that We, reposing great trust and confidence in your knowledge and ability, have authorised and appointed, and do by these Presents authorise and appoint you the said Walter Edward, Baron Moyne (Chairman); Sir Reginald Edward Stubbs (Vice-Chairman); Dame Rachel Eleanor Crowdy; Sir Walter McLennan Citrine; Sir Percy Graham Mackinnon; Ralph Assheton; Mary Georgina Blacklock; Frank Leonard Engledow; Hubert Douglas Henderson; and Morgan Jones to be Our Commissioners for the purposes of the said investigation:

And We do hereby authorise and require you with all convenient despatch and by all lawful means to enter upon, and to collect evidence respecting the subject matter of, such enquiry, and to render a Report and make recommendations in accordance with the terms of this Our Commission:

And We do by these Presents authorise you to visit and inspect personally such places as you may deem it expedient so to inspect for the more effectual carrying out of the purposes aforesaid:

And We do further require you to conform in all things to such instructions as shall be addressed to you through one of Our Principal Secretaries of State:

And We do hereby charge and command all Our Officers, Civil and Military, and all Our faithful subjects and all others inhabiting the said Colonies that in their several places and according to their respective powers and opportunities they be aiding to you in the execution of this Our Commission:

And We do further ordain that you, or any five or more of you, are at liberty to report your proceedings under this Our Commission from time to time if you shall judge it expedient so to do:

And, for the purpose of aiding you in your enquiries, We hereby appoint Our Trusty and Well-beloved Thomas Ingram Kynaston Lloyd, Esquire, to be Secretary, and Charles Young Carstairs, Esquire, to be Assistant Secretary, to this Our Commission.

Given at Our Court at Saint James's this Fifth day of August, One Thousand Nine Hundred and Thirty-Eight, in the Second Year of Our Reign.

By His Majesty's Command,

MALCOLM MACDONALD.

Note.—The United Kingdom share of the cost of the Royal Commission is estimated at approximately £13,454. The cost of printing and publishing this Report is estimated by the Stationery Office at £705

WEST INDIA ROYAL COMMISSION, 1938–1939

To the King's Most Excellent Majesty.

May it please Your Majesty.

Your Majesty's Warrant, bearing date the 5th day of August, 1938, appointed us Commissioners with the following Terms of Reference:—

"To investigate social and economic conditions in Barbados, British Guiana, British Honduras, Jamaica, the Leeward Islands, Trinidad and Tobago, and the Windward Islands, and matters connected therewith, and to make recommendations."

We now humbly beg leave to submit to Your Majesty the following Report.

PREFACE.

Your Majesty's Warrant appointing us to be Commissioners was signed on the 5th of August, 1938. We held our first meeting on the same day, in order to determine our procedure. We deemed it desirable to hear evidence in this country before leaving for the West Indies, and on the 9th of August notice was given in the Press making known this decision, and inviting persons interested to submit memoranda of evidence to our Secretariat. Between the 20th of September and our departure, we met on seven occasions for the purpose of taking formal evidence from 20 witnesses or groups of witnesses. Similar notices to that made public in this country were also issued in the West Indian Colonies, and intending witnesses were asked to submit memoranda to us through the various Colonial Secretariats.

With the exception of our Chairman, who had already left for the West Indies via the United States of America, we embarked at Liverpool on the 13th of October on R.M.S. *Orbita* and reached Kingston, Jamaica, on the 1st of November. We made our headquarters at the Constant Spring Hotel, near Kingston, where office accommodation and facilities for holding public meetings were available. In Jamaica, as elsewhere, the number of persons desiring to give evidence was so great that we could not find time to hear all of them without seriously limiting our opportunities of travelling about the Island and making ourselves familiar with conditions at first hand. We therefore made it a rule to give preference to evidence submitted on behalf of groups of persons and organisations, and to avoid the repetition of evidence already given. All memoranda received were, however, carefully considered, and we made it clear that our decision not to call a particular witness to give oral evidence did not mean that we were not alive to the views expressed in his written submission. Lists of the witnesses who appeared before us and of those who submitted memoranda are given in Appendices A and B respectively.

A party headed by our Chairman left Kingston for Belize, British Honduras, in his yacht M.Y. *Rosaura,* on the 25th of November, 1938, reaching Belize on the 28th of November. Evidence was heard in Belize and in various other centres in British Honduras which were visited by the Commission and the party left on the 9th of December for Puerto Rico, calling at Kingston en route on the 12th of December. Those who had remained in Jamaica continued to take evidence and conduct first-hand enquiries, and a visit was paid to Montego Bay, the second town of Jamaica, and evidence heard on the 2nd of December. On the 6th and 7th of December this party left Jamaica by air for Cuba, en route for Puerto Rico. The opportunity was taken to obtain information about comparable problems in Cuba, and representations were received in both Cuba and Hayti from groups of British West Indians resident there. The Commission reunited in Puerto Rico on the 14th of December, and the composition of the two parties was then changed. On the following day the Vice-Chairman's party left by air for Martinique, proceeding thence on the 17th of December in H.M.S. *Dundee* to St. Lucia. In Martinique the opportunity was taken, through the instrumentality of Your Majesty's Vice-Consul and the courtesy of the French authorities and proprietors concerned, to obtain information regarding labour law, medical organisation and the sugar industry. This party remained in St. Lucia from the 17th to the 29th of December, and, besides hearing evidence in Castries, travelled about the island so far as communications and time permitted. Evidence was heard at Soufrière, on the western coast, and a visit paid to Vieuxfort, at the extreme south, the scene of a proposed settlement of Barbadians. The party left St. Lucia in H.M.S. *Dundee* on the 29th of December for St. Vincent, and arrived on the same day at Kingstown, where they stayed until the 5th of January, 1939. The same procedure was followed as in St. Lucia, although better communications rendered possible somewhat more extensive travels. On the way to Grenada a visit was paid on the 5th of January to Bequia, a small island in the Grenadines under the administration of St. Vincent, where evidence was heard from the Commissioner in charge and members of the public. In Grenada, headquarters were established at the capital, St. George's, and as before evidence was heard and visits conducted as widely as possible. Visits were also paid to Carriacou and Union in the Grenadines, on the 12th of January, the former a dependency of Grenada and the latter of St. Vincent, and on the 14th of January the party left in H.M.S. *Dundee* for Barbados, which was reached on the evening of the same day.

Meanwhile, on the 15th of December, 1938, the Chairman's party had left Puerto Rico in M.Y. *Rosaura* for the Leeward Islands, calling on the way at the American islands of St. Croix and St. Thomas on the 16th and 17th of December. This party visited Tortola in the British Virgin Islands on the 19th of December and Anguilla, which is an island in the Presidency of St. Kitts-Nevis, on the following day: in both places evidence was heard from a number of witnesses. Periods of from three to six days were spent in each of the other principal islands in the Leewards group and evidence was heard at Basseterre in St. Kitts, Charlestown in Nevis, St. Johns in Antigua, Plymouth in Montserrat, and Roseau and Portsmouth in Dominica. In each island visits were made to all the other principal centres of population and members of the party inspected schools, institutions and those estates and factories which were readily accessible by road. On the 24th of December a visit was made to the Dutch island of Saba and the party spent the 12th and 13th of January, 1939, in Guadeloupe where they received every facility from the French authorities and were much assisted by Your Majesty's Vice-Consul. On the 14th of January, after taking the Governor of the Leeward Islands from Guadeloupe to Roseau in Dominica, this party left for Barbados. They called at Martinique on the 15th of January and spent one day in each of St. Lucia, St. Vincent and Grenada. They rejoined the Vice-Chairman's party in Bridgetown, Barbados, on the 19th of January.

The Chairman's party left for Georgetown, British Guiana, in M.Y. *Rosaura* on the 25th January, arriving on the 27th of that month; the Vice-Chairman's party followed in H.M.S. *Dundee* on the 4th of February. While making our headquarters in Georgetown, we also visited other parts of the colony, including New Amsterdam, the Canals Polder area, the Essequibo Coast, the headquarters of the bauxite industry at Mackenzie on the Demerara River, and the hinterland area adjoining the Brazilian border at the Takutu River. In British Guiana one of our number, Mr. Morgan Jones, M.P., had to return to England on account of serious illness from which he later died. We take this opportunity of placing on record an expression of our deep sympathy with his bereaved family, and of our appreciation of the knowledge, sympathy, single-mindedness and unflagging industry which he brought to our common task. It may truly be said that he spent himself in the prosecution of our enquiry into conditions in Your Majesty's West Indian possessions, and we hereby acknowledge the great value of the contributions to our work which he was able to make before being compelled to abandon it.

Again we left in two parties, by M.Y. *Rosaura* and by air, arriving at Port-of-Spain, Trinidad, on the 20th of February, and most of us remained there for slightly more than one month. Visits were paid to all the principal centres of population and to Tobago; and although the bulk of our formal evidence was heard in Port-of-Spain, we took numerous opportunities of familiarising ourselves with conditions and the state of feeling in all parts of the Colony. The majority of our number arrived in England in s.s. *Aquitania* on the 7th of April.

We were everywhere received with cordiality, and our task was much facilitated by the readiness with which the people of the West Indies rendered us all assistance in their power and furnished us with information, often at considerable inconvenience to themselves. We would mention especially the large number of private persons, often in poor circumstances, who went to considerable trouble to furnish us to the best of their ability with views and information to assist us in our enquiry, and we wish here to record our appreciation of such public-spirited action.

The work of the Commission was followed with great interest, and the rooms available for our sessions were frequently not large enough to accommodate the numbers wishing to attend. In Barbados and British Guiana arrangements were made for our proceedings to be relayed to neighbouring open spaces by means of microphones and loud-speakers, and packed crowds stood for hours each day to listen to them.* The keenness of public interest in our proceedings is in itself a sign of the importance attached by the people of the West Indies to the appointment of a Royal Commission, and of the great hopes which are entertained of assistance from Britain to deal with West Indian problems. We have also great pleasure in stating that we everywhere found strong evidence of devoted loyalty to Your Majesty's Person and Throne and to the British connection.

On our return to Great Britain we proceeded to take further evidence, mainly on various technical points which had arisen during our enquiries on the spot. We also continued the task of studying in detail the vast mass of memoranda and evidence accumulated during our enquiry, and proceeded to the preparation of our Report, which we now humbly beg leave to submit to Your Majesty. It is our earnest hope that our recommendations may commend themselves to Your Majesty's Government even in the dark days which have now befallen us.

Our debts of gratitude are too numerous to detail fully. We wish, however, to place on record, first, our high appreciation of the way in which the Governments of the colonies which we

---

* See Plate I.

visited made arrangements for our stay and for free transport, and for the readiness and speed with which our large demands for information were met. The Colonial Office, both before our departure and since our return, have readily furnished us with material on many subjects, as have in various degrees other Government Departments in this country.

Our thanks are due also to Your Majesty's Diplomatic and Consular Services for assistance rendered to us in visits undertaken by members to foreign territories, and to the Cuban, Haytian, United States, French and Dutch authorities for the facilities afforded and hospitality shown to us on our visits to Cuba, Hayti, Puerto Rico, the Virgin Islands of America, Guadeloupe, Martinique and Saba. We also wish to place on record our appreciation of the action of the Lords Commissioners of the Admiralty in placing at our disposal Your Majesty's Escort Vessel *Dundee,* without the services of which our travelling arrangements would have been very much complicated. We were much indebted, also, to the Commanding Officer and Officers of H.M.S. *Dundee* for their ready co-operation in facilitating our visits to the smaller islands.

We feel justified in calling attention to the magnitude of the task which we have attempted to fulfil during the last 15 months. We were charged by our terms of reference to enquire into all aspects of life in the West Indies, and there were few subjects which could not by some process of argument be represented as requiring our attention. Few Royal Commissions can ever have had to cover so wide a field of subjects—the West India Royal Commission of 1896-7, for example, was concerned principally with the plight of the sugar industry, as was the Olivier-Semple enquiry of 1929-30—and few have had to cover so many scattered communities and conditions so diverse in spite of an apparent uniformity. Apart from our journeys of 6,000 miles to and from the West Indies, we covered some 9,000 miles by one means or another. Formal evidence was heard in 26 centres from 370 witnesses or groups of witnesses, including many large delegations, most of whose members took a part in the proceedings. We had further to consider 789 memoranda of evidence, several of which rival this Report in bulk; and in addition we received some 300 other communications relating to individual grievances or other matters which we could not treat as falling within our terms of reference. We felt bound to investigate personally conditions in housing, agriculture, hospitals, schools, prisons, factories, docks, lunatic asylums, orphanages, leper homes, land settlements, and in addition we lost no occasion, apart from the hearing of formal evidence, of making ourselves acquainted with all shades of opinion on the matters which fell within our terms of reference. Our task in this Report has been to attempt to bring all our diverse information and impressions into some sort of coherent whole.

At the outbreak of war most of our Report was already in draft, and we were faced with the choice either of completing it on the basis of the evidence in our possession and of the decisions reached at our discussions during the summer of 1939, or of attempting to take into full consideration the influence of war conditions on the West Indies. It has not of course been possible, particularly in the Chapters dealing with the export trade of the West Indies, to overlook the immediate consequences of a state of war, and although we decided to adopt the former alternative we have nevertheless been obliged to make certain consequential changes in the appropriate sections of our Report. Our decision to report as soon as possible on the basis of the evidence before us was taken partly because the adoption of the second alternative would have involved the reopening of many questions and a considerable and needless prolongation of our enquiry; but in a much greater degree because we believe that the early publication of our Report and, as we hope, action, by Your Majesty's Government in the spirit of our recommendations, will be a valuable earnest of the good intentions of the citizens of the United Kingdom towards the colonial peoples in their charge. We were also influenced by the view that the fundamental problems of the West Indies will remain, and cannot be permanently affected by abnormal war conditions. It is to the solution of these fundamental problems that we have directed our enquiry.

On the 6th of September, 1939, Mr. Ralph Assheton, M.P., was appointed Parliamentary Secretary to the Ministry of Labour. He accordingly consulted the Secretary of State for the Colonies and it was decided that, since he had become a member of Your Majesty's Government, it would be inappropriate that he should participate in recommendations on which Your Majesty's Government will later have to reach their own conclusions. It was solely for this reason that Mr. Assheton withdrew from the deliberations of the Commission. He consequently tendered his resignation from the Commission and this was accepted by Your Majesty. We much regret that it should have been found necessary for Mr. Assheton thus to discontinue his collaboration in our work, in which, up to the date of his resignation, he had taken an active and constructive part.

PART I

THE GENERAL BACKGROUND

CHAPTER I.

HISTORICAL SURVEY.

1. General.

1. The British West Indian Colonies which came within our terms of reference are scattered over an area covering 35° of longitude (2,200 miles) from British Honduras in the west to British Guiana in the east, and 18° of latitude (1,200 miles) from the most northerly point of British Honduras to the most southerly boundary of British Guiana. These two Colonies are the largest in area and are both on the mainland of the American Continent; the group also includes two islands of moderate size in Jamaica and Trinidad, and a large number of small islands in the Lesser Antillean chain. All these Colonies lie within the tropical belt: beyond this similarity, there is great diversity of climate and opportunity. Density of population varies enormously, ranging from 3·8 per square mile in British Guiana (where settlement for practical purposes is confined to a narrow alluvial coastal strip) and 6·62 in British Honduras, to 663 in Grenada and 1,210 in Barbados, where all land available is cultivated.

2. The history of the Colonies is as diverse as their configuration and degree of settlement. Barbados has been in uninterrupted British possession since it was first colonised early in the 17th century and Jamaica since the middle of that century; most of the others suffered more or less frequent changes of ownership between Britain, France, Holland and Spain until the present position was stabilised after the Napoleonic Wars. Strong traces of these influences are visible in the Dutch planning of Georgetown, British Guiana, and Dutch influence on the drainage and sea-defences on which the Colony depends for its life, in the French patois of St. Lucia and other islands, the French and Spanish families in Trinidad, the solid French architecture of St. George's, Grenada, the robust British characteristics of the comparatively large European population of Barbados, and in many other less obvious matters of law, custom and social tradition.

3. By far the greater proportion of the population of the West Indian Colonies are the descendants of the negro slaves brought from West Africa during the 17th and 18th centuries. But in those Colonies, where development was comparatively backward or population comparatively sparse at the time of the abolition of the slave-trade, the shortage of labour led to the importation under the indenture system over a prolonged period of large numbers of labourers from India. In British

Guiana and Trinidad, the " East Indians," as natives of India or their descendants are known in contradistinction to " West Indians," form a very important element in the community, amounting to about half the population in the former Colony, and about one-third in the latter. In Jamaica also they are of appreciable though much less, importance. There are also smaller groups of Chinese and Syrians, and also, in British Honduras, British Guiana, Dominica and to some small extent in St. Vincent, remnants of the aboriginal inhabitants, Mayas, Caribs, Wapisianas and other Amerindian peoples. Apart from the very numerous coloured population, of mixed African and European ancestry, who are to be found all over the West Indies, there are many other racial mixtures, some well enough established to form a distinctive type, such as the so-called Caribs of British Honduras, who are the result of inter-marriage between negro and Amerindian.

4. These racial differences complicate the problems of the West Indians in several respects. The East Indians in Trinidad, British Guiana and Jamaica form a distinct element in the community, retaining their own customs, traditions and aspirations, and mixing comparatively little with the population of negro race. We shall consider in Chapter XXIV various questions that especially concern them. The Chinese and Syrians, again, are engaged almost entirely in retail trade, in certain branches of which they have acquired in some Colonies something approaching a monopoly that evokes considerable jealousy and resentment.

2. Economic Aspects.

5. The early settlement of the West Indies was undertaken with the object of using them as sources of valuable tropical products, such as spices, sugar and logwood. The production of sugar-cane soon became of predominant importance; and, as the consumption of sugar in European countries increased rapidly, the industry became extremely profitable. Adam Smith, writing in 1776, was struck by the ease with which large profits were earned on sugar plantations:—

> " It is commonly said," he wrote in the Wealth of Nations, " that a sugar planter expects that the rum and the molasses should defray the whole expense of his cultivation and that his sugar should be all clear profit. If this be true, for I pretend not to affirm it, it is as if a corn farmer expected to defray the expense of his cultivation with the chaff and the straw and that the grain should be all clear profit. We see frequently societies of merchants in London and other trading towns, purchase waste lands in our sugar Colonies, which they expect to improve and to cultivate with profit, by means of factors and agents,

notwithstanding the great distance and the uncertain returns from the defective administration of justice in those countries. Nobody will attempt to improve and cultivate in the same manner the most fertile lands of Scotland, Ireland or the corn provinces of North America, though, from the more exact administration of justice in these countries, more regular returns might be expected."

In the eighteenth century indeed the ownership of sugar estates in the West Indies was the main foundation of the fortunes of many wealthy British families. West Indian Colonies were regarded by the state-craft of the day as an asset of the first importance; hence the prominent part played by expeditions to the Caribbean in the naval warfare between France and Britain. Despite sharp fluctuations of fortune, as the result of wars, the financial prosperity of the sugar industry continued into the nineteenth century.

6. In the last century, however, it underwent a series of adversities. From the standpoint of the sugar planters the abolition first of the slave-trade and then of slavery was an injury which was only partially made good by the generous compensation voted by the British Parliament. They were left with a depleted and uncertain labour-force; and their costs of production were increased as a consequence to a level which made it difficult for them to compete with other countries in free markets. For a brief period they continued to enjoy a virtual monopoly of the British market as the result of the prohibitive import duties that were still imposed on foreign sugar. The Free Trade movement in the 'forties, however, entailed the gradual removal of this protection; and from 1854 the British Colonies had to compete in the British market, without any preferential assistance, with the slave-grown sugar of Brazil and Cuba. This was a severe blow to the fortunes of West Indian sugar estates. Gradually the industry, aided by the rapid expansion of the world demand for sugar, adapted itself to the new market conditions, partly by means of the amalgamation of estates and improvements in factory machinery, partly by reductions of wages.

7. But the return of financial prosperity proved short-lived. A new and formidable competitor arose in the beet-sugar industry of the European Continent. Stimulated by prohibitive import duties, and by export bounties, the production of sugar-beet underwent a huge expansion in many European countries in the last two decades of the nineteenth century. Between 1882 and 1891, the imports of beet-sugar into the United Kingdom rose from 400,000 tons to over 1,000,000 tons per annum, while the imports of cane sugar from the British West Indies fell from 200,000 tons to 50,000 tons per annum. Indeed the United

States which imposed countervailing import duties on bounty-fed sugar, displaced the United Kingdom during this period as the principal market for British West Indian sugar.

8. Under these conditions, the price of sugar fell rapidly and steadily, until in 1896 it was only about one-half what it was in 1881; and the troubles of the West Indian sugar planters were further aggravated in the 'nineties by a serious outbreak of cane disease. The closing years of the last century represented indeed perhaps the most critical period which the West Indian sugar industry has had to face. Bankruptcies among estate proprietors were widespread; in many areas the production of sugar-cane was abandoned; and it seemed for a time as though the continued existence of the industry, which still accounted for over four-fifths of the exports of the West Indian Colonies, was in danger. It was in these circumstances that the Royal Commission of 1897 was appointed.

9. The main prescriptions of this Commission for the economic troubles that have been described were the substitution of peasant cultivators for estates by a policy of land settlement, and the substitution of other tropical products for sugar-cane. In several of the West Indian Colonies, the production of other commodities had already developed on a considerable scale. Bananas had been introduced into Jamaica in the 'sixties; cocoa was already established in Trinidad and Grenada. The cultivation of these and other products, such as coconuts and citrus, was now greatly increased in place of sugar-cane, and in some islands products new to the West Indies, such as sea-island cotton, were introduced. The extent to which the development of alternative products took place varied greatly from one Colony to another; in Barbados, in British Guiana, and in some of the Leeward Islands sugar remained the predominating industry; in other Colonies, notably Jamaica and Trinidad, it declined to a secondary rôle; in some of the smaller islands, it virtually disappeared. Thus a marked diversity between the agricultural life of the different West Indian Colonies took the place of the essential uniformity which had hitherto prevailed.

10. The abolition of the system of beet-sugar bounties was secured by the Brussels Convention of 1903, and the improvement of the sugar position which ensued, coupled with the turnover to other products in the Colonies that were least suited for the economical production of sugar, restored a measure of financial prosperity to the West Indies in the decade before 1914. During the war of 1914-18, with the British market cut off from its chief sources of beet-sugar supply, the West Indian sugar industry experienced a boom, and made large profits, reminiscent of the spacious days of the eighteenth century.

11. But the high war prices stimulated the production of cane in other countries; when the war was over, Great Britain herself adopted the policy of subsidising the development of a beet-sugar industry; and the expanding productive capacity throughout the world, accentuated by a marked increase in the technical efficiency of sugar production again began far to outstrip the steady growth of world demand. The concession of a substantial Imperial Preference on sugar did much to mitigate the injurious consequences of this state of affairs for Colonial producers. None the less a serious crisis arose in 1929, leading to the appointment of the West Indian Sugar Commission consisting of Lord Olivier and Mr. Semple. The sequel was the concession of increased preferential assistance to Colonial sugar producers and the negotiation of the International Sugar Agreement, under which the export of sugar from the British Colonies, as from other producing countries, is limited by a system of quotas.

12. Meanwhile misfortune had overtaken the producers of most of the alternative agricultural commodities in which the West Indies had found relief from the sugar depression of the 'nineties. In almost every case, a similar tendency towards a marked surplus of productive capacity over world demand made its appearance, prices fell to unremunerative levels; and the situation was aggravated in many cases by plant disease or hurricane damage. The adverse trend of market conditions which it was at first hoped might prove transient has persisted; and the position of the producers of such commodities as cocoa, coconuts, citrus, limes, bananas, coffee, rice and nutmegs has become so serious that in recent years there has been a decided movement back to sugar, though this has lately been checked by the operation of the International Sugar Agreement.

3. Social Aspects.

13. The social structure of most of the West Indian Colonies is dominated by the fact that the agriculture which is their mainstay was founded and long continued on an estate basis, involving the existence of a comparatively small number of proprietors and managers, usually European, and a very large number of negro labourers. Emancipation gave rise to a movement towards small-scale peasant farming. Wherever possible, the freed slaves purchased land of their own, in some cases joining together to purchase abandoned estates for subsequent sub-division among themselves. In several Colonies, the movement towards peasant settlement made steady progress, and was closely associated, both as cause and effect, with the introduction of new crops, notably bananas in Jamaica and cocoa in Grenada, that lent themselves more readily than sugar-cane to small-scale cultivation. This process has been for the most

part of an unorganised character—owing comparatively little to Government land-settlement schemes. But the intense desire of the West Indian people for the personal ownership of a piece of land, however small, has found some means of satisfying itself, wherever facilities for land purchase or for squatting have existed, with the result that even in the crowded island of Barbados, a considerable portion of the land is now in peasant hands.

14. The estate, however, whether a large estate owned by a London company and administered by paid managers, or a small estate of some 300 acres, owned by a locally resident planter remains almost everywhere in the West Indies the predominant economic unit. Nor is the distinction between the estate labourer and the small peasant proprietor so wide or so clear-cut as may be supposed. There are, it is true, numbers of small peasants, particularly in Jamaica, Grenada and Nevis, who depend entirely on their holdings for their means of livelihood, and who may be themselves employers of labour on a small scale during the crop season. But these are a minority. The normal peasant holding is too small to provide the means of an independent existence, and most peasants are accustomed to supplement their income by wage-work on the estates. Thus the great majority of the negro population depend at any rate in a large degree on wages for their livelihood, however much they may supplement them by work on land that they own or rent.

15. When the negro population were introduced into the West Indies, no attempt was made to substitute any kind of social organisation or moral standard for the somewhat elaborate tribal codes of the areas whence they were brought. The benefits of education and the institution of marriage were alike discouraged, and on emancipation a large number of persons were left to shift for themselves without the support of traditions of self-help or mutual co-operation. In the period that followed, the best friends of the negro labourers were the missionaries and the churches; and it is difficult to speak too highly of the devoted services of many of the missionaries, who even before emancipation had done all in their power, often in the face of bitter and violent opposition, to ameliorate the moral and the economic position of the negro population. The work of the religious bodies during this period served to win for the churches and religion a special place in the hearts and the lives of the people. In developing education in particular the religious bodies have played a noteworthy part. But they were unable to exert more than a limited influence on either the moral standards or the social conditions of the community; and, with *laissez-faire* established as the dominant social philosophy in the Victorian age, it was only very gradually that the improvement of social

conditions and the provision of what are called social services came to be recognised as appropriate functions and obligations of Government.

16. Under these conditions, and with their economic life exposed to the vicissitudes that have already been described, social progress in the West Indian Colonies was slow and chequered. In certain directions, none the less, decided progress has been made; indeed some of the major problems that have now arisen are largely attributable to this progress. Birth-rates have always been high in the West Indies; but until comparatively recently death-rates were high also. In the last generation however a great improvement has been effected in health conditions, with the result that death-rates have fallen substantially. As a consequence, the population is now increasing far more rapidly than ever before; and this rapid increase of numbers, coupled with the unfavourable trend of markets, has given rise to a serious problem of unemployment and under-employment. Again, education, inadequate and unsatisfactory though it still is, and the participation of the people in public affairs and corporate activities, have at any rate developed sufficiently to have given rise to an articulate public opinion, conscious of its grievances and insistent on improvement.

17. Serious discontent was often widespread in West Indian Colonies during the nineteenth century, as is indicated by the occasional uprisings that occurred, leading sometimes to considerable loss of life. But the discontent that underlies the disturbances of recent years is a phenomenon of a different character, representing no longer a mere blind protest against a worsening of conditions, but a positive demand for the creation of new conditions that will render possible a better and less restricted life. It is the co-existence of this new demand for better conditions with the unfavourable economic trend that is the crux of the West Indian problem of the present day.

CHAPTER II.
THE ECONOMIC POSITION AND OUTLOOK.
1. The Growth of Population.

1. The populations in all the British West Indian Colonies are now increasing with great rapidity. It is not very easy to measure accurately the size of the populations, since the Census that would ordinarily have been taken in or about 1931 was omitted in most of the Colonies owing to the spirit of public economy that then prevailed, and it is necessary, therefore, to calculate on the basis of 1921 figures, the accuracy of which moreover is in many cases open to considerable criticism. The system of registering births and deaths is, however, in most Colonies stated to be reasonably efficient and comprehensive; and a fairly accurate picture of the annual number of births and deaths and of the natural rate of increase can therefore be given. It should be observed in this connection that it is probable, as was stated to us in evidence in Jamaica, that a larger number of births than of deaths escapes registration, so that in so far as the figures are deficient they probably under-estimate the rate at which the population is increasing.

2. The following table gives the estimates that are generally accepted of the populations of the different Colonies at three different dates: (1) in 1896 or just before the appointment of the Norman Commission, (2) in 1921, and (3) in 1936.

Estimated Population.

Colony.	1896.	1921.	1936.
Jamaica	695,000	858,000	1,139,000
Trinidad and Tobago	248,000	367,000	448,000
British Guiana	279,000	298,000	333,000
Barbados	186,000	166,000	188,000
Windward Islands	146,000	162,000	210,000
Leeward Islands	131,000	122,000	140,000
British Honduras	34,000	45,000	56,000
Total	1,719,000	2,018,000	2,514,000

3. For the reasons already given, these figures must be taken as subject to a large margin of error. In Barbados we found keen statistical discussion as to whether the population of that island may not be materially greater than 200,000. But the main impressions conveyed by the table as to the relative magnitudes of the populations of the different Colonies and as to their different trends since 1896 may be accepted as at least broadly true. In Jamaica and Trinidad it will be observed, there was a huge increase in population in the 40 years covered; in the Windward Islands a smaller but still large increase; while in British Guiana, Barbados and the Leeward Islands,

the increase was much smaller, the expansion since 1921 doing little more in the case of the last two Colonies than make good the decline in the preceding 25 years.

4. These differences are largely attributable to the contrast between the depression of the sugar industry in the earlier part of the period and the comparative prosperity that prevailed until recent years in many other branches of tropical agriculture. The growth of numbers in Jamaica was made possible by the expansion of the banana trade; that in Trinidad by the expansion of cocoa-growing and in a lesser degree by the petroleum industry; the Windwards were also helped by the expansion of cocoa (in Grenada), by sea island cotton and arrowroot (in St. Vincent) and by bananas. In Barbados, on the other hand, in British Guiana and in some of the Leeward Islands, it proved less easy to introduce alternative crops, and sugar remained the predominant industry.

5. But it is interesting to consider how it was that the differences in economic opportunity between the different Colonies led to these varying rates of population growth. Migration was a very important means. Until comparatively recently, there were many emigration outlets in other parts of the Caribbean area open to West Indians who found little scope for their energies at home. They might move at one period to Panama for work on the building of the canal. They might go to Costa Rica to grow bananas; or they might go at certain periods to Cuba to cut sugar-cane. At one time they might even enter the United States. Moreover labourers in one West Indian Colony, where the population was redundant, might move to another where there were larger opportunities. Emigrants from Barbados, where the pressure of population has been acutely felt for a long period past, are to be found in considerable numbers in most of the other Colonies. Conversely, in Jamaica, Trinidad and British Guiana, the sugar estates often found it difficult before the war to secure a supply of labour sufficient for their purposes, and were allowed to import indentured labour from India. It is noteworthy that this system of indentured immigration was not terminated until 1917, and then at the instance of the Government of India.

6. For some 10 years or more the emigration outlets that previously existed have been virtually closed. The other Caribbean countries have, like the West Indian Colonies, experienced growing difficulties in marketing their products. Unemployment has taken the place of an unsatisfied demand for labour as the dominating fact throughout the Caribbean area; and every country has taken drastic measures to exclude fresh immigrants. Cuba has gone further and is endeavouring to secure the repatriation of immigrants who may have resided in the country for a considerable period. So far as concerns

·the exclusion of fresh immigrants the British Colonies have adopted the same policy and have applied it to immigrants from other British Colonies, in some cases with such rigour as to prohibit purely seasonal movements of labour. One of the complaints made to us, for example, in the small Grenadine Islands was that their inhabitants were no longer able to supplement their livelihood by working in Trinidad during the crop season. A scheme, it is true, is in course of development for the settlement of a limited number of Barbadians in St. Lucia, to which we shall have occasion to make reference in subsequent Chapters. This represents practically the only opportunity that exists to-day for West Indians, unless they can command a substantial sum of money, to move even from one British Colony to another. The average West Indian labourer is indeed more strictly confined to his own island, which may be no larger than an average British county, than the English labourer was tied to his parish in the most rigid phase of the Settlement Laws. We had indications that this extreme difficulty of movement, which is as we have seen an essentially modern phenomenon, creates a sense of being shut in, of being denied opportunity and choice, and of consequent frustration in the minds of many young men of adventurous disposition, particularly in the smaller islands. It may be a more important element than appears at first in the psychology of discontent.

7. Thus emigration no longer relieves the growth of population. On the contrary, in some Colonies, the return of many of those who had previously emigrated is now an important aggravating factor. This is particularly true in Barbados where, over the last eight years, the return of emigrants has contributed even more to the growth of population than the excess of births over deaths. Yet almost everywhere the excess of births over deaths is both high and increasing The following table, the figures of which relate to the year 1937, gives a general picture of the position:—

	Birth Rate.	Death Rate.	Crude Rate of Increase.
Jamaica	32·4	15·3	17·1
Trinidad	32·9	17·4	15·5
British Guiana	35·0	21·9	13·1
Barbados	29·9	18·5	11·4
Windward Islands:			
Grenada	32·0	14·3	17·7
St. Lucia	32·7	14·4	18·3
St. Vincent	39·1	15·3	23·8
Leeward Islands:			
Antigua	42·9	20·6	22·3
St. Kitts	44·4	36·5	7·9
Nevis	23·6	14·9	8·7
Anguilla	24·8	13·6	11·2
Dominica	31·6	14·5	17·1
Montserrat	39·3	15·4	23·9
Virgin Islands	31·0	10·9	20·1
British Honduras	32·9	18·5	14·4

Chapter II.

8. It will be seen that in Jamaica, in the Windward Islands and in many of the Leewards, the number of births was in 1937 more than double the number of deaths. The rate of natural increase is in nearly every case much higher than it was 10, 20 or 30 years ago, as the result of a large and steady fall in the death rate. From many standpoints there is indeed no more encouraging fact in the West Indies than the immense progress that has been made within the last generation in reducing the death rate. This progress is still continuing, particularly in the field of the reduction of infantile mortality; and there remains much scope for further improvement. Throughout the West Indies, except in Anguilla, the infantile mortality rate is still over 100 out of every 1,000 children born, in some Colonies it is over 200, as compared with an English infantile mortality rate of under 60.

9. Taking the West Indian Colonies as a whole, the figures in the above table indicate that the population is increasing at a rate of somewhere between $1\frac{1}{2}$ per cent. and 2 per cent. per annum. If the present rate of improvement is maintained in the reduction of mortality rates, as there is good reason to expect, while the birth-rates remain unaltered, the rate of increase will be fully 2 per cent. within a very few years. It may be observed that a population increasing at the rate of 2 per cent. per annum doubles itself in 35 years.

10. There is at present no indication that a decline in the birth-rate may be expected to follow the reduction of the death-rate. Anything in the nature of a deliberate limitation of the size of families is made peculiarly difficult by the character of social life in the West Indies—the prevalence of temporary and often casual unions between the sexes, the absence too often of any settled family life, and the lack of knowledge of, or facilities for, birth-control. It is possible perhaps that the comparatively low birth-rates in Barbados, Nevis and Anguilla may be regarded as representing in some degree a response to the very limited economic opportunities that those islands afford; there is greater reason to fear that the abnormally high infantile mortality rate in Barbados is largely attributable to the overcrowded condition of that island. But no clearly marked tendency towards a reduction of birth-rates can at present be discovered; if anything the prevailing tendency is the other way. As we shall argue later, we regard a reduction in the number of births as an indispensable condition in the long run of improving or even maintaining the standard of life in the West Indies. But it is obvious that a change in this direction can only be effected very slowly. For a long period to come it is inevitable that the population of working age will become materially larger in each successive year. It remains to consider the condition and prospects of the principal occupations in which these rapidly growing numbers must seek a livelihood.

2. Non-Agricultural Activities.

11. The great majority of the population of the British West Indies is engaged in agriculture. Only in Trinidad and British Guiana are mineral resources of any importance to be found. Trinidad has extensive petroleum deposits and a famous pitch lake from which asphalt has been produced for many years. The petroleum industry is of great value to the island in many ways. It makes a large contribution to the public revenue, partly through the taxation that falls upon it in respect of income tax and of customs duties levied on the equipment that it imports, and partly by royalties paid to the Government in respect of the oil produced on crown lands. Over three-fifths of the oil is so produced. Altogether the oil industry provides directly not far short of one-quarter of the public revenue; and its contribution has hitherto increased steadily with the expansion of the industry. For this reason, the Government of Trinidad, alone among the West Indian Governments, is in easy financial circumstances, and in a position to undertake fairly extensive programmes of expenditure without external aid.

12. The petroleum industry also exerts a general stimulating effect on the economic activity of Trinidad as a result of its substantial and growing expenditure on wages, salaries and the purchase of local materials. The exports of oil amount in value, it may be observed, to nearly 60 per cent. of the total exports of Trinidad. As an employer of labour, on the other hand, the petroleum industry is not nearly so important as might be supposed. The oil companies and contractors in the oilfields employ less than 15,000 operatives in a population of over 450,000 persons. The asphalt industry employs only a few hundreds.

13. In the interior of British Guiana there are large deposits of bauxite, the ore of aluminium. Bauxite mining is at present carried on near MacKenzie about 65 miles up the Demerara River from Georgetown by the Demerara Bauxite Company, a subsidiary of the Aluminum Company of Canada. This is an up-to-date and efficient enterprise, which has taken considerable pains to secure the health of its staff and labourers in the face of difficult natural conditions and provides some of the best housing accommodation to be found in the West Indies. It supplies the greater part of the bauxite requirements of the Canadian aluminium industry, and it accounts altogether for an important fraction of the total world supply. In recent years its production has undergone a remarkable expansion, increasing from 110,000 tons in 1935 to 447,000 tons in 1938. This is a reflection of the increased world demand for aluminium, arising partly from the steady extension of peace-time uses,

but largely from European rearmament. Even so, the industry only employs about 1,300 workpeople. It contributes considerable sums to the public revenue of British Guiana, since in addition to ordinary taxation, bauxite is subject, like gold and diamonds, to an *ad valorem* export duty. But its operations are not on a sufficiently large scale to make its rapid expansion a dominating factor in the financial position of British Guiana, as that of the oil industry is in Trinidad.

14. Gold and diamonds have also been found for a long period past in the interior of British Guiana. But neither is easily obtained. As a consequence of the fall in the price of diamonds, the output of the diamond industry has fallen to a small fraction of what it once was; the exports being less than 35,000 carats in 1937 as compared with 214,000 carats in the peak year of 1923. Gold mining received a certain stimulus from the rise in the price of gold that followed the breakdown of the gold standard; but it has not proved very profitable, either to the companies that operate on a substantial scale with modern dredgers, or to the " pork-knockers " as the individual prospectors are called who recover gold by alluvial washings. Gold and diamonds contribute about 10 per cent. in value to the exports of British Guiana, and bauxite about 13 per cent.

15. The possibility cannot, of course, be excluded that fresh mineral resources may at any time be discovered in British Guiana. Since our return from the West Indies, it has been announced that deposits of manganese, one of which it is hoped may prove of commercial importance, have been found there. But such speculative possibilities cannot at present provide the basis for any considerable expectations.

16. In none of the other West Indian Colonies have any mineral resources been found on a scale that is commercially important, though trifling quantities of oil have been produced in Barbados, copper-ore is to be found in Jamaica, and known deposits exist of gypsum, molybdenum and phosphates in some of the Leeward Islands. Lacking mineral resources, it is hardly to be expected that small communities, living in considerable isolation from the outside world, and with climates and traditions that are perhaps uncongenial to regular industrial life, would have developed manufacturing industries on an important scale. Most of the industries that exist belong indeed to one or other of the two following categories:—(*a*) industries like electric power stations and gas-works, printing works and ice factories, that must necessarily be situated in the localities where their products are consumed and (*b*) industries concerned with the " processing " of agricultural commodities that are produced locally.

17. In one sense the sugar factories, in which cane is converted into sugar and various by-products, form the most important example of the latter type of industry. For, though the sugar factories in one or two Colonies are somewhat primitive, in most they are large and highly mechanised undertakings, approximating more closely in character than anything else in the West Indies to the typical machine industry of a modern industrial country. But most of the sugar factories are carried on as an integral part of the work of the sugar estates; and there is obviously no scope for increasing the employment given by the sugar factories apart from an increase in the export sales of sugar. Rum distilleries are another type of industrial establishment associated with the sugar industry.

18. Some of the products of tropical agriculture are, however, the raw materials of manufacturing industries which may be, but need not be, carried on in the Colonies where the agricultural commodities are grown. Coconuts which are widely grown throughout the West Indies are of especial interest in this connection. From coconuts, or from the copra into which they are converted by a simple process, a considerable range of commodities may be manufactured; soap, margarine, edible oils, lard substitute. These are commodities that are consumed on a considerable scale by the West Indian population; and local factories have been established, which in Trinidad and Jamaica supply practically the whole of the local demand for edible oils, and part of the local demand for other coconut products. The possibility of extending the local manufacture of coconut products is a subject much discussed in the West Indies and raises an important issue of official policy. The existing local industries have been made possible by duties or restrictions upon competing imports; these consist partly of the ordinary customs duties imposed for revenue purposes, but the import of edible oils into Jamaica is prohibited except under licence, while Trinidad imposes prohibitive tariffs upon them. We have had representations made to us that the local manufacture of other coconut products should be stimulated by similar means; and we shall consider the question of policy that arises in Chapter XIII. But it should be observed here that such schemes are advocated primarily for the purpose of raising the price of copra for the benefit of the coconut growers. The number of workpeople employed by the coconut products industries is not considerable and can hardly become so. The same observation holds good of such undertakings as citrus packing stations and citrus canning plants and the condensed milk factory which is shortly to be established in Jamaica. They may serve to improve the market for agricultural products; but they cannot become important as employers of labour.

19. Apart from the two categories that have been indicated, a few miscellaneous manufactures are carried on in the West Indies. Aerated water factories are to be found in most Colonies; and match factories in several. In Jamaica there are a few tanneries and leather works, a chemical works and a tobacco factory. But the extent of the industrial development, regarded as a whole, is slight. By far the greater part of the manufactured goods, including the clothes, consumed by the West Indian populations is imported from abroad, chiefly from Great Britain and the United States. Despite the considerable extent of the peasant population in many Colonies, there is a marked lack of peasant industries. The peasant earthenware industry in Barbados is one of the few instances.

20. In small island communities, it might have been supposed that fishing would be an important occupation. But fishing villages are rare, and do not seem to have been successful. Fish forms an important element in the diet of the populations; but this is mostly salt fish imported from Canada and Newfoundland. Few people in the West Indies appear to take any serious interest in fishing, and we found it impossible to obtain any definite information that would enable us to judge how far future development might be feasible.

21. British Honduras and British Guiana have important forest resources. The export of forest products, especially mahogany, is indeed the main basis of the economic life of the former Colony; but the demand for mahogany has, subject to ups and downs, been declining for a considerable time. The greenheart timber of British Guiana is of great value for many purposes owing to its exceptional durability; and the small industry concerned with its exploitation has been expanding fairly steadily. It was represented to us that a profitable industry for the manufacture of woodpulp from wallaba trees might be established in British Guiana.

22. The tourist trade is a factor of some importance in the economic life of Jamaica, Barbados and Trinidad. It affords in various ways a considerable amount of employment, though this is mainly, like the traffic itself, of a highly seasonal character; and being in effect an " invisible " export industry, it helps to maintain the balance of payments of these Colonies. This tourist trade has grown materially in recent years. It is promoted in Trinidad and Jamaica by Tourist Boards, which are financed by Government grants, and in the case of Jamaica by the proceeds of a small tax on tourists. Some of the smaller islands, particularly the Windwards, have also considerable attractions to offer tourists; but the difficulty of getting to and from these islands with the limited means of transport at present

available is a serious obstacle to the development of any important trade. None the less, in St. Vincent and Antigua, enterprising individuals are sinking money in the erection cf bungalows and hotels for the attraction of visitors. It is difficult to estimate the extent to which the tourist trade is capable of further extension and development: it is a trade which is subject to fashions and is easily frightened away and it is liable to sharp fluctuations in accordance with the ups and downs of economic prosperity in the countries from which the tourists come. None the less it is a trade of considerable importance, which is expanding and capable, under peace conditions, of further expansion; and there are unfortunately not many trades in the West Indies to-day of which this can be said.

23. An important fraction of the population in the West Indies, as everywhere else, is engaged in retail trade, commerce, professional occupations, and transport. But an expansion in such forms of employment is obviously dependent on an expansion of the general economic activity of the community.

24. Agriculture is the main basis of the economic life of the West Indies; and, as will be evident from the foregoing survey of other activities, it must necessarily remain so. The possibilities of establishing new types of industry are being keenly discussed in several Colonies, particularly in Jamaica; and various proposals have been submitted to us, raising issues of policy, which we shall consider in Part III of our report. But even if the most optimistic hopes of the advocates of new industries were to be realised, the essential dependence of the West Indies upon agriculture would not be materially affected.

3. The Agricultural Export Outlook.

25. Agriculture in the West Indies is mainly directed to production for export. This holds good not only of estate agriculture, but in almost equal degree of the agriculture of small peasants. It is true that what are called " ground provisions " (i.e., starch foods, such as yams, sweet potatoes, tannias, eddoes, etc.), which form part of the local diet, are extensively grown throughout the West Indies. But, except that in Barbados sweet potatoes are cultivated in a systematic manner by the sugar estates, these are not grown to a very large extent for sale. The average estate labourer grows his own ground provisions on the small plot of land allowed him by the estate. The peasant equally grows ground provisions on part of his holding. But so far as production for sale is concerned, both the estates and the peasants think mainly in terms of export markets, so much so that " cash crop " and " export crop " are virtually interchangeable terms in the West Indies. The

Chapter II.

greater part of the food requirements of the population other than ground provisions, is met by imports; flour, salt fish, meat and condensed milk all being imported in substantial quantities.

26. The following table shows the value of the principal agricultural exports from the West Indian Colonies as a whole for the year 1937:—

	Value. £
Sugar and Sugar Products	6,895,000
Bananas	2,715,000
Cocoa	896,000
Nutmegs and other Spices	393,000
Coconuts and Coconut Products	322,000
Grapefruit and Oranges	203,000
Coffee	177,000
Rice	163,000
Cotton	127,000
Limes and Lime Oil	104,000
Arrowroot	90,000
Tobacco	26,000

The predominance of sugar in the agriculture of the West Indies as a whole will be apparent. But in several Colonies other crops are of major importance; and it will be convenient first to review the position of these other commodities.

27. Bananas have been for many years past the principal crop of Jamaica. In 1937, the exports of bananas from Jamaica amounted to £2,657,000 or to over 50 per cent. of the total exports from the island; the exports of sugar and rum being no more than £1,131,000. It is true that banana exports were abnormally large in 1937, as a consequence of deferred production in the previous year due to hurricane damage; but banana exports have over a long period far exceeded those of sugar. The growing of bananas is, moreover, in a large degree a peasant industry. It was as a small settler's crop that the banana was originally introduced into Jamaica; and, though it is now grown extensively by large and medium-sized estates, it is still the crop to which the majority of small settlers mainly devote themselves. The banana industry is thus of fundamental importance in the economic structure of Jamaica.

28. For several years, moreover, it has been on the whole a comparatively prosperous industry. As the result partly of tariff preferences in the British and Canadian markets and partly of a favourable agreement which has been made with the shipping companies, the Jamaican growers are able to sell their bananas on relatively advantageous terms, receiving prices that are usually at least one-third higher than those received by growers in foreign countries like Costa Rica and Colombia. Subject moreover to a minimum price of 2s. 3d.

per count bunch, the prices received by the Jamaican growers are related to the current wholesale price in London in accordance with a sliding-scale, so that the growers are assured on the one hand of sharing promptly in the benefits of a rise in the London price and protected on the other against the possibility of a severe fall. With the prices secured under this arrangement, the Jamaican producers, both estates and peasants until recently earned very satisfactory returns, subject to the vicissitudes of hurricane damage.

29. The rapid spread of leaf-spot disease within the last few years and especially within the last few months has however transformed the situation. The greater part of the island is now seriously affected by this disease, and it must be expected that for some time the output of bananas will be substantially reduced in quantity and also impaired to some extent in quality as a consequence. Leaf-spot disease can, it is true, be controlled, and, for this reason, it is argued by a section of agricultural scientists that it will prove in the long run a less serious menace to the industry than Panama disease, a disease residing in the soil, which spreads much more slowly, but which renders it impossible to grow bananas again for several years on the lands that it has once touched. But leaf-spot disease represents by far the more urgent problem: the method of controlling it entails spraying the banana trees with chemical mixtures, and it is now evident, if the Jamaican banana industry is to be saved, that spraying must become a normal part of the routine of cultivation. But spraying is an expensive process, costing even in the case of large estates operating on level land about 8d. per count bunch, or something like one-quarter of the price normally received by the Jamaican grower. For the small peasant, growing his bananas up hill-sides, the high-pressure methods of spraying, entailing the use of pipe-lines, that have been evolved in Central American countries, are altogether impracticable; but it is hoped in Jamaica that low-pressure spraying, with the chemical mixture carried in knapsacks, may prove a satisfactory alternative. A scheme for the organisation and supervision of spraying operations is being adopted in Jamaica, with financial support from public funds.

30. On the most optimistic view, however, the control of leaf-spot disease will add materially to the costs of banana production in Jamaica; so that had it not been for a substantial rise in the prices received by growers above the level prevailing during our visit to the island, it would be inevitable that the earnings of both estates and peasants would be seriously reduced, and that many of the less efficient producers would be forced to abandon cultivation. The smaller output of bananas serves as an influence making for higher prices; and the London wholesale price had in fact risen appreciably before the war began.

Chapter II.

If peace had been maintained this rise of prices might have proved transient in view of the desire of the fruit companies to maintain the policy of the penny banana in the British market, and the possibility of importing supplies from foreign countries. Under war conditions, on the other hand, it seems reasonable to assume, if only on account of the increase in transport costs, that the London wholesale price will remain at a high level. In these circumstances the Jamaican growers may expect to receive a good price under the sliding-scale referred to above. Thus war conditions are likely to bring a much-needed relief to the Jamaican banana industry, and it is to be hoped that it will succeed in using this breathing-space to work out an effective system of leaf-spot control. But the long-run outlook for the industry is far less favourable than it was a few years ago.*

31. The growing of bananas is also of some importance in British Honduras, where they form the principal agricultural export. But the soils of this Colony are not well-suited for the crop. In the Windward Islands and in Dominica, they are fairly extensively grown; and in Grenada, in particular, the industry offers possibilities of expansion, which though limited for reasons of suitability of soil, might provide a slight measure of compensation for the probable decline of the cocoa industry. In these islands, the crop has the attraction at present of a definite and assured price to the growers though not so high a price as obtained in Jamaica.

32. Cocoa is grown chiefly in Trinidad and Grenada. It was for a long period the major agricultural export of Trinidad, though it now takes second place to sugar. In Grenada, it is still the main export, though it no longer greatly exceeds the export of nutmegs and mace. Like bananas, cocoa is in a very large degree a peasant crop; and the prominent part played by peasants in the economic structure of Grenada is closely associated with the development of cocoa-growing. For many years, though always liable to severe fluctuations of price in accordance with the ups and downs of general trade activity, cocoa was an exceptionally profitable crop. The rapid expansion in the consumption of chocolate and cocoa by the peoples of Europe and United States led to a prevailing tendency for the world demand for raw cocoa to exceed the supply; and prices fluctuated accordingly about a level that was very satisfactory to growers.

33. But in the last 10 years, this favourable price position has been radically changed. The world production of raw cocoa has undergone so large and rapid an expansion in this period as to outstrip the expansion of demand, and prices have fallen as a consequence. The increase in supply is mainly due to an enormous growth in the production of two British Colonies,

---

* See also note at end of Chapter XVI (page 312).

the Gold Coast and Nigeria, which, unimportant as producers a generation ago, now grow 20 times as much cocoa as Trinidad and Grenada together, and supply nearly 60 per cent. of the world's requirements. The cocoa of Trinidad and Grenada is of a superior quality, which enables it to command a premium over African cocoa. But this premium, which has been substantial in the past, has markedly diminished in recent years, owing largely to new methods of chocolate manufacture. On the other hand the costs of production in the West Indies are much higher than in Africa or indeed in Brazil owing partly to the higher West Indian standard of life and partly to other causes. Accordingly, prices that are ruinous to West Indian growers will not necessarily check the expansion of world production. In these circumstances, there is no solid basis for expecting prices to recover materially from their present level. It seems unlikely, moreover, that the influence of the war, which cuts off German consumption, without doing anything to curtail world production, will be favourable to cocoa prices.

34. At the present level of prices, most of the planters and peasants engaged in cocoa poduction are unable to make ends meet. Many of them have made losses for several years, and have carried on by borrowing, hoping for a recovery of prices. A substantial recovery of prices did in fact occur in the latter part of 1936, forming part of that year's general upward movement in the prices of primary products: but it quickly disappeared; and prices are down again at about their lowest levels. It has now become clear that the majority of West Indian cocoa growers cannot continue in business, without either financial assistance or a radical change in their present system of cultivation.

35. The possibilities of improving the system of cultivation are discussed in Chapter XXI of the *agricultural report. But even if the most optimistic hopes of the advocates of new methods are realised, it is unlikely that the cocoa industry will continue to provide a livelihood for as many persons as are now engaged in it. As regards financial assistance, the Government of Trinidad already pays a subsidy to its cocoa-growers, on a complex and frequently changing plan, which is directed partly to the purpose of encouraging improved methods of cultivation and partly to supplementing the price of cocoa. But the Government of Grenada lacks the means to give any similar assistance. Indeed the unfavourable outlook for the cocoa industry confronts Grenada with an extremely formidable problem, since its other main industry, nutmegs, though less seriously depressed, suffers from increasing competition from the Dutch East Indies, while the population of the island is increasing very rapidly.

---

* See also paragraphs 62 and 63 of Chapter XVI.

Chapter II.

36. The peace time outlook for coconut producers, though far less desperate than that for cocoa growers, is decidedly unfavourable. The confectionery and allied trades constitute a market for a limited quantity of fresh nuts; and Jamaica whose coconuts are of good quality does a fairly considerable trade in supplying this demand at prices that are not unprofitable. But for the most part coconuts are converted into copra, and form one of many competing sources of the supply of oil nuts and seeds. The price of copra has followed in recent years a very similar course to that of cocoa, falling heavily in the slump years of 1930-2, experiencing a short-lived recovery in the latter part of 1936, and having since fallen back to a very low level. In view of the prevailing tendency towards an enlarged supply of oil seeds and nuts of various kinds, any large and sustained recovery in the price of copra seems improbable under peace conditions, though a temporary improvement during war may be expected. Unless the price of copra improves, it is improbable that employment in the coconut industry can be increased, if indeed it can be maintained. Faced with unremunerative prices, producers endeavour, however unwisely, to reduce their costs of production by stinting their expenditure on cultivation; and this entails a diminution in the number of labourers they employ. The industry, moreover, is one that involves a long capital lock-up in trees that do not yield a return for several years; and the investment of fresh capital cannot be expected so long as the market outlook remains unattractive.

37. The growing of both oranges and grape-fruit in Jamaica, and of grape-fruit in Trinidad, represents an industry of some importance, with possibilities of development that are not negligible though they are at present highly uncertain. In Jamaica, special encouragement was given to the industry in 1930 by a Government grant to the Jamaican Citrus Producers' Association, a co-operative organisation of producers, for a central packing house for the purpose of improving the preparation of the fruit for the market. Much progress was made in the ensuing years in developing a trade in oranges with Canada, New Zealand and the United Kingdom. But the trend of prices was unfavourable. The Producers' Association, which was unable owing to differences about marketing policy to secure the adhesion of certain of the most enterprising growers in the island, found itself in financial difficulties, with the result that in 1935 the Government decided to give it further assistance and took over the packing house. At the same time, Government loans were made available to planters for laying out new citrus orchards of standard varieties; and the ability of many of the less skilful planters to repay these loans is regarded as doubtful unless they can secure better financial returns from their production. Thus, while the Jamaican citrus industry has

expanded steadily in the last 10 years, its financial position is by no means satisfactory.

38. The future of the citrus industry raises questions of much interest. It is an industry in which organised and up-to-date methods of marketing are of vital importance; and there remains much scope in Jamaica for rationalising and improving the present marketing methods. Plans to secure this object were being actively considered during our stay in the island. The world demand for citrus is large, and has steadily expanded in recent years; and it is not therefore outside the range of possibility that some development of the Jamaican citrus trade might be secured by raising the general standard of cultivation methods and by adopting more orderly methods of marketing, coupled with an energetic and resourceful sales policy. On the other hand, the productive capacity in the world is also being increased very rapidly; large numbers of trees have been planted in Palestine, for example, in recent years, which have still to bear fruit; and it is not unlikely that a serious excess of supply over demand leading to a slump of prices may before long disclose itself. Difficult questions of policy in regard to preferential tariffs arise in this connection, which we must defer for later consideration. War conditions are not likely to be helpful to the citrus industry.

39. The growing of limes has been for a long period the staple industry of Dominica; but this industry has been afflicted by a series of adverse influences—a succession of hurricanes which caused widespread damage, an outbreak of wither-tip disease, and the virtual disappearance of the market for natural lime juice, owing to the use of synthetic substitutes. Inasmuch as lime-juice and lime-oil are, or used to be, in some degree joint products, this has been a severe blow to the industry, despite the maintenance of the market for lime-oil. The lime industry is also of considerable importance in Trinidad, St. Vincent and British Guiana but it has been adversely affected by the decline in purchases by the United States. Jamaica has in the last two years built up a small trade in fresh limes to the London market, largely through the agency of the newly-established Agricultural Marketing Division; but it remains to be seen whether this trade can be extended sufficiently to become of real importance.

40. The substantial figure in the table in paragraph 26 above for the export of rice represents almost entirely exports from British Guiana to the neighbouring colony of Trinidad. This is at present a declining industry. British Guiana has to compete in the Trinidad market with rice from Burma and India; and it has become evident that an improvement in the quality and efficiency of milling, which it is proposed to effect by establishing

central mills under a Government scheme, is essential to maintain this trade.

41. Arrowroot and sea-island cotton are the staple products of St. Vincent; and sea-island cotton is also grown in some of the Leeward Islands. The arrowroot industry experienced prolonged adversity in the early post-war period; but, owing mainly to a compulsory marketing system, by which all the arrowroot of the island is processed and sold by a single organisation, the Arrowroot Association, it is now in a fairly satisfactory condition with a steady increase in its volume of sales at prices which, though not highly profitable, are remunerative. The market for arrowroot, however, though increasing slowly, is very limited in extent; and any successful attempt to introduce arrowroot into other West Indian Colonies could only serve to deprive St. Vincent of its present trade. The world demand for sea-island cotton underwent a severe contraction after the war of 1914-1918, owing partly to the decline of the lace industry and partly to the competition of artificial silk. In the last five years there has been a recovery, due mainly to demands of a rearmament character; and the West Indian crops have been marketed at profitable prices. The outlook for this industry is, however, precarious, particularly in view of the likelihood of increasing competition, and it offers little hope of material expansion. Coffee which used to be grown largely in Jamaica for export has been for many years a declining industry; and at the present level of prices, there is little hope of recovery. Tobacco for commercial manufacture is grown in Jamaica, mainly on larger peasant holdings, and has been introduced recently on a smaller scale in Dominica and the Virgin Islands. Expert inquiry and advice (see para. 8 in Chapter XI of the agricultural report*) should precede any considerable expansion of this development.

42. It will be apparent from this survey that the present outlook for the export agriculture of the West Indies, apart from the sugar industry, is extremely discouraging. Only the citrus industry offers a reasonable hope, and that a highly uncertain one, of material expansion. A diminishing volume of employment is the prospect in most of the other branches of agriculture; and the outlook for the two most important of them, the Jamaica banana industry and the cocoa industry of Trinidad and Grenada, is grave in the extreme. Great importance attaches therefore to the prospects of the sugar industry which we shall now proceed to examine.

4. The Sugar Position.

43. Barbados, British Guiana, St. Kitts and Antigua depend almost entirely upon sugar. It is once more the principal crop of Trinidad; it is the main crop of St. Lucia, and it is beginning

---

* See also paragraph 23 (*a*) of Chapter XVI.

again to rival the importance of bananas in Jamaica. The production of sugar in the West Indies has undergone a great expansion in the past ten years, as is indicated by the following table which includes all the territories whose output of sugar was of any significance:—

Sugar Production.

	1928	1938-9 (*estimate*)
	Tons	Tons
Barbados	63,100	151,000
British Guiana	116,100	188,000
Trinidad	81,600	115,000
Jamaica	62,500	106,000
St. Kitts-Nevis	19,400	29,000
Antigua	19,700	23,000
St. Lucia	4,800	8,000
Total	367,200	620,000

44. This remarkable increase has been made possible by a combination of two factors, (1) a great reduction in production costs, both in the field and in the factory, (2) substantial preferential assistance in the markets of Great Britain and Canada. The progress that has been made under the former head is noteworthy. Ten years ago, the sugar industry was faced with a serious crisis that led to the appointment of Lord Olivier's Sugar Commission. Lord Olivier and his colleague reported (Cmd. 3517) that " present costs of reasonably efficient production, excluding provision for profit, depreciation, maintenance, or progressive improvement, exceed preferential market prices by amounts up to £2 per ton "; and they recommended that the price of colonial sugar should be stabilized at the figure of £15 per ton, c.i.f. London, by means of a revolutionary change in marketing arrangements that would substitute a single buying agency for the present London sugar market. In recent years, the price received by colonial producers has been nearly always materially below £12 per ton, c.i.f. London, which was the lowest point it touched at the time of the Olivier Commission. Yet the reduction effected in costs has been sufficient to enable the industry, not only to continue in existence, but to increase its production to the extent that has been shown. This reduction of costs has been effected by greater efficiency.

45. But the preferential assistance which the industry has received has been a vital factor. Since the early post-war period the Colonies have received the advantage of an Imperial Preference in the United Kingdom market amounting to £3 15s. per ton. As a sequel to the crisis of ten years ago and the recommendations of the Olivier Commission, a supplementary preference, limited to colonial producers, has since been given under a complex scheme of Colonial Sugar Certificates, the value of which is equivalent on the average to about £1 per ton of sugar

exported. The total preferential assistance now amounts to fully 40 per cent. of the price received by colonial producers. During most of the period during which we were in the West Indies the world price of sugar was about £6 10s. per ton, c.i.f. London. This was the price, that is to say, obtained by Cuban and other foreign producers, for the sugar which they sold in the London market. But the effect of the preferential aids was to make the corresponding price received by British colonial producers about £11 5s. per ton. It should be observed that the preferential prices paid by the United States and by France to their respective colonial producers, are very much higher than this, amounting to nearly £16 in the former case, and to about £18* in the latter. It may be added that Canada also gives a preference to West Indian sugar of £4 13s. 4d. per ton, the main significance of which is that it relieves the British Exchequer of the financial burden in respect of that part of the West Indian output which is exported to Canada.

46. With this large preferential assistance, added to the rapid improvement in their technical efficiency, the sugar producers of the West Indian and other British Colonies succeeded in increasing their exports to the British market at the expense of those of foreign countries like Cuba, which had previously enjoyed the advantage of lower costs. But this process entailed a continued fall in the world price of sugar, and along with it of the preferential price, and a serious injury to the interests of foreign sugar-producing countries. Eventually, accordingly, an international regulation scheme of the familiar type was negotiated under which the principal producing countries agreed to limit their exports in accordance with a schedule of quotas. By virtue of this International Sugar Agreement, which came into effect in 1937, and which was to run in peace until 1942, the further expansion of sugar exports from the British Colonies was limited to a proportionate share of any increase that might take place in the demand of the United Kingdom or the rest of what is termed the " free market ".

47. Thus, until the situation was transformed by the outbreak of war, a serious obstacle had been placed in the way of a further expansion of the sugar industry. Adventitious circumstances in fact occurred to permit unexpected and welcome increases in the quota allocated to the colonial empire in the last two years. None the less, the expansion of the industry was checked in many Colonies; on the basis of the provisions of the Agreement, there would be a very serious danger that the output of sugar might have to be restricted in the near future, in which case the volume of employment in the industry would probably undergo a more than proportionate contraction.

---

* *Note.*—It would not be safe, of course, to assume that the Colonial populations secure the whole benefit of these higher prices.

48. For, in this connection, it is important to observe that the big reduction in the costs of production which has enabled the industry to supply a steadily increasing quantity of sugar to the British consumer at a falling price has necessarily entailed a reduction in the amount of labour employed per ton of sugar. The technical improvements have indeed mainly taken such forms as the use of higher-yielding varieties of cane, and the extraction of more sugar in the factory from a given quantity of cane. The volume of employment in many instances has increased materially but not proportionately to the increase in the output of sugar. A limitation of the exports of sugar from the West Indies to their present level would probably entail a gradual decline in the volume of employment. Inasmuch as the expansion of the sugar industry has been the chief means in recent years of absorbing the rapidly growing population of working age, this would be a most serious matter. An appeal for larger sugar quotas was one of the most widely and most strongly pressed of the demands we encountered in the West Indies; and we shall consider in Part III how far it may be practicable and expedient to meet it.

5. The World Economic Background.

49. The economic outlook, so far as we have already sketched it, is sufficiently depressing; but there is something more to be said before the picture is complete. The West Indies, as our introductory Chapter has made plain, have passed through many serious vicissitudes of fortune. The sugar industry has apparently been ruined on several occasions and widespread distress has often ensued but sooner or later, from one quarter or another, the economic life of the West Indies has received a fresh impulse; and, though the general standard of living has remained low, trade and economic activity again have moved rapidly forward. There may be many who will assume instinctively that this experience will once more be repeated.

50. It will be our object in the recommendations that we make in this report to do our utmost to secure that this optimistic state of mind is justified by the event. But it would be dangerous in the extreme to place any reliance on a spontaneous process of recovery. There is a radical difference between the economic difficulties that face the West Indies to-day, and those that they had to encounter in the nineteenth century. Then the world demand for almost every tropical product was increasing so rapidly as to outstrip, subject to the ordinary ups and downs of trade, the available supply, and to require for its satisfaction the opening-up, one after the other, of new productive areas. Even the set-backs to the West Indian sugar industry did not represent a prolonged condition of world over-production. They reflected rather the vagaries of the fiscal policy of Great Britain

and other European countries. Though the West Indian producers might find themselves in difficulties, the price of sugar was sufficiently profitable to stimulate a large extension of production in other parts of the world, including other countries in the Caribbean area, such as Cuba.

51. But, in the case of many, if not most, tropical commodities, the development of new productive areas has been carried so far that the productive capacity seems now to be greatly in excess of the requirements not only of the present world demand but of any expansion of that demand that is probable in an early future. For it must be remembered that agricultural technique is now improving more rapidly than it did formerly, so that a given productive capacity is now capable of taking care of quite a considerable rate of increase in demand. There is as a consequence a prevailing tendency towards the oversupply of most tropical agricultural commodities, and a prevailing tendency towards a depression of prices. The present economic difficulties of the British West Indian Colonies are in no way peculiar to them. They are difficulties common to the Caribbean area as a whole. Indeed they are more acutely felt in sovereign countries that do not receive the benefits that Colonies derive from the preferential systems of their mother countries. Hence the new rigid restrictions on immigration imposed by countries that used to welcome immigrants. The war may cause a passing improvement in the prices of some tropical products. But not only will the relief so afforded be temporary: it cannot be expected to be so substantial as it was in 1914-18, when the outbreak of war found Great Britain drawing a large part of her normal sugar supplies from what was then the Austro-Hungarian Empire.

52. The trend of world conditions, which was generally favourable in the nineteenth century, has become generally adverse to-day to the development of tropical communities basing their economic life on the export of agricultural commodities. This fact both adds to the gravity of the economic difficulties of our West Indian Colonies, and complicates, in ways that will become apparent later, the problem of relieving them.

CHAPTER III.

SOCIAL STRUCTURE AND CONDITIONS.

1. In this Chapter our main concern will be the conditions of life of the non-European populations—the negroes, whose ancestors were brought to the West Indies in a condition of slavery, and the East Indians, who came in circumstances which cannot be regarded as equivalent to the immigration of free settlers. Many of our comments will obviously relate to the negro population alone; but most of them apply to all non-Europeans whose livelihood lies in work on the land or in the towns for wages—in fact to the labouring classes. Certain matters specifically affecting the East Indians will be dealt with in Chapter XXIV below.

2. The negroes were taken from lands where they lived no doubt in a primitive state, but at any rate under certain social traditions and subject to customs and usages which modern anthropology increasingly shows to have definite social, economic and cultural value. Their transfer to the West Indies, unlike most other large-scale movements of population, did not involve the transfer of any important traces of their traditions and customs, but rather their almost complete destruction. The negroes had one function only—the provision of cheap labour on estates owned and managed by Europeans for the production of their valuable export crops. They lost their language, customs and religion, and no systematic attempt was made to substitute any others. Even in the 18th Century there were not wanting well-intentioned planters, such as Foster and Barham, who introduced into Jamaica the Moravians, and the work of the negro preachers Lisle and Baker, dating from 1783, survives to this day in the flourishing negro Baptist Church. After the turn of the century, other and better-known efforts were made for the amelioration of the lot of the slaves, and the names of the Baptists Knibb and Burchell stand out in the campaign for the abolition of slavery. But the heroic efforts of many denominations to Christianise the slaves, and teach them, met on the whole with great opposition, and could not in the nature of things touch more than a fraction of the populations involved. Marriage among slaves was discouraged, if not completely forbidden.

3. These things have left their mark. The coming of emancipation gave a strong, if temporary, impetus to such forces as were working for the betterment of the negro populations. From an early date both Government and churches embarked on the provision of educational facilities, and Governments have for

some time recognised that their duties include care for the health and general welfare of all sections of the community. But emancipation saw also a disintegration of West Indian society. Itself a blow to the prosperity of the West Indian sugar industry (though mitigated by the payment to slave owners of compensation of some £20,000,000 from the British Exchequer), it was followed by fiscal changes in the United Kingdom which had the effect of transferring a large part of English custom to cheaper producers such as Cuba where slavery continued, and the industry was impoverished just at that time when planters and owners had ceased to have even a proprietary interest in the welfare of their workers. Simultaneously, there was on the part of the workers a drift away from estate labour. Even during slavery, many negroes had escaped from the plantations and in Jamaica after much bloodshed and struggle had established themselves in the remoter and more mountainous parts in self-contained communities with which the central Government interfered but little. To these nuclei were added thousands of recruits attracted by the freedom for which independent land-ownership has traditionally stood. Some land settlement schemes were encouraged both by Government and by the churches; but land settlement in its social aspect has always had a connotation of independence from economic and political thraldom, which makes it more difficult than would otherwise be the case to control and guide it along the most satisfactory social, economic and agricultural lines.

4. The circumstances following emancipation, therefore, lacked the solid economic foundation which would be necessary for the emergence of any very definite social pattern. The population was divided into those who tended to escape from the influence of the estates and from contact with Europeans into often remote and inaccessible holdings of small parcels of land, and those—a diminishing number—who remained on the estates under conditions little, if at all, superior to those prevailing under slavery. The settlers probably formed then, as they do now, the solidest and most enterprising section of the negro population. But uncertainties of land tenure helped to maintain the practice native to African tradition of following a system of destructive shifting cultivation (especially persistent to-day in the Windward and Leeward Islands under the title of " squatting ") which militates against sound agricultural practice, the conservation of soil fertility and the attainment of any degree of prosperity and social security. Among the estate labourers, the depression in the sugar industry which followed emancipation prevented the use of their new-found liberty to attain better wages and higher standards of living, and the subsequent introduction of indentured labourers from India has helped to keep wages down ever since.

5. The best endeavours of the churches, together with what Governments saw fit to do from time to time, did not reach the bulk of the population, and it is not surprising that, for example, the institution of marriage continued to be exceptional. More or less faithful extra-legal unions and illegitimacy rates of between 60-70 per cent. have remained the rule. Several witnesses assured us that there is at present no tendency towards an increase in marriages, and that among the extra-legal unions, casual and promiscuous practices were on the whole gaining at the expense of what is described as " faithful concubinage ". To these factors may be added developments in transport which make it easier for the unscrupulous or improvident father to evade his responsibilities towards his children and their probably unmarried mother. The task which confronts the reformer and the social worker is therefore more complex than ever before, and the times find the churches, who have done and are doing much for the mass of the people, with diminished and diminishing resources.

6. It has become increasingly necessary for Government itself to assume active responsibility in social matters. In the field of public health progress has been considerable, as the trend of vital statistics suggests, although very much remains to be done particularly in the fields of preventive medicine and the inculcation of knowledge of hygiene and nutrition. The State is also having to take over the financial responsibility for education and in general to undertake on a comprehensive scale work that has here and there been started by the enterprise and devotion of private individuals and institutions. Social reform in the West Indies has had to come from above, as the mass of the population have had insufficient experience of conditions elsewhere to be in a position to formulate demands. This state of affairs is rapidly changing, owing to the influence of education and the press, broadcasting, the tales of emigrants returned from Cuba and the American mainland, but the stage has not yet been reached when the demands of the people themselves have definitely crystallised. It remains for the State to initiate, plan and guide, although it does well to take careful heed of the expressions of opinion of a populace rapidly reaching a state of social self-consciousness.

7. It is necessary at this point to consider the social implications of wage rates and the labour market, which are discussed with fuller detail in Chapter X below (Labour and Trade Unions). In investigating these matters, we had before us the material prepared by the various West Indian Governments for Major G. St. J. Orde Browne, Labour Adviser to the Secretary of State, whose report on Labour Conditions in the West Indies was published in July, 1939, as Cmd. 6070. We also had the advantage of a discussion with Major Orde Browne himself

Chapter III.

during our stay in Trinidad, as well as with officials and private persons in the Colonies which we visited. To take first wages, we find that the rates paid, while varying from Colony to Colony, from industry to industry and even from estate to estate within the same Colony, can only be described as very low indeed for the vast majority of the labouring population, namely, those employed on the land. In some parts of the West Indies, notably the smaller and poorer islands, rates for agricultural labourers have advanced little beyond the shilling-a-day introduced after emancipation. Examples are the 1s. 2d. a day in St. Kitts (subject to a very recent 25 per cent. increase), the statutory minimum of 1s. 3d. (1s. for women) in Grenada and St. Lucia, 1s. 1d. and 10d. in St. Vincent. In the larger and more prosperous Colonies, wages, starting from this basic level, have shown some advances, examples being 2s. 2d. per day in British Guiana (1s. 6½d. for women), 1s. 10d.-3s. 4d. in Trinidad (1s.-1s. 10d. for women), 1s. 10d in Jamaica (3s. 3d. in Kingston being a corresponding rate). These figures apply to ordinary field and unskilled labour; other and much higher rates are paid in other circumstances.

8. Low as these rates may be, the history of wage rates during the period since the war does not suggest that they are the only cause of the rising discontent which has latterly found violent expression in more than one Colony. To take Jamaica again as an example (since comparable statistics are there more readily available than elsewhere), the movement of wages for the last 25 years shows a rise from pre-war rates to a peak in the years immediately following the war, followed by a decline which even in the worst year, 1932, did not touch the low pre-war level. Since that year there have been general rises, in some cases preceding but more often succeeding the disturbances. The course of events in other parts of the West Indies is not dissimilar: the years since the worst of the depression have shown an upward tendency varying in degree from place to place. But it does not appear that such increases as have been granted have done much to allay the discontent which in part brought them about: in Jamaica at least that discontent is to-day more pronounced than ever, and not least among the dock-labourers, whose rates of pay when they can get work are among the best in the Island.

9. This points to what we consider to be the most serious problem in the labour situation and consequently the life of the vast majority of the people of the West Indies—namely, the problem of intermittent employment, both in towns and in the country. The actual wages paid may or may not be reasonably satisfactory for persons in full employment—we consider that in many cases they are not—but at the present time the question

does not arise for a tragically large proportion of the labouring population: full employment and regular wages are not available for them. It may be possible for a Jamaican wharf labourer, for example, to earn 10d. or 11d. per hour, but he cannot rely on working on more than one steamer a week, and that for a period from 6 to 14 hours. Similarly, in Barbados, a stevedore may earn 8s. 4d.-10s. for a 9-hour day; but it must be remembered that by far the greater proportion of the island's export of sugar is shipped in a period of a few weeks, apart from which there is little or no work for the army of labourers needed to handle it.

10. This problem of intermittent labour is traditional in the towns and ports: to it has recently been added an equally serious problem of rural under-employment. The effects of low prices and limitation of output under the International Sugar Agreement, and of the rise in wage-rates itself, calling for economy of management and the curtailment of activity, have restricted the volume of work available for the estate labourer, and the difficulty of securing an adequate cash income from the cultivation of export crops has caused many more peasants than before to seek to supplement their incomes by wage labour in a labour market already overcrowded. Rural conditions of employment have thus tended to approximate more closely to those prevailing in the towns, with the important difference that even taking into account recent wage-increases, there remains a large disparity between the town *rate* and the country *rate*. The more regular employment which in the past tended to equalise actual earnings as between town and country is becoming a thing of the past.

11. The consequences of this depression in rural areas are obvious. It is next to impossible for the men to earn enough to support a family with the result that the women have also to work and cannot devote themselves to the maintenance of the home and the care of their children. The children themselves may be set to work to supplement the family's income when they should be at school, or the older children of school age are kept at home to look after their younger brothers and sisters. Only the prevalence of " food-gardens " even among estate labourers mitigates the severity of conditions in rural areas. Accurate facts are more than usually difficult to obtain in this matter; but we were satisfied that malnutrition due to insufficient and ill-balanced diets was common.

12. The increase in rural under-employment and the comparatively greater urban wage-increases have intensified the drift to the towns which is a characteristic of the West Indies as of practically all countries in the world. This tendency is most notable in Jamaica, where the lure of work at the docks

loading bananas, which is carried on all the year round, is potent and evil in its effects. But it is to be found as well wherever there is a centre of population and even the most illusory prospect of casual labour somewhat better paid than that available in the country. To Castries, in St. Lucia, once an important coaling centre, peasants will walk for many miles on a rumour that some work may be available at the docks. This tendency is vicious in its long-term effects. There is no economic possibility for large additional populations to establish themselves in conditions sufficiently stable to enable them to form and perpetuate a healthy community. Further, each influx dilutes the amount of employment available for the original inhabitants and drags down standards of life for others than the newcomers themselves.

13. The condition of many of the townspeople, as we saw for ourselves, is pitiable. Of the condition of much of the housing we speak in Chapter IX; other circumstances are little better. The poorer quarters of towns such as Kingston (Jamaica), Georgetown (British Guiana), Bridgetown (Barbados), or Port-of-Spain (Trinidad), show all the obvious consequences of hunger, disease, ignorance and crime, and of shiftless improvidence. Evidence was submitted to us that gambling was rife in certain of the larger towns, and that quite an appreciable proportion of the exiguous earnings of many labourers disappeared through this channel. It is easy to condemn, and one cannot but regret, the futility of such expenditure; but it is impossible not to recognise it as the result of a natural craving for excitement in lives whose amusements are few, and an expression of the dream of pennies from heaven so appealing to those whose best efforts fail to provide them with a tolerable competence. Another problem is that of casualisation, consequent on a large surplus of labour over the supply of work. The system of part-time relief-works adopted by some Governments in a well-meant effort to alleviate the unemployment problem also tends in this direction, and this evil, like others, can be said to be a growing one. The position is further complicated by the disparity between urban and rural wage-rates: in Jamaica the daily wage of the Public Works Department labourers has been raised to 3s. 3d., and the Government has been presented with demands by those on relief to be paid at the same rate. As such relief-workers would normally be in rural employment at lower rates, Government is naturally reluctant to pay them more on relief than they would be obtaining in their normal employment. The cure for the evils of casualisation, and the attendant ones of thriftlessness and slackness, can only in the long run be to assist the workpeople to obtain through their own efforts a reasonable standard of living, including the opportunity of having a satisfying leisure life.

14. Peasant proprietors with fairly substantial holdings engaged in the production of a remunerative export crop constitute the only section of the working class which can be said to have attained anything like an adequate degree of security and prosperity. In Jamaica, for example, such peasants have hitherto formed an important element. But, apart from the threat that arises from the adverse trend of export markets, they appear now to be a diminishing element, owing to the sub-division of holdings into excessively small units, which is a natural consequence of the growth of population, and compels an increasing proportion of small settlers to supplement their incomes with wage-work. Where, however, the size of the holdings remains adequate, the peasants form the solidest element in West Indian society, and it is among them that the social virtues of forethought and the care of children are most commonly to be found.

15. The relatively satisfactory aspects of a section of peasant settlement and the parlous plight of most export industries have led some to advocate subsistence holdings as a means of solving the problems of unemployment and under-employment and the establishment of a healthy peasantry. The majority of our witnesses, however, held that such a development would be quite insufficient under present organisation without either the opportunity to grow some cash crops in addition or to obtain work for wages; although conversely the value to the community of opportunities for as many labourers as possible to grow some at least of their own food is inestimable.

16. This leads us to one final point of vital importance. One of the strongest and most discouraging impressions carried away by the investigator in the West Indies is that of a prevailing absence of a spirit of independence and self-help, the lack of a tradition of craftsmanship and pride in good work, and a tendency on all matters to appeal to Government for assistance with little or no attempt to explore what can be done by individual self-help. Isolated individuals may rise above this—many do—but the spirit is lacking except in some of the very small island communities. Without some such tradition, no amount of external and governmental help will create a sound and self-perpetuating social tradition. It is true that the history of the West Indies explains and accounts for this pauperisation; and we feel that it is incumbent upon the people of Britain to do what they can to help. But in the last resort the success or failure of any programme of social reform and betterment will depend on a definite and prolonged effort on the part of West Indians to help themselves even while accepting help. The material betterment of the West Indies must be accompanied by, and is to a large extent conditional on, a moral resurgence among the people themselves. We do not believe that the mere

removal of the causes of poverty, uncertainty and casualisation will of itself suffice to remove the evil consequences of these evils —improvidence, theft (in the very prevalent form of praedial larceny of crops), promiscuity, inefficiency. The history of reform shows again and again how easy it is for such traits to be retained even when the circumstances which gave them birth have been removed. They, like their causes, must be energetically attacked, and not least by the people themselves. It is here that we feel that the Churches in the West Indies will find a future to match their past.

CHAPTER IV.

THE AGRICULTURAL SYSTEM.*

1. General Remarks.

1. In the Colonies with which we are concerned a population of less than three million people is dispersed over an area of slightly more than sixty-eight million acres, of which over fifty-seven million acres are in British Guiana, where the population is estimated at less than 350,000, and nearly six million acres are in British Honduras, of which the population is less than 60,000. Considerably more than one half of the total area of all these Colonies is forest and the use of much of the remainder for agricultural purposes is made impossible by the nature of the soil. Nowhere can there be found any substantial area of agriculturally useful land which is not already under cultivation, and in all the Colonies the density of population in relation to cultivable land is high. Moreover population is steadily increasing at an average rate of over $1\frac{1}{2}$ per cent. per annum, and in the absence of any great possibilities for the establishment of manufacturing or other industries which would be capable of absorbing a substantial part of the people in a paying occupation, it is clearly imperative that agricultural production should be intensified in order to support this growing population even at the existing standards of life. (Chapter I, paragraph 8.)

2. The general level of agriculture in these Colonies is low in technical knowledge, business organisation and managerial efficiency; systematic agriculture, by which is meant mixed farming on a plan suited to the inherent circumstances of the area, is unknown. The basic types of agriculture in the West Indian Colonies are shifting cultivation, under which land may be used for, perhaps, two years in every eight or ten, and the continuous growing of one crop on the same land over a long period. Livestock are never the effective complement of crops and the connection between them is frequently adventitious or totally absent. So long as these methods continue it will be impossible for agricultural production to provide even the essentials of life for the growing population of the West Indian Colonies and comprehensive reform of existing agricultural methods is therefore inevitable.

---

* *Note.*—This Chapter is based upon those parts of Professor Engledow's full survey of agricultural resources and needs (Cmd. 6149) which are descriptive of the agricultural systems of the Colonies which we visited. Chapters XVI and XVII of this report are based upon the remainder of that survey, which is being published in a separate volume. It will no doubt be available to many readers of our report and it is for their convenience that in many places in this Chapter we have inserted references to the paragraphs of the survey in which the points here made briefly are more fully developed.

3. While it must be recognised that shifting cultivation is characteristic of vast areas in the tropical world and single crop agriculture prevails widely in North America, it must equally be recognised that a higher standard of living will not be possible in any of those areas until agricultural systems have been substantially improved. This is particularly true of the West Indian Colonies with their acute problem of providing for a dense and rapidly growing population. (Chapter I, paragraphs 10 and 11.)

2. Inherent Agricultural Circumstances.

4. Though the West Indian Colonies lie within the tropics the climate of most of them is sub-tropical and, owing mainly to the influence of prevalent sea breezes, the temperature is equable and its maximum is much lower than that of large land masses in the tropics. These conditions, when accompanied by the abundant rainfall which is normal in many of the territories, are very favourable to plant growth, but everywhere a dry period is characteristic and in several Colonies prolonged drought is not uncommon. The occurrence of a regular and marked dry season, with occasional droughts, is a serious handicap to agricultural development, especially on light soils, and a further climatic disability is the frequency of hurricanes which from time to time have done serious damage to crops in several of the islands and in British Honduras. From the evidence afforded by the growth of crops and from the limited scientific information which is at present available, it is reasonable to conclude that the soils of the West Indian Colonies as a whole are not outstandingly good and their average " condition ", by which is meant the component of its quality affected by agricultural treatment, is in many cases certainly very low. While great depth of soil is found in some parts, there are considerable areas of thin soil on a very poor sub-soil and others, especially on steep hillsides where shifting hand cultivation is often practised, in which mere pockets of soil are separated by a profusion of rocks. In short it can safely be said that neither the climate, nor the topography, nor the soil of these Colonies make for an easy affluence under any agricultural system; nor are they such as to sustain dense population without intensive and well-directed work. (Chapter III, paragraphs 1 to 8.)

5. Water supply, and problems connected with it, call for special mention. Although the rainfall is generally abundant there are areas in which water supplies are inadequate for human needs or preclude beneficial agricultural development, such as the practice of animal husbandry. In others the rainfall, though sufficient for these purposes, is such that it severely restricts the use of the land; in a third group, either

through an excessive rainfall or other natural causes, much land which would otherwise be cultivable is too swampy to be agriculturally useful. (Chapter III, paragraphs 12 and 13.)

6. The attitude of the West Indian people towards agriculture must be regarded as another circumstance affecting the possibilities of that development which in our view is essential. The general level of technical knowledge is low and a narrow outlook is typical of many sections of the agricultural community. These failings can be corrected by better education, but it will be more difficult to overcome the noticeable lack of enterprise and self-help which has been fostered, in part, by the frequency and form of assistance from Government by way of provision for relief from hurricane damage or subsidy for certain crops. The consequent reluctance to embark on any novel agricultural enterprise is in marked contrast to the misplaced enthusiasm with which, under the stimulus of one favourable year, the growing of an existing crop is often unduly extended, sometimes with the aid of borrowed money. It is, in our view, only too unfortunately true that in all such matters as enterprise, good judgment, deliberate policy and working efficiency, the general standard among the agriculturists of the West Indies is regrettably low: to this general conclusion we can make only the one exception that in seeking and promoting technical knowledge, in the enterprising conduct of their businesses and in efficient management, many of the sugar estates, though invariably producing but the one crop, stand out as an example of what can be done under West Indian conditions. (Chapter III, paragraph 14.)

7. It was represented to us by some witnesses, but denied by others, that the West Indian labourer, whether working for wages or cultivating land for himself, is often lazy and negligent. The admitted reluctance of the field labourer in most Colonies to work for more than three or four days in each week represents a long-established social tradition but it is now, perhaps, reinforced by the fear that the widespread unemployment from which he and all his kind suffer must be aggravated by the general working of a full week at any time of the year. Where, as in factories, work is more regular and wages are higher, this difficulty is not experienced. The failure to maintain a full working week is much more serious when it occurs among peasant proprietors. Their zeal is, in our view, largely governed by their knowledge and mastery of their work and the quality of the land with which they have been provided. It must, however, be brought home to peasant cultivators that nowhere in the world has the small holding succeeded, under land settlement schemes, or any other system, except through the hard work of the individual; it is equally important that the need for industry, initiative, and a proper attitude towards their

occupation should be understood by every section of the community which is engaged in agriculture in the West Indies. (Chapter III, paragraph 14.)

3. Survey of West Indian Agriculture.

8. The failure to evolve a balanced system of agriculture in the West Indian Colonies has resulted in a generally poor standard of production. Both crops and stock are produced without method and in consequence the fertility of the land is now, with a few exceptions, most of which are found on sugar estates, at a low level. (Chapter IV, paragraphs 1-2 and 16.)

9. Most West Indian agriculture is in the hands of peasant cultivators or estates, and the two are connected through the custom whereby many smaller peasant farmers work for wages on estates whenever they can spare the time and this form of employment is available. The division of the labour of such men between wage work and cultivation of their own lands shows very wide variations. (Chapter IV, paragraphs 3-6.)

10. Cultivation by hand is the general rule among peasant farmers and is largely practised by estates although many sugar estates use cattle or mechanical power for ploughing. For transport some peasants keep bullocks or a mule, but in hilly districts pack donkeys are used. All classes of livestock are found in these Colonies but their numbers are generally small on both peasant holdings and estates, and as a result insufficient attention is paid to the feeding, management and breeding of the stock which is regarded, under both forms of agriculture, as incidental to, and not part of, the business of producing crops. There is undoubtedly room for a considerable improvement in the quality of livestock, and this depends to a greater extent on better feeding and management, particularly by peasant owners, than it does on more scientific breeding. A more extensive keeping of livestock by peasants would raise the standard of soil fertility, would allow them to use surplus crops more effectively as fodder, and might lead, on suitable land, to the displacement of hand cultivation by ploughing. (Chapter IV, paragraphs 6, 14 and 16.)

11. Grazing is found in the main from derelict or resting land; in some Colonies (particularly Jamaica) large properties are permanently under grass of good quality, which is, however, used unintensively. In paragraph 15 of Chapter IV of the agricultural report several ways are indicated in which desirable improvements in resources for grazing can be brought about. In particular a greater use of fodder crops, and especially cut fodder grasses, would make for the more productive employment of the land.

12. Crops are discussed later in this Chapter but no general survey of West Indian agriculture would be complete which did not draw attention to the domination of sugar. Almost from the beginning of European occupation the prosperity of the British West Indian Colonies has been based on sugar, and of the many other crops which have been tried, only bananas, cocoa, coconuts and citrus fruit are substantially important to-day. Sugar is, for many reasons, a valuable crop in the West Indian Colonies. It shows wide adaptation to environment and it affords a rate of employment which, though not well-distributed throughout the year, is so high in times of crop that wages form a very substantial proportion of the total costs of production. A further advantage is that sugar may safely be grown continuously on the same land for it causes no erosion, suffers from no serious diseases and maintains the organic matter of the soil. But even if substantially larger markets could be found for West Indian sugar, an increase in the continuous growing of sugar cane could not alone solve the problem created by the increasing population of these Colonies. The growers of sugar can justly claim that their interests should be considered as a matter of Imperial and Colonial policy; but it is equally just that they should recognise their obligation to assist in providing properly for the occupation and needs of the West Indian peoples. (Chapter IV, paragraphs 17-21.)

13. Specialisation or concentration on a single crop—which in many of these islands is sugar—is agriculturally undesirable and is dangerous on economic and biological grounds. The great dangers of specialisation stand out clearly in West Indian experience, and their avoidance should be a cardinal point of future agricultural policy. (Chapter IV, paragraphs 22-24.)

4. Land Ownership and Use.

14. In most of the West Indian Colonies the acreage of land which has been alienated exceeds that of land now the property of the Crown, and large areas still in the possession of the Crown often consist mainly of forest land or of steep slopes, neither of which is suitable for cultivation. Both the policy hitherto followed in disposing of Crown lands and the practical steps taken to give effect to that policy have often been defective. (Chapter V, paragraphs 1-2.)

15. While nominally agricultural land (known locally as " ruinate ") is lying idle in most of these Colonies, investigation has shown that, as we have stated earlier in this Chapter, nowhere in the West Indies can there be found any substantial area of agriculturally useful land which is not already under cultivation. Not even in British Guiana are there large areas now idle which could be made usable for agriculture without

Chapter IV.

substantial expenditure on drainage or some other form of improvement in the absence of which their cultivation would be either impossible or unprofitable. (Chapter V, paragraphs 4-7.)

16. Exact figures showing the division of agriculturally usable land between estates and peasant holdings are not always obtainable, but it is a reasonable conclusion from the information available that estates, which are generally in freehold occupation, form the greater part. Sugar estates are of two types. One group consists of those owned by individuals or local companies; these are found chiefly in Barbados, Antigua, St. Kitts and, to a less extent, in Jamaica. In other places, notably British Guiana and Trinidad, the sugar estates are in the hands of larger companies most of whose shareholders live in Great Britain. In size sugar estates commonly range between 2,000 and 10,000 acres. Estates used for the growing of other crops are chiefly under individual ownership, and they normally range in size between 100 and 2,000 acres. (Chapter IV, paragraphs 9-10.)

17. The question of the owning of land by peasants in the West Indian Colonies is likely to assume an increasing importance in social policy. In every Colony there are representatives of a limited class owning properties of between 15 and 100 acres, but there is a definite tendency towards the reduction of the size of such holdings through division between the children of the proprietor on his death. Few peasants have been able to accumulate sufficient money to purchase the land which they cultivate, and the majority are therefore lessees or tenants at will. We found a general desire among the peasantry to own land in preference to any form of lease or rental, but there are arguments on the other side and the problem of policy thus raised is considered in Chapter XVI of this report. (Chapter V, paragraph 14.)

18. From our inquiries the number of absentee owners of estates appears to be comparatively small, but absentee landlordism, though not of great extent, sometimes results in severe neglect of the land, even when, as is often the case, the absentee landlord is an individual actually resident in the same or a neighbouring Colony. The social and agricultural future of these territories is dependent to a large degree upon a wise exercise of the influence of landowners, and the lack of interest which some of them display is much to be regretted. (Chapter V, paragraph 15.)

19. Frequent complaint was made in evidence that excessive rentals are charged to peasants. Some figures are given in paragraphs 17 and 18 of Chapter V of the agricultural report, and as is there concluded, the question is not at present one of equity or quality of the land, but is dominated by a general

ignorance among all classes of the proper systematic use of land, coupled with a lamentable lack of trust between owner and tenant. Another frequent complaint relates to the absence of definite security of tenure. Reform is urgently required in this matter, but the problem cannot be tackled effectively until the full facts of peasant agriculture have been surveyed, as we recommend in Chapter XVI of this report. (Chapter V, paragraph 19.)

20. In many territories an arrangement is common under which peasants pay rent in the form of a share of the crops which they grow from the land hired on this basis. Examples of the way in which this system may be abused are given in paragraph 20 of Chapter V of the agricultural report. While land is available for purchase by peasants in almost every district in all of these Colonies, estates which are reasonably prosperous have shown a natural reluctance to sell any but mediocre land. Some peasants have undoubtedly been charged unconscionably high prices, especially for small parcels of land. (Chapter V, paragraphs 22 and 23.)

5. Peasant Agriculture.

21. The West Indian Colonies between them show a diversity of peasant agriculture which is too great to be strictly classified, but in paragraph 2 of Chapter VI of the agricultural report a detailed description is given of the representative types of peasant farming.

22. One of the largest classes is made up of peasants who depend mainly on wages but rent small food plots. Two factors which contribute to the general dissatisfaction among this class are the insecurity of their tenure of land and the poor results which they obtain, often through their own lack of skill. Their situation offers an admirable opportunity for social reform. For their part the peasants must show more initiative and self-help: on the other hand the estates for which many of them work can, and should, offer them better facilities in the form of land and more advice and encouragement in working it. (Chapter VI, paragraph 2 (a).)

23. The best type of peasant farming in the West Indian Colonies is to be found among the occupiers of holdings of from 1 to 5 acres of land who also rent other small areas away from their houses. Many among this class combine skilfully the growing of both food and cash crops and the management of small numbers of livestock. These people and their children, with appropriate education and guidance, could provide a most useful foundation for an expanded and improved system of peasant agriculture. (Chapter VI, paragraph 2 (c).)

Chapter IV.

24. Other peasant proprietors specialise in some form of cash crop; they grow little, if any, food and as a rule keep no livestock. Even when these people concentrate on the growing of sugar cane, yields are poor and their specialisation shows little of that efficiency which is sometimes claimed for it. Other specialisation by peasants is thoroughly to be deprecated since, as experience with cocoa in Trinidad has recently shown, its effects may be wholly bad, exposed as it is to the triple risk of low prices, disease and weather. (Chapter VI, paragraph 2 (*d*)-(*f*).)

25. Even more injury is caused by banana specialisation among peasants, which deters them from adopting a balanced system of agriculture and from the growing of sufficient food to provide for the needs of themselves and their families. The fact that this crop brings in a cash return each week has enticed great numbers of peasants to become banana adventurers. They cultivate rented plots until Panama disease appears and then move on to fresh holdings where their previous experience is repeated. In many Colonies the plots thus rented are on hillsides and much soil erosion has been caused through the activities of this class of peasant. The practice which we have described is most common in Jamaica, but it is also on the increase in some of the other Colonies. (Chapter VI, paragraph 2 (*g*).)

26. Yet another type of peasant cultivation is the intensively worked small holding near a town which is generally used for the growing of vegetables. Examples of this type are comparatively rare, but one of special interest is found in Barbados among artisans who divide their time between these small holdings and the plying of their craft in Bridgetown. (Chapter VI, paragraph 2 (*j*)-(*k*).)

27. In this great diversity of peasant holdings certain general characteristics are clear. Husbandry is not systematic, the productivity of land is low, shifting cultivation is often the basis, livestock are few and poorly managed, while indebtedness is almost universal. Though many peasant holdings are on poor land, the soil of some is equal in quality to that found on adjoining estates. Composite holdings of as many as four widely separate pieces are not uncommon. In the marketing of his produce, a question with which we deal later, the peasant is often at the mercy of the middle-man. In spite, however, of the disadvantages and weaknesses of the existing system, there is to be found among every type of peasant proprietor a number who are well fitted in every respect to profit handsomely from encouragement. (Chapter VI, paragraph 3.)

Chapter IV.

6. Estate Agriculture.

28. While sugar estates dominate the agriculture and the whole economic life of the West Indian Colonies, there are, however, other estates of considerable importance, especially in areas where sugar has ceased to be the main crop, and it will be convenient to discuss them first. These estates usually have a considerable area of nominal pasture on which livestock, mainly cattle, are grazed in varying numbers. Their tendency is to concentrate mainly on a single crop, but many of them grow one or more subsidiary products, usually on a small scale and not always wisely chosen. The average standard of husbandry among these estates is low as is also the figure of labour employed by them on each hundred acres of their holdings. (Chapter VIII, paragraphs 2-3.)

29. The most striking examples of decay of private estate agriculture are found among those specialising in the growing of limes and cocoa, many of which have been swiftly reduced from prosperity to great distress by the outbreak of disease and by the low price now obtained for these crops. These estates offer an extreme example of the dangers of specialisation. The present position and prospects of the lime industry are discussed in paragraph 11 of Chapter VIII of the agricultural report (and also in paragraph 39 of Chapter II of this report); and certain recommendations in connection with the cocoa industry are made in Chapter XVI of this report.

30. We have already referred, when discussing grazing in our brief survey of West Indian agriculture, to the existence of large areas of permanent grass. The pens of Jamaica and the savannah ranches of British Guiana are the only examples of estates of this kind. A part of this grassland in Jamaica is of mediocre quality but much of it could probably be used more intensively, and an attempt should be made to induce owners to experiment with a combination of grazing with cultivation in the form known in Europe as alternate husbandry. In British Guiana while some improvement can be brought about in savannah ranching, substantial development is not at present to be expected. (Chapter VIII, paragraphs 6-7.)

31. We come now to sugar estates. They vary widely both in size and other characteristics, but it is possible to summarise their general features and our conclusions upon them. These are:—

    (a) The yields of sugar cane have greatly increased during the past two decades through the use of better varieties and more scientific husbandry, though the figure on some estates is still low. (Chapter VIII, paragraph 19.)

Chapter IV.

(b) The full and proper use of arable land by sugar estates is impeded by the accepted practice of single crop agriculture and through the operation of the International Sugar Agreement which prevents the growing of more sugar for export. So far as those limitations permit, arable land in the main is well employed by sugar estates. Pasture land is generally poor and much of it is almost unusable waste; nevertheless it could, as a whole, be put to better purpose if mixed farming were adopted. (Chapter VIII, paragraph 20.)

(c) The larger sugar estates range in size between 2,000 and 10,000 acres. In Jamaica the amalgamation of small properties is still in progress; small estates are characteristic of Barbados and of those of the Leeward and Windward Islands which grow sugar cane. In those groups numerous small private estates are often served by a central factory. In many places even more amalgamation is required and should lead to increased efficiency in both field and factory; in some cases, however, geographical difficulties, especially in connection with transport, preclude further amalgamation. (Chapter VIII, paragraph 21.)

(d) The practice of husbandry on sugar estates, bearing in mind the limitations from which they suffer through being devoted to a specialised crop, is on the whole satisfactory, but new knowledge is clearly necessary, particularly in regard to drainage. (Chapter VIII, paragraph 22.)

(e) There is now a general realisation of the importance of choosing the varieties of cane which suit local circumstances, and the number of varieties grown, which was at one time excessively high, is now limited to a few of the best proved types. For much of this improvement thanks are due to the work of the Central Cane Breeding Station at Barbados, which is now, after many years of necessary preparatory work, beginning to distribute its own new varieties. (Chapter VIII, paragraph 23.)

(f) On many sugar estates cattle are kept for transport and ploughing only, and when, as often happens, they are regarded in this light alone, their quality is generally poor. In contrast with this attitude a few large estates have established fine dairy herds, and this promising development may help to inaugurate a widening of the policy of estates. (Chapter VIII, paragraph 25.)

(g) It is our opinion that the equipment and technical management of the sugar estates in general are good and that they have now attained a reasonable level of productivity from the land. There are, however, marked exceptions to this generally favourable judgment, and it is important that the proprietors of estates which are not well-conducted should be brought to realise that their inefficiency cannot, in the existing circumstances of the West Indian Colonies, be taken as affecting only their own interests. The justification for any form of preference or assistance to the sugar industry must be partly measured by its efficiency which is an integration of the soundness of the methods of all the individual estate managements. (Chapter VIII, paragraph 26.)

(*h*) As the efficiency of the field work of estates steadily advances, partly through the increased use of mechanical power, employment per ton of cane produced must diminish. Any increase in sugar quotas that might be found possible will, therefore, not give a corresponding permanent increase in the number of workers employed. Under-employment and the lack of balance of employment throughout the year are already urgent problems which cannot be overcome so long as estates continue the policy of growing cane only; those problems must become still more acute as population increases. While the immediate concern of sugar estates is naturally to find wages for work done, they cannot stand aloof from the problems caused by the inadequacy and unbalance of employment. By developing a policy of mixed farming for themselves and by encouraging small-holders in every possible way, they would benefit themselves agriculturally and would help to secure for their own work an adequate supply of labour drawn from contented people. (Chapter VIII, paragraphs 27 and 29.)

(*i*) In some cases the subordinate supervisors of labour on sugar estates fall below a reasonable standard of knowledge of their business and show a lack of consideration for the labour under their control. (Chapter VIII, paragraph 28.)

(*j*) The wide range of factory efficiency in the West Indian Colonies is described in paragraph 31 of Chapter VIII of the agricultural report. In general, factory efficiency, if measured by the ratio of tons of cane required to make one ton of sugar, is highest in the larger factories. The only other comment that we would offer on this subject is that in Barbados overabundance of labour resulting in low wages and a fear of reducing employment have prevented the adoption of such measures to increase efficiency as the greater use of mechanical power and the further centralisation of factories.

(*k*) Research on sugar production is partly financed by estates which, in many places, collaborate in this respect with Departments of Agriculture. The practicability of diverting the work of sugar estates in the direction of mixed farming, with cane as the main product, will depend fundamentally on the results of a thorough investigation for the discovery of suitable agricultural systems and practices. (Chapter VIII, paragraphs 33-4.)

32. This will be a convenient point at which to refer again to cane farmers, i.e., peasant growers of sugar cane, who, though not engaged in estate agriculture, are an important and increasing element in Jamaica, Trinidad, British Guiana and Barbados. We have already said that, largely owing to the low level of their husbandry, the yields secured by growers of this class are usually low; in consequence their standard of life is also low. While an increase in the number of cane farmers and a higher yield from their holding could be brought about by instruction and assistance, any advance thus obtained would be trivial in relation to the problem of supporting ever-increasing population. We have already indicated that a complete reform of peasant agriculture is essential and this, in the case of cane farmers, means the adoption of mixed farming with cane as the main component. (Chapter VIII, paragraph 35.)

33. It is often urged that the growing of sugar cane under the Fiji system, which is described in paragraph 38 of Chapter VIII of the agricultural report, should be adopted in the West Indian Colonies. That could only be done by the displacement of sugar estates of which the enterprise, policy and working efficiency appear to us to stand out in marked contrast to all other agricultural undertakings in the West Indian Colonies. Moreover, a transformation to the Fiji system would tend to perpetuate specialisation in a single crop to which many objections have already been pointed out. We feel unable, therefore, to recommend the adoption of the Fiji system in these territories.

7. Soil Erosion.

34. Soil erosion is the term used to denote removal of top soil through its being blown away by wind or washed away by water flowing unchecked over the land. It is now regarded throughout the world as the greatest danger to agriculture, and a full survey of the extent to which it has already caused damage in the West Indian Colonies is given in the first part of Chapter IX of the agricultural report. The various forms of erosion which are to be found in these territories are there described in detail, and the conclusion reached is that while soil erosion is to be found everywhere it is either not immediately significant or confined to a small distinctive area except in the Leeward and Windward Islands and in Jamaica. In the two groups of islands soil erosion is widespread and severe, while in

Jamaica its effects are more serious through their close connection with the growing of bananas which are the principal export of the Colony. So far nothing has been done anywhere in the West Indies to counter this evil. The continuation of neglect, which means a continuation of existing agricultural practices, must inevitably have the gravest consequences. Increasing population requires greater productivity from the land, and that is definitely precluded in any closely populated area subject to soil erosion which involves an ever diminishing yield.

35. While the neglect of soil erosion is as world wide as its occurrence the necessity for action is particularly urgent in areas such as the West Indies where the density of population, in relation to cultivable land, is high.

8. Maintenance of Soil Fertility.

36. The question whether the existing agricultural system in any territory is satisfactory and well suited to its needs must be judged more by its ultimate effects than by its immediate results. The cardinal long-range test is whether the system, if it does not improve soil fertility, at least prevents it from declining. This test can be applied, so far as the known facts permit, to each of the three principal categories of agriculture in the West Indies—namely peasant holdings, sugar estates, and other estates. Shifting cultivation, which is adopted only when an agricultural system cannot maintain the fertility of the land with continuous cultivation, is now a basic principle in peasant agriculture in the West Indies. In general, therefore, it must be concluded that by the test which we have described, peasant agriculture fails alarmingly, a fact which offers further proof of the necessity for developing mixed farming among this class of cultivator. (Chapter X, paragraphs 2 and 3.)

37. Sugar estates have steadily improved their yields for several years. This is due in part to the planting of improved varieties of cane, but the maintenance of soil fertility at a higher level is another important cause. The traditional method of securing this was by burying trash and by applying at planting time pen manure from bullocks used for ploughing and transport, but that method is now being disputed by those who, having abandoned the use of animals for both transport and work, rely on chemical fertilisers for manuring. (Chapter X, paragraph 6.)

38. Other estates are concerned mostly with permanent tree crops or bush crops. The statistical evidence available is not sufficiently reliable to be used as the basis for any definite conclusion on the question whether soil fertility is being maintained by these estates. There is conflicting evidence and the

only certain fact is that the question of soil fertility has generally been neglected by this category of estates. (Chapter X, paragraph 4.)

9. Export Crops.

39. An examination of the tables of statistics appended to the agricultural report will show plainly the dominating position of sugar in the export trade of the West Indian Colonies. For all the group it accounts in value for more than half the total of the agricultural exports. In four of the six Colonies (i.e. excluding British Honduras and treating the Windward Islands as a single Colony) which have a considerable export trade, the value of sugar comes to more than two-thirds of the total agricultural exports. The distribution of other export crops, their agricultural suitability and market prospects, are all reviewed in paragraph 8 of Chapter XI of the agricultural report, and we propose here to record only the principal conclusions reached there. They are:—

(*a*) The undue dependence of many of the Windward and Leeward Islands on a single commodity—in some cases sugar, in some limes and in some cotton—is strikingly shown in the recent history of their export trade.

(*b*) The smallness of the output of all crops, except sugar and bananas, from the several Colonies—and indeed from the British West Indian Colonies as a whole—is an inevitable handicap to the marketing of these crops.

(*c*) So much hope has been based on seeking for markets that producers have tended to lose sight of the importance of reducing the costs of production by a general improvement of methods.

(*d*) The growers of cocoa in the West Indian Colonies are suffering from the intense competition to which they are subjected by larger producers in other parts of the world. It is, however, possible that some of the competing areas will be afflicted by those difficulties, such as disease of trees, which have recently been so serious a handicap to growers in the West Indies. If those growers can bring about improvements, particularly by lowering their costs of production, they may well be able, as time goes on, to regain part of the ground which they have lost in the world market. These are strong reasons for taking active steps to maintain the present output of cocoa.

(*e*) The most favourable line of development for oranges and grapefruit lies not in a continued expansion of exports to markets already over-full, but in the supply of these commodities at special seasons to North America.

(f) The development of secondary industries based on the production of coconuts gives rise to important questions which are considered elsewhere in this report; the prospect of profitable sale outside the West Indies of vegetable oils manufactured there is not such as to encourage the hope of any great increase in the production of coconuts for export.

(g) The growing of tobacco has been successfully developed in Jamaica; interesting experiments in this branch of agriculture are in progress in other territories (e.g. Dominica and the Virgin Islands) and in every Colony there are some prospects for this crop.

(h) The demand from North America at special seasons for certain vegetables and luxury fruits, such as avocado pear and mango, may increase; good marketing arrangements to ensure a regular supply of reliable constant grades would be particularly necessary in this class of trade.

(i) Present production is in many places by no means sufficient to satisfy local demand for vegetables, ground provisions, eggs, poultry, plantains, maize, pulses and other common products.

(j) Although conditions in the West Indian Colonies are suitable for the production of a wide range of agricultural commodities, no new crop is known which would be likely to grow well in those territories and of which the demand throughout the world substantially exceeds existing supplies.

10. Economic Organisation.

40. There is a growing realisation, based on experience all over the world, of the importance to primary producers of the proper marketing, transport, storage and processing of agricultural commodities. The marketing arrangements for sugar cane in the West Indian Colonies are those to be expected from an efficient industry; in the case of bananas, the marketing position, which shows a number of well-marked peculiarities due to the domination of the trade by the United Fruit Company of Boston, is also technically efficient. Other agricultural products are marketed by three forms of agency—merchants, associations of producers, and co-operative organisations arranged or supported by Government primarily for the handling of peasant produce. (Chapter XII, paragraphs 1-2.)

41. Several classes of merchants may be distinguished, including producers who purchase the crops of others and sell them for export, and merchants on a small scale who buy produce for local consumption and control its retail sale. Some of the producers who act as merchants for the crops of others commonly deal with commodities such as limes, rice and coffee,

which have to be processed before they are exported. They may buy the raw product outright or undertake the work of processing either for cash or for a percentage of the price realised by sale. Disputes about these charges are not uncommon. Another complaint made by peasant growers is that they often receive unjust treatment from small merchants of the " huckster " class. They are in a particularly weak position when they attempt to dispose of livestock, and it is plainly evident that the interest which some peasants, especially in the Leeward and Windward Islands, show in livestock is severely checked by their helplessness in marketing. (Chapter XII, paragraphs 3-4.)

42. Associations of producers for marketing are active bodies in the West Indian Colonies, but too often they have proceeded on independent lines in different territories and attempts to secure co-operation between them have sometimes failed after prolonged effort on the part of Government. (Chapter XII, paragraph 5.)

43. Co-operative associations and other arrangements made by Government for the marketing of peasant produce show very varying success but are unquestionably necessary. At the same time co-operation should not be regarded as the only possible basis on which peasant produce can be satisfactorily handled. (Chapter XII, paragraphs 7-11.)

44. Most of the evidence put forward to us in connection with the improvement of transport took the form of criticism of the existing facilities for export to Europe and North America. That question is examined in the earlier part of Chapter XIX of this report; as there stated, the primary need, for the very small islands, is the provision of better communications between them. (Chapter XII, paragraphs 12-14.)

45. Difficulties of storage arise most urgently in connection with foods; many householders have at present no facilities for storage and no means of protecting grain and seed from weevils and other pests. The provision of storage, whether domestic or central, for local-grown foods is of the greatest importance as an encouragement to that increased local production which we regard as essential. (Chapter XII, paragraph 15.)

46. Cold storage is available in many of the territories but is not always employed to the best advantage. The local production of both fish and meat could be encouraged through the wise use of cold storage, and the aim should be to keep cold storage plant in operation throughout the year. (Chapter XII, paragraph 16.)

47. We have referred above to the existence of separate organisations of growers of such products as coconuts, grapefruit and limes, each working in its own interests and disregarding the possibilities of joint action with similar associa-

tions in other Colonies or islands. Orderly marketing is clearly one of the needs of the West Indian Colonies, but still more necessary is the rationalisation of production. Irrationality has gone to an inexcusable length and is perhaps seen at its worst in the proposals of at least three other areas to compete with St. Vincent in the peculiar and limited overseas market for arrowroot. What can be done in the way of allocating production is illustrated by the successful activities of the West Indies Sea Island Cotton Association. Any plan for rationalising or allocating production among the different areas must, we consider, be on a voluntary basis. (Chapter XII, paragraphs 18 and 19.)

48. Secondary industries based on agricultural produce have already been developed on a small scale in some of these Colonies. Generally speaking, manufacturing costs are likely to be higher there than they are in Europe or North America. Moreover, the profit from such secondary industries normally goes to a limited number of manufacturers rather than to a large number of primary producers. The question of the principles which should be followed, when considering applications from promoters of secondary industries for assistance from Government, is considered in Chapter XIII of this report. (Chapter XII, paragraph 22.)

11. Agricultural Credit and Finance.

49. In view of the general necessity for the reform of agriculture on many estates, the prevalence of financial difficulty among the owners of estates growing crops other than sugar and bananas must be looked upon as one of the major economic problems of the West Indian Colonies. Indebtedness and lack of capital are severe handicaps to all owners of estates other than those mentioned above and to the great majority of peasant proprietors. We agree generally with the inferences which are drawn in paragraph 5 of Chapter XIII of the agricultural report. The most important of these, so far as they relate to the existing situation, are:—

(a) A tendency to over-reach in years of prosperity has saddled some proprietors, both of estates and of the larger peasant holdings, with more land than they are likely to be able to maintain at a level of husbandry which would ensure success.

(b) Through frequent financial relief from Government funds in aid of distress caused by hurricane and other disaster, an unwholesome reliance on official aid has been engendered to the detriment of that personal initiative and self-help without which agriculture can nowhere thrive.

(c) In credit and loan schemes it should be a principle to assist men of proved merit rather than to give help to everyone.

(d) No general measures for improving credit facilities and dealing with the question of debt can be evolved until factual knowledge has been obtained by the surveys recommended in Chapter XVI of this report; early action is, however, essential, and the survey of the financial problems of agriculture should not be over-meticulous.

12. Agricultural Departments.

50. The main functions of any Colonial Department of Agriculture can be classified under three heads—investigation, instruction and administration. Investigation, by which is meant the obtaining of new knowledge likely to be of benefit to agriculture, is the primary function. Instruction, unless based on the results of thorough and up-to-date investigation, may be of little value to agriculturists. These two functions involve the third—administration—the scope of which ranges from the control of official agricultural staff and finance to such matters as the enforcement of legislation relating to agriculture and the supply of planting materials. Administration is not creative work, and every extension of that side of the activities of any Agricultural Department must reduce the time which its staff can give to the two major and creative functions. A clearer appreciation of this fact in the West Indies might help to divert public attention from criticism, which is all too common, of details of the work of Agricultural Departments and instead concentrate it on assisting that work by defining the problems to which investigation and instruction can most usefully be directed. (Chapter XV, paragraphs 1-3.)

51. The comments which are made in paragraphs 5-10 of Chapter XV of the agricultural report on the history and organisation of the Agricultural Departments of the several Colonies will no doubt be studied by the Governments concerned. We would commend to particular attention the suggestion that the system of district organisation now employed in most large Colonial Agricultural Departments should be adopted in Jamaica.

52. The work of Agricultural Departments throughout the British West Indies has suffered in the past from a tendency to help estates rather than peasants. No doubt the explanation is to be found in the fact that problems can be studied, and new methods tested, with far greater ease on large agricultural units. Nevertheless both investigation and instruction should be spread over all types of agricultural activity, and the importance of giving similar treatment in this respect to estates and peasant cultivators should be everywhere realised.

53. There has also been a marked tendency on the part of Agricultural Departments to neglect food crops and to concentrate their attention on export crops.

CHAPTER V.
THE ADMINISTRATIVE BACKGROUND.

1. We do not consider it to be part of our task to discuss the organisation of the public services generally nor, though we heard evidence about salaries and other conditions of employment from several delegations representative of branches of the services, do we propose to examine here the points of detail thus raised which appear to us scarcely to fall within the purview of our inquiry. The adoption of the recommendations which we make, in Chapter X of this report, for the establishment of Whitley Councils would provide means whereby the grievances laid before us could be thoroughly investigated.

2. It is, however, essential, as part of the background of the problems of the West Indies, that we should attempt a description of the relationships between the administrations on the one hand and, on the other, public opinion as represented particularly by the Legislative Councils and the Press. This description leads naturally to the examination, towards the end of this Chapter, of the major criticisms of the administration which were made to us.

1. Brief Description of Constitutions.

3. The details of the political constitutions of the various territories differ considerably. In all there are representative institutions but none has yet reached the stage of responsible government. The nearest approach to this is found in Barbados where the representative element in both the legislative and executive parts of Government is considerable. The former consists of the Legislative Council of nine members appointed by the Crown and the House of Assembly of 24 members elected annually. The executive part of the Government is vested in a Council, appointed by the Crown and composed at present with a majority of officials, and in a Committee which consists of the Executive Council, one member from the Legislative Council and four members nominated by the Governor from the House of Assembly. All money votes are introduced in the legislature and all Government measures initiated there by, and with the advice of, the Executive Committee, but the executive has no means of ensuring the passage of legislation, or the provision of funds, by the wholly elected House of Assembly whose members therefore have a vital place in the scheme of government.

4. In British Guiana the position until 1928 was not unlike that now obtaining in Barbados, but a new constitution was then introduced as the result of recommendations by two Commissions, of which the first went out from this country, and

the second was appointed locally. The visiting Commission reported that the financial situation was one of the greatest impediments to the development of the Colony and that an alteration in the constitution would be necessary in order to give to Government the power in the last resort to carry into effect measures which they considered to be essential. The local Committee reported in favour of a change of the constitution and under instruments made in 1928 a Legislative Council was created on which the nominated element (including officials) has a bare majority over the elected members. The Executive Council which was established at the same time is composed of two ex-officio members, not more than four other nominated official members and not more than five nominated unofficial members. Under the existing constitution no legislation may be enacted which was not proposed to the Council by, or with the sanction of the Governor, and the initiation of all money votes is subject to a similar limitation. In addition the Governor has a reserve power under which he, in Executive Council, may decide any matter requiring a vote or enactment to the Legislative Council in a sense contrary to the vote of a majority of the legislature; the exercise of this power is, however, limited to matters in regard to which the Governor declares in writing that his decision is, in his opinion, necessary in the interests of public order, public faith, or other first essentials of good government. Though the Governor is bound by the constitution to consult his Executive Council before using his reserve power, he need not accept their advice.

5. It is not our intention to examine here the constitutional position in the West Indies (to which we return in Chapter XXII) in any greater detail than is necessary for our present purpose of discussing the relationship between the executive and legislative authorities. It may suffice, therefore, to say that while the position in the other Colonies not so far mentioned in this Chapter varies on details, such as the relative proportions of component elements of the Councils, from that in British Guiana, it is similar in essentials, though in the case of Jamaica the elected members have certain special powers of veto. The features which are peculiar to the Windward and Leeward Islands do not call for comment in the present connection and are considered in Chapter XVIII (Closer Union).

2. Relation of Executive and Legislature.

6. We have already remarked on the fact that the elected House of Assembly in Barbados may bar the passage of any legislation and has complete freedom to withhold the provision of money votes moved by the executive. The system appears on the whole to have worked reasonably well: although it was represented to us in evidence that the absence of certain

social legislation and services was due to opposition by the Assembly, an official witness assured us that there had been no recent evidence of obstruction, on the part of either branch of the legislature, to any social measures which the Government had introduced, and we received no indication of any wish, on the part of the executive, for a reform of the constitution of Barbados. Any uneasiness that may be felt about the power of the legislature to impede the pursuit in Barbados of a policy designed to improve social and economic conditions throughout the possessions of the Crown in the Caribbean area would, we consider, be met if, after the local inquiry suggested in Chapter XXII of this Report, the franchise in the island is widened.

7. The other Colonies are still administered under what is known as "the Crown Colony system". That is neither an autocracy nor a democracy. It is true that, as we have shown, the Governor can impose his will in the interest of public order, public faith or other first essentials of good government and, in the last resort, the decision whether those vital needs are affected rests with him alone. In practice, however, the force of public opinion can effectively prevent arbitrary decisions and the known unpopularity of the reserve power is a safeguard against its frequent use. It should be—and, we believe, that in the West Indies it is—the aim of every administrator under the Crown Colony system to give full weight to the expressed views of all responsible sections of public opinion, the more so in that some of these may have no share in any sphere of government, and to balance carefully the claims of every interest before a decision is reached and executive action is taken. The weakness of the system, as it operates in most of the West Indian Colonies, seems to us to lie not, as is so often alleged, in the autocracy which it apparently involves but in the opposition which it engenders between Government, on the one hand, and, on the other, those, among whom must often be counted elected members of the Legislative Council, who so vehemently and constantly criticise Government in speeches and in the Press. Even these critics recognise that the Governor is not an autocrat, inasmuch as they will usually admit that he and his administration are open to influence; the complaint most frequently heard is, rather, that Governments are dominated by vested interests and that only the representatives of such interests are successful in exercising their influence.

8. Before considering the effects of the position which we have described upon individual officers and upon their relations with the public, we should mention another defect which—so we were told in evidence—is inherent in the Crown Colony system. This point of view was put by a witness whose opinion

is the more valuable by reason of his knowledge and experience of several Colonies. He told us that not only are the people, when they become politically conscious, compelled through that system to resort to permanent opposition to Government, and their elected representatives forced into the position of vehement and continual critics of Government, but those representatives are left with no responsibility for practical alternative measures and their criticism, when it becomes perpetual and irresponsible, often leads to a static position and prevents constructive action by the executive.

9. The outstanding features of the evidence tendered to us by elected members of the Legislative Councils in the West Indies —apart from their wish for constitutional reform, with which question we deal in Chapter XXII—were the complaints of the inaction of Government and of their own inability, under the present system, to take the initiative in measures designed to secure an improvement of social conditions. That evidence may, therefore, be regarded as supporting the opinion which is summarised in the preceding paragraph.

3. Public Opinion and the Civil Service.

10. It will be realised that the difficulties of administration, which in many of these Colonies is inevitably complicated through the admixture of their problems and the diversity of their people, cannot but be intensified when the business of Government has to be conducted to an accompaniment of criticism which is often of a distasteful character. It is an unfortunate feature of public life in the West Indies that attacks are all too often directed not so much against the policy of the Government as against individual officers who are thus treated as the designers and not the instruments of that policy. At times these criticisms, particularly in the Press, are ill-informed and amount to personal abuse, while other public attacks on officials may be actuated by motives of spite or personal gain.

11. Where matters of policy are involved, officers are debarred by regulation from replying in the Press to attacks upon them: in meeting criticism in debate in Legislative Council many officers—particularly of professional and technical services—are naturally handicapped by the absence of political training, while in other cases considerations of loyalty to subordinate staff may restrict their freedom of reply. In this unfortunate position members of the public service have to look to Government to defend them from the worst forms of unjustifiable criticism. Public taste must be so educated that it will no longer tolerate irresponsible attacks on public servants when they are striving to the best of their ability with a difficult task and will recognise the distinction between abuse of the

agents of Government and reasonable comment on matters of policy. It is important that, as a first step towards that end, Government should employ every available means of influencing public opinion and, where the means now available are inadequate, should introduce new methods of explaining their policy and the reasons underlying it, the limitations placed upon it by finance and the aims to which it is directed. Much more active steps can, and should, be taken to make known to the mass of the people the point of view of Government on all the major problems of the day.

4. Colour Prejudice and Colour Discrimination.

12. The question of racial feeling raises issues which fall outside the scope of a discussion strictly limited to the background of administration in the West Indies, but, in some of its phases, it is connected with the problems described immediately above and it has, as we will show, an important bearing on the relationship between Government and the people.

13. Those witnesses whom we questioned on the point were practically unanimous in the view that racial feeling had intensified during recent years, though by one of them a good point was made when he said: " If one is comparing the economic interests of the workers with the economic interests of the employers of labour it can always be interpreted to be promoting ill-will among the different classes." Where people of one colour are predominant among employers and the workers are found almost wholly from those of another colour, it is perhaps inevitable in times of labour troubles that racial and economic issues should be confused. Be that as it may, there is ample evidence, in the form of Press articles, memoranda of evidence submitted to us by unofficials and information received from Governments, that in all responsible quarters in the West Indies there is a widespread feeling that colour prejudice is seriously on the increase. The causes of this are economic, social and political. The desire for a higher standard of life can lead to strikes for improved labour conditions and these, as we have indicated above, may come to, or be represented as, a clash of colour interests. In the social sphere the spread of education has opened the way to greater contact between the white people and the better informed among the coloured sections of the community and we feel that it is essential that Governors should do their utmost to break down old barriers and should not limit to formal occasions the hospitality which they extend to the leading unofficials of mixed or coloured descent. Finally, on the political side, increasing racial prejudice arises from the position, with which we have already dealt, whereby the executive is dominated by officials and it frequently takes the particular form, which is discussed

later in this section, of antagonism to, and bitter attacks on, white officers appointed to the service from outside the West Indies.

14. It is satisfactory to be able to record that the growth of colour prejudice was deplored by every witness who gave evidence about it. The representatives of organisations whose immediate interests might be served by this unfortunate development assured us that they were not, and would not be, any party to a campaign of racial propaganda. Such persons should be taken at their word and their active assistance should be enlisted in the utilisation of broadcasting and other means of publicity in an organised attempt to prevent any further extension of racial feeling.

15. Reference has been made above to the resentment frequently caused by the appointment of officials from elsewhere to the public service in the West Indies. Even the most hostile opponents of such appointments will usually admit that in present circumstances Governors, Colonial Secretaries and other senior administrative staff must generally be found from outside the group. Their claim is that with these few exceptions, all official posts in the West Indies can be filled satisfactorily by local candidates who should have priority of claim to all vacancies for which they are qualified. It is indisputable that of two candidates who are equally suitable for an appointment one of West Indian origin should be given the preference over one of other extraction. But the proper organisation of Government services in a world of increasing administrative and technical complexity clearly demands that experience shall be pooled and that the selection for any vacancy shall be the one which is best on grounds of qualifications and merit alone. The application of those tests in making promotions within the Colonial Service has, in fact, resulted in the move to other Colonies of many officers of West Indian origin, some of whom have gone far in the Service. The fact that they have been of white or mixed descent is not to be taken as implying a rigid colour prejudice but reflects the absence, from most branches of the Service, of coloured officers with qualifications equal to those of officers entering from this country. In so far as colour is a bar to the entry of well qualified West Indian candidates to the Colonial Service outside the Caribbean area it is only reasonable that every opportunity should be given to them to secure suitable appointments within that area. The creation, which was suggested to us by one Governor, of posts carrying terms designed to attract such people who have taken an honours degree is at least worthy of serious consideration. Due regard would no doubt be had to such problems as the effect of any reorganisation along these lines on the position and prospects of those civil servants, locally recruited, to whom all but the highest posts in West Indian Secretariats are now open.

16. In their present stage of development the West Indies cannot supply all their needs for experienced staff, particularly in professional and technical branches of the Service, and local opinion must recognise that, so long as the principle of selection on a basis of qualifications and merit is followed, officers from other parts of the world will be needed for many appointments, and if more constructive work, calling for specialised advice, is to be undertaken, the needs in this direction must increase.

17. It cannot be too strongly stressed that irresponsible and unmeasured criticism of imported officers, whether on the ground of colour or as part of a political campaign, detracts from their usefulness, takes up in the answering of it time which could be more profitably employed on constructive work and is a potent cause of that racial prejudice which was so strongly deprecated by all with whom we discussed it. The interests of every section of the community would be well served if all the energy and talent now devoted to unconstructive criticism could be diverted to co-operation.

18. The racial or colour problem would be completely misunderstood if it were supposed to arise simply from the differences between a racially homogeneous white people and a racially homogeneous coloured people. In every West Indian Colony the population shows a wide racial heterogeneity, that is a wide range from completely white to completely coloured. Moreover degree of wealth and degree of colour are by no means completely associated and exceptions to even their general correspondence are frequent and striking. Between racially intermediate grades and the two extremes of racial homogeneity there are prejudice and clash of interest at least as strong as those to be found between the two racial or colour extremes themselves. The existence of this very marked racial heterogeneity is, in itself, one of the most powerful reasons why complete renunciation of colour prejudice is fundamentally necessary to social progress.

5. Other Criticisms of Administration.

19. Complaint was made in evidence that senior officers in the service of West Indian Governments are often inaccessible to private individuals of position and influence. Suggestions made earlier in this Chapter should secure closer touch between Governments and the people and a better understanding of the aims of policy. That is not, however, a complete answer to this complaint, of the force of which it is hardly possible for anyone who is not permanently resident, or serving, in a Colony to form an accurate opinion. The point is certainly worthy of serious attention, and if any Governor is satisfied that the griev-

ance is substantial, it would be well that he should consider what measures can reasonably be taken, or what instructions issued, to remove it.

20. We heard on many occasions from unofficial witnesses allegations of insufficient co-operation between Departments of the Government. There appears to be room for improvement in this respect, particularly in regard to better co-ordination of the efforts of the Departments whose work is connected with social problems. The establishment of social welfare committees, which is suggested in Chapter XI of this Report, would go far to meet this complaint.

21. It was represented in several Colonies—and specially emphasised in British Guiana—that changes among the holders of the highest offices, including Governorships, are so frequent in the West Indies as to be a serious handicap to the formulation and application of a constructive and comprehensive policy. It has even been implied that any officer who does well is quickly promoted from the West Indian Colonies, which are thus left with an undue proportion of men whose work falls below the average.

22. The following table (which is based on information supplied in May, 1939) shows the number of persons who, during the last 20 years, had held substantively some of the senior appointments in each territory which are often filled by transfer:—

Chapter V.

	Governor.	Colonial Secretary, Administrator or Commissioner.	Chief Justice.	Attorney General.	Treasurer.	Head of Medical Department.	Head of Education Department.	Head of Agricultural Department.	Head of Police Department.
Barbados	5	6	4	4	3	3*	—	4	3
British Guiana	7	5	4	3	4	5	3	2	5
British Honduras	4	5	4	5	5†	5	2	2‡	3
Jamaica	6	4	5	4	5	3	3	3	3
Leeward Islands:—									
Federal staff	4	5§	6	7	—	—	—	—	2
Antigua	—	5§	—	—	—	—	—	—	—
Dominica	—	6	—	—	—	—	—	—	—
Montserrat	—	4	—	—	—	—	—	1	—
St. Kitts-Nevis	—	4	—	—	—	—	—	—	—
Virgin Islands	—	5	5	6	—	—	—	—	—
Trinidad and Tobago	6	5	—	—	5	2	4	2	3
Windward Islands:—	5	—	—	—	—	—	—	—	—
Grenada	—	4	5	4	—	—	—	—	—
St. Lucia	—	4	5	9	—	—	—	—	—
St. Vincent	—	6	6	9	—	—	—	—	—

* Vacant since 1935. † Now combined with Colonial Secretaryship. ‡ Post created in 1928. § These posts are combined.

Chapter V.

23. The figures given above indicate the average tenure of office; in the following table the information supplied by Colonial Governments is set out in another form in order to show the variations in the time for which individuals have held their offices:—

	Number of persons thoroughout the group who have held the office in question for the period stated below :—							Total Number.
	Less than a year*	Between a year and 2 years	Between 2 and 3 years.	Between 3 and 4 years.	Between 4 and 5 years.	Between 5 and 6 years.	Over 6 years.	
Governor	5	3	8	3	4	4	10	37
Colonial Secretary, Administrator or Commissioner	9	2	8	12	9	4	19	63
Chief Justice	1	2	11	8	9	2	11	44
Attorney General	4	9	10	13	5	0	10	51
Treasurer	0	2	2	5	2	3	8	22
Head of Medical Department	3	2	3	1	1	3	5	18
Head of Education Department	1	0	0	2	2	0	7	12
Head of Agricultural Department	2	1	0	0	1	1	8	13
Head of Police Department	1	1	0	3	1	1	12	19

* Includes many officers still serving.

24. One comment that we would offer relates to the offices of Governor and Colonial Secretary (with which we include the Administrators and Commissioners in the Windward and Leeward Islands) as it is in their case that the question of continuity of policy assumes most prominence. On an average throughout the group of Colonies both Governors and Colonial Secretaries during the last 20 years have held office for slightly less than four years. It can seldom have happened, therefore, that the head of an administration and his executive chief have remained together for more than two years. These periods, in the circumstances of the West Indies which present special problems on the complexity of which we have already commented, appear to be too short; and even when all due weight is given to the unquestionable desirability of providing and using outlets for the best officers from what is not a popular area of employment, it is difficult to resist the conclusion that it would be judicious, as it would certainly be in the interests of these Colonies, to avoid the transfer of successful and acceptable Governors before they have completed what was, until recently, the normal full term of six years. Colonial Secretaries are not appointed for any specified period, but in their case also an effort to secure greater continuity would be advantageous.

25. The position that we found, upon our arrival in British Guiana, is an illustration of the inconvenience to which an administration may be put when senior officers are transferred without reasonable regard to the number of other recent changes among the holders of higher appointments. The Governor had held his office for 14 months and the Colonial Secretary had been transferred to British Guiana, of which, however, he had considerable experience in a lower capacity, four months before our arrival. The Director of Medical Services had been in British Guiana, where he had not previously served, for the same length of time. The Chief Justice was a newcomer, and the two Puisne Judges had been appointed in 1937. The Attorney-General was on leave pending transfer to Ceylon, and his successor had not arrived. A new Postmaster-General reached the Colony two days before our arrival, and the Director of Education and Commissioner of Police, both of whom had previously served for some years as the Deputies in their respective Departments, had recently been promoted to their present posts. The Director of Public Works and the Commissioner of Labour (a post which was created in 1938) also had experience in other appointments in the Colony but are now engaged on work of some novelty to them. Of the holders of senior appointments normally filled by transfer, only the Treasurer and the Controller of Customs (both local officers), the Director of Agriculture and the Conservator of Forests had held their present appointments for more than three years. In contrast to this series of rapid changes in British Guiana we would mention the cases, which were brought to our notice, of officers who had been expected to serve for unduly long periods, running up to 15 years, in difficult and unattractive conditions.

26. The position in British Guiana which we have described may be an extreme example of the results of the system of inter-Colonial transfer, but it is an indication of the extent of the dislocation of public business which may be caused by too frequent changes, and we would subscribe to the view of the Royal Commission which recently visited other Colonial territories in emphasising " the importance of taking precautions to guard against a recurrence of transfers upon so ill-considered a scale which can only prejudice the ability of the Civil Service to enlist the sympathy and active co-operation of unofficial residents in measures for the development of the country ".

27. Finally our opinion that many of the major problems of the West Indies differ materially from those encountered in most other parts of the Colonial Empire leads us to urge that more regard should be paid to experience in that group when appointments to West Indian Governorships are made. We consider that any senior administrative officer who has done good work in the West Indies and is suitable for a Governorship should be given preference over candidates from other Colonies.

Chapter V.

6. Work of the Civil Services.

28. The dissatisfaction which was expressed in some of the territories, and the allegations made, sometimes not without good reason, that leadership and authority were lacking, should not be allowed to obscure the valuable work which is being done by many persons of all grades of the public service in the Caribbean area. Senior officers have often to carry out their daily business, as we have already pointed out, to an accompaniment of personal criticism which ought to be directed against the policy of the Government and not against those who give effect to it. This inevitably produces a distaste, which is on the increase, for employment in the West Indies. The work of many officers is further handicapped by considerations of finance, often by poor office accommodation and inadequate staff, and by inevitable delay involved by the system of Treasury control (which is discussed in the following Chapter) in those territories which are in receipt of grants from Imperial funds in aid of the general expenses of administration. Moreover, the salaries of senior appointments in the West Indies and the other conditions of service attaching to them are, on the whole, much less attractive, even when full allowance is made for climatic and other conditions of life, than those of appointments of similar status in other parts of the Colonial Empire. Bearing all these factors in mind, we feel that a large majority of the Civil Service deserve great credit for the standard of work which they have been able to maintain under difficult and testing circumstances.

CHAPTER VI.
THE PUBLIC FINANCES.
1. Public Debt.

1. The following table gives for each of the Colonies which we visited the total net indebtedness on the 31st December, 1938, and the amount of that debt per head of the estimated population; it also shows the average over the last three financial years of the annual expenditure on debt charges and expresses that expenditure as a percentage of the total expenditure, exclusive of that of self-balancing Departments:—

Colony.	Total Net Indebtedness at Dec. 31st, 1938.		Average over last 3 years of annual expenditure on debt charges.	
	Total Amount.	Amount per head of estimated population.	Amount.	Percentage of that expenditure to total expenditure.
	£	£ s. d.	£	
Barbados	377,256	1 19 1	22,891	5·3
British Guiana	4,394,914	13 0 9	244,860	21·1
British Honduras*	641,708	11 3 6	43,402	20·0
Jamaica	4,303,162	3 13 4	230,579	11·1
Leeward Islands† :				
Antigua	69,207	1 19 6	3,849	4·6
Dominica	85,441	1 13 9	1,573	2·5
Montserrat	7,563	0 11 0	917	3·0
St. Kitts–Nevis	26,656	0 14 3	3,464	3·7
Virgin Islands	nil	nil	nil	nil
Trinidad and Tobago	3,940,167	8 9 6	196,511	9·5
Windward Islands :—				
Grenada	365,907	4 2 9	13,594	10·2
St. Lucia	102,276	1 9 7	11,069	12·4
St. Vincent‡	86,081	1 9 6	4,791	6·2

* The currency of British Honduras is linked to that of the United States of America but, for convenience, the dollar has been taken here, and elsewhere in this Chapter at 4·80 to £1 which is the fixed rate of conversion in British Guiana and Trinidad where the dollar currency is linked to sterling.

† Figures supplied exclude following amounts lent by H.M.G. in aid (except where otherwise stated) of costs of administration :—
    Antigua £30,000.
    Dominica £95,142 (of which £22,142 was on account of hurricane damage).
    Montserrat £30,000 (of which £9,000 was on account of reconstruction following an earthquake).

‡ The figures of net indebtedness include loans totalling £28,045 (9s. 7d. per head of estimated population) for which Colonial Government is responsible only in event of default.

Chapter VI.

2. It is clear from these figures that the burden of the public debt of British Guiana and of British Honduras, in its relation to both the population and the total expenditure of the Colony, is already so heavy that no margin for expansion remains. In each exceptional circumstances have contributed to the size of the debt.

3. A large part of the outstanding loans raised by the Government of British Guiana was spent on sea defences which, owing to the necessity for constant repair, are regarded locally as having a crippling effect on the finances of the Colony and as being a proper charge on Imperial funds.

4. The largest of the outstanding loans of British Honduras were devoted in the main to the building of the Stann Creek railway (of which the approximate cost was £137,000) and the reconstruction of Belize after the hurricane of 1931. Owing to the failure of banana crops, caused by Panama disease, the Stann Creek railway proved to be a costly burden to Government and it is now being converted to a road from monies raised by loan, the charges on which would, under the original estimate, have been less than the deficit on the railway: we understand, however, that the estimate will be exceeded by an amount which will convert the expected saving into an additional recurrent cost. A sum of over £242,000 was raised, under a Loan Ordinance enacted in 1932, principally for expenditure on the repair and replacement of both Government and private property damaged or destroyed in the hurricane of the previous year. Unfortunately (since the currency of British Honduras is linked to the United States dollar) this money was borrowed in the United Kingdom when the exchange was low and the Colony lost heavily on the transaction; moreover the advances made to individuals from the proceeds of this loan were usually secured on the property thus to be repaired or rebuilt and through the effect of weather and insects on wooden houses that security has deteriorated and is deteriorating rapidly. In short it can be said that neither British Guiana nor British Honduras has much in the way of assets to show for a public debt which is obviously a serious drain on the financial resources of both Colonies.

5. A happier example of exceptional circumstances is to be found in Trinidad, where also the public debt is high in relation to population and will be increased by the raising of a loan recently authorised. Owing in the main to the increasing prosperity of the oil industry, the revenues of Trinidad have maintained during recent years a buoyancy noticeably absent in the case of the other West Indian Colonies. The decision to raise the new loan was, we were told, taken in part in the expectation that the annual charges thus incurred could be met

by setting aside for this purpose, though not hypothecating them, one-half of the revenue from oil royalties. The amount authorised to be raised is approximately £2,500,000, but the Treasurer of Trinidad expressed to us the view that only two-thirds of that sum will be required and that the net additional charges arising from this transaction would be about £58,000. By 1945 the annual charges on existing loans will have been reduced by over £50,000 and the liabilities of the Trinidad Government in this respect will then be approximately the same, assuming that no further commitments are undertaken, as those shown in the table at the beginning of this Chapter. It is at least possible, therefore, that the Government of Trinidad would be in a position to raise an additional loan, should the need occur, in or even before 1945.

6. The burden of debt charges in relation to total expenditure is also severe in the cases of Jamaica, Grenada and St. Lucia, although the amount of debt per head of the population does not, in any of these Colonies, approach the similar figures for British Guiana and British Honduras, nor have exceptional circumstances contributed, save in a small degree, to the size of their debts. In Jamaica an additional loan has been raised since the date for which figures are given in the table at the beginning of this chapter and any further substantial increase in the liabilities of the Colony in the near future would raise the total debt to a figure not previously attained. Here, as in British Honduras, a substantial proportion of the outstanding public debt was raised for capital expenditure on a railway which, owing in part to competition from road transport, is now a charge on public funds.

7. The loans which make up the public debt of both Grenada and St. Lucia at the 31st of December, 1938, were raised for a variety of purposes. In St. Lucia a loan of over £70,000 was incurred to fund overdrafts with the Crown Agents for the Colonies and with Barclays Bank, and in Grenada the bulk of indebtedness is in respect of minor public works. The position in these islands does not call for any special comment, but the burden of debt in both is already so severe that no addition to it for any purpose should be contemplated.

8. Of the remaining Colonies or Presidencies, in each of which the outstanding debt at the 31st of December, 1938, was less than £2 per head of the population and debt charges during the last three years have accounted for a comparatively small percentage of the total net expenditure of Government, only Barbados could view without cause for serious alarm any proposal which involved an addition to existing liabilities. Neither St. Vincent nor any of the Presidencies in the Leeward Islands could afford, without detriment to essential public services, to charge its own present resources with additional debt and in all

those places any new sources of revenue can most profitably be utilised for the improvement of existing services. In Barbados the public debt, having regard to the comparative wealth of the Colony, is low and the burden of annual debt charges is not serious. Here, as in Trinidad, the possibility of financing suitable capital expenditure by loans should not be excluded.

9. This examination of the position has been made solely from the point of view of the degree of ability of the several Governments to undertake from their own resources to bear additional loan charges. Our conclusion that, with few exceptions, those Governments cannot themselves now, or even in the near future, accept any such liabilities is not to be taken as precluding the development of the territories by wise loan expenditure. On the contrary, it is our view that the financing of development by the provision of capital on a much larger scale than has previously been employed may often be both desirable and judicious. While the financial position of most of the Governments clearly precludes them from participating in this work of development, that position should not be allowed to stand in the way of progress along sound lines. There is scope for both private enterprise and broadly conceived measures entailing Imperial assistance.

2. Revenue and Expenditure of Government.

10. Statistical tables, which the Governments of the Colonies within our terms of reference have completed at our request, are included in the following Appendices to this Report:—

C.—Average annual revenue and expenditure of self-balancing Departments during the three years ending on the latest date up to which financial returns had been completed when the statistics were prepared.

D.—Analysis of average annual revenue (excluding that of self-balancing Departments) during the same period and the percentage which revenue under each item bears to the total revenue.

E.—A similar analysis of expenditure.

11. Another table was supplied covering the same period of three years and showing the percentage of average annual revenue (excluding that of self-balancing Departments and any loans-in-aid made by Your Majesty's Government) which was obtained from (a) direct and (b) indirect taxation. In view of the differences between both the systems of taxation in the several Colonies and the basis on which returns of revenue are kept, it has been necessary in compiling this table to make certain arbitrary classifications. Direct taxation has therefore been taken as including income tax, export duties, estate and any other death duties, land and house taxes and fees for licences,

while indirect taxation has been taken as including any import duties, package tax and excise. As the ratio between the yield of the two forms of taxation is of interest, this table is given below.

Colony.	Percentage of average annual revenue during last 3 years obtained by	
	(a) direct taxation	(b) indirect taxation
Barbados*	12·6	73·8
British Guiana	17·2	67·0
British Honduras	15·6	58·1
Jamaica	12·5	69·5
Leeward Islands:		
Antigua	16·6	68·4
Dominica	13·5	56·6
Montserrat	14·0	57·3
St. Kitts-Nevis	17·1	63·9
Virgin Islands	36·8	33·4
Trinidad and Tobago	25·5	56·8
Windward Islands:		
Grenada	20·0	61·0
St. Lucia	12·8	61·2
St. Vincent	22	55·7

12. Revenue not included under either of the heads in the foregoing tables is obtained from a variety of sources of which the most important are tonnage dues, fees of court and office, rents of Crown lands, reimbursements and (in a few cases) surplus on the working of self-balancing Departments, namely, those engaged with postal services, supply of electricity, etc.

13. It will be seen that, with the exception of the Virgin Islands (of which the average annual revenue for the period in question was only £4,526), these Colonies rely on indirect taxation as the principal source of their revenue.

14. On an average about 80 per cent. of indirect revenue is provided by import duties. Any marked change in the spending power of the people of a West Indian Colony is therefore likely to be reflected at once in the revenues of their Government. That power depends in the main upon the sale abroad of agricultural produce and it follows that the necessity for the relief of distress is liable to be greatest, through the failure of crops or inability to find a profitable market for them, at a time when the Government, through the consequent curtailment of their revenue, are least able to meet that need.

15. The following table shows, for all the more important services in each Colony, the percentage which the average annual expenditure during the last three completed financial years has borne to the total expenditure (excluding that of self-balancing Departments):—

* Parochial authorities in Barbados are responsible for services the cost of which elsewhere in the West Indies normally falls on central funds. If parochial taxation were included the figures given above for Barbados would become 29·7 per cent. from direct and 56·9 per cent. from indirect taxation.

Chapter VI.

Percentage of total expenditure which was devoted to:—

Colony.	Debt Charges.	General Administration (including Governor, Legislature, Secretariat, Audit).	Law and Justice.	Security (Military, Police and Prisons).	Social Services (Health, Education, Poor Relief).	Finance and Revenue Collection (Treasury and Customs).	Technical Services (Agriculture, Forestry, Veterinary, Survey).	Public Works.	Pensions and other non-effective charges.	Subventions and Subsidies.
Barbados	5·3	3·6	4·1	15·3	26·8	4·2	3·9	15·2*	7·6	5·8
British Guiana	21·1	4·5	2·6	9·3	20·8	3·0	3·8	14·5	8·0	3·5
British Honduras	20·0	7·2	1·8	12·7	17·8	6·0	8·7	9·3	7·5	3·3
Jamaica	11·1	2·7	3·5	12·9	21·2	4·8	3·7	20·0	5·6	3·9
Leeward Islands:—†										
Antigua	4·6	6·9	3·6	9·5	27·4	4·9	5·9	18·6	10·1	1·2
Dominica	2·5	6·4	4·6	11·0	29·1	5·7	7·8	16·2	8·8	1·3
Montserrat	3·0	7·6	1·5	8·5	20·1	4·6	7·3	30·2	7·1	—
St. Kitts-Nevis	3·7	6·4	4·4	8·8	31·3	6·1	6·7	13·5	9·7	1·2
Virgin Islands	—	10·5	1·3	2·8	29·5	21·5	8·7	8·9	11·0	3·0
Trinidad and Tobago.	9·5	3·6	2·7	10·0	19·9	3·4	4·0	24·5	6·3	1·9‡
Windward Islands:—										
Grenada	10·2	5·2	4·3	8·1	31·7	5·4	2·9	17·6	7·4	2·2
St. Lucia	12·4	6·7	3·8	9·8	22·8	4·2	5·6	17·2	9·0	2·1
St. Vincent	6·2	7·2	4·0	9·7	35·7	5·4	3·7	15·1	7·2	2·1

Notes.—* Includes grant to Central Road Board equivalent to 7·7 per cent. of average total expenditure.
† The contributions made by the Presidencies of the Leeward Islands towards the cost of Federal Services have been allocated locally between the various services and in every case the sum thus allocated to a particular service has been included in the Presidential analysis given above.
‡ Excludes cocoa subsidy which accounted for 4·5 per cent. of average total expenditure.

16. An examination of this table of statistics discloses the following facts:—

(*a*) Apart from Trinidad, which has lately devoted to public works a large share of its available funds, the percentage of expenditure on social services is lowest in British Guiana and British Honduras where, for reasons which have already been discussed, debt charges are highest.

(*b*) If the Virgin Islands (which have no public debt) are omitted, the percentage of the combined expenditure on debt charges, social services and public works covers the comparatively narrow range from 47·1 (in British Honduras) to 59·5 (in Grenada) and for only four other places besides Grenada is the figure over 52 per cent. It is therefore a fair generalisation to say that the extent to which each West Indian Government has been able during recent years to meet two of the needs most frequently brought to our notice—namely, the provision of social services and the improvement of communications—has been governed throughout, so far as local revenues are concerned, by the relative indebtedness of the several Governments.

(*c*) The amount spent on agriculture (which is included under technical services) is everywhere surprisingly low seeing that, as we have endeavoured to show, it is on this branch of their activities that the prosperity of the West Indies depends.

(*d*) The cost of general administration is relatively high in British Honduras (owing to the inevitable necessity for maintaining a scale of administration capable of meeting the needs of a far larger population) and in the Leeward and Windward Islands, the federation of which is discussed in Chapter XVIII of this Report.

3. Imperial Assistance and Treasury Control.

17. The following table shows the issues made from the Colonial Development Fund to the Governments of West Indian Colonies during the period from the 1st of April, 1930, to the 31st of March, 1939, to finance schemes approved by the Colonial Development Advisory Committee:—

Colony.	Grant. £	Loan. £
Barbados	23,489	16,300
British Guiana	103,964	193,674
British Honduras	224,139	53,950
Jamaica	42,206	50,000
Turks and Caicos Islands ...	1,371	—
Cayman Islands	3,100	—

Chapter VI.

Colony.	Grant. £	Loan. £
Leeward Islands:—		
Federal Government	628	—
Antigua	75,448	41,928
Dominica	50,570	36,263
Montserrat	3,120	7,284
St. Kitts-Nevis	19,014	14,862
Virgin Islands	1,700	—
Trinidad and Tobago	106,578	2,175
Windward Islands:—		
Grenada	37,241	61,177
St. Lucia	50,802	23,028
St. Vincent	8,000	56,060

18. The scope of the Colonial Development Fund is limited and it is not available for expenditure on social services. While one of its main purposes was the encouragement and development of industry and agriculture in the Colonial Empire, it was intended also to promote trade between the Colonial Empire and the United Kingdom, and the measure of relief of unemployment which would result from purchases made out of the Fund in this country was one of the factors leading to its establishment by an Act of Parliament in 1929 under which the annual revenue of the Fund may not exceed £1,000,000. The demands made on the Fund from other parts of the Colonial Empire, and its limitation both in amount and scope, have prevented the use of it to relieve in any large measure the financial needs of West Indian Governments. Nevertheless, as the table shows, British Guiana, British Honduras and, to a smaller extent, some of the Leeward Islands have derived substantial benefits from its operations.

19. The following table shows the grants and loans in aid of expenses of administration made from Imperial funds to Governments of the West Indian Colonies during the period from the 1st of April, 1929, to the 31st of March, 1939:—

Colony.	Grant. £	Loan. £
Barbados	Nil	Nil
British Guiana ((a) and (b))	264,493	549,500
British Honduras (c)	22,000	199,500
Jamaica	Nil	Nil
Leeward Islands:—		
Antigua (d)	32,635	30,000
Dominica (e)	36,700	77,750
Montserrat	—	28,000
St. Kitts-Nevis (f)	9,251	10,000
Virgin Islands	Nil	Nil
Trinidad and Tobago	Nil	Nil
Windward Islands:—		
Grenada	Nil	Nil
St. Lucia (g)	76,849	—
St. Vincent	Nil	Nil

Notes.

(a) Includes grants and loans amounting to £326,033 made during the years 1930–33 for the relief of unemployment.
(b) Includes a grant of £2,460 and a loan of £35,000 made in 1935 in aid of the development of the resources of the Colony.
(c) Includes a loan of £50,000 made in 1937–38 in aid of the development of the resources of the Colony.
(d) Includes grants of £21,635 made in 1930–31 for the relief of unemployment.
(e) Includes grants and loans totalling £20,200 and £4,250 respectively in aid of the development of the resources of the Colony.
(f) The grant of £9,251 was made in 1930–31 for the relief of unemployment.
(g) Includes a grant of £349 made in 1931 for the relief of unemployment.

20. Where a Colonial Government is in receipt of a grant in aid, or of a loan in aid, of recurrent expenditure, this relief from Imperial resources is usually conditional upon Treasury control of the finances of the Colonial Government. That control is exercised through the scrutiny and approval by the Treasury of the annual estimates of the Colony and the requirement that their approval shall also be obtained for supplementary expenditure not covered by savings and for other expenditure if, under any item, it exceeds an amount laid down by them. Complaint was made to us of the delay which this system inevitably involves. We are of the opinion that Treasury control may have to be retained, in the interest of the taxpayer in the United Kingdom, in so far as concerns direct grants in aid of recurrent expenditure on general administration. But we make, in Chapter XXI of this report, recommendations which would ensure less rigid arrangements for the control of funds to be spent on improving the social conditions of the West Indian peoples and we feel that thereby more enterprise in administration might be promoted.

4. Taxation.

21. We have already indicated the percentages of Government revenues which, during the last three years, have been obtained from indirect and direct taxation and the figures which we have given show that in most of the West Indian Colonies the ratio between the yields from the two sources is between four and five to one. The question naturally arises whether it is not possible, as was suggested to us by several witnesses, to increase the revenue derived from direct taxation by raising the rates of duty, or by improving methods of collection, or by both devices. Of the various forms of direct taxation only income tax and estate duty require consideration in detail. Each of these is discussed below.

Chapter VI. 76

(a) INCOME TAX.

22. Income tax is levied in all the territories, with the exception of the Virgin Islands, within our terms of reference. In none of them is there any arrangement comparable to the standard rate of income tax which forms the basis of the system prevailing in the United Kingdom. Instead each Government has adopted a complicated table of graduated rates no two of which are identical throughout. Everywhere these tables start with a very low rate of tax, such as a penny or twopence, on each £1 of the first £100 or £200 of taxable income, i.e., income after the deduction of reliefs (including personal allowance) and, in Jamaica and Dominica, the amount of exempted income which in effect is a personal allowance. All of the tables then proceed by different stages, each involving a higher rate of tax on income in excess of that covered by the preceding stage, to such varying levels as 4s. on each £1 of taxable income above £10,000 (in Jamaica), 5s. on each £1 of taxable income above £1,000 (in Dominica) or £7,500 (in Barbados), 6s. on each £1 of taxable income above £3,000 (in St. Vincent) or £9,750 (in British Guiana) and 38 cents in each dollar, plus an additional 10 per cent., i.e., over 8s. 4d. on each £1 of taxable income over £7,917 (in Trinidad). This is, in effect, the adoption throughout the whole range of income tax of the principles upon which the system of surtax in this country is based.

23. The reliefs from income tax which are granted by West Indian Governments follow generally the principles adopted in the United Kingdom. They take the form of personal allowances, and allowances (in a few Colonies only) for earned income and relief in respect of a wife, children, dependent relatives and life insurance; the full amount of any premium paid in respect of insurance on the life of the taxpayer or his wife may be deducted from his taxable income subject to a limit which, as a rule, is fixed at one-sixth of the chargeable income before any other reliefs are deducted from it.

24. The effect of these varying systems is best shown by the following tables which give the amount of tax payable at various stages of income by (i) a single person and (ii) a married person with three children in the United Kingdom and in each of the territories with which we are concerned:—

Chapter VI.

(i) *Amount of Tax payable by a single person.*

Amount of Tax Payable when Taxable Income before Deduction of Reliefs is:—

Territory.		£150.	£250.	£500.	£1,000.	£5,000.	£10,000.
		£ s. d.	£ s. d.	£ s. d.	£ s. d.	£ s. d.	£ s. d.
United Kingdom*	(a)	1 13 4	8 6 8	56 12 6	166 12 6	1,591 6 3	4,227 11 3
	(b)	4 3 4	15 7 6	84 2 6	221 12 6	1,673 16 3	4,310 1 3
Barbados		Nil	1 5 0	6 5 0	28 2 6	540 0 0	1,650 0 0
British Guiana		Nil	3 0 0	12 0 0	41 5 0	641 5 0	1,773 15 0
British Honduras ...		10 6	2 0 0	6 10 0	21 10 0	581 10 0	1,771 10 0
Jamaica		Nil	Nil	2 5 10	17 18 4	422 12 1	1,222 12 1
Leeward Islands:—							
Antigua		1 0 0	2 10 0	10 8 4	39 7 6	865 4 2	1,990 4 2
Dominica		1 0 0	2 10 0	12 14 2	68 19 2	1,037 1 8	2,287 1 8
Montserrat		7 1	2 1 8	9 3 4	37 1 8	792 1 8	1,804 11 8
St. Kitts-Nevis ...		4 2	1 9 2	8 19 2	41 9 2	893 2 6	2,018 2 6
Trinidad and Tobago		Nil	Nil	4 3 4	22 18 4	572 10 0	2,202 18 4
Windward Islands:—							
Grenada		17 6	3 2 6	10 0 0	37 10 0	885 0 0	2,260 0 0
St. Lucia		16 8	2 18 4	11 13 4	44 3 4	911 13 4	2,286 13 4
St. Vincent		1 11 0	3 17 4	12 18 4	44 3 4	1,009 3 4	2,509 3 4

* The figures for the United Kingdom include super tax which is not levied in any West Indian Colony; they are based on the rates of tax prevailing in August last.
(a) Income wholly earned.   (b) Income wholly from investments.

Chapter VI.

(ii) *Amount of Tax payable by married person with three children.*

AMOUNT OF TAX PAYABLE WHEN TAXABLE INCOME BEFORE DEDUCTION OF RELIEFS IS:—

Territory.		£150.	£250.	£500.	£1,000.	£5,000.	£10,000.
		£ s. d.	£ s. d.	£ s. d.	£ s. d.	£ s. d.	£ s. d.
United Kingdom*	(a)	Nil	Nil	3 6 8	95 2 6	1,519 16 3	4,156 1 3
	(b)	Nil	Nil	12 12 6	150 2 6	1,602 6 3	4,238 11 3
Barbados		Nil	Nil	2 7 6	22 10 0	525 0 0	1,625 0 0
British Guiana ...		Nil	Nil	3 15 0	26 5 0	596 5 0	1,715 12 6
British Honduras ...		Nil	Nil	4 0 0	16 10 0	556 10 0	1,740 5 0
Jamaica		Nil	Nil	18 9	17 18 4	422 12 1	1,222 12 1
Leeward Islands:—							
Antigua		1 3	18 4	6 16 8	35 5 0	855 1 8	1,980 1 8
Dominica		Nil	18 4	7 6 8	61 1 8	1,025 16 8	2,275 16 8
Montserrat		Nil	6 8	6 0 0	29 10 0	770 14 2	1,783 4 2
St. Kitts-Nevis ...		Nil	9 2	6 12 6	37 6 8	883 0 0	2,008 0 0
Trinidad and Tobago		Nil	Nil	7 6	12 13 4	525 5 0	2,117 3 4
Windward Islands:—							
Grenada		Nil	12 6	6 5 0	30 0 0	885 0 0	2,260 0 0
St. Lucia		16 8	2 18 4	11 13 4	44 3 4	911 13 4	2,286 13 4
St. Vincent		10 0	2 5 10	9 16 4	41 2 10	998 1 4	2,498 1 4

* The figures for the United Kingdom include super tax which is not levied in any West Indian Colony; they are based on the rates of tax prevailing in August last.

(a) Income wholly earned.   (b) Income wholly from investments.

25. Before considering, in the light of the comparative information given by these tables, the question whether the system of income tax obtaining in the West Indies ought to be revised, we must mention another important aspect of that system. Although, as has been shown above, there is no standard rate of income tax in the West Indies, much the same effect is secured by taxing the chargeable income of companies in most Colonies at a fixed rate. This is usually 2s. or 2s. 6d. in the £, but is often still lower in the case of life insurance companies which, in some Colonies, are taxed at a rate equivalent to the average applicable to an individual whose chargeable income is £1,000. Jamaica, however, is an exception, and the anomalous system prevails there of taxing companies according to the graduated scale applicable to individuals. This arrangement is a direct encouragement to the formation of subsidiary companies.

26. There is also variation in the treatment of income arising abroad and not brought into a Colony. In British Honduras such income is entirely exempt from tax. We recommend that, as in this country, taxpayers who are permanent residents should be compelled to show in their returns all income wheresoever arising and that such income should be made liable to tax with corresponding relief from double taxation.

27. This completes the account of the major differences between the two systems of income tax, and it remains to consider whether, and, if so, to what extent the existing arrangements in the West Indies should be altered. It would be difficult to resist the conclusion that there is justification for the complaint, which was put to us in evidence, that the sacrifice required from the limited class now liable to income tax in the West Indies is not as onerous as that made, through indirect taxation, by the less prosperous sections of the community. It would be still more difficult to resist the argument that, if the taxpayer in the United Kingdom is called upon to provide additional assistance for the West Indian Governments, the level of direct taxation imposed by them ought to be brought nearer to its standard in this country. Absolute equality of direct taxation would be difficult to justify since, as a form of return for his contribution to revenue, the direct taxpayer in the United Kingdom receives the benefits of services far more diverse and better organised than any that in present circumstances can be provided in the West Indies. We do consider, however, that participation by any West Indian Colony in the additional financial benefits which are recommended later in this Report should be conditional upon an undertaking by the Government of the Colony to overhaul their system of taxation in order to bring it more closely into line, as regards the

standardisation of the income tax, the level of taxation (including surtax), the liability to tax of income wheresoever arising and the taxation of both companies and land, with the system obtaining in the United Kingdom.* Further reference to the question of land taxation is made in part 5 of this Chapter.

28. When, as in Barbados, a heavy parochial tax is payable to defray expenses which elsewhere would be met from central revenues, it would be reasonable, if that form of taxation cannot at once be remitted, to take into account the additional burden thus borne by the direct taxpayer when the question of the new standard rate of income tax is under consideration. The equity of the principle of approximate equality of sacrifice by persons of equal wealth in the West Indies and at home is unquestionable and that principle should be the governing factor.

29. It is not possible to give an accurate estimate of the effect which the adoption of these proposals would have upon the revenues of the West Indian Governments. Owing to the operation of the normal arrangements for the grant of relief from double taxation the imposition in the West Indies of any higher rate than one-half of the standard rate prevailing at the time in the United Kingdom would not result in any increase in the revenue thus secured either from the profits of companies registered in the United Kingdom but engaged in business in the West Indies or from the dividends received by individual shareholders in such companies. For the same reason the new arrangements might have only a limited effect upon the revenue derived directly or through individuals from the profits of companies registered in other parts of the British Empire with which arrangements for relief from double taxation exist. It must also be borne in mind that the number of persons liable to taxation in the West Indies who are in receipt of substantial incomes (from which alone could greatly increased yields be secured) is nowhere large and outside Barbados, Jamaica and Trinidad is small even in relation to population. Tables of assessments for the year 1938, which were supplied at our request, show that in the remaining territories the numbers of returns by individuals of a taxable income of between £2,500 and £5,000, between £5,000 and £10,000 and over £10,000 were only 21, 4, and 1 respectively. For Barbados, Jamaica and Trinidad combined the corresponding figures were 158, 49 and 26. But unless it can be demonstrated by any of the Governments concerned that the revision of taxation which we suggest would not increase their revenues, all of these should make the change for the sake of the principle which we have mentioned and in the interest of uniformity within the group. Later in this Report the appointment

---

* We have here in mind the rates of tax prevailing in August, 1939.

is suggested for the West Indies, as a whole, of a person with expert knowledge of the administration of income tax in this country. There are many ways in which his services and advice would be useful. Apart from assistance in securing uniformity, which is clearly desirable, his experience should enable him to suggest methods whereby income tax could be more efficiently and effectively collected and additional safeguards could be provided against evasion of tax of which complaint was made in evidence to us although this was not supported by proof.

(b) ESTATE AND LEGACY DUTIES.

30. There is no estate, legacy or succession duty in any of the Presidencies of the Leeward Islands.

31. In Barbados estate duty is payable on the death of any person whose property in the Colony would be liable to a duty in England under the Finance Act of 1894, and the duty charged is the amount which would have been payable in England in respect of that property under the Act of 1894 or any Acts amending or altering it. No estate duty is payable in respect of the property of any deceased person who was domiciled in Barbados, and there was no provision for either legacy or succession duty as recently as May last though it was understood that this might be made in the near future.

32. In British Guiana also, no legacy or succession duties are imposed, but estate duty is charged on the net value of all property as defined in the provisions of a complicated Ordinance, and the duty is fixed at a percentage of the net value of the property, the minimum rate being $\frac{1}{2}$ per cent. where the value is between $500 (about £104) and $2,500 (about £520), and the maximum rate being 50 per cent. where the value exceeds $10,000,000 (about £2,083,000). Property abroad is taken into account for this purpose, subject, however, to an allowance of the amount of any estate duty payable to the Government of the country where the property is situated. Relief in respect of quick succession is granted, and the rate of duty on the first $25,000 (about £5,200) of the property may be halved if it passes to the widow of the deceased or to his minor male children or unmarried female children, or to children certified as unable, through infirmity, to earn a livelihood.

33. There is no legacy or succession duty in British Honduras, but estate duty is charged upon the principal value as defined by Ordinance, of all property, real and personal, passing on death, and " the estate " is defined by law as including property of the deceased situated outside the Colony, the usual provision being made for relief from double taxation. The rates at which duty is charged rise from 1 per cent. where the value of the estate is between $100 (about £21) and $500 (about £104), to

15 per cent. where the value of the estate exceeds $50,000 (about £10,417). The rate of duty is halved in respect of property passing to the wife or other close relatives of the deceased.

34. In Jamaica estate duty is charged on all property or interest in property, whether real or personal, passing on death and amounting to over £1,000. The rates charged vary from 3 per cent. where the value of the estate is between £1,000 and £2,000 to 20 per cent. where the value exceeds £500,000. Reciprocal arrangements are made between Jamaica and certain other British possessions for relief from double estate duty. In addition, legacy duty is collected on personal property and succession duty on real property at rates which vary from 1 per cent. to 10 per cent. according to the degree of consanguinity. These duties are payable on bequests exceeding £20 except in the case of lineal issue and their descendants and lineal ancestors and their descendants, all of whom enjoy an exemption up to £200 for adults and £500 for minors. Complete exemption from both legacy and succesion duty is granted to a surviving spouse and in the case of estates of a net value of £50 or less.

35. In Trinidad estate duty is charged on the principal value of property passing on death and amounting to over £100. The minimum rate is $\frac{1}{2}$ per cent. where the value of the estate is between £100 and £1,500 but estates of small gross values (up to £500) may be exempted on payment of fixed rates of duty of 15s. or 25s. The maximum rate is 10 per cent. and that is charged on estates of which the principal value exceeds £25,000. In addition succession duty is collected on any interest acquired by a person, as the successor of the deceased, in property passing on death; the rates vary from $\frac{1}{2}$ per cent. (where a husband, lineal descendant or ancestor succeeds to an interest of which the value is between £20 and £500) to 20 per cent. (where a distant relative or stranger in blood succeeds to an interest of more than £10,000). Exemption from this duty is granted to a surviving wife and for certain charitable bequests.

36. In each of the Windward Islands only one form of duty is levied, and although this is known as estate duty in Grenada and St. Vincent and as succession duty in St. Lucia, the arrangements in force are practically identical in the three islands. The duties are levied on all real and personal property passing on death, subject to certain exemptions which include property situated out of the Colony unless it is personal property of a person who, at the time of his death, was domiciled in the Colony and no duty is payable in respect of the property under the laws of the country in which it is situated. Provision is also made for relief in respect of quick succession, and only one half of the normal rate is charged on property passing to the wife or other close relatives of the deceased. In all the territories the minimum rate of duty is 1 per cent. where the value of the

estate is between £100 and £300, and the maximum rate (12 per cent. in Grenada and St. Lucia and 10 per cent. in St. Vincent) is imposed on estates of a value exceeding £80,000.

37. These particulars have been given in detail in order to show the wide variations between the existing systems in the several Colonies. The table below shows the average annual amount thus collected during the last three years in each of the Colonies concerned and the percentage of the total net average revenue obtained from this source:—

	£	Percentage.
Barbados	1,838	0·4
British Guiana	27,183	2·4
British Honduras ...	662	0·3
Jamaica	47,316	2·2
Trinidad and Tobago ...	20,199	0·9
Windward Islands:—		
Grenada...	980	0·7
St. Lucia	820	0·9
St. Vincent	53	0·1

38. It will be seen that only British Guiana and Jamaica collect more than 1 per cent. of their total revenue from this form of internal taxation. The legislation in force in the former Colony, where the yield is highest in relation to both population and total revenue, is modelled closely on Acts of Parliament, and the rates of estate duty correspond nearly to those imposed in this country. The arguments for assimilating the rates of estate duties in the other West Indian Colonies to those prevailing in this country are less strong than they are in the case of income tax, for, in the West Indies, agricultural land is the chief form of property, and it is coming to be recognised in the United Kingdom that the imposition of high death duties on agricultural land has unfortunate consequences. Indeed the main reason why high duties are found practicable in British Guiana is that much of the land in production there is owned by companies which escape this form of taxation.

39. In these circumstances we do not feel able to apply, without qualification, to estate and other death duties the recommendation made in regard to income tax that the system in the West Indies should be brought more closely into line with that prevailing here. We feel, however, that the question whether the rates of these duties could not be increased, subject to a suitable measure of exemption for agricultural land, is one which deserves the serious attention of the Governments of all West Indian Colonies where the rates are now substantially below their levels in the United Kingdom.

(c) RELATIVE BURDENS OF DIRECT AND INDIRECT TAXATION.

40. The relation between direct and indirect taxation was mentioned to us by witnesses in several Colonies and in almost every case the complaint was made that the burden fell most

heavily on those least able to bear it. The figures which we gave when discussing earlier in this Chapter the sources of Government revenues in the West Indies show that on an average about 60 per cent. of these annual revenues has been obtained during recent years by indirect taxation. But with the adoption of the suggestions made in regard to income tax, the burden of the direct taxpayer, though it may not thereby be substantially increased in several of the territories, would at least be weighted, by standards recognised as appropriate in this country, according to his ability to bear it. Moreover, it must be remembered that nowhere in the West Indies is there to be found a middle class comparable in size or wealth with the one which provides the larger part of the direct revenue of this country and it would be unreasonable to impose upon the limited wealthy class in the West Indies a scale of taxation even more onerous than that prevailing at home for the purpose of securing a closer relation between the yields of the two forms of taxation. If our proposals are adopted no reasonable ground will remain for the complaint that in the West Indies the direct taxpayer is specially favoured by comparison with the treatment accorded to the payer of indirect taxation.

41. Any comparison between the weight of direct and indirect taxation would be incomplete without an examination, however brief, of the possibilities of raising additional revenue through indirect means or, alternatively, of lessening the existing scale of that form of taxation. Since import duties provide on an average 80 per cent. of the yield of indirect taxation the problem is, in effect, whether those duties can be increased or whether they should be reduced. The customs tariff has recently been simplified in most of these Colonies but is still complicated and more could be done in this direction by the removal of existing surtaxes. Everywhere a preference is granted to most Empire produce which is usually taxed at between one-third and two-thirds of the rate applicable to imports from foreign sources. All goods are subject to import duty unless specifically exempted by a table which as a rule does not include the imported foodstuffs most commonly in use, or, indeed, any of the principal imports of the Colony. During the last three years for which figures are available the revenue from import duties, expressed as a percentage of the value of total imports, varied from 29 in British Guiana and 23 in Antigua and St. Kitts-Nevis to 14 in British Honduras and the Virgin Islands and 12 in Barbados. Some further idea of the scale of taxation on what are now regarded by many West Indians as essential imports can be gained from the following table, which shows the duties imposed in all these Colonies on nine of the commodities figuring most prominently in their trade statistics:—

Chapter VI.

IMPORT DUTIES, ETC., ON VARIOUS COMMODITIES IMPORTED INTO CERTAIN WEST INDIAN COLONIES.

	Wheat Flour.		Rice.		Canned Meat.		Salted Fish.		Condensed Milk.		Lard.		Refined Sugar.		Edible Oil.		Boots, etc.	
	British Preferential Tariff.	General Tariff.	British Preferential Tariff.	General Tariff.	British Preferential Tariff.	General Tariff.	British Preferential Tariff.	General Tariff.	British Preferential Tariff.	General Tariff.	British Preferential Tariff.	General Tariff.	British Preferential Tariff.	General Tariff.	British Preferential Tariff.	General Tariff.	British Preferential Tariff.	General Tariff.
(g) (h) Barbados	Whole-meal: Free. Other: 3s. 9d. per 196 lb	2s. per 196 lb. Other: 5s. 6d. per 196 lb.	1s. per 100 lb.	2s. per 100 lb.	4s. 2d. per 100 lb.	8s. 4d. per 100 lb.	1s. 6d. per 112 lb.	4s. 6d. per 112 lb.	Free to 10s. (f) per case of 48 lb.	2s. to £1 (f) per case of 48 lb.	2s. 1d. per 100 lb.	8s. 4d. per 100 lb.	8s. 4d. per 100 lb.	16s. 8d. per 100 lb.	2d. per gallon	4d. per gallon	3d. per pair or 10 per cent. to 12½ per cent. ad valorem.	1s. 1½d. to 2s. 6d. (e) per pair or 30 per cent. ad valorem.
(a) British Guiana	4s. 2d. per 196 lb.	5s. 9¾d. per 196 lb.	2s. 1d. per 100 lb.	4s. 2d. per 100 lb.	6s. 3d. per 100 lb.	12s. 6d. per 100 lb.	Morocut: 4d. Other: 3s. 1¾d.	Morocut: 2s. 1d. Other: 9s. 4¼d.	£1 per 48 lb.	£3 per 48 lb.	2s. 4¾d. per 100 lb.	7s. 2d. per 100 lb.	12s. 6d. per 100 lb.	£1 5s. per 100 lb.	2s. 6d. per gallon except mustard and olive oil	5s. per gallon	50 per cent. ad valorem.	16⅔ per cent. ad valorem plus 24 cents per pair.
(a) (j) British Honduras	1s. 0½d. per 196 lb.	3s. 1½d. per 196 lb.	1s. 0½d. per cwt.	2s. 1d. per cwt.	10 per cent. ad valorem	20 per cent. ad valorem	10 per cent. ad valorem	20 per cent. ad valorem	Free	5 per cent. ad valorem	2d. per 100 lb.	8s. 4d. per 100 lb.	6s. 3d. per 100 lb.	10s. 5d. per 100 lb.	10 per cent. ad valorem	20 per cent. ad valorem	5d.— 1s. 0½d. per pair or 12½ per cent. ad valorem.	1s. 5¼d.—2s. 1d. (e) or 12½ per cent ad valorem plus 2s. 1d. per pair.
(k) Jamaica	1s. 6d. per 100 lb.	2s. per 100 lb.	2s. 3d. per 100 lb.	3s. per 100 lb.	10 per cent. ad valorem	25 per cent. ad valorem	3s. 6d. per 100 lb.	7s. per 100 lb.	1s. 6d. per 48 lb.	3s. per 48 lb. or 1s. 6d. per 48 lb. plus 10 per cent. ad valorem whichever is the higher	6s. 3d. per 100 lb.	12s. 6d. per 100 lb.	6s. 3d. per 100 lb.	8s. 4d. per 100 lb.	1s. per gallon	1s. 4d. per gallon	15 per cent. ad valorem	25 per cent. ad valorem.
(l) Antigua	7s. per 196 lb.	9s. per 196 lb.	3s. per 100 lb.	4s. 6d. per 100 lb.	8s. 4d. per 100 lb.	12s. 6d. per 100 lb.	2s. per 100 lb.	4s. per 100 lb.	6s.—12s. (f) per 48 lb. (f) or 10 per cent. ad valorem	9s.—18s. per 48 lb. (f) or 15 per cent. ad valorem	4s. 2d. per 100 lb.	12s. 6d. per 100 lb.	2s. per 100 lb.	8s. 4d. per 100 lb.	10 per cent. ad valorem	15 per cent. ad valorem	10 per cent. ad valorem 1s. to 2s. per pair.	10 per cent. ad valorem plus 1s. to 2s. per pair.
(m) Dominica	8s. 4d. per 196 lb.	12s. 6d. per 196 lb.	2s. 6d. per 100 lb.	3s. 9d. per 100 lb.	10s. per 100 lb.	15s. per 100 lb.	5s. per 100 lb.	7s. 6d. per 100 lb.	1s. (d.— 3s. (f) per 48 lb.	2s. 8d.— 5s. (f) per 48 lb.	5s. per 100 lb.	12s. 6d. per 100 lb.	4s. 2d. per 100 lb. (b), 14s. 7d. p. 100 lb.	4s. 2d. per 100 lb. (b), 20s. 10d. p. 100 lb.	9d. per gallon	1s. 2d. per gallon	10 per cent. ad valorem (e) plus 3d.—1s. per pair.	10 per cent. ad valorem (e) plus 2s. per pair.
(n) Montserrat	7s. per 196 lb.	9s. per 196 lb.	3s. per 100 lb.	4s. 6d. per 100 lb.	8s. 4d. per 100 lb.	12s. 6d. per 100 lb.	2s. 6d. per 100 lb.	4s. 2d. per 100 lb.	6s.—12s. (f) per 48 lb. (f) or 10 per cent. ad valorem	9s.—18s. per 48 lb. (f) or 15 per cent. ad valorem	4s. 2d. per 100 lb.	10s. 5d. per 100 lb.	2s. per 100 lb.	8s. 4d. per 100 lb.	10 per cent. ad valorem	15 per cent. ad valorem	10 per cent. ad valorem	10 per cent.— 20 per cent. (e) ad valorem 1s.—2s. per pair.

Chapter VI.

	Wheat Flour.		Rice.		Canned Meat.		Salted Fish.		Condensed Milk.		Lard.		Refined Sugar.		Edible Oil.		Boots, etc.	
	British Preferential Tariff.	General Tariff.	British Preferential Tariff.	General Tariff.	British Preferential Tariff.	General Tariff.	British Preferential Tariff.	General Tariff.	British Preferential Tariff.	General Tariff.	British Preferential Tariff.	General Tariff.	British Preferential Tariff.	General Tariff.	British Preferential Tariff.	General Tariff.	British Preferential Tariff.	General Tariff.
(o) St. Christopher and Nevis	7s. per 196 lb.	9s. per 196 lb.	2s. 10d. per 100 lb.	4s. 3d. per 100 lb.	8s. 4d. per 100 lb.	12s. 6d. per 100 lb.	1s. 6d. per 100 lb.	3s. 6d. per 100 lb.	6s.—12s. per 48 lb. (f) or 10 per cent. ad valorem	9s.—18s. per 48 lb. (f) or 15 per cent. ad valorem	4s. 2d. per 100 lb.	10s. 5d. per 100 lb.	2s. per 100 lb.	4s. 2d. per 100 lb.	10 per cent. ad valorem	15 per cent. ad valorem	10 per cent.—20 per cent. ad valorem plus 1s.—2s. per pair.	General Tariff.
(p) Virgin Islands	3s. per 196 lb.	5s. per 196 lb.	2s. per 100 lb.	3s. 6d. per 100 lb.	6s. 8d. per 100 lb.	10s. per 100 lb.	4s. 2d. per 100 lb.	8s. 4d. per 100 lb.	4s.—8s. (f) or 8 per cent. ad alo em	6s.—12s. (f) or 12 per cent. ad valorem	2s. 1d. per 100 lb.	6s. 3d. per 100 lb.	2s. per 100 lb.	3s. per 100 lb.	8 per cent. ad valorem	12 per cent. ad valorem	6 per cent.—10 per cent. ad valorem	12 per cent.—20 per cent. ad valorem
(q) Trinidad and Tobago	1s. 6d. per 196 lb.	3s. 6d. per 196 lb.	1s. per 100 lb.	2s. per 100 lb.	4s. 2d. per 100 lb.	8s. 4d. per 100 lb.	1s. per 100 lb.	3s. per 100 lb.	6¼d.—10s. per 48 lb. (f) or 10 per cent. ad valorem	2s. 2d.—£1 per 48 lb. (f) or 20 per cent.	1¼d. per lb.	5½d. per lb.	2d. per lb.	4d. per lb.	Certain oils 3s. 6d. per gallon Other 9d. per gallon	specified —. 7s. per gallon oils.:—1s. 6d. per gallon	6s. 8d. per doz. pairs (e) 10 per cent. ad valorem	£1 per dozen pairs (e) or 30 per cent. ad valorem or 10 per cent. ad valorem plus 3s. per pair, whichever is the higher.
Grenada ...	5s. per 196 lb.	7s. 6d. per 196 lb.	2s. per 100 lb.	3s. per 100 lb.	4s. per 100 lb.	6s. per 100 lb.	1s. 8d. per 100 lb.	2s. 6d. per 100 lb.	Free	2s. per case not exceeding 48 lb.	8s. 4d. per 100 lb.	12s. 6d. per 100 lb.	10s. per 100 lb.	15s. per 100 lb.	1s. per gallon	1s. 6d. per gallon	15 per cent ad valorem	22½ per cent. ad valorem (e) and 1s. per pair to 25 per cent. ad valorem
(r) St. Lucia ...	6s. per 196 lb.	9s. per 196 lb.	2s. per 100 lb.	3s. per 100 lb.	6s. 8d. per 100 lb.	10s. per 100 lb.	2s. 6d. per 100 lb.	3s. 9d. per 100 lb.	5s. 4d. per 48 lb.	8s. per 48 lb.	10s. per 100 lb.	15s. per 100 lb.	4s. 2d. per 100 lb.	6s. 3d. per 100 lb.	6d. per gallon	9d. per gallon	15 per cent. ad valorem	15 per cent. ad valorem plus 1s. to 2s. (e) per pair to 22½ per cent. ad valorem
St. Vincent ...	5s. per 196 lb.	7s. 6d. per 196 lb.	1s. 3d. per 100 lb.	3s. per 100 lb.	6s. 8d. per 100 lb.	10s. per 100 lb.	1s. 3d. per 100 lb.	3s. 4d. per 100 lb.	4s. 2d. per 100 lb.	8s. 4d. per 100 lb.	5s. per 100 lb.	12s. 6d. per 100 lb.	6s. 6d. per 100 lb.	9s. 9d. per 100 lb.	1s. (c) per gallon 10d. (d) per gallon	1s. 6d.(c) per gallon 1s. 3d.(d) per gallon	12½ per cent. ad valorem	12½ per cent. ad valorem (e) plus 1s. to 3s. per pair to 18¾ per cent. ad valorem.

NOTES.

(a) The customs tariff of these Colonies are expressed in dollars which have been converted to sterling at 4/80 to £1.
(b) The manufacture of the Colony.
(c) Lucca, olive and other similar refined table oils.
(d) Cotton seed, soya bean and other similar oils.
(e) Varying duties according to the type of footwear.
(f) According to butter fat content.
(g) Surtax of 10 per cent. of the duty is charged on all goods subject to customs duty.
(h) Package tax of 1d. per package is charged on all dutiable goods.
(j) Package tax of 10 cents.
(h) Package tax of 1s. per package is charged on all dutiable goods subject to a variation of the rate in the case of certain commodities.
(l) Trade tax of one quarter of one per centum on the value is charged on all dutiable goods except goods imported for private use or not exceeding a value of five pounds.
(m) Trade tax of ⅜ per cent. on all dutiable goods imported for sale.
(o) Surtax of 25 per cent. of the duty is also charged.
(p) Surtax of 2 per cent. of the duty is also charged.
(q) Surtax of 15 per cent. of the duty is also charged in the case of canned meat, some condensed milk, lard and some boots.
(r) Surtax of 25 per cent. of the duty is also charged except in the case of wheat flour.

42. Although, as will be seen from this table, the rates of import duty are high, it is only in British Guiana and Trinidad (for which the figures are about £2 5s. and £2 16s. respectively) that the total yield of indirect taxation of all forms exceeds £2 per annum per head of the population and the similar average over the whole of the West Indies is 33s. When regard is had to the standard of living of those people who pay the greater part of this taxation, an average annual contribution to revenue of 33s. is admittedly high, but the figure is so much lower than that (about £7 per person per annum) paid by the indirect taxpayer in the United Kingdom that it would be difficult to justify any substantial reduction of the existing rates of import duties and excise in the West Indies, if financial assistance from Imperial funds is now to be provided for those territories. On the other hand, no material increase in any form of indirect taxation that falls on the necessities of life in the West Indies should be contemplated in present circumstances.

(d) Miscellaneous Taxation Questions.

43. In the course of evidence several suggestions were made for increasing the revenue of particular Colonies. Only the more important of these need be examined here. Some of the suggestions—for example, one that a high rate of duty should be imposed on all imported cement—had as their primary object the protection of existing or projected local industries rather than the increase of Government revenue. Any such proposals raise important questions of policy which are considered, in connection with problems of employment, in Chapter XIII of this Report, and for present purposes it will suffice to point out that in so far as projects of this nature secured their principal purpose of protecting local industries, they would fail as a means of additional revenue and might in fact deprive Government of some revenue already received.

44. Another suggestion was that where tourist traffic is considerable a tax—or an increased tax if a small levy is now made—should be imposed on tourists. Any moneys thus obtained could be paid into a reserve fund to be used only in times of adversity when the number of visitors to the Colony might decline. A special tax on tourists already operates in Jamaica, but the proceeds of it are there expended on the improvement of services intended to attract a larger number of tourists to th Colony. The suggestion is one which may well be left for consideration by the several Governments directly concerned.

45. Witnesses in Trinidad proposed that substantial additional taxation should be imposed upon the oil industry of that Colony. The contribution which that industry already makes to the revenues of the Colonial Government, mainly through

the payment of royalties and income tax, is considerable, and no reason was put forward in evidence which would justify the singling out of the oil companies for a special additional liability.

46. In some Colonies considerable difficulty has been, and still is, experienced in the collection of taxes, and the amount of arrears is often now substantial. The question is one upon which guidance from outside can be of little use to the local authority, but where the arrears are due in the main to the levying of house or land tax upon properties of little value, and the cost of collection approaches, and may sometimes exceed, the proceeds of the tax, Colonial Governments may be well advised to give serious thought to the possibility of raising the minimum point at which these taxes operate to a level at which the labour and expense involved in bringing them into revenue would be more clearly commensurate with their yield.

5. Finance of Local Authorities.

(a) INDEBTEDNESS.

47. There are no local authorities in the Presidencies of Antigua, Montserrat, St. Kitts-Nevis and the Virgin Islands.

48. The following table shows the total net indebtedness of the local authorities in the other territories on the 31st of December, 1938, and the extent to which that indebtedness was in the form of loans or advances from the Colonial Government:—

Territory	Total net indebtedness at 31.12.38 £	Total of sums included in preceding column which are owed to Government £
Barbados	21,267	nil
British Guiana	878,540	744,900
British Honduras	68,599	68,599
Jamaica	1,619,314	1,611,474
Leeward Islands:		
Dominica	1,232	612
Trinidad & Tobago (including Central Water Board).	261,562	233,971
Windward Islands:		
Grenada	89,077	7,076
St. Lucia	15,013	2,618
St. Vincent	2,693	2,693

From a comparison of the figures in the last column of this table with figures given in the first table in this Chapter it will be seen that the debts of local authorities to Government on the 31st of December, 1938, were in Jamaica 37 per cent. of the net indebtedness of the Colonial Government on that date while the similar percentages in the cases of British Guiana and British Honduras were 17 and 11 respectively. Only in British Guiana.

has any serious problem arisen in connection with the due payment to Government of the charges on loans made by them to local authorities. In that Colony the financial position of certain drainage areas, with particular reference to the liabilities of local authorities for the capital cost of drainage works and their maintenance, was recently the subject of a prolonged inquiry by an authoritative Committee of the Legislative Council which has recommended the remission of certain debts and the readjustment of others. Further reference to this matter is made in Chapters XVI and XXIV of this Report.

(b) REVENUE OF LOCAL AUTHORITIES.

49. The following table shows the average annual revenue of local authorities in each of the territories over the latest period of three years for which completed accounts are available and states the percentage of local revenue which was derived from (a) rates, (b) Government grants and (c) all other sources.

Territory	Average Revenue £	Rates	Govt. Grants	Other Sources
Barbados	134,771	68·0	5·6	26·4
British Guiana	201,300	75·0	3·6	21·4
British Honduras	21,548	65·4	15·7	18·9
Jamaica	538,902	67·2	4·5	28·3
Leeward Islands:				
Dominica	3,053	87·5	nil	12·5
Trinidad and Tobago (including Central Water Board)	258,149	52·3	4·3	43·4
Windward Islands:				
Grenada	8,113	46·5	8·5	45·0
St. Lucia	13,030	34·0	nil	66·0
St. Vincent	3,867	74·1	6·2	19·7

In St. Lucia the principal items contributing to the revenue under " other sources " are water dues from shipping (19·4 per cent.), sale of electric current (19·2 per cent.) and market dues (11·8 per cent.); in Trinidad they are fees for licences (9·9 per cent.), receipts from institutions (7·1 per cent.) and sale of electric current (6·0 per cent.); in Grenada they are market dues (16·0 per cent.) and overland dues (10·9 per cent.) Elsewhere, as in the United Kingdom, much the greater part of the revenues of local authorities is raised by rates on real property, i.e. land and buildings. But the value of agricultural land represents in the West Indies a far higher proportion of the total value of real property than it does in the United Kingdom. Moreover, the system in vogue in many West Indian Colonies of valuing houses and buildings is one which underrates their assessment in comparison with that of agricultural land and from the limited examination which we were able to make, there appear to us to be good grounds for believing that in some territories (particularly Barbados) the burden of rates may bear too severely upon owners of land. When to this is added the fact that in many of the Colonies a land tax is imposed for purposes of both central and local revenue, it will be realised that landowners may be called upon to make a contribution to the expenses of the administration which is unreasonable when compared with that made by other payers of income tax.

50. The basis of the system of rating and its scope vary so widely between the several Colonies that it was not possible for us thoroughly to explore the question on which we have touched above, and we can only suggest therefore that the Government of each Colony should consider the advisability of instituting, as suitable opportunity offers, a thorough inquiry into the prevailing system of land and local taxation with a view to its simplification and to its readjustment, where necessary, upon a basis which will secure a more equitable allocation of its liabilities. The contribution of land to central revenues ought normally to be obtained through the payment of income tax upon the basis of an assessment of its net annual value. Whether such a change is practicable is a point which could no doubt be borne in mind both during the inquiry which we have suggested above and when the system of income tax is overhauled in the way proposed earlier in the Chapter.

(c) NEW SOURCES OF REVENUE.

51. Representatives of certain local authorities suggested in evidence that in order to improve their financial position the Government should hand over public utility services to them, or should secure these for them by purchase from private enterprise. The particular case of the telephone concession in Trinidad is discussed in Chapter XIX. In none of the others was the evidence tendered so conclusive as to justify a more positive recommendation than that Governments ought to keep constantly under review all possible means of increasing the revenues of local authorities and so widening their activities which, when properly conducted, deserve every encouragement as a most useful form of training in public administration.

52. The expenditure of local authorities covers a range of purposes which varies so widely from territory to territory that no general survey can readily be given; nor does it call for any comment.

PART II

SOCIAL SERVICES
EXISTING POSITION AND NEEDS

CHAPTER VII.

EDUCATION.

1. Descriptive.

1. In theory the British West Indies possess a fairly complete educational system. Primary and Secondary Schools have long existed, there are institutions for the training of teachers and higher education in certain subjects is available at Codrington College in Barbados and the Imperial College of Tropical Agriculture in Trinidad. Efforts have been made to establish institutions of university rank in the West Indies from time to time but, apart from the exceptions mentioned above, and in spite of a frequently expressed feeling that this lack should be remedied, these projects have come to nothing.

2. An examination of the working of the educational systems, however, reveals serious inadequacies in almost every respect. There is not nearly enough accommodation for the children who attend schools; and these include by no means all the children of school age. Existing accommodation is frequently badly planned and in a chronic state of disrepair and insanitation. Teachers are inadequate in number, and are in most Colonies not well paid. Their training is largely defective or non-existent, and far too great reliance is placed on the pupil-teacher system—theoretically a means of training teachers, but all too often simply a means of obtaining cheap staff.

3. Curricula are on the whole ill-adapted to the needs of the large mass of the population and adhere far too closely to models which have become out of date in the British practice from which they were blindly copied.

4. The administration and finance of schools are often so divided between Government and private institutions (notably the Christian Denominations) as to render difficult the formulation of an educational policy, let alone its vigorous and consistent execution.

5. These conditions, which admit of numerous exceptions in individual cases, have come about after a period of more than a century, during which it has been an accepted policy to extend the benefits of education to the entire population irrespective of race or creed. Before emancipation, education was in effect denied to the labouring population. The first few years which followed saw great activity and a good deal of expenditure by the Imperial Government and the local Governments as well as by private humanitarian organisations and

by the Churches. By the '50's and '60's of the nineteenth century, the first burst of enthusiasm waned and education fell into the doldrums, as is shown by the strictures passed by contemporary enquiries. It is interesting to note that then, as now, the questions of the relation of curricula to the future life of the pupils, and of the adjustment of the relations between the denominations and Government took a prominent place in discussions of educational policy.

6. From the first, Governments followed, as in England, a dual policy of, on the one hand, granting conditional assistance to denominational schools, and on the other setting up schools under complete Government control, sometimes as models, sometimes to provide facilities where no denominations could or would do so. With continual modification and in an atmosphere of constant debate, this system has lasted to the present day and is an integral part of the educational provision of the West Indies. The proportionate part played by the denominations and Government schools varies, an extreme example being St. Lucia, where among 47 primary schools no single one is managed by the Government.

7. The most important factor which has led to the gradual modification of the relations between Governments and the denominations is finance. With occasional exceptions, the period has ended when the Churches could look outside the Islands for any substantial support, and Government assistance has increased until, at present, the denominations' functions are mainly confined to management and the provision and maintenance of school buildings. Even in this respect it is increasingly usual for Government to grant assistance for building, books and equipment. Government normally provides the whole of the cost of teachers' salaries, and in return has a say in the appointment and dismissal of staff, curricula and management, and the right of inspection, thus possessing a financial sanction against gross inefficiency. The efficacy of such a sanction depends, of course, on the possibility of improvement being effected whether by the denominations or by Government itself; and does not render impossible the existence of many schools where the standard of accommodation and teaching leaves much to be desired.

8. The natural criticism is frequently made that, however valuable their services to education may have been in the past, the denominations have now played their part, and that Government, which already provides such a large proportion of the cost of education, and which in effect controls it already, should formally assume the whole responsibility. There are numerous complaints, some to our minds justifiable, that schools are housed in buildings primarily adapted for religious exercises,

with the result that many consist of a more or less large single room,* crammed with children, where one or more teachers have to attempt to teach different subjects to over-large classes of children of all ages under conditions of the utmost difficulty and distraction. That the educational results of such a system are slight cannot be a matter for surprise: that they exist at all simply shows that human ingenuity, enthusiasm and devotion in the West Indies as elsewhere often exceed what it is reasonable to expect, a factor on which it would not be proper to base an educational or any other policy. Further, the teachers' associations frequently complained to us that the denominational managers paid undue attention in matters of appointment to such educationally irrelevant considerations as the applicants' religious affiliations and their willingness to undertake church duties at the weekends or during the week. We are not in possession of any conclusive evidence on this point—the religious bodies denied that such considerations played an important part in their decisions—but there is no doubt that this feeling is widespread, and of itself must detract from that harmonious working of the educational system which is necessary if it is to have the best effect.

9. On the other hand, we believe that the denominational system has the support of a large proportion of the population, and any attempt to abolish it would give rise to serious opposition. And there are certain considerations which lead us to the conclusion that its retention in some form is of positive educational value. One characteristic of the West Indies is the regrettable absence of those factors and traditions which elsewhere make for social cohesiveness and a sense of membership of a community. Almost the sole integrating agency has been the religious influence exercised by the Churches. Religion plays an important part in the life of a large proportion of the population and if, as we hope, education is to perform its proper function of the creation and transmission and continual improvement of a social tradition, it would be most unwise to cut it completely adrift from the Churches. We hope to see education, in its broadest sense, come to be regarded not as something extrinsic to the life of the people but as a part of it in which they have a lively interest, and for the running of which they may in time come to share the responsibility. This development will be much facilitated if it can be carried out in close collaboration with the Churches, the one important institution having intimate knowledge and the confidence of large sections of the community. It is true that certain modifications regarding the details of denominational control are desirable in the interests of educational efficiency. We believe

---

* This is by no means the universal rule with regard to denominational school buildings. An example of a good type of school room is given in Plate II.

that the removal of causes of mistrust and criticism at present existing can be effected without divorcing education from an organic connection with the Churches; and that this would result in an enhancement of the prestige of the Churches and of their consequent value in education as in others of their fields of activity.

10. Reference has frequently been made above to " education in the West Indies ", and to educational policy. The deduction must not be drawn that there is any agency which formulates such a policy, or that such a system exists, for the Caribbean area as a whole. Similarity of history has almost alone produced such uniformity in organisation and practice as there is: until very recently there was little or no attempt to effect any form of continuous inter-colonial co-operation in this or in other spheres. One recent development, however, points the way to the future and is greatly to be welcomed. This is the appointment in 1936 (as a result of a recommendation of the West Indies Education Commission*) of Education Commissioners for the Windward and Leeward Islands. Two Commissioners were appointed whose function it was to inspect and report to the Governors concerned and to the Secretary of State on educational problems, and to render all assistance possible in the execution of policies approved as a result of their recommendations. This appointment has been made possible by the generosity of the Carnegie Corporation of America, and is but one of the manifold benefactions to social development in the West Indies as elsewhere for which that body is responsible. Both Commissioners have repeatedly toured the Islands under their purview, and we have had the opportunity of studying their Reports for 1937 and 1938†; Mr. S. A. Hammond, the Senior Education Commissioner, also submitted to us a separate memorandum, on which we had an opportunity of questioning him during our stay in Trinidad.

11. It is difficult to exaggerate the value, particularly in the smaller and poorer Colonies, of such a system. None of them can afford from its own resources very much more than its present expenditure on education; and without some external stimulus and advice it is almost impossible for Governments to avoid falling victim to a sense of discouragement which renders unlikely the best and most economic use of available resources. This system has the great advantage over the occasional *ad hoc* enquiry, in that it enables the Commissioner to follow up his inspection by advice as to the detailed application of his recommendations in varying circumstances and for varying needs, and to effect running modifications in his policy through

---

* Colonial No. 79 of 1933.
† Colonial No. 164 of 1939. The 1937 report was not published.

Chapter VII. 96

seeing how it works out in practice. We do not propose here to detail the Commissioners' proposals, but to indicate the nature of an existing means of providing expert advice to a group of impecunious Colonies independently of political federation. We are strongly of the opinion that this organisation should not lapse, whether or not the Carnegie Corporation decide to continue the grant of assistance which has made possible its inauguration.

12. Educational facilities and the amount spent on them vary from island to island. The following table is appended giving some statistics regarding primary education for the year 1937.

Chapter VII.

PRIMARY EDUCATION.

(Statistics for 1937 except where otherwise stated.)

1. Colony.	2. Schools.	3. Teachers (excluding pupil teachers).	4. Pupil teachers.	5. Estimated number of children of school age.	6. Enrolment.	7. Enrolment as percentage of number of school age.	8. Average attendance.	9. Average attendance as percentage of enrolment.	10. Enrolled pupils per teacher.*
Barbados	126	614	35	30,000	26,397	88·0	19,582	74·2	43
British Guiana	243	924	162	†	52,318	†	38,978	74·5	58
British Honduras	79	165	44	15,000	10,431	69·5	7,791	77·5	63
Jamaica	661	2,180	188	196,000	158,418	80·8	103,325	65·0	73
Leeward Islands¶ :—									
Antigua	23	57‡	44‡	8,000	6,124	76·6	3,874	62·8	107
St. Kitts-Nevis	33	107	78	9,000	7,867	87·4	5,519	70·1	74
Montserrat	12	33	28	3,700	2,873	77·0	2,085	73·1	87
Dominica	33	87	51	12,400	7,723	62·3	5,138	66·5	89
Virgin Islands	11‡	19‡	14	1,550	1,268	81·8	824	64·1	67
Trinidad and Tobago	293	1,333	555	88,740	72,766	82·0	50,799	69·8	55
Windward Islands :—									
Grenada	60†	112‡	119‡	26,000	13,391	51·5	8,757	65·4	120
St. Vincent	47	99‡	105‡§	21,850	10,159	46·5	6,995	68·9	103
St. Lucia	37	81‡	83‡	14,500	10,457	72·1	5,972	57·1	129

Notes.

* In arriving at these figures, pupil teachers have been ignored. Hence, the figures for some, especially the smaller and poorer colonies, are very large, as pupil teachers there form an important part of the teaching strength (see columns 3 and 4).
† Not ascertainable.
‡ 1936 figures.
§ Including 69 probationers.
¶ In some of the Leeward Islands, the figures in column 3 include Assistant Teachers some of whom were paid as, and had the qualifications of, pupil teachers.

Comparable figures for secondary education are not available. Some of these figures are estimates only, e.g., those of the population of school age, owing to the absence or unreliability of recent census figures. It will be seen that the average attendance varies between 60 per cent. and 75 per cent. of the enrolment, with a few exceptions. In no case is the average number of enrolled pupils per teacher (ignoring pupil teachers) less than 43, and in several Colonies it is very much more. (The corresponding figure for England and Wales is 30 and that for the average of 26 European countries is 36·6.) It must also be remembered that it is usual for several classes to meet simultaneously in one unpartitioned room, which greatly increases the strain on the teachers. It is difficult adequately to describe in words what these conditions can mean; Plate III shows a school-building of the single-room type, and Plate IV the extremes to which overcrowding in schools can go. Public expenditure on education is also far from uniform, but low, a medium figure per child in average attendance being £2, and per head of the population about 4s. Corresponding figures for England and Wales quoted by the West Indies Education Commission were about £15 and £2s. 10s. Although this expenditure is extremely low, the additional cost of providing even the same standard of education for say 95 per cent. of the children of primary school age would be well outside the financial powers of practically all of the West Indian Colonies either at present or at any time within the measurable future. For this reason, while primary education is free and open to all, it has not been made compulsory except in certain limited areas. Schools which are at present overcrowded when attended by 50 per cent. or 60 per cent. of the children of school age would be totally inadequate to accommodate the whole; and only the provision of adequate accommodation and—still more—of teaching staff adequate in numbers and attainments could justify such a step.

13. Linked with the question of compulsory attendance is that of absenteeism which, as figures show, is a very serious problem. The figures for average attendance vary between about 60 per cent. and 75 per cent. of those actually enrolled in the primary schools (as compared with a figure of over 90 per cent. for the secondary school enrolments). This represents a very serious educational loss. The causes of chronic absenteeism are mainly social and economic: children stay away from school on Mondays because that is by custom washing-day and it is unusual for members of poor and large families to possess a change of clothes; and towards the end of the week to help with the cultivation of food-crops or with the preparation of their parents' produce for market. Economic improvement will doubtless do much to remove these causes, but the habits are deeply ingrained and will themselves have to be dealt with.

Constant propaganda will be necessary, and later in this Chapter we recommend that where school meals are being inaugurated a beginning should be made with meals on the later days of the week, to induce parents to send their children to school at what are often the lean times before pay-day. The clothing difficulty may be met by the provision of clothes for children from the poorest homes. But the best method is the introduction and enforcement of compulsory attendance wherever accommodation, etc., warrant the measure. In order that such a campaign may have the widest possible effect, the provision of adequate accommodation should not be confined to the urban areas but spread throughout the country districts as well, so that the example of the consequent improvement in attendance may be as widespread as possible, even although it may not be practicable at once to provide sufficient accommodation to warrant the introduction of universal compulsory attendance.

14. Secondary schools exist in the West Indies many of which provide an excellent classical education, but they provide for only a very small proportion even of the children who pass through the primary schools. As it is, unemployment is rife among the products of secondary education, owing to the lack of suitable "white-collar" jobs and the disinclination of the pupils to take employment in agriculture as at present organised.

15. Inadequate as the teaching staff is in numbers, it is still more inadequate in training. Very few have had more than a primary education, followed by a period as pupil teachers where, in theory, they learn the technique of teaching under supervision and sit for examinations leading to certification. In practice, the shortage of staff is such that the supervising teacher has quite enough to do in looking after his or her own classes, and may often be ill-qualified to give any very useful instruction. The pupil teacher therefore in effect works as a full teacher and picks up what he can by trial and error. Training colleges exist in several of the Colonies, but in the case of Trinidad only can it be said that there is an early prospect of trained teachers being the rule in all schools. In Jamaica, where there are no less than four training Colleges, 58 per cent. of the primary teachers have received College training, although here too steady progress is being made. It would be beyond the finances of the Governments of the smaller islands to establish teachers' training institutions, nor, owing to the smaller numbers of students who would pass through them, would it in any case be economic for such Governments to do so. Schemes have therefore been adopted whereby students from the Windwards and Leewards are admitted for training at the Government Training Colleges in Trinidad, a move which is certainly on the right lines.

16. In this connection the question of salaries is relevant. Without attempting to estimate what might be a valid relationship between English and West Indian salaries, it is clear that, with the exceptions of Barbados, Trinidad and Jamaica, primary teachers' salaries are low. They have, however, been regraded in the recent past in many islands, and any substantial improvement would not be within the financial compass of the smaller Colonies. There is scope, however, for so arranging scales as to give incentives for improvement, and some measure of regional uniformity is strongly desirable if a healthy interchange of staff is to be encouraged.

17. The summary table here given shows the salaries until recently paid throughout the West Indian Colonies. In certain Colonies there have recently been some though not considerable changes and regradings. The wide range of emoluments for the same type of teachers in the same Colony (e.g., Barbados, head teachers' salaries range from £80 to £340 per annum) is accounted for by the fact that salaries vary according to the qualifications of the teacher and the grade (normally = size) of his school. This table excludes pupil teachers, whose allowances are frequently from £6 to £24 per annum according to Colony, seniority and qualifications. In several Colonies head teachers receive in addition free quarters (or allowances in lieu up to £24 per annum) and " result grants " based on the examination records of their schools.

Primary School Teachers' Salaries (£.p.a.).

	Head teachers	Assistant teachers
Barbados (men)	80—340	35—100
(women)	60—290	35—75
British Guiana	75—275	41—69
British Honduras	56—191	38—77
Jamaica	96—200	36—100
Leeward Islands (average)	65—120	24—42
Trinidad (men)	85—275	45—125
(women)	80—228	40—120
Windward Islands:		
St. Lucia	15—125	17·10*—25
St. Vincent	25—150	40—75
Grenada	30—150	12—60

* Refers to registered assistant teachers. Unregistered assistant probationers (junior in standing to pupil teachers) received £4. 16s. per annum.

18. It will be seen that there is a marked difference between Barbados, British Guiana, Jamaica and Trinidad on the one hand, and British Honduras, the Leewards and the Windwards on the other. It is this kind of disparity which in the past has rendered impossible any plan for a joint West Indian or even regional teaching service; and it is not within the financial powers of the smaller islands to bring up their standards to those of, e.g., Trinidad.

19. We have mentioned earlier in this chapter (paragraph 4) that the control of educational policy is uncertain. This is true particularly of the smaller islands, where finance has not permitted the establishment of strong educational departments. By virtue of the extent of Government financial assistance the control of curricula and staffing does ultimately rest with Government in the primary schools; in the secondary schools the pressure of the external examination and popular demand for teaching leading up to it is sufficient to ensure as good academic teaching directed to that end as resources will allow. It is seldom that primary and secondary education are supervised by the same authority, although there may be an overlap. In Jamaica the Department of Education is directly responsible for primary education; whereas secondary education is under the aegis of the Jamaica Schools Commission, a statutory body with a strong unofficial element, and having executive functions. The present Director of Education happens to be Chairman also of the Jamaica Schools Commission, but is not so in virtue of his office. In the smaller islands the Inspector of Schools, the sole Government officer dealing with education, deals with primary education alone, and is normally so fully occupied with inspection and routine administrative work, that he has little leisure or opportunity to devote his mind to the broad lines of educational policy. The desirability of co-operation with other departments, notably those of agriculture and health, is almost universally recognised; but such actual collaboration as we saw depended more on the energy and imagination of individuals working under adverse conditions than on the existence of any organised machinery for that purpose. However, the possibility of such collaboration, as for the adequate direction of educational policy, exists in virtue of the financial sanction in the hands of Government; and the question is one of its proper organisation. For the smaller islands it appears to us to be unnecessarily expensive to attempt to set up elaborate educational departments, and that much greater benefit is likely to be drawn from a permanent organisation on the lines of the Educational Commissioners for the Windwards and Leewards. There should, however, be in each island an officer who can devote his time to the supervision of education as a whole and not be submerged in routine administration and inspection. This officer could usefully have other functions in connection with social welfare.

20. We observed in the first paragraph of this Chapter that, apart from the Imperial College of Tropical Agriculture in Trinidad and Codrington College in Barbados, there is in the West Indies no institution of university status. At the present time those who wish to pursue university studies have either to follow postal courses or to go overseas either to the United Kingdom or to the United States or to Canada. Some students are

assisted by Government and other scholarships; but these are necessarily few in number, and the expense of going abroad for a number of years makes it quite impossible for all but a very few West Indians to go to a university on their own resources. Also, the very handsomeness of the available scholarships causes them to exercise an influence on the type of secondary education given which is far from being wholly good. The prospect of a degree of affluence even for three or four years much in excess of what the large majority of secondary school leavers can expect in their homes tempts many to compete unhealthily for the few scholarships, with little thought of what they will do with them and less of what they will do in the probable event of failure. The subsequent careers of scholarship-holders have, on the whole, been somewhat of a disappointment considering the amount of public money which has been spent on many of them, and this gives rise to the feeling that a university education is desirable which does not cut off the student from his own people so completely as at present. One group of witnesses informed us that the present system bears most hardly on the girls: that most parents given the choice will sooner spend money on their sons' higher education than on their daughters', with the result that there is a great scarcity of educated women to undertake social work.

21. Witnesses repeatedly advocated to us the desirability alike in the interests of education and of the political development of the West Indies of the establishment of an institution or institutions of university status to serve the area as a whole. Our evidence on this point was not, however, unanimous, several witnesses, including officials, holding that an effective demand does not yet exist in the shape of sufficient potential students to render worth while the large expense which would be involved, and pointing to the difficulty of finding employment for the graduates. It is, however, most difficult to base any firm conclusion on conditions as they are at present. It may well be that the supply of facilities would in fact evoke the demand.

22. One of the chief difficulties is the dispersal of the population of the West Indies over a large area, for the most part in fairly small communities with poor and expensive inter-colonial communications. It is almost as easy and as cheap for a Jamaican student to travel to the United Kingdom as it would be for him to travel to, say, Trinidad; and on the whole the purely geographical advantages of having a university in the West Indies are not so great as they might at first sight appear.

23. A further difficulty is that of locality. There can be no doubt that any attempt to centralise all faculties in one Colony, which, for this purpose, would mean Trinidad, Barbados or Jamaica, would arouse great resentment elsewhere, and

jeopardise the prospects of that harmonious inter-colonial co-operation which it would be one of the objects of such an institution to foster. But many of our witnesses felt that this difficulty could be met by constituting a West Indian University on the basis of some central controlling and examining authority with faculties or colleges in different parts of the group. The possibility of higher classical studies clearly exists in Codrington College in Barbados, of agricultural study and research in the Imperial College of Tropical Agriculture in Trinidad, and in the evidence of the Director of Education of Jamaica it was suggested that the centre for higher science teaching in the Island, for which proposals have been put forward, might form the basis for a faculty of science. From various quarters it was also suggested that there is a need for a medical training college for West Indians, although some doubts were expressed whether the teaching and training in such an institution could be of the quality at present available to students proceeding overseas. Experience in other parts of the world, however, suggests that some such institution would be of great benefit to the area as a whole. Such an institution would, of course, have to be located in one of the larger centres of population where there is adequate clinical material, and it might at the same time be a most valuable centre of research into tropical diseases and conditions of living.

24. We consider that the establishment of institutions of collegiate rank is an entirely laudable object to be pursued when funds are available. In view of other more urgent developments involving heavy financial demands, we do not feel that we are in a position to make detailed recommendations on this matter; but we agree that a system of faculties in different centres is an object which should be borne in mind, rather than the establishment of a comprehensive university in some single Colony. Educational development is in fact spontaneously tending in this direction, and we recommend that when any projects are under consideration for the establishment of institutions for advanced training in any subject, the possible place of such an institution in a collegiate framework should be borne carefully in mind. Wherever possible, such projects should be considered in consultation with other Governments, and care should be taken that they do not overlap unnecessarily with developments elsewhere.

25. There remains a further subject of vital importance which has not so far received in the West Indies the attention which it deserves—education in health and hygiene. " Hygiene " figures in practically all curricula, good text-books are now available on tropical hygiene, and most of the new school readers contain chapters dealing with health matters. But the relation of the subject to the life of the community is defective,

and its teaching almost invariably theoretical only. If this teaching is to be of effect, the school buildings and arrangements must not as at present negative by example the precepts there enjoined. Inadequate water supplies, bad latrines, pools of water in grounds strewn with refuse, leaking roofs, overcrowded classrooms, ill-designed furniture and lighting arrangements which cause eyestrain are all too common, although there are encouraging exceptions.

26. Bad conditions are largely but not entirely due to poverty on the part of the authorities responsible for buildings and equipment: ignorance also plays a part; and many of the worst features could be eliminated with little additional expenditure, given the necessary knowledge.

27. There is a great need for clear, definite guidance for the education authorities themselves in such matters as school sanitation; vague recommendations have long been familiar and are useless. The formulation of such guidance in explicit and detailed terms should be one of the first preoccupations of the Committee of which we recommend the establishment at (2) in paragraph 100 below; as should the clear explanation to education authorities and teachers of the way in which the teaching of hygiene should be tackled. Teaching on such subjects as diet, the prevention of hookworm and malaria must be related as carefully as possible to local conditions and customs if it is really to be carried over into the lives of the people. The teaching should be closely associated where appropriate with such subjects as civics, domestic science, child welfare, nutrition, agriculture and house construction. In this connection the possibility should not be overlooked of following the practice increasingly adopted in many parts of the world including Great Britain of making available for school purposes specimen dwellings similar in type to those in which the children will later live. These might be built partly by the older boys under competent supervision and could be used as demonstrations of healthy habits of living, and notably for girls' domestic science training, small numbers of girls being taken in turn for tuition.

28. Before concluding this section, we feel it necessary to mention one further factor of vital importance in West Indian education, the continued and rapid growth of population. The resources of the Colonies are rarely adequate to enable them to cope with the existing child population, and do not permit of any very substantial improvement without external aid. West Indian Governments are faced in addition with the demand for educational facilities for a growing child population, an increasing percentage of which is attending the primary schools. The implications of this for education are twofold:—

(1) a heavy direct burden is placed on educational budgets through the pressure of numbers;

(2) indirectly, through the strain thrown by population growth on the standards of living of the community, and the consequent diminution of economic opportunities, the difficulty of preparing pupils for life in the West Indies is greatly enhanced.

29. The population problem in its broader social and economic aspects is more fully discussed in Chapter XII: it suffices here to mention it in order to show its important bearing on the task of educational advance.

2. Previous Expert Reports.

30. In the preceding paragraphs we have discussed in broad outline the existing general system, indicated some of its main deficiencies and hinted at some remedial measures. In this section we shall mention briefly the main recent inquiries into education in parts of the West Indies and discuss their chief recommendations. We wish here to place on record our great appreciation of the value of these reports for the future of education in the West Indies. They have also greatly simplified our task in this respect, not only because of the intrinsic value of the surveys and recommendations which they contain, but because the public debate which they have aroused has given us invaluable clues to the intricacies of the existing position and to the local attitude towards educational problems of all kinds.

31. First in time and fundamental in importance of these reports is that of the West Indies Education Commission* to which we have already referred and of which the members were Mr. F. C. Marriott, then Director of Education, Trinidad, and Mr. A. I. Mayhew, joint secretary to the Advisory Committee on Education in the Colonies which is attached to the Colonial Office. The territories with which they concerned themselves were Trinidad, Barbados, Grenada and St. Vincent. To these were added during their travels St. Lucia and the Leeward Islands, on condition that their recommendations would not involve additional expenditure.

32. Their most important recommendations may be briefly summarised as follows:—

    (1) the restriction of primary schooling to children of age 6-12;

    (2) provision of crèches, play-centres, etc., for younger children;

    (3) provision of new post-primary " modern " schools for ages 12-15, having vocational and practical bias, to supplement existing secondary schools;

---

* Colonial No. 79 of 1933.

(4) appointment of educational commissioners for **Windwards and Leewards**;

(5) central training in Trinidad of teachers from the smaller islands;

(6) institution of a Central Library system based on Trinidad and in connection with the teachers' training institute, to serve adult education;

(7) the better association of local opinion in the formulation of educational policy by the creation of Advisory Boards, including unofficial representatives of all sections of the community, notably agricultural and industrial interests; these Boards to have no executive functions;

(8) simplification of primary curricula, with the aim of giving an adequate grounding in essentials such as correct use of language and arithmetic, and interest in surroundings.

33. We had an opportunity of discussing these proposals with Mr. Mayhew before we left for the West Indies, and he made it clear to us that what was recommended was not a diminution of the educational provision but a pruning of what has become a sprawling, ineffective growth. By dividing education into well-marked stages, it is hoped to attain a greater efficiency within each stage than is possible when the primary schools are used at one end as crèches or kindergartens and at the other as a means of obtaining a rudimentary intermediate education. These proposals of the 1932 Commission aroused a good deal of local opposition, on the mistaken ground that they were designed to lower the standard of education for the people; we have satisfied ourselves, firstly, that there was and could be no such intention on the part of the authors of the report, and, further, that their proposals were well conceived to lay the foundations of a better-articulated and more comprehensive structure. An unbiased reading of their report shows that it was not intended to reduce the present opportunities for secondary education on the traditional " classical " lines, but to supplement it, as has notably been done in this country, by " modern " schools. These schools would at once provide post-primary education for many who to-day get none, and an alternative to the " classical " education which numbers of pupils in secondary schools at present have to take for want of choice. For our part, we should not for a moment countenance any attempt to reduce educational facilities from their present low level. We do not however consider that there is any danger of any responsible authority in the West Indies attempting to do so, and we trust, in the consideration of the complex needs of the West Indian education, no further attention will be paid to this imaginary danger. Care must, however, be taken to guard against any tendency for the modern school

to be treated in respect of buildings, staff and equipment as less important than the existing secondary schools.

34. Certain of the recommendations of the 1932 Commission are now bearing fruit, and their general findings may be said to form the basis of educational reconstruction at any rate in the Eastern Caribbean area. Advisory Boards are being set up on the lines which they suggested, which provide for certain powers of initiation, and also for the delegation to such Boards of certain executive functions. The Trinidad Government Training College is taking students on a fee basis from the Windwards and Leewards, and its capacity in this respect will presently be greatly enhanced, through the munificence of the Carnegie Corporation. The same body have also made a grant for a Central Library system, which is to cover the Windwards and Leewards as well as Trinidad. A beginning has been made with the provision of intermediate schools* for children of 12-15 and having a practical bias. Lastly, and again (as we have already stated) through the agency of the Carnegie Corporation, Education Commissioners for the Windwards and Leewards were appointed in 1936 for a period of three years. This is to our minds the most important single result of the 1932 Commission, as it provides a means of supplying the Governments of the smaller islands with continuous expert advice, without which it is doubtful whether any valuable progress could have been made with the other recommendations of the Commission. The development is important, not only in the value of the services which have thereby been rendered to education in the Windwards and Leewards, but as an experiment in the technique of supplying advice on specialised subjects to units of government too small individually to afford staff of adequate experience and calibre. To this matter we shall return in later Chapters.

35. The first report of the Education Commissioners, based on an inspection of the Windwards and Leewards during 1937, contains a most valuable survey of the educational systems as they then existed. The general tenor of their observations tally with those of the 1932 Commission, and with our own as set out above. A most valuable feature of this first report (which, though not published, is summarised in the earlier pages of the 1938 Report†) is an attempt to relate educational policy to social conditions in the islands, and to point out in what respects the efficacy of even the best system of education is dependent on the social and economic environment from which the child comes and in which he will subsequently have to make his living. In particular, it is rightly stressed that the

---

* For an example of the excellent building associated with some of these new intermediate schools see Plate V.
† Colonial No. 164 of 1939.

provision of post-primary education with a practical or agricultural bias will be of little avail if the conditions of life which the pupil may expect remain as uninviting as they have traditionally been and, with slight improvement, continue to be. In his evidence before us, Mr. Hammond remarked that in one island the ex-pupils of a school where agricultural and practical subjects were best taught contained the lowest percentage of agriculturists: the highest percentage was shown by one of the most backward schools concentrating on the traditional curriculum unrelated to the life of the community. It is difficult not to share his view that in present social and economic conditions the best-taught children, in whatever school, will be the least likely to take to life on the land. If education is to fit the West Indian to make the most of the opportunities afforded by his own country, those opportunities in their turn must be sufficient to attract those who have had a good education. Educational and social progress, indeed, must go hand in hand if either is to be of permanent value, and cannot in fact be separated from one another.

36. This approach made it essential for the Commissioners to treat of education in its broadest sense, and to include not only primary and secondary education as ordinarily conceived but the care, both at home and in play-centres, of the pre-school child, adult education and the place of the school as a community centre and as a training in civics for persons of all ages. For the development of healthy societies, encouraging the qualities of self-help and a sense of social responsibility so lacking in the West Indies to-day, much more is needed than the mere exercise of a vote and the right to stand for election to a central legislature. The West Indies are practically devoid of all the multifarious institutions, official and unofficial, which characterise British public life and bring a very large proportion of the population into some living contact with the problems of social importance. It is the view of the Education Commissioners, which we share, that whatever else may be done in the more strictly political sphere, the educational system can be made the framework of much social activity, especially in remoter parts, to the immense benefit both of itself and of the life of the community which it serves. This will be particularly important in connection with developments in land settlement, discussed in Chapter XVII. Although from its earliest inauguration as much stress has been laid on the social as on the economic value of land settlement, little or no provision has been made to ensure the emergence of real community life; and this omission has played a part in the relative failure of many of the land settlement projects of the last 35 or 40 years. The school, as the centre for adult education, talks and demonstrations on agriculture and hygiene, mothercraft, wireless or the broadcast

programmes, cinema shows, as well as for the ordinary education of the children of school age, suggests itself as the best means of attaining this end; and the possibility should not be overlooked of associating the community, whether through parent-teacher associations or otherwise, in responsibility for the running of the schools, in order that they may come to regard them as their own and to take a real interest and pride in them.

37. It is not to be thought that none of this has hitherto taken place. Sporadically some of these activities have been initiated throughout the West Indies, through the energy and enthusiasm of departments, managers, and, not least, teachers and groups of teachers themselves. Instances are the lively parent-teacher associations in parts of Jamaica, and the praiseworthy efforts of the Tobago Teachers' Association: many more could be mentioned. But these functions are far too important to be left to the unco-ordinated enthusiasm of individuals, and we agree that definite steps should be taken by Departments of Education in regular consultation with the Agricultural, Health, Labour and Land Settlement Departments to promote their establishment as an integral part of the social and educational system.

38. The Education Commissioners also stressed the unsuitability of the curricula of most of the primary schools, the chief faults being over-elaboration and lack of touch with the lives of the children. Insufficient importance is placed on the formation of habits of clear and connected speech, and the correct use of words, which is all the more important in view of the prevalence throughout the West Indies of patois of varying degrees of unintelligibility and imprecision. In the official memorandum on education submitted to us in British Honduras it was stated that the children whose vernacular was a totally different language (such as Spanish or Carib) seem to learn to speak and write " correct " English more readily than those who speak " Creole ", the local name for a kind of pidgin-English which is spoken by many. The same difficult problem —of effecting drastic repairs on a degenerate form of English rather than imparting knowledge of a completely new language —faces teachers all over the West Indies and requires the most careful handling. The Commissioners pointed out also that the teaching of hygiene and, where it existed, of nature-study and the elements of agriculture, was too often half-hearted and theoretical. The difficulties of teaching the importance of habits of cleanliness are admittedly great in schools which are often overcrowded and ill-provided with the most elementary sanitary equipment; but even so there is wide scope for valuable work by teachers who are alive to the importance of these subjects, and who have received some instruction in suitable teaching methods.

As regards the elements of agriculture, beginnings have been made with school gardens and simple biology all over the West Indies; but the results have on the whole been discouraging in the area covered by the Education Commissioners. The experiment of appointing a special agricultural instructor to the staff of the Education Department in Grenada has, we were informed, lessened the teachers' sense of responsibility and interest in this work instead of increasing it. Much more hopeful is the carefully elaborated experiment in British Guiana, where the Departments of Education and Agriculture have collaborated in selecting certain schools and training the teachers for this work. The results here have been good, and the increasing number of home gardens started in response to this stimulus is a sign of the lively interest aroused. This indicates the importance of making a very careful start, and of collaborating to the full with the technical departments concerned. (For further discussion of this matter see the Agricultural Report, Chapter XVI, paragraph 3.)

39. The Commissioners criticised the teaching of history and geography as being based upon text-books which are quite unsuitable for children in the West Indies. Some knowledge of the outlines of the history of the Caribbean Colonies, and of their relation to the British Empire and its constitutional development, is obviously desirable; but it is difficult to justify any study of minor details of English history.

40. The Education Commissioners stressed, as they could not fail to do, the inadequacy and unsuitability of very many of the school buildings in the Windwards and Leewards; but stated that, in their view, there was a danger that the very prominence of these defects might lead to a disproportionate concentration on fabric, and prejudice the even more important task of improving the teaching staff in quality and number. Many of the present one-room schools could, they felt, be made reasonably suitable by means of movable screens, which would afford better ventilation than more substantial divisions, and also make easier that supervision by head teachers which will be necessary until a much higher standard of teaching is generally attained. They deprecated the erection of imposing concrete structures, both on grounds of initial expense, and because such materials can never become indigenous to the West Indies. In the almost total absence in the country districts of buildings which can set standards for the rural population, they felt that there was much to be said for cheaper structures, erected by local craftsmen from local materials in styles and by methods which could be copied. They stressed that the major effort must be reserved for the improvement of the teaching force, and to this end they recommended:—

(1) that increasing use should be made of the facilities for training of new entrants in Trinidad;

(2) the improvement of the existing staff by means of specially-trained supervisory teachers, each of whom would be in charge of a group of schools and function as an adviser and instructor rather than as an inspector only;

(3) the regrading of salaries to give greater incentive to self-improvement among assistant teachers.

41. Progress is being made on all these lines, and it is interesting to note that in British Honduras, outside the scope of the Education Commissioners, the Jeanes technique of training supervisory teachers for rural schools has been started.

42. This summary by no means exhausts the many points of interest which emerge from the reports of the Education Commissioners. We have concentrated on those which have the widest bearing, and shall not attempt to deal in such detail with their second report, partly because it has been published, and partly because it consists largely of an elaboration of the considerations set out in the first and of an account of the steps taken to put their recommendations into force.

43. It is appropriate here to make some mention of the evidence submitted to us in Jamaica and Trinidad which, with Barbados, are markedly in advance of the other West Indian Colonies, and which possess strong Education Departments. The evidence which we there obtained was more detailed than that obtainable elsewhere, and we feel justified in dwelling on it also because the larger and more advanced communities must necessarily set standards for their neighbours—and indeed, through the teachers' training colleges, have a direct influence on them.

44. In the case of Jamaica, the Director of Education made it plain to us how far even one of the more prosperous of the West Indian Colonies is from being able to provide accommodation and teaching staff for the whole population of primary school age. In the financial year 1938-9, expenditure on education was estimated to be £300,000 (inclusive of some £13,000 on buildings charged to the Public Works Extraordinary Vote, and expenditure from loan funds of about £20,000). The amount chargeable to the Education Department is slightly over 10 per cent. of the total ordinary expenditure of the Colony. While no striking increase in the funds available for education can be expected, and while Jamaican expenditure is quite up to the standard for the West Indies, it is illuminating to compare this figure of £300,000 with the amount which would be spent per year if English standards were adopted, namely, £2,500,000. Even allowing for differences in salaries and much lower expenditure on buildings than in England, these figures illustrate the enormous difficulties under which West Indian Governments labour in setting before themselves substantially the same objectives as in England.

45. As elsewhere, the denominations in Jamaica are playing a less and less important part financially even in the maintenance of school buildings. In the five-year period 1933-8 Government provided £20,000 to assist the denominations in building. Government has on the whole been driven to undertake the provision of further Government schools.

46. Secondary education is well catered for in Jamaica, and none of the secondary schools are under direct Government management. As we have observed in paragraph 19, control of secondary education is vested in a statutory body, the Jamaica Schools Commission, with executive powers. It is noticeable that although there is a good deal of unemployment among those who leave the secondary schools, the number of them who enter the teaching profession is very small indeed. That profession is largely recruited from the ranks of the pupil-teachers, who have had a primary education only, but who now have to undergo a period of training in one of the four training colleges in Jamaica. The supply of trained teachers from these colleges was stated to us by the Director of Education to be adequate to the demand of the educational system under its present financial limits.

47. There are no facilities in Jamaica for higher education beyond the secondary stage; but scholarships are awarded to Universities in the United Kingdom or the British Empire; and one Rhodes Scholarship annually is allotted to Jamaica. From such information as we could obtain, it seemed to us that, on the whole, those Jamaicans who have benefited by these scholarships have not made the contribution to the public life of the Colony which might have been expected of them. Practically none of them are to be found among the teachers, or in Government service, where it is plain that persons of their ability and training could render services of the utmost value to the Island.

48. Vocational education is not neglected in Jamaica. There are seven industrial schools, and valuable experiments are being carried out at the Vocational Centres at Dinthill and Holmwood, where two- and three-year courses in agriculture are given to youths of 15 years and upwards. The teaching is effective, and great keenness is shown; but there is some reason to doubt whether these elaborate courses are well suited to the needs of the Island, and do not compete unnecessarily with the excellent facilities available at the Government Farm School at Hope, near Kingston. It is clear that centres such as Holmwood and Dinthill cannot by any conceivable expansion serve the very large class of peasant farmers, and in fact few of those who have completed courses there have returned to the land as independent cultivators. The need in this respect seems to be for short courses on the practice of farming for young men who

have just begun their career as peasant farmers. (See also the Agricultural Report, Chapter XVI.)

49. Interesting developments are taking place in the field of practical training for girls as well as boys. A new needlework syllabus was introduced in 1936, and the appointment of a Supervisor and Assistant has made much more guidance possible. Exhibitions, competitions, refresher courses and a regular bulletin for teachers have all helped to raise the standard of work. In 1938 financial provision was made to supplement what is done for domestic training in the elementary schools. There is a domestic training centre attached to the Kingston Technical School; one is in the course of erection at the new Kingston Senior School, and another is planned for Montego Bay. The first post-primary practical training centre for girls was opened in January, 1937, and further centres are planned. Fees are charged of £5 per term, and subjects include, in addition to the ordinary " cultural " subjects, domestic science, dressmaking and handicrafts.

50. A most important point of general significance was raised in the evidence of the Director of Education, namely, the question of the stage at which a practical bias may best be introduced into education. On the one hand, it is clear that unless this is done at some stage in the primary course, the great majority of schoolchildren, who do not proceed beyond the primary stage, will receive none at all. On the other hand, the authorities are reluctant to do anything to diminish the not very large amount of " cultural " education at present afforded in the primary schools, and any such tendency would be strenuously opposed by public opinion. Fundamentally, the question is a social rather than an educational one, and is connected with the relative prestige and economic advantages of clerical and manual work, our observations on which are given elsewhere.

51. When giving oral evidence, the Director of Education was asked what in his mind was the order of priority in which educational problems should be tackled. His reply was as follows:—

    (1) Continuance of school building and increased accommodation in existing schools.
    (2) Replacement of obsolete and unsuitable school furniture and equipment.
    (3) Improvement of the salaries of the lowest-paid teachers.
    (4) Expansion of post-primary practical training.

In response to a further request, the Director estimated the additional cost of effecting desirable improvements to the educational system as being £570,0000 capital and £450,000 per annum recurrent expenditure.

Chapter VII.

52. In Trinidad we were able to observe the results of the recommendations of the Marriott-Mayhew Commission, and of the Disturbances Commission* of 1937. The former we have summarised above (paragraph 32); the latter are as follows:—

(1) Education in hygiene, food values and simple horticulture to be maintained and vigorously expanded in primary schools, and teaching in mothercraft for older girls. These subjects to be obligatory.

(2) Establishment of a central school for simple agricultural training for boys of 12-15, success to be followed by further similar schools.

(3) Effect to be given to the Marriott-Mayhew recommendation for modern secondary schools.

(4) Short courses for settlers or intending settlers at Government River Estate and Stock Farm.

(5) Education authorities to keep close touch with industry, to ensure that they turn out boys suitable for industrial requirements.

(6) Industries with the necessary facilities to be urged to take on apprentices, and Board of Industrial Training to institute in San Fernando continuation classes on the lines of those in Port-of-Spain.

53. With regard to the Marriott-Mayhew proposals, the Trinidad Government have proceeded with the establishment of " modern " post-primary schools in Trinidad and Tobago, and have made nature-study and school gardening compulsory in all rural schools. Close co-operation exists between the Education and Agricultural Departments, and entries for the school garden and other competitions have shown that a satisfactory degree of interest has been aroused. Three handicraft centres have been established in Trinidad and one in Tobago, for boys between 12 and 15. Eleven domestic science centres were in operation in 1938, and it was proposed to provide ten more in the country districts, in connection with which special transport arrangements will be made. State-aided vocational education is under the management of the Board of Industrial Training, which is responsible under Ordinance for the control of apprenticeship, and which provides evening classes.

54. Efforts have been made to remodel the curricula of the primary schools in the light of the observations of the Marriott-Mayhew Report, so that the material from which the " cultural " subjects are taught shall be as nearly related as possible to the general knowledge and environment of the pupils.

55. Since 1933 there has been a series of Ordinances regarding the functions of the Education Board, the powers and

---
* Cmd. 5641 of 1938.

responsibilities of Boards of Management, East Indian schools, Primary Education Regulations, compulsory education in Port-of Spain for children from 6-12, Private Schools, Building Grants and the compulsory registration of all schools whether assisted or not, and the imposition of certain sanitary standards.

56. In the summer of 1938 a special local Committee was appointed by the Education Board to consider in the light of the recommendations of the Marriott-Mayhew and of the Disturbances Commissions the question of vocational education. The Chairman was the Director of Education, and the membership included the Professor of Economics at the Imperial College of Tropical Agriculture, and representatives of the Board of Industrial Training and of the oil and agricultural industries. An interesting feature of the report of this Committee is a table showing particulars of pupils who left primary schools during 1938. Of a total of 5,902 boys and girls, only 864 completed the Standard VII course and passed an examination therein, whereas 3,612 did not complete Standard V. Of those who passed Standard VII, 210 proceeded to higher education, 109 became pupil teachers, and only 95 are recorded as having taken to any form of work on the land. No particulars were available for 106 out of this total of 864.

57. The main recommendations of the Committee were:—

(1) Support for the development of " modern " secondary schools in Tobago, Port-of-Spain and San Fernando. Establishment of an additional Agricultural Modern School on a suitable site, pupils for which to be carefully chosen, preferably from those whose parents or guardians are owners of small estates or have small holdings, or who would for other reasons be likely to take up practical agriculture.

(2) The apprenticeship system conducted by the Board of Industrial Training should be extended to cover the oil and sugar industries, and a qualified Superintendent of technical classes appointed, and technical classes started where warranted by the number of apprentices. The Committee did not consider the time ripe for the establishment of a whole-time technical school.

(3) Continuation classes in general education should be established throughout the Colony.

(4) Agricultural courses should be organised in selected primary schools and the teachers trained accordingly, and a Farm School established where 6-12 month courses could be given by the Department of Agriculture to those already engaged in agriculture.

(5) A school for domestic training should be established where girls of about 15 could receive a two years' course;

and where girls already in employment could receive part-time instruction during the day.

58. It is notable in Trinidad that there is a preponderance of boys over girls in the primary enrolment figures (40,000 as against 33,000). This is due in the main to the conservatism as regards the education of women of the East Indian population, who form 33 per cent. of the whole. East Indian girls rarely go to school after the age of about 9 or 10. It is hoped that the work of the Naparima Girls' High School will help to rectify this position, and also to supply the necessary women teachers.

59. In giving oral evidence, the Director of Education expressed himself as being on the whole satisfied that the provision of new and enlarged accommodation is keeping pace with the increase in the population of school age, and in enrolment and average attendance. In the case of 244 denominational primary schools, however (out of a total of 287), assistance is provided on a dollar-for-dollar basis, and no denomination except the Canadian Mission has a central fund for this purpose. Thus building and improvements depend on the possibility of raising funds locally before a school can qualify for the 50 per cent. Government grant. In other respects, however, denominational control in Trinidad is among the most centralised in the West Indian Colonies.

60. The Director of Education stated that the present output of the three teachers' training colleges at 64 per annum was sufficient to ensure within a few years that all elementary schools will be staffed with trained teachers. When the new Central Training Institute is in operation, this number will be raised to 100 per annum, and accommodation will be provided for a larger number of students from the Windwards and Leewards, for whose benefit special curricula having regard to their predominantly agricultural background will be devised.

61. There is in Trinidad an active Teachers' Association which has benefited by contact with the English National Union of Teachers. The relations of this body with the Department are good, and they have been taken into consultation at appropriate stages on matters of major importance such as the revision of the Primary Educational Code. There has from time to time been some controversy about the liberty of teachers to take part in politics. While it is obviously undesirable to limit unnecessarily the citizens' rights of this influential section of the community, it is also clear that a teacher who might become a member of the Legislative Council could not retain his post as a teacher without scamping one or other of his duties. It is also desirable that teachers should be wary of giving rise to the impression that they are using their position for the advocacy

of political views to which as individuals they are entitled. This is a matter on which it is very difficult to lay down hard-and-fast rules without curbing legitimate political activity, and in the end reliance must be upon the good sense and responsibility of the teachers themselves.

62. As elsewhere, the teachers of Trinidad were critical of denominational control, on grounds of discipline, appointment and promotion rather than on the broader grounds of educational efficacy. We do not consider that their opposition is shared by the majority of the people of Trinidad, nor that the objections which are still raised despite the action lately taken by the Government to meet this difficulty cannot be met without the abolition of the system itself.

63. As regards the place of the school in social welfare work, the Director of Education stated that he would like to see the rural schools developing into community centres, where library and adult education work, and possibly community listening and other social activities could be carried on.

3. Assessment of the desirable Aims and Objects of Education in the West Indies.

64. So far we have attempted to set out in broad outline the position of education in the West Indies as we saw it, and as revealed by previous enquiries and by evidence. We have not refrained from giving our opinion on various points as they arose; but before we proceed to set out our general conclusions on the educational needs of the West Indies, we feel it appropriate here to set out briefly what we consider its aims and objects should be.

65. We wish to emphasise at the outset that we have not taken into account any theories regarding variations in intellectual capacity between different races. That such theories are widely held is common knowledge; but they are too often used in support of claims for economic, political and social domination of one race by another to be regarded otherwise than with suspicion. It is not possible at the present stage of anthropological knowledge to dismiss the possibility that some such differences may exist; but we consider that it is far too early yet to take such theories into consideration in formulating an educational policy. It is, we consider, far more profitable to concentrate attention on environmental rather than inherited factors, on climate, conditions of work, nutrition, health, social conditions and customs.

66. The function of education we take to be the systematic transmission from one generation to another of the knowledge,

customs, traditions and aptitudes which have been evolved in any given community, and their conscious improvement and modification, both to meet changing environments and the better to adapt the community to deal with existing conditions. In other words, it should teach people how best to make use of the resources of their country, of the opportunities of social organisation and of their individual talents to enable them to lead lives as healthy, as satisfying and as prosperous as possible. Education in this sense begins at birth, and perhaps takes place most powerfully for good or ill in the first four or five years. Hence the great significance rightly attached to the influence of the home, and the importance in any community of intelligent interest on the part of mothers. Further, education in this sense is never finished. The man, of any age, who ceases to learn and to adapt becomes a burden to himself and a liability to the community of which he is a member.

67. Education, in the everyday sense of the word, limited to the activities of the schoolroom, consists mainly in training in the accurate use of the means of communication—speech and writing—and of computation, some factual knowledge of the world into which we are born, and of the nature of the society of which we are members as seen by an inspection of some parts of its history. It is also hoped at the same time to inculcate habits of concentration, accuracy and intelligent curiosity. It is further hoped to stimulate the formation of character, which may be described as a courageous and informed independence of mind, readiness to play a part in improving conditions when they are capable of improvement and to accept them without bitterness when they are not. The school not only attempts to impart knowledge, but to impart a willingness and aptitude for the acquisition of knowledge as a permanent component of personality.

68. It is clear that these objects are not to be attained by a concentration on " book-learning "; but we should deplore any tendency to regard their pursuit as in any way prejudicial to " book-learning ". Western society having long since outgrown conditions of tribal simplicity where an adequate knowledge of tribal usage and of mechanical skills could be passed on by demonstration and word of mouth, ability to profit from the written word is an essential part of the aptitudes of the modern man. It is unfortunately possible to attain quite a considerable skill in the technique of words without at the same time learning to make a judicious and critical use of this skill. Thus, education has a moral as well as a technical aspect. The school must impart not only a knowledge of various techniques, but of their right use. By their right use, we mean their use for the mutual benefit of the individual and of the community.

69. It is obvious that education neither in the West Indies nor in England can claim to come up to the standard thus set. In England, long tradition has lent prestige to the purely scholastic side of education and insufficient attention was paid to the modification of systems of education to meet changing needs. The results have been twofold: on the one hand a reaction in favour of concentration on character-training sometimes took the form of instilling an incurious loyalty to accepted standards and the production of many adjutants but few leaders. On the other, the coming of universal education found the schools ill-equipped to meet the needs of many of those who now came under their influence for the first time. Those who had opposed popular education advocated a severely practical training in the arts of the mechanic; those who supported it rejected such proposals as an attempt to deny to one class what was afforded to another. Few thinkers, until comparatively recently, paused to consider whether the traditional education was in the best interests of the whole population, or whether a much greater variety of teaching was not needed to meet the suddenly increased variety of needs. The debate has raged for many years, and still continues. But it has come to be more and more generally recognised that to concentrate on a literary education is to produce a number of applicants for white-collar occupations far in excess of the demand, and steps are being taken to supply training of a practical kind for the many who would benefit by it rather than by a strictly literary curriculum.

70. There is also the consideration that there are very many children in any country who find far greater satisfaction in practical than in clerical work. There are many in England who, for reasons of social prestige and tradition, struggle with distaste through a prolonged literary education, and either spend their lives in an uncongenial if " respectable " post or find their way to the exercise of their natural bent after irreparable waste of time and effort.

71. The relevance of these observations to West Indian conditions is apparent when we recall that the West Indian educational system was modelled on that of England in the nineteenth century, and that it has only recently begun to undergo the changes now well established here. Furthermore, and not unnaturally, West Indians have always looked to England for their model, and have opposed any attempts to treat the West Indies differently from England as designed to keep them in an inferior position. In fact, the England which many West Indians keep before their eyes is dead; and even were it not, there can be no possible objection to varying English practice to meet West Indian conditions, provided the general objects of education remain the same. Indeed, a readiness to adapt itself to changing needs is one of the attributes of a living educational system; and

the attention of critics should be directed not to the fact of adaptation but to the suitability or otherwise of the system to the needs of the population.

72. There is no need to labour the point that the past, present and, so far as one can see, the future of the West Indies are predominantly agricultural. It is plain, therefore, that a system of education suited for a society with much more varied activities may not be equally suited for the West Indies; and even less so if we agree that in England, for historical reasons, education still tends to have too pronounced a " literary bias ". No one could wish to reduce the amount of literary and cultural education available in the West Indies. There will always be a demand for the products of the secondary schools as they are at present; and as regards the primary schools we should like to see an improvement in the quality of the literary education given. But we wish to see an end of the illogical and wasteful system which permits the education of a community predominantly engaged in agriculture to be based upon a literary curriculum fitting pupils only for white-collar careers in which opportunities are comparatively limited. Far from reducing the educational facilties available to the mass of the population, we feel that an expansion on the practical side would, by better fitting the people to play a part in the major industries of the West Indian Colonies, increase their prosperity and consequently the opportunities for careers more varied than exist at present.

73. For the success of such a change, two things are necessary. First, the opportunities of earning a decent living on the land, given reasonable industry, must be increased, and for this we must look outside the sphere of education to land settlement, the raising of standards for estate labour and the development of a satisfying way of life particularly in the rural areas. Secondly, the people of the West Indies must appreciate that such a way of life is in no way inferior to any other, and must adjust their ideals to the opportunities afforded by their own territories. Constantly to look to other countries for their standards is to postpone indefinitely the emergence of a real sense of independence and self-respect.

74. In the meantime, we feel that it may allay West Indian suspicions to know that active developments are taking place in England and elsewhere in the sphere of practical education particularly for rural areas. The Village College System in Cambridge and similar developments in Suffolk and elsewhere have taken firm root and are arousing a great deal of interest in the world of education. Similar experiments are proving successful in the United States. In addition, the Young Farmers' Clubs of England and corresponding organisations in the United States are also playing an important part in fostering interest in

agriculture and in improving its efficiency. We do not, however, wish to commend such developments to the West Indies simply because they are taking place elsewhere. We consider, and many of our more responsible and thoughtful witnesses, both official and unofficial, agreed, that such developments would be to the unqualified advantage of West Indian communities.

75. There remains the question of the manner of the introduction of the practical and more particularly of the agricultural bias into the present educational system. Several witnesses, including officials, felt that too early an introduction of, say, agriculture was to be deprecated, partly because it might cut into time available for the teaching of the cultural subjects recognised on all sides to be necessary; and partly because agricultural techniques are no simple matter and are beyond the mental and physical capabilities of children of primary school age. With the idea underlying these criticisms we are in agreement; but we would draw a distinction between definite training for a given practical vocation and teaching calculated to lead on to such a vocation by arousing interest in it, and instilling some of the fundamental aptitudes which it requires. It should not be forgotten that the traditional "literary" education, while broadly speaking "cultural", also has its roots in a strictly "vocational" training, having grown out of a system primarily designed to produce clergymen and lawyers. It does not seek to teach law and theology, but to impart habits of industry and accuracy, and a knowledge of the literary tools of those professions. Traditional education has, in fact, been "pre-vocational" in a narrow sense, and in a sense unsuited to the conditions prevailing in the West Indies. We wish to see it become "pre-vocational" in a much broader sense, to include a preparation for vocations other than clerical, and more important for the great masses of the population of the West Indies than these. For these reasons, therefore, we consider that the curricula of primary schools should be remodelled to include the elements of practical instruction and the maximum possible training of hand and eye. We feel that most of the cultural subjects can so be taught as to reinforce this practical bias without losing their cultural value. Indeed if they are thereby more closely related to the environment of the children, to life as they know it, it may well be that these subjects will arouse far more interest and be of far more value than at present.

76. In concluding this section we wish to emphasise that by far the most important factor in education in the West Indies as elsewhere is not accommodation, equipment, or curricula, but the personality and training of the teacher. We have had much evidence to show that the qualities of a head teacher are carefully scrutinised by parents and guardians, who will often send children to a comparatively distant school where

another is more conveniently situated, in order that they may come under the influence of a teacher whom they respect. Considering the difficulties under which they work, we consider that the teachers of the West Indies deserve generous praise, and we feel sure that their co-operation will be readily given for well-considered programmes of educational advance. Their position is one of vital importance and influence, without as well as within the school itself, and disinterested work for the good of the community in which they live brings them a rich reward in public gratitude. It has been stated in evidence that some teachers do not show much interest in the attempts which have recently been made to add practical subjects to the primary curriculum. This we believe is true, and is to be deplored. But it would not be altogether fair to blame the teachers alone for an attitude which is widespread in all sections of the community, and which is part product of the traditional educational and social system of those Colonies. Where careful and systematic efforts have been made, as in Trinidad and British Guiana, though not only there, to devise suitable methods of practical education, teachers have co-operated well; and when such methods have been elaborated and form part of the regular training of teachers, we feel confident that this tendency will become a thing of the past.

4. Deficiencies and Remedies.

77. In this section we propose to set out concisely our general conclusions and recommendations on education, some of which have unavoidably been anticipated in earlier sections of this Chapter.

(a) TEACHING STAFF.

78. Teachers in the West Indies are inadequate in number and in training, especially in the smaller islands. Too great reliance is placed on the pupil-teacher system, too little effort is made to attract into the profession those who have received a secondary education, and there is an almost complete lack of transfer between the islands, which prevents the profession from broadening its scope to include the Caribbean area as a whole.

79. The most effective means of improving health education is by giving the teachers a thorough and really practical training in the subject, and this imposes on the staff of Training Colleges themselves the necessity of having a clear understanding of the subject and its application to local conditions. The planning of the fabric of the Colleges themselves, and of the attached residential quarters, their sanitary arrangements, the meals provided and the general habits of life imposed should all be related to this training and exemplify it. Instruction in domestic science and the care of infants is important for women teachers.

Chapter VII.

80. *Recommendations.*

(1) Perseverance with reforms to secure that all teachers have received a systematic training.

(2) Training colleges to include as compulsory subjects certain practical subjects such as gardening and elementary botany, domestic science and handicrafts, and hygiene and physical training.

(3) Pupil-teacher systems to be reduced as speedily as possible, and steps taken to ensure

(*a*) that such as remain are in fact not overtaxed with teaching duties and are provided with adequate regular instruction,

(*b*) that pupil-teachers are treated as students and their pay readjusted accordingly, to avoid attracting persons not desiring to enter the teaching profession but using the system as a means of earning a little money while looking for a more congenial post.

(4) Establishment of supervisory teacher system (as recommended by Mr. Hammond) at any rate until the bulk of teachers have been adequately trained; and institution of refresher courses for teachers already in employment. It should be considered in each case whether such courses should not be made compulsory.

(5) Government to assume more complete and effective control over appointment, transfer, promotion and dismissal of teachers in denominational schools, and to initiate such action as well as control it where necessary.

(6) Governments in similarly situated Colonies (e.g., Windwards and Leewards) to consult with a view to approximating teachers' salaries and conditions of service, with the ultimate object of establishing joint educational service.

(7) Definite attempts to be made to popularise the teaching profession among pupils at secondary schools.

(8) In order to enhance the effectiveness of the system of school medical inspection which we recommend in Chapter VIII teachers should be given a short course of instruction in the detection of the diseases most commonly met with among children, and also in the treatment of minor ailments by simple remedies.

(*b*) Accommodation.

81. Schools are deficient in accommodation, planning and sanitation, and only less so in number. In remedying this, it should be borne in mind that the recent tendency in England is against locking up capital in elaborate structures—such as the heavy and unsuitable stone edifices built in the nineteenth

century with which many English education authorities are burdened—and towards the provision of much simpler accommodation capable of easy expansion and alteration as need arises and educational policy develops. Educational methods are developing too fast to render it advisable to sink capital in expensive structures which may soon be found to hamper the application of new methods.

82. *Recommendations.*

(1) Building programmes to be actively proceeded with, bearing in mind the greater importance of providing some schools for *all* areas than of erecting a few showy and expensive structures in the main centres of population. The aim should be that no child should have to walk more than three miles to school, instead of as much as six as is possible at present; but it should be borne in mind that in some of the islands even a distance of three miles may be excessive.

(2) In building new schools, careful attention to be paid to the possibility of using simple and inexpensive local, in preference to imported, materials, and to enlisting where possible local interest and assistance in construction.

(3) Close consultation to be observed between Education Departments and Advisory Committees on the one hand, and on the other the actual building authority on questions of design.

(4) Provision of adequate playground space for *every* school.

(5) Provision of water-supply, and adequate and properly segregated sanitary equipment in all schools.

(c) Equipment.

83. This is almost universally inadequate in quantity and ill-suited, particularly for the younger children. A severe hardship is frequently imposed on the poorer parents and guardians by the need for providing schoolbooks and stationery.

84. *Recommendations.*

(1) Immediate attention should be paid to the question of the design of school equipment, on which much information is available in the United Kingdom and elsewhere.

(2) Determined efforts should be made to replace out-of-date and unsuitable equipment by new designs, and in effecting this the maximum possible use should be made of local materials and craftsmanship. Much of the simpler equipment could be constructed by older pupils in handicraft centres.

(3) Attention should be paid to the provision of the equipment necessary for physical training, at present almost totally absent.

(4) Steps should be taken to decide upon an approved list of suitable schoolbooks, and these should be provided free. This, we consider, should be taken in hand as a matter of urgency and with the least possible delay. Economies could be effected if Government dealt direct with the publishers and eliminated the wholesaler and retailer who inevitably add much to the cost of the books.

(5) Similar steps should be taken as regards stationery.

(*d*) CURRICULA.

85. Although much thought has recently been expended on this matter, and some developments have taken place, curricula are still out of touch with the needs and interests of the vast bulk of the population. There is too great stress on purely literary work, and on rote as against training in clear speech and thought.

86. *Recommendations.*

(1) The introduction, in the late primary stage, of practical and agricultural subjects, the courses to be designed in close and constant consultation with the Agricultural and Public Works Departments.

(2) The establishment of further junior secondary schools with a practical bias (as recommended by the West India Education Commission and the Education Commissioners). These new units, where wholly paid for by Government, to be wholly controlled by Government.

(3) The revision and simplification of the cultural curriculum, concentrating on clear and connected speech and thought, and giving subjects where possible a West Indian background rather than an English one.

(4) More definite introduction of hygiene and health teaching, to be made as practical as possible, and to be linked with e.g. elementary science instruction.

(5) Systematic physical training (to be linked with provision of playgrounds and food for undernourished children).

(6) Teaching of history and geography with special reference to the West Indies and radiating from there; and use of local topography and historical monuments.

(7) Domestic courses for girls, together with instruction on cooking and child welfare.

(8) Lessening of dominance of the Cambridge examinations, by abolishing the Junior Cambridge examination,

(e) Films.

87. Although the technique of the film in education is still at an experimental stage, its great value is everywhere recognised.

88. *Recommendations.*

(1) The possibilities of this aid to education should be energetically explored, and consideration given to the various means of showing films—e.g., by the Schools Cinema Month method, as in Trinidad, or by small portable apparatus, or by cine van. We recognise that different methods will be suitable for different colonies.

(2) The establishment at some one centre of a Library of suitable educational films, as it is too expensive to hire films from the United Kingdom. The Library might be in conjunction with the new Central Library in Trinidad, for which assistance is being furnished by the Carnegie Corporation of America.

(3) The production locally, if found practicable, of films dealing with agriculture, hygiene, physical training, etc., with the collaboration of departments concerned. The guidance might be obtained of an expert on documentary films who could be engaged to tour some or all of the West Indian Colonies for this purpose. This might result in the acquisition at comparatively little cost of a number of officers of sufficient technical knowledge to enable them to proceed unaided with the production of further films. These locally-made films might also be stored at the Library and be available for all the Colonies.

(f) Broadcasting.

89. Elsewhere in this report we recommend the establishment of at least one broadcasting transmitter to serve the whole Caribbean area. We feel that this transmitter would largely be wasted if it were not used for educational as well as for other purposes, and we recommend the complementary provision as speedily as possible of suitable receivers, particularly for outlying schools, and the systematic use of school broadcasts as an integral part of the educational system of the Islands. A discussion of the financial and technical aspects of this proposal will be found in Chapter XIX (7) below.

Some instruction will be necessary for teachers in the care and maintenance of the receivers: this could be conveniently undertaken at the Training Colleges.

(g) Adult Education.

90. Very little is attempted at present, and what is done in various fields is unco-ordinated and of no very deep effect. There is scope for much good work in this field, owing to the large proportion of the population who have little or no regular schooling.

91. We recommend that this work in all its aspects should be co-ordinated and that the Departments chiefly concerned should act together. In rural areas at any rate, the school should as far as possible be the centre for these activities, thus enabling full use to be made of facilities for the use of wireless and films.

92. It is doubtful whether, at the present low state of general education, anything very elaborate in the way of formal instruction can be attempted—certainly anything as advanced as the work in England of the Workers' Educational Association would fail to touch the vast majority of those whom we wish to help. For a number of years it will be sufficient to foster the habit of looking to whatever is the recognised centre for information and interest, and the appeal, to be wide, must be simple. For a people with the gifts of the negro race, drama and music would be potent means of arousing interest, as they have proved in England.

93. Steps should also be taken to provide reading matter so that the practice of reading should not as so often at present be abandoned within a short time after leaving school. Projects are on foot for supplying books from the proposed Central Library in Trinidad to the Windwards and Leewards; but this, together with any possible Government expenditure, cannot effect nearly all that should be done, and affords an excellent opportunity for voluntary effort to supplement the work of Government, etc. We commend to philanthropically-minded persons both in the West Indies and in England the provision of suitable books and magazines in large quantities for distribution particularly to rural centres throughout the West Indies, and we are sure that if the need is realised the response will be proportionately generous. The machinery of the Trinidad Central Library might be used for this purpose, and some centre established in England for the reception and despatch of reading-matter. We are sure that shipping companies would co-operate by transporting these books for low freights.

94. On the more practical side, there is a great need for simple instruction in agricultural methods for peasants and especially for newly-established settlers, and we consider that this work would be most effective if planned and executed in relation to other branches of adult education, such as instruction on food values, housing and hygiene.

95. We refer in Chapter XVI to the value of agricultural shows as a means of spreading knowledge of many matters affecting the health and prosperity of the community. An account is also given in the First Report* of the Committee on Nutrition in the Colonial Empire of various propaganda devices, many of which could no doubt be adapted for other purposes than nutritional campaigns. They include suitably phrased circulars and leaflets, the establishment of reading circles, lending libraries, adult classes, posters, broadcasting, the cinema and magic lantern, the gramophone, demonstration plots, etc., model houses, and competitions. No doubt other means will occur to those engaged in this work, and some of those mentioned above will prove more efficacious or practicable in given circumstances than others. The organisation of such work would be a suitable subject for action by the Committee of which we recommend the establishment in paragraph 100 (2) below.

96. A means which suggests itself to us for bringing together the varied activities which come under this heading is the publication of a periodical, edited either from the Central Training Institute or from the Central Library, in which there could be simple articles on matters of agricultural, social, educational and general interest. This experiment has been successfully started in various African Colonies, where contributors have included teachers and agricultural instructors, and where the subjects discussed have covered a very wide field. Such a periodical or periodicals—which would be of value and interest to the general public as well as to teachers and social workers —would have the great advantage of providing reading matter of topical and immediate West Indian interest, of which there is at present a notable lack.

(*h*) ORGANISATION OF EDUCATION DEPARTMENTS.

97. The existing organisation varies widely from Colony to Colony. In some, the Inspector of Schools, the sole Government education officer, concerns himself with primary education alone, and is generally unable owing to lack of assistance to undertake more than inspection and the routine details of government control.

98. There is need in this as in other fields for the co-ordination of action by Government departments, and for the determination of policy in the light of the experience not only of the education department itself but of others whose work concerns the life of the community.

99. The need is also apparent (as was recognised by the West Indies Education Commission†) for the better association of unofficial opinion with the work of education at the

---
* Cmd. 6051 of 1939. † Colonial No. 79 of 1933.

centre as well as locally. The existing committees and boards are either dormant, in many cases, or else exercise executive authority, which as we state in Chapter XXII may be on general grounds an undesirable system, leading in this case to too great division of responsibility and cumbersomeness in action.

100. *Recommendations.*

(1) In each Colony there should be an officer with the function of supervising education as a whole, who should have sufficient staff to free him from the more mechanical details of administration. Whether this officer could in the smaller islands also undertake some secretarial or administrative duties is a matter for consideration in the light of local circumstances.

(2) The standing interdepartmental committee on social welfare, the establishment of which we recommend in Chapter XI below, should in respect of education act as a Committee of Public Instruction. Its functions as such should include the proper evolution of educational policy to meet the economic and social needs of the community. It should co-ordinate schemes of adult education both cultural and practical, consider questions of school building extension and design, ensure the proper provision of educational and social facilities in land settlement areas, and organise the proper provision of health services to children of school age. In many cases these duties could be assumed by the Committee itself or by a sub-committee, and powers should exist to co-opt if necessary additional members with special educational qualifications.

(3) In order to associate unofficial opinion with the formulation of educational policy, we recommend the general institution of Committees on the lines recommended by the West Indies Education Commission. Such Committees should be purely advisory in character, as their primary function is not to control educational activities but to inform public opinion on educational matters, and to provide a means for keeping Government in touch with unofficial opinion on such matters.

(*i*) GRADING OF SCHOOLS.

101. We agree with previous enquiries that the range of primary schooling, in one case as much as 4-16, is unmanageably large, and that the attempt to teach children of widely different ages within the same system results in indifferent education for all.

102. *Recommendations.*

(1) Reduction of primary school age to 6-12, conditional on and side by side with

(2) Estabishment of junior secondary schools for ages 12-15 and

(3) Establishment of play-centres or, in certain cases, of nursery schools for the children under six, to be attached to primary schools, under the supervision, where numbers warrant it, of a qualified infant-mistress and staffed by the older girls from the primary schools, who would thereby acquire some knowledge of child welfare methods.

(*j*) EDUCATION FOR GIRLS.

103. So far no specific mention has been made of the education of girls. The present low status of women in the West Indies makes it the more important to secure essential equality of educational opportunity between the sexes. If there are to be happy marriages girls must be able to be companions to their husbands and therefore need every opportunity for as wide a cultural education as possible. In the early age-groups, there is no marked difference between boys and girls as regards school attendance; but in the older classes the numbers of girls fall off, partly because girls are kept at home to look after the younger children. This falling-off is very marked among East Indians, but is perceptible throughout; and the introduction of play centres for infants as recommended at (*i*) (3) above will mitigate but not remove the tendency. It is therefore necessary that vocational training should begin earlier for girls than for boys, and might best take the form of using the specimen dwellings the use of which we have recommended earlier in this Chapter.

104. We consider that education of this nature could be usefully supplemented by employing girls of school-leaving age as assistants in the infants' play-centres which we recommend ((*i*) (3)) should be attached to the primary schools. The Education Commissioners have suggested that such girls might receive a small fee for their services; on this suggestion we offer no comment, but feel that this point would have to be decided in the light of local circumstances.

105. In the matter of secondary education, girls are at a disadvantage as compared with boys. The number of girls enrolled in secondary schools is generally (though not universally) well below that of boys; and it must be borne in mind that these figures include those for preparatory sections to which small boys are admitted. Government provision for girls' secondary education is much lower than for boys; there is no Government Secondary School for Girls in British Guiana or Trinidad and only one (St. Vincent) in the whole of the Windwards and Leewards.

106. It is also essential that girls anxious to enter the professions and capable of doing so should not be denied the necessary

preliminary education. Complaints were made to us in evidence also of the difficulty of obtaining girls with the education necessary to enable them to enter the nursing profession. Further, many girls find it very difficult to obtain the teaching in subjects such as mathematics, Latin, physics and chemistry demanded by the scholarship regulations: in justice either the regulations should so be modified as not to discriminate against girls, or the appropriate teaching should be made as readily available to them as to boys.

107. Outside the sphere of secondary education in the ordinary sense there is room for vast improvement in the vocational education of girls. The great success which has attended the Carnegie Trade School for girls in British Guiana, the long waiting-list of applicants and the readiness with which its students find employment show that it fills a real need. Similar institutions could be established with great profit in the other large Colonies.

108. Domestic science should of course form a part of the curriculum in all girls' schools, as it does already in many.

(k) Health, Nutrition and Clothing.

109. Among the more important causes of non-attendance and irregular attendance are bad health and lack of clothing due to poverty. It is plain that even if children attend school, they can only be expected to profit from instruction if they are reasonably well nourished. Our recommendations regarding the medical inspection and treatment of school children will be found in Chapter VIII below.

110. *Recommendations.*

(1) School meals should be cooked and served for all schools, wherever possible, by voluntary help or by trained social workers. Government subsidies should provide the funds, and the children themselves might well take some part in the preparation of these meals. A small charge would be made in the case of all children whom the social worker reported as able to pay, whereas the necessitous child would receive free meals. Owing to the deficiency of animal protein in the diet of the children, milk or fresh fish should be included. It was represented to us that under-feeding was often noticed on the later days of the week, i.e. before pay day. Where this is established it might be best, in the first instance, to provide school meals on Thursdays and Fridays, which would also give the advantage of attracting children to come to school on Fridays, a day on which absenteeism is common.

(2) Supply of clothes for children from impoverished homes—the aid of voluntary organisations to be enlisted in

this as in other welfare activities, and the possibility to be borne in mind of making some suitable clothing in needlework classes.

(*l*) DENOMINATIONAL CONTROL.

111. As we have seen above, this system, traditional in West Indian education, has been subjected to much criticism, but has certain very definite advantages which to our minds render it inadvisable to take any steps to hasten its demise. Much of the criticism would be met if Governments make it their business to take the administrative responsibility for matters of discipline, as they already have the financial responsibility for salaries and for a large and increasing proportion of the cost of fabric and equipment. Where new schools are provided, wholly from Government funds, Government should certainly retain control and not share it with other institutions.

112. Existing facilities must be maintained for the giving of religious instruction in Government schools by representatives of the denominations.

(*m*) EDUCATIONAL ADVISER FOR THE WEST INDIES.

113. We recommend the appointment to the staff of the Comptroller of the West Indian Welfare Fund, of which we recommend the establishment in Chapter XX, of an educational adviser.

5. Finance.

114. In the foregoing section which includes our recommendations we have not dealt with the question of finance. It is plain that the financial implications of our proposals will be considerable, as is shown by the figures which we quoted in paragraphs 44 and 51. But we do not consider that any attempt on our part to assess the cost of these proposals would be of value, for the following reasons:—

(1) The nature of our investigations and the material at our disposal have rendered it impossible for us to arrive at figures which would have any reasonable claim to accuracy.

(2) The reactions of the developments which we propose on the community at large, particularly in the fields of public health and of agriculture, would probably enhance the wealth of the West Indies and render them more able to bear such burdens than they are at present, but to a degree which it is quite impossible to estimate.

(3) Although some of our proposals will, we hope, speedily be put into effect (e.g., the free provision of

school books and stationery, and the establishment of wireless transmitters) many can only come about gradually, and may require drastic modification in the light of new experience. We trust, in fact, that educational policy will cease to be regarded as something that can be laid down once for all, instead of being a process, developing with the changing needs and standards of the communities of whose life it is a function.

(4) We hope to see education become the special care of the Comptroller of the West Indian Welfare Fund. We have not attempted to indicate which of our recommendations should be financed from that fund as we would not desire to limit the Comptroller's discretion in any way.

(5) In general, we would emphasise that educational advance is a matter in which it is unwise too carefully to count the cost. Failure to provide educational facilities on the right lines (our view of which we have indicated above) must inevitably bring retribution in numberless ways, not least among which will be loss in prosperity and financial stability far outweighing any temporary savings which may thereby be achieved.

CHAPTER VIII.

PUBLIC HEALTH.

1. Descriptive.

1. We propose in the first part of this Chapter to describe in broad outline the conditions and factors which appear to us to be the most important of those affecting public health and medical services in the West Indian Colonies and, in the second part, to put forward proposals for the improvement of those conditions. In the final section we give our views about defective diets and malnutrition.

2. In any comparison of the general standard of health in the West Indies with that in other tropical parts of the Colonial Empire the climatic advantages which are enjoyed in all the islands bounding the Caribbean Sea must not be overlooked. Normal tropical heat is here tempered by prevalent winds and by the cooling effect of the sea on small masses of land. Even in the two Colonies with which we are concerned on the mainland of Central and South America the temperature is fairly equable and in the coastal strips, where most of the people live, never rises to heights which are common in other territories lying so near to the equator. Rainfall, though variable, is generally abundant and the areas in which the natural supply of water is inadequate for human needs are few and limited, although in others where the supply is ample, conservation and purification by artificial means are sometimes required. Periods of drought are seldom so prolonged as to cause anxiety about their effect on the health of the people but, particularly in British Guiana and British Honduras, heavy rainfall, coupled with the absence of natural drainage, has resulted in the formation of large swamps which are a source of malarial infection and partially account for the generally less healthy conditions in those Colonies. In short it may be said that the natural characteristics and inherent health circumstances of the British West Indies are particularly favourable for countries lying within the tropics and their good fortune in this respect is a factor which must contribute at all times to the health of their people.

(*a*) VITAL STATISTICS.

3. There is, unfortunately, no definite standard by which health conditions in the British West Indies can be compared with those of other countries. The general death rate and infant

Chapter VIII.

mortality rate may, however, be used to make a rough comparison; these figures, together with the birth rate, and, where available, the maternal mortality rate, are given in the following table for the West Indian Colonies and a selection of other countries:—

Country.	(1) Birth rate.	(2) Death rate.	(3) Maternal Mortality rate.	(4) Infant Mortality rate.	(5) Estimated population per square mile.
England and Wales	14·9	12·4	3·3	58	703
Scotland	17·6	13·9	4·8	80	159
Northern Ireland	19·8	15·1	5·0	77	235
Eire	19·2	15·3	3·6	73	110
U.S.A. (1936)	16·6	11·5	5·7	57	36
Germany	19	11·8	4·9	64	353
France	15	15·3	2·5	65	197
Italy	22·7	13·7	3·0	150	360
British India (1936)	35·4	22·6	*	162	211
Ceylon	37·8	21·7	19·9	158	208
Mauritius	35·2	28·8	11·0	154·5	555
Malta	34·3	20·0	*	242·7	2,519
Gold Coast (certain districts only).	33·7	25·3	16·6	117	35
Uganda	26	20	11·2	159	38
Gambia	25	31	*	370	52
Malaya (1936)	44	24·9	7–10	170	86
Hong Kong	32·1	34·4	*	361	2,500
Porto Rico (1936)	40·6	20·5	*	—	457
Venezuela (1936)	32·7	17·9	*	135	8
Mexico	39·9	23·8	*	140	21 (1935)
British West Indies					
Barbados	29·9	18·5	*	217	1,210
British Guiana	35·0	21·9	12·8	121	3·5
British Honduras	32·9	18·5	8·5	122·6	6·6
Jamaica	32·4	15·3	5·3	118·5	254
Leeward Islands:—					256
Antigua	42·9	20·6	⎫	171·1	320
St. Kitts	44·4	36·5		209·0 ⎫	
Nevis	23·6	14·9		107·1 ⎬	254
Anguilla	24·8	13·6	*	77·7 ⎭	
Dominica	31·6	14·5		114·3	304
Montserrat	39·3	15·4		158·1	413
Virgin Islands	31·0	10·9	⎭	130·4	117
Trinidad and Tobago	32·9	17·4	6·4	120·5	230
Windward Islands:—					
Grenada	32·0	14·3	4·14	115·0	663
St. Lucia	32·7	14·4	9·1	101·1	238
St. Vincent	39·1	15·3	5·0	117·8	384

Note.—Unless otherwise stated figures given are for 1937; * denotes that figures are not available.

4. It will be seen from this table that the birth rate throughout the West Indian Colonies is much higher than it is in the European countries for which figures are given. The death rate is generally slightly higher than that of the European countries, but, with the exception of St. Kitts, the figure for which is seriously high, is less than in many tropical countries. The most unsatisfactory feature is the high rate of infant mortality in these Colonies; the substantial margin by which it exceeds that of most European countries is more than sufficient to account for the difference between the general death rates in the two areas. In the West Indies, as in other parts of the world, a high birth rate and a high rate of infant mortality go together. The maternal mortality rates are low in comparison with most tropical countries, but to this generalisation British Guiana is an exception owing to the high maternal mortality among East Indian women. Comparison of West Indian figures with those for the African colonies is not, however, of great value since the collection of vital statistics in the latter is still very incomplete and figures are often available for only a few districts and larger towns.

5. While the figures given for the death rate, and to a less degree those given for the infant mortality rate, in the British West Indies are considered to be fairly reliable in most cases, yet care is necessary when drawing deductions based upon those figures. For example, in England and the United States of America a much higher proportion of the population comes into the higher age groups; a difference in the general death rate figures cannot therefore be used as a just index of the respective health conditions. The comparison would show the West Indies in a too favourable light. The infant mortality rate can be used as an indication of the comparative chances of survival of infants in the different countries but cannot be used as a health index for other ages of the population. In the West Indies the very high rate of illegitimacy—a factor which always tends to increase infant mortality—limits the value of the deduction which can be drawn from the infant mortality rates as an index of general health conditions.

6. The following table shows the death rate per 1,000 of the population and the infant mortality rate per 1,000 live births for the various West Indian Colonies for the past 10 years:—

Chapter VIII.

	1928.	1929.	1930.	1931.	1932.	1933.	1934.	1935.	1936.	1937.
BARBADOS.										
Death rate	30·1	23·7	23·1	25·9	19·0	20·1	23·0	20·2	18·5	18·5
Infant mortality rate ...	331·0	239·0	251·0	298·0	198·0	235·0	256·0	220·0	198·0	217·0
BRITISH GUIANA.										
Death rate	27·9	23·5	23·0	21·8	21·1	24·4	24·7	20·6	20·4	21·9
Infant mortality rate ...	185·0	146·0	146·0	139·0	139·0	154·0	168·0	122·0	120·0	121·0
BRITISH HONDURAS.										
Death rate	18·2	20·9	19·2	36·7	20·3	20·8	19·2	24·8	20·2	18·5
Infant mortality rate ...	113·1	129·5	109·5	151·7	104·8	124·6	102·8	170·1	152·7	122·6
JAMAICA.										
Death rate	19·7	18·4	17·0	18·6	17·2	19·3	17·0	17·7	17·3	15·3
Infant mortality rate ...	157·0	160·0	141·0	153·0	141·0	149·0	131·0	137·0	130·0	118·5
LEEWARD ISLANDS :—										
Antigua—										
Death rate	31·4	21·4	24·8	22·8	20·6	19·4	19·7	18·4	20·4	20·6
Infant mortality rate	*	*	*	*	93·0	174·6	125·5	105·2	111·2	171·1
St. Kitts—										
Death rate	39·8	40·1	37·2	27·6	27·5	27·1	30·7	29·2	33·2	36·5
Infant mortality rate ...	308·3	200·2	186·0	185·5	166·7	180·4	229·0	169·5	164·1	209·0
Nevis—										
Death rate	19·4	19·0	24·2	17·1	11·1	10·1	12·3	16·6	14·5	14·9
Infant mortality rate	286·6	203·7	155·9	155·9	102·2	73·0	103·9	168·0	177·4	107·1

* Not available.

Chapter VIII.

	1928.	1929.	1930.	1931.	1932.	1933.	1934.	1935.	1936.	1937.
LEEWARD ISLANDS cont :—										
Anguilla—										
Death rate	17·3	13·9	17·5	10·0	8·8	12·8	11·2	17·9	15·4	13·6
Infant mortality rate	114·2	70·8	130·1	130·1	52·8	76·1	109·4	74·3	124·1	77·7
Dominica—										
Death rate	21·8	24·0	17·2	19·2	15·9	17·1	15·4	14·6	13·7	14·5
Infant mortality rate	134·9	186·0	141·3	170·6	87·8	126·0	106·8	97·6	99·6	114·3
Montserrat—										
Death rate	25·1	17·2	19·5	23·1	15·3	14·4	14·3	13·9	14·7	15·4
Infant mortality rate	135·0	105·0	145·0	216·0	82·0	79·5	121·9	130·3	118·7	158·1
Virgin Islands—										
Death rate	18·6	10·1	14·8	10·6	23·3	18·4	17·4	13·6	14·7	10·9
Infant mortality rate	157·3	97·7	30·1	31·3	129·2	164·7	68·8	98·4	109·4	130·4
TRINIDAD AND TOBAGO.										
Death rate	19·9	19·4	18·9	20·0	17·1	19·1	18·6	17·5	16·3	17·4
Infant mortality rate ...	128·6	127·9	127·0	144·1	108·9	131·3	127·4	99·4	96·8	120·5
WINDWARD ISLANDS :—										
Grenada—										
Death rate	16·5	16·8	15·8	17·2	13·8	14·3	13·6	14·3	15·4	14·3
Infant mortality rate	110·0	109·0	119·0	129·0	84·4	94·0	100·8	84·0	104·0	115·0
St. Lucia—										
Death rate	19·8	20·5	16·1	18·2	18·3	16·1	14·4	15·8	14·9	14·4
Infant mortality rate	125·7	150·1	85·6	134·1	121·0	92·0	106·3	109·0	97·9	101·1
St. Vincent—										
Death rate	18·1	17·4	15·1	21·2	16·3	15·2	14·5	15·4	16·3	15·3
Infant mortality rate	134·0	149·0	94·0	162·0	94·0	73·0	109·2	111·2	119·3	117·8

7. It will be seen that in most of the Colonies there has been a gradual improvement, which is reflected more by the general death rate than by the infant mortality rate.

(b) Nature of Ill-Health.

8. From the evidence placed before us and from a study of the Annual Medical Reports it appears that though the general mortality rates are not very high, yet chronic sickness among the people of the West Indian Colonies is common. Random surveys which have been made show that a large percentage of the population is infested with hookworm. Throughout the West Indies the numbers suffering from some form of venereal disease or from yaws are so high that the incidence of those complaints constitutes a serious economic and social problem. The amount of malarial infection varies in the different Colonies; malaria is common in British Guiana and British Honduras but is relatively rare in St. Kitts, while such sporadic cases as occur in Barbados are imported. In most of the West Indian Colonies, however, malaria is without doubt one of the most widespread and debilitating diseases and it constitutes a serious economic problem, as does hookworm also.

9. The number of cases of well marked deficiency disease, such as scurvy, beri-beri and rickets, is very small, but there can be no doubt that many of the poorer people, more especially those living in the large towns, are suffering from an ill-balanced diet consisting mainly of carbohydrate foods and lacking in fresh vegetables, animal protein and fat and certain vitamins. A lowered resistance to disease results, as do also certain forms of ill-health not yet clearly defined. There is abundant evidence of malnutrition among infants and young children, due in some cases to poverty, in others to ignorance or neglect on the part of the parents and in many others to the difficulty of feeding their children which is experienced by mothers who work; fatal cases of marasmus result from these conditions. There appears also to be a lack of adequate food for many old people, sometimes caused by poverty but in many cases due to that lack of family life and family responsibility which gives rise to one of the most serious of the health and social problems in the West Indies.

10. The unsatisfactory housing of many of the poor people is one of the main causes of ill-health and the general level of sanitation in these countries, judged by English standards, is low: in some of the larger towns much improvement has taken place in recent years, but in the smaller towns, and in most rural areas, sanitation is often still very primitive. One of the worst examples is to be found in some villages in those parts of St. Kitts where no effort has been made to provide even the most rudimentary forms of sanitation and the labouring

people, living in closely crowded areas, have still no other method of sewage disposal than the use of gullies, which run at the back of their dwellings and are often dry for long periods each year. The prevalence in the West Indies of bowel diseases (such as dysentery, enteric fever and worm infection) which are in most cases due to lack of proper conservancy systems and of pure water supplies, is an indication of this low standard of sanitation. The very serious amount of malaria in some Colonies is evidence of insufficient preventive measures against that disease; the occurrence of many cases of tuberculosis, leprosy and yaws, and to a certain extent, venereal diseases, points to the existence of overcrowded housing conditions.

11. The diseases mentioned above are responsible to a great extent for filling the dispensaries and the hospitals in the West Indies. It should be noted that they can all be classed as preventible diseases; and again that most of them can be described as social diseases in the sense that they arise mainly from adverse social conditions. Their relatively high incidence also reveals a lack of education in health matters among the inhabitants.

12. Tuberculosis is a very serious problem in most West Indian Colonies. The negro section of the community shows little resistance to this disease and the overcrowded housing accommodation makes for its rapid spread.

13. The amount of leprosy which now exists cannot be accurately stated. The numbers of known lepers and of those in the leper institutions vary from colony to colony. There is much need for surveys of the extent of leprosy among the populations and for the detection and isolation of early infectious cases. While it is considered that leprosy is not a major medical problem in these Colonies, and that it is diminishing in extent, nevertheless constant vigilance is required if it is to be further reduced. The arrangements made for the unfortunate sufferers from tuberculosis and leprosy should be such as to encourage them to enter the special institutions and not such as to cause them and their relatives to conceal the diseases. To those of us who are more particularly interested in the social aspects of institutions the leper centres which we visited appeared to fall into three groups. Some consisted of dark and crowded huts in which no education is provided and no facilities exist for any form of recreation. In another group of centres neither funds are apparently available nor knowledge nor imagination existent to cater for the mental and psychological needs of the patients. In the best centres everything possible is done to occupy their time and energy.

14. The existing arrangements for dealing with epidemics seem fairly satisfactory. Port Health Officers have been

Chapter VIII.

appointed in the larger ports and Medical Officers of Health in some of the larger towns; notification of a number of serious diseases is enforced. Yellow fever has disappeared; smallpox rarely occurs, and the health authorities are generally able to get epidemics of infectious diseases under control in a reasonable period of time.

(c) Expenditure on Medical Services.

15. In the tables below we show the average annual expenditure in the different West Indian Colonies on medical work during the last three completed financial years as a percentage of the total average expenditure (excluding that of self-balancing Departments) during the same period; in the case of those Colonies which could provide the information, the total expenditure is divided between preventive and curative work:—

	Percentage of Medical Expenditure to Total Expenditure.	Percentage of Preventive to Total Medical Expenditure.	Percentage of Curative to Total Medical Expenditure.
Barbados	11·3	8	92
British Guiana	10·2	12	88
British Honduras	8·9	Not available.	
Jamaica	9·8	18	82
Leeward Islands :—			
Antigua	17·1	22	78
St. Kitts-Nevis	18·6	31	69
Dominica	15·6	8	92
Montserrat	8·9	25	75
Virgin Islands	16·9	Not available.	
Trinidad and Tobago ...	9·2	18	82
Windward Islands :—			
Grenada	16·9	9	91
St. Lucia	12·7	10	90
St. Vincent	19·6	15	85

16. It will be noted that medical expenditure is exceptionally high in St. Vincent and St. Kitts; there is not, however, always the expected relationship between the amount spent on medical work and the health conditions revealed by death and infant mortality rates. Even after due allowance has been made for any unreliability of available statistics, the fact remains that St. Kitts, with the highest death rate, and the second highest infant mortality rate, devotes a relatively high percentage of its revenue to medical work; this contrast raises the questions whether the money is being spent in the most effective way, whether more expenditure on the improvement of social conditions might not have had a better effect, and whether, indeed, it is possible for Medical Departments to raise the standard of

the health of the people until social conditions have been improved.

17. While the percentage of total revenue expended on medical work in many Colonies is relatively high, yet the actual amount of money available per head of population is small in proportion to the amount of disease present; scarcity of funds for medical work is undoubtedly one of the major causes of the continuance of unhealthy conditions. When it is considered that so much of the disease in these countries is of a preventible nature the percentage of money available which is devoted to preventive work appears to be disproportionately low. This is due partly to the fact that the medical services were built up before preventive medicine had been developed; partly to the insistent demand of local public opinion that diseased members of the community should have better treatment; partly to the education and experience of the present medical staff, many of whom have been trained mainly for curative work, while some of them have not the preventive outlook which is so necessary in the West Indies to-day; and partly to the opposition of vested interests, such as the owners of house property, to needed preventive measures.

18. It ought to be recognised in the West Indies that expenditure on curative work can never effect a permanent improvement in the health conditions of a country. The whole revenue of a colony might be spent on the alleviation of disease and the cure of the sick and the most up-to-date and costly methods might be used, without much evidence of improvement in the general health conditions. No very marked lowering of the numbers of those who become diseased owing to faulty environment can be expected from purely curative medicine. Cure of the sick is important from a humanitarian point of view, but the allocation of the available funds between that service and the prevention of illness, which also has a humanitarian aspect, must at all times be carefully watched.

19. It is significant that Directors of Medical Service, most members of the medical profession who gave evidence before us, and the parent body of the British Medical Association, all stressed strongly the very great need for an increase in preventive medicine The problems are to decide how this need can best be met and how, as the result of careful study, the present hindrances to progress can be overcome

(*d*) THE EXISTING MEDICAL ORGANISATION.

20. Each colony has its own medical organisation; in each colony there is at least one hospital, and separate institutions generally exist for lepers and for mental cases. There is at present no central medical organisation and there are no central medical institutions shared by a group of colonies. The

types of building and the number of staff employed depend largely on the funds which the Colonial Government can afford to spend on them. The standard of medical work done is apt to vary for the same reason. The smaller and poorer colonies accordingly suffer.

21. The charge of the medical organisation of each Colony or Presidency is in the hands of a Director of Medical and Sanitary Services, or a person known by some other title such as Chief or Senior Medical Officer; by the term " Director of Medical Sevices ", when used in this Chapter, we mean the officer at the head of the Medical Department in any territory.

22. The Director of Medical Services has in many cases an extremely difficult and onerous position. Owing partly to shortage of trained clerical staff, and partly to the existing political system, much of the Director's time is taken up in office work, in attending the meetings of committees and boards, and in sitting in the Legislative Council. When, as is the case in Jamaica, meetings of the Legislative Council extend over several months in each year, the demand thus made on his time may be so great as to interfere seriously with his professional duties. The Director of Medical Services may therefore have comparatively little time to tour the rural areas of his colony and to get into real touch with the medical necessities and problems in outlying districts, to inspect the hospitals and dispensaries, and to advise the local staff. In some of the colonies he is subjected in the local press and in the local councils to fierce criticism, which may amount to personal abuse. This criticism is often ill-informed, and at times appears to be actuated by personal motives. The Director of Medical Services is in many cases unable to reply to the criticism partly because he is a Government servant and is debarred from replying in the press; and in some cases because of his loyalty to his staff. As we have said in Chapter V, one remedy is the education of public taste so that it will no longer tolerate irresponsible attacks on public servants. Proposals which we make in Chapter XXII for limiting the appointment of Heads of professional Departments to the Legislative Council may also alleviate the difficulties of Directors of Medical Services.

23. In several colonies part of the medical organisation is in effect controlled by Sanitary Boards which have executive powers. It is clearly essential that organisations empowered with the control of local affairs should be composed, as they are in this country, of disinterested persons. That is often not possible among the small communities in the West Indies, and, as we point out when discussing this problem in a wider aspect in Chapter XXII, the proper course then is to limit the powers of the local authority to the giving of advice. We are satisfied that through motives of self-interest on the part of members, some

Chapter VIII.

Sanitary Boards have impeded the passage of legislation or other measures designed to secure sanitary improvements. We consider, therefore, that in present circumstances the boards should be converted to advisory bodies save in those larger towns where experience has shown that they are capable of undertaking executive responsibility. Even when limited to the giving of advice, such boards can play a useful part by interesting public opinion in health measures and in sanitary improvements.

(e) STAFF OF MEDICAL DEPARTMENTS.

24. Most of the medical officers are West Indian and have been trained either in Great Britain or Canada. Some of them have obtained high medical degrees and many of them are efficient doctors. Usually their training has been mainly in the treatment of disease since the general medical education in this country has still a strong bias towards curative medicine. There is no doubt that in many ways it would be preferable to provide facilities for a good medical education in the West Indies; ultimately a medical college should be established as a faculty of a West Indian University. Until that is practicable the bias can be corrected to some extent by insisting that all doctors in Government service should take the Diploma in Tropical Medicine and Hygiene, and that the holders of certain appointments should possess the Diploma in Public Health. The lack of facilities for post-graduate education in this country, of which West Indian doctors complain, is a very serious handicap and arrangements should therefore be made, wherever it is possible, to increase the facilities for post-graduate training in the West Indies; we also suggest that at the same time the Colonial Office might try to arrange for West Indian doctors to obtain elsewhere any post-graduate training which cannot be provided within these Colonies.

25. Most of the time of the medical officers is occupied by the treatment of established disease in the individual. With the exception of those appointed to special institutions, in whose case duty allowance is generally given, they are all permitted to engage in private practice. This right to private practice was severely criticised in many of the memoranda which were sent to us. We were told that it diminished the attention paid by these medical officers to the poor; that it interfered with the performance of such public health work as was required of them; and that it prevented purely private practitioners from setting up in practice in districts in which they were often much needed. An extreme example of the possible conflict of duties and interests which may be caused by the system of private practice is to be found in the arrangement whereby some Government

Doctors are employed by industrial undertakings or estates, the conditions on which they have to inspect and may have to criticise in their official capacities. We strongly support the view expressed in the report (Cmd. 5641) of the Commission of Inquiry into the disturbances which occurred in Trinidad in 1937 that such arrangements are open to great objection.

26. Insufficient attention has been given to the training of nurses and midwives and to their conditions of service. Until recent times there were no sister-tutors to train them, residential quarters were often lacking and the salaries and conditions of service, both during and subsequent to training, were unsatisfactory. In several of the larger Colonies improvements have been made in the last few years, a few sister-tutors have been appointed and residential quarters built but in many of the Colonies conditions are still definitely bad, and the training now given to those who become district nurses and health visitors is perhaps the most deficient. It is of course difficult for the poorer Colonies to provide the funds required to effect improvements. Some centralization of training at the larger hospitals is therefore required.

27. All the sanitary inspectors are trained in the West Indies, but some of them take locally the examination of the Royal Sanitary Institute of Great Britain. As there is no Central Training School for them the standard of proficiency varies. In some of the smaller Colonies in which training staff is not available training may be deficient or absent. The fact that sanitary inspectors are usually confined to one Colony, and, in some cases even to one district of a Colony, throughout their working life, is a drawback to efficiency which admission to a larger unified service might help to overcome.

28. Everywhere the establishment of the Medical Department appears to us to be uneconomic in that the proportion of auxiliary staff, of all grades, to each doctor is too low.

(f) Medical Institutions.

29. Each Colony has one relatively large hospital, and in some there are several. Most of these institutions are overcrowded; the buildings are frequently old and in disrepair, and the arrangements for the nursing staff are often inadequate. In Jamaica good modern hospitals with up-to-date equipment have been or are being constructed in both Kingston and Montego Bay. In Trinidad arrangements have been made in the "Five-year-plan" to provide modern hospitals in Port-of-Spain and in San Fernando.

30. The general surgical work done in these hospitals, both old and new, is usually of a high standard; the medical work is seldom as good. Facilities for bio-chemical, bacteriological, and pathological examination are in many cases inadequate; in Trinidad, Jamaica and British Guiana those facilities exist, but the laboratory buildings are unsatisfactory. The standard of maternity work varies in the different hospitals; in most of them ante-natal work is neglected. More children's wards and separate maternity wards are needed and another serious defect of many of these hospitals is the lack of isolation wards or blocks for cases of infectious diseases: at present patients suffering from tuberculosis, enteric fever, and even diphtheria, may sometimes be accommodated in a single ward.

31. The Directors of Medical Services in these Colonies are constantly being pressed by local public opinion in the larger centres to improve the facilities in the hospitals. This, unfortunately, is an expensive undertaking. Special departments for various branches of curative medical work are being increasingly developed. When there are specialist medical officers in a Colony, they demand modern equipment for the scope of their talents. The lay visitor to the hospital adds his voice to the criticism as does also the patient who has had experience of conditions abroad. With such pressure brought to bear upon him it is sometimes difficult for a Director of Medical Services to balance fairly the relative medical needs of the community. There is no doubt need for larger and more up-to-date hospitals and for the development of special departments. The relative value of these improvements, as compared with that of providing medical aid for outlying areas where large sections of the population have now no medical provision at all, and that of extending preventive measures, is difficult to determine. Where a hospital could be used as a training or post-graduate school the justification for extension is naturally greater. On the other hand much of the disease treated in special departments is preventible and the question therefore arises whether it is justifiable at the present time to spend more money on specialities when preventive measures are still so inadequate.

32. In most of the West Indian Colonies there is a mental hospital and also an institution for the accommodation of lepers. Several Colonies, but not all, make separate provision for patients suffering from tuberculosis. When there is a keen and specially trained Medical Officer in charge and the accommodation is adequate, these institutions are doing good work. Unfortunately such conditions are to be found in very few of the institutions; many of them are of value only in so far as they isolate their inmates from the rest of the community. Here again, the cost to the smaller and poorer Colonies of providing

and maintaining these special institutions, and the staff which is required if treatment is to be effective, would be out of proportion to the money available for the general medical services of the Colony. Central institutions, which would be shared by groups of Colonies, are therefore needed; where this is impossible arrangements might be made for several Colonies to share the services of officers with special training.

33. Complaints of their diet in medical institutions were made at times by the patients and more often by the staff. In some cases the diet sheets are out-of-date and should be revised according to more modern ideas of food requirements; the frequent criticism that the diets are monotonous was sometimes justified. In a number of hospitals, even when residential quarters are provided, the system prevails of giving ration allowances to the nurses who have then to supply and cook their own food. This, although popular with some of the nurses, is not a satisfactory arrangement. The nurse may try to economise and as a result provides herself with quite inadequate food; if she has already done a day's work it is unreasonable to expect her to buy and cook her evening meal herself, as so often happens now.

34. Visiting committees, the members of which interest themselves in the improvement of the hospital, have been appointed for several medical institutions. Such committees can be of great value provided their criticism is constructive, and that they assist in providing better amenities for the welfare of the patients and of the staff.

35. In the small rural hospitals the conditions are frequently far from satisfactory; in many cases the building, equipment, staff quarters and sanitation are defective. When these institutions are used as general hospitals for the district, the medical work suffers since the small staff cannot cope with the diversity of disease which presents itself. The policy of making them merely clearing stations for the larger hospitals, as adopted in some of the Colonies, is obviously the better one; this would necessitate the provision or improvement of ambulance services.

(g) DISPENSARIES.

36. The dispensaries throughout the rural areas are devoted entirely to the treatment of the sick; nowhere has any attempt yet been made to transform them into health centres of the type which can be seen nowadays in parts of Africa and the East. They are visited by a doctor at intervals, generally of about a week; usually at other times they are closed. Frequently no nurse is in attendance to assist the doctor; the need

for this assistance in the treatment of women patients was urged by the East Indian community in Trinidad.

37. Many of the ailments treated at these dispensaries are of a trivial nature and should not require the attention of a doctor if adequate subordinate staff were available; there is, therefore, a lack of economy in the use of the doctor's time and skill.

(h) Special Clinics.

38. The high infant mortality rate, and, in British Guiana, the high maternal mortality rate, show clearly the need for good maternity and child welfare clinics. Yet, in the West Indian Colonies, with certain praiseworthy exceptions, this important branch is seriously neglected. In those cases where a few ladies devote their spare time and energy to voluntary work in these clinics, they are generally handicapped by scanty funds and inadequate staff. Much of the work at the clinics, moreover, consists of supplying milk to poor mothers and children and giving simple drugs for minor ailments. There is often little real educative health work, and in many cases no properly trained health visitors are provided to assist at the clinics and to visit in the homes. Very few ante-natal clinics have yet been established and so far few women doctors are employed, though their work, more especially among the East Indian women, and in maternity and child welfare work, would be valuable.

39. Special clinics for the treatment of venereal diseases which, with yaws, account for such a large amount of the sickness in the West Indies, have been opened in the last few years in buildings constructed for the purpose. Specially trained doctors are in charge of some of these clinics which are proving to be very useful institutions. There are, however, a number of ways in which the services thus provided in many places could be improved; they are considered in the second half of this Chapter.

(i) Availability of Medical Treatment for the People.

40. It is difficult to state precisely what proportion of the people are now able to obtain medical treatment, what is the nature of the treatment they are now given, or how much the cost of illness is to the individual. Some information which is relevant to the first of these questions will be found in the following table which shows, for the West Indies and some other Colonies, the number of Government doctors for each hundred thousand of the estimated population and the number of beds

in Government hospitals which are available for each thousand of the estimated population:—

Country	Number of Government doctors per 100,000 of estimated population	Number of Government hospital beds per 1,000 of estimated population
West Indies:		
Barbados	6·4	1·35
British Guiana	7·0	7·20 (with estate hospitals)
British Honduras	14·3	2·34
Jamaica	6·1	1·53
Leeward Islands:—		
Antigua	14·3	2·59
St. Kitts-Nevis	18·4	4·26
Dominica	8·2	2·94
Montserrat	14·6	2·55
Trinidad	13·2	2·30
Windward Islands:—		
Grenada	9·1	2·57
St. Lucia	9·1	1·81
St. Vincent	12·1	1·45
Other Colonies:		
Nigeria	0·7 (including all practitioners, 1·0)	0·18
Tanganyika	0·6 (including all practitioners, 2·0)	*
Gold Coast	2·0	0·38
Cyprus	10·0	0·92
Ceylon	5·0	2·00

* Not available.

41. In the large towns, and in those villages at which a doctor is stationed, most sick persons can have medical treatment, the type of treatment varying naturally with the skill of the medical staff and also with the institutional facilities available. In rural areas remote from a medical station it is sometimes very difficult for a sick person to obtain aid; we received many representations about this and about the lack of ambulances which often causes great hardship.

42. In an effort to extend medical benefits to a greater number of the people the Governments of some Colonies have adopted the plan of placing district nurses in rural areas, but as a rule they are inadequately trained for the work which they are expected to undertake and in practice most of them do little except midwifery. The total number of district nurses in the British West Indies is certainly insufficient for the needs of the Colonies; their salaries, their housing accommodation and the arrangements for their transport are often quite inadequate, as is also their training. There is a very real need for more district nurses who have had a thorough training in public health nursing, and for the improvement of their conditions of service. Some Colonies, for example, British Guiana, employ

dispenser-dressers in remoter areas where there is a scarcity of doctors; in none of the Colonies, however, are officers employed corresponding to the sub-assistant surgeon in India.

(j) Payment for Treatment.

43. We have so far considered only the case of those for whom the difficulty of obtaining adequate medical attention is caused by the distance of their homes from the nearest doctor: a different problem is that of the sick person who is too poor to pay a doctor's fees. Such people, on the production of a pauper certificate, are given free treatment throughout the West Indies, but the definition of a pauper varies in the different Colonies. Destitute persons suffering from chronic illness receive attention in almshouses, up to the limit of the available accommodation.

44. It was often represented to us that persons of limited means, such as artisans, labourers, peasant farmers, shop assistants, clerks, chauffeurs, and domestic servants, suffer hardship through having to pay the fees charged for their own medical treatment and that of their dependants. It was urged that the fees demanded by doctors for visits by the patient to the doctor's surgery were excessively high and that when a doctor is required to visit at the patient's home the charges were often exorbitant.

45. In British Guiana, Jamaica, Trinidad and the Windward Islands regulations have been made limiting the charges which Government medical officers who are allowed private practice may make to their private patients. For each attendance at the residence of the doctor or at medical institutions the charges thus laid down are (i) in British Guiana, 1s. if the patient has a " poverty certificate " and 2s. for such people as artisans, labourers, small farmers, and sempstresses, (ii) in Jamaica, for those who are not covered by the ticket system, 4s., (iii) in Trinidad, if the patient is a working person and is not in receipt of salary or wages of more than £52 per annum, 2s., and (iv) in the Windward Islands, 1s. for labourers, as defined in the regulations, and subject to an income limit of £25 per annum in Grenada and St. Vincent.

46. For each special call, if at a place within a mile of the doctor's residence, the authorised maxima for the classes of persons mentioned above are (i) in British Guiana, 1s. 6d. and 4s. 2d., for the two classes respectively, (ii) in Jamaica, 6s., (iii) in Trinidad, 4s. 2d., and (iv) in the Windward Islands, 2s. These rates are for special visits by day and usually an additional charge of at least one-half or more of those rates may be made for visits at night: also a mileage fee may be charged for any distance over one mile in each direction which the doctor

has to cover. To take a case which would not be exceptional, an artisan in British Guiana who required a visit at night from a Government doctor living six miles from his home would be liable to be charged for that service as much as 13s. 4d.

47. These fees, moderate though some of them appear to be in comparison with those charged to paying patients in Great Britain, are, in many cases, very high in relation to the income of the people who have to bear them and payment of them by a sick person who, while sick, would seldom be earning money, must often entail unwise economies in food and clothing and housing during his illness and convalescence.

48. Only a small percentage of the population of the West Indies can afford to pay for any private medical treatment, and the cost of adequate treatment during a prolonged illness is beyond the means of a still larger section of the community. The problem is thus a serious one and the difficulty experienced in paying the fees demanded has caused bitter resentment against the medical profession in some places; this was particularly shown in Grenada where almost every memorandum placed before us contained an attack upon the doctors. It is obviously not in the interest of either the people or the medical profession that this state of feeling should continue, and some system must be evolved by which the people may obtain skilful medical treatment and, at the same time, the doctors may receive an adequate return for their services.

49. There are no voluntary hospitals in the West Indies, and private nursing homes are found in only a few of the larger towns. Poor housing accommodation, and the shortage of trained nurses, often make it impracticable for patients to be nursed in their own homes. The position is therefore very different from that in Great Britain where medical treatment is provided under a National Health Insurance Scheme and many large voluntary hospitals are available.

(k) Schemes for supplying Medical Care.

50. There are in almost all these Colonies Friendly Societies, some of which give a limited amount of sickness and medical benefit. Some allow free choice of doctor, others retain one doctor or a panel of doctors to treat their members. The most highly appreciated advantage of many of these Societies appears to be the provision of funeral benefits, although a bonus paid by some at certain periods of the year is an additional attraction. The idea of such Societies is undoubtedly popular among the West Indian people, but, as is shown by statistics supplied to us, their scope is extremely limited. In Kingston, Jamaica, an organisation called the New City Dispensary, to which a limited number of people subscribe about 3d. a week in order to obtain

medical treatment, employs a panel of doctors for the care of its members and also gives sickness benefits.

51. In Jamaica a system for supplying medical care, known locally as the " Ticket System ", has been organised by the Government. Under this system the members of the population are graded according to their means and the fees which are to be charged by the Government medical officers are laid down in accordance with this grading; the fees are retained by the medical officer. The estimate of the means of the patient may be made by one of several local persons, e.g., clergymen, shopkeepers, members of the Legislative Council, magistrates. The income of the patient is generally well known to these persons, but their judgment may not perhaps always be as disinterested as is desirable. Two complaints were made about the working of this system. The private practitioners, who are opposed to it, said that many persons were now obtaining free treatment who could well afford to pay something; that others were paying much less than their income warranted; that it was impossible, in many cases where a worker owned land, to assess his income satisfactorily; and finally, that certain distributors of the tickets might find it in their interest to give as many free tickets as possible. If there is force in these complaints, they can only be met by a more careful selection of those empowered to distribute tickets; they should be disinterested and trustworthy persons, chosen not because they hold certain positions but for their knowledge of the people of a particular locality and because they command the respect of both those people and the medical profession.

52. The other complaint, which was made on a few occasions, is that the doctors gave priority and more careful attention to those who could afford to pay. This could be overcome to some extent by restricting Government medical officers from private practice and arranging that all fees should go to Government. Finally, some beneficiaries under the present system dislike the necessity, which it may involve, of making a fresh application whenever they want a ticket. In many cases it should not be impossible to settle once and for all the question of ability to pay and to give the man a permanent ticket, or one for a long period, regulating the payment which he is to make for medical treatment.

(*l*) Private Practitioners.

53. There are usually several private practitioners in the larger towns throughout the West Indies and in a few of them there are private nursing homes. The economic depression in the West Indies, the improvement in public hospital facilities, and the development of preventive medicine are now restricting

the profits to be obtained from private practice. For example, the principle is now generally accepted that in order to cope with venereal disease effectively, it is essential to provide free treatment. Since much of the illness formerly seen in the surgery of the private practitioner was venereal in origin, this departure necessarily results in the loss of many of his patients. The extension of maternity and child welfare work and of school medical services also affects his practice and the development of other measures of prevention, such as anti-malarial work, improved sanitation, better diet and the education of the people in health matters, must restrict it in an increasing degree as those measures progress. In addition the private practitioners have to face competition from Government medical officers who are now allowed to engage in private practice.

54. There is no doubt that, in consequence of these developments, some private practitioners are finding it difficult to earn an adequate living; they are naturally discontented and hostile to the official medical policy. Recognising their difficulty, the British Medical Association has suggested that these doctors should be given further employment as part-time officers, not only in the Government hospitals and dispensaries, but also on public health services such as school medical inspection, maternity and child welfare clinics and venereal disease clinics. The Association suggested that these practitioners should be subsidised and that in some cases they should be eligible for pensions from Government funds. The advantages and disadvantages of this system are now being widely debated in this country. The arguments against its adoption in the West Indies seem to us to be stronger than those now urged against it in England, and are considered in the second part of this Chapter.

(*m*) OTHER DEFECTS OF WEST INDIAN MEDICAL SYSTEMS.

55. In addition to the limitations of finance and other handicaps to which we have drawn attention, the present medical arrangements everywhere suffer from two important general defects. First, there is a great need for expert medical advice on many aspects of health work, more especially in the smaller and poorer Colonies. Advice is required on housing, on anti-malarial work, on the treatment and prevention of tuberculosis, leprosy, venereal diseases, and mental disease; also on nutrition and on general sanitation. Moreover, surveys of the health of the people—to investigate, for example, the extent of malnutrition, of leprosy, and of tuberculosis—cannot be undertaken unless expert assistance is available, and that cannot be provided without some sharing of staff and pooling of money by different Colonies, and, indeed, without financial assistance from outside the Colonies.

56. Secondly, the medical work in many of these Colonies seems to be too much isolated from the work of other Departments. We consider that a general social welfare policy should be laid down, of which the health policy will form part. There appears to be need for more consultation and co-operation between various Departments not only on the general social welfare work, including health work, but also in regard to the expenditure of the available revenue which is to be devoted to the social services.

(*n*) Conclusions.

57. We will end the first part of this Chapter by stating briefly the main conclusions which either have been reached in the course of the foregoing description of existing conditions or follow from the facts recorded above:—

(1) The health of the people in the West Indies, while on the whole better than in some other British Colonies, is still unsatisfactory.

(2) Two of the most serious aspects of the ill-health are, first the very high infant mortality, and secondly the large amount of morbidity (chronic sickness).

(3) The cure of disease has received much more attention than has been given to its prevention.

(4) The facilities for the cure of the sick nevertheless are still inadequate, more especially in rural areas.

(5) Much of the ill-health arises from poverty—poverty of the individual, of the medical departments, and of the Governments.

(6) Much of the ill-health is of a preventible nature and most of it arises from ignorance and adverse social conditions. There is need, therefore, for a united effort by many Departments and sections of the community to improve matters.

(7) The high rate of illegitimacy combined with large families, and the lack of parental responsibility are very serious factors in the causation of ill-health and death, more especially among young children.

(8) Housing accommodation for the poorer people in the West Indies is generally deplorable, general sanitation is often primitive in the extreme, and the diet of the poorer people is often insufficient and usually ill-balanced. Little improvement in the health of the people can be expected —however extensive the hospital facilities—until these serious defects are remedied.

(9) The training of all classes of medical personnel in the prevention of disease is inadequate.

(10) There is great need for a better education of the general public and of school children in health matters.

(11) The medical departments are to be congratulated on the fact that the death rates in many Colonies have been lowered to their present levels, on having obtained control of several of the more serious epidemic diseases, and on having provided a curative medical service of the present standard. The two greatest hindrances to their work are undoubtedly lack of money, and bad social conditions.

(12) The major defects of the medical services are:—

(a) that relatively too large a proportion of the available funds and of their efforts is expended on curative medicine and too little on prevention;

(b) that they tend to neglect rural districts in favour of urban areas;

(c) that the interests of efficiency and economy suffer through the dispersion of medical institutions and from the attempts on the part of each separate Colony to maintain its own complete medical department;

(d) that the number of well-trained personnel of the subordinate medical staff is everywhere low in proportion to the number of fully qualified doctors;

(e) that little attempt is made to co-ordinate health and social welfare policies in a way designed to improve conditions; and

(f) that insufficient attention is given to research into the causation, distribution and control of disease.

(13) Expert advice and financial assistance from outside these Colonies is needed in order to reorganise medical work on a better preventive basis and to assist in correcting the adverse social conditions.

2. Recommendations.

58. Our proposals for the improvement of the medical services and of the medical conditions affecting the health of the people of the West Indian Colonies can conveniently be grouped under the seven headings mentioned below, each of which is followed by a brief statement of the benefits which, in our opinion, should ensue from its adoption:—

(1) *The Appointment of a Medical Adviser for the West Indian Colonies.*—The Medical Adviser, whose duties are described later in this Chapter, should be of the greatest value in organising the unification of medical services and co-ordinating the other activities mentioned below.

(2) *The Unification of the Medical Services.*—The interchange of personnel and the advice of specialists, which

should more readily be available under a unified service, should help to advance both curative medical work and preventive measures.

(3) *The Centralisation of Medical Institutions.*—This reform should secure greater efficiency and economy in the treatment of the sick and should also make possible the provision of very much better training facilities, for all classes of medical personnel, in curative medicine.

(4) *The Creation of at least one School of Hygiene.*— This should be a centre for both the widening of knowledge of, and research into, the prevention of disease; auxiliary medical personnel could here be given a thorough training in preventive medicine.

(5) *The Development of long-term Health Policies.*— These should form part of a larger social welfare policy which should be so framed as to co-ordinate the efforts of all Government Departments and to secure co-operation from various sections of the public.

(6) *The Reorganisation of the Medical Services.*—The aims of reorganisation should be better balance between preventive and curative activities, an increase in the number of auxiliary medical staff and the improvement and extension of the facilities for medical attention which are available to the general mass of the people, especially in rural areas.

(7) *An Increase in certain Preventive Measures.*—These should include action designed to improve housing and general sanitation, more anti-malarial measures, and the extension, or establishment, of maternity and child welfare clinics, clinics for the treatment of venereal diseases and school medical services.

59. We propose now to give a more detailed explanation of each of these seven groups of recommendations.

(1) APPOINTMENT OF MEDICAL ADVISER FOR THE WEST INDIES.

60. In Chapter XXI of this report the appointment is recommended of a panel of experts who would be given, under the control there described, certain duties and responsibilities which they would discharge for the whole of the British West Indian Colonies. These experts should include a Medical Adviser, and one of his first duties should be to secure the establishment of a unified medical service for the West Indies along lines discussed in the following section of this Chapter. If, after the proposal to organise such a service has been accepted in principle, it is desired to appoint a Director General to control it, the Medical Adviser should undertake that duty in addition

to the others which should be placed upon him from the beginning. They are:—

(*a*) to consider, in consultation with the Governments concerned, the question of the centralisation of medical institutions, and to arrange for this so far as it may be found practicable;

(*b*) to advise on the planning of long-term health policies for the various Colonies;

(*c*) to advise on the education of all medical personnel and of teachers, school children and the people generally, in public health matters;

(*d*) to supervise the analysis of the vital statistics and returns of diseases in the different Colonies and to report on general health conditions;

(*e*) to arrange for the provision of such expert and medical advice in connection with surveys and research as may be required;

(*f*) to arrange, in consultation with the Colonial Office, for visits by lecturers to different medical centres in the West Indies;

(*g*) to investigate the possibility of health insurance schemes for the West Indies as a whole or for separate Colonies.

(2) UNIFICATION OF MEDICAL SERVICES.

61. This proposal should be considered in the light of the second part of Chapter XVIII of our report, where, after an examination of the question of the unification of services in the West Indies, we conclude with a recommendation that the Governments of the West Indian Colonies should be invited to accept the principle of local unified services, and that, if it is generally accepted, they should address themselves to the task of putting that principle into practice at the earliest possible date. We there say that, given good will, it should not be difficult to make a start by establishing a medical service in the West Indies. In our view this is one of the most important medical recommendations, and many advantages should be secured by its adoption and general application.

62. For the doctors the benefits of unification will include greater possibilities of advancement, more opportunity for gaining wider experience, and a better prospect of congenial work, including specialisation and individual research. Increased facilities for taking study leave might thus be made possible, and the centralisation and improvement of certain of the medical institutions, which should accompany unification, would open up better possibilities of providing post-graduate

training. For the Governments and peoples of the West Indian Colonies, the advantages of unification will include the widening of the range of selection for both first appointments and promotions and the general improvement of the efficiency of the service through the greater scope thus offered for the employment of its individual members on work best suited to their talents. The prospects of being able to make proper medical surveys and of carrying out research into specific health problems should be improved, and through the centralisation of medical institutions, which, as we have said, should accompany unification, more efficient medical care for particular diseases could be provided in well-equipped hospitals shared by several Colonies. Unification might also lead Colonies to share the services of visiting specialists such as surgeons, ophthalmologists, malariologists, sanitary engineers and housing experts.

63. Most members of the medical profession in the West Indies who gave evidence before us strongly supported the idea of unification. The parent body of the British Medical Association, in the memorandum which they submitted to us, wrote as follows:—

> "A unified West Indian Medical Service commands considerable support amongst the medical profession in the West Indies."
>
> *   *   *   *   *
>
> "The Council of the Association believes that unification, properly organised and safeguarded, would result in many improvements in the medical services, but it also considers that the difficulties, especially with regard to administrative control, are not to be minimized."

64. These administrative difficulties should now be clearly stated and examined, and it is time also that the administrative machinery should be made capable of giving practical effect to what appears to us to be a very desirable and necessary reform.

65. While unification should be limited in the first place to posts held by qualified members of the medical profession, its advantages in the case of the subordinate medical staff would be considerable, and its scope might well be extended later to include them, a start being made with the more senior posts.

(3) CENTRALISATION OF MEDICAL INSTITUTIONS.

(a) *Mental, Leper and Tuberculosis Hospitals.*

66. The most striking need is for the centralisation of some of the leper and mental hospitals, and this is particularly noticeable in the case of the smaller Colonies, where the lot of the inmates of the existing institutions is often hopeless and their treatment alien to all ideas of modern therapy. In some of the leper and mental hospitals the arrangements which now exist as regards general sanitation, opportunities for work

and recreation, and the provision of up-to-date methods of treatment are distressing. We consider that an improvement of the conditions in these hospitals is one of the most urgent medical requirements. Although most of the Governments of these territories are trying to make the best of difficult circumstances, they cannot afford to provide skilled medical treatment and nursing or suitable accommodation, and the problem of providing appropriate work and recreation in some of the smaller institutions is obviously one of great difficulty. The advice of experts in the organisation of these institutions on an efficient and economic basis is clearly necessary.

67. We do not advocate either the erection of institutions of an expensive type or the establishment of one home either for all the mental patients or all the lepers of the West Indies. Our proposal is that one central mental hospital and one central leper colony should cater for all the smaller islands and for any other territories which cannot efficiently undertake treatment and provide other facilities from their own resources for the limited number of patients of either class found from among their own people. The policy should be to make both mental and leper hospitals as nearly self-supporting as may be possible, and Governments should actively encourage Medical Departments to work to that end.

68. The centralisation of hospitals for the treatment of patients suffering from tuberculosis presents greater difficulties but may be found practicable in some degree for the smaller islands.

(b) General Hospitals.

69. Centralisation of these institutions is not possible, but with a unified medical service a certain amount of sharing of some of the special services of a general hospital and of expert staff could be effected. Inside each Colony at least one large general hospital should be made as efficient and complete as is financially possible, and outlying hospitals should be used solely as feeders or clearing stations for these central hospitals. This plan could not be worked effectively unless a better ambulance service were provided and were supplemented by stretchers of a modern pattern and suitable for use in hilly country served only by tracks or inadequate and rough roads. Everywhere the ambulances should be attached to the Medical Departments and the stretchers should be kept at convenient and well-known centres, such as the Police Stations, in all districts to which access by ambulance is impossible.

70. Under the system of indentured labour estates were required to maintain hospitals for their resident workers; though that system has long been abandoned and the obligation has

lapsed, many estates still continue this provision. While due credit must be given to those employers who have undertaken this responsibility, we consider that it is desirable that ultimately Governments should themselves provide hospital accommodation for all sections of the community, thus relieving estates of a burden which they cannot reasonably be expected to bear indefinitely.

71. By gradually improving the large general hospitals and with their growth extending the area served by each they could be made of much greater use as teaching institutions. They would thus become centres at which recently qualified West Indian doctors could be given locally that post-graduate experience which is so necessary and, as we were told, is difficult for them to obtain in Great Britain. Visits by specialists from teaching hospitals in this country to lecture and demonstrate in central hospitals in the West Indies could also be arranged and would be very helpful.

72. These large well-equipped hospitals would provide a much better training-school for nurses also. We were impressed by the fact that very few West Indian nurses hold senior positions in the Nursing Services. We consider that this is a real grievance which should be remedied as soon as possible. The present training of nurses in the small hospitals and the accommodation and conditions of service there are, as we have said earlier in this Chapter, often unsatisfactory. It would be far better to have a few good training centres in the large hospitals with adequate residential quarters, and above all a good type of sister-tutor should be appointed, and a training syllabus of lectures and practical work suitable to the health conditions of those Colonies should be carefully arranged at each centre. Particular attention should be paid to preparing the student nurses to assume responsibility by gradual promotion to higher grades. Until by these or other means more attention is given to training, the claims of the majority of local nurses to promotion cannot be entertained and their very natural dissatisfaction at the slowness of their progress to responsible positions must remain. We also recommend that a few scholarships should be instituted to enable those nurses who have shown special capability to take post-graduate training overseas. The registration of nurses and midwives and the formation of Nursing Boards are also important matters to which in some Colonies more attention might be given.

73. Special consideration needs to be given also to the training of district nurses to fit them to be of real value as members of the auxiliary medical staff in rural areas. The aim should be to turn out people of the type of those who now combine in the country districts of Scotland the duties of district nurses and

health visitors. Training in these cases should be provided partly in the hospitals and partly at the School of Hygiene.

74. More maternity wards and children's wards are required at general hospitals. These wards would be useful in giving a more adequate training to both midwives and nurses, as would also a district midwifery service which should be conducted in association with the hospitals.

75. Another matter demanding attention is the training of dispensers, which can best be undertaken in large hospitals. None of the West Indian Colonies will be able for many years to come to afford the salaries of the staff of fully qualified medical officers which would be wanted in order to make their services available to the whole population. It is essential, therefore, both that the numbers of dispensers and district nurses should be substantially increased and that the standard of their training should be much improved and its scope widened. In the large general hospitals dispensers should be given full instructions in such matters as the administration of injections for yaws and venereal disease, the dressing of ulcers and the treatment of minor ailments, so that they can relieve the fully qualified medical officer for more skilled work; for those dispensers who are to work in rural areas extra tuition would be required in the preventive side of medicine, and this could be provided in the School of Hygiene. In many of the British Colonies training on these lines has been given to dispensers who are now very useful members of the auxiliary medical staff. Definite training in a limited number of special subjects, followed by continual supervision, should be the aim.

(c) *Medical Laboratories.*

76. At present many small islands in the West Indies suffer from lack of laboratory facilities for diagnosis and would benefit by advice from laboratory experts. So far as is practicable these services should be centralised. It is unfortunately true that, owing to the long distances by which so many of these Colonies are separated, the amount of centralisation must be limited, but, if communications are improved as we suggest in Chapter XIX, it should be possible for all of the islands to make more frequent and more rapid use of any central medical laboratories, which should therefore be established in the smallest number of places likely to provide adequate and effective facilities for the whole area.

(4) THE CREATION OF A SCHOOL OF HYGIENE.

77. It is doubtful whether any great advance in preventive medicine can take place in the West Indian Colonies until at least

one School of Hygiene has been established there. The recommendation which we now discuss is therefore intended to meet one of the greatest necessities of that area. A School of Hygiene would be used as a training centre for sanitary inspectors and health visitors and would also supply one part of the training which would equip dispensers and district nurses for subsequent work in rural areas. The School should also provide instruction in health matters both for school teachers and for other persons who are to lecture on those matters to the general public. It would increase the value of the School in this latter connection if it contained a museum so planned as to demonstrate the method of improving health conditions to all sections and classes of the people. Later the School could provide the training for medical graduates for the Diploma in Public Health.

78. The staff of the School would be available to assist the West Indian Governments and their medical Departments in all health problems. They would carry out surveys, conduct research, study conditions and advise on the best methods of improving them. The School would also provide accommodation in which visiting health experts could conduct their work, and which might be used as a central bureau for the analysis of vital statistics and returns of diseases.

79. The School would, in short, act as a centre for the promotion of knowledge of the prevention of disease and should eventually prove to be an agency of the greatest value in the improvement of health in the West Indies. The theoretical work in the School should be linked up with practical training, which should take such forms as instruction in maternity and child welfare clinics for health visitors and district nurses, and instruction in the field for sanitary inspectors. Co-operation would also be necessary between the hospitals, the laboratories, and the School of Hygiene, and this could be readily arranged under a unified medical service.

(5) THE DEVELOPMENT OF LONG-TERM HEALTH POLICIES.

80. In the past medical work in the West Indies has consisted mainly in supplying relief to the sick, if and when they presented themselves, and does not appear to have been based on any very clearly defined long-term policy. Little attention has been given to the study of the fundamental causes of ill-health, more particularly when those causes were of a social nature. It is, in our view, essential that a long-term policy should now be laid down for each of these Colonies and that in every case it should aim at removal of the fundamental causes of ill-health. Much preliminary work may be required before a new policy can be properly framed. This will include more complete surveys

of existing diseases, their nature, their prevalence and the amount of mortality which they cause. The reasons for the occurrence and prevalence of those diseases will have to be studied and a critical analysis should be made of both vital statistics and returns of diseases over a period of years. Finally, it will be necessary to consider the question of the most economical and effective method of effecting improvement.

81. Most of the Governments of the West Indian Colonies cannot carry out this programme unless they are given financial assistance and experts in such subjects as housing, nutrition, malaria, tuberculosis, venereal diseases and leprosy are appointed to undertake investigations and frame the recommendations which will be required.

82. It is equally desirable that the Colonial Office, after collecting information, should advise the Governments of these Colonies in the planning of their future health policies. Information about methods and organisations which have proved successful in other parts of the world—not only in the British Empire but in such other territories as Java and the French and Belgian Colonies—is required, as are also suggestions of possible methods for dealing with the particular problems of the West Indies.

83. The policy to be followed would naturally vary in the different Colonies. In the first place a scheme should be prepared by the Director of Medical Services in each territory and submitted by him, through his Government, to the Medical Adviser for his comments. Those schemes should then be discussed by the Social Welfare Committee, the creation of which is recommended in Chapter XI of this report, and that body would decide the extent to which different departments in the territory concerned could co-operate in carrying out the health policy, which is only one part of a programme for the improvement of the general social welfare in the territory.

(6) THE REORGANISATION OF THE MEDICAL SERVICES.

84. In the reorganisation of medical work in the West Indian Colonies four aims must be kept in view. The first may be described as the development of the preventive outlook; the second is to provide for a relative increase in well-trained auxiliary staff such as sanitary inspectors, health visitors, district nurses and dispensers; the third is to arrange, as far as possible, for more centralisation of medical institutions, a matter which we have already discussed* in both its curative and teaching aspects; the last is to make better facilities available for medical treatment in rural areas and for certain sections of the people of the towns.

---

* See paragraphs 66-76 above.

(a) Development of Preventive Outlook.

85. The first of these aims can best be secured by giving a more adequate training in preventive medicine to all medical personnel. Government medical officers, without exception, should be required to take the Diplomas in both Tropical Medicine and Hygiene. The courses for those Diplomas would be of greater practical use to doctors serving in the West Indies if, in them, increased attention could be given to modern methods of diagnosis and treatment of venereal diseases and tuberculosis, and if emphasis could be laid on their prevention. The present courses of training for nurses, health visitors and dispensers should be revised so that they may receive much more training in preventive work than is now given to them; as we have already said, the establishment of a School of Hygiene would be of great help in bringing about this change.

86. It would remain the duty of the Director of Medical Services to co-ordinate curative work with these expanding activities on the preventive side; in the larger towns the two branches might be separated to a certain degree and appointments made of special health officers. In the rural areas the District Medical Officers would continue to be responsible for both branches of the work; they should have attached to them, and should supervise the work of, a subordinate staff of well-trained district nurses and dispensers, who would treat minor ailments, and of equally well-trained sanitary inspectors. The areas allotted to District Medical Officers could then be enlarged. Wherever possible the rural dispensaries should be transformed into health centres which could serve as the headquarters of all health activities for the district.

(b) Increase of Auxiliary Staff.

87. The second of the four aims mentioned at the beginning of this section was the relative increase in auxiliary staff whose duties have been discussed immediately above. The better and more systematic training which these officers will require, if they are to undertake the more responsible duties proposed for them, can more easily be provided if, as we have suggested, teaching hospitals are centralised and at least one School of Hygiene, with special teaching staff, is established.

(c) Better Facilities for Medical Treatment.

88. We come next to the problem of providing better facilities for medical treatment in the rural areas and for the poorer people in the towns. Several suggestions for effecting improvements in the existing arrangements have been made to us. The first of these is the " Ticket System " now in force in Jamaica. this has been described in the earlier part of this Chapter,

where we have made suggestions for meeting the complaints about the operation of that system which were brought to our notice.

89. Another arrangement was recommended by the British Medical Association in the following paragraph of their memorandum:—

> " The Association therefore suggests that wherever possible environmental public health work should be undertaken by whole-time officers and the clinical work now performed by District Medical Officers should be performed by private practitioners who are willing and able to undertake this work on a part-time basis for the Government. . . .
> . . . The part-time work which the private practitioner could perform for the Government would include not only attendance on those patients who are unable to afford private fees but also attendance at maternity and child welfare clinics and perhaps certain hospital sessions. The method of payment of the private practitioner for his government work would vary with the local conditions. It may be by salary, by sessional or capitation fee, or per item of service. Usually these part-time appointments would not be pensionable, but in districts where prospects of private practice are small and payment is made by salary provision for pension should be made."

The arrangement described in this quotation appears to us to have several disadvantages. It involves an increase in qualified medical staff which the West Indian Colonies cannot afford. It would go far to prevent that close co-operation between all forms of medical work which in our view is very necessary in the West Indies. It would increase the difficulty of maintaining discipline and of transferring staff of the unified medical service. Finally, it cannot be overlooked that there is a very real danger, as was brought out by numerous and serious complaints made to us in evidence, that the interest of the private practitioner would be centred on his private work and the attention that he would give, and the time that he would devote, to official duties, including the care of pauper patients, would be diminished.

90. The existing contributory schemes which we have briefly described in the first part of this Chapter can reasonably be regarded as evidence both of a desire for some co-operative and mutual scheme whereby medical benefits could be obtained on moderate terms, and of the ability of a limited section of the West Indian people to participate in such a scheme. We have, therefore, considered the possibility of recommending the introduction of some arrangement, of a contributory character and controlled by Government, similar to the National Health Insurance Scheme in Great Britain. Such a system would be of great benefit to the people of the West Indies, but unfortunately there are practical obstacles to its introduction. That irregularity of work which is so marked a feature of the lives of the poorer people in the West Indies would make it impossible for them to pay regular contributions; even when they were in regular employment they could not afford to set

aside for this purpose out of the present wages more than 1d. or 2d. a week. It is a fair deduction from experience in this country, where administration costs 1½d. per person per week, that the whole of the worker's contribution in the West Indies would be absorbed by administrative expenses, including the cost of collection, which among these communities is certain to be high. A final consideration is that until a better and wider system of education is available in the West Indies, a very large proportion of the working people cannot be expected to accept and discharge such obligations as the keeping of stamped insurance cards. We have, therefore, come with reluctance to the conclusion that such a Health Insurance Scheme as that operating in this country is not at present practicable for all these Colonies.

91. An extension of contributory schemes, with a carefully selected membership, may, however, be possible, and we suggest that among the first duties of the Medical Adviser, whose appointment we have recommended, should be the careful examination of this possibility in consultation with all the West Indian Governments and Medical Departments. Meanwhile the medical services now provided, with extensions through the appointment, which we have recommended, of more and better trained dispensers and district nurses, should be available for all sections of the community, and charges for those services should be graduated according to the means of the individual and should be imposed only when authorities appointed by the Government are satisfied that the patient is in a position to make some payment. The general policy should be for Government to employ only full-time medical officers, the fees for any treatment given by them being paid to the Government.

92. The question whether the salaries paid to medical officers in the West Indies are too high is another matter which was frequently raised in evidence before us and is one which can appropriately be considered here, since the level of those payments is one of the factors governing the possibility of the provision by Governments of more extensive services staffed by fully qualified doctors.

93. Until a local Medical College has been established the demand for salaries of a comparable order to those paid to doctors in Government or Municipal employment in England is likely to be maintained, since the claim is based mainly on the ground of the expense of obtaining medical training overseas. Whether this is a justifiable demand when the wages of workers in the West Indies are so much below those of workers in this country is doubtful. Moreover, some of the salaries paid on first appointment in the West Indies are considerably higher than appears to be necessary. An extreme example is the initial

salary of £500 per annum which, with a travelling allowance of £75 per annum, is now paid to a District Medical Officer in British Guiana, who has also the right to private practice and, if confirmed in his appointment, is eligible for a pension.

94. In our opinion there is a case for very careful reconsideration of the scales of salary of Government doctors in the West Indies in the light of the admitted fact that the medical profession is now financially the most attractive to young West Indians leaving secondary schools. Another and relevant consideration is that the salaries of Government doctors ought to be kept reasonably in line with those paid to other professional officers in Government employment. Without wishing to prejudge the outcome of any inquiries which may be made, we would record the opinion that if a unified medical service is established in the West Indies some correlation of salary scales throughout the group would be necessary; it may be desirable to fix the initial salary at some lower figure than £500 per annum, to provide for the grant of study leave and to make the attainment of the higher ranges in the approved scale of salary conditional upon post-graduate study and the passing of efficiency bars. While initial salaries should be such as to attract a good type of candidate they should not be so high as to lead the majority of promising students to train for the medical profession—often with the aid of scholarships granted by the Government. Nor should the level of salaries be so high as to make the employment of an adequate number of doctors beyond the resources of some of the West Indian Governments.

95. Unification will, as we have pointed out, bring to the doctors such benefits as greater possibilities of advancement, more opportunity for gaining wider experience and a better prospect of congenial work. These advantages, coupled with the higher rate of salary to be attained after post-graduate study and the passing of efficiency bars, should, we consider, compensate for the lower initial salary in those few territories where, in the interests of uniformity, this will have to be fixed below the present figure. We feel confident that the fact that the new standard conditions of initial employment must be less attractive than the best terms now offered in a few Colonies will not lead doctors in the West Indies to oppose the whole principle of unification. Through any such antagonism to the scheme an opportunity of reform, intended to benefit the West Indian peoples as a whole, might be missed, and it would be difficult to resist the conclusion that the time is still far distant when a common and constructive effort by those Colonies will be possible.

96. A number of points relating to the salaries and conditions of service of auxiliary medical personnel were also raised in evidence. Those questions are too closely related to the wider

issue of the terms of service of all subordinate Government officers for us to discuss them separately. In any case that matter appears to us to be one which, as a rule, should be left for consideration by Colonial Governments, but, as we have already said, the salaries and other conditions of service of district nurses and their housing accommodation and transport arrangements must be improved in many of these Colonies if staff of the right quality is to be obtained in numbers adequate for the new organisation which we have recommended.

(7) INCREASE IN PREVENTIVE MEASURES.

97. Before we make proposals for the extension and improvement of the limited work which is now being done by West Indian Governments in the field of preventive medicine, we wish to pay tribute to the very valuable assistance which has been, and is still being, given by the Rockefeller Foundation. Their successful efforts to develop this branch of medical activity have been greatly appreciated by all thoughtful people in the Caribbean area. We trust that West Indian Governments will always take advantage with alacrity of any offers by the Foundation to place this invaluable assistance at their disposal and give every encouragement to their work and co-operate with them fully. At the same time, those Governments should themselves, as finances permit, increase preventive work, and in the following paragraphs of this section we indicate some of the directions in which, in our opinion, that work could most usefully proceed.

(a) *Housing.*

98. The measures suggested in the following Chapter of this report for the improvement of housing in the West Indies are among the most important steps which could be taken there for the prevention of disease.

(b) *General Sanitation.*

99. Throughout the West Indies much more attention should be given to general sanitation. For example, the rarity of the " bore hole " type of latrine is surprising; admittedly it would be unsuitable for some parts owing to the nature of the soil but in many others it would be most useful. It is cheap and generally popular among rural communities and can be constructed by the people themselves if they are given a little advice and assistance.

100. Too little attention has been given to sanitation of schools and it is not surprising, therefore, to find a high incidence of such preventible diseases as hookworm, dysentery and

typhoid fever, which may be attributed to the defective sanitation to be found in most parts of the West Indies. In particular it cannot be too strongly emphasised that the treatment of hookworm must be ineffective unless full preventive measures are also taken. That disease is so widespread that it must be regarded as a serious economic factor in these Colonies. Considerable improvement of the sanitary arrangements in the schools and a better education in sanitary requirements at the teachers' training colleges are steps which can, and should, be taken at an early date to correct that ignorance which is so marked among children, teachers, and even school managers themselves.

101. Water supplies and systems of sewage disposal are often unsatisfactory in the towns. The installation of modern services for these purposes in urban areas is expensive, but in many cases some improvement should be practicable at a reasonable cost. In some towns where the local authorities have been assisted from the Colonial Development Fund to make the initial provision, proper supervision of the services has not been maintained. Rural water supplies also require attention in many districts and in many cases the cost of improvement need not be high.

102. In all these matters there is need both for initial expert advice and for subsequent continuing supervision which everywhere can best be obtained—and in some of the smaller Colonies can only be obtained—if our earlier recommendations are adopted. Several of the Colonial Governments concerned must be assisted financially if the problems which we have described are to be effectively tackled.

(c) Anti-Malarial Measures.

103. Although, as we have already said, malaria is one of the most widespread and debilitating diseases in a number of the West Indian Colonies, and constitutes a serious economic problem, less care, time and money have been expended on its prevention there than in many other British Colonies, and certainly it has not received the attention warranted by the serious nature of its effects on the people. If anti-malarial measures in the future are to be economical and more effective, it is essential that experts should be appointed to study its prevalence, to ascertain the breeding places and habits of the local mosquito vectors and to give advice on the best method of controlling the disease. This programme is quite beyond the financial resources of the smaller islands, in many of which the problem is serious. The institution of a unified medical service and the advice of visiting experts would in this case also be of much value not only for research but in the execution of anti-malarial measures such as the drainage or filling up of swamps.

(d) *Maternity and Child Welfare Work.*

104. The fact that infant mortality rates are seriously high in most of these Colonies points to the need for an improvement in the standard of maternity and child welfare work. With the exception of a few places this important branch of medical activity has been much neglected. The creation of at least one School of Hygiene, through which adequate training, now unobtainable, for local health visitors should be provided, would be of immense importance to this work. In the meantime it is essential to secure the services of qualified women who could be employed to supervise a number of infant welfare clinics in which they could help with the training of local health visitors. There is great need for an increase in the number of well-trained health visitors not only in connection with child welfare centres but for home-visiting in villages and also on estates. It cannot, however, be too strongly emphasised that no amount of attention at child welfare centres will bring about an appreciable lowering of the high rates of infant mortality until social conditions have been improved and the mothers of young children are enabled to feed and care for them.

(e) *Venereal Diseases Clinics.*

105. Since venereal diseases are so widespread and transport is often so difficult to obtain, the campaign against them should be organised on a wider basis; it is essential to combine with treatment a better education of the public in the prevention of these diseases. Moreover, consideration should everywhere be given to the possibility of having separate sessions at the clinics for the two sexes, or separate entrances, when separate sessions cannot be arranged, and of having treatment in the evening.

(f) *School Medical Services.*

106. The Governments of Jamaica and Trinidad have made a start with these services, but considerable extension is necessary in those Colonies, and elsewhere similar facilities should be provided as rapidly as finances permit. Where possible these services should be operated by full-time Medical Officers, with the assistance of school nurses, and save in exceptional cases no charge should be made for treatment ordered as the result of the medical inspection of children in the schools. There is abundant evidence that, when charges are made, many children in fact do not receive treatment. The responsibility of seeing that the orders of the doctor are carried out should rest on the school or district nurse, or on the social welfare worker in the nearest village.

107. Where it is financially impossible for a Colonial Government to provide a school medical service controlled in the way

suggested above, by qualified doctors, much improvement could be effected by giving special courses of training to selected teachers. Those courses should cover both the general health requirements of school children and the detection of medical defects and, as we have already suggested, education in sanitary matters. Teachers so trained could be authorised to send children who, in their opinion, need treatment to special school clinics—to be held on certain days, preferably Saturdays—where they could be examined and treated by doctors or trained nurses.

(g) Employment of Women Doctors.

108. In our opinion the employment in the West Indies of a larger number of well-trained women doctors would be most valuable. Where school medical inspection and maternity and child welfare work are to be expanded, every effort should be made to obtain the services of women doctors. They would also be of great assistance in gynaecological clinics and in treating female patients at venereal disease clinics. The local supply of women doctors is now small and we suggest that through the grant of scholarships West Indian Governments should encourage promising girls who are leaving secondary schools to train for the medical profession.

(h) Education of the Public in Health Matters.

109. It is not necessary to repeat here the remarks made in the preceding Chapter on the subject of health education, but the importance, from the preventive point of view, of widespread knowledge of the elements of hygiene must be strongly stressed.

3. Defective Diets and Malnutrition.

110. In 1936 the Secretary of State for the Colonies addressed to all Colonial Governments a circular drawing attention to the importance of nutrition in public health work and in general adminstrative policy, and calling for a comprehensive report upon every aspect of that question. In consequence of this circular most Colonial Governments appointed local Nutrition Committees to study the subject; the replies received by the Secretary of State setting out the information collected by those Committees have now been summarised and are fully discussed in the report of the Committee on Nutrition in the Colonial Empire (Cmd. 6050 and 6051), which contains a most interesting and complete account of nutrition in the Colonies in all its varied aspects—economic, social, educational, agricultural and medical. The following comments are based on those reports and on our own observation and investigations.

111. With the one exception of milk, nutritious foods of all kinds necessary for health can be produced to-day without much difficulty in almost every West Indian Colony; under a proper organisation, therefore, all malnutrition should be avoided. Nevertheless malnutrition does exist, especially among the poorer and unemployed people, and occurs most severely among infants, young children, old persons and the poor mothers of large families. It was particularly noticeable in the cases of infants and small children. Ignorance, neglect and poverty are probably its causes and the most obvious, the simplest, and yet perhaps the most neglected remedy is that mothers should have the opportunity of breast-feeding their babies. Secondly, mothers should have the financial assistance of the father of their children. Thirdly, women should be educated in child welfare as girls at school, later in maternity and child welfare clinics and through the advice of health visitors. Finally, a better supply of milk should be made available for children.

112. Cases of well-marked deficiency diseases such as scurvy, rickets and beri-beri are not common among the West Indian people; cases of less well-defined forms of deficiency disease were to be seen in several Colonies, chiefly among poor urban school children. Their condition is probably due to deficiency of animal protein and fat, combined with the lack of vitamin A and/or some of the vitamin B complex. The East Indians in Trinidad and British Guiana appeared to suffer even more severely from similar deficiencies, the remedy for which is an increased supply of cheap animal food, such as milk, eggs, poultry and fish, and of fresh vegetables. The adoption of the recommendations made in the agricultural Chapters of this report for the introduction everywhere of systems of mixed farming would go far to satisfy these needs within a short space of time and we propose here only to indicate particular ways in which that process might be stimulated.

113. Through the increase of livestock, and the improvement of their breeding, management and feeding, the available supply of local milk could be brought more nearly into line with admitted needs. Meanwhile the cost of imported milk and milk products should be kept as low as possible and the removal of any tariffs on such imports from within the Empire should be considered. The pasteurisation of milk, about which we heard evidence, tends to raise the price beyond the reach of the majority of the people. There is also the danger that the supervision of pasteurisation might be inadequate and epidemics of infectious disease might result. For the wealthier classes in the larger towns a supply of pasteurised milk, hygienically produced, may be practicable, but poorer people may find it more satisfactory and more economical to boil their

milk, and for school children in present circumstances the supply of imported dried milk or condensed milk may in most cases be advisable. The extension of milk supplies should be accompanied by arrangements for adequate supervision of herds, of dairy equipment and of means of collection and distribution. In the agricultural report reference is made to the possibility of increasing the supply of milk through the use of goats. The danger of the introduction and spread of Malta Fever can be minimised by such measures as the regular examination of stock and the boiling of milk before consumption.

114. We recommend in Chapter XVI of this report an immediate expert inquiry into the possibility of rapid expansion of the existing local fishery industries in the West Indies. The purpose is so to cheapen costs that it will be possible for all sections of the community to improve their diets by the greater consumption of fish.

115. Another matter to which attention should be given, in the interest of the health of the people, is the training of women in poultry keeping and the introduction of strains of fowl which are good layers and are known to do well under West Indian conditions. Women should also be given adequate instruction in the growing of vegetables. Whenever land settlements are established, training and encouragement in this branch of agriculture for both men and women are just as important from the medical standpoint as they are necessary to the success of the settlers as agriculturists.

116. A more practical type of education in schools, with the teaching of domestic science to girls and of diet requirements to children of both sexes, would be one effective method of solving the problems of malnutrition.

117. In short, the fundamental cause of such malnutrition as exists appears to be the divorce of the people from the land without the provision of compensatory arrangements which would help to ensure adequate food supplies for the displaced population. The immediate remedies which we have suggested are designed to meet that fundamental cause. But the causes of malnutrition are complex and before a more comprehensive policy can be framed to deal with them, inquiries involving many Departments in each Colony must be made in order to determine with accuracy such questions as the extent of malnutrition, and the exact nature of the major deficiencies. Persons trained in the study of those questions are not now always available in the West Indian Colonies and it may be found that help from outside is required.

CHAPTER IX.
HOUSING.

1. We now come to a subject on which our principal conclusions and recommendations will be founded mainly on our personal investigations. We made a point in every Colony of visiting the areas in which the housing conditions were said to be worst, of inspecting model buildings and any other local efforts to tackle the problems of slum clearance and rehousing, and of seeing the experiments which some Colonial Governments, and private persons, are making in the hope of being able to evolve cheap methods of construction based on the use of local materials. In addition, both in the West Indies and since our return to this country, we have heard much oral evidence on the subject of housing.

1. Existing Conditions.

2. In both town and country the present housing of the large majority of the working people in the West Indian Colonies leaves much to be desired; in many places it is deplorable; in some the conditions are such that any human habitation of buildings now occupied by large families must seem impossible to a newcomer from Europe. It is no exaggeration to say that in the poorest parts of most towns and in many of the country districts a majority of the houses is* largely made of rusty corrugated iron and unsound boarding; quite often the original floor has disappeared and only the earth remains, its surface so trampled that it is impervious to any rain which may penetrate through a leaking roof; sanitation in any form and water supply are unknown in such premises, and in many cases no light can enter when the door is closed. These decrepit homes, more often than not, are seriously overcrowded, and it is not surprising that some of them are dirty and verminous in spite of the praiseworthy efforts of the inhabitants to keep them clean. In short, every condition that tends to produce disease is here to be found in a serious form. The generally insanitary environment gives rise to malaria, worm infection and bowel diseases; leaking roofs, rotten flooring and lack of light encourage the spread of tuberculosis, respiratory diseases, worm infections, jigger lesions and rat-borne diseases; overcrowding, which is usually accompanied by imperfect ventilation, is an important agent in contributing to the high incidence of yaws, tuberculosis, venereal diseases and, to a certain extent, leprosy.

3. Two examples—one from a town, another from a rural area—may help to form a picture of these conditions at

---
* See Plate VI.

their worst. In part of Smith's Village, on the outskirts of Kingston in Jamaica, we found large areas covered by ruinous shacks, none of which could have escaped instant condemnation in this country even under standards long since abandoned. The conditions of squalor almost beyond imagination are accentuated by appalling overcrowding. Whole families—father, mother and numerous children—have their meals and sleep in one small room; such is the pressure of poverty that when a second room is available, it will often be sub-let for the sake of the few shillings which are thus to be obtained each month. Often the only available source of water supply for large numbers of these dwellings is cut off for long periods of each day. Not unnaturally many of these " properties " are focal centres of disease and crime, and all of them appear to be neglected by their owners who spend nothing on even the crudest maintenance.

4. In the island of Anguilla—one of three comprising the Presidency of St. Kitts-Nevis in the Leeward Islands—we came across a " trash " house* (i.e., one constructed of leaves and other vegetation intertwined with rough poles) which covered about 200 sq. ft., divided into two sections by a similar construction. Gaps in these rough walls were filled by iron, the galvanising of which had long since disappeared, and by torn strips of blanket; the floor was earth and light penetrated only by the doorway. Sanitation is unknown in Anguilla; all the water supply is brackish and the nearest well was some miles distant from this house, which, we were told, was occupied by five adults and 15 children.

5. It has been said by previous Commissions which visited the West Indies that the low standard of housing there, especially in agricultural districts, can be traced to historical conditions and in particular to the system under which indentured Indian immigrants, employed as labourers on sugar and cocoa estates, were accommodated in long ranges of single rooms, the floors of which in many cases rested on the ground. That there is justification for this view is shown by the present condition of many of the old ranges or barracks which are still occupied. Some of the worst examples are to be found in British Guiana where, both near estates within a mile of the capital and along the Essequibo Coast, once the centre of a thriving sugar industry which has now deserted that area, East Indians are closely crowded in ranges on the verge of collapse, lacking every amenity and frequently almost surrounded by stagnant water. These people either themselves are, or are the descendants of, immigrants whose contracts of indenture entitled them to free housing as part of their conditions of service and, although that system of employment has

---

* See Plate VII.

long since lapsed, the feeling of the people that employers should continue to bear this obligation makes it difficult—and in present circumstances impossible—to eject them from these dilapidated buildings.

6. These examples and the general description which we have given of the housing of many of the poorer people are, of course, only one side of the picture: on the other are, first, the practice of some employers who have constantly tried to improve the housing conditions of their resident labourers, and, secondly, the efforts, limited by their financial position, which some Governments have made, particularly within the last year or so, to provide new dwellings at rents within the means of working people. We were glad to note, for example, the work of reform which is being attempted on the estates of the West Indian Sugar Company in the Westmoreland district of Jamaica, on the Caroni and Waterloo estates in Trindad,* on the Blantyre estate in British Guiana, at Roseau in St. Lucia,† and by a number of firms outside the sugar industry, such as those working a bauxite concession at Mackenzie‡ in British Guiana and the Asphalt Lake in Trinidad. In short it may be said that, in the majority of cases in which a firm of substance and repute employing resident labour in considerable numbers is making, or hopes to make, a reasonable profit from its activities, a greater realisation is now being shown of the responsibility for seeing that employees are properly housed. Some of the modern cottages which we inspected on the estates of such firms set a new standard for working-class houses in the West Indies, and the condition of many of those cottages is a clear contradiction of the story, so often repeated, that the labourer in the West Indies neither wants, nor is capable of taking proper care of, a better type of accommodation.

2. Nature of the Housing Problem.

7. It will be clear from what we have said that the housing problem in the West Indian Colonies is so acute that no means which makes for a solution of it should be neglected; however partial or limited its immediate results may be, every line of constructive action should be adopted and pursued with vigour. A sustained and complementary effort by Government, local authorities, private enterprise and the people themselves is not merely necessary but of pressing urgency.

8. The problem is, however, of a dual nature and its differing aspects in urban and rural districts must be described. In urban areas it is similar in kind, though comparatively worse in degree, to that which has confronted many local authorities in

---

* See Plate VIII. † See Plate IX. ‡ See Plate X.

this country since the War. Its main features, apart from the generally poor quality of most existing houses, are the overcrowding which is now being accentuated by the drift to the towns, the lack of sanitation and absence of water supplies, and the failure to work to any organised plan of development. In other parts of this report we stress the great need for checking in the West Indies that movement into towns which in so many parts of the world is a characteristic of this age; even if no other reason existed, the fact that that drift seriously increases the difficulty of housing the townsfolk would justify the taking by Governments of effective action against it, even at the risk of an apparent infringement of the rights of personal liberty. That apart, the issue in the towns is one of the clearance of slums and the provision of solid structures on a rental basis. These changes, including the necessary provision of adequate arrangements for sanitation, cooking and washing, cannot be carried out at a cost which would bring the economic rent within the means of the slum dweller. We agree therefore with the view expressed by Major Orde Browne in his recent Report (Cmd. 6070) on Labour Conditions in the West Indies that it should be frankly recognised that any slum clearance scheme should be undertaken as an essential social service rather than an economic proposition. Outside the towns it is necessary to distinguish between the housing of estate labour and that of the peasant proprietor or cultivator. On most estates, so long as the labour force is maintained at its present level in order to alleviate distress by distributing the available work as partial employment, not even the most prosperous companies could afford to re-house all their resident labour. The cost of replacing the whole of the existing unsatisfactory accommodation by cottages would certainly be prohibitive, and even the provision of quarters in some improved form of range, if permitted by Government, would be too serious a liability for most proprietors of estates. So long as they continue to shoulder the burden of housing labour which is really superfluous to their needs, these people have a reasonable claim to financial assistance for this purpose from Government funds.

9. The case of the peasant proprietor or cultivator is different in that, until he is settled permanently on land as the owner or tenant of the Government, or unless he is engaged on a system of farming based on tree crops, the most suitable form of structure may often be a small movable house provided on terms of hire purchase. Here again Governments can reasonably be expected to give some measure of financial assistance unless it is clear that the small sums of money required can be borrowed elsewhere at fairly low rates of interest. It is also reasonable that people in this class should be expected—as they should certainly be encouraged—to undertake themselves

much of the work of constructing their new dwellings, provided that simple plans for doing this are made available and explained to them by officers of Government or local authorities, who might also be able to assist by giving advice on the spot.

3. Siting and Types of Houses.

10. In the interests of health the nature of the site of any housing scheme is of primary importance and equal consideration should be given to the following suggestions when Government can control the choice of the site for isolated dwellings. First, land on which houses are to be built should be remote from anopheline-breeding swamps; the selection of elevated and cleared sites will diminish the risk of the contraction of malaria. Easy access to a good water supply, and, whenever possible, to land available for the growing of food, is very desirable. The lay-out should be such that both the house and the immediately surrounding area can be effectively drained, thus preventing the breeding of mosquitoes and that dampness of the dwelling which so often is a cause of disease in the West Indies. It is equally important especially in rural districts, that the site should lend itself to the use of one of the simple sanitary types of latrine. By co-operative arrangements between the Government and villages it has been found possible in some other British Colonies to supply satisfactory bore-hole latrines to each household for the sum of a few shillings. In all these matters the medical reforms recommended in the previous Chapter, including the appointment of experienced sanitary engineers, should be of great assistance.

11. Before we consider the debatable issue of the most suitable materials, of which there is a wide choice, for West Indian housing, we will state briefly the elementary principles which, in our opinion, should be observed in the construction of all new homes in these Colonies. They should be raised from the ground and should have damp-proof floors which can be kept clean and are unlikely to harbour insects and vermin. The roof and walls should be impervious to rain and wind; the roof should overhang more than is usual in order to give the maximum protection to the walls against both sun and rain.* While the size of houses must vary, as does the size of families, and separate rooms should be provided for the segregation of older children of different sexes, the floor space for each occupant need not be large; it must be remembered that most West Indians spend much of the day out of doors and use their houses mainly as sleeping quarters. Better arrangements than are usual for ventilation in cold countries should be made in

---

* Plate XI shews how this feature has been naturally evolved by unassisted peasants.

the West Indies in view of the absence of chimneys; spaces should therefore be left between the top of the walls and the roof. Verandahs and galleries are useful when the occupants can be prevented from enclosing them in boards. The essential facilities for cooking and washing should be adequate and conveniently planned; whenever possible water should be made available by stand-pipes placed at frequent intervals. The absence of most of these features is shewn in Plates XII and XIII, which illustrate very common types.

12. Whenever possible the opinion of local women should be sought on such questions as the type and arrangement of houses and, where this can be obtained, it should be carefully considered. We would also call to notice the desirability of appointing a woman on any local Housing Committee.

13. There is, as we have said, a wide choice of building materials and many experiments have been, and are being, carried out to test the suitability, under present conditions and with existing tastes, of several compositions both old and new. Thus, in British Honduras, a model house was constructed in the autumn of last year from a mixture of which a material known as " pipeshank ", extracted locally from the sea, was the principal ingredient. This house, of attractive design and well-equipped with all the necessary services, contained three rooms and had been erected at a cost of about £180*; it was suggested that this figure might be reduced by production in quantities. In British Guiana one of the sugar companies was experimenting with lignocrete, a composition made partly of cement and partly of sawdust from local timber; the results had been satisfactory over a brief period of trial. In some Colonies an attempt is being made to restore to favour, through an improvement of its form, the local method of building known as " tapia ". We saw in one Colony an attractive small dwelling† built by this method at a cost of under £40. In Jamaica we were told that a house of three rooms, with a verandah, could be built from clay blocks for about £80, and that some sugar estates had been able to design and build small cottages at an average cost of £60, which could be substantially reduced if mass production became possible and cement and tiles could be manufactured locally at cheap prices. In contrast to these figures, it should be mentioned that the cost to the Jamaica Government of tenements of blocks of six rooms, with a communal kitchen, bath and sanitary arrangements, worked out at the high figure of £500; these tenements are made of native

---

* This figure and the other statements, or estimates, of cost which follow relate to a period before the present war.

† See Plate XIV. Plate VIII gives an example of a more elaborate tapia structure.

hard-wood with walls of concrete nog. The Trinidad Lake Asphalt Operating Company had constructed family apartment houses—in ranges of six, with two rooms to each house—at an average cost of about £110 a house; the same Company had erected single family cottages, including bathrooms and lavatories which are detached from the cottage, at a cost of a little over £180. In both cases the construction is mainly wooden. It was estimated by a Committee of the Legislative Council of Trinidad, which reported last year, that the sum of £1,000,000 there set aside for the building of houses for the working classes would provide for the acquisition of land, for road construction and for the building of between 6,000 and 6,500 houses; the total capital cost of each new dwelling, including overhead charges, would therefore be at least £150. We have given these examples of the figures of cost supplied to us since this is clearly a most important factor in any scheme of housing on the scale of the one which ought to be undertaken in the West Indies. The relative cost of construction in different types of materials is a consideration which must go far to influence the choice between them; it is, in our opinion, important that these costs should not be so high that the rent, although uneconomic, has still to be fixed at a figure which might force the tenants to make unwise economies on food.

14. The only definite conclusion which we have been able to reach on this aspect of the housing problem is that no single model could be found which would be suitable to meet all the varying conditions in the different territories. The wide diversity of the views expressed to us about both types and costs of suitable houses points, in our opinion, to the need for an investigation of the problem by an expert to whom full reports should be made on all the many experiments to which we have referred; those reports should cover such matters as the relative costs of building in different materials, the suitability of houses so constructed to the West Indian climate, their ability to withstand every form of climatic condition known there and the extent to which each satisfies local taste in housing. In the course of our inquiries we received promises of assistance in any more detailed investigation of methods of building and types of houses in the West Indies from the Building Industries National Council, Associated Portland Cement Manufacturers Limited and the Building Research Station of the Department of Scientific and Industrial Research. These generous offers we gratefully acknowledge and we commend full acceptance of them, and close study of the information with which some of these bodies have supplied us, to any expert appointed to make a special investigation of the housing problem in the West Indies. That investigation is justified by the magnitude of the problem,

the scale of expenditure involved and the consequent imperative need for economy which will be the more easily secured if, through the inquiry, some measure of standardisation of design and materials is found to be possible. Meanwhile much progress can, and should, be made without waiting for the outcome of this investigation, and the suggestions which we put forward in the following sections of this Chapter are intended for immediate adoption.

4. Government Housing Schemes in Towns.

15. The problem in the towns is, as we have said, largely one of the clearance of slums. It is essential that where powers are not already available to issue clearing and demolition orders in respect of insanitary property, they should at once be taken and a definite authority should be appointed to exercise them. When buildings are condemned as no longer fit for habitation and their demolition is ordered, compensation, if the land is to be acquired by Government, should be on the basis of valuation as house spots—i.e. on the value of the land as a building site—and no account should be taken of the abandoned dwellings. Even when the site of buildings ordered by proper authority to be demolished is not acquired by Government for rehousing or other public purposes and is therefore to be left in the possession of its owner, no compensation should be paid for the condemned property and protests of injustice or hardship should not be allowed to impede the execution of the demolition order. One exception to this may be found desirable. Where people who are the owners of leased property which is condemned have no means of subsistence apart from the rents which they thus received, small *ex gratia* payments might reasonably be granted. Proper safeguards should be attached to this concession and should be rigidly enforced.

16. In many towns the first practical step to be taken after the issue of a demolition order will be the provision of quarters to which slum dwellers can be removed temporarily while their present dwellings are cleared and the sites used for their permanent re-housing. In the climate of the West Indies, and having regard to the need for economy, it would be unreasonable to demand that those quarters should be more substantial or more expensively equipped than is necessary for their temporary purpose. Any discomfort and inconvenience should be accepted with good grace for the sake of the subsequent benefits and desirable progress should not be stopped by unreasonable objections to removal based on the nature of the alternative accommodation which is offered by the Government or housing authority. The powers of that authority should be wide enough to allow them, in all suitable cases, to provide this

alternative accommodation and to charge for it rentals within the means of the individuals displaced, even when those charges are uneconomic.

17. In all matters of procedure Governments, and Municipal Councils when they are used by Governments as housing authorities, should follow the lines which have been so successful in this country, and any defects in their legislative powers, as compared with those given here by Act of Parliament and bye-laws, should be remedied unless it is certain that the powers thus conferred in Great Britain are inappropriate to the circumstances of the particular Colony or are not wholly applicable there. In particular, overcrowding should be clearly defined and its occurrence in new housing provided by the State should be made an offence, a course for which there is precedent in this country. Such a provision would prevent the use of increased space to accommodate a lodger when, by proper standards, it is required for members of the re-housed families.

18. Peculiar points of procedure, outside the experience of this country, may arise at times but can usually be solved by the exercise of common sense and goodwill. For example, in two islands it has been found difficult, owing to complications of ownership due to an old legal system, to prove the title to land required for a housing scheme. We can see no objection to the issue of a regulation providing that, in such cases, subject to the allowance of a limited period for appeals, occupation of land for five years will be accepted as proof of ownership. Another matter on which special provision may be required in the West Indies, owing to the habits of many of the people, is that of preventing the boarding up of verandahs or stoppage of other ventilation provided in new dwellings in the interests of health.

19. It is essential that all the West Indian Governments should have easily applied powers to enable them to acquire compulsorily land which is needed for housing purposes. As we say in Chapter XVI, when dealing with compulsory acquisition for land settlement, it may be found appropriate in some Colonies to decide upon a definite basis for the valuation of land which is required by Government; for example, it could be laid down that the price should be a certain number of years' purchase of the net average annual return from the land over a specified period of years. In other territories the price might be left to be determined by valuation, but in that event it might be desirable, in the smaller territories at least, to provide by law that when the Government and the owner of the land cannot agree on a price an independent valuation shall be made by some authority from outside the island.

20. We have already expressed in this Chapter our concurrence with the view that it should be frankly recognised that any

slum clearance scheme should be undertaken as an essential social service rather than an economic proposition. Private enterprise is unlikely therefore to be attracted to this work unless induced thereto by substantial grants or subsidy: it follows then that the burden of financing most of the housing schemes in the towns must fall on public funds and in many cases a continuing subvention in the form of uneconomic rents must be borne from the funds which finance the scheme.

21. Another recommendation to which attention in many rural districts, particularly on estates, will be as desirable as it is obviously necessary in the towns, is that powers should be taken, through town planning legislation where it does not already exist, to control the siting and lay-out of new housing. Apart from the considerations which we mentioned when discussing the question of types of houses, it will be important to ensure that all new construction conforms to an approved plan and takes account of such requirements as the provision of adequate gardens.

22. Finally, under this section, we would emphasise the importance of a planned housing policy in which one element, perhaps the most important, would be the maintenance of a balance between the work done in towns and on rural housing. Imperative as the needs of the townsfolk are, it would be disastrous to concentrate attention mainly on the meeting of those needs; the provision of new urban houses, unless accompanied by a parallel programme in the country districts, could not fail to accelerate the already undesirable rate of movement into the towns.

5. Estate and Company Housing.

23. For the sake of brevity and to avoid repetition the word " estate " is used throughout this section to cover all undertakings which employ resident labour.

24. The first important question is that of the division of responsibility between Government and private enterprise for the housing of estate labour. It is not difficult to find arguments with which to support the view that the liability should be undertaken by Government. Not only would that relieve employers of an obligation, the burden of which increases with the quite legitimate demands for an improved standard of housing by a body of people whose numbers often exceed greatly the actual labour requirements of the estate, but it would remove the complaint, so often made to us in evidence, that the right to evict gave the employer an unfair hold over his resident labourers. In fact, examination of such complaints normally showed that the right was seldom exercised and then only in extreme cases of neglect or disregard of duties. Nevertheless the feeling is genuine and cannot be disregarded.

25. The taking over of the liability by Government is not, however, a feasible solution. Apart from the great expense involved, many practical difficulties would be certain to arise if all resident labour were housed by Government on land within an estate. For example, if a workman is discharged by the Company, must he give up his house or is the Company to find accommodation elsewhere for any person whom they wish to employ in his place? Again, resident labour is unaccustomed to the payment of rent and would not readily accept an obligation to make such payments to Government even if wages were slightly increased. Thirdly, it would be difficult to justify this course of action in the case of estate labour unless Government were prepared to undertake a similar responsibility for all other rural people, and that is clearly outside their means unless they are to be given financial assistance beyond any that we contemplate.

26. In our view the responsibility will be fairly divided between estate proprietors and Government if the former provide the land and give reasonable security of tenure to the occupants of houses built thereon under schemes financed by Government in the form of loans at low rates of interest. The provision of sites by the estates is of particular importance in areas where they possess a monopoly of the land suitable for housing purposes. The claims of the peasants should clearly have priority over those of agriculture, and estate owners can reasonably be required, therefore, to contribute in this way to the rehousing of their employees, and indeed to that of residents in villages bordering their property who do not work for them but for whose housing needs no other land is available. It should be a condition of the grant of loans by Government at low rates of interest that, as regards methods of construction, lay-out of the scheme and all other necessary requirements, the housing built by estate proprietors should conform to approved standards, which should include the provision of land for the growing of vegetables unless the Government are satisfied that this would be impracticable. It would also be reasonable to make this assistance conditional upon the grant of that additional security of tenure to which we attach much importance. In our view it is desirable that this grant should be given a practical significance by the charging of rent in return for a corresponding increase of wages when, as is usually the case, no rent or a nominal sum, such as 1d. per week, is now charged for the occupation of housing provided by the estates. The obligation to make this payment to the Company, which could deduct it from wages before they are issued, would not be likely to give rise to the difficulties which we mentioned when discussing the question whether Government should undertake responsibility for the housing of all estate labour.

27. Whatever may be decided on the question of responsibility for new housing there can be no doubt that in most of the Colonies a more extensive survey of the buildings now used to accommodate estate labour is required. This survey should be undertaken by persons appointed by the Governor, usually from the staff of the Medical Department, and the principles which we have suggested to govern the issue of demolition orders and the payment of compensation in the case of slum property in the towns should apply generally to condemned housing on estates. There is, however, this material difference. The issue of orders for the demolition of ranges or other quarters on estates must be done with care and with due regard for the problem which would be created if no alternative accommodation is available within easy reach of the only work for wages in the district. For example, the authorities may sometimes find that it is expedient to require only the repair of property which they would have condemned if its occupants could be housed elsewhere in the neighbourhood. In such cases this less stringent requirement should be recognised from the outset as a temporary measure and should be subject to an undertaking by the proprietors to build new accommodation, with such Government assistance as we have suggested, within a specified period of time.

28. A controversy which has aroused much interest is whether all new housing on estates should be self-contained or whether ranges may be continued in a modified form. We were informed in British Guiana that our appointment was one of the reasons which led the Government to defer their decision on this issue, and that in consequence some estates had suspended all building activity. It is important, therefore, that the question should be definitely settled and that an official policy should be laid down in all the West Indian Colonies with the minimum delay. Substantial arguments can be put forward in favour of both types of housing. The range is less expensive in cost and occupies a smaller area, which is an important consideration when land is valuable and scarce. Some medical authorities prefer that system on the ground that it involves less work in the control and clearing of the surrounding land, and thus lessens the difficulty of taking adequate anti-malarial measures. The attractions which ranges may have for some of their occupants were mentioned in Major Orde Browne's report (Cmd. 6070), where he said that they " find that it militates against fire and theft, while a semi-communal existence has advantages in the care of children ". The main arguments, on the other side, are that estate labourers in the West Indies value increasingly the privacy which is denied by the occupation of quarters in a range, and secondly, that the range system is associated in their minds with conditions from which they are now trying to escape. We

agree with the view expressed to us by one witness that for historical and psychological reasons every effort should be made to break with that system and to provide detached or semi-detached cottages for all married labourers. But to lay it down that the construction of ranges should now cease would add materially to the cost of the rehousing programmes and would postpone still further the time when all the working people of the West Indies will be properly accommodated. We consider, therefore, that the construction of ranges in the greatly improved form which we saw in British Guiana should certainly be permitted for the accommodation of unmarried men employed by estates. Houses of the cottage type should usually be provided for family occupation, but we think that ranges of the new pattern may continue to be built for this purpose also, provided that the number of dwellings should be limited to four. This form of construction should not, however, be sanctioned unless either it will secure a substantial saving of cost or is recommended by medical or other public authorities as being specially suited to the needs of a particular area.*

29. Nomadic labour is most common in Trinidad where exploratory work, known as "wildcatting", is carried out on behalf of oil companies, and in British Honduras where the collectors of chicle, known as "chicleros", and mahogany fellers live, during the season of their employment, in camps which are moved frequently. In the report (Cmd. 5641) of the Commission which inquired in 1937 into disturbances which had occurred in Trinidad, it was recommended that the oil companies should make temporary provision for their workers engaged on "wildcatting", paying particular attention to sanitation; or, alternatively, unless distance makes such an arrangement impracticable, they should provide the necessary transport to and from work. We support this recommendation, which is equally applicable to nomadic labour in British Honduras except that distance will there usually preclude the adoption of the alternative arrangement.

6. Other Rural Housing.

30. The case with which we are here concerned is mainly that of the peasant proprietor or cultivator, but the suggestions which we make may be found to be equally applicable to the inhabitants of some of the smaller villages.

31. Most of these people own the poor dwellings in which they now live. Their houses are, however, often built on land belonging to their employers. Here, again, the question of

---

* The barrack method is not confined to estate housing. Plate XV shews urban barrack tenements, better in some respects than those described in paragraph 5 of this Chapter, but presenting many of the same undesirable features.

eviction, to which we have referred when discussing the housing of estate labour, must be considered. The degree of protection which should be given to "tenants at will" must vary with the circumstances of their employment, but it is, in our view, particularly important that any peasant cultivator, or other person who has given time and attention to the growing of food crops, should at least be secured against dispossession without the payment of adequate compensation for any existing crops or other work that he may have put into the land. Moreover, reasonable notice to quit should be required unless summary removal can be justified by special circumstances which should not normally include the owing of arrears of rent.

32. Whenever such a course is practicable the survey of housing conditions on estates, which we have suggested, should include other rural houses. But the demolition of the house of a peasant proprietor or cultivator should not be ordered unless either he can afford to replace it or Government are prepared to grant financial assistance which will bring that task within his means. All new building should be subject to the approval of Government, but, particularly in the case of isolated dwellings, the requirements should be kept to those which are essential in the interests of health and hygiene. Moreover, the grant of financial assistance should be conditional on a right of inspection by authorities appointed by the Government, which should also be empowered to insist upon a proper standard of maintenance and to take appropriate action—such as the seizure of the property—in any case of flagrant disregard of these requirements by persons who have not repaid loans granted to them for the building of their houses.

33. The general aim of policy in rural districts should be to encourage the undertaking by the people themselves of much of the work of building their new dwellings. The attainment of this end will be assisted, as we have already said, if simple plans are made available and explained to the peasants by officers of Government or local authorities who might also be able to assist by giving advice on the spot. Both for this reason and in view of the paramount importance of keeping to the minimum the cost of what must in any event be an expensive undertaking, the use of local materials, and of methods of construction known to the ancestors of the West Indian people, should receive every encouragement. Some of us are in favour of wooden houses for villages and isolated dwellings for peasants throughout the West Indies. Where that form of construction is adopted, it should be possible for Governments to speed up the work by the purchase of housing material in bulk and by arranging for the mass production of suitable lengths of wood and of such finished articles as door and window frames and ventilators. Wherever possible the wood should be specially

preserved before it is distributed to the peasants or others who are to use it. Every encouragement should be given to the use of local timber; should it prove to be generally suitable for this purpose a substantial demand might be established for the timber of the three West Indian Colonies in which there are forests capable of commercial exploitation.

7. Finance and Supervision.

34. It will be clear from the preceding sections of this Chapter that, in our opinion, the task of bringing conditions of housing in the West Indies up to what we regard as a satisfactory level will entail expenditure of a very substantial order from public funds. It is equally clear to us that, under present economic conditions, most of that financial assistance must be provided by Parliament. It is not possible, on the information now available, to frame an accurate estimate of costs. That half the population of the West Indies should be rehoused is certainly an understatement of the position, but to get an approximate idea of the scale of expenditure involved we will make that assumption. For the accommodation of that number of people, taking the average family at six persons, about 225,000 new houses would be required. In towns the average cost of each new house is certain not to be less than £125: in country districts as low a figure as £50 may be attainable when production of materials expands and skilled advice is everywhere available. If it is assumed that for every new house in the towns two are built in country districts, the total cost would amount to more than £16,000,000. Such a programme would, of course, be spread over a period of many years, and long before it was completed substantial returns by way of rent might reasonably be expected; moreover in many cases part of the expense could be met by estates, peasant proprietors and others. But, when every allowance has been made for these and other factors which will help to reduce the figure given above as a rough estimate, it must be assumed that the total capital expenditure from public funds on building alone could not well fall below £10,000,000 and, when the cost of land and services has been added, would probably exceed that sum by a substantial margin.

35. An undertaking on this scale would call for direction and control by a person with qualifications and experience not to be found within the West Indies themselves. We have already suggested that such questions as methods of building and types of houses should be investigated by an expert, who ought to be temporarily attached to the central organisation proposed in Chapter XXI of this report. In addition that organisation should include an officer with a knowledge of town planning which would fit him to advise on the layout of approved housing

schemes in the West Indies. Finally—and this we regard as of the utmost importance—the supervision of the new housing programme throughout the West Indies should be entrusted, subject only to administrative control on issues of major policy, to an officer who has the initiative, drive and experience which are required if works of this order of magnitude are to be carried through with economy and expedition. For this last appointment every endeavour should be made to obtain the services of a person who has proved his worth on similar work on a large scale in this country.

CHAPTER X.

LABOUR AND TRADE UNIONS.

1. General.

1. No examination of labour conditions in the West Indies could be adequate unless the general character of employment there was first considered. In the main these Colonies are engaged in the production of agricultural commodities and industries are of comparatively new growth. As we record in Chapter XIII of this report, there is little prospect that industry can be developed in the near future in any of the West Indies on a scale which would influence the problem of employment. Such industries as now exist are usually ancillary to some branch of agriculture or forestry. Typical examples are the factories at which cane is crushed and sugar extracted from it, the mills in British Guiana and British Honduras where the timber brought down from the forests is sawn, the plants where citrus fruit and similar products are graded and packed and the transport services associated with all of these enterprises. Trinidad, where the production of both oil and asphalt has assumed very considerable dimensions, is the only Colony in which any substantial population can be said to be supported directly by industries not associated with agriculture in some form.

2. Owing to absence of any recent occupational census, and indeed of accurate labour statistics of any kind, it is not possible to give in tabular form a picture of the distribution of the West Indian people between their various occupations. But the following information, based on the figures and estimates which we have been able to obtain, shows how the people of the four territories with the largest populations depend upon agriculture for their employment:—

(a) *Barbados.*—At the census of 1921 only 34 per cent. of wage-earners were directly engaged in agriculture, but even now there is no industry on a large scale in this island and a large proportion of those then returned as industrial or commercial employees (36 per cent.) must have been dependent on the milling, packing and transport of sugar for their earnings. The only other large group was made up of domestic servants (25 per cent.).

(b) *British Guiana.*—In 1931, when a census was last taken, 46 per cent. of the wage-earners were agricultural labourers and 40 per cent. of the independent workers were landed proprietors or agriculturists. Domestic servants came next and accounted for 15 per cent. of the wage-earners.

(c) *Jamaica.*—In Major Orde Browne's Report (Cmd. 6070) on Labour Conditions in the West Indies it is stated that 61 per cent. of the labourers who, at the time of his recent visit were employed by the various industries in this island, were engaged in agriculture. Peasant proprietorship is an important feature of the agricultural life of this Colony, and though no estimate of the numbers of this class is available, it is certain that the proportion of the population which is dependent, either directly or indirectly, upon agriculture is very large indeed.

(d) *Trinidad.*—The only recent figures which are available relate to the number of employees in certain branches of agriculture and in industry. They show that while the oil and asphalt industries normally employ less than 15,000 operatives and labourers, the sugar and cocoa estates alone provide an occupation for more than 41,000 workers. It may fairly be assumed, therefore, that in this island, as elsewhere in the West Indies, the working people as a whole are mainly dependent upon agriculture for their earnings.

3. In the Leeward Islands and Windward Islands any form of industry unconnected with agriculture is practically nonexistent. In most of them peasant cultivators or peasant proprietors form a large proportion of the population and agriculture dominates the whole field of employment. It is only in British Honduras that agriculture takes the second place. Here the forestry industry has provided the principal occupations for the people but, as is pointed out elsewhere in this report, that industry is declining and rapid development of agriculture is essential.

4. Three other branches of employment have to be considered, all of which are connected, in a varying degree, with public administration. The first is the teaching profession, some members of which are for all purposes, including discipline and pay, servants of the Crown. In other cases teachers are employed through managers representing the various religious denominations, although the Colonial Governments meet the whole cost of the salaries of practically all of these teachers. The second group is composed of people serving in public institutions such as hospitals, infirmaries and asylums, who are usually direct employees of Colonial Governments. The third and last group is made up of members of the Colonial Service in these islands. The total number of persons engaged in the three branches of employment is, however, extremely small in relation to the gross adult population and the existence of those forms of occupation has but little effect on the general question now under discussion.

5. We do not propose in this Chapter to deal in detail with the conditions of service of teachers which have been considered in Chapter VII, where reference is made to the salaries paid in the different Colonies. Our concern here is to consider the conditions of the labouring population as a whole. By labouring population is meant those ever-growing sections of the people who are either completely or almost completely dependent upon paid employment for their livelihood.

6. In most of the West Indian Colonies there are substantial numbers of peasant proprietors who subsist independently of paid employment, or to whom such employment is a subsidiary means of augmenting the receipts from the cultivation of their land. Thus in Dominica, at the end of 1937 only 1,050 people out of a total estimated population of nearly 50,000 were believed to be wage earners. In Montserrat also the small community of about 14,000 people is preponderatingly one of peasant proprietorship, and in Grenada, of which the population is about 88,000, there are believed to be 18,000 small holdings covering about 25,000 acres of land. Nevertheless the present general tendency throughout the West Indies as a whole is for an ever-increasing section of the adult population to become dependent upon work for wages or other earnings derived from employment.

2. Character of Employment.

7. The exact form of employment in agriculture varies from Colony to Colony, but everywhere task work is characteristic. Task work is the West Indian term for what is described in Great Britain as " piece work " or " payment by results ". By far the greater proportion of agricultural workers in the West Indies are paid for the amount of work they actually perform and not according to the length of time they take to do it. Payment by the day and not by the task is the rare exception for field work in West Indian agriculture and the rates, though varying greatly from one Colony to another, are extremely low.

8. In sugar factories, where duties consist largely of the operation of machinery, most of the workers are paid at daily rates, though there also some of those employed are paid upon a basis of task work. Twelve-hour shifts are generally worked in these factories, but in a few instances eight-hour shifts have been instituted. Thus, generally, when sums paid to labourers are quoted these are normally *earnings* and not *wages*. This is an important consideration and it cannot too often be repeated that most West Indian labourers employed on agricultural work are paid for what they actually do. This system of task work has certain consequences. The rates of pay for particular tasks are not fixed by any general agreement or collective bargaining

but are usually decided on the spot. Frequently we heard complaints that labourers did not know the rates at which they were to be paid until after they had begun their task. On other occasions, when rates were being fixed on the spot because innumerable variations in soil and other conditions were likely to affect the time taken to complete a set piece of work, the discussion developed into a haggle between the labourers and the overseers. Or, more frequently, the task rates were arbitrarily decided by the overseers.

9. Owing to the variations mentioned above, it was nearly impossible in the majority of cases to obtain any satisfactory definition of what composed a reasonable task. As a consequence the rates fluctuated in apparently the most arbitrary fashion. Not only did those variations occur from Colony to Colony but they were sometimes noticeable between one estate and another in the same Colony, though the rates paid by neighbouring planters were, as we remark in a later paragraph, generally similar.

10. It is generally recognised in this country that in the absence of collective bargaining the worker is at a decided disadvantage in that he is not a free agent to bargain with his employer. The whole system of collective negotiation which exists in Great Britain and in most western countries rests upon the principle that the worker is entitled to entrust the care of his interests to officials of an organisation of his own choice. The owner of an estate which employs five thousand people is in an infinitely stronger position than is any one of those employees when a question arises which involves negotiation between them over conditions of work. Particularly is this true when there is a known surplus of labour and the employer can easily replace any dissatisfied worker from the ranks of the unemployed.

11. It is this principle of collective bargaining which has led to the combination among British workers now typified in the modern trade union with the negotiation and conclusion of agreements between associations of employers and workers. To say that the West Indian labourer is placed at a disadvantage in bargaining with his employer, who in all probability owns the range in which he lives, and could evict him at short notice, is to under-state the case. Devoid of any effective protection by means of trade unionism, the labourer is helpless and, if he wishes to live, must accept the rate of pay offered to him. In the light of this it is not surprising to find that earnings have remained extremely low, even in periods when planters were making good profits.

12. Full particulars of rates of pay and hours of work in all those Colonies for which the information is readily available were given in Major Orde Browne's Report (Cmd. 6070) on

Chapter X.

Labour Conditions in the West Indies. Those tables are too detailed to be summarised here, but the following figures, some of which are taken from his Report, of the prevailing rates of pay for work on the sugar plantations, are given as an indication of the typical earnings of the West Indian agricultural labourer. Substantially higher rates than those given below are paid to, for example, stevedores, employees on the oilfields, skilled staff in factories, and, in some cases, labourers in the service of Public Works Departments of Governments, but agricultural labour forms by far the greater part of the wage-earning population of the West Indies and these statistics therefore give a fair general impression of the earnings of the working men and women in these Colonies. While the rates are typical, they cannot be taken as the basis for any comparative estimate of conditions in the different Colonies owing to the variations in the cost of living and the availability of work.

Barbados.—Daily rates vary between 1s. and 1s. 6d. for men; a normal rate for women is 1s. a day. Earnings from task work may be substantially higher than the daily rates when sugar cane is " in crop " but the difference over the whole year does not appear to be large.

British Guiana.—Male workers engaged on the weeding of land earn on an average 2s. 2d. a day for a working period of between 7 and 9 hours and are usually employed for four days in each week. Female weeders earn on an average 1s. 6½d. for the same work.

Jamaica.—Daily rates vary from 1s. 6d. to 2s. 6d. for men and from 10½d. to 1s. 6d. for women. On task work average earnings in 1938 varied widely in different parishes. They ranged between 1s. 3d. and 4s. for cane cutting, between 1s. 6d. and 4s. 3d. for forking and between 1s. and 1s. 9d. for weeding.

Antigua.—Daily rates vary from 1s. to 2s. for men and from 7d. to 8d. for women. On task work men can earn between 2s. and 4s. a day and women between 1s. and 1s. 6d. a day.

St. Kitts.—The average daily wage for an unskilled labourer was 1s. 2d. a day at the time of our visit, but an increase of 25 per cent. has since been granted; to this wage must be added an annual bonus which in the past has fluctuated between 6s. and 30s. for each worker.

Trinidad.—The average daily rate for men varies between 1s. 10d. and 3s. 4d. and for women between 1s. 0½d. and 1s. 10½d. The average weekly earnings vary between 10s. 5d. and 14s. 7d. in the case of men and between 6s. 10½d. and 9s. 4½d. in the case of women.

St. Lucia.—Men earn on an average between 1s. 3d. and 1s. 6d. for each day of 9 hours and women are paid on an average 1s. for the same period of work.

13. Low as these earnings are, they do not, when taken by themselves, furnish the only, or the truest, indication of the standard of life of the West Indian labourer. The availability of employment is at least an equally important consideration, and the part played by unemployment and under-employment must be taken into account if a true valuation of the position is to be made.

3. Unemployment Problems.

14. The problem of employment in the West Indies is considered, as one of the major issues affecting policy, in Part III of this Report. Here it will suffice to say that unemployment is a question of increasing importance and that, aggravated as it is by the economic factors which we discuss elsewhere, its extent and effects are already very formidable in most of the West Indian Colonies. Such are its proportions that demonstrations and processions of unemployed are the causes of growing concern to the Colonial Governments; this was particularly noticeable in Jamaica where, during our stay in the Colony, large numbers of the unemployed marched to the headquarters of the Public Works Department on several occasions and even to one of the prisons in the hope that the Superintendent would be able to provide them with work. It is understood that, since we left Jamaica, powers have been conferred on the Governor to prohibit public meetings and demonstrations. Whatever may be the wisdom of this step it certainly does not dispose of the cause of the demonstrations, which arise from the inability of many labourers to secure work. Some of the Colonial Governments had embarked upon various schemes for the relief of unemployment. These usually took the form of road making, bridge building or the reclamation and settlement of land, but all had the character of hastily devised expedients and nothing in the way of a long-range policy to deal with the problem of unemployment emerged during our investigations.

15. The plight of the unemployed, aggravated as it is by the seasonal character of employment, is serious to the point of desperation. There is no unemployment insurance in the West Indies and public assistance in the form of poor law relief is usually confined to the old and infirm. If an applicant is able-bodied and so does not fulfil the latter condition, there is normally no means of assisting him from public funds, no matter how desperate his position may be. The meagre character of the relief which is granted may be judged from the fact that in several of the Colonies the average payment is only 1s. 6d. per week. The belief that land is always available on which

poorer people outside the larger towns can eke out a living is often illusory. Large numbers of labourers have a piece of land on which they can grow food crops. On the other hand, there are many cases in which no food plots are obtainable or in which the land available is so rocky or hilly as to make cultivation almost impossible. With charitable organisations completely unable to do more than touch the fringe of the problem, the lot of the unemployed with no means of income to sustain life can well be imagined. When rates of earnings are inadequate, employment is seasonal and generally scarce, and public assistance is thus limited, there can be little wonder that the standard of life of many of the working people throughout the West Indies is deplorably low.

16. We have considered the possibility of recommending that a system of unemployment insurance should be established in these Colonies similar to that in force in this country. The difficulties are formidable, but we feel that the Governments of the larger Colonies should examine carefully the possibility of establishing some arrangement for unemployment insurance in the case of those undertakings which are organised on a system of regular employment and with exemptions for those industries where, owing to the intermittent character of employment, a scheme based on that obtaining in Great Britain would be impracticable.

4. Regulation of Wages and Conditions.

17. One outstanding phenomenon in the history of the West Indies during the last few years is the occurrence of public disorders of such magnitude as to have led in all except three cases to the appointment of a Commission to investigate the causes and character of the outbreak. A list of these disturbances in order of date is given below:—

May-July 1934	Disturbances on sugar estates in Trinidad.
January 1935	Disturbances in St. Kitts.
May, 1935	Strike of wharf labour at Falmouth, Jamaica, followed by disturbances.
September–October, 1935	Disturbances at various estates in British Guiana.
October, 1935	Rioting in Kingstown and Camden Park, St. Vincent.
June, 1937	General disturbances in Trinidad.
July, 1937	Disturbances in Barbados.
May, 1938	Disturbances on the Frome Estate, Jamaica.
May-June, 1938	General disturbances in Jamaica.
February, 1939	Disturbances at Leonora Plantation and neighbouring areas in British Guiana.

18. Those disturbances can only be regarded as a symptom of which the principal causes are low earnings and irregular employment. The situation was accurately described by the Secretary of State for the Colonies, Mr. Malcolm MacDonald, when on the 14th June, 1938, he said: "These feelings of unrest are a protest against the economic distress of the Colonies themselves, a protest against some of the consequences of that economic distress: uncertainty of employment, low rates of wages, bad housing conditions in many cases, and so on." The growing concern expressed in Parliament and in the country generally at the troubles in the West Indies which were ultimately responsible for our appointment has focused attention on the need for orderly arrangement in industry to regulate the relations of employers and workpeople and to promote a better standard of living.

19. Practically all the witnesses who came before us readily agreed that collective bargaining is both necessary and desirable and nowhere did we encounter opposition to the principle that relations in industry should be governed by agreements between the employers and trade unions similar to the representative organisations which are found in this country. It appears to be recognised on every side that under present conditions the interests of the workers have been virtually unprotected. On the other hand, employers in the West Indies have long been associated for purposes of trade and in some cases—for example among the sugar manufacturers—their organisation has attained a high state of efficiency. As far as can be ascertained no *formal* arrangements exist among planters and sugar manufacturers generally for the fixing of rates of wages by agreement between them. Admittedly there is *informal* consultation on that subject, and that this achieves the same purpose is shown by the similarity of the rates paid by neighbouring planters.

20. It is a fair generalisation to say that while agricultural employers are comparatively well organised, the workers are either completely unorganised or at best are only partly organised. In this position collective bargaining in the British sense has been virtually an impossibility, and wage rates have followed standards laid down by the employers alone.

5. Trade Unions.

21. The need for trade unions is generally admitted in the West Indies, and during recent years there has been a move to establish them. Considerable numbers of emigrant West Indians have returned to these Colonies from North and South America and from Cuba, partly in consequence of economic depression in those areas. Many of these emigrants have brought with them some knowledge of the working of trade unionism in

other countries; that knowledge has spread and the attempts which have been made to form trade unions in the West Indies are therefore not surprising.

22. Successive Secretaries of State for the Colonies have spoken publicly of the need for the encouragement of trade unions in the Colonial Empire, and from time to time over the last decade they have made representations to Colonial Governments in the West Indies drawing their attention to the desirability of facilitating the development of trade unions. Despite this, and the repeated statements of the present Secretary of State that Your Majesty's Government would welcome the establishment of trade unions, we were unable to discover that any real effort had been made until quite recent times to assist their formation and development.

23. One explanation of this may be that the influence of powerful vested interests has stood in the way; whatever may have been the cause, the fact is that even to-day the obstacles to the successful working of trade unions have not been removed by legislation in most of the West Indian Colonies.

24. The inherent right of free men to refuse wages and conditions of employment which they deem to be inadequate has long been recognised. Whether the refusal is an individual one or concerted does not disturb the principle; for generations the right to strike has been possessed by trade unionists in democratic countries and has been admitted by their governments. Any restriction of this liberty of action fetters the workman in his dealings with the employer and is tantamount to industrial servitude. Little purpose can, however, be served be conceding this right to strike and at the same time removing all possibility of its effective use by making a union liable for loss or damage caused to employers as the consequence of a strike. That position is fully accepted in Great Britain, where it is now axiomatic that the operation of trade unionism would be impossible were it not for the protection which the unions are given by law against actions for damages. Nevertheless, that right, so fully safeguarded in English law, is rendered completely nugatory in several of the West Indies. Up to the time of our appointment trade unions were protected against actions for damages consequent upon strikes in British Guiana alone of the West Indian Colonies. In Jamaica this protection was expressly omitted at the instance of the Government of the Colony from the Trade Union Law of 1919.

25. A second fundamental right is that of peaceful picketing, by which is meant the right peacefully to persuade workers to take part in a strike. In Jamaica alone of these Colonies

peaceful picketing is legally permissible. A Law enacted in December, 1938, included provisions which protected trade unions against actions for damages and legalised peaceful picketing.

26. It is not surprising that, when confronted by such legal obstacles, the formation of trade unions in the West Indies has been slow. There are, however, signs that the legislative difficulties which we have mentioned are now appreciated and will be removed. We welcome the attempts which are being made in some of these Colonies to rectify an unsatisfactory position; the legislatures of most of the larger territories have already considered the course of action which they should take, but we would urge the need for the adoption of uniform principles which should follow, in the main, the lines of the Jamaica Trade Union Law of 1938. Among other things that Law, which we regard as generally satisfactory, provided—in addition to the protection of the funds of trade unions against actions for tort and the legalisation of peaceful picketing—for the compulsory registration of trade unions and the auditing of their funds; we believe that all of these conditions are essential to the proper development of trade unionism in the West Indies.

27. We desire, however, to make one observation on the auditing of the funds of trade unions. In Trinidad we were told in evidence that an audit of six months' accounts, undertaken by professional accountants, had entailed the payment of a fee of £40 by the trade union concerned. While not questioning the professional justification for this fee, we think it unreasonable that a small and struggling union should thus be legally saddled with what to them was an extremely heavy charge. We feel that the audit of the accounts of trade unions might quite properly be undertaken by Colonial Governments. It should be recognised that the audit of such simple accounts is not a highly intricate task necessitating the services of a skilled accountant. Even in this country the accounts of many large registered trade unions are audited by lay members and in the present stage of development of trade unions in the West Indies, the audit could reasonably be undertaken by officers of the Labour Department free of charge to the union.

28. We have said that we regard the principles of the Jamaica Trade Union Law of 1938 as generally satisfactory and we have advocated the adoption of those principles in the other West Indian Colonies. The exercise of peaceful picketing is complicated, however, in some of the Colonies by the difficulty which we explain below. Many of the workers employed in the sugar industry live on estates far removed from the public highways and inaccessible to members of the public, and most

sugar factories are also situated on estates. Any picket who attempted to gain access to the workers, either at their place of employment or at their homes, would render himself liable to an action for trespass. In the past admission has been denied in some Colonies. As will be realised, to confer the right peacefully to picket the workers, and at the same time to withhold from the pickets all means of approach to many of those workers, is misleading and unsatisfactory. We consider it proper, therefore, that pickets in reasonable numbers should be given access to the workers both at the gates of the factory and at their homes, whether these be situated on private or public property.

29. Even if the legal obstacles to the formation and development of trade unions and the exercise of their normal functions were removed, there would still be other difficulties to consider, not the least of which is the attitude of many employers towards trade unions. In evidence every body of employers proclaimed a readiness to welcome responsible trade unions. In practice, however, considerable difficulty attended the recognition of trade unions, both in private and public employment. Naturally employers are reluctant to recognise organisations other than *bona fide* unions led by responsible men and the absence of responsible leadership was the ground of complaint by several employers. We do not take the view that there was no justification for these complaints, but we cannot avoid the conclusion that more ready recognition of the trade unions would help to evolve the type of responsible leadership which is undoubtedly desirable. It is not to be expected that experienced leaders can be evolved overnight, among either the employers or the workers. Admittedly educational and other disabilities due to the lack of training and experience place the workers under a handicap in this respect, but the generous tribute paid, during our proceedings in Trinidad, to the value of the work done by officials of trade unions in that island encourages us to believe that responsibility will come with growth and experience.

30. On this point, Major Orde Browne, in his recent report (Cmd. 6070), records his view that " a marked change for the better has appeared in the industrial relations in the Colony during the last eighteen months. In 1937 feeling ran very high, culminating in riots attended by a deplorable loss of life in June. The progress made since then reflects credit on all concerned; all considerable employers are in favour of responsible trade unions and collective bargaining; similarly the leaders of the workpeople have mostly proved themselves capable and responsible." The only official in the West Indies possessing extensive and first-hand knowledge of the handling of labour problems in the United Kingdom spoke in terms of high praise

about the quality and capacity of the officers of trade unions with whom he had worked in the Colony where he is serving. With proper encouragement by Governments and employers we hope that trade unionism in the West Indies will develop into a responsible institution beneficial to the workers and the community alike. Official witnesses everywhere attested to the readiness of their governments to recognise trade unions, but little or nothing appears to have been done in most Colonies to give practical effect to the policy which Secretaries of State for the Colonies have laid down time and time again.

31. We feel that it is our duty equally to impress upon trade unionists the need for them to make every effort to develop their activities in a way which will enable their organisations to play a constructive part in the life of the community.

32. We encountered suspicion among trade unions that there was an underlying hostility not so much from those in higher governmental posts as from others occupying administrative posts in Government Departments. There is a real need for Colonial Governments to set an example not only in the encouragement of trade unionism outside the Civil Service, but within it also. The formation of Whitley Councils, properly organised by Departments on the model of the constitution of the National Council for the Civil Service in the United Kingdom, would do much to regularise and harmonise relationships between Governments and their employees. No opposition to this principle was expressed to us anywhere, but we had no evidence that any active steps had been taken by West Indian Governments to encourage the formation of trade unions either inside or outside the Civil Service. A pronouncement by the various Governments that this was an aim of their policy might well be decisive. Moreover, Governments could give material assistance by allowing public offices or other premises owned by them to be used, whenever possible, for the holding of meetings of trade unions. In other cases they could use their influence to obtain preferential terms for unions wishing to hire premises for their meetings. Yet another way in which they could help is by the grant of scholarships to young workers who had the experience and capacity to fit them to study in this country both industrial legislation and the practical working of trade unions.

33. The prospects of establishing trade unionism vary considerably from Colony to Colony and, as might be expected, it is in the larger Colonies (Jamaica, Trinidad and British Guiana) that they appear most hopeful. But it is true of all the West Indian Colonies that, with the best will in the world, several years must elapse before the organisation of trade unions can be developed to the point at which they will play a decisive part in the regulation of wages and conditions of

employment. In present circumstances and for some time to come, therefore, the need must be recognised for Governments to assist by every means in the proper regulation of labour relations. For that reason the establishment of Labour Departments in the different Colonies is a matter of great and immediate importance.

6. Labour Departments.

34. For some years the policy of Your Majesty's Government has been to encourage the appointment of Labour Officers by the Governments of all except the smallest Colonies. In our view this policy should now be carried one stage further in the West Indies by the establishment of Labour Departments in each of the principal Colonies in that group. Each Department should be in the charge of a Labour Commissioner assisted by such Labour Officers and subordinate staff as may be found necessary. In Trinidad and British Guiana, where large numbers of the workers are East Indians, one member of the Labour Department should specialise in questions affecting their welfare and conditions of employment. He should, of course, be thoroughly familiar with the languages commonly used by East Indians and he should, if possible, have other departmental functions in addition to this advisory work.

35. We also support the proposal of Major Orde Browne that there should be attached to each Labour Department an advisory Labour Board or Committee composed of representatives of employers and workers with an impartial chairman. This body should have power to co-opt additional members, as the occasion arose, in order that it may represent all the best available authority on each aspect of labour problems. These Boards or Committees would have no executive powers; those would remain with the officers of the Labour Department working in direct responsibility to the Government of the Colony.

36. The duties of the Labour Department* should include all questions relating to the regulation of wages, conciliation, arbitration, the establishment and working of wages boards and trade boards, the inspection of wage lists, the obtaining and collation of such data as statistics of unemployment, hours and wages and cost-of-living, the inspection of conditions of work in factories, workshops and agriculture, and measures for the protection and safety of the workers. The functions of Registrar of Trade Unions should be undertaken by a member of the Department and, as we have already suggested, the responsibility for the auditing of their balance sheets.

---

* Here, and subsequently in this Chapter, the term "Labour Department" should be taken to include the Labour Officer in those Colonies or islands where no such Department is established.

37. One of the most important of these duties is the work of conciliation and the adjustment of disputes between employers and workpeople. In discharging this task Labour Departments in the West Indies should follow closely the lines on which similar work is carried out in this country. Those Departments should also prepare, in consultation with the advisory Board or Committee, panels of names from which arbitrators and assessors could be drawn whenever recourse to arbitration is requested by both parties to an industrial dispute.

38. In the summary of the duties of Labour Departments we mentioned measures for the protection and safety of the workers. These, in so far as they call for new or improved legislation, are discussed in the following section of this Chapter. Here we shall only give examples of the measures which Departments can, and should, take in the protection of the interests of the workers. They should be given compulsory powers of inspection and access to all books and wage lists kept by employers. They should undertake prosecutions in cases where employers have infringed the provisions of legislation providing for the payment of minimum wages or where officers of the Department are satisfied that wages are being withheld from workpeople, whether employed under a collective or individual contract of service. It should be part of their duty to advise workpeople about their legal rights, and to make public information on that subject whenever, as may occur from time to time, it appears that sections of the workers are unaware of their rights. Officers of the Department should also be available to address gatherings of workers on such matters either through trade unions or direct. Finally, where workers are employed under written contracts of service, the Department should endeavour to incorporate uniform principles into those contracts and to secure legislative enforcement where that is desirable.

39. We have also considered the question of the working relations between the local Labour Departments and the Labour Adviser, who will be a member of the central organisation of which the creation is recommended in Chapter XXI of this report. Those Departments will be responsible to their Governments alone, but they should maintain close touch with the Adviser and so assist him in the considerable tasks of forming a general picture of labour conditions in the West Indies and of securing a greater degree of uniformity in both labour legislation and the handling of the labour problems of the different Colonies. To this end the Adviser should be furnished with copies of all principal and subsidiary legislation bearing on labour questions at the earliest possible date after that legislation becomes available for distribution. The Adviser and his staff, with the assistance of the statistical officer on the central

organisation, will be responsible for the final collation of labour statistics for the whole of the West Indies. It will be the duty of the local Labour Departments to collate partially all statistical information which they are able to obtain in the territories where they are serving, and to forward copies of those statistics to the Adviser.

40. From this description of the duties of Labour Officers it follows that their calibre should be high and that they should be men of character, experience, capacity and integrity. Their duties would be of such a nature that they should be protected against undue pressure from any quarter. Wide experience is clearly essential and the difficulty of obtaining from within the West Indies men who satisfy this qualification is self-evident. For this reason it would probably be necessary in present circumstances that the Labour Commissioners, who will undertake the charge of new Departments in the larger Colonies, should be recruited from the United Kingdom. It is to be hoped, however, that in the future it may be possible to find from the Colonial Service officers competent to carry on this work. With the exception of the Labour Commissioners the staff required could be recruited locally.

41. We understand that considerable difficulty has been experienced in filling satisfactorily the few senior Labour appointments which have already been created in the West Indies. This appears to be due in part to the fact that the salaries offered have not been sufficiently attractive and in part to the absence of prospects of advancement similar to those available in the services from which staff for these appointments would normally be recruited. To the right type of man this latter consideration might be partially counter-balanced by the opportunities for creative work which await him in the West Indies, but we are satisfied that unless the salaries offered are comparable with those paid to men in responsible posts in this country, it will continue to be difficult to secure candidates with the qualities which, to us, seem so much to be desired. We do not consider that the search for Labour Commissioners and others who may be appointed from the United Kingdom need be confined to members of Your Majesty's Services. Within the ranks of the trade unions and organisations of employers and from those engaged in industry and commerce generally, it should be possible to find men with the necessary qualifications. The success which has already attended the efforts of the Industrial Adviser in Trinidad is an outstanding indication of what can be achieved by an experienced officer.

42. We were impressed by the capacity of some of the native-born West Indians who are now serving as Labour Officers in the Windward Islands. We would also commend the work of

the Department of Labour and Local Government in British Guiana whose chief has exhibited considerable resource and courage in the face of great difficulties. It is essential, however, that the training of such men should be undertaken in this country through the Ministry of Labour, the Home Office and the Ministry of Health, working in conjunction for this purpose, and that facilities for this training should be afforded by these Departments. In course of time this training in the United Kingdom could be supplemented by a period spent in one or other of the Labour Departments which by then should be well established in the larger West Indian Colonies.

43. In Chapter XXII of this Report we recommend that Heads of technical Departments should be relieved of what is, to many of them, the distasteful task of membership of the Legislative Council. We regard it as essential that the Labour Commissioner or Labour Officer should not be nominated as a member of such bodies, nor even required to attend their meetings. We consider that the amount of time occupied by the former duty and the atmosphere of dispute in which they might become involved through attendance at meetings would both be likely to impair seriously the effectiveness of their work.

44. While both Labour Commissioners and Labour Officers should spend the maximum amount of their working time on duties outside their offices, a considerable amount of administrative work will be inevitable for them. They should therefore be provided with better office accommodation and more adequate clerical staff than had been made available, when we were in the West Indies, to most of the Labour Officers then serving. The poor quality of the arrangements so far made in this respect may have been due to a feeling that the needs of a newly created branch of Government were the least urgent, but we consider it necessary to state clearly that the work of Labour Departments is certain to be severely handicapped unless proper and adequate facilities are forthcoming.

45. The organisation which we have recommended would, in our view, be incomplete unless a Labour Department is established within the Colonial Office itself, and in this connection we desire to emphasise the need for early action. It will not be sufficient merely to require officers to devote the major part of their time to the labour problems of the Colonial Empire. Very much more than this is necessary if the Department is to keep under constant review the major developments in connection with labour and is to act with expedition, instead of with the protracted delays which in the past have characterised the conduct of matters relating to labour questions. The Department would have to be adequately staffed and contain at least one officer seconded from the Ministry of Labour, the Ministry of Health and the Home Office, in order that Colonial developments

and labour affairs can be kept in close touch with current practice in the United Kingdom. It would be the function of this Department continually to stimulate Colonial Governments to progressive policies and to keep constant contact with Labour Departments overseas. It is recognised that the duties of the new organisation which we propose would cover a wider field than the West Indies alone, but that fact, to our minds, strengthens the case for its creation. The considerable diversities in native conditions throughout the Colonial Empire with its 60 million inhabitants are surely sufficient to warrant specialised treatment through an efficient Labour Department within the Colonial Office.

46. We consider it essential that there should be attached to this Department an Advisory Committee composed of persons with expert knowledge of labour and Colonial questions and matters directly related thereto. The members of this Committee would be appointed by the Secretary of State for the Colonies in consultation with other Ministers of the Crown whose Departments would be interested, with the Trade Union Congress, and with the West India Committee and other similar organisations representative of industrial, commercial and native interests in the Colonies. The Advisory Committee would no doubt appoint sub-committees, one of which would be mainly concerned with labour problems arising in the West Indies. The duties of the new Labour Department of the Colonial Office should include the submission of regular reports on labour developments in the appropriate area to each sub-committee which, in turn, would submit observations and recommendations thereon to the Advisory Committee. An appendix giving an account of the work of the Advisory Committee might, with advantage, be added to the Report on the Administration of the Colonial Empire which the Secretary of State for the Colonies now presents each year to Parliament in connection with the Estimates for the Colonial and Middle Eastern Services.

7. Industrial and Protective Legislation.

47. Generally speaking, industry is in its infancy in the West Indies, although sugar factories have been in operation for some generations. This may explain partially the almost complete absence of legislation to provide for the protection of the worker, whether he is engaged in a factory, in a workshop, or on such services as transport. Only in Trinidad, where the duties devolve on the Inspector of Mines, are arrangements made for anything in the nature of regular inspection of factories. There was no compulsory or systematic reporting of accidents in any of the Colonies which we visited, and often machinery

was completely unguarded; in the majority of cases the employers are not under any obligation to fence and guard plant, although that is a normal provision in industry in this country.

48. In this connection it may be pertinent to observe that it is the usual practice of makers of machinery in the United Kingdom to fix on it, or provide with it, adequate protection in accordance with specifications laid down by the Home Office. It should be easy to establish, through the proposed new Labour Department of the Colonial Office, a liaison between the Home Office and Labour Departments of Colonial Governments by means of which the latter could be kept in touch with current home practice and requirements. It should be realised that even the most modern machinery obtained by West Indian firms from other countries would not necessarily conform to standards and specifications prescribed by the Home Office. It would be desirable, therefore, that after the home practice in this matter has been adopted in any Colony, local firms in the West Indies, when ordering machinery—particularly if it is to be obtained from other countries—should take steps to ensure that it is fitted with the necessary guards and other devices to bring it up to these standards.

49. The importance of adequate inspection of factories need not be stressed when it is remembered that West Indians are by habit and tradition more accustomed to outdoor life. In consequence the health, protection and welfare of those who are now working in factories call for the exercise of an even greater care on the part of employers and the authorities than would be sufficient and reasonable for people among whom industrial occupation had been the rule for generations.

50. It is important to distinguish between legislation on paper and legislation in practice in the West Indies. Time and time again we found that laws passed by the Legislative Council had never been put into active operation. No doubt this failure was due in part to administrative difficulties, themselves caused by inadequate staffing, and the prospects of improvement in this respect should be greatly assisted by the establishment of the Labour Departments which we have recommended. None the less, the presence on the Statute Book of legislation not applied in practice is apt to be misleading to public opinion, particularly that in the United Kingdom, and to savour of " window dressing ". We also felt that it was unsatisfactory, where the need for legislation was long overdue, to be assured so often that " the matter was under consideration "; from its constant repetition, that phrase began to bear the appearance of a stock expression.

51. Factory legislation should be closely co-ordinated with laws and regulations relating to public health, and we consider that it is essential that the enforcement of both, in so far as each affects the worker in industry and agriculture, should be under the control of a single authority. This authority should, as we have said, be the Labour Department in each territory, but we suggest that, in order to secure effective supervision of all conditions of employment which may be detrimental to the health of the workers, a medical inspector should be seconded to the Labour Department in each of the larger territories. Elsewhere special staff may not be needed, but the closest co-operation should be maintained between the medical and social welfare authorities and the Labour Department.

52. We come next to the question of the regulation of wages, hours and other conditions of labour. In several of the West Indian Colonies minimum wage legislation has been enacted during recent years, but we consider that the basic rate thus laid down has usually been too low to be of any real value. Generally speaking, the device of a legal minimum wage fixed by Ordinance is too inflexible and we prefer the system under which questions relating to rates of wages and hours of employment are considered by Boards composed of representatives of employers and workers and members of the general public who are appointed by the Government. Experience in this country of both Agricultural and Trade Boards has shown that they provide a most satisfactory means of fixing and imposing a legal minimum for wages and a standard for hours of employment. We are not in favour of the creation of a large number of separate Wages Boards in any West Indian Colony. For each of the smaller territories a single Board might well suffice. In each of the larger territories—British Guiana, Jamaica and Trinidad—we suggest that Boards should be established for suitable groups of industries.

53. In Chapter XV of this report we make recommendations designed to assist the West Indian sugar industry. We consider that the participation of any Colony in the arrangements there suggested should be made conditional on the enactment by its Government of satisfactory legislation providing for the establishment of Wages Boards and that no payment of a share in the benefits secured by those arrangements should be made to estates or individual owners which are not carrying out fully the decisions of Wages Boards.

54. We have already intimated that Governments could do much to encourage the development of trade unionism in these Colonies if they would set an example by forming Whitley Councils for the Civil Service. We recommend that they should

take that step, and that the principle should extend to subordinate staff, such as that of the Medical Departments. We suggest also that a Whitley Council should be established in each territory for the teachers, though in many cases its composition on the employers' side would be a matter for arrangement between the Government and any denominations which would have a claim to be represented through their connection with the administration of schools.

55. Any differences arising in industries not covered by Wages Boards should be handled by members of the staff of the Labour Department acting as conciliation officers or by the arbitration panels, of which we have already suggested the formation. Where, however, the differences are such, either in magnitude or in character, as to make it essential that the tribunal should not be composed entirely of local persons, we consider that an Industrial Court should be established in accordance with the recommendation made in paragraph 298 of the Report (Cmd. 5461) of the Commission which inquired in 1937 into the disturbances in Trinidad. In our opinion, however, the scope of the Court should be extended to cover the whole of the West Indian Colonies and its President should be nominated by the Labour Adviser in the central organisation to which we have already referred. He should be responsible also for maintaining a panel of persons, drawn from both employers and workers, who are capable of acting as assessors in disputes outside their own Colony and are willing to undertake that duty.

56. The status of women in the West Indies, as illustrated by the conditions under which they are employed in shops, as domestic servants and on manual work, is examined under Social Welfare in the following Chapter of this report, where examples are given of the wages which they sometimes earn, and the hours for which many of them have to work. Recommendations already made in this Chapter should go far to remedy the present poor conditions of many women workers. They would benefit from the inspection of the factories and shops in which they are employed, from the establishment of Wages Boards, in cases to which that machinery would be appropriate, and in others from the work of conciliation officers. There are in addition certain special measures which might reasonably be taken in the interests of women workers. The hardship which may be caused when women are unable to draw any wages for the proportion of task work which they have completed at the end of the week, should be examined by the Labour Officers and, if possible, some remedy should be devised. If it is anywhere the case that, as we were told, domestic servants can be discharged without wages in lieu of notice, payment should be made compulsory, subject to the

exceptions allowed in this country. If at any time Labour Departments undertake the duty of supplying workpeople to fill vacancies notified to them by employers, they should refuse to send domestic servants to houses when they have reason to believe that conditions of employment are bad.

57. Evidence which we heard in the West Indies leaves us in no doubt that children under the legal age of employment are in fact employed from time to time in both agriculture and industry. We strongly deprecate this practice, and recommend that everywhere the employment of children under the age of 14 years should be prohibited and that stringent penalties should be inflicted for infringement of this prohibition, the sole exception to which should be employment on work, or in an undertaking, shared only by members of the same family. That is, in effect, a provision of one of the Washington Conventions of 1919 which, however, applied only to industrial employment. As regards the employment of women and children generally, we consider that the provisions of the various international conventions on that subject should be taken as the minimum standard for the West Indies.

58. Another form of protective legislation is that regulating the hours of shop assistants. At present the hours during which shops may be open are fixed by law in many of the West Indian Colonies, but no limit is set to the hours of work of the assistants, whether male or female. Complaints were made to us that assistants were often kept at work long after the shops had closed. In our view this is most undesirable, and we consider that the weakness of the existing legislation ought to be remedied by providing in it a maximum weekly period for the employment of shop assistants; that period should bear a direct relation to the hours during which shops may be open. In Colonies where no restriction is at present placed on shop hours, legislation should nevertheless be enacted to fix a limit to the working week of assistants; powers should also be taken, wherever they do not now exist, to inspect the conditions under which shop assistants work.

59. Although legislation providing for workmen's compensation has been in force for several years in a number of the West Indian Colonies, its effect in practice is still limited. Large numbers of workers are excluded from its operation and an unusually long term is prescribed as the period during which an accident must deprive a worker of employment before he is eligible for compensation. In almost all of the West Indian Colonies the following persons, amongst others, are not covered by this legislation—persons employed in agriculture (unless employed in connection with machinery), domestic servants, clerical workers, shop assistants and drivers of motor vehicles.

The effect of these exclusions in Colonies which are predominantly agricultural, and where many thousands are engaged in domestic service, may easily be imagined, and it was not surprising to find that, in some of the territories, approximately four-fifths of the total working population was ineligible for compensation. Considerable exclusions have been maintained even in recent legislation such as that passed in Jamaica at the end of 1937. We see no valid reason why the laws in this subject should not be made of general application; in particular we regard the inclusion of agriculture within the scope of this legislation, with proper facilities for insurance, as a primary and necessary reform. With rare exceptions, witnesses who appeared before us in a representative capacity on behalf of bodies of employers were not opposed to this extension of the law. At the same time we recognise that certain exclusions may be necessitated by difficulties of administration, particularly in relation to small producers and peasants. We recommend, therefore, that persons who, on an average taken over the whole year, employ five people or less, should not be brought at this stage within the compass of legislation providing for the payment of workmen's compensation. We are also of the opinion that the period for which incapacity must last before compensation becomes payable should be reduced to three days. That recommendation was made at the end of 1937 by the Commission which inquired into the Trinidad disturbances, but it has not yet been implemented in any of the West Indian Colonies, although the Governments of all have, we understand, been invited by the Secretary of State for the Colonies to give the matter their favourable consideration.

60. We are impressed by the need for a simple system of recovery of compensation under which litigation would be reduced to a minimum in the West Indies. Insurance should be compulsory and it is necessary to provide for the case of those employers in several of the Colonies who may find it difficult to cover these liabilities through Insurance Companies. We are of opinion that these three requirements would be satisfied by a State scheme based upon the principles of the one which has operated in the Province of Ontario since 1915 and became a model for systems in other Canadian Provinces. That scheme is compulsory and covers manual and non-manual workers in public and private undertakings and in a wide range of industries, including mining, lumbering, manufacture and construction, and both rail and water transport. Exclusive administrative authority is vested in a "Workmen's Compensation Board", which consists of three members appointed by the Lieutenant-Governor in Council. This Board determines the industrial and occupational classification of employers for the purposes of their contributions and determines all claims. The

costs of workmen's compensation are a charge on employers covered by the scheme, but the Provincial Government contributes towards the costs of administration. Where the arrangement made is one of collective liability, the contributions of all employers are paid into an Accident Fund, the rates being assessed for the several industries according to the risk of accident in each. Employers are required to furnish returns which are needed in connection with the fixing of the amounts of their contributions. Undertakings which enter the scheme on a basis of individual liability have to contribute towards expenses of administration and may also be required to insure their liability, or to deposit adequate security with the Board.

61. The benefits which are provided under this scheme include (a) medical and surgical treatment, (b) cash allowances during temporary incapacity, (c) occupational rehabilitation facilities, (d) pensions for permanent total disablement, (e) pensions or lump sum payments to dependent survivors in cases of fatal accident or disease, and (f) funeral benefits.

62. Two passages of comment on this scheme may be quoted as showing the view of it which is taken by persons who have been concerned with its working. In 1927 a special committee of the Trades and Labour Congress of Canada wrote as follows in its report: —

> "The system proved of inestimable benefit to the 450,000 workers coming under it. . . . Few employers or workers would desire to return to the old system. Procedure is simple, litigation and expense is eliminated, wide protection for workmen and their dependents, and payment of benefit, are secured."

In 1934 the Secretary of an association of employers in Canada wrote as follows: —

> "The present law and methods of administration have great advantages over other systems. Adjudication is placed in the hands of a Board instead of the Courts, and the simple and speedy method of handling cases has eliminated enormous expense and delay. . . . The present system gives absolute security of payment, whereas recovery from individual employers was previously often impossible."

63. We recommend that the West Indian Governments should be invited to consider carefully the possibility of the adoption of a scheme based on the one which we have described. If this suggesion is favourably received, a choice must be made between one central scheme for the whole group and separate arrangements for each of the larger Colonies and, probably, for groups of the smaller islands. In the former case control of the Accident Fund might be entrusted to the Labour Adviser on the central organisation. Whichever choice is made, the local Labour Officer in each territory could act as an agent of the Compensation Board in dealing with claims.

64. While, as we have said, we desire litigation, and with it, expense, to be eliminated from the administration of workmen's compensation, we recognise that it may be desirable in any scheme adopted for the West Indies to give workmen, many of whom are illiterate, the right to be accompanied before the Compensation Board, or its officers, by an adviser who need not, however, be a member of the legal profession.

65. Another valuable feature of the present system in the Province of Ontario is its preventive work Great good would result in the West Indies from suitable propaganda to educate the workers in habits whereby accidents might be reduced to a minimum, and the Governments of those Colonies might, with advantage, study the methods which have been adopted for this purpose in Ontario.

8. Local Welfare Levies.

66. During the hearing of evidence in the West Indies we asked the representatives of all associations of sugar manufacturers who appeared before us whether they agreed that, in the event of increased assistance being granted to the sugar industry, a portion of the proceeds should be earmarked for the welfare of the employees. It was explained to these witnesses that in Great Britain a levy is imposed on every ton of coal raised at the pithead and that the proceeds of this levy (which is now at the rate of $\frac{1}{2}$d. per ton and yielded last year the sum of £819,458) are devoted exclusively to the welfare of the mining community. In every case the witnesses accepted the principle of such a levy but no attempt was made to lay down the precise manner in which it should be applied.

67. In our opinion the best method of giving effect to the principle that workers shall share in any additional benefits to be granted to the sugar industry will be to impose a levy on the output of sugar from all factories in the West Indies. If that method is adopted a rate of levy must be fixed which would be reasonable, having regard to the receipts of the producer from the sale of sugar. During the time of our visit to the West Indies the price obtained by colonial producers for their sugar was about £11 5s. 0d. per ton c.i.f. London. This figure has since increased slightly and a further upward trend of prices might be expected to follow from the adoption of the recommendations made in Chapter XV of this report. After careful consideration we suggest that a levy at the rate of 2s. a ton would be reasonable. On the basis of the estimates of production for 1938-9 which were given in Chapter II of this report a levy at that rate would yield about £62,000. The benefits to be provided from any funds thus financed would have to be confined in the main to employees in the sugar industry and their relatives, in the same way as the benefits of the Miners' Welfare Fund are confined in Great Britain to the mining community. The amounts available would be too small to permit

of general disbursement. Moreover, the British taxpayer, who gives direct assistance on a generous scale to the West Indian sugar industry, can reasonably expect that part of the profit resulting from that assistance shall be expended in securing a better standard of life for the workers engaged in the sugar industry of those Colonies. That aim is most certain to be secured through the imposition of a levy on the basis which we have suggested.

68. Following the principles adopted in the case of the Miners' Welfare Fund the control of money raised by this means should be vested in each Colony in a Central Committee working under the Labour Department or, where no such Department exists, under the Colonial Secretary or Administrator. The Central Committee should, where necessary, establish District Committees which would be empowered to submit schemes involving expenditure from these local funds. All these Committees should be composed of representatives of employers and workpeople nominated by organisations of employers and trade unions respectively. Where there are no trade unions in existence, or they are insufficiently representative, the responsibility for nominating suitable persons to represent the workers on Committees should fall on the Government. They should also nominate to every Committee suitable representatives of the general community. If, at a later date, the principle of a levy on output to provide for the social needs of workers in a particular industry should be extended to other forms of industry in the West Indies, one Central Committee, suitably subdivided, could be established in each Colony.

69. As examples of the purposes upon which these funds could properly be expended we may mention the provision of buildings for purposes of recreation, and of playing fields and sports grounds; in the educational field payment might be made for classes and lectures and funds used to establish scholarships, including industrial scholarships the holders of which could be trained in this country in the principles of industrial legislation, collective bargaining, etc.; finally, money from these funds might properly be expended on meeting such social needs as the provision of village institutes and community centres. In no case should the cost of housing workers be defrayed as part of the scheme since that would be too heavy a burden and would involve the undertaking of responsibility which should properly be borne by employers or Governments.

70. We regard it as most desirable that a scheme based on the principles which we have outlined above should be established by the Government of each sugar-producing Colony or island, in consultation and co-operation with the sugar producers, and we recommend that each of those Governments should be invited to take early steps to that end.

CHAPTER XI.

OTHER SOCIAL NEEDS AND SERVICES.

1. Social Welfare.

1. In the preceding chapters in this part of the Report we have considered social conditions in the West Indies from four points of view, each of which is directly connected with a branch of public administration. There remain to be examined a number of needs and services all of which, taken together, can be described as " social welfare work ".

2. In Chapter III of this Report we have described the social structure of the West Indies in general terms but, before we discuss how far and in what way the work of social welfare can best proceed in those Colonies, it will be convenient to examine here social conditions from the standpoint of the ordinary West Indian man and woman.

(a) SOCIAL CONDITIONS.

3. Little can be said for the social conditions which exist in the West Indies to-day. The child, so often reared in an ill-built and overcrowded home, passes from it to what is, all too frequently, an overcrowded school. If he has been fortunate enough to continue his education until school-leaving age, which is usually 14 in the towns and 12 in the rural districts, he enters a world where unemployment and under-employment are regarded as the common lot. Should he find work as a manual labourer, his wages often provide only for bare maintenance and are far from sufficient to enable him to attain the standard of living which is set before him by new contacts with the outside world. If he is fitted by education and intelligence for clerical posts, competition for which is intense, he will have the prospect, at best, of a salary on which, even in Government employment, he will find it a serious struggle to keep up the social position and appearances which he and his friends expect. He will have leisure hours but few facilities for recreation with which to fill them.

4. The position of women is more unfortunate. We deal later with the status and conditions of female employment. At this point we are concerned only to give a picture of the daily life of the woman in the home. Generally she has a large family and, whenever employment is available, must work to support them or to eke out the slender earnings of her man. Most commonly her work is in the fields; after feeding her family she must start out from her home in the early morning, often leaving little or no food in the house for her children whose main

meal may have to wait for her return in the evening. Her difficulty in securing work is at least as great as that with which the West Indian man is faced. If she alone is responsible for the support of a family, her position is indeed difficult and there can be little cause for wonder that a combination of economic circumstances and natural irresponsibility so often leads a woman, even if she already has the sole responsibility for several illegitimate children, to seek the uncertain help afforded by association with yet another man, although she must realise only too well the temporary nature of that assistance and that eventually, perhaps after her responsibilities have been increased, she may again be abandoned.

5. It has been said that social conditions in the West Indies are better than those of the African in his own country, but it may be doubted whether the comparison is in fact valid. The West Indian is not living a simple life among his own people under a tribal organisation. He has lost his native background and culture and is now touching elbows with modern civilisation. What would have seemed to him years ago to be luxuries quite beyond the means of all but the rich have become the necessities of to-day. Many of his people, leaving the West Indian Colonies to work in Panama, Cuba and the United States of America, have returned with accounts of higher wages and better conditions in other countries. The British West Indian, from his insanitary or inadequate home, has seen beside him the building of good houses out of their savings by these returning friends. He knows that on his own low wages he cannot save. In the nineteenth century there was little except food and house rent on which the West Indian could spend his money. To-day for the better off townsfolk such amenities as the cinema, motor transport and imported clothes are available and everywhere a far greater variety of imported foodstuffs is now offered; to all these things the poorer people naturally aspire. Everywhere the urge is being felt for better housing, better education and other amenities normally associated with modern civilisation. The desire for education, particularly noticeable in the case of parents anxious to secure a better future for their children, cannot always be satisfied and compulsory education is beyond enforcement owing to lack of school buildings. Many of the other improvements and services for which the West Indian now wishes are often not provided for him and poverty puts them beyond his power of purchase.

6. On many of the estates the labourer is given free housing, but he has no security of tenure and may feel that, should he complain, he will be in danger of dismissal. He has gained his freedom but his employer is not under an obligation to give him good living conditions, and what he receives to-day is not a right but is an act of a benevolent autocracy.

7. The Churches, such social welfare organisations as exist and, in many cases, the local Governments, within their very limited means, have done something to ameliorate these conditions, but clearly much more, and better organised, effort is still required.

8. Three questions call especially for consideration as affecting social conditions in the West Indies. They are the status accorded to women, the lack of family life and the absence of a well-defined programme of social welfare. In addition, Governments, while alive to these needs, often show an ignorance, in which the people themselves share, of the best means of meeting them, and in some of the West Indies there is a marked apathy on the part of those classes with higher incomes who in most countries of Western civilisation are available for voluntary services among those less fortunate than themselves.

9. We propose now to examine these three main factors. In doing so we must touch at times on matters which are mentioned elsewhere in this report, but some repetition is inevitable if we are to give here a complete picture of a fundamental problem.

(b) THE STATUS OF WOMEN.

(i) *In Public Administration.*

10. Women can take but little part in the administration of the West Indian Colonies. When they are eligible to exercise the vote on equal terms with men or to stand with them for election to representative institutions, the prescribed qualifications are usually such that few women possess the property or income to satisfy them. In three Colonies woman is debarred from candidature at elections for the Legislative Council. In Jamaica, where women are eligible for election or nomination to the Legislative Council, none has yet sat in that body. In Barbados women are not eligible for the vote. Another inequality is that in three Colonies women, otherwise qualified for the vote, may not exercise it until they reach an age higher by some years than that at which a man is entitled to vote. A recommendation that women should be put on an equal footing with men in these matters is made in Chapter XXII. Women should also be eligible for service on any Boards or Local Authorities which are concerned with education, housing, medical, land settlement or social welfare schemes; their special interest in these problems and the value of the advice which some women may be able to give on them are considerations which should be borne carefully in mind when any question arises of nominating individuals for appointment to these bodies. We heard of only one woman who is a member of a Municipal Council in the West Indies.

11. The administration of justice is another field of public service from which the women are in practice excluded. Women magistrates, who have proved elsewhere to be of great assistance in dealing with cases of juvenile delinquency, are unknown in the West Indies and women appear to be debarred also from jury service. In these respects also, women should, we consider, be put on an equality with men.

12. Few senior administrative offices are held by West Indian women who are employed in the Civil Service mainly as teachers or clerks, etc., and in Postal departments. It was alleged that in some cases there is a difference of procedure in the selection of male and female candidates for the Civil Service. We consider that the same procedure should be adopted for both.

(ii) *The Shop-girl.*

13. The hours of the shop-girl are not so long as those of the domestic servant but her work is exacting and tiring. In some shops pay varies between £1 and £5 a month. There are shops in which substantially higher wages are paid; on the other hand, in small shops wages are sometimes as low as 16s. a month. The hours of work are often unsatisfactory in these small shops and there is said to be evasion of the law by " back-door trade ". Evidence given before us indicated that wages are lowest and hours are longest in the small provision shops.

14. Working conditions in the stores, with few exceptions, appear to be unsatisfactory. Rest rooms for the staff are rare: food is not provided and there is seldom a suitable place where an assistant can eat her meal; sanitary accommodation, when it exists, is often shared with a large number of men. More than one delegation, representative of the Churches or of social welfare workers, submitted to us typical budgets of the shop-assistant showing that her wages were inadequate, and we were told that those having responsibility for the support of others are sometimes obliged to supplement their wages by undesirable means. There is a great need for an increased number of hostels with rooms at low rents for the single woman worker.

(iii) *The Domestic Servant.*

15. The normal working day of the domestic servant is from 6 a.m. to 9 p.m. She depends upon the goodwill of her employer for any sick leave, annual holiday or other time of release from duty. Workmen's compensation legislation, where it exists, does not apply to her. Her lot, which is often a hard one, might be relieved in many cases if she would live in, but we were told that few servants will accept that condition of employment and there are many homes which do not offer it.

16. The wages of the domestic servant range between 6s. and 12s. a week, out of which she has usually to feed and house herself; they are sometimes as low as 1s. 6d. a week in rural districts when food is supplied. The average rent of the poorest room in the city is about 2s. a week; many domestic servants are therefore left with little margin from which to meet other necessary expenses, and it is not surprising that some of them are "helped" by men, who make a small contribution to the weekly budget and share the room as "visitors". For those who, growing old, get no such assistance, undernourishment amounting to starvation is inevitable.

(iv) *Factory and Manual Labour.*

17. The position of women employed in factories does not differ materially from that of men so employed and is therefore covered by the observations and recommendations made in the preceding Chapter with regard to the inspection by Labour Officers of working conditions in factories.

18. By far the largest number of women are employed on agricultural work. They are usually assigned such tasks as weeding and are engaged on a basis of piece work, payment for which is not normally made until the task undertaken has been finished. We have referred in the preceding Chapter to the need for inquiry by Labour Officers into the hardship which may be caused by this practice.

19. Women in the West Indies are employed on other manual labour which would often seem to the onlooker unsuitable for women, besides demanding more than their physical strength justifies. For example, when unloading coal and sand barges, women are required to carry very heavy weights; this form of work is particularly undesirable for people who are in a constant condition of child-bearing. A load of sand, which is carried in a basket from the hold of a ship to the dock on the head of a woman, may weigh as much as 72 lb. A load of coal may weigh 50 lb. Work for more than two days, or at the most three days, in any week is seldom available for the dock-worker who is dependent entirely on the number of ships entering the port. In view of the intermittent character of this form of employment, the work is poorly paid and the average earnings of the woman labourer engaged in the carrying of sand or coal, after she has paid a percentage of those earnings to the gang-leader who engaged her, amounts to only a few shillings a week. The same comment applies to the carrier of bananas on the docks, who is paid $\frac{1}{4}$d. for each stem and is usually under-employed, and to the carrier of stones on the road, who in some places earns as little as 9d. for a day's work.

20. Generally throughout the West Indies, although the level of pay for men is low, an even lower standard is adopted for women, who often receive less than a living wage. The argument that man is the head of the household and is responsible for the financial upkeep of the family has less force in the West Indies, where promiscuity and illegitimacy are so prevalent and the woman so often is the supporter of the home.

(c) Lack of Family Life.

21. In considering this question a clear distinction must be drawn between promiscuity and permanent unmarried cohabitation. It is the promiscuous union which creates a grave danger to the social stability of the West Indies and has those unfortunate consequences which we shall attempt to describe. Permanent cohabitation between the unmarried—or, as it was described to us in evidence, " faithful concubinage "—at least leads to a home life and to the establishment of a family group which is little different from the married state. This system appears to have little or no effect on the social standing of the unmarried mother or her children, and no stigma appears to be attached to illegitimacy. We were told in evidence by both social workers and representatives of the Churches that permanent cohabitation to-day is on the wane and that promiscuity is on the upgrade. The percentage of illegitimacy varies in the different Colonies; it is seldom less than 60 per cent. and often is in the neighbourhood of 70 per cent. of the population.

22. This lack of family life has a bearing on every aspect of social conditions in the West Indies and its effects from a health standpoint are particularly serious. It is possibly the chief contributory factor to the high rates of infant mortality in these Colonies, little reduction in which can be expected until the family is recognised as the normal unit of human existence and the responsibilities of parentage are accepted in the West Indies. Nor, until that position is reached, can any marked success attend efforts to fight venereal disease or to improve the standard of nutrition among young children. In present circumstances full value cannot be obtained for money spent on the treatment of that disease or on the provision of free meals in schools. Nor again can the misery and ill-health of old people be substantially alleviated until a feeling of family responsibility has been more securely established.

23. The effect of existing conditions on the welfare and well-being of children is particularly marked. If the father can evade the application of legislation under which he would be made financially responsible for his illegitimate children, the whole of that responsibility falls on the mother, whose earnings must provide for the maintenance of what may often be a large

number of children. In such circumstances cases of extreme poverty are inevitable, for the standard of living must be lower than it would be in a family group where, even if both parents were not employed, more money would be available, since the wages of men are normally higher than those paid to women.

24. Great stress was laid by many witnesses on the high rate of mortality among children born of promiscuous unions. Some School inspectors emphasised the fact that there is a marked difference, in both mental and material condition, between children from promiscuous homes and others attending the schools; as one of them has said—"There can be no moral training by the mother, nor discipline by the father." Prison authorities and those who have the care of the delinquent child state that a large number of them come from these shifting households; they complain that such children on discharge have no home to fall back upon and no family traditions to uphold. From the hospitals and from the homes for neglected and abandoned children came the same story. As was to be expected, in view of the preponderance of illegitimate children, a majority of those admitted to these institutions were born out of wedlock. The effects of promiscuity are clearly shown in the greater degree of ill-health which is found among children of such passing unions. That is indeed inevitable when the father, who has gone on his way, cannot be traced and the mother is left as the sole earner of wages and the supporter of the household. The task of caring properly for her children is then beyond her, and her consequent neglect of them is bound in time to react upon herself, for the child who is himself neglected by his parents will have no feelings of responsibility for them in their old age.

25. What then are the fundamental causes of this grave social evil, without redress of which the West Indies must continue to lack the civic strength of the family group? Some witnesses averred that the West Indian prefers cohabitation without marriage, but no convincing evidence on that point was put before us. Other witnesses alleged that the failure of the West Indians to marry is a legacy from the time when the institution of wedlock was discouraged among the slaves. This historical basis was often quoted to us, but there are many other factors, first among which should perhaps be placed the absence of a strong opposing public opinion among a people whose immature minds too often are ruled by their adult bodies. Other causes follow from conditions already described. Unmarried cohabitation and illegitimacy are the sequels of bad housing, with overcrowded rooms shared by adults and children of both sexes; of the absence of education in civic responsibility and sex hygiene; of the poor facilities for the occupation of hours of leisure; and of the

denial, through poverty, of that display which the love of the West Indian for colour and gaiety leads him to associate with the ceremony of marriage.

26. Perhaps the most important step, apart from a general raising of the standard of life, which could be taken in an attempt to bring about reform in this matter would be an organised campaign against the social, moral and economic evils of promiscuity. In this work an important part should be played by the Churches and they should recognise that much of the success of their efforts will depend upon the extent to which they combine and show a common front. Other remedies, which have already been discussed or will be examined in more detail later in this Chapter, include the training of boys and girls in domestic crafts, the better education of all sections of the community in civic responsibility coupled with sound propaganda on sex hygiene, the providing of more and better opportunities for organised recreation, the building of hostels for domestic servants and shop-assistants, and an increase in the number of social workers in both towns and rural districts. In addition, we consider that certain changes should be made in existing legislation. The age of marriage should be raised to not less than 15 years for girls, and the age of consent should at least be brought up to the same level where it is not already higher; the penalties for infringement of the law on this point should be severe. The law providing for the issue of maintenance orders against the fathers of illegitimate children should also be amended and strengthened. Maintenance Officers should be appointed and empowered to enforce the collection of money of which the payment has been ordered by the courts. Men against whom orders have been made should be compelled to report to the Maintenance Officer before they leave his district and on arrival in another. Men who have been sentenced to imprisonment for failure to comply with maintenance orders are not normally required to work in prison. Imprisonment, without the necessity of working, has, however, little deterrent effect in the West Indies.

(*d*) NEED FOR A WELL-DEFINED PROGRAMME OF SOCIAL WELFARE.

27. It is against this background that we need to consider the part which might be played in the West Indies by the development of social welfare work. Expanding the formula adopted by a recent international Committee of official delegates, we may define that term as the work of specially-qualified persons " who are engaged in activities for promoting the welfare of other members of the community by close and friendly contact, which may involve direct assistance to the individual or have in view the improvement of his environment ". These activities are far-reaching and at times must

overlap with those of Departments of Government administering services which we have already discussed. Close co-operation between the social welfare worker and such authorities as those in charge of medical, education and labour services is therefore essential; at the same time the social welfare worker has his own angle of approach to problems affecting the well-being of the people. He takes as the basis of his work the social, cultural and moral background of the family and his efforts are directed towards the improvement of the surroundings of the common people and the raising of their standard of life above their environment. His primary responsibilities are to understand from within the problems of the poor, the mal-adjusted and the unfortunate, and to help in the solution of those problems. The range of his activities must therefore be wide. He should be a friend and adviser in the home; he should cater for the leisure of the worker, and he should take a lively interest in the care or aftercare of people in all public institutions, from the hospital to the prison, in the relief of distress and in conditions of employment wherever workers are to be found in large numbers.

28. The social conditions in the West Indies make it specially desirable that a full programme of social welfare work should be planned by each Colonial Government, but so far no Government has been able to undertake that planning. Busy as they are with problems of labour, health and education, they have naturally been content to leave the work of social welfare to any who were willing to undertake it. As we have shown in the first Chapter of this report, the denominations have played a leading part in this work in the West Indies from the days when, it is said, Moravians sold themselves into slavery in order to bring religion, teaching and pity to an oppressed people, up to the present day when a large number of the schools are still controlled by the Churches. But they have not been able to do more than touch the fringe of the problem, and that is equally true of the efforts of certain voluntary organisations to which great credit is nevertheless due. The Salvation Army, which sent its first mission to the West Indies more than fifty years ago, still continues its work of prevention and rehabilitation, its institutions for the blind, its hostels and its depots for the supply of cheap food. Other bodies, such as the Y.M.C.A. and the Y.W.C.A., offer friendship and recreation to the young man and woman and to the child. In certain Colonies Women's Societies maintain child welfare centres and crèches and provide meals for necessitous children. But the work of all has been confined to the large towns and in rural areas little or nothing is being done. Subsidies from public funds are granted to many of these enterprises, but each year their accounts show large deficits and the raising of money to cover them is a most difficult task in

countries where active public opinion is either non-existent or unorganised and people of leisure show little interest in social welfare. Moreover the work of both voluntary organisations and the Churches has suffered through the lack of collaboration. A combined campaign on the part of the Churches would accomplish far more in the way of social reform than could ever be achieved by the separate efforts of the denominations. Through union they could speed up social progress; they would be in a position to bring pressure to bear on Governments, Legislative Councils and Parochial Boards and on the people themselves.

29. The direction of the main schemes of reform must, however, rest with Government, and the primary need is that they should establish the machinery and the administrative organisation through which policies and programmes can be evolved and put into practical effect. From what we have already said it will be clear that these activities must involve joint endeavour in many fields of public adminstration by several departments of Government. To take one example, it is now generally accepted that improvement of health is no longer the sole concern of Medical Departments, and that it is essential to secure the co-operation of the educational, agricultural, labour, social welfare and administrative authorities. The time has come when a mere recommendation that this co-operation should be effective is no longer sufficient; definite means must be adopted to attain it.

30. Our first recommendation, therefore, is that each Colonial Government should appoint a Senior Social Welfare Officer and, in addition, should form a Social Welfare Committee composed of representatives of each Department which is interested, however indirectly, in the evolution of a programme of social welfare. We consider that the Colonial Secretary should normally be the Chairman of these Committees and that the chief financial adviser of the Government should also be a member. In the larger Colonies the Senior Social Welfare Officer should be a member of the Committee, and in the smaller territories it may be convenient that he should also undertake the duties of Secretary to it. Each Committee should meet at regular intervals to consider the long-term policies of the Departments represented upon it and to frame a general social welfare policy which would be submitted to the Government of the Colony, for approval, with proposals for the exact role that each Department should play and for the allocation of available revenue between the various Departments. The special functions of the Social Welfare Officer, in addition to those falling upon him as part of the work of this Committee, would be to advise the Government upon, and to develop, those aspects of social welfare which are not the sole interest or concern of other

Departments. For example, he would be responsible for co-ordinating the efforts of voluntary organisations with those of any official social workers who would come directly under his control; he should be able to bring to the notice of the Colonial Secretary, either directly or through the Committee any ways in which the activities of other Departments ought to be supplemented in order to provide, as completely as the funds available permit, for the needs of the people. In short, the repair of the social fabric will be his particular concern.

31. In Chapter XXI of this report we recommend the creation of a new organisation, the head of which would be assisted by a panel of experts, one of whom should be a person of outstanding experience in the work of social welfare. In addition to the duty of advising the head of that organisation about the general social welfare programme to be followed for the West Indies as a whole, that officer would be available to visit the different Colonies, on the invitation of their Governments, and to advise them on the planning and the execution of any special social reforms in that territory. The appropriate persons from the panel of experts, including the Social Welfare Adviser, should be constituted into a Committee which would be a counterpart in the central organisation of those local Committees of which the establishment in the bigger Colonies has been recommended above. The duties which, in our opinion, should fall to that Committee are mentioned in Chapter XXI of this report.

32. With the appointment of the local Committees and the establishment of a counterpart to them in the central organisation, the administrative machinery would be complete, but additional staff will be required to give executive effect, under the direction of the Social Welfare Officers, to those parts of new programmes of social welfare which are not carried out by members of other Departments. Trained social welfare workers should be appointed to the additional posts, but such persons are not at present available in the West Indies. It will be necessary, therefore, either to import trained staff or to send students from the West Indies to other countries for this special training, or to establish in the West Indies a central training school for this purpose. In our view the last of these three courses should be adopted. The establishment of a training school in the West Indies has the great advantage that the practical part of the curriculum could be given under conditions comparable with those in which the students would later work. To bridge the gap while the first students are still being instructed, the services should be obtained on a temporary basis of persons who have completed their training in some of the excellent schools for social workers which now exist in the British Empire and the United States.

33. The course of instruction should include practical training in community work in both rural and urban districts. The curriculum should cover child welfare and juvenile recreation, the visiting of homes, probation and after-care, factory welfare work, and the organisation of clubs (with cultural, social and athletic branches), women's institutes and libraries. The theoretical instruction should include lectures on first aid, home nursing and mothercraft. In addition, there should be classes in handicrafts with special emphasis on what is known in America as Homecraft. The valuable work which is now being done by voluntary organisations in the West Indies should be supplemented and supported and not be displaced; they may be willing to allow these students to take part in their practical work and thus to gain the benefit of their long experience which has helped them to understand the problems of the West Indian people.

34. The giving of this training in the West Indies should help to create among the people themselves a desire to raise the standard of their daily life; it should also do much to arouse an interest in social welfare work among persons of leisure, most of whom seem so far not to have realised their opportunities for social service.

(e) SPECIAL DUTIES OF SOCIAL WELFARE WORKERS.

35. The division of responsibilities between this special staff and the officers of other Departments will vary in different Colonies and everywhere will undergo a steady process of modification in which administrative convenience and a growing experience will be important factors. But certain duties must always be the particular care of the social worker, and we propose next, as an illustration of the service which they can give, to describe the defects in such arrangements as now exist for the care and leisure of the child and adolescent, and the benefits which organised social work could bring.

(i) *Care of Infants.*

36. In chapter VIII attention was drawn to the need for improved and extended child welfare centres; here we are concerned with the daily well-being of infants and young children. In the typical poor house in the West Indies the elementary needs of suitable feeding, healthy housing and cleanliness are seldom obtainable. Those mothers who are working in the fields or as domestic servants—and there are many of them—can neither look after nor feed their children, who are usually left in the charge of a neighbour or older child. The nourishment then given may often be quite unsuited to the child's digestion; its home may be a house of the type which

we have already described; most probably its whole environment, far from inducing habits of cleanliness, is a deterrent to their practice.

37. In addition to more child welfare centres, more crèches are required, more funds for their proper maintenance and trained staff with the knowledge and experience to direct and assist the efforts of voluntary workers in ways which would make for sound and economical administration. Both nurses and volunteers are showing whole-hearted and unselfish interest in the work of existing crèches, but their efforts are often hampered by unsuitable buildings and shortage of funds and they would certainly benefit by guidance from qualified social workers.

38. In one of the Colonies a Baby Week is held annually and during it lectures and demonstrations are given to mothers. This institution, which is very popular among them, might with advantage be copied in other territories. Another praiseworthy enterprise is the provision by some estates of free crèches for the small children of their workers. Some of these consist merely of a bare room, a tin bath and a " granny " in charge, but others are more modern in their equipment. It would be well if good crèches could be provided on estates under proper supervision.

(ii) *The Child and the Home.*

39. Next after food the child of any age needs in its home the light and air which bring health of body, the privacy which will give it an opportunity for thought and the development of mind, a healthy and intelligent occupation for its leisure hours and the discipline which will fit it to take its place as a helpful member of the community. In the poorer homes of the West Indies the child gets none of these. It may know only a small unlighted hovel with wooden shutters tightly closed by night in order to shut out evil spirits or thieving neighbours. Privacy of any kind is impossible when a family of ten or twelve have to sleep in one small room, some on the floor, some under the bed, some in it, and all in a stifling and foul atmosphere. The best that a child of such a family can hope for is that it will find in its school life and in organised social centres compensations for its home conditions. Only the understanding help and advice of the trained social worker, known in these homes as a friend, could induce the parents to make an effort to improve the lot of their unfortunate children.

(iii) *The Deserted and Orphaned Child.*

40. The conditions under which deserted and orphaned children are brought up are sometimes even worse than those described above. As a rule the destitute child is in the care

of the Poor Law Authorities and may be found in the Almshouse with the senile and the sick, or in the Reformatory sleeping and working and playing with the delinquent child. There are in some Colonies children's institutions known as Rescue Homes to which deserted children are sent. Here elementary reading and writing are taught, but practical training is seldom given and the children leave these homes, as a rule at 14 years of age, with no occupational equipment. Inevitably some of them soon become applicants for poor relief and join the company of those who are permanent occupants of Poor Law institutions. When a deserted female child is adopted, as often as not she becomes a household drudge. Adopted children are not registered and the homes to which they go are seldom inspected and never supervised. In British Guiana, however, where there are a number of orphans of Indian immigrants, the Agent-General is responsible for appointing a guardian who is bound to visit once in each quarter the home into which any of these children have been adopted. The lot of the deserted and orphaned child could be greatly improved by establishing for them Homes in the country where an agricultural bias should be given to their education. By this means they might be trained to be the farmers and farmers' wives of the future. Better still might be the boarding out of children in good residential homes in the country under the foster mother system, which has been so successful in this country and in the Dominions; these homes could be grouped into units under trained social workers.

41. The adopted child is often exploited, morally by the male members of the adopting family, physically by the work he or she is expected to do. No Societies for the Prevention of Cruelty to Children exist in the West Indies, and the steps that can be taken to prevent this exploitation are therefore limited to any action that is possible under Ordinances for the employment of women, young persons and children.

42. We consider that in each Colony legislation should be enacted to provide for the registration, supervision and inspection of all homes where legally adopted children are placed. Deserted children should not be accommodated either in almshouses or in reformatories but under one of the alternative systems suggested above. Some Government officer, preferably a social welfare worker, should be made responsible for inspecting the conditions under which all these children live.

(iv) *The Leisure Hours of the People.*

43. The services of the trained social worker can be invaluable in showing the child and the adolescent how to continue their education and in helping all sections of the people to make the best use of their hours of leisure. Regimentation in any form

should be avoided; the purpose must be not to organise the leisure of the community but to offer facilities which will allow individuals who care to use them the chance of both recreation and cultural development. To this end a social centre should be provided everywhere under the supervision of a social worker, and in each place it should be appropriate to the needs of the community which it is intended to serve.

44. In country districts the centre at first may be only a barn containing a small library, or a church hall made available on two or three evenings of each week for meetings at which a local social worker could discuss with young people their problems and give them simple advice. From small beginnings much may in time be possible particularly if, from the outset, Committees are established to attract the active help of those villagers or land settlers who are interested in social reform.

45. In the larger towns and at the centres of all land settlement schemes the ultimate goal should be an institution so designed and constructed that it could cater fully both for the education of people through reading or through lectures and for the amusements of those who have no wish for systematic instruction. The multiplication in the West Indies of centres modelled on that established in Kingston by the Jamaica Welfare League would go far to satisfy the reasonable requirements of communities for which nothing is now done. In this case also a less ambitious start will often be necessary, but much can be done even when expenditure has to be kept within narrow limits. At least rooms could be rented, if no friendly owner could be found who is prepared to forgo any charge, and in them wireless could be installed, a library could be housed and a consulting room provided for the social worker. Here community singing might be encouraged, indoor games might be played and the tastes of those who wish to continue their education by private reading might be guided. Whenever such a plan is practicable—and particularly in country districts—adolescent boys and girls should be encouraged to build a model house, from local materials and at a cost bringing it within the means of the people, to be attached to the centre for demonstrations by social workers in domestic crafts. In addition, the centre should be used by those workers to encourage the formation of troops of Girl Guides and Boy Scouts; one obstacle to their establishment to-day is the difficulty of finding persons who are fitted for leadership in these organisations, but with the new knowledge of the personal qualities of individuals which may be obtained through the work of the centres it should not be impossible to overcome that difficulty.

46. It is obvious that many years must pass before the problem of finding occupation for the leisure of townsfolk in the West Indies can be completely solved. The day must still be far distant when libraries, technical schools, clubs and playing fields will be provided on a scale commensurate with reasonable need. Nevertheless an organised effort must at once be made along the simpler lines which we have indicated if the young and the adolescent are to be offered some alternative to the spending of their hours of leisure in the woods or in overcrowded homes.

(f) Conclusions.

47. This completes our review of a social welfare policy to serve the general communities of the West Indian Colonies, and it may be convenient, therefore, to restate briefly our conclusions before we pass on to an examination of the few special questions which remain to be discussed in this part of the report.

48. Those conclusions are:—

(a) Undesirable features of West Indian social conditions are the low status accorded to women, the lack of family life and the absence of a well-defined programme of social welfare.

(b) The status of women in the West Indies might be improved by making it possible for them to take a greater part in the administration of those Colonies, by improving the conditions under which they work and their pay, and by giving them a better training in domestic duties. Detailed recommendations on some of these points have been made in Chapters VII and X and others will be found in Chapter XXII; those made in this Chapter are:—

(i) women should be eligible for appointment to all Boards and Local Authorities;

(ii) where nominations may be made to those bodies and representation of the interests of women has not been secured through elections, the desirability of nominating a woman or women for membership, if well-qualified persons can be found, should be borne carefully in mind;

(iii) women should be equally eligible with men for appointment as magistrates and service as jurors;

(iv) the same procedure should be adopted in selecting both male and female candidates for appointment to the Civil Service; and

(v) more hostels should be provided for single women workers.

(c) An organised campaign should be undertaken against the social, moral and economic evils of promiscuity; in this work the Churches should play an important part, the success of which will mainly depend upon the extent to which they combine. In addition, certain changes should be made in existing legislation relating to the age of consent and of marriage and the issue and enforcement of maintenance orders against the fathers of illegitimate children.

(d) An organisation should be created and staff should be appointed through the agency of which a well-defined social welfare programme can be planned and executed in each West Indian Colony. Locally this organisation should operate through Social Welfare Committees, of which the Senior Social Welfare Officer should be a member; in addition a Social Welfare Adviser should be appointed to the central staff, of which the creation is recommended in Chapter XXI of this Report, and the central machinery should include a Committee which would be a counterpart to the local Social Welfare Committees in the Colonies.

(e) Social welfare workers must be trained for service in the West Indian Colonies; when they are available their special duties will include:—

> (i) The direction and assistance of the efforts of voluntary workers in crèches and child-welfare centres, and the supervision of the work of any crèches established on estates;
>
> (ii) An attempt to improve conditions in the homes of the poorer people by gaining their confidence and becoming their friend and adviser;
>
> (iii) The responsibility for the welfare of adopted and deserted children and the inspection of homes to which legally adopted children are taken;
>
> (iv) The supervision of community centres at which they would guide the occupation of leisure hours, would give advice to young people and would promote such activities as the formation of troops of Girl Guides and Boy Scouts;
>
> (v) Welfare work arising out of recommendations made elsewhere in this Report in connection with factories, prisons, hospitals and other institutions; and
>
> (vi) Other duties which to-day in progressive communities are allocated to social workers.

(f) In addition to creating the new local organisations West Indian Governments should assist all these enterprises by supplementing, when necessary, from public funds any voluntary subscriptions which may be raised for those purposes.

(*g*) Policy should be directed to supplementing and supporting, and not to replacing, the valuable help of the many voluntary organisations now working in the West Indies. It is vitally important to attract still more interest in that work from people of leisure who are in a position to help both financially by subscribing towards the cost of these activities and by personal service.

2. Prisons.

49. We would first acknowledge the valuable help which we received in this part of our inquiry from the results of an investigation into the reformatories and penal establishments of the West Indian Colonies a few years ago.

50. The standard of conditions in many of the prisons in the West Indies is reasonably good, and those found in the penal establishment in an island off Trinidad call for particular commendation. In other prisons, where conditions are less satisfactory, efforts are being made to give effect to recommendations made as a result of a recent inquiry, and gradual improvements may be expected. But there are still some institutions the inmates of which suffer serious hardships; these are due in part to the requirements of economy which have so far prevented the adoption of reforms which entailed expense, and in part to lack of imagination and knowledge among some of those who control West Indian prisons. Another noticeable feature to be found in most of these Colonies is the want of any sustained or intelligent public interest in either the fate or the treatment of the offender. To most people in the West Indies prison is a place of punishment alone and designed for the protection of the community from the criminal; it is not an opportunity for rehabilitation, nor is its purpose to create a good citizen from the offender. The authorities in charge of many prisons are experienced men who realise this unfortunate position and do their utmost to spread the doctrine that prison administration has a positive function; all too often opinion outside the prison weights the scales against them.

(*a*) THE YOUNG OFFENDER.

51. Particularly unfortunate is the case of the young offender whose detention may sometimes be traced to the surroundings in which he was brought up. That lack of family life to which we have already referred cannot result in a proper discipline in the home; housing conditions in general are not conducive to the training of the child for citizenship, nor do they, or the poverty so prevalent in many homes, make for a sound moral

outlook or for personal honesty. Bad habits acquired in this environment cannot be eradicated by education when classes are so overcrowded as to be beyond the capacity of buildings and staff. It is not unusual to find several hundred children of the seven grades and the infants' section working in one unpartitioned building under the supervision of a few distracted teachers. The delinquent child committed often for some small offence, is brought, as a general rule, before a juvenile court or magistrate. We have already recommended that, when suitable persons are available, women should be appointed as magistrates; they should be of great value in the West Indian Colonies, as they have been found to be elsewhere, in dealing with young offenders.

52. The usual punishments ordered when young offenders have been convicted are probation, whipping or committal to, in theory, a Reformatory or Industrial School. Probation is applied all too infrequently and, as a rule, is carried out by an overworked officer of the Salvation Army who sometimes receives a small payment from Government for this work. Much more use should be made of the system of probation, subjection to which should be the punishment for all young offenders for whom it is the best method of treatment. The probation system will therefore need considerable expansion and increased aid from Government.

53. Though the principle is accepted that the delinquent boy should be sent to a Reformatory or Industrial Home and not to prison, in practice some of us found children of 14 and 15 years of age imprisoned in general penitentiaries as a punishment for such minor offences as the stealing of empty flour sacks, empty bottles and school primers.

(b) INDUSTRIAL SCHOOLS FOR BOYS.

54. The number of Industrial schools is too small. They are, in general, many years behind the times. Frequently they are under the control of superintendents who have neither the special training nor the knowledge of child psychology that could fit them for their task. Discipline seems to be their motto, and education and recreation play little part in the life of their schools. It should be realised that the control of an Industrial school is a specialised profession; persons for such posts should be carefully selected and, when selected, should be given a period of training, preferably within the West Indies.

55. The Industrial school is often in some inaccessible place. Visitors are few and far between, official inspections are rare and the boys are entirely at the mercy of the superintendents. With rare exceptions the technical training in these schools

is indifferent and its scope is governed by the wish to meet the internal needs of the school, such as cooking and the making of uniforms to clothe the inmates, rather than by the idea of instructing the boys in a trade which may be useful to them when they return to the outside world. In the better schools, however, the importance of training is realised; sometimes a boy is supplied, when he leaves, with the tools of the trade which he has learned in the school, and he may also be sent away with a small sum of money in his pocket.

56. These problems of staffing and training are particularly difficult in the smaller islands, and we strongly support the suggestion that federal action is required. In our opinion, the Governments of the Leeward Islands and the Windward Islands should consult and attempt to draw up a scheme for the establishment of a Central Industrial School to accommodate delinquent boys from all those territories.

(c) THE DELINQUENT GIRL.

57. The offence of the delinquent girl is usually one which arises from sex problems, and the fact that the number of young girls detained in most of the Colonies is small adds to the difficulty of providing adequately for these cases. Ultimately it should be possible to establish a Central Industrial School to which the more serious offenders could be sent from all the West Indian Colonies; for the present every effort should be made to find foster parents who would be prepared to undertake the care of the less serious offenders.

58. Many of these girls are now in institutions belonging to religious orders; they are given some education, but little attention is paid to their needs for recreation. Corporal punishment may be too frequently administered in some of these institutions. In one case a punishment book seen by two of us recorded the whipping of ten girls in one day at a time when there were less than 30 girls in the home. We consider that it should be made the rule that all whippings in private homes are to be reported, at frequent intervals, to Colonial Governments.

(d) THE ADULT PRISONER.

59. The system of probation is rarely applied in the case of adult offenders in the West Indies. Its cost is much less than that of imprisonment, the gross figure for which was given in a recent estimate as varying between £36 and £84 per annum for each inmate. If more first offenders were bound over and placed in the care of a probation officer, much money would be saved to Colonial Governments and could be utilised

for more useful purposes such as after-care and the aid of prisoners. It should be recognised that first offenders can seldom be kept completely apart from recidivists and, where probation is not readily applied, many of the former are turned into hardened criminals by what they learn from prison inmates of that type.

60. In a few of the prisons which we visited excellent training is given in a variety of trades and an issue of the tools of his trade was usually made to each prisoner on his discharge. Our inquiries showed, however, that the more general practice is for male prisoners to be employed on such occupations as quarrying and the making of sacks.

61. In most of the prisons for men some elementary education is given to the illiterate who generally number about 60 per cent. of the occupants of the prison. It was, however, exceptional to find that facilities for recreation, either in or out of doors, were provided, although in two Colonies excellent arrangements had been made both for games and gymnastic exercises.

62. The conditions in prisons for women are usually even more dreary than those to be found in the prisons for men. In few of them are handicrafts taught or any trade which might be of use to the prisoner on discharge. Her time is occupied, as a rule, by cooking, washing and mending; no open-air exercise, beyond the daily round of the prison yard, is provided. Arrangements for the education and recreation of female prisoners are even less adequate than those provided for the men, and they receive no payment for their work.

63. The woman in charge of a female prison has seldom received any form of training which would fit her for her responsibilities. More often than not the grounds for her selection are that she is the deserving widow of some minor Government official, or is willing to accept conditions of employment under which payment is made only when there is a woman prisoner in the gaol. In the larger prisons for women conditions of service are better. Speaking generally, however, the conditions of women prisoners cannot be materially improved unless staff of a higher quality, and engaged on some permanent basis, is provided.

(e) Prison Treatment and Accommodation.

64. It was a frequent practice in some of the prisons which we visited for the inmates to be locked in their unlit cells on public holidays and during week-ends in order that warders might be allowed longer periods away from duty. On the other hand in one small island the warder took the only inmate of his prison

for walks in the country. Everywhere the authorities should aim at an arrangement of the hours of duty of the warders to prevent the confinement of prisoners in their cells at times of public holiday and week-ends.

65. In some places the accommodation for prisoners on remand is quite inadequate. In one we found a girl, barely 15 years of age, who was being detained for a time while awaiting trial on a charge of being concerned in the death of her illegitimate child. She was the only inmate of a temporary gaol; her one visitor was the temporary wardress who brought in her meals twice daily; at night-time she was alone in the prison, the key of which was not available to the resident prison authorities as the wardress took it away with her each night. This was no doubt an exceptional case but conditions under which it could happen clearly call for immediate attention.

(f) The Ticket-of-Leave System.

66. The discharged prisoner, of whose sentence a portion has been remitted for good conduct, is required for a certain period to report to the police who may seek for him in his home or in his place of employment. In consequence he may lose the friendship of his neighbours and be thrown out of work. This system is often a cause of hardship, particularly to the first offender who is trying to make a new start. Most prison authorities with whom the question was discussed in the West Indies were inclined to agree that the abolition of this system would be justified. The police might then lose sight of a few hardened criminals, but many first offenders would have a far better opportunity of making good.

(g) After-care.

67. Well-organised Prisoners' Aid Societies, supplied with adequate funds, are greatly needed in several of these Colonies. At present the functions which should fall to such a Society are usually carried out by officers of the prison and by representatives of the Salvation Army who are known to supplement from their own private means the small funds made available by the Government. In one prison some of us saw nine men, the larger number of whom had received 2s. 3d. on their previous discharge; the highest amount then paid to any of these men was the sum of ten shillings received by one who had served a sentence of seven years. If a Board of Visitors could be appointed for each prison and its members would co-operate with those who are now administering aid to discharged prisoners, public opinion might be aroused to take more interest than at present appears to be shown in the fate of the unhappy offender.

(*h*) Recommendations.

68. Before we deal with the few remaining social problems, we will state briefly the measures which we consider to be desirable in order to secure reform of prison conditions in the West Indies: —

(1) The system of probation should be used more frequently, especially in the case of both young and first offenders, and the probation service should be strengthened and further subsidised.

(2) Young offenders should not be sent to a general penitentiary unless they are unsuitable cases for probation and no special accommodation is available for them.

(3) The Superintendents of all institutions dealing with young offenders should be carefully selected and should be given a period of training, preferably within the West Indies, to fit them for their responsibilities.

(4) The Governments of the Leeward and Windward Islands should consult and attempt to draw up a scheme for the establishment of a central industrial school to accommodate delinquent boys from all those territories.

(5) All whippings of young offenders detained in private homes should be reported at frequent intervals to Colonial Governments.

(6) Both education and recreation should be regarded as essential parts of the penal system and amenities accorded to men should be made available for women. Staff of a higher quality, and engaged on some permanent basis, should be provided at prisons for women.

(7) The aim should be so to arrange hours of duty of the warders that prisoners need not be confined in their cells at times of public holiday and week-ends.

(8) The ticket-of-leave system should be abolished.

(9) Every penal establishment should have connected with it a Prisoners' Aid Society and a Board of Visitors.

3. Remaining Social Problems.

(*a*) Poor Law Relief.

69. In certain of the Colonies of the West Indies Poor Relief forms part of the Medical Department, or is under the Police. In others it is administered by a Charitable Advisory Committee which is responsible for the administration of Government grants. This Committee deals with outdoor and casual relief and with the organisation and operation of Homes of Refuge

for destitute and ailing people, and is composed of representatives of all district boards, government officials and prominent citizens. In Jamaica, where expenditure is relatively high, poor relief is financed and administered by thirteen local government boards, each of which provides its own staff and its own almshouse. This is an uneconomical arrangement, and does not lead to efficiency of administration, though it may be argued on the other hand that it has the advantage of enabling the inmates to keep in touch with their friends.

70. In one or two of the Colonies the poor law relief is entirely a parochial matter and is not supervised by the Government.

(b) Poor Law Homes and Asylums.

71. Although the inmates of these institutions include persons suffering from tuberculosis, venereal disease, malaria, hookworm and other tropical diseases, the medical attention seems to be very inadequate. There are frequently no wards for the sick and it is not often that any one with trained medical or nursing knowledge is in charge of the institution. Special wards are badly needed. It is not uncommon to see advanced mental cases for whom there is presumably no room in the Mental Hospital sharing the common wards with other paupers. Some of the buildings visited by members of the Commission were good but as a whole the standard of accommodation and food left much to be desired and better provision should be made for the care of the destitute and ailing.

(c) Outdoor and Casual Relief.

72. Owing to the prevalence of illegitimacy throughout the Colonies a large portion of the relief funds is spent on behalf of children for whom the father pays no maintenance.

73. The sums allowed for outdoor relief are very small, varying from sixpence a week to one and sixpence in rural areas and rising sometimes to two shillings and sixpence in large towns. It is understood that the Government of Jamaica has under consideration proposals for the removal of all sick poor to a Central institution, by which means the overhead cost may be so reduced as to make financially possible adequate nursing care. It also proposes to provide in rural areas for farm residential schools for destitute children. To meet the needs of outdoor relief it is suggested that there should be an increase in the number of medical outstations and of the public health and district nursing services.

74. It is recommended that this example should be followed by other Colonies. Such a scheme carried out, together with

(d) Prostitution.

75. Commercialised prostitution is not common as a profession in the West Indies. The high percentage of promiscuity in the Colonies puts prostitution in the category of a luxury profession. When this profession is followed, it is usually for economic reasons and because the wages earned by the woman in her other occupation are often too low to obtain the necessities of life for her. She is therefore to be found by night at the docks when ships put in, while carrying on her own work as well in the daytime.

76. The small boys from the wharfs—the wharf rats as they are called—who so often find their way to Juvenile courts are, we were told by police authorities, the offspring of these temporary prostitutes.

77. In some of the cities of the bigger Colonies there are open brothels, not " tolerated " by the Government but under private enterprise. They are a known source of venereal disease for the passengers and crews of the cargo and passenger ships calling at the West Indies. Laws exist for the suppression of these brothels, but there is difficulty in securing sentences under these laws, because it has been thought necessary by West Indian Administrations to get first-hand evidence of a recent client in order to convict.

78. Inquiries into the existence of traffic in women in the West Indies showed that, although cases may sometimes occur, it is by no means widespread.

(e) Other Social Evils.

79. Gambling (as we have indicated in paragraph 13 of Chapter III) and certain peculiar cults also take their toll of the wages of the working man as well as vitiating his outlook. Lotteries and the Chinese games of Drop Pan and Peaka Peow divert the earnings of many from the purchase of necessaries as well as of such luxuries as might otherwise be afforded. The incidence of gambling varies, but it is naturally most prevalent in the larger towns, where earnings are most precarious and the desire for excitement and interest most insistent. Precise information as to the extent of gambling is difficult to obtain, as the authorities are not inactive in its suppression and most of it is consequently driven underground. Nevertheless, it was put to us that in Jamaica the sale of Peaka Peow tickets throughout the Island brought in sums amounting to thousands of pounds weekly to the organisers of the game.

80. It is even harder to arrive at any precise information regarding the extent and nature of the many peculiar cults said to flourish in the West Indies, and not only in the remoter parts. The term obeah is given to the most widespread of these, which seems to consist of a variety of witchcraft, administered by obeahmen or witchdoctors, and akin to the much more powerful Voodoo cult prevalent elsewhere in the Caribbean area. Information as to the identity of these obeahmen and as to their methods is very hard to obtain, as those under their influence are reluctant to speak and in any case mystery, secrecy and intimidation are of the essence of the cult. It does appear, however, that the psychological effects of their activities may be serious, leading now and then to unrest, madness, violence and even murder. From a social standpoint, perhaps the greatest danger is the preaching of hatred and fear, and it is on these emotions that the obeahmen depend for their profits. The charges which they exact are said to be relatively large and out of all proportion to what a labourer could afford to pay.

81. Certain other cults, related to obeah, are Pocomania, Balmism and Ras Tafarism. Of these the first has features akin to those of a highly excitable revivalism, accompanied by dancing, chanting and the beating of tom-toms, and show some Christian influences grafted on to a purely African stock. Balmism, probably the least harmful of all, is a combination of faith-healing and herbalism, and is associated with skilful emotional oratory and the parading of " cures ". Ras Tafarism, a comparatively recent manifestation, is, as its name indicates, political and pan-negro in tendency, with a strong dash of mysticism.

82. Irrational, primitive, and often thoroughly noxious as these practices may be, the experience of the effects of the legal prohibition of obeah in one Colony shows that they cannot be eradicated by simple suppression, since to a large extent they are the result of ignorance, poverty, a sense of insecurity and of a craving for emotional outlets among people whose lives are otherwise lacking in interest and leisure occupations. Their danger was stressed by several responsible witnesses, and various methods of coping with them were suggested, including the legislative suppression of the peculiar cults, in addition to obeah. Apart from the technical difficulty of so wording an enactment as to safeguard generally recognised denominations, such measures would not go to the root of the matter. We concur with the view, expressed by the Christian bodies, that better education and the healthy occupation of leisure hours can alone in the long run meet the needs of which these cults are a symptom, and thus bring about their disappearance.

PART III

PROBLEMS OF POLICY

CHAPTER XII.

THE PROBLEM OF POPULATION.

1. In this part of our report, we consider what measures are desirable to relieve the economic difficulties and to meet the social needs that have been described in the preceding Chapters. But before discussing the many detailed questions that arise, we wish first to emphasize the extreme and fundamental importance of the question of the growth of numbers. The main facts have been already set out in Chapter II. Though the rates of increase of population are very different in the different Colonies, the prevailing rate of increase in the West Indies may be taken as being fully $1\frac{1}{2}$ per cent., and, on the basis of present tendencies, it is likely to approach 2 per cent. in the near future. This is a far larger rate of increase than countries, lacking for the most part any important mineral resources, with limited supplies of fertile land, and confronted with an adverse trend of selling prices for their principal products, can afford. The indefinite continuance of the present West Indian birth-rates would seriously endanger the maintenance of even the present standard of living, and might render nugatory any attempts to improve that standard.

2. Behind the various economic and social defects that have been described in the preceding Chapters, the rapid increase of population is to be found, sometimes as a major cause, and almost always as an aggravating factor. It has contributed more than any other single influence to the formidable increase of intermittent employment in the towns and of under-employment in the country, and has thus gone far to nullify the effects of wage advances in improving the standard of living. It has led in areas where an independent peasant proprietorship had previously been established to the sub-division of holdings into plots so small that their owners are compelled to rely largely on wage-work for their livelihood. It has contributed in two different ways to the difficulty of providing adequate housing accommodation. Dwellings containing space that might be more or less sufficient for families of a moderate size become palpably overcrowded when they are inhabited by families containing eight, ten, twelve or more children. At the same time, there is a steady increase in the number of family units requiring to be housed. Again the difficulties of providing adequate school accommodation are greatly aggravated by the large annual increase in the number of children of school-age; for in many Colonies it is difficult to find money for school-building on a scale sufficient to keep pace with this increase. Nor is it easy to see how malnutrition in childhood can be prevented when the number of children in the average household is as large as it is to-day.

3. In later Chapters, we make proposals which we trust will help materially to increase the volume of employment, to raise the standard of living and to promote the development of the social services. But it is well to recognise that the adoption of these proposals would prove only a superficial palliative, a mere postponement of the evil day, if the present growth of numbers continues unabated. So far as can be foreseen, whatever may be done to increase preference or sugar quotas or to grant financial assistance from Imperial funds, it will not be many years, if the present West Indian birth-rates are maintained, before unemployment is again as acute, housing as overcrowded and nutrition as deficient as we found them in one Colony after another in the autumn of 1938 and the spring of 1939.

4. We lay our stress, it will be observed, on the excessive rate of increase, rather than on the absolute size of the population. For the former phenomenon is found almost everywhere in the West Indies. But in some Colonies absolute over-population also exists in an acute degree. In Barbados, as we have seen, the population is over 1,200 to the square mile, or nearly two persons to each acre. This represents a much greater density than that of the United Kingdom with its immense industrial development. Yet, apart from the assistance given by the tourist trade, the population of Barbados is almost entirely dependent upon agriculture. Under these conditions, there is little scope for suggestions such as we make in connection with the West Indies generally for mitigating the excessive dependence upon export markets by the development of mixed farming and increased production for the domestic market. For it is essential in Barbados, if even a tolerable standard of living is to be maintained, to secure the maximum possible yield per acre; and the specialised production of sugar-cane has the great advantage that its yield per acre and the employment it provides are high.

5. The pressure of population has been felt in Barbados for many generations past; but the large possibilities of emigration that existed before the war of 1914-18 afforded such relief that the total numbers in the island actually declined by some 20,000 between 1896 and 1921. Now, however, as was explained in Chapter II, all the former emigration outlets have, unfortunately, been closed, and Barbadians who had previously emigrated are finding conditions made so uncomfortable for them abroad that they are returning to the island in large numbers. In recent years, indeed, the repatriation of emigrants has contributed even more than the process of natural increase, though the births outnumber the deaths by more than 50 per cent., to swell the total numbers of the population. The total rate of increase arising from these two sources is about as high as anywhere else in the West Indies.

6. The remedy for this state of affairs that commends itself to all sections of opinion in Barbados is to secure somehow new outlets for emigration. A scheme is actually in progress for establishing a settlement of Barbadians in St. Lucia. An abandoned sugar estate at Vieuxfort has been taken over and and is being re-equipped by a company owned by the Barbadian Government; and it is hoped that eventually a few thousands of Barbadians may be settled there. This scheme is of interest as a rare example of practical inter-island co-operation; but its success is contingent on the adoption of effective methods of malaria control and on the allocation to St. Lucia of a larger sugar quota. At the best, it can only bring a comparatively small relief to the pressure of population in Barbados. We found that vague hopes were popularly entertained in Barbados of the possibilities of settlement on a large scale in British Honduras and in the interior of British Guiana; but, so far as we are able to judge, there is no solid basis for these hopes. Another possibility that is perhaps worth consideration, if the St. Lucia experiment proves successful, is that of settling Barbadians in the coastal belt of British Guiana in the district known as the Essequibo coast. This is a district where sugar used to be grown, but which is now seriously distressed, with drainage and sea-defences in a derelict condition, and with rice-growing as practically the only occupation of its inhabitants. The fact that sugar production was abandoned there during the last depression, while it continued in Demerara and Berbice, appears not to have been due to any differences in soil fertility or inherent suitability of the different areas for economical sugar production. A revival of sugar production on the Essequibo coast, would, of course, require the allocation of a larger sugar quota to British Guiana. But, if this proviso could be met, it would make possible the rehabilitation of an area, the present condition of which is most unsatisfactory; and it is at least conceivable, if the lines of the St. Lucia analogy were followed, and if the necessary capital could be supplied from Barbadian sources, that scope might be found for the services of Barbadian immigrants, while doing benefit rather than injury to the existing inhabitants. This must be regarded, however, as a very speculative possibility; and the general prospects of securing a revival of emigration from Barbados on any considerable scale are not encouraging. The outlook for the island is accordingly extremely grim, if the present rate of natural increase is maintained.

7. Several other islands are nearer to the Barbadian position of absolute over-population than the ratio between their numbers and their areas might suggest. Most of the West Indian islands are mountainous; much of their land consists of steep hill-sides,

which cannot be brought into effective agricultural use without the risk of soil erosion. Much land of this type is actually cultivated to-day with unfortunate results; the disastrous landslide in St. Lucia in November, 1938, was admittedly attributable to the cultivation of bananas on unsuitable hill-sides.* There is much less land in the West Indian Colonies capable of more intensive utilisation than is frequently supposed. In Colonies where such land exists in considerable quantities, there is an opportunity for introducing new agricultural practices and for extending land settlement along lines that will reduce their dependence upon export agriculture. But reorganisation of this kind can only proceed slowly; and can hardly be expected, on the most optimistic view, to provide additional employment at a rate that will keep pace with the present rapid increase of numbers.

8. Yet, as we have seen, the steady trend of world economic conditions is unfavourable to the maintenance of an expanding export trade in tropical agricultural commodities. The growth of a surplus of world productive capacity for most of these commodities has led the West Indian Colonies to rely increasingly in recent years on the United Kingdom market; and the hopes that they entertain of future development mostly presuppose that they may be enabled to obtain a larger share of this market by the aid of preferential tariffs. The question of further preferential assistance raises many serious difficulties as will be seen in Chapter XIV. But, apart from these, the idea that a solution of the West Indian problem might be found along these lines raises a fundamental difficulty. The population of Great Britain is no longer increasing rapidly; the British birth-rate, like that of most Western European countries and the United States of America, is far below a replacement level; and unless there is a speedy and substantial recovery, it will not be long before the population of the United Kingdom enters a phase of contraction. This will necessarily reduce the power of the United Kingdom market to absorb increasing quantities of West Indian produce.

9. We therefore regard a reduction of the birth-rate as in one sense the most pressing need of the West Indian Colonies. This raises a problem which is far too difficult and complex to form the subject of concrete recommendations. High birth-rates are not a West Indian peculiarity; birth-rates about as high prevail, so far as statistical evidence enables us to judge, in Africa, in India, in the East generally, and throughout the whole tropical and sub-tropical world. The sharp contrast between the present birth-rates of tropical peoples and those

---

* See Plate XVI.

Chapter XII.

of most peoples of European stock is indeed a phenomenon of the most profound importance, with far-reaching implications. It is not to be supposed that a phenomenon, so widely spread, so long established, so deeply rooted in social customs, and in the case of the East Indian population, so intertwined with religion, can be quickly and easily corrected in the West Indies. Where public opinion is in a mood to appreciate the importance of the question, it is possible that the establishment of birth-control clinics might fulfil a useful purpose. With a different outlook higher wages, better housing conditions, or an extension of peasant settlement might help to secure a reduction in the number of children born; but experience does not suggest that any of these measures would be likely in practice to have the desired effect, unless at all events public opinion in the West Indies becomes widely and vividly conscious of the need for a limitation of the birth-rate.

10. An awakening of public opinion is indeed the indispensable condition of a solution of this problem; and every body and organisation that seeks, in whatever sphere, to guide or influence opinion should recognise the responsibilities that rest upon it to assist and not to obstruct the process of public enlightenment. We fully recognise the difficult position in which many Church leaders find themselves upon this matter. But we should regard it as a tragedy if the religious bodies, many of which played so courageous and constructive a part in the darkest period of West Indian history, were now to feel themselves unable to modify an attitude which would set them in opposition to one of the plainest and most pressing needs of the present day.

11. It is obvious that a reduction in the average size of the family can only come as a very gradual process. Moreover, throughout the West Indies, the birth-rate has been high during the last ten or fifteen years, so that whatever may happen henceforward to the birth-rate, the number of young persons of working-age must be expected to undergo a rapid increase for a considerable time to come. This fact carries a twofold moral. On the one hand, it adds to the urgency of securing a general recognition of the need for a limitation of the birth-rate. On the other hand, it is no less essential to seek other means of solving the formidable problem of how to absorb the West Indian population of working age in useful activity.

CHAPTER XIII

THE PROBLEM OF EMPLOYMENT.

1. If a serious aggravation of the twin evils of unemployment and under-employment is to be avoided, a substantial and steady increase in the volume of economic activity in the West Indies is essential to keep pace with the growth in the population of working age. This increase in economic activity can only be secured in one or other of two ways; (1) through an increase in the external demand for West Indian products, (2) through an increase in the proportion of the population engaged in producing agricultural commodities or manufactured goods for West Indian consumption. Our review of the position in Chapter II has shown how discouraging is the prospect, on the basis of existing arrangements, under the former heading; and, whatever steps may be taken to improve this prospect, we are convinced that it would be disastrous in the long run for the West Indies to continue to depend so largely, indeed so nearly exclusively, on production for export. It may be that in some islands, notably Barbados, it will always be necessary to rely almost entirely upon sugar but, speaking generally, a reorientation of West Indian economic life in the direction of greater production for the domestic market is an indispensable objective.

2. The possibilities of increasing production for the West Indian market are partly agricultural and partly industrial, though as will appear there is no very sharp line between them. It will be convenient first to examine the possibilities of an industrial character, and to consider the issues of policy that arise in this connection.

1. Industrial Development and Local Protection.

3. The present very limited extent of industrial development has been described in Chapter II. In several of the larger Colonies we found keen interest in the idea of developing new industries. This was especially true of Jamaica, where the problem of unemployment is particularly acute, and where it would be natural to find greater possibilities of industrial expansion than elsewhere, in view of the comparatively large extent and population of the island. The most definite suggestions that were made to us in Jamaica were for the establishment of a cement factory, a condensed milk factory, a cornmeal industry, and for the extended manufacture of soap, margarine and lard substitutes. Of these proposals, it should be observed that all except the first are designed primarily to extend the markets or improve the prices of agricultural products.

4. The project of the condensed milk factory is in course of being realised. The factory is to be set up by the well-known concern, Nestlé's, under an arrangement by which they agree to sell milk at its present price, pay no excise duty for several years, and subsequently pay a small excise duty less than the present customs duty. The scheme thus involves the principle of moderate protection, the burden of which falls upon the Jamaica Government, in the form of loss of existing revenue, rather than on the consuming public.

5. Protection against external competition is a feature of most of the proposals for industrial development under discussion. Most of them also entail the further principle of Government enterprise or Government finance. Thus the scheme submitted to us for a cement factory in Jamaica was that the Government should provide the funds and conduct the enterprise through a nominated Board. It seemed to be regarded as hardly practicable to induce private individuals to risk their money in the enterprise, although the calculations as to costs, etc., that were put forward, indicated that the enterprise should be highly profitable, if secured, as was proposed, against competing imports. On our return to England we discussed the question of a cement factory in Jamaica with representatives of the Associated Portland Cement Company. We found that they had lately examined the possibility of putting up a works in the island. They informed us that the result of their investigation was that, on the basis of the present consumption of cement in Jamaica, a local works should be able to cover costs of production and capital charges, while selling at present prices and paying an excise duty equivalent to the existing customs duty; but allowing for the loss of the contribution to their British overheads that their present export sales provide, the proposition was not sufficiently attractive and assured to make them inclined to proceed with it. They agreed that the prospect might become materially more attractive if a much larger consumption of cement in Jamaica, as the result possibly of a continuous public works programme, could be assumed.

6. A cement works in Jamaica would not provide very much employment; it seems that only between 100 and 200 men would be directly employed. But the growth of urban unemployment is so serious that even small contributions to its solution should not be neglected; and the addition of even a small number of factory workers to the limited industrial element in the Jamaica population might serve an educative purpose, helping to make easier other forms of industrial activity. It will be observed that a local cement works should be able to pay an excise duty equivalent to the customs duty, as well as selling at existing prices, so that in this case no burden would

be thrown on either the Government or the consuming public. From the standpoint of Jamaica, therefore, the establishment of a cement works is a clearly desirable objective; and we do not think that the interests of the maintenance of British export trade, or employment in Great Britain, should be allowed to stand in the way of a development of which this can be said.

7. We are unable, however, to support the proposal that the Government should own and control the cement works, or provide the capital for it. A measure of uncertainty must necessarily attach to the success of the enterprise from the financial standpoint; and the financial outlook for the Jamaican Government is not such that it can afford to risk even comparatively small sums of money without good reason in speculative ventures. In our opinion, the most satisfactory means of establishing the cement industry in Jamaica would be that the enterprise should be established by one of the leading cement companies in this country. This would be the best way of ensuring that the enterprise was conducted with the requisite technical knowledge. We suggest therefore that the Government of Jamaica should enter into negotiations with such a company with a view to persuading them to establish a branch works.

8. It may be convenient to refer at this point to the project submitted to us in British Guiana for manufacturing wood-pulp for high-class paper from waliaba trees. In this case, there was no suggestion of Government conduct of the industry; the advocates of the project were themselves prepared to undertake it; but they asked for Government financial assistance to provide the necessary capital. We do not consider that an enterprise of this character, which is necessarily highly speculative, and the merits of which we cannot attempt to assess, forms an appropriate subject for assistance either by the Government of British Guiana or from Imperial funds. Generally, we regard it as undesirable that Governments in the West Indies should either conduct or finance speculative industrial enterprises.

9. But the same considerations do not apply to undertakings the primary purpose of which is to improve the markets for agricultural products. The projects to which we have already referred for the manufacture of corn-meal and coconut products in Jamaica belong to this category. The local manufacture of corn-meal is advocated with the object of displacing the imported corn-meal and flour which are now among the principal food imports in the West Indies and thus developing a market for locally-grown maize. The object of stimulating the local manufacture of soap, margarine and lard substitutes

is to improve the prices received by the coconut producers for their copra. These are both important objectives; the former represents one of the possible means of developing agricultural production for the home market; the latter, a means of improving the position of a depressed branch of the existing export agriculture. But both projects entail the application of protection, from which either the Government or the consuming public is likely to suffer; and it becomes important to consider how far it is appropriate that protectionist measures should be carried in the West Indies for the purposes that we have indicated.

10. We shall consider first the proposals for stimulating the manufacture of coconut products. For some years, in both Trinidad and Jamaica, the home market for edible oils has been secured for local production by prohibitive tariffs or prohibition of imports. In Trinidad, the protection given was conditional upon an arrangement under which the factories were required (1) to pay a fixed minimum price for copra, materially above the world level that has ruled for most of the intervening period, (2) to supply edible oils to the public at prices not exceeding those obtaining at the time the arrangement was made, and (3) to pay an excise duty equivalent to the customs duty on the edible oils previously imported. These various conditions have been fulfilled; and the only cost to the Trinidad public or Government of establishing the edible oil industry has been that arising from the fact that the prices of edible oils in other countries and in other West Indian Colonies have fallen materially since the arrangement was made, so that the public are now paying more than might otherwise have been the case. In Jamaica, the results have been far less satisfactory. The Government has suffered a substantial loss of revenue from the exclusion of imports, while the coconut growers, on the other hand, have failed to derive any material benefit. Statutory conditions as to the price of copra were not imposed, with the result that competition forced the price down to a level little better than that obtainable in export markets. The chief beneficiaries of the scheme have been a number of competing edible oil factories each operating on a scale far too small for efficiency, but succeeding none the less in making profits. Measures for the rationalisation of edible oil production and for the regulation of the price of copra appear to be essential in Jamaica if the main objectives of the exclusion of imports are to be secured. Proposals for effecting the needed reorganisation were receiving serious consideration during our visit; and it was out of these proposals that the idea arose of extending the reorganisation to include all the coconut product industries and of enlarging the range of the protection afforded correspondingly.

11. It was seriously claimed by the Development and Marketing Officer of Jamaica that if the coconut product industries were reorganised as proposed and assured of the local market, it would be feasible in the case of laundry soap, and margarine and lard compounds, as well as edible oils, to fulfil the three conditions which on the surface at least have been satisfied by the edible oil industry of Trinidad; i.e., to sell to the public at existing prices, to pay a fixed price for copra remunerative to the growers and to pay excise duties that would yield as large a revenue as the import duties obtained from coconut products before the edible oil industry was established. We do not possess the expert knowledge that would be necessary to decide whether this claim could be made good. But it does not seem to us prima facie improbable that it could. If so, the project is clearly a very desirable one from the standpoint of Jamaica; and, as in the case of cement, we do not think that considerations of employment in the soap and margarine industry of the United Kingdom should be allowed to stand in the way of its adoption. We think it important, moreover, that the consideration of the project on its merits should not be unduly prejudiced by the unfortunate past record of the edible oils experiment in Jamaica. If the project is held to be feasible, it might well be that the best way of giving effect to it would be a scheme which would provide for the participation of British manufacturing interests. On the other hand, we are of opinion that it should be an essential condition of any project for increasing the range of protection for the coconut product industries that there should be a fair prospect of realising the three conditions mentioned. The primary object of such proposals is to raise the average price of copra for the growers; and it is uncertain how far this would stimulate additional output or employment. This is not an object for the sake of which it would be justifiable in our judgment for the Government to incur a substantial loss of revenue which would have to be made good in other ways, or to impose substantial burdens on the consuming public. The volume of employment that would be provided in the factories would be far too small to be a material factor.

12. In the smaller West Indian islands, the local consumption of coconut products is insufficient to provide an economic basis for a factory. But in the Windward Islands we found considerable discussion of the idea that the Windwards should co-operate with Trinidad in a scheme under which part of the copra of the Windwards would be sent to Trinidad for conversion into coconut products, which would then be returned to the Windwards for sale in the local market in place of the coconut products or similar commodities now imported from

Great Britain and elsewhere. Any proposal for inter-island co-operation deserves sympathetic consideration; but the economic feasibility of this project appears to depend on the assumption that the Governments of the Windward Islands would forego the revenue they now derive from duties on imported coconut products. These Governments are not in a position to afford this loss of revenue; and in any case, for the reasons given above, we do not think that they ought to incur such a loss for the purpose in question.

13. We next consider the possibility of establishing mills in Jamaica for the manufacture of corn-meal from maize. This idea comprises large, though necessarily uncertain, potentialities. The development of maize-growing might conceivably play an important part in the reorientation of West Indian agriculture in the directions of mixed farming and a greater production for the home market, the desirability of which we urge in other Chapters. But maize-growing on any extensive scale, and the manufacture of corn-meal, would both represent essentially new undertakings in the West Indies; and a considerable period must be expected to elapse before they could be established on a strictly economic basis. At present, moreover, the public is accustomed to consume wheat-flour, and it is only gradually that a natural reluctance to accept corn-meal as a satisfactory substitute could be overcome. A strong case can thus be made out on the lines of the ordinary " infant industry " argument for fostering the development of corn-meal manufacture by some degree of protection.

14. But flour forms an important element in the dietary of the West Indian population; and no plan that required the public to consume corn-meal, instead of flour, at an appreciably higher price could in our opinion be justified under ordinary peace conditions. Whatever may be done to develop production for the home market in the West Indies, the majority of the population must continue to depend, for a long period, if not indefinitely, on export agriculture; and this export agriculture is unlikely to be able to command high prices for its products, or consequentially to provide high earnings for its labourers or peasants. It is important, therefore, that the cost of living should be kept as low as possible. A very high proportion of the revenue of all West Indian Colonies is derived, as has been shown in Chapter VI, from import duties on articles of popular consumption; and these import duties are a material factor in increasing the cost and lowering the standard of living. The tendency, moreover, in most Colonies, under the pressure of adverse economic and consequently financial conditions, is towards an increase in these duties. In these circumstances we regard it as an essential condition of any acceptable scheme for

encouraging corn-meal manufacture that the corn-meal should be sold to the public at a price equivalent to that at which imported flour is sold.

15. We think, however, that it would not be unreasonable for the Government of Jamaica (or any other West Indian Government) to refrain from imposing an excise duty on corn-meal to compensate for the loss of revenue on imports of wheaten flour or corn-meal. The present import duties on flour in Jamaica are about 2s. per 100 lb. on foreign flour and 1s. 6d. per 100 lb. on Empire flour. Exemption from excise duty would thus give the corn-meal industry a moderate measure of protection. In proportion as the industry developed and succeeded in displacing imports of flour, the Government would of course lose revenue; but having regard to the potential value of the industry to the economy of the island, and to the possibility that it might eventually become sufficiently economic to enable it to pay an excise duty without raising the price to the public, we are of opinion that assistance to this extent would be fully justified. We have sought in these paragraphs to indicate the limits of the protection that would be justifiable. We cannot attempt to pronounce as to whether it would be practicable to establish a corn-meal industry with this measure of assistance. Nor do we suggest that ordinary tariff protection is necessarily the best method to employ. We understand that in July, 1939, the Government of Jamaica, with the assent of the Legislative Council, took the necessary steps to erect a corn-meal factory which is to be financed by public funds and to be operated by the Development and Marketing Division of the Department of Agriculture. This new venture is, it appears, to be supported, for the time being at any rate, by prohibiting the import of corn-meal except under licence. This represents a very interesting experiment, which war conditions may do something to assist. In the long run, however, its success should, we suggest, be judged by the criterion that we have indicated.

16. The principle which we have just suggested for corn-meal may be extended so as to supply a general indication of the maximum amount of protection that it is expedient to give for the promotion of West Indian industries. Exigencies of revenue have already led all West Indian Governments to impose duties as high as they think expedient on most imported commodities that are widely consumed; and it follows, as a general presumption, that it would be unwise to raise the prices of such commodities to the public any further for the necessarily speculative purpose of establishing new industries. These import duties provide a moderate degree of protection to local industry when corresponding excise duties are not imposed. Where excise duties are imposed, it is a legitimate matter for consideration in

each case whether they should be removed or reduced so as to encourage local industry, having regard to the possible importance of the industry and the ability of the Government of the Colony to incur a sacrifice of revenue. This principle should apply, we think, even in the case of dress-making which, on broad social grounds, it is particularly desirable to develop so as to provide more varied employment openings for women.

17. But there is something to be added as to the methods by which in certain cases protection may most appropriately be given. West Indian manufacturing industries must necessarily be small and weak, whereas their external competitors are often large and powerful. In certain lines of industry there is an obvious danger that local factories established behind no stronger shelter than revenue import duties might be destroyed by a few years' campaign of intensive underselling from overseas, undertaken for the purpose of destroying them. It was for this reason that the methods of prohibition of imports and prohibitive duties were adopted in Jamaica and Trinidad to establish the edible oil industry, although the interests of the consumer were safeguarded by requiring the local industries to sell at prices no higher than those prevailing at the time the schemes were introduced. It is possible that the method of the quantitative limitation of imports, with similar safeguards for the consumer, may prove the most satisfactory method, from the local West Indian standpoint, for developing certain other industries, such as the manufacture of corn-meal. We are aware that it has been for some years an object of British commercial policy to secure the modification, and if possible the abandonment, of the quantitative restrictions imposed by foreign countries on imports of manufactured goods. At the same time, the system of quantitative restrictions maintained by many Colonies, including the West Indies, on the import of Japanese textiles, was imposed at the request of the British Government and has proved of great value to the British textile industry. In these circumstances, we are of opinion that schemes for the development of local West Indian industries, based on the method of the quantitative limitation of imports, provided they contain safeguards for the consumer against an undue increase of price, ought not to be disallowed on the ground that they appear to run counter to a general principle of British commercial policy. Nor, we would add, should a general dislike of this method be permitted to prejudice a fair consideration of such schemes upon their merits.

2. Public Works and the Tourist Trade.

18. As we have previously observed, most of the proposals to establish new industries, whether by protective means or otherwise, are directed to the purpose of improving the market

for agricultural produce; and it is unlikely that any of them would employ more than a trifling number of labourers. A far more substantial possibility of increasing the amount of employment of a quasi-industrial character, at any rate for a limited period, is that which would arise from the development of public works programmes, whether for the improvement of roads or housing, or for new schemes of irrigation, drainage, etc. The embarrassed financial position of most West Indian Governments makes it difficult for them at present to undertake extensive programmes of this character, though in Jamaica the formidable growth of unemployment, particularly of urban employment, has compelled the Government in the past year to spend considerable sums of money on relief-works. The Government of Trinidad, on the other hand, is in an exceptionally strong financial position, thanks to the expanding revenue which it derives from the oil industry. It has thus been able to spend substantial sums in recent years on road improvements, housing schemes, etc., and it has lately undertaken a larger development programme, known locally as the Five Year Plan. It is doubtless largely owing to this developmental expenditure that the problem of unemployment is far less acute in Trinidad than in any other important West Indian Colony: and that the serious plight of the cocoa industry expresses itself in the form of localised distress, rather than in a general overcrowding of the labour market.

19. Some public works may contribute, of course, to productive capacity or future development. But the direct employment that is provided by other programmes of public works, however desirable, that are financed by borrowing and concentrated into a limited period of years, is likely to be of a correspondingly limited duration. The Trinidad Five Year Plan is apparently, at any rate, of this character. But vast scope will still remain, when the present programme has been completed, for further useful developmental expenditure. Finance, however, is necessarily a governing factor; and though the scope for useful development expenditure is as great elsewhere, no other West Indian Government could prudently undertake a programme on similar lines, unless something were done to strengthen its financial resources.

20. We propose later, in Chapter XX, the establishment of a West Indian Welfare Fund to be financed by a substantial annual grant from the British Exchequer, for the purpose of assisting the improvement of social services in the West Indies. If this plan is put into effect, the West Indian Colonies should be able to undertake larger programmes, for such purposes as improved housing, than are now within their resources. In addition to its primary object of promoting the development of social services, the plan should thus do something to provide more employment.

21. The development of the tourist trade, comprising as it does a demand for hotel services, transport facilities and the like is another possible means of increasing the volume of employment outside agriculture. In the main West Indian opinion seems fully alive to the potentialities of an increased tourist trade; in some Colonies, indeed, it is perhaps inclined to exaggerate them. In several of the smaller islands, the present scale of the tourist traffic is far less than the attractions that they have to offer would justify, largely owing to the scanty means available for getting to and from these islands. The proposals that we make in Chapter XIX for improving communications may help to overcome this difficulty.

3. General.

22. If any substantial increase in the volume of production for the home market is to be secured, it is evident that this must come mainly from agriculture. For this purpose, we believe that the substitution, wherever possible, of mixed farming methods for the single-crop system of agriculture now predominant in the West Indies and the extension of peasant agriculture along appropriate lines will be required. We consider in later Chapters how these ends can best be promoted.

23. But progress in these directions must, on the most optimistic view, be slow. The successful application of new farming methods will require the widespread diffusion of greater agricultural knowledge; and this must depend largely on the improvement and extension of the services for agricultural instruction. Peasant settlement, moreover, particularly if it is to be adapted to production for the local market, must be carefully planned, and cannot without grave risks, be pushed forward at a rapid pace.

24. In the meantime, the West Indian populations have to live; and openings must be found for the rapidly growing numbers of working age. For a long period to come, these openings can only be found in the staple branches of export agriculture. It is thus an urgent and inexorable necessity for most of the West Indian Colonies that they should be enabled somehow to secure an expansion of the volume of their export sales in face of the discouraging market prospects that have been described in Chapter II. Nor is this all. The standard of living in the West Indies is at present lamentably low; and any material improvement in this standard would require both a reduction in under-employment and an upward movement in wage-rates. Yet, at the present level of selling-prices, the maintenance of even existing rates of wages in several branches of export agriculture would be a matter of considerable difficulty

without special measures of assistance. The aim must therefore be twofold; to increase the volume of exports of West Indian agricultural commodities, and to improve the prices at which these commodities are sold.

25. The principal suggestion made to us in the West Indies for accomplishing these ends was that the preferential assistance given to West Indian products in the United Kingdom market should be increased and extended, or as regards commodities for which it was recognised that preferences would be futile, that assistance should be given in other ways. We shall consider how far it is practicable and reasonable to give such assistance in the two immediately following Chapters. It is convenient at this stage to consider other possible means of increasing the volume of export sales.

4. Marketing.

26. The first of these is an improvement in the marketing of some of the minor agricultural commodities. Efficient marketing is perhaps especially important in regard to citrus fruit and limes. If the fruit is to find regular purchasers in overseas markets, its quality must be reliable; and to ensure this, efficient methods of selection, grading, preparation, packing and inspection are essential. Failing these, a large proportion of the fruit shipped may be wasted. How important a factor wastage may be can be gathered from the following extract from a report issued in March, 1939, by the Food Products Sub-Committee of the Colonial Empire Marketing Board, dealing with the possibility of increasing the sale of fresh limes:—

> "The experimental consignments of limes from Jamaica to this country last year, covering 4,105 cases, disclosed a lamentable state of affairs in the matter of wastage. From figures furnished to the Board, it appears that, out of a total of 505 cases drawn from cold store in London for purposes of re-packing, 262 cases were lost owing to the bad condition of the fruit, i.e., over 50 per cent."

27. It is also essential that those responsible for the export of the fruit should maintain close contact with the markets of the importing countries, in order that the fruit may be packed in the manner best suited to the market requirements, that shipments may be made at the most favourable times, and that knowledge of changes in the varieties of the fruit required may be communicated quickly to the growers. These considerations make it important to maintain an agency or office in the consuming countries, capable of providing reliable intelligence.

28. When a trade is on as small a scale as is the export from West Indian Colonies of citrus or limes, it is impossible to expect such services to be efficiently rendered by ordinary

Chapter XIII.

export merchants. By far the most desirable arrangement is that the whole business of export should be in the hands of a single organisation. There are two possible forms that a single organisation may take, (1) a co-operative organisation of producers, (2) an organisation financed and controlled by the Government.

29. Various co-operative organisations of agricultural producers are to be found in the West Indies; and in Jamaica at one period special steps were taken by the Government to encourage the formation of co-operative organisations in several branches of agriculture. But these organisations have not fulfilled the hopes that were placed in them, largely for two reasons; first, that they never succeeded in including all or nearly all the producers, or indeed in commanding the wholehearted loyalty of all their members; second, the co-operative principle entails the keeping of separate accounts with each member, and when, as is usually the case with the minor agricultural products of the West Indies, the output of the average producer is extremely small, this means a heavy overhead expense.

30. The recent tendency in Jamaica has been accordingly to move away from the co-operative method to that of marketing organisations financed and controlled or supervised by the Government. A special Marketing Division has been set up under the Department of Agriculture, with the functions of promoting orderly marketing in established trades and of developing markets for new or neglected products. Under the former heading, it is hoped to evolve acceptable schemes for both citrus fruit and coconuts, by which the advantages of a single export organisation may be secured. Practical difficulties arising from the divergent interests and views of different producers have still, however, to be overcome. Under the latter head, the Marketing Division does not confine its attention to export commodities. It has done useful work in stimulating the production of potatoes ("Irish potatoes" as they are called in Jamaica in contrast to sweet potatoes) for the Kingston market, by supplying suitable seed potatoes and giving short-term credit facilities to growers, and by making special arrangements with retailers for the sale of the product. It is clear that energetic marketing activities of this character will be essential in the West Indies generally to the success of policies aiming at increased production for the local market.

31. In connection, however, with marketing organisations designed to increase export sales, it is important to avoid mutually destructive competition between the different West Indian Colonies and also indeed with other parts of the Colonial Empire. This object can best be secured by the maintenance

of close contact between the marketing organisations of the West Indian Colonies and the Colonial Empire Marketing Board.

5. Inter-Island Trade.

32. The development of trade between the different West Indian Colonies represents another possible means of increasing the outlets for their produce. At present, however, the commodities that one West Indian Colony imports are not mostly of a type that other West Indian Colonies produce on a scale sufficient to satisfy their own requirements. Apart from petroleum, the most important instance to the contrary is rice, which Trinidad imports on a substantial scale, and which British Guiana grows extensively. It was suggested to us in the latter Colony that Trinidad might be asked to give British Guiana preferential treatment for its rice as compared with Burma and India. But such a step, even if it were acceptable to the Government of Trinidad, would be contrary to the accepted principle against the discriminatory tariff treatment of goods from different parts of the Empire. The same principle precludes the adoption of a larger idea which from some points of view is attractive, namely, that there should be complete free trade between the different West Indian Colonies. It is one of the arguments that can be urged in favour of the political federation of the different West Indian Colonies, or of some of them, that this obstacle to mutual Free Trade would thereby be overcome. But for the reason already given, namely, that one West Indian Colony seldom produces what another imports, it is improbable under existing economic conditions that the advantage that would result would be very substantial.

33. But the position may become very different if considerable progress is made with the development of West Indian agriculture along the lines of mixed farming and greater production of foodstuffs for local consumption. It is possible, for example, that Jamaica might develop the production of meat and the growing of maize for corn-meal manufacture on a scale sufficient to supply not only the greater part of her own needs, but the needs of other Colonies such as Barbados, which may continue to depend more largely upon export agriculture. The development of local food production and the development of inter-island trade may thus go hand in hand with one another and assist one another.

34. The difficulties of communications in the West Indies are at present an obstacle to trade not only from Colony to Colony but between different islands forming parts of the same Colony, notably the different Leeward Islands. Between these very small islands there are perhaps relatively greater possibilities of developing mutually advantageous trade, as for example by

the export of cattle from Tortola to Anguilla, than exist as between the larger Colonies. Certain of the proposals which we make in Chapter XIX for improved communications are designed to overcome this obstacle.

CHAPTER XIV.

PREFERENTIAL ASSISTANCE.

1. Great Britain is the principal market for West Indian exports; and several branches of West Indian agriculture derive substantial benefits from the preferential tariff treatment that Great Britain accords to imports from the Empire. Many proposals were submitted to us during our tour of the West Indies for increasing existing preferences or for granting new ones. Such proposals deserve in our judgment sympathetic consideration. It must not be forgotten that the preferences which Great Britain gives to the Colonies form part of a reciprocal system, and that the West Indian Colonies in particular give preferences to British manufactures which are of great benefit to hard-pressed British exporting industries. The cotton industry, in particular, benefits not only from West Indian preferences, but from the quota restrictions on competing imports from Japan.

2. But preferential duties are not always a practicable means of giving effective help to colonial producers. In the first place, there is a fundamental economic factor to be considered, namely the relation between the production of a commodity in the British Empire, and its consumption in Great Britain or other Empire markets. When the Empire production of a commodity greatly exceeds the Empire consumption, preferences in the United Kingdom market are likely to prove futile.

3. The point can be illustrated by the example of cocoa. A preference of one-sixth of the full rate of duty is actually given to imports of cocoa from Empire countries. But the Gold Coast and Nigeria together produce more than four times the amount of cocoa that is consumed in the United Kingdom. The greater part of the colonial output of cocoa has accordingly to be exported to other markets, notably the United States, where it has to compete on equal terms with the cocoa of foreign countries, such as Brazil. In these circumstances, the British preference fails to secure a higher price even for that part of the colonial output which is sent to the United Kingdom. For British purchasers have only to offer colonial producers a price as high as that which can be obtained from sales to foreign markets in order to secure, under competitive conditions, all the cocoa that they require to buy. In practice, therefore, the British preference serves merely to exclude foreign supplies (apart from certain special qualities) from the British market, and to divert them to foreign markets, without exerting any effect on the price of cocoa.

4. The position is very different as regards commodities of which the British public consume much greater quantities than the Empire produces. The normal effect of a preference on such commodities is to raise the price received by Empire producers above that received by foreign producers by the full amount of the preference. It is possible, of course, that the world price itself may be somewhat reduced, if the preference has the effect of increasing Empire production and thereby adding to the total world supply. But though the benefit accruing from the preference in the form of a higher price may thereby be reduced, the increased volume of production is itself an advantage to Empire producers, particularly to those faced like the West Indies with a serious unemployment problem. There is thus no question as to the real advantages which Empire producers derive from preferences on commodities of which Great Britain consumes much more than the Empire produces. When Empire production and British or Empire consumption are fairly equally balanced, the efficacy of a preference becomes an uncertain matter, depending on the technical details of the market for the particular commodity.

5. Apart from the question of their efficacy, the concession of new or increased preferences may be open to serious objection on the ground that they would conflict with the aims of British commercial policy or perhaps run counter to the express provisions of commercial treaties. The Trade Agreement of November, 1938, between the United Kingdom and the United States is of especial importance in this connection.

6. With these general considerations in mind, we turn to consider the various proposals for increased preferential assistance that were submitted to us in the West Indies. Sugar is a commodity of which Great Britain consumes much more than the Empire produces, and in respect of which colonial producers already derive large benefits from preferences. The question of the policy that should be pursued in regard to sugar is, however, so important and so complex that we think it well to devote a separate Chapter (Chapter XV) to its consideration. Cocoa, as we have already pointed out, is an outstanding example of a commodity upon which preferences of the ordinary type are futile; and we found that this fact was fully appreciated by the cocoa growers of Trinidad and Grenada. In the latter colony, however, the suggestion was made that it would not be unreasonable to give preferential treatment to West Indian cocoa as compared with that of the Gold Coast and Nigeria; and a proposal was submitted to us on behalf of the Agricultural Association of Grenada that British cocoa manufacturers should be required by law to use a specified proportion of West Indian cocoa, the price of which would also be fixed by law at a level sufficient to ensure a reasonable return to

growers. Any scheme upon these lines would necessarily entail discrimination between the West Indian Colonies on the one hand and the West African Colonies on the other; and we are unable to recommend the adoption of so novel and so dangerous a principle. We make suggestions in Chapter XVI upon other lines, for giving some external assistance to the Grenada cocoa industry.

7. An increase in the preference on bananas was strongly urged upon us both in Jamaica and since our return to England, but before the outbreak of war, by the Jamaica Banana Producers' Association. No duty is imposed on imports of bananas from Empire countries, so that the proposal made is that the duty on foreign bananas should be increased from its present figure of £2 10s. 0d. per ton to £5 per ton. This proposal has been endorsed by the unanimous vote of the Legislative Council of Jamaica.

8. The ground on which this proposal is urged is the importance, in view of the rapid spread of leaf-spot disease, of securing to the grower, by excluding bananas from foreign countries, a better price than he has obtained in recent years. Leaf-spot affects the grower in two ways; it reduces the quantity and impairs the quality of his crop, and it makes it necessary for him to incur heavy expenditure on spraying in order to check the further progress of the disease. There can be no doubt that unless helped by a rise in the price of bananas above that of recent years, or by substantial assistance in some other form, a considerable proportion of producers, particularly those of the small settler type, would be unable to defray the costs of spraying and would be forced before long to abandon cultivation.

9. As a consequence, however, partly of the diminished supply of bananas and partly of war conditions, the price has already risen by more than the desired amount since the representations to which we have referred were made. Under the arrangements that have been made for the determination of prices, the growers are paid a price for their bananas in Jamaica which moves up and down (subject to a minimum) with the wholesale price in London. Thus every increase in shipping costs serves automatically to increase the price received by the Jamaican growers. Since May, 1939, the London price has increased by nearly £4 per ton, as against the suggested increase in the rate of duty of £2 10s. 0d. per ton; and the grower in Jamaica is now receiving as a consequence a substantially higher price per count bunch than was contemplated as the result of an increased preference when the demand for it was put forward. Under war conditions a fall in the London price seems unlikely. In these circumstances there remains no good reason for increasing the duty on

Chapter XIV.

foreign bananas, which indeed have only been imported on an inconsiderable scale since the war began. The question is one which may well deserve reconsideration on its merits when peace is restored, if the London wholesale price should then undergo a sharp decline. It is impossible at this stage to foresee all the factors that may then be relevant. It is worth noting, however, that bananas belong to the intermediate category of commodity, the Empire production of which does not differ greatly from the amount consumed in the British and Canadian markets. If it were not, therefore, for the special conditions affecting the marketing of bananas, the efficacy of a preference might be somewhat doubtful. But bananas are a fruit which cannot easily be transported over long distances in good condition. They require a special type of ship, with special facilities for refrigeration; and in order to justify the maintenance of a service of ships of the required type, the collection of supplies in adequate quantities from regular sources must be assured.

10. In developing the necessary organisation for shipping and marketing, as well as in developing the consumption of bananas in our British market, the United Fruit Company of Boston played a valuable constructive rôle, and this company, together with a connected company, the Standard Fruit Company, enjoyed for a long period a virtual monopoly of the trade. Dissatisfaction with the prices paid to growers led to the formation of the Jamaica Banana Producers' Association, which in its original form was a co-operative organisation of growers, and which built up a rival marketing organisation. After a period of competition, the so-called Tripartite Agreement was concluded, which provides for co-operation in the use of ships between the three companies, and which fixes the prices paid for bananas in Jamaica on a basis which is recognised to be very favourable to the growers. The existence of the British preference on Empire bananas was undoubtedly a factor of great importance in promoting an agreement upon such satisfactory terms. This was not so much because imports of foreign bananas were penalized by the comparatively small duty of £2 10s. 0d. per ton, as because the duty was accepted by the United Fruit Company as a sign of the determination of the British Government to safeguard the interests of colonial producers. Since the conclusion of the agreement, the United Fruit Company have accordingly displayed a helpful and constructive attitude in matters concerned with the welfare of the Jamaica banana industry and have worked in co-operation with the Banana Producers' Association. The maintenance of this spirit of mutual co-operation is a most important matter for the future of the industry; and it is in this light that questions as to the alteration of the duty on foreign bananas should be considered.

11. In the meantime it is probable that war conditions will ensure for Jamaican growers a price which will bring them substantial compensation for the ravages of leaf-spot; and it is important that the favourable conditions should be utilised to establish an efficient system of spraying and leaf-spot control. If further assistance to the industry should prove desirable, this should be given, as we suggest elsewhere, in the form of financial help to meet the costs of spraying.*

12. It should be observed that in regard to bananas Canada, also, gives a preference of 50 cents per count bunch which is of value to West Indian producers. It is to the Canadian market that the bananas produced in Dominica, Trinidad and the Windward Islands are mainly shipped, through the agency of a subsidiary of the United Fruit Company.

13. The citrus industry was another on behalf of which representations were made to us in Jamaica for increased preferential assistance. So far as fresh fruit is concerned, Palestine is the chief competitor of the West Indies in the British market, and as an " A " Mandated Territory, Palestine is not eligible for the preferential treatment which Empire countries receive. West Indian citrus thus already enjoys a preference over Palestine citrus in the British market equivalent to about 2s. 10d. per case. It was urged in Jamaica that the advantage of this preference is practically cancelled out by the high freight-rates that must be paid on fruit shipped from the West Indies; but, in the main at least, this must be regarded as natural disadvantage, attributable to the need for refrigerated space when fruit is shipped over a long distance. Although Palestine does not rank for preferential purposes as part of the Empire, Great Britain has a responsibility for her welfare; and she is confronted with economic problems which are in some respects not dissimilar to those of the West Indies. We are unable, therefore, to support the appeal for an increased duty on fresh citrus from foreign sources.

14. It was also suggested that an increased preference should be given upon canned grapefruit, in order to enable Jamaica to build up an export trade in canned fruit to the London market. The principal exporter of canned grapefruit is the United States; and the Anglo-American Trade Agreement provides that canned grapefruit as well as grapefruit juice shall be admitted free of duty to the British market. For the time being, at all events, this must be regarded as a fatal obstacle to the proposal.

15. Two further proposals that were made to us for preferential assistance are also precluded by the terms of the Anglo-American Trade Agreement. The Agreement provides that cotton shall be admitted free, and this makes it impossible to

---

* See also note at end of Chapter XVI (page 312).

give preferential aid to the West Indian Sea Island cotton industry. It also provides that the preference given to Empire tobacco shall not be increased, and foreshadows the possibility that it may be reduced after 1942. In these and in all other cases, however, where the United States is the principal competitor, the fall in the exchange-value of the pound should serve to improve the competitive position of West Indian and other colonial producers.

16. For most other West Indian exports, as for example, coconut products and arrowroot, preferences would be nugatory for the basic reason that Empire production greatly exceeds Empire consumption. The field in which it is feasible to assist the West Indies by additional preferences is thus extremely narrow, and for the reasons we have given, we find ourselves unable to make any definite recommendation in favour of increased preferences upon any of the commodities that we have so far considered. We have still, however, to examine the question in relation to the most important commodity of all—namely sugar.

CHAPTER XV.

SUGAR POLICY.

1. The International Sugar Agreement.

1. The present position has been described briefly in Chapter II. Colonial sugar producers receive substantial preferential assistance in the United Kingdom market and also in the Canadian market. Partly as the result of this assistance, there was a very large increase in the production of sugar in the West Indies between 1932 and 1937. But this expansion has since been checked by the operation of the International Sugar Agreement, which came into force in 1937, and which limits the amount of sugar that can be exported from the Colonial Empire to an assigned quota.

2. We have shown in preceding Chapters how vital it is to secure expanding employment outlets for the rapidly growing populations of the West Indies, how difficult it must be for a long time to come to provide such outlets on a sufficient scale except by an increase in the exports of agricultural commodities, how unfavourable is the outlook for most branches of export agriculture other than sugar, and how limited are the measures that we are able to recommend for assisting them. In these circumstances the restriction on the further expansion of the sugar industry imposed by the International Sugar Agreement is, or at any rate would have been but for the outbreak of war, a most serious matter for the West Indian Colonies.

3. The sugar agreement is one of many international regulation schemes, which have been put into effect in recent years, and which apply to commodities as diverse as rubber, tea, tin and copper. The object of these schemes is to raise the prices of the commodities concerned to a remunerative level; and the general policy of trying, in the case of primary commodities, to achieve this end by means of agreements between the various producing countries to regulate their output or their exports received the blessing of the World Economic Conference of 1933. The schemes have succeeded in varying degrees in raising prices; and, inasmuch as British Colonies are important producers of all the restricted commodities, the international regulation schemes, regarded as a whole, have proved of great advantage to the British Colonial Empire.

4. But the sugar scheme differs in material respects from the others that have been mentioned. In the first place sugar is a commodity the production of which has long been artificially fostered by many countries by means of protection, subsidies, preferential tariffs, and other expedients; and since the war of

1914-18, and more especially since 1930, there has been a wide extension and a marked intensification of these measures of state assistance. A position has been reached which was thus described in 1935 by the Wilfrid Greene Committee* that inquired into the position of the United Kingdom Sugar Industry:—

" To-day, therefore, practically the only countries which are producing sugar without state assistance in one form or another are Java, Peru, and Santo Domingo, and these together provide not more than 5 per cent. of the world's current output."

Nor is this all. Most of the principal countries of the world have closed their markets almost altogether to sugar imports from foreign countries. This is true not only of countries like Germany, Russia and Italy, that pursue self-sufficient economic policies. France reserves her market for her domestic beet-sugar production and for the cane-sugar of her colonies. The United States similarly reserves her market by means of a system of import quotas for her domestic production and for imports from her colonial territories, from the Phillipines and from Cuba, whose sugar she admits at preferential rates of duty. It is true that she allocates a trifling quota to imports from " foreign countries other than Cuba," but this amounts to less than two-fifths of one per cent. of the United States consumption. The so-called " free market " for sugar, limited as it is to those countries that normally obtain an appreciable part of their supplies from foreign countries on non-preferential terms, accounts for only a small fraction, perhaps about 12 per cent. of the total world production. Great Britain is by far the most important single element in the " free market," and Empire countries constitute about half of it.

5. Great Britain during the last 17 years has adopted the continental policy of subsidizing a beet-sugar industry: but the greater part of the British requirements of sugar is met by imports which come partly from foreign countries, partly from the Dominions of Australia and South Africa, and partly from the Colonial Empire. The following table shows the relative importance of the domestic beet-sugar output and of imports from these three sources, during recent years:—

UNITED KINGDOM—PRODUCTION AND IMPORTS OF SUGAR.

	1934 Tons	1935 Tons	1936 Tons	1937 Tons	1938 Tons
Production of Beet Sugar	615,000	487,000	537,000	391,000	298,000
Imports from Foreign Countries	969,000	1,113,000	1,161,000	891,000	1,179,000
Imports from Dominions	423,278	395,167	452,396	572,798	595,695
Imports from Colonial Empire	520,154	407,344	598,417	752,517	602,934

* United Kingdom Sugar Industry Inquiry Committee. Report published in 1935 as Cmd. 4871.

6. Three observations should be made upon these figures: —

(1) It will be observed that there are large variations from year to year in the amounts of sugar obtained from these different sources.

(2) Canada is a large importer of colonial sugar, taking about 400,000 tons per year from Empire countries. The total exports of sugar from the British Colonies are therefore much larger than the figures in the final row of the above table.

(3) The United Kingdom exports each year a substantial quantity of refined sugar; and for the purpose of this export trade the refineries are allowed in effect (by a system of drawbacks) to import sugar free of duty. They naturally import foreign sugar for this purpose. It would be difficult indeed to retain the export trade in refined sugar, unless the raw sugar required for it could be obtained at the lowest world prices. Thus a large part of the foreign sugar imported, amounting in most years to rather more than 350,000 tons, is subsequently re-exported in a refined form.

7. None the less, the amount of foreign sugar retained for consumption in the United Kingdom remains substantial. In these circumstances, the leading part which the British Government took in promoting the international agreement entails something of a paradox. For we were endeavouring thereby to raise the price of foreign sugar against ourselves. A reasonable price for Empire producers could, in theory at all events, have been secured in other ways at less expense to the combined interests of the British revenue and the consuming public. There were, however, various considerations appealing in different degrees to different interests, that secured general support in Great Britain for the policy of an international regulation scheme. Since these considerations represent essential factors in the sugar problem, of which account must be taken in considering future developments of policy, it will be useful to enumerate them.

8. First, there was the prevalent view that the raising of the world prices of primary commodities was an essential condition of economic recovery. At the World Economic Conference of 1933 this view had been generally endorsed, and international restriction schemes had been indicated as the most appropriate and practicable remedy. The International Sugar Agreement thus appealed, as a constructive measure, inspired by an international outlook, to those who were uneasy at the strong trend throughout the world towards economic nationalism or economic imperialism.

9. Secondly, the Agreement, while limiting the amount of colonial sugar that could be produced, offered the hope of improving its price; and as prices had been barely remunerative for some years previously, this consideration naturally made a strong appeal to the sugar producers of the West Indies and other British Colonies. It is true that a better price for colonial sugar might conceivably have been secured in ways that would not have checked the expansion of production, as for example by readjusting the preferences given to colonial sugar, perhaps on a sliding-scale basis related to the world price. But as will appear in a moment, there was no possibility of inducing the British Treasury to accept any such plan. In these circumstances, most colonial sugar producers were inclined to welcome the International Agreement.

10. Thirdly, the restriction on the expansion of colonial sugar production served to safeguard the revenue accruing to the British Exchequer from the import duties upon sugar. The steady increase in colonial production during the preceding years had been costly to the Exchequer, which lost the amount of the Imperial Preference, i.e., £3 15s., upon every ton by which Empire sugar displaced foreign sugar in the British market. Moreover, Your Majesty's Government had recently agreed to provide additional assistance for the colonial sugar industry, through the system of colonial sugar certificates which will be described later. This supplementary assistance had been granted in the belief that it was essential in order to avert a large-scale abandonment of sugar production in the West Indies and perhaps elsewhere in the British Colonies, with grave social consequences. Yet no sooner was the life of the industry thus saved than it proceeded to display astonishing powers of growth at a serious cost to the pocket of its benefactor. The fact that an international regulation scheme would check this growth was thus a strong argument in its favour from the standpoint of the British revenue.

11. Fourthly, the Treasury dislike of an indefinite increase in colonial sugar production was shared, from a different standpoint, by the London sugar market. In respect of sugar as of many other commodities, London has long filled the rôle of an international market, in which buyers and sellers from all parts of the world are brought together. Sugar, for example, that is produced in Cuba or other foreign countries may be sold to purchasers in the Baltic or the East through the medium of the London market. Various British interests, including banking, insurance and shipping, in addition to the sugar-brokers, receive remuneration for the services that they render in connection with these transactions. The international business of the London sugar market has undergone a serious decline since 1930; and it was feared in Mincing Lane that the position of

London as an effective international market might be destroyed altogether, unless a substantial part of the British requirements of sugar continued to be met by imports from foreign countries. If this were to happen, preferential assistance might become powerless to avert a fall in the price of colonial sugar to a ruinous level, for reasons which the argument in paragraph 22 will make clear.

12. The International Sugar Agreement came into force in September, 1937, and was to remain in operation for five years. The Agreement permits withdrawal by any party that is involved in hostilities; so that its provisions no longer possess the same binding force that they had when we were in the West Indies. But, whatever happens to the Agreement itself during the war period, the problems and difficulties which it was designed to meet are likely to re-emerge after the war is over. It is important therefore to examine how much weight should properly be attached to the considerations that have just been outlined.

2. The Disadvantages of Increased Colonial Sugar Production.

13. It will be convenient to review those considerations in the reverse order to that in which they have been set out, and to begin with the apprehensions of the London sugar market. The most essential condition of an effective market is that it should be *wide*; that the transactions undertaken in it should be so numerous and so frequent that both buyers and sellers can feel assured that they can deal at any time at the prices quoted, and that these prices are likely to be as favourable to them as those that they could obtain elsewhere. In regard to sugar, this means that if foreign purchasers are to continue to make use of the London market, they must feel sure of finding there at all seasons of the year large quantities of *foreign* sugar, since Empire sugar owing to our preferential duties commands a higher price. The use of the London market by foreign buyers and sellers helps, of course, to bring the necessary supplies of foreign sugar there; but the leaders of the London market fear that the market would not remain sufficiently wide to retain this business, unless a firm basis is provided by the importation of large quantities of foreign sugar for British use.

14. British imports of foreign sugar are still, as has been seen, substantial. But they are much smaller than they used to be, and there are several points to be borne in mind in considering their apparent magnitude. First, as has already been observed, a considerable part of the foreign raw sugar imported is re-exported as refined sugar. It is true that so long as the export trade in refined sugar continues, these imports contribute, just as much as retained imports, to the width of the London market. But in certain circumstances, particularly if anything in the

Chapter XV.

nature of a world price for sugar were to disappear, the export of refined sugar might be jeopardised. If these imports are deducted, the net imports of foreign raw sugar retained for British consumption have been as follows in recent years:—

	Tons.
1934	595,000
1935	755,000
1936	784,000
1937	542,000
1938	791,000

But before 1937, the imports of sugar from the Empire had not reached the magnitude they have since attained, while since 1937, various abnormal factors, such as the purchase of war stores by the British Government, have helped to swell the volume of foreign imports. In the opinion of a leading London sugar broker, the annual imports of foreign sugar for British consumption that could be expected under normal conditions on the basis of the present arrangements would be only about 400,000 tons, if the British beet-sugar industry were to produce its full quota of 560,000 tons of white sugar. Moreover the foreign sugar does not arrive evenly throughout the year. The seasons of the heaviest shipments are different for the different producing countries. We have been informed that even with the large imports of foreign sugar during recent years, there have been periods when the available supplies of foreign sugar in the London market have sunk to a very low figure. If accordingly colonial sugar were to displace foreign sugar to a materially increased extent, there might often be periods when no foreign sugar was available.

15. Finally, it is important not to overlook the vital contribution that Canada at present makes by importing some 400,000 tons of colonial sugar annually on preferential terms. If Canada were to withdraw the preference she gives, or were even to reduce it to a level materially below that of the United Kingdom preference, these 400,000 tons would be diverted to the London market, with the inevitable effect of displacing a corresponding quantity of foreign sugar. If this were to happen, the British retained imports of foreign sugar would shrink to a low figure, and if British beet-sugar production were to approach its permitted quota, might become of negligible importance. The Canadian preference is linked up with the Canada—West Indies Trade Agreement, of which Canada has given notice of termination, and the renewal or revision of which has recently been under discussion.

16. There are thus solid grounds for the apprehensions of the London sugar market; and though we do not think that dangers to the interests of Mincing Lane should be allowed to overrule

the vital necessities of the West Indian Colonies, it is well to recognize that such dangers are involved in the further expansion of colonial sugar production. It is still more important to appreciate that, even if such dangers are disregarded, the scope which the British market provides for absorbing increased colonial production is both limited and uncertain. The apparent scope might indeed disappear altogether if a reduction of the Canadian sugar preference were to be accompanied by a return of the output of British beet-sugar to the level of 1936.

17. The force of the revenue objection to a further increase of colonial sugar production can be assessed more precisely. Under the existing preferential arrangements, the British revenue loses £3 15s. per ton on sugar that comes from the British Colonies instead of from foreign countries. Thus every 100,000 tons by which colonial sugar displaced foreign sugar in the British market would cost the revenue £375,000. The preference indeed amounts to well over 50 per cent. of the price of foreign sugar in the London market in recent years. In a sense, therefore, the colonial sugar industry is heavily subsidised; and if the industry were either technically inefficient, or essentially uneconomic, in the sense that it could not hope to stand on its own legs in fair and equal world competition, we should find it very difficult to justify its further expansion, despite the urgency of West Indian needs.

18. But, in respect of both the points indicated, the West Indian and other sugar colonies can make a good case. Though at times the West Indies may have lagged behind other parts of the world in the technical efficiency of their methods of sugar production, that is not generally true at the present day. Lord Olivier's Commission* in 1930 paid a tribute to the high level of efficiency that prevailed in most colonies at that time; and since then there has been a steady increase in technical efficiency both in the field and in the factory which explains the remarkable expansion that has taken place in the output of sugar per acre and per labourer employed. The sugar industry is indeed by far the most efficient industry to be found in the West Indies.

19. It is true that some other countries, notably Cuba and Java, possess natural advantages for sugar production, such as geographical conditions that are consistent with larger central factories, that enable them to produce sugar more cheaply than the West Indian Colonies can do. None the less, the West Indian sugar industry cannot properly be regarded as essentially uneconomic. For, as has already been indicated, most sugar production in the world to-day is subsidised in one form or another, and a large part of it is subsidised far more heavily

---

* Cmd. 3517 (1930).

than is British colonial production. If the different sugar producing countries were ranged solely in accordance with the cheapness at which they can produce sugar (leaving all other considerations out of account), the West Indies, though they would not head the list, would appear fairly high up in it. They produce far more cheaply, for example, than the beet-sugar industry, or South Africa, or Australia, or France or the United States; and it is contended in the West Indies that if all artificial measures of stimulating sugar production were abolished throughout the world, and sugar was bought and sold on a free trade basis, the relations between demand and supply would be such that their sugar would command a materially higher price than it does to-day. This contention must be regarded as doubtful, in view of the immensely greater volume of production of which Cuba and Java have shown that they are capable. But the point is at least arguable. In these circumstances, it seems to us unfair to regard the assistance that the West Indian sugar industry receives from preferences and colonial sugar certificates as a kind of charity, bolstering up an uneconomic industry at the expense of the British taxpayer.

20. A further point should be borne in mind in this connection. The prices of both foreign sugar and colonial sugar are far lower than they were at any period prior to the last few years. Despite the displacement of the cheaper foreign supplies by the dearer colonial supplies, we buy our imported sugar nowadays on much more favourable terms than we did formerly. The nature of the sacrifice that the British people would incur by a further substitution of colonial for foreign sugar would be only that of the partial loss of the benefits derived from the downward trend of prices in recent years. The loss of revenue could be made good, as indeed has been done in 1939, by raising the level of customs duties.

21. There is next to be considered how the price received by colonial producers would be affected by an expansion of the volume of colonial production. If a sufficient increase in the quota of the British Colonies could be secured, without disturbing the general scheme of the International Agreement, there would be no reason why the price should be adversely affected. It is possible to imagine circumstances in which this might be done. If the British beet-sugar subsidy were abolished, as the Wilfrid Greene Committee recommended, or if the volume of beet-sugar production were substantially reduced, foreign sugar producing countries might be willing to agree that the greater part of the increase in export quotas that would then be made available should be allocated to the British Colonies, though a modification of the terms of the existing agreement would be necessary for this purpose. It is even possible that foreign

countries might be induced to submit to a transfer of part of their existing quotas as an alternative to the collapse of the agreement. But this is only a possibility. It is very likely that insistence on a substantially larger quota for the colonial Empire would entail the breakdown of the international regulation policy. If this were to happen, the huge excess of productive capacity over world demand makes it probable that the world price of sugar would again fall materially, and drag down with it the preferential price received by colonial producers.

22. If the increase in colonial exports were confined within moderate limits, it would be possible, as we have already indicated, to provide against the danger by adjusting the effective rate of colonial preference in accordance with the movement of world prices; and later in the Chapter we make a definite proposal of this character. But this expedient might fail to maintain the price of colonial sugar if exports from the colonies increased sufficiently to displace foreign sugar altogether from the British market at certain seasons. For in that event the link between the preferential price and the world price would be broken, and the competition of Empire sugar might force down the preferential price without any limit. Short of this, moreover, the disadvantages of a return to chaotic conditions of world prices would not be removed, though they might be mitigated, by the method we propose. In an economic world in which the producers of all commodities are subject to the risks of price fluctuations, it would be difficult to justify carrying the adjustment of the colonial preference so far as to guarantee complete stability for the price of colonial sugar; and the plan that we suggest would leave the colonial producers liable to suffer, though less than at present, from a fall of world prices. From the standpoint of the British Treasury, the adjustments that we propose are open to the objection that they entail some degree of uncertainty as to the yield of an important source of revenue. These considerations supply an argument for confining the expansion of colonial sugar production within such limits as may conceivably prove compatible with the continuance of the international restriction scheme.

23. Finally, there is the broad international aspect of the question. There is already a large excess of productive capacity in the world for sugar as for other tropical commodities. A substantial increase in the sugar production of the British Colonies, while it would relieve their immediate difficulties, would aggravate correspondingly the similar difficulties of other very similar communities. If it should lead to the disappearance of the International Sugar Agreement, it might deal a blow to the general policy of international regulation schemes, several of which are of the utmost value to the British Colonial Empire,

and might administer a setback to attempts to solve world economic problems by methods of international co-operation, as opposed to those of economic nationalism or imperialism.

24. This might be a cogent objection, if it were not for the extreme artificiality of the economic conditions that govern the production of sugar. But, as has already been mentioned, only about 5 per cent. of the sugar of the world is produced without some form of State assistance. Other countries, moreover, give far more substantial assistance to their sugar-producing colonies than does Great Britain. Both France and the United States, as has been explained, reserve their sugar markets almost wholly for their home and colonial or other favoured producers; and their fiscal arrangements are such as to give their colonial producers a price for their sugar so much higher than the British preferential price, as to make the whole difference between ample profit margins and constant financial anxiety. It is true that the larger volume of production in the British Colonial Empire makes the problem a more difficult one for Great Britain. None the less, there is a contrast of treatment to the disadvantage of the British Colonies, which geographical propinquity brings into strong relief; for the French sugar-producing colonies of Martinique and Guadeloupe, and the American territory of Puerto Rico lie interspersed among the British West Indies in the same Caribbean Sea. So long as these conditions obtain the treatment of the sugar question on genuinely international lines must be regarded as impracticable.

3. Proposals regarding Increased Production.

25. This completes our review of the dangers and disadvantages that would attach, under peace-time conditions, to an expansion of the volume of colonial sugar production;/ and though the outbreak of war has thrown them for the time being into the background, they must be expected to reappear, with whatever modifications in detail, as essential factors in the problem when the war is over. But the war transforms the immediate outlook, and is likely to leave enduring consequences behind it. It is reasonable to assume that no artificial restrictions will be retained during the war period upon the output of colonial sugar. The war is likely to entail a heavy drain upon our gold reserves and foreign exchange resources; and it becomes important therefore to concentrate our purchases of imported goods as far as possible on countries that form an effective part of the " sterling area ". The substitution of colonial sugar for foreign sugar in the British market will thus assist the prosecution of the war.*

---

* Another important war-time consideration is that it is more economical in respect of shipping to import sugar from the West Indies than from other Empire countries at a greater distance from Great Britain.

26. The problem of world over-production will be aggravated when peace is restored by any increase of colonial production that takes place in the meantime. It is impossible at present to foresee how large this increase of production is likely to be. For the expansion of sugar production is a slow process, with a time-lag of 18 months or more between a decision to plough up more land for cane and the resultant sugar; and war conditions are likely to hamper the process of expansion in various ways. But the extent to which production is increased during the war will obviously be a material factor in the problem that subsequently emerges.

27. It may perhaps be useful, none the less, to indicate the views which we had formed under conditions of peace as to the extent to which the claims of the West Indian Colonies for increased sugar quotas should be met. These claims were based on a variety of grounds; but it is possible to distinguish, if not very sharply, between two broad purposes by which they were inspired:—

> (a) to avert the under-employment of labour (and of plant) where sugar is at present grown;
>
> (b) to provide increased employment openings in districts which are either actually distressed or threatened with a serious decline in other branches of export agriculture.

28. In general, the case for claims of the latter type is relatively weak. There is a presumption that districts in which sugar production either has never been attempted, or has at some period been abandoned, are not well-suited for the industry, and that its establishment in such districts would be relatively uneconomic. Having regard to the various difficulties that have been indicated earlier in this Chapter, the limitations of the British sugar market, the standpoint of the British revenue, and the large excess under peace-time conditions of world productive capacity, it would be difficult as a rule to justify the erection of new sugar factories in such districts, particularly where financial assistance from public funds would be required. But the presumption to which we have referred is of a very general character; and in some instances a fairly strong case can be put forward for re-establishing sugar factories in districts where the industry has previously failed. The Barbadian settlement scheme in St. Lucia is the outstanding instance of this type; and we regard it as essential if this project is to have a fair chance of succeeding that the Vieux-Fort factory should receive a quota sufficient to permit operations on an economic scale, without restricting production in the other districts of St. Lucia. We have also already suggested, in paragraph 6 of Chapter XII, that the possibility of re-establishing sugar-growing on the Essequibo Coast in British Guiana deserves serious examination.

29. But there is obviously a much stronger case for allowing such an expansion of production in districts where cane is already grown as would permit the fuller utilisation of the existing factory equipment and the fuller employment of the labourers or cane-farmers already attached to the industry. To secure these objects, it would be necessary in most Colonies to allow a substantial increase in the average annual volume of exports in excess of the quotas hitherto allocated.

30. In British Guiana, the representatives of the Sugar Producers' Association expressed the view to us that the output of sugar could be increased by 20 per cent. without establishing any new factories or drawing additional workers into the industry. In Jamaica the West Indies Sugar Company, with the completion of its new modern factory at Frome, is capable of an output perhaps double that of the quota to which it was limited at the time of our visit to the island. In Barbados, where the output varies greatly from year to year in accordance with the rainfall, the prevailing tendency in recent years has been for the output available for export to exceed the permitted quota by a substantial amount. In all these Colonies and in many of the smaller islands under-employment among estate labourers was already a serious phenomenon, and, on the basis of the quotas fixed for the last pre-war year, likely to become rapidly worse. Trinidad was the only important Colony in which the sugar industry would require additional plant and additional labour in order to increase its output.

31. After surveying the needs of the various Colonies in the light of the criteria that we have indicated, we had reached the conclusion, before the outbreak of war, that it was vitally important to increase the export quotas allocated to the West Indian Colonies by about 120,000 tons. An increase of this magnitude would be mainly required to avert the under-employment of plant and labour in districts where sugar is already grown. It would contribute comparatively little to the solution of the problem of finding employment outlets to compensate for the decline of other branches of export agriculture. Even in sugar districts it would only serve for a few years to absorb the steady growth in the population of working age. In allocating this increased quota among the various West Indian Colonies, regard should be paid, of course, to their varying needs. The claims of Jamaica to an increased quota are, in our judgment, especially strong, and we think that Jamaica should be allotted an additional quota of not less than 50,000 tons. The claims of British Guiana rank next in importance, while at the other end of the scale we do not consider that there is any urgent need to increase the quota of Trinidad. In general, however, we think it best to leave over for subsequent consideration the manner in which the increased quota that we have suggested should be allocated.

32. Having regard, however, to the various difficulties that have been examined earlier in this Chapter, we do not feel justified in pressing for a larger increase than the above. Our inquiry has been limited to the West Indian Colonies; but we are bound to recognise that a very similar case can be made for increasing the permissible volume of sugar production in Mauritius and Fiji. The increase that we have suggested for the West Indies works out at about 20 per cent. of the combined export quotas of these Colonies. If the other sugar Colonies were treated on an equal footing, it would be necessary to secure an increase in the total quota for the Colonial Empire of fully 200,000 tons. It remains to be seen how far this expansion will be effected under the unrestricted conditions which we assume will prevail during the course of the war. But on the basis of the knowledge at present available, an increase of 20 per cent. in the exports of the Colonial Empire as compared with the basic quotas laid down in the International Agreement represents in our judgment a reasonable objective of policy, provided that the expansion of sugar production goes hand in hand with an increase in the production of foodstuffs for local consumption.

4. Prices and Preferences.

33. We turn from the question of the volume of sugar production to that of price. During recent years, colonial producers have received a price for their sugar in the British and Canadian markets something like 70 per cent. in excess of the so-called world price, which has undergone considerable fluctuation. In most West Indian Colonies steps have been taken to secure a price substantially above the export price for the sugar that is sold in the local market and to distribute the benefits of this higher local price equitably among the different sugar producers. In some Colonies similar steps have been taken to pool the proceeds of high-priced sugar products, such as rum in Jamaica, and "fancy molasses" in Barbados. Over the average of recent years, the export price of sugar, as supplemented by these various expedients, has sufficed to enable efficiently managed estates to make profits; but in most cases these profits have fallen short of an economic return upon capital, if adequate allowance is made for depreciation, while the wages paid to labourers and the prices for cane paid to peasant "cane-farmers" have been insufficient for a satisfactory standard of living. We regard it as important in these circumstances that the West Indian sugar producers should be enabled in future to obtain better prices for their sugar than those that have prevailed in recent years.

34. Shortly after the outbreak of war, the British Government contracted to purchase the export surplus of the West Indian sugar crop at a price representing a moderate increase

over that which prevailed in the previous year. We may assume that, so long as the war lasts the price of sugar will be determined by similar bargains for bulk purchase, which will take account of all the relevant factors. It is possible moreover that the war will leave behind permanent changes, as, for example, in the exchange rates and the purchasing power of sterling, which will vitally affect the level of prices that will subsequently be appropriate. It is possible again that the system of central buying now in operation will survive the war. On the other hand, the world surplus of capacity for the production of sugar is likely to be aggravated by the expansion of colonial production that may be expected during the war period; while the claim of the colonial producers to arrangements that will ensure them a reasonable price will be greatly strengthened. In these circumstances it will be important to be prepared with reasonable arrangements to come into operation if and when the method of bulk purchase is abandoned. Moreover, the war-time contract for bulk purchase is based, we understand, on an assumed world price for sugar of 7s. 6d. per cwt., and leaves untouched the arrangements, which we are about to describe, in regard to the Imperial Preference and Colonial Sugar Certificates. We think it well, therefore, to set out the proposals which, in the light of pre-war conditions, and on the basis of the pre-war value of sterling, we had intended to make, leaving open the questions as to how far they can be applied under war-time conditions, and how far they may require modification when the war is over.

5. Peace-time Proposals.

35. For this purpose, it will be convenient to begin with a description of the arrangements that existed before the war. All Empire sugar, Dominion as well as Colonial, receives in the British market the benefit of a preference equivalent to £3 15s. per ton of 96° sugar. In addition, a supplementary preference is given to Colonial as distinct from Dominion producers upon a limited quantity of " certificated " sugar. This supplementary preference is of the nominal value of £3 per ton, but the certificated sugar upon which it is payable is limited to a fixed quantity for each Colony, which represents only a small proportion of its actual exports, the aggregate of certificated sugar for the Colonial Empire being 360,000 tons. In 1934, when this system was introduced, the exports of the Colonies had been ranging in the immediately preceding years between 750,000 tons and 800,000 tons; so that the preference on certificated sugar was then equivalent to about £1 7s. 6d. per ton of Colonial sugar exported. But this value has diminished as the volume of exports has increased. On the basis of the basic export quota, approximately 950,000 tons allocated to the Colonial

Empire under the International Sugar Agreement, the average value of the certificate is about £1 2s. 6d. per ton of sugar exported. For the last crop year (1938-39), when the Colonial Empire's export quota was increased materially to meet an unexpected market shortage, the certificates were worth about £1 per ton averaged over the exports of the Colonial Empire. It should be added that the value of the certificates regarded as a supplementary preference, varies greatly from Colony to Colony, and also from factory to factory, in accordance with the differing changes in the volume of production that have occurred since 1934.

36. Though the amount of certificated sugar is fixed and does not increase or decrease with a change in the volume of exports, the preference payable on the certificated sugar is liable to be reduced in the event of a rise in the world price of sugar. The arrangement is that if the world price of sugar should exceed 6s. 6d. per cwt. (or £6 10s. per ton) for the first six months of any calendar year, the supplementary preference is reduced by one-quarter for each complete 6d. of such excess. The reduction thus does not take effect unless the world price of sugar averages over 7s. per cwt. or £7 per ton. As soon as it does so, the supplementary preference is reduced by one-quarter. If the world price averages over £7 10s. per ton, the preference is reduced by one-half; while it would disappear altogether if the world price rose to £8 10s. per ton. The broad effect is to deprive the sugar producers, by reductions in the preference on certificated sugar, of roughly one-half of the benefits of a rise in the world price of sugar. But there is at present no similar provision for compensating the sugar producers for an abnormally low world price by increasing the preference on certificated sugar.

37. It will be evident from this description that the system of Colonial sugar certificates is one of considerable complexity. There was, however, a good reason for adopting the plan of a substantial preference on part only of the Colonial exports rather than the simpler method of an ordinary preference at a lower rate on all Colonial sugar imported by the United Kingdom. The latter method, in the form of an additional preference of £1 per ton on Colonial sugar, was in fact employed between 1932 and 1934 as one (though not the only) means of giving further assistance to Colonial sugar producers. But this had the effect, when a fall occurred in the exchange value of the Canadian dollar, of making the British price for Colonial sugar more attractive than the Canadian price, and thus diverting supplies from the Canadian to the British market. The present system of Colonial sugar certificates was introduced as a safeguard against this danger; and we think it desirable to retain the general framework of this system.

38. We propose, however, various detailed modifications with a view to improving and stabilising the price received by Colonial sugar producers. We are, of course, concerned only with the sugar industry in the West Indies, which accounts for less than two-thirds of the total Colonial production. But we assume that it would be impossible to differentiate, in any arrangements that are made, between the West Indies and other sugar Colonies; and our proposals and calculations relate accordingly to the Colonial Empire as a whole.

39. In the first place, we propose that certificates, bearing their present value of £3 per ton, should be issued, not as now for a fixed quantity of sugar, but for a varying quantity representing *one-half* of the total exports from any Colony in any year. This change would have the following consequences. First, the value of the supplementary Colonial preference would become £1 10s. per ton of sugar exported, as compared with the present average value of from £1 to £1 2s. 6d. Second, the value of the preference would remain at £1 10s. as the volume of Colonial exports increases, instead of falling as it does under the existing arrangements. Third, the value of the preference would be equalised as between the different Colonies, instead of varying as it does now in accordance with the changes that have occurred in the volume of exports since 1934.

40. We would add as a corollary to this proposal that the certificates issued to any Colony should be distributed among the different sugar factories in accordance with either their current production or their current exports, as may be most appropriate. The system of Colonial sugar certificates was introduced some years before the exports of sugar from the different Colonies were restricted by the International Agreement, and the arrangements made were influenced by a desire to avoid stimulating increased production in the Colonies. For this reason, not only was the amount of certificated sugar allocated to each Colony limited to a fixed quantity; it was also laid down that the distribution of the sugar certificates within each Colony among the different sugar producers should also be stereotyped with reference to production in the past, so that an estate which increased its output of sugar would not thereby obtain additional certificates. Actually this rule was not universally applied. In Barbados, the certificates have always been distributed among the factories, with the agreement of the Colonial Office, in proportion to current production. In British Guiana, we found that they were distributed, owing apparently to a misunderstanding of the Colonial Office instructions, in accordance with a moving average of the output of the three preceding years. But in other Colonies, the principle of a stereotyped distribution on the basis of output in certain specified years in the past was strictly maintained, with results that seemed to us in many cases anomalous and inequitable.

41. When the International Sugar Agreement came into operation, and the output not only of each Colony but of each factory within each Colony was limited by a statutory system of quotas, the purpose of these rigid arrangements for the allocation of Colonial sugar certificates disappeared. Under war conditions, it seems definitely undesirable to maintain arrangements designed to discourage increased production. The anomalies and inequalities that the arrangements entail must necessarily increase with the passage of time. We therefore recommend that for the future the distribution of the certificates among the different producers or factories in a Colony should be based on current production or current export. These changes would make the system of certificates conform more closely to its central purpose of giving a supplementary preference in the British market to Colonial producers, without diverting supplies from the Canadian market.

42. Our next proposal is that the value of the preference on certificated sugar should not only be reduced when the world price of sugar rises above a defined par figure, but should be increased in similar proportions when the world price falls below that figure. We suggest that this par figure should be £7 per ton, or 7s. per cwt. on the basis of the pre-war purchasing-power of sterling. This seems to us an appropriate figure to adopt, in view of the fact that it has been, we understand, the objective of the International Sugar Council in administering the International Agreement to raise the world price to this level. We would emphasise, however, in this as in other similar connections where prices are mentioned, that the suggestion of 7s. per cwt. is based on the pre-war level of prices and costs. A higher figure may be required after the war to effect the purpose in view if there should be a substantial fall in the meantime in the purchasing-power of sterling.

43. For every complete 3d. per cwt. (or 5s. per ton) by which the world price of sugar, for the average of the first six months of any year exceeds or falls short of the defined par value, we propose that the preference given on certificated sugar should be reduced or increased by one-ninth, i.e., by 4d. per cwt. Since the certificated sugar will amount under our proposals to one-half of the total exports, this is equivalent to altering the effective rate of preference by 2d. per cwt. for every complete 3d. by which the world price changes. This arrangement would provide Colonial sugar producers with a considerable measure of protection against the consequences of a fall in the world price to low levels, though it would fall short of a stabilised price. It would leave the sugar producers to bear the full brunt or reap the full benefit of fluctuations in the world price between 6s. 9d. and 7s. 3d. per cwt., and to bear one-third of the brunt or to reap

one-third of the benefit of fluctuations outside those limits. But so long as producers generally are exposed to price vicissitudes, the arrangements we propose represent as large a measure of stability as seems to us reasonable, especially in view of the fact that greater security to the Colonial producers must be accompanied by greater uncertainty to the United Kingdom revenue.

44. The above proposals may be summarised as follows:—

(1) The amount of certificated sugar eligible for the supplementary Colonial preference shall be calculated in future for each Colony in any year so as to represent one-half of the total exports from that Colony in that year.

(2) The certificates shall be distributed among the different factories in each Colony on the basis of their permitted production or exports for that year, whichever may be most appropriate.

(3) The amount of the supplementary preference payable on certificated sugar shall be 3s. per cwt. as at present, but shall be reduced or increased in any year by 4d. per cwt. for each complete 3d. per cwt. by which the world price of sugar, for the average of the first six months of the year, exceeds or falls short of 7s. per cwt. This figure of 7s. per cwt. should be regarded as subject to adjustment from time to time in accordance with changes in the purchasing-power of sterling.

45. These proposals would effect an improvement in the position of the Colonial sugar producers, which we are agreed in regarding as the minimum that is required. If they were adopted, the producers would receive an appreciably higher price for their sugar than hitherto, and, unless world prices should undergo much greater vicissitudes, a less fluctuating price. But it is important to avoid conveying an exaggerated impression of the benefits they would obtain. The price received by Colonial producers would still depend largely on the world price of sugar. If the objective of the International Sugar Council were realised, and the world price of sugar reached an average level of 7s. per cwt., or £7 per ton, Colonial producers, under the arrangements we have suggested, would receive an average price of £12 5s. per ton, c.i.f., London, corresponding, on the basis of pre-war freights, to about £11 5s. per ton f.o.b. This, it will be observed, is far below the figure of £15 c.i.f., which the Olivier Commission* regarded as essential ten years ago. At a price of £12 5s. per ton c.i.f., most efficient sugar estates should succeed, on the basis of pre-war wage-rates and pre-war costs generally, in making satisfactory

---

* Cmd. 3517 (1930).

though not exorbitant profits, and with their position thus strengthened, they should be able to make some improvement in wages and afford opportunities for expenditure on purposes designed to improve the social conditions of their labourers. If, as we have proposed earlier in this Chapter, the volume of permitted sugar production is also substantially increased, the financial position of most estates will be further strengthened by a reduction of overhead costs, while the standard of life of the labourers should be directly improved through an increase in the amount of employment afforded. The majority of us would like to go further, and establish a price for Colonial sugar which would render more immediately practicable a substantial improvement in the wage-rates of the sugar workers.

46. We have to recognise on the other side that the proposals elaborated above would impose a heavy burden on the British Exchequer. The increase suggested in the volume of Colonial sugar production would be particularly costly. If an additional 200,000 tons of Colonial sugar were to displace an equal quantity of foreign sugar in the British market, there would be a loss of revenue amounting to £750,000 in respect of the ordinary Imperial Preference, and (under the arrangements we propose) to a further £300,000 in respect of additional Colonial sugar certificates. This, it is true, is to place the possible cost of this particular change at its highest, since part of the increased imports from the Colonies might be absorbed by increased British consumption, rather than by displacing imports. The cost of our proposal to increase the amount of certificated sugar to one-half of the exports from the Colonies is included, so far as concerns additional production, in the above item of £300,000. But this proposal would entail a further burden on the Exchequer, in respect of the existing basic Colonial export quota, of £360,000.* The cost of the arrangements we suggest for adjusting the preference payable on certificated sugar in accordance with changes in the world price would depend on the course of the world price. But it seems not unlikely that it might work out at an average of between £200,000 and £400,000 per year.

47. Altogether, therefore, it seems probable that our proposals with regard to sugar would cost the British Exchequer upwards of £1,500,000; though it should be observed that less than two-thirds of this sum would be attributable to the West Indies. This represents as large an expenditure as it seems to some of us reasonable to propose for the benefit of a particular branch of export agriculture.

---

* i.e., £3 multiplied by the difference between one-half of 960,000 tons or 480,000 tons, and the present fixed quantity of 360,000 tons.

6. Objects and Conditions of Proposals.

48. Our main object in making the recommendations contained in this Chapter is to facilitate an improvement in the conditions of the West Indian population employed in the sugar industry. An increase in the volume of employment may be expected, as a matter of course, to accompany an increase in the permitted volume of sugar production. But we think it important to ensure that the labouring population share the benefits of any increase in the effective price of Colonial sugar that may result from our recommendations. With this end in view we have already proposed in Chapter X that a cess of 2s. per ton should be levied to finance welfare funds for the benefit of sugar workers. We have also proposed the establishment of Wages Boards for determining wage-rates. We have further suggested that it should be made a condition of the payment to any West Indian Colony of Colonial sugar certificates on the more generous basis proposed that that Colony should enact legislation for the establishment of Wages Boards that is satisfactory to the Colonial Office; and further that within each Colony it might be made a condition of the payment of the certificates due to any estate or factory that it should observe such regulations with regard to wages as may be laid down by the Wages Boards.

CHAPTER XVI.

AGRICULTURAL POLICY.*

1. General Remarks.

1. We have pointed out in Chapter IV that the outstanding agricultural need in the West Indies is the increased production of food in order to support even the existing low standard of life among a population which is increasing rapidly. The most helpful line is the development of peasant agriculture, but substantial progress among both peasants and estates is dependent upon far-reaching reform of the basic methods now in vogue. The practice of shifting cultivation by peasant farmers must be abandoned and replaced by an organised system of permanent mixed farming: the present policy of those larger proprietors who grow a single crop continuously must be modified by the development of mixed farming in a measure which will vary from place to place with local circumstances. Neither of those reforms can be successfully carried through until new knowledge, which is obtainable only by scientific investigation, has been secured. War conditions will give an opportunity, of which advantage should be taken, for making an immediate start with both measures of reform.

2. Food Supply.

2. The aim of agricultural policy in the British West Indies should, we consider, be the greatest possible measure of self-sufficiency in essential foods. At present these Colonies import large quantities of food and maintain their balance of trade by the export of such commodities as sugar, bananas and cocoa. Even when increased local production reaches a level at which imports of food can be reduced, the export trade of these Colonies need not be affected. There are many needs, such as clothing, shoes and domestic equipment, on the importation of which all the money likely to be obtained from the sale of exports could most usefully be expended.

3. In thus advocating the making of a serious effort to bring about greater self-sufficiency we have in mind other factors in addition to the geographical and agricultural circumstances which we describe in the early sections of Chapter IV of this

---

* *Note.*—This chapter is based upon those parts of Professor Engledow's full survey of agricultural resources and needs which relate to the future agricultural policy of the West Indian Colonies with which we are concerned. That survey, which is being published in a separate volume (Cmd. 6149), will no doubt be available to many readers of this Report, and it is for their convenience that in many places in this chapter we have inserted references to the paragraphs of the survey in which points here made briefly are more fully developed.

Report. As we there pointed out, crops produced for export are in jeopardy from many causes, including climatic fluctuations, such as drought and hurricanes, and loss of those crops when, as is often now the case, they are intended to pay for essential food imports, may clearly be disastrous. The dependence of the West Indian Colonies on imported foods lays them open to other risks of a strategic and economic character. In time of war or other major disturbance their lines of communication would be liable to attack; experience has shown that a general economic crisis, or even a great decline in the world price of their exports, adversely affects the interests of communities which are too small to exercise much influence in world trade. (Chapter II, paragraph 1.)

4. Considerations of health point unmistakably to the same conclusion. A better balanced diet is much to be desired and cannot be brought within the means of the poorer people except through organised reform of the agricultural system. The definition of an exact policy for the improvement of food supply in every territory must naturally depend on its special circumstances, but maize, rice, beans, peas, milk, beef, goat meat, pork, eggs, chickens, green vegetables and fish are the best products for general development; fresh fruit is generally available at almost all times of the year, a fact which is of great nutritional advantage. Some of the ways by which policy might be directed towards the aim which we suggest are described in the Agricultural Report (Chapter II, paragraphs 22-28, and Chapter XX), and we do not propose here to discuss the detailed proposals there made beyond saying that, from the point of view of health, special importance should be attached to securing larger supplies of milk, fish and green vegetables at prices which would enable all sections of the community to improve their diets by the greater consumption of these foods. Every encouragement should therefore be given by Governments to householders who wish to produce their own milk, and an immediate expert inquiry should be made into the possibility of rapid expansion of the existing local fishery industries.

5. While reliance for the greater part of the increased production of food crops must be placed upon peasant cultivation, it is essential to introduce those crops into every part of the agricultural system. Estates must play an important part in the scheme; for example, in most Colonies, they should undertake much more extensive growing of food crops between successive bouts of sugar cane, and they should realise that it is in their own ultimate interests to offer generous facilities, including the provision of land and skilled advice and assistance with supplies of seeds and fertilisers, to any of their labourers who wish to grow food for the consumption of themselves and their families. (Chapter II, paragraph 29, and Chapter VI, paragraph 2 (a).)

6. Before concluding this section we would refer to paragraph 20 in Chapter II of the Agricultural Report, where the effect of praedial larceny on food production is examined. This theft of growing crops and even of small or young animals is so common in most of the West Indian Colonies that it has come to be accepted as inevitable. Both the practice and this attitude towards it are clearly severe handicaps to the scheme of development which we have recommended. Severe punishment of the few thieves who are caught and convicted does not appear to be a sufficient deterrent; its efficacy might be increased and more general co-operation in eradicating praedial larceny might be secured through an organised campaign, by the use of the wireless and through the Press, to arouse among the West Indian people the feeling that this is an offence against the community.

3. Soil and Land Surveys.

7. One of the immediate agricultural needs of every West Indian Colony is a comprehensive soil survey, which should be planned so that its results may be used as a guide in such matters as the inherent manurial needs of various soils, the suitability of different areas to various crops and farming systems, the prevention of soil erosion, the selection of suitable sites for land settlement, the alignment of roads and the proper development of both forest and agricultural policy. So far as is possible this survey should be combined with a similar comprehensive review of the ownership, use and agricultural condition of land, and we recommend that both branches of this work should be entrusted to the Imperial College of Tropical Agriculture as part of the general scheme of investigation suggested later in this Chapter.

4. Land Ownership and Use.

8. As we have stated in Chapter IV of this report, the policy hitherto followed in disposing of Crown Land and the practical steps taken to give effect to that policy have often been defective. Although it is a normal requirement that parcels of Crown Land when sold or leased should be surveyed and registered, surveys in some Colonies are several years in arrears, and the boundaries between Crown and private property are often in doubt or the subject of dispute. Topographical survey as a basis of recording ownership is essential, and should be undertaken as rapidly as possible. (Chapter V, paragraphs 2 and 3.)

9. The increasing pressure of population makes it essential to bring all land into the fullest possible use, and attention will therefore have to be given not only to the eradication of the evil of shifting cultivation, which is the real extravagence to-day

in the use of land, but also to the restoration to cultivation of much of the ruinate land in spite of its inherent poverty. (Chapter V, paragraph 6.)

10. The insistent demands of peasantry for the freehold tenure of the land which they cultivate can well be understood, but the dangers of small freeholds are considerable and cannot be ignored. Among those which have already become apparent are the fragmentation of land at death or by sale, the serious damage which may be caused to land through bad husbandry, against which there is no remedy when purchase is completed, and the cramping effects of the freehold system if, as often happens, the owner has exhausted his capital in the purchase of the land. We consider that, particularly in connection with land settlement, Government should experiment with both leasehold and freehold systems. Full security should be given to tenants subject only to the maintenance of a reasonable standard of cultivation. The grant of freehold rights should be subject to appropriate conditions to prevent fragmentation of the land and to suitable safeguards of good husbandry which might take the form of a remission of the final instalment of purchase in cases where cultivation had been satisfactory. (Chapter V, paragraph 14.)

11. The system, especially prevalent in distressed areas, under which peasants pay rent in the form of a share of the crops should be replaced by land settlement or in any other way which may be considered more appropriate to the circumstances of a particular territory; where this reform is not immediately possible, and the system of share cropping must continue for a time, contracts should be controlled by Government in order to protect the interests of tenants. Draft legislation recently prepared in Antigua might be a guide in this matter to other administrations. (Chapter V, paragraphs 20 and 21.)

12. It is essential that all the West Indian Governments should have easily applied powers to enable them to acquire compulsorily agricultural land when this is needed for agricultural purposes such as land settlement. In some Colonies it may be found appropriate to decide upon a definite basis for the valuation of land thus acquired; for example, it could be laid down that the price should be a certain number of years' purchase of the net average annual return from the land over a specified period of years, though this procedure might be rendered inapplicable by substantial changes in the value of money. In other territories the price might be left to be determined by valuation, but in that event it might be desirable, in the smaller territories at least, to provide by law that when the Government and the owner of the land cannot agree on a

price an independent valuation shall be made by some authority from outside the island. (Chapter V, paragraphs 22 and 23.)

5. Peasant Agriculture.

13. Efforts made in the past by the Governments of the West Indian Colonies to help peasant agriculture are open to the criticism that they have been insufficient in scope and based upon inadequate information. Experience in other parts of the Colonial Empire has long made it clear that the first stage in any attempt to improve peasant agriculture should be the study of the existing structure; better systems cannot be satisfactorily devised except through specific investigation. We recommend, therefore, that a comprehensive survey of peasant agriculture throughout these Colonies should be undertaken by the Imperial College of Tropical Agriculture. This should deal not only with size of holdings, systems of cropping and other purely agricultural matters, but also with the economics of peasant life. (Chapter VI, paragraphs 4 and 5.)

14. While plans for the future development of peasant agriculture must vary to take account of the differing local circumstances of Colonies, the aim should everywhere be a steady transition to mixed farming which involves permanent, as opposed to shifting, cultivation, and the complementary use of stock and crops; this should ultimately result in much higher productivity of the land. (Chapter VI, paragraph 7.)

15. Another point at which general policy should aim is the increase of the best types of existing holdings in preference to the development on a large scale of any form of holding hitherto unknown in the territory. To this general conclusion there must be an exception where, for example, share cropping is the universal system; abrupt development will then be necessary in accordance with the recommendation which we have made in paragraph 11 above. (Chapter VI, paragraph 9.)

16. The development of peasant agriculture cannot be ensured solely by the investigations and other steps which we have recommended; it must be made complementary to estate agriculture. The measure of the success of peasant holdings, which are essentially family farms, will be an index to social conditions among the peasantry generally, and in this connection it is noteworthy that many experienced observers are convinced that peasant agriculture will be greatly influenced by the extent to which the legitimate family becomes the established social unit. It must be realised, however, that many people of the peasant class prefer work for wages to complete independence. It must not be assumed that every man can find happiness on a peasant holding and it is of primary importance that the people selected for family settlement should be of the right type and should be

given every encouragement and support. (Chapter VI, paragraphs 10 to 13.)

6. Estate Agriculture.

17. Although efficiency on sugar estates has greatly increased since the war, the policy, which has been followed for the last 150 years, of growing sugar cane only and growing it continuously on the same land, still remains. Social needs, in particular the growth of population, make it essential to consider at once the question whether cane growing cannot, with profit to the community, be changed so as to make the land more productive while not lessening the whole output of sugar. This question cannot be satisfactorily settled except through specific investigation, coupled with trials by estates. It is thought that some enterprising sugar estates would be willing to give a trial to agriculture on a wider basis, and we recommend that the work of investigation which is required should be centred in the Imperial College of Tropical Agriculture. Those investigations would be directed to the possibility of displacing the existing system by one of mixed farming, which, while it will everywhere be based on sugar cane as the major product, would otherwise vary with local climatic and other conditions. (Chapter VIII, paragraph 40.)

18. The future development of other estates must, we consider, also be in the direction of mixed farming with permanent tree crops as the most important component of the system, which would thus correspond to the system now followed when fruit is grown in quantity on mixed farms in England. It is, however, impossible to make definite suggestions, or even to begin for these estates the practical investigations and tests which will be required, until the circumstances of their financial and working policy have been comprehensively surveyed. Such a survey should be put in hand without delay, for the present situation of the owners of many of these estates is one in which they can only despair for their future. (Chapter VIII, paragraph 41.)

19. The present research on sugar production, which is partly financed by estates, should be extended in range and should in future include factory technology, not merely with the object of securing increased efficiency from existing methods by providing mechanical and chemical control in the factory, but also with the purpose of devising new and better methods. (Chapter VIII, paragraph 34.)

7. Soil Erosion.

20. The erosion of soil is perhaps the greatest danger to West Indian agriculture and unless checked will certainly stand in the way of the greater productivity of the land which an

increasing population requires. The prevention of erosion can proceed in any of three ways. The first is through the control of very steep slopes; the second by protecting the surface of the soil, especially at times of intense rainfall, by suitable vegetation and through sound husbandry; the last through the provision of adequate drainage for that part of the very heavy rainfall which must run off the land. The West Indian Colonies can with great profit draw on the experience now becoming available from other countries which have experimented in various methods of combating soil erosion. But if each Colony and island attempted, without some central direction and control, to tackle its own problems, much of the effort might be misplaced and the benefit of experience gained in one territory might be lost to the others. For these reasons we recommend that an initial survey and investigation of preventive methods against soil erosion should be centralised at the Imperal College of Tropical Agriculture, local investigation and final executive action being left to each Government. The initial survey should be made as part of the soil survey already recommended and the investigations into this problem cannot be separated from those inquiries which we have proposed into mixed farming by peasant proprietors. One word of warning is, however, necessary. It would be most unfortunate if action against soil erosion, which is a matter of urgency, was not put in hand at once without awaiting even the preliminary results of the survey.* Governments in the West Indies should do everything within their power to show, and to make clear to the people, that they realise that the tackling of this important problem is not merely an agricultural matter but affects vitally the general interest and is, and should be, the business of Government, the administration generally and the individual cultivators. (Chapter IX, paragraphs 15 and 16.)

8. Maintenance of Soil Fertility.

21. We have pointed out in Chapter IV that the system of peasant agriculture now practised in the West Indian Colonies is such as rapidly to exhaust the fertility of the soil and that the remedy for this lies in the development of mixed farming by peasant cultivators. We have also mentioned there the existing controversy, which is described in detail in paragraphs 6 and 7 of Chapter X of the Agricultural Report, between those who advocate the use of chemical fertilisers on sugar estates and those who prefer still to rely on the established and proved method of burying trash and applying pen manure at planting

---

* Apart from the rapid loss of cultivable soil caused by erosion, it is a powerful contributory factor to such disasters as the St. Lucia landslide of November, 1938, the scene of which is illustrated in Plate XVI.

time. The controversy can only be settled through experimental investigation, but it must be emphasised that, whatever may be the outcome of those experiments, it will still be important, in our view, that all sugar estates should keep livestock, not merely in the interests of maintaining the fertility of the soil, but as one stage in the advance towards a proper system of mixed farming in which sugar cane would continue, as we have said, to be the most important element.

22. While it seems likely, from some of the available evidence, that the fertility of the soil is not being properly maintained by estates devoted to crops other than sugar, it is almost impossible to reach reliable conclusions in this matter. Until specific recommendations can be made upon a basis of knowledge gained by adequate experiments it would be unreasonable to expect owners of estates in this category to make substantial alterations in their agricultural practice in the interests of maintaining soil fertility. Proper experimental investigation should therefore be undertaken as part of the scheme of centralised work which will be entrusted to the Imperial College of Tropical Agriculture if our recommendations are adopted.

9. Export Crops.

23. The examination of the market prospects of West Indian export crops which was made briefly in Chapter IV of this Report and at length in Chapter XI of the Agricultural Report, suggests two main lines of investigation apart from those which we have recommended elsewhere. These are:—

(a) The appointment of a person who has experience in the production and manufacture of tobacco and, preferably, with a knowledge of West Indian conditions, to investigate and report upon the present situation of the tobacco industry in all of these Colonies, with particular reference to the future increase of production and the stabilisation and expansion of the export trade. An expert in the growing of tobacco was employed, until quite recently, in Jamaica.

(b) An inquiry should be undertaken by Your Majesty's Government into the part which the West Indian Colonies might play as sources of supply of cellulose to be used for such purposes as the manufacture of paper and artificial silk.

10. Economic Organisation.

24. Our conclusions on this subject (which can be taken to cover marketing, transport, storage, processing, inter-island trade and competition and the development of secondary industries) may conveniently be summed up as follows:—

(a) A survey of the systems of marketing and a study of the activities and profits of intermediaries should be undertaken centrally for all the West Indian Colonies; the points to which this investigation should be specially directed are mentioned in paragraphs 6 and 8 of Chapter XII of the Agricultural Report.

(*b*) Endeavours should be made to arrange for selected estates to act as central agents for their districts in the matter of the processing and selling of such products as coffee and limes.

(*c*) When, under the arrangement suggested immediately above, work for peasants is undertaken by estates, the charge to be made should be fixed by Government.

(*d*) Control and assistance by Government is particularly necessary in the marketing of meat; provision should be made for the sale of livestock to be based on their live weight.

(*e*) The work of associations of producers should be centrally studied and the arrangements made by Government and by co-operative and other organisations for the marketing of the produce of peasants should also be surveyed.

(*f*) An investigation of the possibilities of the development of cold storage should be made for the whole area by a member of the staff of the Imperial College of Tropical Agriculture.

(*g*) Hand-mills and other devices, to be used in the domestic preparation of such products as maize and cassava, should be available for purchase at low prices and domestic storage of food crops should be investigated.

(*h*) The unification of associations of producers should be encouraged. In this way arrangements for the marketing of produce overseas could be improved and the help of the Colonial Empire Marketing Board would be more effective if they could negotiate with a combination of these associations and not with each singly. The Board might also help with rationalisation in the form of voluntary allocation of production between territories; this suggestion is not intended to interfere with existing production, but to prevent further disastrous competition. (Chapter XII, paragraph 23.)

11. Agricultural Credit and Finance.

25. As we have said in Chapter IV, no general measures for improving credit facilities and dealing with the question of indebtedness can be satisfactorily evolved until factual knowledge has been obtained through the surveys which we have recommended. Immediate action appears, however, to be necessary in the Leeward and Windward Islands and in the case of growers of cocoa in Trinidad and Grenada. The question of assistance to

the cocoa industry is considered, with other special problems, at the end of this Chapter. In the two groups of smaller islands special action will be required to meet the distressing financial situation of both peasants and estates. Surveys are already in progress or under discussion, and tentative estimates, as a guide to financial policy, should be made as these surveys proceed. In any measures which they may decide to take, Governments should give no encouragement to agriculturists to expand their enterprises unduly in years of exceptional prosperity. It is equally important to awaken a proper sense of obligation to repay debts promptly, and to bring it home to the people of the West Indian Colonies that in the long run the measure of their success depends on their own exertions. (Chapter XIII, paragraphs 4 and 5 (*h*).)

26. Above all, it should be clearly understood that no arrangement for the grant of financial assistance to peasant agriculture in the West Indies is likely to be successful unless the standard of agricultural knowledge and ability is substantially improved. The individual cultivator must be instructed in improved systems and brought to a better understanding of the elements of husbandry. (Chapter XIII, paragraph 5 (*i*).) When the time comes to frame a general policy on the question of relief from debt and the provision of credit facilities, it will clearly be important not to overlook the financial obligations which many of these Colonies will have to undertake in connection both with measures against erosion and, as investigation of present agricultural systems paves the way, with land settlement.

12. Veterinary Matters.

27. Although many diseases of livestock are known in the West Indian Colonies, the severe outbreaks common in most tropical countries are here very rare, and widespread loss from disease does not occur. It is generally true throughout the British West Indies that when stock are in poor condition, the cause is normally not disease but poor management and bad husbandry. The major problems of livestock in these Colonies are therefore the practical issues of breeding, management and feeding. (Chapter XIV, paragraphs 1-2.)

28. In general it may be said that existing veterinary arrangements in all but the smallest territories are sufficient for such formal duties as the notification of animal diseases. Better facilities are, however, required for diagnosis and advisory work in difficult cases, and provision should also be made for pathological and other researches on veterinary problems. For each Colony to undertake this work would clearly be uneconomical. Moreover better results should be obtained by joint effort, and we therefore recommend that the work should be entrusted to a

Department of Veterinary Science to be established at the Imperial College of Tropical Agriculture. The new Department would provide central facilities for diagnosis, advisory work and veterinary research, the results of which should be available to Veterinary Officers throughout the area. The Department should work in the closest touch with those Officers and should enlist their help with investigations into the improvement of breeding and other connected questions. Its work, particularly in the field of animal experimentation, would be much assisted by the transfer of the Government Stock Farm in Trinidad to the Imperial College of Tropical Agriculture. We suggest that if a Department of Veterinary Science is established, the Government of Trinidad should be invited to consider the possibility of making that transfer as a contribution towards re-organisation and for the general benefit of the British West Indian Colonies. (Chapter XIV, paragraph 4.)

13. Agricultural Departments.

29. We are convinced that very substantial changes are vitally necessary in all the main forms of agriculture in the West Indian Colonies. Those changes amount to an agricultural revolution which must be based on a new policy and on investigation. In our view it would be impracticable and even dangerous to leave the different Governments to frame and implement agricultural policy independently and in complete isolation. The Colonies, though differing in numerous geographical and agricultural characteristics, are alike in fundamental circumstances. All have to face the problem of a rapidly growing population and of developing a peasant agriculture long neglected and very backward. All have the same two main agricultural elements— estate and peasant—and between them a relationship of great social and economic significance. In framing agricultural policy, therefore, these Colonies should be in concert, and it is no less necessary that they should act jointly for the purpose of agricultural investigation, the expense of which, if it is to cover a reasonably wide range, would be outside the means of any of those Governments. (Chapter XV, paragraphs 21-22.) In our view concerted action can best be secured by the following arrangements:—

> (a) An Inspector-General of Agriculture should be appointed for these Colonies. His principal duties would be to advise the Colonial Governments on agricultural policy and on the organisation and working of their Agricultural Departments; to decide which problems should be investigated centrally at the Imperial College of Tropical Agriculture under the scheme recommended later; to take steps to ensure the fullest utilisation of the results of those investigations; to act in these and other matters as **directed** by the

Agricultural Adviser to the Secretary of State for the Colonies and to report regularly on all those matters to him. To meet contingencies of leave or other absence, the Inspector-General of Agriculture should be given an assistant who, at the outset, might specialise in questions of marketing, co-operation and other connected matters.

(b) If, as suggested later, arrangements are made for long-term investigation of all the major agricultural problems to be carried out for the whole group at the Imperial College of Tropical Agriculture, the specialist staffs of Agricultural Departments should be gradually reduced, the personnel being employed, if they have the requisite qualifications and experience, on the central work at the College. A number of specialist Agricultural Officers will, however, always be required in the larger Colonies to study problems and to undertake duties peculiar to the Colony or of special importance to it.

(c) The work of Colonial Agricultural Departments should be concentrated on local replications of the central investigations and on advisory and educational work.

(d) The duties of the Director of Agriculture in Barbados should be enlarged to include responsibility for the Leeward and Windward Islands, and he should be provided with three Assistant Directors residing in Barbados, Antigua and St. Lucia.

(e) The charge of the Agricultural Department in British Honduras should be taken over by the Director of Agriculture in Jamaica.

(f) Agricultural Conferences, at intervals of two or three years, should be arranged for the West Indian Colonies on lines which have proved advantageous in Africa. (Chapter XV, paragraph 23.)

14. Agricultural Education.

30. The question of the part that agriculture should take in the primary and post-primary stages of the educational system of the West Indian Colonies has been examined in Chapter VII of this report, and we shall here discuss only more advanced courses in agriculture.

31. Special schools for agricultural education appear to us to be inappropriate to the needs of the West Indian Colonies. The two vocational agricultural centres at Dinthill and Holmwood in Jamaica hold out great promise, but it will probably be found that such institutions can most profitably be used to give courses, extending for a few months only, to youths and young men between 16 and 25 years of age such as the sons of small-holders, who are already working on their own or their fathers' land. (Chapter XVI, paragraphs 5-8.)

32. Boys studying science at the Harrison College in Barbados, whose science masters come under the Director of Agriculture of the Colony, generally take the course for the local Diploma in Agriculture. Few of those who complete the course find employment in agricultural pursuits. It appears desirable to discontinue this agricultural teaching and to make use of the Hope School of Agriculture in Jamaica, or of the Imperial College of Tropical Agriculture in Trinidad, for the instruction of all classes of young men in the science of agriculture. All facilities for higher agricultural education could with advantage be centralised in these two institutions, the activities of which should be closely concerted. The Hope School would serve admirably for the training both of the sons of planters and managers and of all subordinates for Agricultural Departments. Other members of the Agricultural Service, or private persons seeking more advanced training, should attend the Imperial College. The greater use by private persons of these two well-equipped training centres would do much to remedy that lack of agricultural knowledge which is at present an important limiting factor to the success of estate agriculture generally, with the exception of sugar estates. (Chapter XVI, paragraphs 10-13.)

33. One way by which an intelligent interest in the improvement of rural life can be encouraged is the holding of agricultural shows. This is already done in several territories, but the shows might well be increased in number and widened in scope. The opportunities which they afford could be taken to disseminate elementary information about the improvement of health, about the nutritional value of the foodstuffs exhibited, and also to arrange displays illustrating various aspects of rural life.

15. Need for Defined Agricultural Policy.

34. We are satisfied from our inquiries that in none of the West Indian Colonies is sufficiently informed attention being given to agricultural policy. We have seen a statement of proposals made recently by a Committee of the Colonial Advisory Council of Agriculture and Animal Health for the formulation of an agricultural policy in the Colonial Empire, and reproduced in a Circular Despatch from the Colonial Office dated the 23rd of August, 1939. That statement is set out in full in paragraph 3 of Chapter XVII of the agricultural report, and it will be sufficient to give here the following summary of its principal recommendations:—

> (a) In each Colony a review should be prepared of the agricultural situation in all its aspects and of the official policy of agricultural action and development; a similar review of the veterinary situation should also be made.

(b) Programmes of executive work of both the Agricultural and Veterinary Departments should next be drawn up and should contain proposals for implementing the policy approved by the Colonial Government. In the preparation of these programmes due regard should be given to questions associated with the proper utilisation of land, soil conservation measures and soil erosion control.

(c) Programmes of investigational work for the two Departments should similarly be prepared by their respective Heads.

(d) By this plan the value of the work of the Agricultural and Veterinary Departments would be greatly enhanced, and it would be more securely linked to the work of other technical departments and of the Administration. A common aim and a sound collaboration would also be induced among all the officers of the Department. Moreover, the statements and programmes would be of use to the Colonial Development Advisory Committee and the Colonial Empire Marketing Board.

(e) Annual programmes of agricultural and veterinary work should be supplied by each Colony and made available to the Council.

(f) Colonial agricultural and veterinary policy should be bold, not shrinking to embrace large groups of territories.

35. We are of opinion that the principles embodied in this statement should be adopted for the West Indian Colonies. One of the duties of the Inspector-General of Agriculture, whose appointment we have recommended, would be to advise the Governments of those Colonies on agricultural policy and on the work of their Agricultural Departments. We believe that both the framing and the implementing of agricultural policy throughout the British West Indies would be substantially assisted by the appointment of such an officer and by connecting him with the central investigation undertaken at the Imperial College of Tropical Agriculture. (Chapter XVII, paragraphs 4-7.)

16. Imperial College of Tropical Agriculture.

36. An Imperial Department of Agriculture for the West Indies was formed in 1898 as the result of a recommendation made by the West India Royal Commission which reported in the previous year. This Department, the expense of which was borne by Imperial funds, was amalgamated with the West Indian Agricultural College in 1922 and soon afterwards the combined organisation developed into the Imperial College

of Tropical Agriculture in Trinidad which is intended to serve the interests of the whole Colonial Empire. In less than two decades the College has made great contributions, of both Imperial and local significance, to the study of the problems of tropical agriculture. Partly through financial difficulties, no attempt has been made to connect the College with the West Indian Colonies in a manner which would enable it to act as a central research station for their agricultural problems. Nevertheless, the authorities of the College, without formal obligation, have given valuable assistance to those Colonies with economic surveys, by their research into soil and other chemical problems, and by experiments with banana breeding. This voluntary activity by the College is, we believe, a good augury for the scheme which we propose below. (Chapter XVIII, paragraphs 1-3.)

37. We recommend that the Imperial College of Tropical Agriculture, while continuing those functions of training and research which it now undertakes for the Colonial Empire as a whole, should become also a special research station for the British West Indies. The work of the Advisory Department of the College would cease if, as we have recommended, responsibility for agriculture in the Leeward and Windward Islands is taken over by the Director of Agriculture in Barbados. It will be clear from the earlier sections of this Chapter that the work of research which, in our view, should be undertaken at the College, would touch upon, even if it did not definitely cover, every important aspect of agriculture in the West Indies. The major problems which call for central investigation are summarised below under the three categories of husbandry, economics and specialist science:—

Problems of Husbandry.

(*a*) Systems of mixed farming for peasant holdings.

(*b*) Comparison of continuous cane with other methods and especially the possibility of linking cane growing with mixed farming on both large and small scales.

(*c*) Cultivation, draining and use of organic manure on sugar estates.

(*d*) Cultivation, draining and manuring for coconuts, limes, cocoa, and other plantation crops.

(*e*) Incorporation of perennial plantation crops into a mixed farming system.

(*f*) Improved breeding, feeding and management of all classes of livestock, for carefully determined objectives.

(*g*) Management of permanent grass; use of fodder grass; alternate husbandry.

Chapter XVI.

Economic Problems.

(*h*) Surveys of peasant agriculture, including cane farming.

(*i*) Surveys of estate agriculture (other than for sugar).

(*j*) Study of agricultural credit and indebtedness.

(*k*) Examination of producers associations and connected enterprises.

(*l*) Marketing.

Specialised Scientific Problems.

(*m*) Survey of soil and of land utilisation.

(*n*) Soil erosion.

(*o*) Maintenance of soil fertility for perennial crops other than cane.

(*p*) Problems in veterinary science.

(*q*) Nutritional standards for livestock and feeding value of local materials.

(*r*) Plant breeding: cane, bananas, cocoa, rice, limes, food crops.

(*s*) Sugar technology, i.e., factory processes.

(*t*) Food storage, including cold storage.

(*u*) Plant diseases and pests: especially of bananas, cocoa and limes.

This recapitulation is an illustration and not a complete list of the questions to which attention should be given; it will be realised that the three categories under which we have set out the problems have been adopted for convenience and that any such sharp delimitation in practical experimentation would not be possible. (Chapter XVIII, paragraph 4.)

38. Detailed proposals for giving effect to this scheme—apart from the creation of a Department of Veterinary Science—were prepared at our request by the Principal of the College with the assistance of his Heads of Departments. Those proposals have not been formally submitted to the Governing Body of the College, whose approval must, of course, be sought for any extension of the functions of that institution. We do not consider it necessary to reproduce here the scheme prepared by the Principal and his colleagues. It is in a form which would allow immediate examination if our recommendation should be accepted in principle. At our request the Principal also made tentative estimates of the cost of the scheme. Those estimates, which make no provision for veterinary work, show that capital expenditure of the order of £70,000 would be required and that when the scheme was in full operation the additional recurren.

annual expenditure would be of the order of £100,000. It should be understood that these are not close and final figures, and that in any event the complete scheme could not be brought into operation at once. Moreover, allowance should be made for savings in the expenditure of certain Colonial Agricultural Departments, and these cannot well be calculated in advance of definite decisions on the programme of work to be undertaken centrally. (Chapter XVIII, paragraph 8.)

39. It would not be possible for the Governments of the West Indian Colonies to finance this scheme, and for administrative reasons it is desirable that the money required should be found from one source and that the continuance of payments should be guaranteed over a period of years; only thus can scientific work be properly staffed and planned. We recommend, therefore, that Parliament should be invited to ensure the continuance of the scheme for a definite term of years. (Chapter XVIII, paragraph 9.)

17. Special Agricultural Problems.

40. In Chapter IV we described the salient features of the West Indian agricultural system, and we have now completed in this chapter our recommendations for the framing of a new agricultural policy for that area. There remain a number of important problems, each of which is peculiar to one or two of these Colonies or islands; we now propose to state briefly our views on those problems of which more detailed accounts are given in Chapter XXI of the Agricultural Report.

(*a*) BANANA INDUSTRY IN JAMAICA.*

41. Bananas account in value for more than half the export trade of Jamaica, and it would not be possible to replace them, either now or in the near future, by any other commodity which commanded a ready sale. The crop is threatened by Panama disease, soil erosion and leaf-spot disease. Panama disease is encouraged in many ways, of which the most common are the continuous use of land for the growing of bananas and the planting of new areas with suckers from infected land; it is essential that the prohibition of the latter practice should be rigorously enforced and all other possible steps should be taken to check these and other actions which are likely to spread this insidious disease. Soil erosion, which may reduce both the yield and size of the fruit, is often caused by the cultivation of bananas on steep slopes; we have already suggested an immediate survey of the problem of soil erosion throughout the West Indies. Leaf-spot disease has been the subject of careful local investigation since we left Jamaica. The results of those inquiries show that it is a most serious menace to the prosperity

---

* See also note at end of this Chapter.

of the banana industry. The disease can be effectively controlled by spraying the trees with Bordeaux mixture, if this work is correctly done at frequent intervals and is started before the infection reaches an advanced stage.

42. The outlook is most serious and we recommend that, if the necessary campaign against the two diseases and for the local control and prevention of soil erosion, pending the outcome of the survey, cannot be financed by the Jamaica Government, more special financial assistance should be given by Your Majesty's Government.

43. Even if, through spraying or unexpected natural check, leaf-spot disease should be brought under control in a few years, the interim period will be one of difficulty, and a recurrence of the outbreak might take place at any time. From an agricultural standpoint it is therefore desirable that the planting of bananas should be limited to areas where high yields and the proximity of water supply combine to bring the cost of spraying within the means of the producer. Any areas on which bananas can no longer be grown should be developed as rapidly and as fully as possible for the production of food crops as part of the programme of mixed farming. The present piecemeal and unskilful growing of bananas should be displaced by well-regulated production in which spraying and every other aspect of the problem of disease should receive constant attention. (Chapter XXI, paragraph 3.)

44. Much progress with the breeding of bananas resistant to Panama and leaf-spot disease has already been made in Jamaica and at the Imperial College of Tropical Agriculture; every encouragement should be given to this work and in particular to efforts to market the immune varieties now available from these experiments. The possibility of introducing other varieties which are resistant to leaf-spot disease, such as the types known to be on trial in Surinam and Guadeloupe, should also be kept constantly under review. (Chapter XXI, paragraph 2 (*e*) and (*f*).)

45. The application made to us for the grant of an increased preference on bananas imported into the United Kingdom has been examined in Chapter XIV of this report.

(*b*) AGRICULTURAL DEVELOPMENT IN BRITISH HONDURAS.

46. The population of British Honduras is increasing but the employment offered by the forestry industry, which is the principal occupation of the Colony, is declining, and this tendency is not likely to be reversed in the near future. Meanwhile numbers of the people are drifting into Belize and many of them are supported by work on the construction of roads undertaken

by Government partly as a measure of relief. The rapid development of agriculture on improved lines is essential. The Carib and Mayan sections of the population between them account for one-third of the total and are self-supporting. It is suggested that a special Commissioner should be appointed to foster their interests and to assist in improving their agriculture. The soils of the Colony are not well-suited for banana growing and special assistance for this purpose cannot be recommended. (Chapter XXI, paragraphs 7 to 10.)

(c) SUGAR FACTORY AND LAND SETTLEMENT IN NEVIS.

47. The present unhappy state of agriculture in Nevis is described in paragraph 11 of Chapter XXI of the agricultural report. An application was insistently made to us by many sections of the people of that island for financial assistance towards the cost of constructing a modern sugar factory; similar requests were put forward in Dominica, Montserrat and St. Lucia. Nevis was at one time the centre of a thriving sugar industry and its entire dependence, until quite recent times, on the growing of sugar cane differentiates it from the other islands mentioned above. It is, in our view, essential to the future prosperity of Nevis that the growers of sugar cane should receive a better price for their produce. One of the several ways through which their receipts could be improved is by the construction of a small modern factory in Nevis, to which, however, there is the objection that it is always difficult to ensure the efficiency and economical working of small units. That objection would be largely met if an arrangement could be made with the sugar company operating in St. Kitts whereby some of their present staff would supervise the operations of any factory which may be established in Nevis, and we suggest that negotiations to that end should be opened as part of any scheme to rehabilitate the sugar industry in the island. We have been informed of the possibility of effecting substantial savings on the equipment of a factory in Nevis by installing in it some of the machinery now available for purchase owing to the recent sale of a factory which is no longer required in Antigua. That is a matter on which we are not competent to express an opinion. The comparative advantages, both in immediate costs and in working efficiency, of re-erecting the old plant or of installing entirely new machinery would need expert consideration. We feel strongly, however, that urgent action is needed to improve the lot of the people of Nevis, and that this can best take the form of a substantial grant from the Colonial Development Fund towards the cost of erecting a small sugar factory, to be managed under an arrangement on the lines suggested above. If the construction of a factory in Nevis should prove to be impossible and the Government of the

Leeward Islands are unable by other means to obtain a better price under existing arrangements for sugar cane grown in Nevis, some measure of special assistance should, we consider, be granted to the growers, even at the cost of a small subsidy from Government funds, which might, for example, take the form of the provision of transport at uneconomical rates.

48. Land settlement should displace share cropping throughout Nevis and should itself be based on a system of mixed farming with sugar cane as the chief crop; as the growing of sugar develops in Nevis, a quota, increasing ultimately to at least 3,500 tons per annum, should be earmarked for that island.

(d) AGRICULTURAL ASPECTS OF POPULATION PROBLEM IN BARBADOS.

49. Estate enterprise must remain the basis of Barbadian agriculture, but an improvement, and some extension, of peasant agriculture is urgently needed. No internal reform can however, overcome the necessity of finding an outlet for part of the rapidly increasing population. This necessity makes it all the more urgent that soil and land surveys should be undertaken rapidly and energetically in British Honduras, and that the possibility of settling Barbadians on the coastal strip of British Guiana, for which extensive drainage would first be necessary, should also be actively investigated. Special financial assistance will be required if rapid progress, which we regard as essential, is to be made. (Chapter XXI, paragraph 15.)

(e) DRAINAGE PROBLEMS IN BRITISH GUIANA.

50. The nature of these problems, the present condition of the system of drainage in British Guiana and its basic deficiencies are described in paragraphs 16-19 of Chapter XXI of the agricultural report. Comprehensive reform is required. No further scheme of drainage should be undertaken until full data for it have been obtained by survey; many of the costly failures of the past have been due to lack of survey and an entirely inadequate sum has been devoted to that side of the work. It is important that in any future programme of drainage attention should first be paid to the areas which are most suitable from the point of view of sea defence drainage and agricultural value. Moreover, grants of Crown land should not be made in undrainable areas; past experience shows that agricultural effort is always wasted when water cannot be properly controlled.

51. Practically the entire coastal area of British Guiana, where the great majority of the population live and work,

depends upon an elaborate system of sea-walls, drainage, irrigation and navigation canals. The front lands are at or below sea-level, and flow drainage has frequently to be supplemented by pumping.

52. Since the British Guiana system does not involve one great outfall like the Fens of Eastern England, the problem of silting at the various small outfalls, with comparatively small discharge and low silt-removing power, is an extremely serious one. Grouping of the drain trenches to feed a smaller number of large outlets with a higher rate of discharge would help to meet this problem.

53. The sugar estates depend for their prosperity on adequate drainage and, since sugar remains the most profitable crop, practically all well-drained land is found to be in sugar. Inability to maintain the drainage system inevitably means, as on the Essequibo Coast, the abandonment of sugar. The areas devoted to rice and to pasture are badly drained and abound in large swamp areas, where almost amphibious cattle, sheep and pigs eke out an unusual existence.

54. The maintenance of the internal drainage necessary for any form of cultivation is often neglected by the persons concerned, on the plea that the main drainage system is defective. While this has been, and in some areas still is, true, occupiers should remember that complete reform of the main channels will not relieve them of the necessity of attending to their own.

55. The Government has in the past been greatly handicapped in dealing with this problem by the absence of the necessary technical information regarding levels, etc. Proper plans have been prepared by the present Director of Public Works, and we recommend that these plans should be supported by adequate financial help.

56. We endorse the suggestions in the agricultural report, namely, the establishment of a central statutory body to control drainage and irrigation in the same way as the existing Sea Defence Board deals with that aspect of the problem, the ascertainment as soon as possible of the survey data necessary for further works (which might, in time of peace, be done by a detachment of the Royal Engineers) and the correlation of agricultural policy with the drainability of the lands in question.

57. The assumption of central responsibilty for drainage is made necessary by the breakdown of the present system. The local bodies, who are responsible for rather less than one-half of the cost of drainage, are entirely unable to pay interest and sinking fund charges. Even present payments are often made at the expense of vitally necessary work on maintenance.

58. We agree that, although the principle of general debt remissions is undesirable, there is a strong case for the remission of these debts, which are in fact irrecoverable. Further, the cost of drainage, etc., is such that in any future development scheme, the initial drainage will have to be undertaken as an irrecoverable Colonial charge.

(f) Rice Industry in British Guiana.

59. The decline in the sugar industry has caused cultivators throughout the Colony, and particularly on the Essequibo Coast, where sugar has disappeared, to turn to rice cultivation, a crop for which the coast lands are excellently suited. The rice grown in British Guiana is among the best in the world, and could form the basis of an important and profitable export trade, and fully supply the local market. Nevertheless, exports have tended to decline, cultivators are not prospering, and there is even an import from distant Burma. During our stay in British Guiana two reports on the situation were made available—that of Mr. H. Parker, Manager of the Government Rice Mill, Perak, Federated Malay States (Legislative Council Paper No. 3 of 1939), whose inquiry which was financed by a grant of £1,000 from the Colonial Development Fund, and that of a local Committee appointed especially to consider the position on the Essequibo Coast. It is agreed that the troubles from which the industry is suffering are bound up with disorderly marketing and inefficient and uneconomic processing of the grain by far too many small out-of-date and often insanitary mills. The result is that the Demerara product has lost reputation in the export markets where it has to compete with the uniform, reliable product of other, better-organised producers, and the grower, not knowing from day to day what price he will receive, except that it will be a low one, has little incentive to take the extra trouble with his grain which will ensure its delivery in the best condition for processing.

60. Mr. Parker himself, and the local committee with which he was in consultation, both recommended the establishment of Government central mills to supersede the existing small inadequate establishments, starting on the Essequibo Coast. The new mill or mills would be financed by Government but operated on commercial lines. A stable price for grain would be guaranteed, thus bringing certainty into the operations of the grower. The new mill or mills would operate more economically with better machinery than the existing mills, and ensure a product of reliable standard which could regain favour in the export market. The local committee worked out a scheme of compensation for the benefit of the millers who would be affected, on a basis which Mr. Parker held to be too generous, since he did not consider that they need go entirely out of

business, but that they could continue under supervision as collecting and drying agents.

61. We consider that speedy development on these lines is strongly desirable, and we trust that the interests of the present inefficient millers will not be permitted to hold up a development for the benefit of the industry and the Colony as a whole, although we do not exclude the possibility of some compensation in suitable cases, bearing in mind the opportunities which will remain for the ex-millers to act as middlemen. We would draw attention especially to Mr. Parker's suggestion that the new mill should at first be under the charge of an experienced manager from Burma or Malaya.

(g) COCOA INDUSTRY IN TRINIDAD AND GRENADA.

62. In paragraphs 28-34 of Chapter XXI of the agricultural report the present situation of the cocoa industry of Trinidad is examined, as are also the form and effect of the subsidy which has been paid to growers of cocoa in that island during the last three years. The conclusion there reached, with which we agree, is that the cocoa subsidy should be put on an entirely new basis, under which its objective would, in fact, cease to be that of relief and would become the rehabilitation of the industry. As part of this plan unsuitable land, on which cocoa is now grown, should be used for other purposes, and on the remainder of the area on which cocoa would continue to be grown the aim should be to secure a general improvement of the standard of cultivation and of the quality of the crop. The replanting of from 20 per cent. to 30 per cent. of the worst trees during the next 10 years would probably be conformable with safety and would greatly promote the rehabilitation of the industry. This objective must also be ensured by laying down definite conditions which receivers of the subsidy are to follow and by the firm enforcement of those conditions.

63. The comments which in the agricultural report are made upon the situation of the cocoa industry in Trinidad apply equally to Grenada, with the exception that witchbroom disease does not occur in that island. The growers of cocoa in Grenada have a reasonable claim to assistance from Government, based on the principles which we have suggested for adoption in Trinidad. The Government of Grenada are, however, without funds from which to provide this measure of assistance, and we recommend, therefore, that, subject to full consideration of any recommendations made as the result of the recent survey of the position of the cocoa industry in that island, it should be granted by Your Majesty's Government. As we have said in Chapter IV of this report, it is possible that, if growers of cocoa in the West Indies can bring about improvements, partly

by lowering their costs of production, they may well be able, as time goes on, to regain part of the ground which they have lost in the world market, and there is, therefore, strong reason for taking active steps to maintain the present output of cocoa from those Colonies.

18. Forestry.

64. Forestry is of no commercial importance in Jamaica, the Leeward Islands and the Windward Islands, in all of which, however, its problems should receive skilful attention if only because of their connection with water supplies and with soil erosion. A Forest Officer is now employed in Jamaica; in those high areas where no form of agriculture could be profitable, the bush should be strictly protected from shifting cultivation and burning, and when the soil has regained sufficient fertility, it should be reafforested and then be permanently reserved. In addition, powers given by existing legislation for the protection of forests should be more rigidly used. (Chapter XIX, paragraphs 3-5.)

65. In the Leeward and Windward Islands property boundaries should be demarcated, the Ordinance affecting forestry should be revised and a larger staff and more effective action are needed to enforce control. The need for staff could perhaps be met by giving a certain proportion of the Agricultural Officers in the two groups a training in forestry sufficient to fit them to take charge of the control of forests under supervision, which would be provided by visits of inspection at intervals of a few years. We suggest that the Government of Trinidad should be invited to undertake both the training of senior forest subordinates for the Leeward and Windward Islands and the arrangements for visits of inspection by a senior member of the staff of their Forest Department. (Chapter XIX, paragraphs 6-7.)

66. In British Honduras, the most important problem is that of safeguarding the future of mahogany, which, at present rates of cutting and regeneration, is a steadily disappearing resource. Many small contractors ignore the felling regulations laid down by the Government of the Colony and show no care for, or interest in, the regeneration of mahogany; the methods of the Belize Estate and Produce Company stand out in sharp contrast to this practice. The three plain needs in British Honduras are better forest protection, the reconstitution of mahogany areas and the continuation and amplification of the forest survey, possibly with the aid of aerial photography. The admirable preliminary survey already completed by the Forestry Department should be a good basis for the latter development. For the past eight years the efforts of that Department to maintain an executive policy have been impeded by fluctuations in the

amount of money available for its purposes. The definition of a clear forest policy for this Colony is an urgent necessity, and when one has been laid down, the funds provided must be sufficient to permit consistent continuity in giving effect to it. It must be understood, however, that in the future forestry, which was the basis of past prosperity, will not be able to meet the needs of all the growing population. While it should be sedulously preserved, agricultural development must, as we have pointed out, be regarded as essential. (Chapter XIX, paragraphs 9-16.)

67. In British Guiana valuation surveys covering 1,800 square miles and preliminary surveys covering another 800 square miles have already been completed. The principal needs in this Colony are continued survey and valuation, more extensive and protected regeneration of greenheart (which is the chief commercial species), the expansion of markets for greenheart and an outlet for sawn lumber both in the Colony itself and in other West Indian Colonies. Of equal importance is the pursuit of a continuous forestry policy which has hitherto been impossible mainly for reasons of finance. We are of the opinion that, if wider markets could be found, greenheart could be exploited on an increased scale at a low cost including that of proper attention to regeneration. Proposals, which would involve substantial financial guarantees by Government, have been put to us for the manufacture of wood pulp from wallaba. We consider that such questions as the world demand for pulp and the relation between factory cost and probable output have not been sufficiently investigated to enable us to express any opinion as to the financial possibilities of this proposal. In any case, as we stated in Chapter XIII of this report, we regard it as undesirable that Governments in the West Indies should either conduct or finance speculative industrial enterprises. (Chapter XIX, paragraphs 17-23.)

68. A well-defined forestry policy has been laid down by the Government of Trinidad. Mora, which is the most valuable species in this island, frequently occurs at high density, and its present utilisation nowhere approaches permissible production. In hard woods the Colony is practically self-supporting, but the importation of soft woods, several species of which are available in the island, will be necessary for several years to come. Although local requirements for timber are on the increase, the dominating problem is to find an outlet for the forest products of the Colony which are certain to show a marked upward trend as the programme of forestry development progresses. (Chapter XIX, paragraphs 24-27.)

69. It is clear that, for the three Colonies in which forestry is of commercial importance, the two problems which have to

be faced are those of defining a policy and of finding markets. In each case the Forestry Department has carried out the survey on which policy must be based and has proposed a policy, but, in practice, owing largely to financial reasons, it has hitherto been impossible to adhere steadily to a policy in either British Honduras or British Guiana. Continuity is of special importance in forestry; without it expenditure on regeneration or protection over one period of years may be completely wasted if followed by neglect. The need for market expansion in all three Colonies is equally clear, and after full consideration of the evidence presented to us about the arrangements made by the Colonial Office for both the supervision of forest policy in these Colonies and the giving of assistance to their Governments in searching for markets for their forest products, we feel that those arrangements are in both cases far from adequate. We recommend, therefore, that both points should be the subject of investigation by an expert. Though the importance of a systematic forest policy does not appear yet to have been appreciated by the Colonial Office, there have been in recent years notable improvements in the standard of forest officers recruited and in their training. We support the suggestion in the Agricultural Report that the duties of the officer in charge of the Forestry Department of one of the three Colonies should be enlarged so as to include a general supervision over the activities of the Departments in the two other Colonies. (Chapter XIX, paragraph 28.)

Further Note on the Banana Industry in Jamaica.

The considerations discussed in paragraphs 41-45 disclose a sufficiently serious situation for the Jamaican banana industry. Since our Report reached the proof stage, we have learnt with much regret of storm damage which is officially reported to have caused loss of bananas averaging 75 per cent. of the bearing trees, and amounting in some areas to total destruction. Advances from already depleted Colonial funds of up to £75,000 each to the Banana Industry Aid Board and to the Agricultural Loan Society, for re-loan to cultivators whose crops have been destroyed or damaged, have been approved by the Jamaica Legislative Council. This development aggravates the banana situation and strengthens the claim of the industry for financial assistance from other than Colonial funds. The opportunity should be taken to foster the rehabilitation of the industry on a sounder basis than hitherto, in the light of the principles enunciated above. Attention has already been called to the danger of undue reliance by a country or by an individual cultivator, large or small, on a single agricultural product.

CHAPTER XVII.

LAND SETTLEMENT.

1. The Nature of Land Settlement.

1. In every place which we visited in the course of our travels in the West Indies, our attention was invited to the possibility of extensive land settlement, and it was clear from the tenor of much of the evidence which we heard that many people in these islands expect from land settlement results and benefits which, in practice, would be found difficult or impossible to realise. The nature and potentialities of land settlement appear not to be properly appreciated in many quarters in the West Indies, and the issues which we are now to discuss will continue to be clouded until there is a clear realisation that it means no more than an orderly plan for settling people on the land in considerable numbers as small-holders and providing them with assistance in marketing, instruction, cultivations and livestock and, at times, credit facilities

2. General Considerations.

2. Land settlement is therefore one aspect of peasant farming, and in the framing of any proposals regard must be had both to its own special needs, which we discuss below, and to the views which we expressed when we examined, in Chapters IV and XVI of this report, the general question of peasant agriculture. For convenience, the conclusions which we then reached are briefly repeated below:—

(*a*) Mixed farming must be the basis, and specialisation should be avoided.

(*b*) The production of foods for domestic use and for local sale should be the main objective.

(*c*) Steps should be taken to ensure the successful marketing of produce and the improvement of livestock.

(*d*) Family life is everywhere a feature of successful peasant farming, and the need for encouraging this should be borne in mind.

(*e*) Peasant agriculture must be made complementary to estate agriculture through the provision of work for wages for those who desire it.

(*f*) Importance should be attached to the selection of suitable types of men.

(*g*) Unremitting attention should be given to agricultural education.

(*h*) Both the freehold and leasehold systems of tenure should be tried.

3. Central Farm.

3. Before we can discuss the factors and requirements which must be specially considered in connection with any scheme of land settlement, it is necessary to examine a form of co-operation which is frequently advocated. This consists of the grouping of settlers around a central farm maintained by the Government. The farm is intended to supply instruction, to grant advances on crops or other suitable credits, to arrange by wholesale buying for cheap supplies of fertilisers, etc., to undertake heavy cultivation for settlers through the use of mechanical power, and to be a centre for the co-operative marketing of produce and the focus of general culture and social intercourse.

4. A system based on a central farm is necessarily elaborate and may be expensive unless the farm serves a large number of settlers. Although the arrangement has great theoretical advantages, in practice it is by no means easy to work. The co-operative marketing of produce from a large number of growers depends for success, as do all forms of marketing, on a reasonably steady output. This means, in practice, that settlers must be constrained or inspired to arrange their cropping plans and their general programme of work upon some common basis. In the present state of agricultural knowledge in the West Indies, and in view of the limited experience which their peoples have of organised action, it is improbable that any attempt to introduce a common cropping plan would be attended with immediate success. This opinion is supported by the proved failure, or very limited success, of schemes already attempted for the marketing of the produce of peasants in some of these Colonies. Moreover, a central service of heavy cultivations by tractors implies a degree of regimentation which is unlikely to be acceptable at present to peasant cultivators in the West Indies.

5. In our opinion, any system of co-operation based upon a central farm demands a greater sacrifice of personal interest and convenience than can reasonably be expected in present circumstances in most parts of the British West Indies; and while we see no reason why any Colonial Government which wishes to make, and can finance, an experiment on these lines, should not be allowed to do so, we feel doubtful whether the system could be applied on a wide scale anywhere in these Colonies. Co-operation among small-holders is, however, highly desirable, and where the method of ensuring this through the establishment of a central farm is not adopted, Governments should consider most carefully the alternative means by which it can be secured, and when they have decided which of them is most suited to the need of any particular settlement, should take every possible step to bring about the active pursuit of that method.

4. Special Considerations.

6. Much attention has been given recently in several parts of the world to the question of the special requirements of land settlement. These special requirements naturally vary on points of detail with local circumstances, and we propose, therefore, to give only the following outline of the more important among them:—

(*a*) A most careful examination of the proposed site from every point of view is necessary to ensure both that the soil is suitable in texture and chemically and is of good depth, and that slopes likely to induce erosion are avoided.

(*b*) Good access from a main road should be provided to the settlement, and in laying out roads attention should be paid to drainage requirements and the need for avoiding erosion.

(*c*) A good water supply should be ensured and particular care should be exercised to avoid both the selection of sites where malaria is prevalent and the introduction of that disease.

(*d*) Proximity to schools, churches and other social amenities should be considered when sites are being selected for settlement.

(*e*) So far as possible each holding should be compact and the arrangement, now common, whereby one man owns or rents a number of widely separated plots should be discouraged.

(*f*) Variations in the size of holdings will depend in part on the nature of the land; the question whether work for wages on estates is available in the neighbourhood of a settlement is another factor which should be borne in mind.

5. Credit Facilities and Other Assistance.

7. The questions of the form and extent of financial and other assistance to settlers during and after their establishment on the land have been widely debated. Formal instruction and occasional advice should be given generously everywhere, and financial assistance will generally be required in the early stages of any scheme of land settlement. It must, however, be remembered that experience has shown that settlers may be spoiled and lose their self-reliance if they are led to believe that they can rely upon Government for financial support whenever they encounter difficulties. It should be firmly impressed on all concerned in the business of peasant farming, whatever its form, that the success of their enterprise depends upon their own exertions.

8. When settlers are given freehold tenure, subject to their repaying the cost of the land by instalments, repayment should not begin for three years, thus allowing the man a reasonable time within which to earn a profit, and should be spread over longer periods than those now customary. Experience has shown that where rapid repayment is required the settler may impoverish his holding in the early years in the attempt to meet this obligation, and that the consequent process of restoring the fertility of the soil is both prolonged and expensive. We would also repeat here the suggestion made in the preceding Chapter that the grant of freehold rights should be subject to appropriate conditions to prevent fragmentation of the land and to suitable safeguards of good husbandry, including the prevention of erosion and the maintenance of soil fertility.

9. Credit facilities are widely demanded, but the evidence which we heard showed that the prospect of repayment is not encouraging unless it is secured on crops which are processed in factories or which pass through a single outlet for export. It must also be borne in mind that the grant of special assistance, in the form of credit facilities to new settlers, is open to objection and creates difficulties, about which we heard evidence, unless Governments are prepared to extend the same measures to established cultivators who are encountering difficulties, such as that of finding a market for their produce, similar to those which led to the grants to the newcomers.

6. Value of Land Settlement and its Financial Aspects.

10. Land settlement in most parts of the world is still in an experimental stage. There is no one perfect or generally applicable plan, and all the West Indian Governments must regard their existing and immediate projects as being in part an endeavour to discover the principles and methods best suited to their circumstances. They must also realise that, as experience everywhere has shown, land settlement usually involves heavy expenditure, only part of which is recoverable through the return of purchase money; it is, however, not unreasonable to reckon against these losses the social and agricultural improvements which should ensue from the organised placing of some of the labouring population in possession, or in secure tenancy, of land.

11. It was represented to us that reluctance to meet such obligations as the repayment of loans or the payment of rent or taxes on small properties is characteristic of the West Indian Colonies. This view is supported by the experience of a number of the Colonial Governments and we feel bound to say that a more general recognition of the duty of meeting debts promptly will be necessary if land settlement in these Colonies is to be rapidly extended.

12. We have stated in the preceding Chapter of this report that we regard it as essential that all the West Indian Governments should have easily applied powers to enable them to acquire compulsorily agricultural land when it is needed for such purposes as land settlement. We there indicated in general terms the various ways by which a basis for valuation might be reached, and we would only add here that when, as was also recommended in Chapter XVI, the system under which peasants pay rent in the form of a share of their crops is replaced by land settlement, the price at which the land is taken over should be based, not on any excessive returns received by its owner under the share system, but on the average of profits made from land of the same type when worked on the plantation system.

7. Existing and Projected Settlements.

13. The Royal Commission of 1897 put land settlement first among the measures of relief which they recommended and the West India Sugar Commission of 1930 (Cmd. 3517) supported their view. Although many attempts at settlement have been made, few have been on a large scale and very few have had unqualified success. We have devoted much attention to the hearing of evidence about land settlement in all these Colonies and we have inspected a number of settled areas. In the course of our investigation examples came to our notice of disregard of most of the requirements which we have described in preceding sections of this Chapter as contributing to the success of schemes of land settlement. We now propose to describe briefly any points of outstanding importance in the schemes or projects of the various Colonies.

(a) JAMAICA.

14. In 1938 the Government of this Colony decided on extensive land settlement at an estimated cost of £650,000 of which £400,000 was to be spent on the purchase of land. The intention is that instalments paid by tenants should be credited to the original fund, thus providing money to be spent on further settlement. The consent of the Legislative Council is required for each separate purchase of land under the scheme, and this leads to both difficulty and delay. Adequate arrangements have not been made for the survey of sites and the study of soil conditions, nor, so far as we know, has a policy been evolved for suitable agricultural systems, choice of crops and marketing. Swift development is contemplated and widely demanded in spite of the fact that many of the settlers will be entirely untrained in agriculture, apart from a comparatively short course upon which undue reliance appears to be placed.

Furthermore, it may not be sufficiently appreciated that the settlement scheme will call either for a substantial increase of the staff of the Department of Agriculture, or for a large Land Settlement Department, and that the administrative costs may therefore be disproportionate to the resulting benefits. It seems desirable, therefore—although the pressing necessity for settlement cannot be questioned—that at the outset action should be cautious, should be preceded by most careful preparation and should be frankly regarded as, in a large measure, experimental. The transcendent necessity of improving existing small holdings, in addition to the creation of new settlements, must not be overlooked.

(b) British Honduras.

15. We have already expressed the view that whatever may be done to conserve and reconstitute the forest resources of this Colony, it is imperative that a considerable number of the people should be diverted to employment on permanent agriculture. The prospects of the successful establishment of any enterprise on a large scale in the form of plantations are not such as to encourage private investment, and in any case the production of food ought to be the first objective of agricultural expansion. Settlement on small-holdings therefore appears to be the inescapable task of Government. An admitted aversion from steady, continuous work on the land, which is natural in a country where forest work has been the normal occupation, will add greatly to the difficulties of this task. That disinclination is a significant and unfortunate feature which has been particularly noticeable among the people settled recently at Rockstone Pond, near Belize. The settlers, who have no previous experience of agricultural work and learn slowly, seem unable to resist the temptation to leave their holdings at frequent intervals in order to visit Belize where they stay for several days.

16. Plans are being considered for the settlement in a valley south of Cayo, which is in the west of the Colony, of selected Barbadians whose traditional agricultural skill should publicly demonstrate the possibilities of land settlement. Access to the area, a survey of soil and the adoption of a suitable agricultural system are essential to the success of this deserving scheme, and we consider that the tentative proposals, of which we were informed, for the preparatory work of soil examination need further consideration. Permanent settlement, based on the considerations described earlier in this Chapter, should be the aim, and the temporary exploitation of holdings through the growing of bananas should be definitely precluded.

(c) ANGUILLA.

17. The success achieved here by settlers on poor land, who have received little assistance from Government, is encouraging, but for any future developments it will be necessary for the Government to acquire new land and we recommend that this possibility should at once be investigated. If the annual migration of labour to San Domingo should be further curtailed, Anguilla would be in a critical state.

(d) ST. KITTS.

18. There is little scope for land settlement in this island, except through the displacement of estate cane growing by peasant cane growing which, if experience elsewhere is a good guide, would involve a considerable drop in yields. It is, however, both possible and desirable for estate labourers to be given more facilities and advice with the growing of food crops. Good progress has already been made in this respect in St. Kitts by comparison with some of the other West Indian territories, but estates should recognise that their duty is not limited to the provision of land, but extends to the giving of assistance and encouragement to the efforts of their labourers to produce their own food. At present food plots on steep slopes are a frequent cause of soil erosion.

(e) NEVIS.

19. Land settlement in this island has been sufficiently successful to augur well for the future, and the tenacity of settlers in places, such as the Hamilton Estate, where they are handicapped by natural conditions, is much to be praised.

20. We have stated elsewhere our conclusion that share cropping should be brought to an end; one method is through the acquisition of estates now used for share cropping and their conversion into small holdings.

(f) ANTIGUA.

21. Many peasants have been settled on the land in this island and have attained considerable success. Unfortunately, however, cane growing is the basis of all the settlements. A system under which Government tractors would plough all peasant land in preparation for cane, might be tried, but we consider that a wiser policy would be the development of peasant mixed farming, including maize, cattle and pigs. It is impossible, as yet, to make a fair judgment of the financial results of the existing land settlement, but these should be constantly scrutinised.

(g) MONTSERRAT.

22. There has been no land settlement in this island, and estates unable to cultivate directly more than a part of their land have been forced into share cropping in association with peasants whose earnings from wage work are insufficient to maintain them. In the framing of any scheme of land settlement for Montserrat it must be remembered that the island as a whole is very mountainous and that much of its soil is poor, shallow, filled with boulders and on steep slopes. In such conditions erosion is hard to overcome and the fertility of the soil is difficult to maintain. On much of the land cane could be grown and would be more suitable than any other crop, but could not be adopted, even as one element in a programme of mixed farming, unless an export quota is allotted to the island. The right course is, in our opinion, the displacement of crop sharing by peasant settlement under a scheme of mixed farming.

(h) DOMINICA.

23. We were told that the wish for land settlement in this island is less keen that it is in the other Leeward Islands. We are not convinced on that point and we think that a decision about future land settlement policy should be guided by the results of the survey of peasant agriculture which we have recommended in Chapter XVI. The Administration have developed about 100 acres of land, which is planted with orange and grapefruit trees, with the intention of dividing it into small holdings when those trees reach full bearing. Such specialised holdings are, as we have made clear, undesirable.

(i) ST. LUCIA.

24. The desire of the Government of this island is to expand land settlement rapidly, but it would be dangerous to disregard the need to determine by preliminary investigation which system of peasant agriculture is best suited to the circumstances and needs of St. Lucia. Any settlements which are developed immediately would have to be based on the growing of bananas and we cannot recommend specialisation in that crop.

25. Before export quotas had been prescribed for the Colonies under the International Sugar Agreement the Government of Barbados were negotiating the acquisition of an estate in St. Lucia for the purposes of land settlement. Unless a special addition can be made to the quota of sugar export from St. Lucia, this scheme must be abandoned, or diverted to another basis.* We are strongly of the opinion that every effort should

---

* The export quota for St. Lucia was fixed in 1937 to allow for this scheme, but a further addition is nevertheless necessary if the settlement is to produce on an economical scale.

be made to arrange an increase in the St. Lucia quota, but that cane growing should not, in any event, be the basis of agriculture in the settlement. Mixed farming with livestock and including cane should be adopted. Special importance attaches to this scheme since it involves a migration of population. If attended by marked success the scheme may provide a precedent for organised plans for settling Barbadians elsewhere in the West Indies, provided that suitable land can be found: failure would seriously prejudice any further efforts in this direction.

(j) St. Vincent.

26. Peasant agriculture is already extensive and produces one-third of the arrowroot, two-fifths of the cotton, and all the food crops grown in this island. Some peasants rent land, some share land, and some have bought land from estates or under settlement schemes. We were told that there is still a keen demand for land among estate labourers, but it does not appear to be known whether this demand is prompted by a wish to be independent of wage work or by the need to supplement their earnings. Here again, more land settlement ought not to be attempted until suitable systems of mixed farming for peasants have been devised. Unless land is acquired from estates, settlement must be on the hills, and terracing or other expensive measures against erosion will be essential. Several estates are financially embarrassed, and it might be possible to acquire some of these for settlement after the full requisite preparatory action. Share cropping is a common practice in this island and is open to the great objections explained elsewhere.

(k) Grenada.

27. This island is remarkable for the large number of its peasant cultivators. In addition to 19 settlement schemes covering 4,000 acres there are believed to be some 18,000 small holdings covering about 25,000 acres of land. The disorderliness and low productivity of many holdings on some of the settlements which have been established for several years are striking illustrations of the need for improved forms of peasant agriculture and we are convinced that this improvement, and not the immediate development of fresh land settlements, is the paramount need in Grenada.

(l) Barbados.

28. Although there is a large number of small proprietors in Barbados, there has been no official land settlement in this Colony and the inevitable dependence of the dense population upon estate sugar production appears to us to preclude future

settlement. We have referred in Chapter XVI and in preceding sections of this Chapter to the possibilities of the migration of Barbadians to, and their settlement in, other parts of the West Indies.

(*m*) BRITISH GUIANA.

29. Committees appointed during recent years by the Government of British Guiana have put forward proposals for various types of land settlement which included the provision of more land for estate labourers, the extended cultivation of village lands and entirely new settlements. Those proposals are, in our view, incomplete, since they leave unsolved fundamental problems connected with cropping, marketing and agricultural systems. The financial proposals made in some of these reports appear to be of doubtful soundness and in particular to make inadequate provision for draining and irrigation. All requirements rightly described as necessary for the new land settlement proposals—including such difficult undertakings as draining—are the common necessity of all existing small-scale agriculture. We consider that these fundamental problems should be tackled not in the limited connection of new land settlement but for the whole of existing and future peasant agriculture. The prospect of the rapid creation of new land settlements in British Guiana is, in our view, remote.

30. In making the above comments we have had mainly in mind the possibilities of settlement along the coastal strip which is the only area at present extensively cultivated. We gave attention also while in the Colony to the possibilities of settlement in the hinterland, but, in view of the visit made between February and April last by the special Commission which has since reported (Cmd. 6014) on the suitability of parts of the interior for Jewish settlement, we do not propose to comment upon those possibilities.

(*n*) TRINIDAD.

31. A Committee appointed by the Government of Trinidad in 1938 recommended an extension of land settlement in the two forms of garden allotments for the growing of food and larger settlements for the growing of economic crops. The Committee stated that the prospects of settlers engaged in the production of cash crops were poor owing to the economic conditions prevailing throughout the world, and they recommended that as much attention and encouragement should be given to existing small-holders as was given to new schemes of land settlement. We are much impressed by the importance of this recommendation, and we consider that it would be far wiser for the Government of Trinidad to spend money on improvements to existing small holdings which (particularly those in

the possession of the numerous cane farmers) are capable of great betterment, than on the purchase of land which has failed when growing either sugar or cocoa. Much land of this kind is in fact available, but its development for small holdings ought not to be attempted until fundamentally improved systems of peasant husbandry have been devised.

8. General Conclusions and Recommendations.

32. A substantial increase in peasant farming throughout these Colonies is necessary to ensure the larger production of food for local consumption and is one way of tackling the problem of under-employment. Both these considerations gain more force each year with the annual increase of population. The method of land settlement is, however, only one of several ways by which the number of peasant holdings could be increased and their yield improved. It must be remembered that land settlement schemes in the West Indies are expensive and throw a charge on the finances of the Colonies concerned that is heavy in relation to the number of persons settled. This necessarily limits the extent to which land settlement is possible apart from external financial assistance. Any plans to improve the husbandry of existing small-holders and to provide additional land for their sons should receive at least the same measure of encouragement from Government as is given to large, formal land settlement colonies, and for some time to come the betterment of existing peasant agriculture will be far more practicable and fruitful than the undertaking of new schemes of settlement.

33. Every Government in the British West Indies should re-examine its existing or immediately projected plans for land settlement in the light of these general considerations and of what we have said about the progress and experience of the schemes already undertaken in particular territories. The next step would be for each Government to make proposals for the improvement of existing settlements and for the establishment of new settlements, but fresh development should not be carried out on an extensive scale until, through the reorganisation of Agricultural Departments and the carrying out of at least preliminary scientific investigations, both of which are recommended in Chapter XVI, the way has been cleared for the planning of settlement on a new and sounder basis of agriculture.

CHAPTER XVIII.

CLOSER UNION AND THE UNIFICATION OF LOCAL SERVICES.

1. History of question of Closer Union.

1. From time to time over a long period the possibility of the political federation of the British West Indies has engaged the attention of the British Government, of the local administrations and of persons, both here and in the Caribbean area, who take an interest in questions of constitutional development.

2. It is not necessary for our purpose to go further back in history than 1922, when Lord Halifax (then Major the Hon. E. F. L. Wood, M.P.) included the following paragraph in the Report (Cmd. 1679) on an official visit which he, as Parliamentary Under-Secretary of State for the Colonies, had made to the West Indies:—

> "The establishment of West Indian political unity is likely to be a plant of slow and tender growth. If any advance in this direction is to be achieved, it can only be as the result of a deliberate demand of local opinion, springing from the realization of the advantages of co-operation under modern world conditions . . . . I am satisfied that, so long as public opinion stands where it does to-day, it is both inopportune and impracticable to attempt amalgamation of existing units of Government into anything approaching a general federal system."

3. Nothing that we need record occurred thereafter until 1929, when Unofficial Members of the Executive and Legislative Councils of Antigua suggested, in a petition to the Secretary of State for the Colonies, that Trinidad, the Windward Islands and the Leeward Islands might be combined under a single Governor with one Legislative Council for the new Colony, the local affairs of each constituent island being left to a Commissioner and Local Council which, in matters of finance, would act under the authority, or subject to the approval, of the Governor in Legislative Council. In the following year the West Indian Sugar Commission, in Part IV of their Report, (Colonial No. 49 of 1930), recommended to the Secretary of State the consideration of the possibilities of an administrative conjunction of the Windward and Leeward Islands which, they said, " would be more conducive to their agricultural progress and prosperity and to the maintenance of a continuous, instead of an intermittent, policy of land settlement and improvement of peasant agriculture and co-operation."

4. Influenced in part by these views and in part by the importance of exploring every possible method of increasing economy and efficiency, Lord Passfield, as Secretary of State for the Colonies in 1931—at a time when retrenchment in public expenditure was a vital consideration—suggested to the

Governors of Trinidad, the Leeward and the Windward Islands that a Commission should be appointed to investigate the possibility of closer union between those territories, or some of them. The suggestion was accepted in principle by the Governments concerned, and in November of the following year a Commission was appointed by Lord Swinton (then Sir Philip Cunliffe-Lister), as Lord Passfield's successor. In its Report (Cmd. 4383) that body, which spent three months in investigating on the spot the problems referred to it, made the following recommendation:—

" The islands at present forming the Colonies of the Leeward Islands and the Windward Islands should be united into one Colony under a Governor, with Headquarters at St. Lucia.

" The present federation of the Leeward Islands should be dissolved and each Presidency should be given in general the same independence as is at present possessed by the three islands of the Windwards Group, each retaining as now its own Executive and Legislative Council under the Presidency of the Administrator or Commissioner, enacting its own laws, and regulating in general its own finance and local affairs.

" The three islands of the Windwards group should similarly remain autonomous as now. We recommend no unification of services at the present stage except in the case of the Police Force and of Agriculture, for which latter a detailed scheme is put forward."

5. The Commissioners also defined their conception of the position and duties of the Governor of the new Colony and laid special emphasis on the need for him to maintain, by frequent tours, the closest possible touch with the constitutional organs in the several islands in the proceedings of which he was, however, to take no direct part. They found it impossible to recommend any form of political union between Trinidad and the smaller islands since they had been convinced that any such proposal would receive no support in Trinidad where the opinion which they consulted was strongly opposed to any undertaking which would involve serious financial responsibilities or commitments.

6. The Leeward Islands differ constitutionally from the Windward Islands in that the former is a federation of units with local autonomy in all matters save those expressly delegated to the Federal Legislature, while the Windward Islands are three separate Colonies united only to the extent denoted by their having a common Governor. The Commission of 1932-3 recommended the extension to the Leeward Islands of the constitutional arrangements then obtaining in the Windwards group. The resulting organisation would have been an association of eight Colonies under one Governor, but otherwise independent of each other and autonomous in every respect. The Commission, after remarking that this appeared " to be a retrograde, rather than a progressive step in the direction of closer union " continued as follows:—

" We desire to make it clear that our proposals do not pretend to be more than a first step—and that a tentative one—towards a real federation, not only of the islands with which we are dealing, but of other units in the West Indies which may eventually be found willing to join. We hope that, partly as a result of the Annual Conferences between the several islands of the group under the chairmanship of the Governor, the early institution of which we regard as of the utmost importance, the islands may themselves evolve a much closer union than the very loose one we are now suggesting. Obviously the next step should be the establishment of Federal Executive and Legislative Councils, dealing with matters of common interest to all the islands, as distinguished from those of purely local concern. In this connection we should like to refer to the West Indies Conference inaugurated in 1926, at which delegates from all the islands meet periodically to discuss matters of common interest. Meetings of this Conference at regular intervals will, we trust, be continued, and by this means the idea of a wider West Indian Federation will be kept in sight, and, it is to be hoped in course of time, be attained."

7. After the Secretary of State had given preliminary consideration to the proposals of the Commission, local Governments were asked to prepare provisional estimates of the cost of putting them into effect. It was found that the amalgamation would involve a net increase in annual expenditure of over £6,000 in addition to certain non-recurrent expenditure. When the proposals were debated in the Legislative Councils of the two groups a considerable divergence of opinion was disclosed, particularly on the question of additional expense. In the circumstances Lord Swinton decided that it was not practicable to proceed with the scheme which the Commission had put forward.

2. Evidence of present local opinion.

8. Although the question of closer union has remained officially in abeyance since the events described above, there is evidence that a lively and growing interest has continued to be taken in it in many political circles in the West Indies, some of which now advocate, as part of their programmes, wide measures of federation to cover all the British Colonies in the Caribbean area. For example, the Guianese and West Indies Labour Congress put before us definite proposals—in the form of a Bill to provide for a federal constitution for the British West Indies—for the appointment of a Governor-General for the Colony of the Bahamas, as well as the seven Colonies falling within our terms of reference, and for the creation of a Federal Executive Council, with an unofficial majority, and a Federal Legislative Council elected in and from the eight Colonies composing the federation. It is true that the meeting of the Congress convened for the purpose of preparing the memorandum submitted to us was attended by representatives from only three Colonies (Barbados, British Guiana and Trinidad), but it is evident that throughout the British West Indies contact is being maintained between those in each Colony who are most interested in securing rapid political progress, and constitutional

developments, such as the widening of the franchise, in any area may be found to reinforce the strength of the movement for federation of the whole group.

9. These considerations became apparent at an early stage of our inquiry, and we therefore put to most of the unofficial witnesses, who appeared before us in a representative political capacity, the question whether they favoured the idea of the closer union of the West Indian Colonies. Almost every witness thus questioned was in favour of closer union, but few of them were able or prepared to define the degree or nature of federation which they considered desirable. Our general impression, from the evidence which we heard, is that while local opinion has made a considerable advance in the direction of political unity since 1932, it is doubtful whether the time is yet ripe for the introduction of any large scheme of federation. Local pride is a most important factor and recent experience has shown that efforts to secure co-operation for the common good from all the West Indian Colonies are still at times frustrated by an insularity which is illustrated by the scepticism felt by even well informed people who freely express the view that nothing beneficial to their Colony could result from institutions established elsewhere in the West Indies. There is room, therefore, for doubting the readiness of West Indian opinion to accept federation in principle. Even if that doubt could be removed, the practical difficulties appear still to be insuperable, and on this question we feel bound in present circumstances to subscribe to the conclusion reached by Lord Halifax in 1922 that " it is both inopportune and impracticable to attempt amalgamation of existing units of Government into anything approaching a general federal system ". Nevertheless, a combination into one political entity of all the British possessions in the Caribbean area is the ideal to which, in our opinion, policy should be directed. With that in view an attempt should be made to overcome local prejudice against federation, both by the exposition of its theoretical advantages and by testing these in practice, as soon as a suitable opportunity presents itself, through the amalgamation of some of the smaller units. Both these points are considered below.

3. Advantages of Federation.

10. The Commission of 1932-33 recorded that the witnesses before them made it clear that for any federation or closer union to be acceptable it must achieve economy in administration. That is, no doubt, a desirable end in itself, but it would be shortsighted policy to reject the principle of amalgamation merely because in its initial stages it would not secure savings on salaries or other administrative expenses. On any long view

it appears unquestionable that monies available for social services can be better and more wisely controlled if those services in a large number of islands are made to work to a uniform plan under common direction. The savings thus obtained should soon outweigh any immediate additional expense. In particular, if Your Majesty's Government are to make more financial provision for the needs of the West Indies, it appears to us to be more important that those monies should be well and wisely spent than that small economies in administration should be obtained. Any measure of closer union, however small, should help in this direction. Moreover through the payment of higher salaries, which could no doubt be made available from the funds of any amalgamated group of Colonies, the services of officers with better qualifications and greater experience should be obtainable and considerable benefits might be expected to result.

11. Other advantages which could be secured by any amalgamation of West Indian Colonies are that the unification of local services, to which we refer later in this Chapter, would be facilitated, and that free trade would be possible, and should in fact be the rule, within any federated group.

4. Amalgamation of Leeward Islands and Windward Islands.

12. A practical test, on a small scale, of what appear to us to be the advantages of federation could most easily be made by combining all the Leeward and the Windward Islands in one federation on the lines of that now existing in the former group. If local opinion is prepared to accept the principle of federation it need not, in our view, be long delayed after inter-island communication has been substantially improved by the methods suggested in the following Chapter of this Report, or by any others which may be found to be more suitable. We recommend, therefore, that subject to the two considerations mentioned above, the advisability of amalgamating the Leeward Islands and the Windward Islands should be borne carefully in mind as a desirable political end to be adopted at the earliest opportunity, both for the benefits which it may be expected to bring to those groups of islands, and as a means of demonstrating the advantages of closer co-operation. This amalgamation should, as we have said, follow in general the lines of the present federation of the Leeward Islands but it is our opinion that the Federal Legislature should be entrusted with wide powers and only questions of local application should be left to the control of the Commissioners in the several islands acting on the advice of Local Councils. The choice of the headquarters may present some difficulty, but they should, we consider, be in St. Lucia or Grenada. It is not our intention to enter into any details of this scheme, in the working out of which legal and other advice

would be required, but we suggest that when the time for it comes consideration should be given to the question whether the officer in charge of the administration of one of the islands composing the federation should be granted Your Majesty's commission as a Lieutenant-Governor and be empowered to act for the Governor during his absence or incapacitation from duty.

13. Amalgamation of the various services would naturally follow as a result of federation, and efforts should be made to get neighbouring Colonies (Barbados, British Guiana and Trinidad) to amalgamate their services with those of the federated group, thus paving the way to political union with those Colonies.

5. Present Extent of Unification of Services.

14. It will clarify the issues which we are now to consider if we first give a brief account of the history of the arrangements already made for the unification of the Colonial Service and indicate the extent to which those arrangements cover the West Indian Colonies.

15. Mr. Joseph Chamberlain, when Secretary of State for the Colonies, instituted an inquiry into the possibility of combining the separate services then existing into a unified Colonial Service, but he found that the objections to this arrangement were at that time insuperable. Both before and in the years immediately after the war of 1914-18 an increasing tendency towards the standardisation of salaries and other conditions of service in several groups of Colonies (which did not include the West Indies) was noticeable, and, particularly in the post-war period, the Service grew rapidly in size while the problems with which its members were faced became much more complex and were found to call for a higher standard of educational and other qualifications. The question of recruitment for appointments normally filled outside the Colonies was therefore brought under review by a Committee appointed in 1929 under the Chairmanship of Sir Warren Fisher. They advised (Cmd. 3554 of 1930) strongly in favour of the unification of the Colonial Service which, they felt, would increase its prestige and by giving more formal recognition to the principle of inter-Colonial transfer would open up the prospect of a wider career and so stimulate recruitment. The second Colonial Office Conference, which was held in 1930 and consisted of representatives of the Governments of most of the Colonies, adopted a resolution in which they said that they considered unification of the Colonial Services desirable if a generally acceptable scheme could be devised. In July of that year Lord Passfield, then Secretary of State for the Colonies, announced his acceptance of the principle of a single Service, and two years later, after details had been worked out in consultation with Colonial

Governments, the Colonial Administrative Service, as the first of the unified branches, was established. At intervals there followed the creation of other unified branches, and the system now covers most higher appointments in the Colonies which can readily be classified and are normally filled by recruitment from outside the Colony by the Secretary of State.

16. In his report (Cmd. 5760) on the affairs of the Colonial Empire for 1937-8, the Secretary of State for the Colonies (Mr. Ormsby Gore, now Lord Harlech) described a unified Service as " one which has a definite membership, based upon a schedule of posts normally filled by members of the Service, a standard method of entry, and a recognised system of transferability throughout the Colonial Empire, entrants to a service after its institution being liable to serve in any Dependency ". The unified services are intended as a source from which the Secretary of State can supply the needs of any Colonial Government for officers with qualifications and experience not likely to be found among their local staff. There is, however, no bar to the admission to a unified Service of persons recruited locally provided that they possess the requisite qualifications, which are usually defined for each branch of the Service in regulations made by the Secretary of State, and are nominated by him for admission to the Service. While posts which are scheduled as part of a unified service are normally filled by its members, there is nothing to prevent the appointment to any such post of a person who is not a member of that Service and who does not wish to accept the liability to transfer which membership now involves. Thus the holding of a scheduled post does not confer membership of a unified service which depends on the nomination of the Secretary of State; on the other hand, members of unified services can be employed, with the approval of the Secretary of State, in posts which are not scheduled offices.

17. The proportion of higher appointments which is included in unified branches varies considerably in different parts of the Colonial Empire and is relatively low in the West Indies where the total strength of the unified services is only about 350, or less than 5 per cent. of the total establishment of the unified branches of the Colonial Service. Moreover, through the application of the accepted policy of allowing fully qualified candidates from any Colony to have the first claim on vacancies in their own public service, more than half of the West Indian appointments in unified services are at present held by officers of local origin. In the West Indies, therefore, these services form only a small, though most important, part of the general structure of administration and the proportion of the total establishment of the Government service which is in practice reserved to be filled by the Secretary of State for the Colonies from outside the Caribbean area is very low indeed.

6. Unification of Local Services.

18. It remains to consider the question of local unification of services in the West Indies as a supplement to, or in substitution for, the general Colonial system which we have described. As we remarked when discussing the problem of colour prejudice, the West Indies cannot in their present stage of development supply all their needs for experienced staff with professional and technical qualifications; also the highest administrative posts there, as elsewhere in the Colonial Empire, must continue to be filled by appointment from outside until there is a regular flow into the service of West Indian Governments of local candidates with educational qualifications equal to those of men now entering the Colonial Administrative Service from this country. Local unification cannot, therefore, in present circumstances be substituted for participation in the wider scheme. This conclusion is not, however, to be taken as implying any dissent from the view, which was put to us in evidence, that the change over, which must be gradual, from the present arrangement to one under which all posts would normally be filled within the Caribbean area should proceed as rapidly as is compatible with the supply of well-qualified local candidates able to discharge efficiently the duties of any appointments from which West Indians are now, in practice, debarred. The rate of progress of this transition will vary in different branches of the Service, and for some of them the time of its completion may still be distant.

19. Meanwhile West Indian Governments should consider most carefully the possibility of combining some of their less senior posts into local unified services. Some progress has already been made in this direction by the amalgamation, which is now in train, of the judicial, legal and police services of the Leeward Islands and Windward Islands, all officers in which —when not already under a wider liability as members of unified services—will thereafter be liable to be posted for duty to appointments of their grade anywhere in the two groups. The Leeward Islands and Windward Islands also share a Commissioner for Agriculture and an Education Commissioner, but no attempt has yet been made to amalgamate the staff employed, under the direction or advice of those officers, in the different islands. It is also worth mentioning that in the Leeward Islands the clerical staff, doctors and police (both men and officers) are already interchangeable between Presidencies at the discretion of the Governor.

20. The arguments which secured the acceptance by the Secretary of State and Colonial Governments of the principle of unifying into Colonial Services those appointments which are normally filled from the United Kingdom are relevant in

a large degree to the problems which we are now discussing, and the practical difficulties encountered in the application of that principle arise here also. The more important benefits of unification to Governments are that (*a*) the range of selection for both first appointments and promotions is widened and candidates of greater experience are often thus made available; (*b*) methods of entry for appointments of any class and the qualifications required in each class can be standardised; and (*c*) the efficiency of the Service is improved through the greater scope thus offered for the employment of its individual members on work best suited to their talents. The advantages to officers are corollaries of those to Governments. Greater possibilities of advancement and more opportunities for gaining experience are thus opened up for many of them, and all have a better prospect of congenial work.

21. Even if public opinion and the public service in the West Indies could be persuaded by these arguments to accept the principle of local unification, formidable practical difficulties would have to be overcome before effect could be given to it. The most important of these is the diversity of salaries and other conditions of service between the several Colonies. In the case of the unified Colonial Services the same difficulty was experienced but is being met by a gradual movement towards standardisation. That solution may not be possible in the West Indies where the Governments of some of the smaller Colonies would need substantial financial assistance, which we do not feel able to recommend, to enable them to pay salaries and to offer other conditions of employment comparable with the standard now obtaining in the larger islands. A definite classification of salaries to be adopted throughout the Colonies concerned would be the first stage in the practical application of local unification, and each participating Colony would then have allotted to it a number of appointments in each class. The proportion of junior posts would be highest, and that of senior posts lowest, in the smaller islands. In its early stages at least local unification would, therefore, entail the posting of an undue proportion of new entrants to the smaller islands, and promotion from those islands to the larger territories would be likely at all times to be more common than promotion in the reverse direction. We understand that it was this latter probability which led to the abandonment of a suggestion that educational posts throughout the West Indies should so far as possible be thrown open to candidates from the educational services of the area as a whole. The feeling among the public servants in the larger Colonies that their prospects would be adversely affected is thus a real obstacle to local unification, and to this must be added the known reluctance of many West Indians to leave their native Colony or island. But both these difficulties must be faced and ways of overcoming them must

be found if the West Indies are to work towards a federation which will have more than a nominal significance.

22. We recommend, therefore, that the Governments of the West Indian Colonies should be invited to accept the principle of local unified services, and that, if it is generally accepted, they should address themselves to the task of giving practical effect to that principle at the earliest possible date. The difficulties which we have mentioned must postpone for a time the creation of some branches of the suggested West Indian Service, but the end at which Governments and the people should aim is clear, and, given goodwill, it should not be difficult to make a start by establishing a Medical Service for the West Indies the need for which has been discussed in Chapter VIII of this Report. In the case of other services in which existing wide variations in salaries or other practical considerations preclude unification in the near future, the possibility of achieving what is undoubtedly a desirable end ought to be kept constantly under review, and nothing should be done in the way of altering scales of salary or other conditions of service without full consideration of the question whether those alterations would increase existing disparities and thus render more difficult ultimate unification.

CHAPTER XIX.

COMMUNICATIONS.

1. Services by Sea.*

1. Although air services for the carriage of passengers and mails already cover several of the British West Indian Colonies, and there appears, as we explain later in this Chapter, to be room for an extension of those services in the near future and their subsequent development as part of a wider plan, the principal need is, and must continue to be, the provision of adequate and cheap facilities for the transport by sea of the agricultural produce upon which the prosperity of the territories primarily depends.

2. The problem of communication by sea naturally falls into two sections, namely the question of external services, mainly to the United Kingdom and North America, and that of transport between the islands. In the following account of the existing position under each head we have not attempted any description of detail beyond that required to give a general picture of the situation or to make clear the recommendations which follow.

(a) EXTERNAL SERVICES.

3. The main channels of external trade are to and from the United Kingdom, Canada and the United States of America, but some Colonies do a fair volume of business with other countries. For example, imports into Trinidad from parts of South America and those into several Colonies from India are far from negligible either in quantity or value. All the evidence which we heard on this question was, however, related to the services with the United Kingdom or North America and it generally took the form of complaint that these services are inadequate or too expensive.

4. Before we examine the services available in the several Colonies we should mention the arrangement whereby, as part of the Trade Agreement concluded in 1925 between Canada and the West Indies, the Government of the Dominion, in return for subsidies amounting in all to £45,500 per annum, undertook to provide:—

> (a) a fortnightly freight, passenger and mail service from Canadian ocean ports all the year round, calling each way at Bermuda, St. Kitts, Nevis, Antigua, Montserrat,

---

* The more important sea communications are indicated on the map appended to this report.

Dominica, St. Lucia, Barbados, St. Vincent, Grenada, Tobago, Trinidad and Demerara;

(b) a fortnightly freight service from Canadian river ports in summer and from Canadian ocean ports in winter calling at St. Kitts, Antigua, Barbados, Trinidad and Demerara;

(c) a fortnightly mail, passenger and freight service between St. Lawrence ports in summer and such Canadian ocean ports in winter as may be designated by the Canadian Government, and calling both ways at Bermuda, the Bahamas, and Kingston, Jamaica, alternating with a fortnightly freight service between the said Canadian ports and Kingston, Jamaica, direct; and

(d) a steamer operating on a fortnightly schedule between British Honduras and Kingston, Jamaica, and connecting with the service in (c) above.

5. The agreement also prescribed the size of the vessels to be used on these services, their speed and, in some cases, the types of accommodation to be provided for both passengers and cargo. Freight rates were made subject to the control of the Canadian Government which undertook to give the fullest possible consideration to any representations made to them in regard to these charges by the Government of any West Indian Colony.

6. These provisions were, as we have said, part only of the agreement, the remainder of which was intended, through the grant of preferences at rates there laid down, to promote closer trade relations between the contracting parties and to extend and enlarge their respective trade. The agreement has undoubtedly been advantageous to the West Indies in that they have thereby been provided with a regular shipping service to Canada at the cost of a subsidy of which the Government of the Dominion has borne the larger part. That service is particularly valuable to the smaller islands since, as will be shown later, many of them have no alternative means of external communication which is equally reliable. Your Majesty's Government in Canada have, however, given notice of their intention to terminate the agreement on the 31st December, 1939, and, pending the outcome of the negotiation of the new agreement which is contemplated in its place, the outlook, as regards this particular branch of the shipping facilities in the West Indies, is obscure.

7. We propose now to comment briefly on the other sea communications of the West Indian Colonies and to sum up the evidence heard in each on that point. In this respect Barbados is the most fortunate of the group. The island lies on a main trade route and in consequence the tonnage of shipping entered

and cleared is high in relation to the volume of the external trade. Reasonable facilities appear to be provided for all forms of traffic and the only substantial criticism made in evidence was that the island is too dependent on foreign lines, particularly for the conveyance of passengers.

8. British Guiana is the turning point of a regular monthly service, provided by steamers of the Harrison Line,* which cater for both passengers and freight and call also at Barbados, Trinidad and a few of the smaller islands. The Colony is on the route of other passenger steamers but communication by some of them is less regular. No complaint was made in evidence about the facilities for the transport of cargo but it was represented to us that the freight charges on sugar shipped to the United Kingdom are excessive in comparison with the rates charged for that commodity when shipped from Trinidad, and that the development of an external trade in rice is seriously handicapped by the inability of exporters to meet the cost of sea transport which is high owing to the absence of a regular and reliable business in that commodity. In addition, representatives of the East Indian community in British Guiana urged that direct communication by steamer should be provided between India and that Colony, but it appeared from the evidence to be recognised that considerations of finance preclude any such possibility.

9. In addition to the fortnightly shuttle service with Jamaica, which is maintained under the agreement with Canada, the Colony of British Honduras is served by cargo boats of the Harrison Line which call at Belize each month, and by small foreign vessels, most of which belong to the United Fruit Company or the Royal Netherlands Lines. All space for the return voyage on the Harrison boats is normally chartered to shippers elsewhere and cargo is not loaded at Belize. Freight for the United Kingdom must therefore be transhipped either in Jamaica, if sent by the shuttle service, or in the United States and Holland if sent on foreign boats. It cannot be said that these services are inadequate for the needs of a Colony with so small an external trade, but the absence of direct communication with the United Kingdom was criticised by witnesses on such grounds as that the additional cost owing to the transhipment of citrus fruit in Jamaica is a serious burden on exporters, and that they had suffered losses through a deterioration of produce which would have been avoided by direct shipments in vessels fitted with refrigerating plant. We were also told that it is not possible to obtain favourable shipping rates by any British line for mahogany, the principal export of the Colony,

---

* At the end of July, 1939, it was announced that this service was to be withdrawn after October, since in the view of the operators it has become definitely uneconomic.

which must therefore be conveyed in foreign bottoms to New Orleans en route for this country.

10. We were supplied with a list of no less than 25 shipping lines (15 of them on the British Register) which provide regular services to Jamaica. There are 13 principal regular connections, calling in Kingston at intervals of a week or a fortnight; two of these are connections with the United Kingdom, six with North America and five to ports within the Caribbean area. The service thus provided was said to be adequate for passenger traffic, with the exception that there is at times a shortage of accommodation between North America and the island during the tourist season. Space for freight is usually obtainable without difficulty or delay but many complaints were made about the charges which were compared unfavourably with those paid by the competitors of Jamaica, particularly in the trade in citrus fruit. The rates have varied from time to time and it seems clear that prior to a fairly recent reduction of them there was good ground for this complaint. From evidence which we received it appears that the rates which were being charged when we were in Jamaica, for citrus fruit exported both to the United Kingdom and North America, are reasonable and, when regard is had to such considerations as distance of carriage and the cost of refrigeration, compare not unfavourably with the rates prevailing for similar transport in other parts of the world. The question of the propriety of the action of the Jamaica Producers' Steamship Company in becoming an associated member of the West India-Trans-Atlantic Steamship Conference was also raised in evidence. The Company is a co-operative organisation and it was alleged that it should not have joined an organisation which some of its members regard as inimical to the interests of producers. We are satisfied, however, that the action of the Company was intended to benefit its members—and has, in fact, been of benefit to them—by obtaining, through membership of the Conference, a share in the carriage of general cargo exported from the United Kingdom to Jamaica and thus reducing the ultimate cost of that transport of bananas which is their principal business.

11. The Leeward Islands and Windward Islands rely for external sea communications mainly on the services provided under the Canada-West Indies Trade Agreement, but the vessels of other lines connecting with North America make calls, at fairly regular intervals of about two weeks, at most of the principal ports in these groups. The larger ships of the Harrison Line proceed direct from London to either St. Kitts or Antigua, and also call at Grenada on the outward voyage. The schedule for return journeys may depend in part on the cargo offered by different islands. Many witnesses from these territories

criticised the existing services on the grounds both of inadequacy and expense.

12. The Trinidad Chamber of Commerce supplied us with copies of a full and helpful report on West Indian shipping facilities which they had prepared in May, 1938, for submission to the Government of the Colony in connection with the inquiry into that subject by the Imperial Shipping Committee. Their comments and suggestions, as amplified in evidence before us, can be summarised under the following main heads:—

(a) Fares to the United Kingdom are high and foreign lines offering an excellent service carry the greater part of the regular passenger traffic between the Colony and Europe, much of which would be diverted to British companies if their ships were quicker and more modern.

(b) The passenger service to Canada is good, but at times is barely sufficient for the traffic available.

(c) Facilities for the transport of all cargo except fruit are adequate and most of the trade with other parts of the Empire is carried in British ships.

(d) More accommodation for the cold storage of fruit was said to be required and complaint was made that freight rates, particularly on sugar, cocoa and fruit, were high and, in the case of the last two commodities, compared unfavourably with the charges payable by the principal trade rivals of the Colony in the home market.

Other evidence which we heard in Trinidad gave general support to these views which may therefore be taken as an accurate presentation of the situation.

13. This description of the external sea communications of the West Indian Colonies and our conclusions on that subject may be summed up as follows:—

(i) Passengers wishing to travel to North America have a choice of services which makes reasonable provision for their needs, but any substantial curtailment of the facilities now provided through the agency of the Canadian Government would create serious difficulties in the smaller islands and in British Honduras which is entirely dependent in this respect on the shuttle service with Jamaica maintained under the Canada—West Indies Trade Agreement.

(ii) The services available for passengers travelling between Europe and the larger Colonies are adequate, but some of the smaller islands and British Honduras have no such direct communication, and everywhere the facilities provided by British lines compare, on the whole, unfavourably with those offered by their foreign competitors, most of which are subsidised directly or indirectly.

(iii) The requirements of these Colonies for space for cargo are met but not always at a time or in a way most convenient for shippers, and particularly in the case of some of the Leeward and Windward Islands the service is at times so irregular and unreliable (owing mainly to the smallness of shipments offered) as to handicap local trading interests.

(iv) Complaints about freight charges are general, but there is no evidence that these are excessive by standards prevailing in other parts of the world or that the Companies concerned are making unreasonable profits from their business with the West Indies.

14. While we were in the West Indies we heard that the Imperial Shipping Committee would begin, early this year, an inquiry into West Indian shipping problems. In order to avoid overlapping between our work and that of the Committee, we arranged to confer with their Chairman after our return to England. We exchanged views with him in August last and in normal circumstances we should have been content to leave his Committee to frame recommendations on this subject. We understand, however, that the work of that body is now suspended owing to the war, and we think it advisable, therefore, to record our opinion that British lines have been under such disadvantage, through direct or indirect subsidy to their foreign rivals, that it has been impossible for them to offer a passenger service to and from the West Indies which could compete with that provided by the modern and luxurious ships of the foreign lines. If, as seems to us to be desirable, the passenger traffic between this country and the West Indies is to be regained by British lines, it will be necessary for Your Majesty's Government to consider whether, on a return to normal conditions, they should not offer to pay a subsidy for the maintenance of a regular passenger service with Trinidad, Barbados and possibly a few of the smaller islands.

(b) INTER-ISLAND SERVICES.

15. While the facilities for passenger traffic between the West Indian islands cannot be regarded as entirely satisfactory, the volume of that traffic is not large enough to offer an economic basis for any considerable extension of the existing services. Although the requirements for the transport of passengers may be expected to increase if proposals made elsewhere in this report are adopted, those needs can, we consider, best be met by the provision of the air services recommended later in this Chapter.

16. It is the lack of adequate means for the transport of produce between the smaller islands which most urgently demands attention. This is well illustrated by the following passage in paragraph 14 of Chapter XII of the agricultural report:—

" But possibly the transport deficiency which most affects peasant agriculture is found in the exceedingly bad communications among the various Islands and Colonies. Some of the lesser islands of the British Virgin group are bound to rely for cash on their miscellaneous export of pigs, goats, sheep, cattle and certain crop products to nearby islands. Veterinary restrictions recently imposed in the American Virgin Islands are likely to rule out this export market for livestock. The only hope will therefore be increased trade with other British islands. The available communication for this, as in a number of other instances, is by local sailing sloops. Livestock, ground provisions, fruit and other kinds of cargo are indiscriminately bundled into these small craft, of which the departure, arrival, and smoothness of passage are very inconstant. The captain of the sloop is himself the merchant for much of this inter-island trade. He is in the strong position of the sole agent of sale. The peasant producer cannot bargain with him and is obliged to accept a share of what he on return reports to be the price at which he was able to sell. The hope of increased production of food products by agricultural changes described in other Chapters depends considerably, especially for the very small islands, on better transport to neighbouring territories."

There can be no doubt that if trade in agricultural produce between the Lesser Antilles is to be encouraged and developed a regular service must be provided by at least two vessels specially equipped for this purpose. Accommodation for a limited number of passengers would be a convenience but is not essential. We consider that, as oil fuel is so easily obtainable from Trinidad, these special ships should be driven by Diesel engines. At the time when we made our inquiries we were informed that a vessel so equipped, of about 650 tons gross registered tonnage and capable of carrying about 400 tons weight of cargo, could be built at a cost of approximately £50,000. That estimate allows for a limited amount of refrigerated storage for fruit, deck space for cattle and one single and 12 two-berth cabins for passengers; the number of cabins might, however, be reduced if air services are provided as suggested later in this Chapter. The expenses of running a vessel of this size cannot be estimated with any precision, but in June last we were told by a witness with wide experience in such matters that those expenses might amount at that time to as much as £25,000 per annum for each ship. Allowing for interest and amortization on a capital expenditure of £100,000 and for insurance and other charges, the annual cost of maintaining a service with two vessels must be put, as a minimum, at £60,000. If that figure is accepted, there can be no prospect that the undertaking could pay its way in the initial stages, and it is therefore unlikely that such a service would ever be provided by private enterprise. We consider, however, that the need for improvement of communications between these islands is so great that the question of expense of the order we have mentioned ought not to be allowed to prevent the execution of measures which, in our view, may be expected to bring substantial benefits to the trading community and to help the work of the administration. No local funds are, or can be made, available for this purpose, and we recommend, therefore, that the initial outlay should be borne by Your Majesty's Government. In addition, if the service is to be conducted under Government control, it would be necessary for Your Majesty's Government to make good the annual deficit on its working. Alternatively, the management of the service might be entrusted to private enterprise already operating in the Caribbean area since overhead charges should thereby be kept at a substantially lower figure than would be the case if the services were worked by Government. In that event, a reasonable subsidy would have to be provided by Your Majesty's Government in return for the maintenance of a regular service by two vessels equipped in the way which we have described. It would no doubt be considered whether the capital cost and the payment of deficits, or the alternative subsidy, could be found from the Colonial Development Fund.

2. Air Services.*

17. Many of the Colonies with which we are concerned already have facilities for transport by air for which they are mainly indebted to the services maintained by Pan-American Airways. The extent to which the principal services of that company cover these Colonies is shown below:—

> (a) Kingston in Jamaica is on the route from Miami in the United States of America via Cuba to the Panama Canal Zone; seven through services are thus provided each week between North and South America; there is also a weekly service to and from Haiti via Santiago de Cuba.
>
> (b) Port-of-Spain in Trinidad is the terminus of a service, on which five flights are made each week in both directions, from the Panama Canal Zone via Colombia and Venezuela; it is also a place of call for machines flying twice a week in each direction between Miami and Brazil and the Argentine, and it is the terminus of a weekly service to and from Miami via Cuba, Haiti and Puerto Rico.
>
> (c) Georgetown in British Guiana and St. John's in Antigua are also places of call for machines flying on the route between Miami and South America, but each has only one through service a week in each direction.

In addition, internal services between Belize and four other centres in British Honduras are operated by Transportes Aereos Centro Americanos, three flights each way are made every week between Barbados and Trinidad by machines belonging to a Dutch company, and during the last four years the British

---

* The more important air communications are indicated on the map appended to this report.

Chapter XIX.

Guiana Aviation Company, Limited, has performed a most useful service by providing facilities for flights, usually arranged by charter, up and down the waterways of that Colony. At the time of our visit to British Guiana most of the capital of that company was held by a citizen of the United States of America, and British aviation was, therefore, unrepresented throughout the area with which we were concerned.

18. Mr. Banks, a member of the staff of the Civil Aviation Department of the Air Ministry, visited, between December, 1938, and March, 1939, the Colonies (except British Honduras) within our terms of reference and several other territories in the Caribbean area. His mission was to investigate, in consultation with the Colonial Governments concerned, the possibilities of the establishment of an inter-island air service in that area, and to advise those Governments on the provision of the aerodromes and other ground organisation which would be necessary for the purpose, and on any other question which might arise in connection therewith. In April last we were informed of the conclusions at which Mr. Banks had arrived as a result of his visit to the West Indies, and that it would be of assistance to certain departments of Your Majesty's Government if we could indicate in general terms whether we supported those conclusions. The effect of the recommendations made by Mr. Banks was that, if, for reasons of administrative convenience, more frequent and speedy communications were desired between the islands of the Leeward and Windward groups, a regular service should be established, ranging from St. Kitts in the north to Trinidad in the south and covering Barbados in addition to all the principal islands in those two groups. The administrative changes which we have suggested in the preceding chapter of this Report and proposals which are put forward in Chapter XXI appear to us to depend, for their proper execution, upon considerable improvement in inter-island communication throughout the Caribbean area. While this need could be met to some extent by a better service of steamers, it would clearly be of great advantage if that improvement could be supplemented by the provision of air communications between the islands, and, therefore, after hearing evidence from Mr. Banks, we informed the Colonial Office in June last that we felt able to support the scheme which he had put forward.

3. Railways and River Services.

19. The Government Railway in Barbados was closed to traffic some years ago and that in British Honduras (which ran from Stann Creek inland for about 25 miles) is now being converted to a road. The running of both these concerns involved a deficit and in neither case has the withdrawal of the

facilities resulted in any public inconvenience. Barbados is well served by road transport, the charges for which are said to compare favourably with the old railway rates; the new road from Stann Creek in British Honduras will clearly be of greater benefit to the general community than was the railway. The only railways in the smaller islands are a few light tracks owned by estates and used for the conveyance of sugar cane from field to factory.

20. In British Guiana the railways are controlled by a Board of Commissioners of the Transport and Harbours Department which also manages coastal and river services throughout the Colony, a system of road transport covering 173 miles and the Harbour and Pilotage Services. The Colonial Secretary is the Chairman of the Board, and of the nine members, all of whom are nominated by the Governor, three must be elected members of the Legislative Council and two must be chosen from a panel submitted by the Georgetown Chamber of Commerce. The Board is therefore an example of the association of unofficial members of the legislature with the administration of Departments of Government and, since that is an arrangement which in a wider form we advocate in Chapter XXII of this Report, we would record here that in this case it appears to have given satisfaction.

21. The railways in British Guiana are confined to the coastal belt where they are faced with severe competition from road transport, but the other services maintained by the Board of Commissioners are outside the field of private enterprise. In order to meet the competition of road transport the rates charged for the conveyance of both passengers and goods on the railways have been fixed at very low figures. Partly for this reason, and partly because the Board have to meet an annual charge of over £30,000 in respect of capital costs incurred when the railways were purchased in 1922 from a private Company, the Department now operates at a loss. During the three years 1936-8 the average deficit on their working was slightly in excess of £31,000. In evidence the Board of Commissioners asked us to consider whether we could make any recommendation which would give their Department some measure of relief from that part of the charge on account of capital costs which takes the form of interest on permanent annuities and perpetual stock. If the Board were relieved of this liability it would still have to be met from the general revenues of the Colony and we feel unable, therefore, to consider the suggestion, except as part of the larger question of indebtedness in British Guiana, with which we deal in Chapter XXIV.

22. In other evidence proposals were made for the construction, at very considerable expense, of a railway which would

serve the hinterland of British Guiana. It was represented that the heavy financial outlay thus involved was justified by the economic and other developments which could not be secured in any cheaper way. This possibility, and other methods of developing the interior of the Colony, had been thoroughly examined by a representative Committee shortly before our arrival in British Guiana and we do not feel able, with the limited knowledge of the problem which we were able to acquire during our short stay, to dissent from the conclusion of the majority of the Committee, only one member of which reported in favour of the construction of a railway.

23. So far as we are able to judge, the system of coastal and river steamer services maintained by the Board of Commissioners is satisfactory and the rates charged appear to be reasonable; special low rates have been fixed for certain agricultural districts to subsidise the export of their products to the markets in Georgetown. The road service provided by the Board of Commissioners extends from Bartica over a distance of 118 miles to the Potaro District in the interior and covers also branch roads of 55 miles. Owing largely to climatic conditions the surface of these roads is poor and we were told that the average life of a lorry used on the service is about two years, with a total mileage of little over 20,000. Nevertheless this part of the activities of the Board showed a small surplus of revenue over working expenditure during the last year for which figures were available.

24. The Government Railway in Jamaica traverses the island by main lines from Kingston to Montego Bay (113 miles) and from Spanish Town to Port Antonio (63 miles). There are also three branch lines of a total length of 34 miles. The railway is a Department of Government and its management is assisted by an Advisory Board of seven members consisting of the Director and six others, most of whom are engaged in business locally. The number of passengers has shown substantial declines during recent years, and the receipts from this source are now less than one-half of their level seven years ago.

25. Bananas account for more than one-half of the normal tonnage of goods carried by the railway. While road transport competes with the railway for the carriage of general merchandise, especially since main roads often run parallel with, or very near to, the railway, it also acts as a feeder for the railway by bringing in goods from remote districts of the island, of which the greater development has been made possible by the advent of the motor lorry. Railway revenue from the conveyance of goods, though it has shown some decline, is on the whole being fairly well maintained. The tonnage carried in 1937-8 was in fact higher than during any of the preceding

ten years, though the revenue thus obtained had been exceeded three times in that period. Owing in part to substantial charges, now amounting to about £90,000 per annum, which have to be met on account of interest on, and redemption of, debt, and in part to the annual expense incurred under a programme, initiated in 1925, of relaying rails, the Jamaica Railways showed during the last three completed financial years an average annual deficit of over £70,000. Problems of railway administration in the Colony have from time to time been the subject of expert inquiry, but a solution has still to be found for the problems caused by the present marked and continual decline in receipts from the transport of passengers and the heavy burden which the railway system imposes upon the general taxpayer.

26. The railway system in Trinidad, which is owned by the Government, consists of four distinct lines, and its total length is 118 miles. A short extension of one of these lines by about four miles is contemplated and provision to meet its cost has been included in an approved programme of works to be defrayed out of reserves. Here, as in Jamaica, the competition of road transport for the conveyance of passengers is intense, but the volume of, and receipts from, both passenger and goods traffic carried by the railway have been well maintained and the railway authorities have recently taken over certain concessions for the running of road services by motor omnibus. The wages of subordinate railway staff were increased in 1937 as part of a general increase throughout the Colony, and in consequence the margin by which gross receipts exceeded operating expenditure (exclusive of debt charges and other capital expenditure) will be reduced unless traffic continues to expand. During the three years 1936-8 the working of the Trinidad Railways, including charges for debt and renewals, resulted in an average annual deficit of over £100,000. Here, as in Jamaica, the possibility of lightening the heavy burden which the Government Railway at present places upon the general taxpayer is clearly a matter which deserves the serious attention of the Government of the Colony.

4. Communications by Road.

27. The road systems of these territories show wide variations both in their scope and their quality. At one extreme are Trinidad and Barbados. In the former Colony all the main roads are of reasonable width, and many of them have an excellent oiled surface; the secondary roads are generally passable throughout the year, and the system as a whole needs only minor improvements and extensions, for several of which provision amounting to over £600,000 is included in the new programme of loan works, to raise it to a standard exceptional in the tropical dependencies. The system in Barbados is still

Chapter XIX. 346

more elaborate, as there are in that small island 533 miles of road suitable for motor traffic and every village is connected to the capital by a daily service with motor omnibus. The surface of the roads is not, however, of so high a general quality as that found in Trinidad and in times of exceptionally heavy rainfall considerable trouble is experienced in some districts through the subsidence of soil and the collapse of the foundations of the roads.

28. Road communications are poorest in British Honduras, British Guiana and some of the smaller islands, of which Dominica is a typical example. In British Honduras the need for roads has been ignored in the past, and until recent years bridle tracks and rivers were the sole means of communication apart from the Stann Creek Railway. Since 1935 nearly 120 miles of main road have been constructed at the cost of grants made from the Colonial Development Fund and, as we have mentioned earlier in this Chapter, the Stann Creek Railway is now being converted to a road. Some of these roads have already been damaged by heavy traffic, but recent experiment in Belize may solve the problem of finding a cheap surfacing material capable of withstanding both the climatic conditions and the toll of that traffic.

29. In British Guiana the system of main roads is still limited to the coastal belt, and apart from the railway and the Bartica—Potaro Road, to which we have already referred, reliance for internal communications is placed on transportation by river. We were informed that a progressive deterioration in the road system has taken place owing to the change in the volume, weight and speed of traffic during recent years, and that this is shown by the increasing rapidity with which road surfaces give way after the onset of the rainy season and the frequency with which stretches of main road become almost impassable in heavy weather. In an attempt to reduce the cost of maintenance, experiments are now being made with concrete strip roadway—i.e., two narrow parallel strips of that material—in the sections subject to the greatest weight of traffic. The average cost of constructing an all-weather road to the interior of the Colony is estimated at over £10,000 a mile; development of the hinterland by this method is, therefore, clearly beyond the resources of the Colonial Government.

30. In Dominica the roads, apart from one of 29 miles recently completed in the north of the island with assistance from the Colonial Development Fund, are so narrow and of such uneven surface that the use of motor conveyances upon them is often difficult and at times dangerous. The total length of road on which motors can be used is less than 70 miles (including the one good road in the north) and the system, such as it is, therefore falls far short of providing adequately

for the needs of an area of over 300 square miles. There is no through communication by road between Roseau, the capital, and Portsmouth, the second town of the Island, and the Administrator has therefore to make this journey by sea.

31. Certain recommendations for the improvement of the road systems of the territories whose needs appear to us to be greatest are made in Chapter XXIV of this Report, and, having given, by the best and worst examples, a general indication of the facilities now available, we do not propose here to enlarge upon this matter. We think it desirable, however, to make one suggestion for consideration by Governments throughout these territories. There is in Trinidad an abundant natural supply of asphalt, of which great use has been made by the Public Works Department of that Colony in connection with the construction of roads. We were told by witnesses representing the company which now leases from Government the rights in this commodity that their trade is suffering from the competition of other materials suitable for the surfacing of roads. It should not be impossible to arrive at an arrangement whereby other British Colonies in the Caribbean area would agree to purchase asphalt from Trinidad in return, where such a course is necessary, for an undertaking by the Government of that Colony to do all within their power to secure an increase of the imports into Trinidad of some suitable products from the purchasing territories.

5. Telephone Services.

32. A detailed description of the system of telephone services in each Colony is not necessary for our purpose, which is to give a brief account of the more important evidence which we heard on that subject and to record the conclusions at which we have arrived.

33. For many years the telephone system throughout the island of Trinidad had been operated by a private company under franchise, due to end in June, 1939, and in 1935 the Governor of the Colony appointed a Committee to advise upon a petition which he had received from the company for an extension of their concession. Four of the five members of this Committee recommended that an extension should be granted, provided that satisfactory arrangements were made between the Government and the company on a number of points, including the right of the Government to purchase the undertaking at prescribed intervals during the currency of the extension. The fifth member recommended that Government should take over the enterprise on the expiration of the original franchise. In November, 1938, after prolonged negotiation with a representative of Telephone and General Trust Limited,

which had acquired a controlling interest in the original concessionary company, the Government presented to the Legislative Council of the Colony a Bill based upon the recommendations of the majority of the Committee. That Bill was strongly opposed by some unofficial members of the Council who were in favour of the transfer of the telephone system, on the expiration of the concession, to the Port-of-Spain City Council, which would thus have been made responsible for a service extending far outside the boundaries of its administrative area. On a division of the Council 16 members (of whom two were elected and two were nominated unofficials) voted for the Bill, and two unofficials, both elected members, voted against it. A request was then made to the Secretary of State for the Colonies that the legislation thus enacted should be suspended until he had received our Report, but, after full consideration of all the circumstances, he saw no ground to intervene in the matter, and that legislation therefore came into effect in December, 1938. It was represented to us, in evidence given on behalf of the Port-of-Spain City Council, that the grant of this extended franchise was not in accordance with the wishes of the people of the Colony, and we were asked to support the request of that body that the control of the telephone services should have been vested in them, as was the operation of the tramway and lighting systems in the city of Port-of-Spain a few years ago after the Council had succeeded in litigation with a private company which had previously maintained those systems under a concession. As the matter had been settled by legislation before our arrival in Trinidad, we do not propose to offer any comment upon this evidence beyond remarking that the control of an island-wide telephone system by one local authority appears to us to be generally inadvisable; the one proper alternative to the extension of the franchise was the taking over of the system by the Government which had been advised against that course.

34. In Jamaica a public telephone service is conducted in Kingston and St. Andrew by the Jamaica Telephone Company acting under licence from Government; private systems, also operated under licence, are maintained by the United Fruit Company, the Standard Fruit and Shipping Company and other smaller concerns. The system of the United Fruit Company included, until the 1st April, 1939, the operation of public telephone exchanges at Montego Bay and Port Antonio. The trunk line connecting these exchanges with that serving Kingston and St. Andrew was the property of the United Fruit Company, and in the absence of public trunk lines, communication by telephone between these centres was dependent upon the goodwill of the company. In 1936 Mr. Hedley, formerly a member of the staff of the General Post Office in this country, visited Jamaica, at the invitation of the Government of the

Colony, to advise them on the subject of the reform of the existing telephone system, which was admittedly chaotic. In consequence of the recommendations made in his report, the Legislative Council of Jamaica in July, 1938, approved a proposal that Government should proceed with the construction and subsequent operation of a public telephone service, including both trunk and toll lines, throughout the Colony. The work of constructing lines required under this scheme began last year, and the telephone service at Montego Bay was taken over by the Government on the 1st April, 1939; it was intended in June last that the service at Port Antonio should be taken over in the near future. We were informed that it is anticipated that by 1943 every important town in the island will be connected by telephone, and that all telecommunication systems, now maintained by private companies or persons, with the possible exception of the one operated by the Jamaica Telephone Company, will be absorbed into a new Telecommunication Department, the creation of which, in order to centralise control, had been advocated by Mr. Hedley. The licence of the Jamaica Telephone Company does not, however, expire until 1965. That company is now identified with Telephone and General Trust Limited, which, in addition to the interests in Trinidad which we have mentioned, has already expended considerable sums on the improvement and modernisation of telephone services in Barbados and is, we understand, prepared to investigate the possibility of developing telephone services in the smaller islands with a view to their inclusion in a comprehensive scheme which might also extend to British Guiana and British Honduras. While the new arrangements contemplated for Jamaica would go far to remedy the deficiencies of the existing telephone system, they would still be unsatisfactory in that, failing an agreement between the Government and the Jamaica Telephone Company for the purchase of the rights of the latter which continue until 1965, the single control, which was recommended by Mr. Hedley and by Consulting Engineers, would be impossible. We suggest, therefore, that the Government of Jamaica should be invited to consider carefully whether it would not be preferable instead to grant a concession in respect of the telephone service throughout the island to Telephone and General Trust Limited, subject to the inclusion in the concession of satisfactory provisions for the restriction of their profits to a reasonable level and to safeguard other interests of the Government and the community. We regard it as important that, as part of any such agreement, the company should undertake to assume the responsibility for the telephone services of the smaller islands on terms which will include a definite obligation to expand and improve those services. It would no doubt be considered at the same time, and in consultation with the Governments of British Guiana and British Honduras, whether the telephone systems of those Colonies should also be brought within this arrangement. We realise that objection to this suggestion may be raised by persons in the West Indies who are opposed to the control by private enterprise of any form of public utility service, but we cannot avoid the conclusion that the interests both of Governments which have other and more urgent calls on their purses and of the public in the Caribbean area will be best served in the long run by securing the active and constructive assistance of an influential company in the provision of a comprehensive telephone system to serve the needs of the whole of the British West Indian Colonies.

6. Wireless Communications.

35. The system of telegraphic communication by cable and wireless is well developed throughout the British West Indian Colonies and with few exceptions they have wireless stations with a range extending to several neighbouring territories through which they can ultimately reach North America and Europe. Only in Jamaica has a wireless telephone service yet been established; speech from that island with London can be obtained by way of radio-telephone to Miami, land line thence to New York and the Trans-Atlantic Telephone Service to this country. We were informed before we left for the West Indies that in 1937 the total receipts from the Wireless Telephone Service in Jamaica were £466, a sum which falls far short of the expenditure incurred upon it during that year; since our return to England we have been told that only four calls were made by telephone from this country to Jamaica, and three calls in the reverse direction, during the six months which ended on the 31st of March last. It is clear, therefore, that in present circumstances a telephone service from the other West Indian Colonies to Great Britain is not required and would not be financially self-supporting. We are convinced, however, that for reasons both of administrative convenience and of economic development there is need to supplement the existing telegraphic services between the West Indian Colonies by providing facilities for communication by speech. One practical objection to the proposals for federation which have been put forward in Chapter XVIII of this Report is the difficulty of securing a representative attendance from the component islands at meetings of the combined legislature, if they are held frequently, or extend over long periods. It is essential that the Governor should have an assurance that, whenever he has to take, between meetings of the Council, executive action which requires subsequent legislative approval, the Council will not withhold their endorsement of his action. The provision of a service of wireless telephones would materially assist the Governor and his advisers to make sure in advance that important executive acts

of this kind command the support of a majority of the legislature. From the point of view of economic development a telephone service might be of great assistance in securing an increase of that inter-island trade for the transport of which we recommended, earlier in this Chapter, the provision of two special ships.

36. We understand that authority was given early this year for an experiment to be made in wireless telephony between Barbados and St. Lucia. We regard the provision of such communications as one of the more urgent needs of the smaller islands and we trust that the experiment will be completed quickly and that the lessons to be learned from it will be such as to make possible the rapid extension of these desirable facilities throughout the area with which we are concerned. The prospect of speedy development in this respect would, we consider, be materially increased by the adoption of the plan suggested in the preceding section of this Chapter.

7. Broadcasting.

37. One of the Empire services provided by the British Broadcasting Corporation is sent out at times and on wavelengths suitable for its reception in the West Indies. We found, however, on all sides a desire that this should be supplemented by a local service which could be better suited to the particular needs of the West Indies than is possible in the case of programmes distributed from London and could be the means of providing facilities, the absence of which is a serious handicap to both Governments and people in the West Indian Colonies. We have specially in mind the desirability of making the views of Government and their policy known among the people, the repair by the use of wireless of some of the considerable gaps in the educational curriculum of many of the Colonies and the meeting in part of the admitted need of the older people for more and better opportunities for recreation. It would indeed be difficult to over-estimate the potential political and social value of a well organised and balanced system of local broadcasting in the British West Indies; in addition the creation of such a system might prove eventually to have anticipated urgent requirements in times of emergency.

38. It would probably be necessary, on grounds of expense, to limit the broadcasting system at the outset to a single service operated from a central point. While the technical opinion which we have consulted agrees that such a service must be given by means of short waves, there is a difference of view on the question of the number and output of the transmitters required at a station to provide an effective service all over

Chapter XIX.

the West Indian Colonies. If a single transmitter with an output of 10 kilowatts should be sufficient, the capital cost of erecting and equipping the station (including the provision of studios) would, we understand, be of the order of £25,000. But if, as in another opinion might be necessary, the station has to be equipped with at least three short wave transmitters with an output of about 20 kilowatts, the cost would rise to over £100,000.

39. We have no ready means of resolving these conflicting opinions, and we can only recommend that such investigations on the spot as may be necessary to determine the issue should be carried out at a very early date and that, in the light of the results of those investigations, Your Majesty's Government should decide what means they will adopt to institute a local broadcasting service for the West Indies. The value of that service to the territories where no transmitting station is established will depend in a large measure on the extent to which it can be used for personal broadcasts by people known to the inhabitants of those territories. We understand that this should normally be possible either through the medium of gramophone records of speeches by such persons, or by the use of wireless telephone in conjunction with the transmitting station. The point is, however, of such importance that it should be brought specially to the notice of any person appointed to make the investigation which we have recommended and the possibility that any wireless telephone service would be used in this way should be borne in mind whenever its establishment is under consideration.

40. According to an estimate with which we have been furnished the running expenses of a single station of 10 kilowatts, exclusive of fees for performing rights and payments to individuals participating in the programmes, would be about £4,000 per annum; if the bigger scheme should be adopted, or more than one station should be established, those expenses might be substantially increased. It would clearly be beyond the resources of the Governments of many of these Colonies to contribute their share of the capital expenditure involved in either plan, and we therefore recommend that Your Majesty's Government should bear the whole of that expense; the Colonial Governments could reasonably be expected, however, to meet the cost of maintaining the service and each should contribute in proportion to its average annual revenue.

41. Questions of expense would also arise in connection with the provision of receivers in schools and of amplifiers and loudspeakers to be used at centres, both indoors and on suitable open spaces, whenever Government wished to disseminate news. We have been informed that the standard receivers used

for the purposes of broadcasting in villages in India cost about £22 and can reach the whole of an audience in a room of 1,500 square feet. This figure includes the expense of providing batteries, the cost of the maintenance of which is, in India, about £6 per annum per receiver. Special arrangements have been made there for the charging of batteries and it would be advisable for any West Indian Colonies where electric mains are not available to profit by the experience of India in this respect; the Government of India would no doubt be willing to prepare, for distribution to those Colonies, a statement showing the special arrangements made there and the lessons to be learned from the working of their scheme. Where electric mains are available the work of maintenance is, of course, greatly simplified, but periodic inspection of the receiving sets would still be necessary. As regards amplifiers and loud-speakers for public addresses, we have been informed that instruments capable of reaching an audience of 500 people when indoors can be provided in this country at a cost of about £25. This figure does not include the cost of batteries which would be required in places where power supply is not available; we understand that in such cases the problem of charging the sets might be serious. The question of the incidence of the expense of providing receivers in schools and additional amplifiers and loud-speakers in other places is one which can perhaps be best decided after each of the Governments concerned had supplied an estimate of its requirements in this respect. But the use of the service in this way for the purposes of widening the educational curriculum and of making known the views and policy of Government, is, in our view, so valuable a measure of social reform that, where it is established that a Colonial Government cannot from its own resources provide adequately for the needs of the people in this respect, the cost might well be defrayed either by a grant from the Colonial Development Fund or out of the special Fund, the creation of which is recommended in the following Chapter.

42. British Guiana is already served by a short-wave transmitter fitted with a specially designed aerial. We heard no evidence about that station when in the Colony, but since our return to England we have been informed that the scheme for its future operation, which includes a limited amount of advertising, is on the right lines and our proposals made above are not intended to interfere in any way with its activities.

CHAPTER XX.

WEST INDIAN WELFARE FUND.

1. We will now recapitulate briefly the more important of the conclusions involving expense which we set out in Part II of this report where we considered the social needs of the West Indian Colonies.

2. In the field of educàtion teachers with better training and a wider background of knowledge are required; the building of new schools, with adequate space for recreation and improved sanitation, should proceed as rapidly as possible; much of the equipment, which is largely out of date and unsuitable, should be replaced. Free text books should be provided; the curriculum needs revision in directions which will entail expense; broadcasting and films should be introduced into the educational system; more attention should be given to the education of girls and to adult education; schools should be regraded and junior secondary schools and play-centres should be established; a proper system of school medical inspection is needed; and some assistance should be given towards the cost of the feeding and clothing of the children of necessitous parents.

3. Our proposals for the improvement of the conditions affecting the health of the people of these Colonies include the unification and reorganisation of the medical services, the centralisation of medical institutions, the creation of at least one School of Hygiene, the better training of medical staff of all grades, the appointment of largely increased numbers of auxiliary medical staff, the bringing of medical assistance within the means of all sections of the community and a great increase in certain preventive measures, including the improvement of general sanitation, the prosecution of a more active campaign against malaria, and the extension, or establishment, of maternity and child welfare clinics and clinics for the treatment of venereal diseases.

4. A very large proportion of the population of the West Indian Colonies needs to be re-housed and the expenditure on building alone, over a term of years, cannot be put at less than £10,000,000 and, when the cost of land and services has been added, is likely to exceed that sum by a substantial margin.

5. The expenditure involved by our recommendations affecting labour questions is relatively low but may amount to a considerable sum if, in time, some form of unemployment insurance is found to be practicable. Meanwhile the provision of machinery for the fixing of wages, the expansion and adequate staffing of Labour Departments, the inspection of factories, and

Government participation in a new scheme of Workmen's Compensation will call between them for a substantial contribution from public funds to the betterment of labour conditions.

6. In the field of other social services there is room for very substantial expenditure. Special staff should be appointed and trained to plan and administer new social welfare programmes; better provision should be made for the care of the destitute and ailing and of deserted and orphaned children; community centres should be established, equipped and maintained; hostels are required for certain classes of people and will often have to be subsidised; the probation and after care services should be strengthened and other reforms connected with prison systems are required including the establishment of a central industrial school for young offenders in the Leeward and Windward Islands.

7. In the framing of the proposals which are summarised above we have endeavoured to formulate a plan, the adoption of which might cater for the needs of the West Indian Colonies for the next 20 years. That plan involves both immediate expenditure on a large scale and commitments of a comparable order over a period which, although it cannot now be precisely estimated, will clearly extend for at least a generation. It remains now to consider how our proposals are to be financed.

8. By the Colonial Development Act, 1929, such sums of money, not exceeding £1,000,000 in any one year, as Parliament may from time to time determine are placed at the disposal of the Treasury to make advances to Colonial Governments. The purposes for which advances may be made are strictly defined by the Act and, as is made clear by the Preamble to it, are intended to be limited to the aiding and development of agriculture and industry in the territories to which the legislation applies. The authorities which administer the Colonial Development Fund could therefore do but little to assist West Indian Governments to meet the social needs of their people. In this respect a clear distinction must be drawn between the proposals now under discussion and those put forward in Chapter XVI of this report for the investigation of agricultural problems in the West Indies. It would be possible for much of the expenditure on the latter purpose to be met from the Colonial Development Fund in its present form, and that method of financing the enlarged activities which we have recommended for the Imperial College of Tropical Agriculture will no doubt be carefully considered. Whatever may be the decision upon the question, which we discuss below, of providing special financial assistance for the West Indian Colonies, their Governments should be allowed to continue to share in the benefits of the Colonial Development Fund in its present limited scope; and

if the purposes for which the monies in the Fund are available should be widened, those Governments should still be at liberty to submit proposals for expenditure from it on services, such as the construction of roads, not covered by any special arrangements for the financial assistance of those Governments which may be made in consequence of this report.

9. Before we consider the problem of providing from other sources funds for the betterment of the social conditions in the West Indies, it is necessary to examine the possibility of increasing the amounts which the local Governments now devote to those purposes. In Chapter VI of this report we described at length the financial and budgetary position of each of the Colonies. We concluded that, with few exceptions, West Indian Governments cannot themselves now, or in the near future, undertake from their own resources to bear additional loan charges. We also expressed the opinion that no material increase in any form of indirect taxation that falls on the necessities of life in the West Indies should be contemplated in present circumstances. Finally, we suggested that participation by any West Indian Colony in additional financial benefits to be provided by Your Majesty's Government should be conditional upon an undertaking by the Government of the Colony to overhaul their system of taxation to bring it more closely into line, as regards the standardisation of income tax, the level of taxation* (including surtax) and the taxation of both companies and land, with the system obtaining in this country. It will no doubt be possible by this means for most of the West Indian Governments to secure an expanded revenue, but nowhere is the increase likely to be large in relation either to the present annual revenue of the Government or to the expenditure involved by the programme of social reform which we have recommended. Even the least poor of these Colonies would not find it possible to finance from additional funds obtained from the reform of the system of direct taxation more than a fraction of the schemes of development and betterment which are undoubtedly needed. We are forced, therefore, to the conclusion that for the period of reconstruction which, in our view, lies immediately ahead of every West Indian Government, each of them will require financial assistance on an unusual scale. The proper aim of all Government policy should, of course, be to bring about conditions in which each territory can support itself financially. We believe that in time our proposals for the improvement of agriculture, on which the prosperity of the West Indian Colonies must always depend, will go far to achieve that end. The partial stabilisation of the price at which West Indian sugar is sold and the increase of sugar quotas would also help. But we are satisfied that there is no way through which economic

---

* We have here in mind the rates of taxation prevailing in August 1939.

conditions in the British West Indian Colonies could be so changed as to avoid the necessity for embarking, if crying social needs are to be met, on a period of wise expenditure from outside resources on the redress of social evils and the rehabilitation of people in distress.

10. The question may fairly be asked whether the grant of assistance to provide better living conditions for the West Indian people is a burden which the British taxpayer can reasonably be expected to bear. The answer is to be found in the change of outlook towards Colonial administration which, after a period of slow but steady development, is now rapidly gaining ground in this country. The Secretary of State for Foreign Affairs in a speech on the 29th June last said:—

> " There was a time when in the British Empire, as elsewhere, Colonies were regarded merely as a source of wealth and a place of settlement for Europeans. You have only to read any of the Colonial literature of those days to see for how little counted the rights and welfare of the natives. But during the last half century a very different view has gained ground, a view which has been finely expressed in Article 22 of the Covenant, namely, that the well-being and development of ' people not yet able to stand by themselves under the strenuous conditions of the modern world ' is ' a sacred trust of civilisation '."

There is undoubtedly a growing sense in Great Britain of an obligation resting upon Your Majesty's Government to assist in the improvement of the conditions of all British Colonial peoples, and there are equally signs on every side of a willingness to shoulder expenditure from Imperial funds for this purpose. Ample evidence of the favour which this trend of thought receives in most circles was given by the reception accorded by the Press and by public opinion to those parts of Lord Hailey's " African Survey " in which emphasis was laid on the need for the adoption in that part of the Colonial Empire of a policy designed to raise the standard of living and to secure the improvement of social services. The tone of the debate in the House of Commons on the 7th June last, when the Colonial Office Vote for the current financial year was being discussed, showed that among all schools of political thought there is wide support for such a policy. The conclusions which we have summarised at the beginning of this Chapter are, we hope, a sufficient indication of our sympathy with this attitude towards future Colonial administration. The policy of Your Majesty's Government must naturally be directed to the achievement of progress in all Colonial territories, the pace in each being determined in part by its immediate needs, in part by the wish to use available funds to the best advantage and in part by the present stage of development of its peoples which must influence their ability to benefit fully from new or extended services thus provided. Our concern is more limited. It is to urge that, notwithstanding the fact that the peoples of the West Indies have to-day social services which are less inadequate than those provided in some other parts of the Colonial Empire, those territories have a special claim to share fully in any measures which may be adopted in pursuit of a new and beneficent Colonial policy. The reasons which, in our opinion, vindicate the claim of the West Indies to special attention may be summed up as follows:—

(*a*) The history of the coloured West Indian peoples differentiates them from the native inhabitants of other parts of the Colonial Empire. Those peoples have entirely lost the benefit of their original native cultures and constructive effort to modify, in their interests, the full economic pressure of their present mode of existence is therefore thoroughly justified.

(*b*) The contact of coloured peoples in the West Indies with white folk puts before them a higher standard of life than is known to Africans, and this, coupled with their greater knowledge of what has been done by way of providing social services among more advanced communities, naturally strengthens their aspirations to similar benefits.

(*c*) The propinquity of the West Indies to North America has a similar effect which has been stimulated by accounts reaching those territories of the endeavours made to improve conditions in, for example, neighbouring American Colonies.

(*d*) The dispersion of the West Indian people over so many islands increases both the difficulties and the cost of administration and differentiates them as a group from any other large section of the Colonial Empire.

(*e*) The handicap from which these people suffer, owing to the persistent tendency towards over-supply of their primary products, is particularly severe. Remedial measures which have succeeded elsewhere are here possible in the case of sugar alone, and the banana is the only other West Indian product which so far has escaped this unfortunate position.

(*f*) Largely through the pressure of the economic conditions mentioned immediately above, some of the smaller West Indian islands have already experienced a serious deterioration in their standard of life and others are threatened with a similar experience which is inevitable in the absence of measures of relief.

11. The last of these reasons leads us to make a comparison between the position in many of these Colonies and that of the areas in this country in which the necessity has been recognised,

and Your Majesty's Government have undertaken the liability, for special treatment to counteract in part the pressure of economic tendencies and factors over which the inhabitants of those areas have no control. In our view the two cases are so nearly parallel as to justify the conclusion that the West Indian Colonies have a good claim to be given treatment similar to that accorded, through Special Area Commissioners, to certain parts of the United Kingdom. This analogy would be strengthened if, as we have suggested, participation by each West Indian Colony in the benefits of any special arrangements for the assistance of this group of territories was made conditional on the bringing of the scale of direct taxation in that Colony approximately into line with that of this country.* The point has already been made that acceptance of this condition would not enable even the less poor of the West Indian Colonies to finance more than a fraction of the schemes of improvement which are undoubtedly needed. The poorest Colonies are those which do not produce sugar for export, and there are at least three reasons why those territories have a special claim on the generosity of Your Majesty's Government. The adoption of the principle of equality of direct taxation can have but little effect on the financial position of the Governments of these territories where taxable incomes are relatively lowest by every standard of comparison. Secondly, these Colonies will not benefit from the limited proposals which we have been able to make for the amelioration of the position of the West Indian sugar industry. Thirdly, the people of the territories in which sugar is not produced for export contend that they are, on balance, losers by the existing system of Imperial preference although they recognise that this system is beneficial to the British West Indian Colonies as a whole. Unless direct financial aid is given, these territories will definitely continue to be distressed areas with no more hope of recovery than must be felt by the inhabitants of those parts of the United Kingdom with which we have compared them.

12. If our conclusion is accepted that the growing sense of responsibility for the well-being of Colonial peoples should be marked in the West Indies by the grant of substantial subventions to meet the cost of relieving distress and improving social services, we have next to consider the exact form which this assistance should take, its amount and the arrangements for the control of the expenditure of those subventions. On the first of these points the choice open to Your Majesty's Government appears to lie between three possible courses of action. These are (1) to make a large capital grant which would be at the disposal of West Indian Governments or of some organisation created for the purpose of controlling it, (2) to vote each year the sum estimated to be required for approved expenditure on

---

* See footnote to paragraph 9 of this chapter.

social welfare in the West Indies, and (3) to undertake to provide annually, and for a specified term, a grant of fixed amount to be expended in that way. We have no hesitation in recommending that the third of these courses should be adopted. Only thus would it be possible to plan wisely a definite programme of social improvements designed to cover the period which we had in mind in the framing of our proposals. That planning on this scale is necessary if reforms now introduced are to have lasting effects is clear to us from the evidence which we obtained during our stay in the West Indies. Many of the benefits expected from programmes of social reform initiated in the past have not been realised either because the schemes then adopted catered only for immediate needs, or because the occurrence of one of those periods of adversity, to which the West Indian Colonies are specially liable, prevented the completion of the original programme. It is only by far-sighted schemes, backed by the security of an assured income, that the deficiencies of past administration can be corrected and adequate arrangements made for the prosecution of policies, the full benefits of which are not likely to be felt during the early stages of their practical application. We recommend, therefore, that Your Majesty's Government should create a special fund to be expended on the improvement of social services and conditions in the West Indies, and that Parliament should be invited to agree to the payment into that fund of a fixed annual amount for a definite term of years. We suggest that the fund into which those monies are paid should be known as the British West Indian Welfare Fund. That title has the merit that it connotes the purposes to which expenditure from the Fund should be limited. Those purposes should be strictly defined and, in our view, should exclude the cost of supervisory staff (the appointment of which is recommended in the following Chapter), the cost of the agricultural research and surveys proposed in Chapter XVI and any subsidies which may have to be paid as the price of the improvement of communications. The definition should cover in general terms those social services which were described at the beginning of this Chapter; in addition, it might include land settlement, apart from the cost of the purchase of land, which should normally be met from some other source, and the equipment of broadcasting services and the provision of loud-speakers which, in our view, will serve a social as well as a political purpose.

13. We come now to the question of the amount to be paid annually into the Fund and the term for which that payment should be made. The present expenditure of the West Indian Colonies on social services has some relevance in this connection. The following table shows the average annual expenditure over the last three completed financial years on education, public health and poor relief, but does not include either capital

expenditure, such as that now being incurred in some Colonies on housing and land settlement, or any other expenditure on major works of construction, which is normally included under the heading of public works in the accounts of Colonial Governments:—

	Education £	Medical £	Poor Relief £	Total £
Barbados	65,961	48,494	45,032*	159,487
British Guiana	98,770	118,529	23,886	241,185
British Honduras†	16,539	18,452	1,952	36,943
Jamaica	236,361	204,869	87,809*	529,039
Leeward Islands:				
Antigua	5,958	14,447	2,466	22,871
Dominica	7,481	10,114	1,000	18,595
Montserrat	2,843	2,759	466	6,068
St. Kitts-Nevis	9,607	17,671	1,934	29,212
Virgin Islands	634	992	75	1,701
Trinidad & Tobago	190,706	189,464	32,460	412,630
Windward Islands:				
Grenada	16,822	22,361	2,893	42,076
St. Lucia	7,030	11,378	1,985	20,393
St. Vincent	11,594	15,218	858	27,670
Total £	670,306	674,748	202,816	1,547,870

* Borne by parochial funds.
† Taking the dollar, which is linked to the currency of the United States of America, at 4·80 to £1.

14. After careful consideration we have decided to recommend that the sum to be paid into the Fund should be £1,000,000 a year and that, subject to the approval of Parliament, the payment should be assured for a term of 20 years. We are satisfied that no lower amount would suffice if the social problems of the West Indies are to be dealt with comprehensively, and since we are, as we have said, planning for a generation, it would be unwise to fix any shorter term for the payment. Large though the sum may seem to be at first sight, even brief consideration of the long and imposing list of purposes to which it should be devoted will establish beyond doubt that, unless assisted, as in time it may be, by substantial sums available from expanded local revenues, it will still fall far short of providing adequately for all the needs which it is intended to serve. On the other hand, the amount proposed for the annual subvention is high enough, in relation to present expenditure on social services, to ensure that, with wise administration, aided and guided in ways which we suggest later, it should suffice to bring about great improvement in those services.

15. The last of the three points which we have mentioned as calling for consideration is that of the arrangements for the control of the Fund. The administrative reform which we consider to be necessary is discussed in the following Chapter where our proposals are described in detail. Here we will only say

that, in our opinion, a new authority must be created to control the Fund and that, while the officer in charge of that authority should be required to work out long-term programmes of social reform for submission to the Secretary of State for the Colonies, to whom he would be responsible for restricting expenditure to schemes which conformed to the approved programme, it is important that he should be given wide power to settle points of detail without the obligation to refer to the Secretary of State. Moreover, any steps which would obviate possible causes of delay, without impairing a proper system of financial control, should certainly be taken. The expert advice which would be needed in connection with many of the purposes which the Fund is intended to meet should be provided in the way recommended in the following Chapter of this report.

CHAPTER XXI.

PROBLEMS OF ADMINISTRATION.

1. No study of conditions in the West Indies to-day would be complete without an examination of the problems of administration in that area, and any policies for the improvement of those conditions, no matter how carefully they are planned, might prove to be of little value unless their execution is guided and controlled in the way and by the means most likely to combine a high level of efficiency with that regard for economy which the people of this country and in the West Indies have every right to expect. The problems of administration which we are now to consider are therefore of fundamental importance. Moreover they cannot be dissociated from the wider issues of Colonial policy which of late have been receiving an increasing attention in Parliament and the Press of this country. It would be idle to ignore the existence of those issues, and when at times in this Chapter we traverse ground which is strictly outside our terms of reference, that has been done solely for the purpose of putting our views in better perspective by relating them to a more general background.

2. The organisation and machinery of Colonial Governments everywhere were originally designed to perform certain elementary functions, such as the preservation of law and order, which are essentially negative in character. This conception of the functions of Government was popular during the nineteenth century and all over the world it was preached by the political philosophers of that age, and accepted by most thoughtful people, as the true and sufficient object of the State. By a process of evolution, of which both the starting time and the rate of progress varied widely from country to country, this theory has lost favour among all the more advanced peoples and has been replaced by a political philosophy which involves an ever-increasing intervention and participation by Government in most spheres of life and work. The effect of this change on the scale and complexity of public administration needs no emphasis here: the mere comparison of the estimates of the Social Service Departments in this country to-day with the similar figures at the beginning of the century will illustrate the point in startling fashion.

3. During the early stages of this period of transition in Europe the old doctrine continued to dominate the field of Colonial administration. In most Colonies little attention was paid by Governments to social needs, and such educational and medical services as existed were still provided in the main by the churches or missions. Gradually the new conception came

to be extended from metropolitan countries to their dependencies, but a process which was certain in any event to be slow has been checked by a number of causes, principally economic and financial. The prosperity of most of the British Colonies depends upon their ability to produce primary commodities at low prices and to find remunerative markets in which to sell them. Never have those tasks been so difficult over a prolonged period as they have during the last 20 years. The excess of supply over demand in a world of reluctant buyers, many of whom are obsessed with the wish to be self-sufficient, has inevitably led to restrictions on output; even so, the price obtained for primary commodities has left no margin either for the payment of better wages from which the workers might improve their own conditions, or for substantially increased taxation which would enable Colonial Governments to undertake these services. Few of those Governments have been in a financial position to follow the new lead of more advanced administrations by planning measures of social reform which involve new liabilities extending far beyond the immediate future. Nor could they count on continuing grants for social services from the British Government, whose general policy in the past has been to avoid long-term commitments, to press for the balancing of the budgets of the various Colonies and to limit financial assistance (apart from capital sums granted or lent for particular purposes from the Colonial Development Fund) to the amounts, fixed annually by the Treasury, needed to ensure that equilibrium.

4. Within the limits imposed upon them by their own financial position, by the uncertain economic outlook and by the prevailing system of Imperial grants, most Colonial Governments in the West Indies have made some effort to follow the modern trend by engaging in State activities unknown a century ago. But those efforts—of which the latest example to be found in most of these Colonies is the creation of Labour Departments—have so far done no more than touch the fringe of the problem, and they must be intensified and extended in scope if Governments in the West Indies are to assume the responsibilities now taken for granted in many other countries. Their existing machinery is, however, barely adequate to serve its purpose under the present far less intricate systems of administration and social services, and there is no expedient through which, without radical reform and expansion, that machinery could be adapted to the new duties which, in our opinion, must in future be undertaken by the Governments of the West Indian Colonies.

5. In the preceding Chapter we have recommended that, in view of the admitted inability of those Governments to finance the measures of social improvement which we consider to be necessary, a grant of £1,000,000 per annum from Imperial funds

should be assured for a definite term of years. Any programme of administrative reform must therefore include, first, the creation of some authority to decide how money thus made available is to be spent in order to bring most benefit to the West Indian people; secondly, it must provide for expert advice in the planning of schemes and expert control over their execution, when approved; thirdly, it must safeguard the interests of the British taxpayer by ensuring that the grants which he is to make are administered with every regard for both efficiency and economy. The first of these functions clearly points to the establishment of an organisation independent of the West Indian Governments, between whose competing proposals the new authority will have to judge. The second function makes it imperative that the new administrative machine should include the best available advice on a variety of problems beyond the capacity of any single organisation yet created to supervise or administer Colonial affairs. Finally, the duty of watching the interests of the taxpayer at home will demand a close supervision at all stages of each project.

6. The existing arrangements for the supply of advice to West Indian Governments and for the exercise of control over their affairs are centred in the Colonial Office, working through the normal machinery supplemented by a system of special Committees advising on such questions as agriculture, education and public health. It is clear that the choice lies between an enlargement of the activities of that Department and the creation of a new organisation. An increase in the higher staff of the Colonial Office appears, in any event, to be unavoidable if new and more constructive policies are to be adopted for the Colonial Empire. We have been informed that, in so far as is possible under existing conditions, contact between that Department and Colonial officers on leave is already taking place to an extent which interferes markedly both with the day-to-day work of the Colonial Office and with the leisure of Colonial servants on leave. We attach much importance to the greater development of that contact and to more frequent interchange of staff between Downing Street and Colonial administrations, and we are satisfied that a larger margin of staff is necessary which will permit more frequent and more extensive travel by members of the Colonial Office. But even if every reform which we consider to be necessary were made in the central organisation, we could not regard that organisation as fitted for the purpose which we now have in mind. We consider that any plan based on an office working at a distance of thousands of miles from the West Indies would fail, both because the supervision required should be closer and more detailed than any that such an organisation could give and because advice ought to be readily and speedily available if proper progress is to be achieved. The supervision

and administration of new social policies should therefore be controlled by machinery to be established within the West Indies themselves.

7. The next questions to consider are those of the form of the new organisation and the source from which it should be supplied. One of its functions, as we have already said, will be at times to decide which of rival schemes submitted by different West Indian Colonies is to be adopted. Not only must it, for that reason, be independent of the local Governments, but in the present state of jealous rivalry between the larger Colonies, it is important to avoid the appointment of officers who, however unjustly, might be suspected of partiality for a Government under which they have recently served. Most of the advisory staff should therefore be found from outside the West Indies. Even if the reason given above had not led us to that conclusion, we should have been forced to it by the practical argument that a better training and wider experience and vision are here needed than are likely to be found among officers who have served for all, or even for most, of their time in the West Indies. Public employment in that part of the world has, at present, a narrowing effect. The geographical range of the West Indian Colonies, the smallness of many of the islands, the present difficulties of communication and the absence of frequent contact have all combined to frustrate any sustained common effort by the Governments of territories, most of the inhabitants of which still regard their fellows in neighbouring Colonies as rivals rather than as potential partners. In time these difficulties in the way of co-operation will be whittled down, and already there are, as we have said in Chapter XVIII, signs of a growing movement in favour of political federation, but the obstacles are still too serious to be readily surmounted and for the present the best hope of securing unity of effort and a proper balance in new activities is through the maintenance of a supervisory organisation controlled by Your Majesty's Government.

8. So far we have considered this question of administrative reform mainly from the point of view of the West Indies and their need for better and more accessible advice in the framing and implementing of future social policy. There is another aspect of the question to which equal regard should be paid. While it might be an over-statement to say that the Colonial Empire has been neglected in the past, there can be no question that its interests and the welfare of its people have received but little attention from Parliament and the Press. To-day, however, an increasing concern is being shown in the affairs of the Colonial Empire. In our view it is very desirable that the changes in the West Indies which we are now discussing should be so devised as to encourage the future growth of that interest.

Not only should the affairs of that group of Colonies be brought under constant review by an authority whose advice would be available to all British Administrations within the Caribbean area, but the functions of that authority should include the submission of an annual report which would help to focus public attention in this country on the progress of social and economic policy in the West Indies.

9. The principal duties of the person in charge of the new organisation should be:—

(1) to work out, with the aid of the experts to be attached to him and in consultation with the Colonial Governments concerned, long-term programmes of social reform for submission to the Secretary of State for the Colonies;

(2) to consider schemes submitted by Colonial Governments—either on their own initiative or in consequence of consultation with the expert advisers—for the improvement of social conditions within the West Indies;

(3) to control the West Indian Welfare Fund, of which the creation has been recommended in the previous Chapter of this report, and to approve grants from it for expenditure by West Indian Governments on schemes which he has accepted as conforming to the general programme approved by the Secretary of State;

(4) to supervise, through his staff, the administration of those grants; this duty will include frequent inspections of works and of schemes financed from the Fund; and

(5) to submit annually to the Secretary of State a report, in a form suitable for presentation to Parliament, on the work carried out under his supervision during the preceding year. If a Parliamentary Committee on Colonial affairs should be established, the annual reports of this officer could be examined by them in his presence on the analogy of the procedure of the Committee of Public Accounts.

10. It will be noticed that all of these duties are connected with the expenditure of the money to be provided for the betterment of social conditions, and we therefore suggest that the officer at the head of the new organisation might appropriately have the title of Comptroller of the British West Indian Welfare Fund. We have considered several other descriptions, including that of Inspector-General of the British West Indian Colonies, but that title seems to us to be more suitable for an officer whose principal occupations would be, as they are under the French colonial system, those of reviewing by tours of inspection, and reporting to a Minister upon, the whole field of administration in a number of Colonies. It may well be found convenient, as the new organisation develops, to attach wider duties of that character to the new office, but at the outset, when most of the

time of its holder should be devoted to the work described above, the title which we have suggested appears to be preferable. Our proposals are in no way inconsistent with the application in the West Indies of any scheme for the inspection of British colonial administration generally, and could readily be adapted to form part of such a scheme provided that arrangements were made whereby the whole time of a senior and experienced officer would continue to be given to the important and responsible duty of stimulating by wise expenditure forward social policies in the West Indian Colonies.

11. The Comptroller should spend most of his time in the West Indies, but, as a rule, he should visit London once in each year to consult the Secretary of State for the Colonies and his visits should be so timed that he will be available in London during the period immediately after the publication of his report for the preceding year. Most of us think that, for reasons of administrative convenience, the Comptroller should be fitted into the machinery of the Colonial Office; some of us, however, consider that he should be independent of that Department and should be responsible to the Secretary of State for the Colonies alone. We are all agreed that, whatever may be decided on that point, the Comptroller should have the right of direct access to the Secretary of State. His salary should be fixed at a figure which will attract the best candidates from the Colonial Service and from any other fields of public administration, experience in which is likely to be valuable in the head of the new organisation. We suggest that the salary, in addition to adequate travelling allowances, should be not less than £3,000 per annum.

12. Throughout this report frequent reference has been made to the need for the appointment of experts who should be available to advise on a diversity of subjects for the whole of the West Indian Colonies. Our intention is that these experts should be attached to the Comptroller of the British West Indian Welfare Fund, and that their work should be conducted in the main under his supervision. At the same time their services should be available to the Governments of those Colonies which would no doubt wish to take advantage of their advice before framing and submitting to the Comptroller schemes involving expenditure from the Fund. They would also advise the Comptroller on the distribution of grants for purposes affecting those aspects of social progress with which they were concerned, and the appropriate persons from among them should be constituted into a Social Welfare Committee to which would fall the duty of considering, and advising on, the question of the extent to which the different departments in any Colony could, and should be required to, co-operate in any schemes of social welfare, most of which will clearly involve joint activity by, for example, medical, educational,

labour and social welfare authorities. That Committee would be a counterpart in the central organisation of the local bodies, the establishment of which in each Colony was recommended in Chapter XI of this report.

13. The panel of experts to be attached to the Comptroller and to work under his supervision will no doubt grow, and be modified, from time to time in the light of experience. For a start it is, we consider, essential that it should include members capable by training and experience of advising on educational, financial, health, housing, income tax, labour and social welfare problems, and a civil engineer. Many of these will require, either at the outset, or at an early stage, assistants who are specially qualified to advise on particular aspects of those subjects. For example, the adviser on housing, who, as we have said in Chapter IX, should have considerable experience of large housing schemes in this country, will need the assistance of an expert in town planning. A statistical officer should also be appointed and be made responsible for the collation and analysis of statistics for the whole of the West Indies under the supervision of the Comptroller. Agriculture appears to us to need different treatment, and we have recommended in Chapter XVI of this report that an Inspector-General of Agriculture for the British West Indies should be appointed and should be mainly responsible to the Agricultural Adviser to the Secretary of State for the Colonies. Full use should, however, be made of his services and advice in connection with land settlement or other schemes forming part of programmes of social reform which are submitted to the Comptroller and by him to the Secretary of State.

14. The value of this panel of experts would not be limited to their work in planning and co-ordinating schemes for social improvement in the Caribbean area. They would also be a clearing house for experience and information throughout that area, and there is no reason why the benefits thus gained should not be made available, in course of time and through some larger organisation, to the whole Colonial Empire. Our proposals might well be regarded as an experiment in method to be extended, if they proved their worth, to some of the other Colonial Dependencies.

15. It is essential, if these administrative changes are to succeed, that the Comptroller and members of his staff should be able to travel between the West Indian Colonies much more freely and more quickly than would be possible with existing communications. The provision of two small ocean-going steamers, as recommended in Chapter XIX, would help in this direction, but its advantages to the new organisation are not to be compared with those of the proposed air service between

St. Kitts and Trinidad which also we recommended in that Chapter. Such a service would reduce considerably the loss of valuable time which regular visits of inspection by members of the panel to the smaller islands would otherwise involve; it would also go far to enable West Indian Governments to obtain at short notice the advice of one of the experts—as, for example, when the Labour Adviser of the Comptroller is wanted to act as mediator in a major dispute over wages or conditions of labour; and it would substantially shorten the delay involved when the Comptroller wishes himself to visit, or to send a member of his staff to visit, the scene of such disasters as the recent landslide in St. Lucia before deciding whether his organisation can effectively help the Colony which has thus been afflicted.

16. It is difficult to frame even an approximate estimate of the cost of these proposals. A reasonable assumption is that at the outset a staff of about ten officers (including a Secretary) of high standing would be required to assist the Comptroller. We consider, therefore, that a sum of approximately £25,000 would be required each year for personal emoluments. As travelling must be extensive, particularly during the early years when programmes are being prepared, provision under this head should be not less than £20,000 per annum. Other charges, including free quarters (or allowances in lieu), passages to and from the West Indies and pensions or pension contributions would probably bring the total estimate up to £50,000 per annum. That figure would certainly increase as the organisation developed and new surveys and other investigations were found to be necessary. It would, we consider, be unwise to put the estimated expenditure, once the scheme is fully developed, at less than £100,000 per annum. That, as we have said in the preceding Chapter, should be definitely additional to the money to be provided for welfare work (which should be free of all charges for central staff), for agricultural research and surveys and for any shipping or other subsidies which may have to be paid. Even if the West Indian Governments could afford to finance this scheme, we should regard it as most undesirable that they should bear any part of the cost of an organisation which is to be completely independent of them and will have at times to criticise their policies and to require that they shall conform to approved plans as a condition of grants to assist their programmes of social welfare. The charge must, therefore, fall on Imperial funds. It is, as we fully realise, a substantial liability to add to those already proposed, but we are convinced that from the standpoint of the public interest this recommendation is vital. Without expert guidance and control, which cannot be secured within the West Indian Colonies themselves and would not, in our view, be equally effective if given from London, much of the effort to improve conditions in those Colonies would be wasted.

17. The question of accommodating the Comptroller and his staff is far from easy. Wherever they are placed—and it is not, in our view, essential, though it would clearly be convenient, that the headquarters of all should be in one island—some new buildings will be needed. We suggest that the possibility of using for this purpose the buildings which the War Office own in St. Lucia should be carefully investigated. But other factors besides the availability of existing premises will have to be considered and we do not wish to make any proposal which might prejudice a free decision in the taking of which the Colonial Governments concerned would no doubt be fully consulted.

18. There remain two questions which can conveniently be considered here though neither is directly connected with the creation of new administrative machinery. Both relate to the conditions of service of officers employed by West Indian Governments. The first is that of the grant of passages to those officers when proceeding on leave to their normal places of residence outside the West Indies. In consequence of recommendations made in the report (Cmd. 4730) by a Committee over which the Earl of Plymouth presided, Colonial Governments, with the exception of most of those of the West Indies, now pay for the passages of officers (and generally their wives and children) both on first appointment and on the occasion of their taking vacation leave outside the Colony. The refusal of most West Indian Governments to come into line with the rest of the Colonial Empire on this point undoubtedly causes hardship. Moreover it lessens the attraction of a branch of the Colonial Service, the salaries and other conditions of which compare unfavourably with those offered in other Colonies of similar standing. It is our opinion that those Governments would be well advised to reconsider their attitude; on a long view nothing but good could result from the grant of a concession which made for the greater contentment of their staff and, by thus improving terms of service, widened the field of selection for posts which, in present circumstances, have normally to be filled from outside the West Indies. We trust that, if Your Majesty's Government undertake to assist the West Indies in the several ways which we have recommended, all the Colonies will see fit, by conceding this privilege, to contribute to the improvement of the standard of administration. Some Colonial Governments now make generous provision for the grant of study leave and the payment of the passages of officers to whom it is granted. It may be beyond the means of the smaller West Indian Governments to make similar concessions, but extended and more generous facilities must be granted if medical, educational and some other officers are to refresh their professional knowledge and keep in touch with modern developments. We recommend, therefore, that the Comptroller of the

West Indian Welfare Fund should be empowered, subject to the consent in each case of the employing Government, to grant a certain number of scholarships each year to serving officers and to meet other costs of their study leave if he is satisfied that this expenditure cannot be borne by local funds.

19. Finally, we come to the question of the salaries of the higher staff in the West Indies. From a full statement which was supplied to us by the Colonial Office we are convinced that the rates in general are low, both for the standard of work expected and by the level of remuneration in other Colonies. We do not feel able to recommend that Your Majesty's Government should undertake the burden of supplementing the emoluments of these appointments. That is properly the liability of the employing Government. We consider, however, that Governments in the West Indies, and particularly in the larger Colonies, would be well advised to review the salaries of their senior officers, bearing in mind that unless those salaries conform to the general scale of emoluments attaching to posts of similar status in other comparable Colonies, it must become increasingly difficult to fill the higher administrative and professional posts by men whose training, experience and ability will fit them to co-operate effectively with the Comptroller and his staff in schemes for the social betterment of those territories. Up to a point a panel of experts can be relied upon to stimulate progress, but no endeavour on their part could completely redress any failure caused by the lack of really capable staff at the head of departments in the Colonies.

CHAPTER XXII.

CONSTITUTIONAL PROBLEMS.

1. Reasons for considering these Problems.

1. Our terms of reference were to inquire into the social and economic conditions of seven Colonies and " matters connected therewith ". The Secretary of State for the Colonies, in reply to questions asked in the House of Commons on the 23rd of November, 1938, made it clear that our mission, thus defined, did not exclude the consideration of constitutional problems and the question of constitutional reform, if we were satisfied that these were relevant to the social and economic conditions which were our principal concern.

2. Rightly or wrongly, a substantial body of public opinion in the West Indies is convinced that far-reaching measures of social reconstruction depend, both for their initiation and their effective administration, upon greater participation of the people in the business of government. Many adherents to this view are prominent in political movements, some of which would not be content with any constitutional change falling short of self-government; others are interested in local politics only in so far as they regard these as the readiest means to the securing of the end of social reform which is their real concern. But all are firmly persuaded that their feeling on the constitutional issue is a correct one, and no amount of argument would change their convictions. An examination of the social and economic problems of the West Indies which, however exhaustive, took no account of this point of view, would therefore be regarded by some sections of public opinion in the Caribbean area as having failed in a primary purpose. Moreover, we are satisfied that the claim so often put before us that the people should have a larger voice in the management of their affairs represents a genuine sentiment and reflects a growing political consciousness which is sufficiently widespread to make it doubtful whether any schemes of social reform, however wisely conceived and efficiently conducted, would be completely successful unless they were accompanied by the largest measure of constitutional development which is thought to be judicious in existing circumstances. We felt bound, therefore, to extend our inquiry to the issues which we are now to consider.

3. A brief description of the existing constitutions was given in Chapter V of this report in order to prepare the way for a discussion of the relationships between the Executive and public opinion as represented by Legislative Councils and the Press. Also, in Chapter XVIII we have recommended that the principle of federation in the West Indies, which we regard as the proper

Chapter XXII. 374

ultimate aim of policy, should be initiated in a practical form, at the first suitable opportunity, by an amalgamation of the Leeward Islands and the Windward Islands. The leading question remaining for examination here is that of increased participation of the people in their own Government by, first, a variation in the composition of Executive and Legislative Councils, and, secondly, an extension of the franchise.

2. Composition of Executive and Legislative Councils.

4. Suggestions made to us in evidence varied from one for the grant of immediate and complete self-government, based on a universal franchise, to a proposal that the authority of Governors should be widened in a way which would come near to converting the existing system into the autocracy which it is so often alleged to be. We cannot support either of these extreme points of view. The claim for independence is irreconcilable with that control which, though not necessarily in its present form, must continue to be exercised, in the interests of the home taxpayer, over the finances of Colonies receiving substantial assistance from funds provided by Parliament. On the other hand, any considerable reduction of the powers of an elected body would be difficult to justify, except as a temporary measure in an emergency, unless it was intended to assist the pursuit of a common policy in the West Indies. That apart, while variation in the numbers and composition of the Executive and Legislative Councils may from time to time be found desirable, any fundamental change in the parts which they play in the public affairs of these Colonies is, we consider, to be avoided. The initiative in formulating policy should remain with the Governor in Executive Council but the representatives of popular opinion can be given more opportunity to influence policy, and some of them may perhaps be converted from criticism to co-operation, if an arrangement can be made whereby they are more closely associated with the work of the executive. At present there is everywhere an unofficial element in the Executive Council but this is normally composed of persons nominated by the Governor who need not have a seat in the Legislative Council. Of only one Executive Council in the West Indies can it be said that it contains any representative of the interests of labour; we consider that, when selecting individuals for nominated appointments on those bodies, Governors should bear carefully in mind the desirability of broadening the basis of their Executive Councils and giving, as far as is possible, representation thereon to all important sections of the community. The question of the appointment to Executive Councils of persons who are elected members

of the Legislative Council is one which deserves careful consideration. There may be difficulties in some cases, but we are impressed with the desirability of thus securing the co-operation of the elected element in the work of the executive, and, wherever the difficulties can be overcome, such appointments should be made. In addition—and this we regard as the more important change—some form of committee system should be adopted in the larger Colonies to give unofficial members of the Legislature, particularly elected members, an insight into the details of administration. These Committees should be advisory and not executive bodies, but should be given statutory sanction. Their range should be wide enough to cover all major branches of Government activity in the Colony. Heads of Government Departments, even if they are not members of the Legislative Council, should be appointed to the appropriate Committees; that apart, their composition would vary but in general it is desirable that the representatives of elected members of the Legislature, chosen by them, should be in a majority on each Committee, the Chairman of which would be nominated by the Governor.

5. In making these suggestions we have not overlooked the defects which are now thought to be inherent in the Committee system as applied during recent years in Ceylon. They are, however, important differences which, in our view, make it unlikely that the experience of Ceylon would be repeated in the West Indies. Conflict of racial interests would seldom be so acute as to disturb the successful working of such a system in the Caribbean area. Our proposal that the Committees should be consultative bodies should avoid the worst of the administrative weaknesses, such as delay and the absence of directing control, which have been criticised in regard to the Ceylon system, where the Committees are executive. One other valuable lesson can be learned from experience in Ceylon and elsewhere. It is that all matters relating to appointments and personnel should remain in the hands of the Governor in Executive Council and of the Secretary of State for the Colonies.

6. Our advocacy of the repetition in the West Indies of an experiment which, notwithstanding those differences, bears much resemblance to one which may now be abandoned, after a full and fair test, in another part of the Colonial Empire, would be incomplete without a brief account of the advantages which, in our judgment, it might be expected to secure. The first, to which we have already referred, is its value in educating unofficials in the business of government. It might also be the means of shortening speeches in Legislative Council; so inordinate has been their length in Jamaica, that during our visit there the Council passed a self-denying resolution

prescribing set limits to them. Thirdly, the appointment of heads of Government Departments on these advisory Committees will enable them there to answer their critics and so permit their release from the unwelcome duty, which now falls on many of them, of appearing publicly at meetings of the Legislative Council in what is in effect a ministerial capacity for which few of them are fitted by training or temperament. We consider therefore that the system is well worth a serious trial in the larger West Indian Colonies.

7. The last of the points made in the preceding paragraph leads to another and more general conclusion. We consider that the nomination of heads of Departments as members of the Legislature should be exceptional and that normally the Colonial Secretary, the Treasurer and the Attorney-General should be the only officials on that body. Between them these three officers should be able to explain the policy and represent the point of view of Government, and all questions should be addressed to the Colonial Secretary who would answer them, on behalf of the Government, unless they raised issues with which one of the two other official members could deal more appropriately and effectively. Not only would heads of other Departments thus be relieved of a distasteful task, but through the release from long hours of attendance during which they are often required only to record their votes, many of them would be able to give much more time to their proper duties.

8. Before we pass on to the question of filling the places on the Legislature which would be vacated by the removal of officials, it is necessary to refer to the functions of that body under the Crown Colony system. The most important of these are the discussion of policy, the passing of legislation and the voting of monies to finance the administration. So far as the first of these is concerned there is much to be said for widening the scope of unofficial representation on the Councils and for increasing its numbers; the two other purposes can be secured, when there is an unofficial majority in the Council, by some such constitutional device as giving the Governor the power to declare any matter to be of paramount importance and to decide it in a sense contrary to the vote of a majority of the Council if he is satisfied that such a decision is necessary in the interest of first essentials of good government. The use of these powers, however, invariably results in popular outcry. To increase unofficial representation in the Council, even to the extent of making it wholly an elected body, without at the same time relinquishing control by the executive, or dispensing with the Governor's special powers, would do little to satisfy political aspirations in the West Indies. The time for self-government, as we have already said, has not yet come. So long as the need for financial control continues,

constitutional reform, apart from the changes recommended earlier in this Chapter, ought to be directed towards making the Legislative Councils more fully representative of all important sections of the community. This can be secured through the wise use of the power to nominate members of the Council. In selecting them the first consideration must, of course, be the enlistment of the help of the individuals, of any race or class, most fitted to offer useful advice on public policy, but the principle of broadening the composition of the Council should be accepted and recognised as second only to that. We will give one example. Women are just beginning to take part in public affairs in the West Indies and, as will be clear from other passages in this report, many reforms are needed on which their advice might be of considerable value. Where representation of those interests has not been secured through the elections to the Legislative Council, the Governor should bear carefully in mind the possibility of nominating a woman to that body.

9. It will be clear from the preceding paragraph that we attach more importance to the representative character of the Legislative Councils than to any more fundamental change in their composition which, unless accompanied by an executive control not practicable in present conditions, could not satisfy those who most pressed for it in evidence before us. It follows therefore that, in our opinion, any appointments to the Council to make good the removal of officials should normally be filled by nomination and not by election. We are anxious, however, that this expression of opinion should not be used as an argument against all other constitutional reform. We understand that proposals for such changes are being, or may be, put forward by some Governors and we wish it to be understood that any reasonable progressive measures would command our support provided that they satisfy two conditions. The first is that they must be consistent with what is, in our view, the primary need of wider representation on the Legislative Council; the second is that they should give the people an increased share in their government without impairing the essential financial and other control by the executive.

3. Extension of the Franchise.

10. The qualifications for registration on the roll of persons entitled to vote at elections to membership of the Legislative Council are summarised below:—

Chapter XXII.

Colony.	Property qualification.	Tax qualifications.	Salary or income qualification.
Barbados	Ownership of property of value of £5 p.a.; rents and profits from land of an annual value of £5; occupation of land or buildings assessed at £15 p.a.	Payment of taxes of £2 p.a. in the City of Bridgetown or £1 p.a. in rural areas.	£50 p.a. or £15 when derived from real estate, securities or dividends on shares of company incorporated in Island.
British Guiana	Ownership of not less than six acres of land. Occupation or tenancy of not less than six acres of land secured by lease or other written document for at least three years; ownership of house or land (or both) of value of not less than £72 18s. 4d.; occupation or tenancy of land or house (or both) of not less than £20 rent p.a. secured by lease or other written document for one year.	Payment of direct taxes (not including licence duty) of £4 3s. 4d. p.a.	£62 10s. 0d. p.a.
British Honduras. (The dollar, which is linked to the currency of the U.S.A., has been taken at $4·80 to £1.)	Ownership of real property situate within the Colony to the value of £104 3s. 4d. Rent in respect of real property situate within the Colony at the rate of £20 p.a.	—	£62 10s. 0d. p.a.
Jamaica	—	Payment of rates on property amounting to 10s. p.a. if a male or £2 p.a. if a female; payment of taxes amounting to £1 10s. p.a. if a male or £2 p.a. if a female, in respect of personal property.	Salary of £50 p.a.; income of £50 p.a. with occupation of premises rented at not less than £10 p.a. (male or female voters).

Colony.	Property qualification.	Tax qualifications.	Salary or income qualification.
Leeward Islands (except Virgin Islands which have no legislature).	Ownership of real property of value of £100; payment of rent of £12 p.a. on real property.	Payment of direct taxes of 15s. p.a.	£30 p.a.
Trinidad ...	Ownership of property of rateable value of £12 10s. in borough or £10 elsewhere; occupation of property rented at £12 10s. p.a. in borough or £10 elsewhere.	Occupation as owner or tenant under agreement of property and paying at least 10s. p.a. land tax.	£62 10s. 0d. p.a.
Windward Islands :— Grenada, St. Lucia, St. Vincent.	Ownership of real property of value of £100; payment of rent of £12 p.a. on real property.	Payment of direct taxes to amount of 15s. p.a.	£30 p.a.

11. Although these qualifications are not high by standards which prevailed in this country when similar tests were applied, they are high in relation to average incomes in the West Indies and in consequence only a small portion of the population is everywhere registered as voters. For example, at the time (January, 1938) of the last election held in Trinidad the registered electorate totalled 30,911, which is only 6·6 per cent. of the estimated population of the Colony, and the corresponding figure for Barbados in the same year was 6,359 or 3·3 per cent. of the estimated population. Even if, as we were told in several Colonies, a number of people who are eligible to be registered as voters either do not understand, or for other reasons fail to comply with, the formalities of enrolment, the figures given above clearly indicate that the present qualifications have had, as they were no doubt intended to have, the effect of restricting the electorate to the comparatively well-to-do.

12. We questioned many witnesses about their views on the extension of the franchise and from most of them received a favourable reply. In some Colonies it may be true that, as stated by opponents of any change, the lowering, or removal, of the qualifications for the exercise of the vote is not at present a live political issue. Nevertheless, the point clearly deserves serious consideration on its merits. The case for an extension of the franchise is founded mainly on the claim that the people of these Colonies have now reached a stage at which they must

either stagnate politically, or move one more step in their progress towards that self-government which is the avowed aim of British colonial policy. The opponents of concession argue that the changes which have taken place, and are still taking place, in labour and other conditions in the West Indies are so far undermining the existing social structure that any step which to-day might accelerate the pace of that process should at least be postponed until the West Indian peoples have had time to adjust themselves to the new circumstances brought about by those changes. Between these two extremes lie many varying shades of opinion, of which only one need be mentioned here. It is the view that the franchise should be extended, but made subject to some form of literacy test from which all voters now registered would be excused. This suggestion is superficially attractive, but experience elsewhere has shown that such tests may be abused, and we understand that it was not considered desirable to adopt them when an extended franchise was introduced a few years ago in India, where the percentage of illiteracy is higher than that of the West Indies.

13. Some of us hold that the time has already come for the introduction of universal adult suffrage throughout the West Indies. We are not all satisfied that this is the case but we are unanimously of opinion that universal suffrage should be the ultimate goal.

14 Those of us who feel that it would be premature to adopt at once so wide a measure of enfranchisement recommend that the Colonial Governments should give early and earnest consideration to the subject with a view to reducing the present qualifications so as to enlarge the electorate to as great an extent as local conditions make possible or prudent.

15. It is suggested that a fully representative committee should be appointed in each Colony to undertake this duty and that these various committees should consult with each other in order to secure the maximum possible degree of uniformity in the qualifications required throughout the islands—a point of some importance in connection with a possible future Federation.

16. In this connection the position of women should come under review. At present, in some Colonies women are debarred from registration as electors, while in others the age at which women become eligible for the vote differs from that prescribed for men.

17. All such discrimination between the sexes should certainly be abolished but even the grant of votes to women on the same terms as to men would not, in the circumstances prevailing in the West Indies, result in the enfranchisement of any large number of women. This is one of the considerations which have

influenced those members of the Royal Commission who advocate the immediate introduction of universal suffrage. Those of us who dissent from that proposal consider that the situation can be met to some extent by the grant of a vote to the wives of registered electors.

4. Qualifications for Membership of the Legislative Councils.

18. The qualifications which candidates for election to the Legislative Councils of the various Colonies must possess are summarised below:—

Colony, etc.	Property qualifications.	Salary or income qualification.
Barbados	Ownership of 30 acres of land with a dwelling house of the value of not less than £300; or ownership of any real property of the absolute value of £1,500; or beneficial interest in a property the rental value of which is not less than £120 p.a.	£200 p.a.
British Guiana	Ownership of immovable property of the value of not less than £1,042 clear of all charges and encumbrances; ownership under a lease for 21 years or more of any house or houses and land the annual rental of which is not less than £250.	£500 p.a.
British Honduras	Ownership of real property within the Colony of value of at least £104.	£208 p.a.
Jamaica	Ownership of lands producing £150 p.a.	£200 p.a. where income derived partly from lands, partly from business, otherwise £300 p.a.
Leeward Islands (except Virgin Islands which have no legislature).	Ownership of real property within Presidency of the value of at least £500. Occupation of land in the Presidency, as tenant to another, of rental value of at least £50 a year.	£200 p.a.
Trinidad	Ownership of real estate of the value of at least £2,500 or from which the annual income is not less than £200.	A clear annual income of £400 from any source.
Windward Islands · Grenada. St. Lucia. St. Vincent.	Ownership of real property in the island of the value of at least £500.	£200 p.a.

19. It will be observed that these qualifications are much higher than those required for registration on the electoral roll. We consider that in many cases they are unnecessarily high, and we suggest that in all the West Indian Colonies a careful examination should be made at an early date into the possibility of reducing substantially the margin between the qualifications for membership of the Legislative Council and those for registration as a voter. If it is thought necessary to guard against freak candidates provision could be made for the payment of monetary deposits which would be forfeited by those who failed to obtain a prescribed proportion of the votes recorded.

5. Representation of West Indian Colonies in Parliament.

20. The complaint was made in several memoranda of evidence, and by witnesses, that the House of Commons does not give sufficient time to the discussion of Colonial affairs, and it was argued that in order to secure proper attention by Parliament to the problems of the West Indies, those territories should be accorded the privilege of direct representation in the House of Commons. The first of these points would be met in part by the establishment of a standing Parliamentary Committee charged with the duty of examining reports to be rendered annually on the administration of each Colonial Dependency. That possibility has recently been receiving active attention both from Parliament and in the Press of this country, and we do not propose to offer any comment upon it here. But we regard it as essential that the House of Commons should devote more time to the discussion of Colonial Affairs and we hope that means will be found, within the limits of Parliamentary procedure, whereby this can be done. The second suggestion springs from the knowledge that each of the neighbouring French islands of Guadeloupe and Martinique sends two representatives to the Chamber of Deputies and one to the Senate in Paris. The contrast between the French and British systems of Colonial administration is sufficiently marked to make it doubtful whether an arrangement which has worked well as part of one of those systems would necessarily be successful under the other. But even if that point of argument is conceded certain difficulties and objections still remain. No reason was put forward which would justify the singling out of the British West Indian Colonies for special treatment in this respect and the suggestion must therefore be considered as one involving the representation in Parliament of other parts of the British Colonial Empire. The appointment of a delegate or delegates by each Dependency would clearly be out of the question and such factors as geographical dispersion and diversity of interests would be obstacles in many cases to their effective combination for this purpose. Moreover the present crowded state of Parliamentary business would make it difficult to find the time for even a limited number of Colonial repre-

sentatives to be given more than infrequent opportunities for the discussion of the affairs which most interest them. We can only conclude that the suggestion is not so likely to help towards a solution of the difficulties of the West Indies as to justify such a novel departure from British constitutional practice. A much more effective step would be the association of the elected representatives of these Colonies with the work of any standing Parliamentary Committee which may be created to consider Colonial affairs by giving those representatives in each Colony the right to seek permission for one or more of their number to participate in the deliberations of that Committee when any report which directly concerns their Government is under examination. We understand that the elected members of the Municipal Councils in the American Colony of the Virgin Islands have certain rights of access to the parliamentary bodies in the United States, and the possibility of conceding a similar, though not necessarily identical, privilege to the British Colonies in the Caribbean area, appears at least to be worthy of serious consideration.

6. Local Government.

21. The terms of reference of any Committee appointed in a West Indian Colony to investigate, as we have suggested in this Chapter, the possibility of a lowering of the existing qualifications for the exercise of the vote at elections to the Legislative Council, might appropriately be extended to include consideration of the reduction of the qualifications for the vote at elections to any municipal or other local authority.

22. It is our view that the improvement of social conditions in these territories depends in a large measure on co-operation between the central administrations and the people through properly constituted and well-conducted local authorities. In the West Indies the basis of representation on such bodies should gradually be broadened and, above all, service on them must be disinterested if this aspect of government is to attain the standard achieved in this country. In present circumstances it is often impossible, particularly among the smaller West Indian communities, to avoid the appointment, or election, to local councils and sanitary or other boards of persons whose private interests might be affected by decisions in the making of which they may share if those bodies have executive powers. In such cases the local authority should, we consider, be limited to the giving of advice and should so remain until there is reason to believe that their members have a proper understanding of the powers and responsibilities of an executive body and are not likely to obstruct, for reasons of self-interest, reforms recommended by technical or professional experts. Ultimately the system should be completely democratic but outside the largest towns the safeguard which we have suggested will, we consider, be necessary for some time to come.

PART IV
OTHER QUESTIONS

CHAPTER XXIII.

MISCELLANEOUS GENERAL QUESTIONS.

1. We have now completed an examination of the main problems of policy affecting economic and social conditions in the West Indies as a whole. It remains to consider here a number of general questions which concern either the whole group or a number of those Colonies and, in the next Chapter, questions of local or sectional significance.

1. Reconstitution of the British West Indies Regiment.

2. During our proceedings in the West Indies it was suggested that we should recommend the reconstitution of this Regiment which was disbanded in 1927. We have given full consideration to this suggestion and we agree that, from the point of view of those Colonies in which the Regiment would be stationed, the re-establishment of this military unit would have many advantages. It served as a most useful training ground for several other occupations. For example, our attention has been called to the value of the tradition of discipline and *esprit de corps* among the Prison Service in the West Indies which had resulted largely from its stiffening by the infusion of Warrant and Non-Commissioned Officers of the Regiment. Moreover, particularly if some of the senior non-commissioned posts were filled for a time from this country, the reconstitution of the Regiment might have been the means of spreading a knowledge of trades and craftsmanship which is so greatly needed in the West Indian Colonies. The primary consideration is, however, that of finance. The cost of maintaining the Regiment is estimated at over £85,000 a year. If, as we understand to be the case, there is no possibility of this charge being borne from Imperial funds, we feel unable to recommend that the Regiment should be reconstituted since, as we have clearly shown, there are other and more urgent demands to be met from the funds at the disposal of West Indian Governments.

2. Grievances of Ex-Service Men.

3. In four Colonies we heard evidence from representatives of associations of ex-service men, and in others we received memoranda setting out their grievances. The more substantial complaints related to the stoppage of disability pensions, the failure of Governments to give preference to ex-soldiers when selecting men for minor appointments in the Public Service and for the allotment of land under settlement schemes, and the withholding of sums of money alleged to be due.

4. Whenever a witness who personally put forward the first of these complaints was examined in detail, it was found that the payment of his pension had not ceased until a competent medical authority had reported either that he was no longer disabled or that the degree of incapacity had fallen below the standard laid down in this country as a qualification for the receipt of a pension. In all cases it seemed clear that the practice followed was based on that of the Ministry of Pensions and we feel unable to suggest that any departure from that practice should be introduced in the West Indies.

5. The complaint of the withholding of money due was found on investigation to be connected with the failure of individuals to make application for payment for many years after the war of 1914-18, by which time no documentary proof of liability could be obtained. The difficulty of now meeting individual claims was recognised by the witnesses who asked that a model land settlement should be established for their benefit. Personal qualifications must, however, be the first consideration in the selection of people to be settled on the land, and we do not feel able to suggest any greater concession to ex-service men than that they should be given the preference whenever a choice has to be made between applicants whose claims on other counts are reasonably equal. At least the same degree of preference should be given to those men in the selection for employment in minor official posts, e.g., messengers, postmen or customs guards.

3. Tourist Trade.

6. As we have said in Chapters II and XIII of this report, the tourist trade is a factor of some importance in the economic life of Jamaica, Barbados and Trinidad, where it has grown materially in recent years. Notwithstanding its susceptibility to changes of fashion and its liability to sudden and sharp fluctuations, it is a trade which should be encouraged. We do not feel able to recommend that any West Indian Colonies should undertake substantial liabilities for this purpose—as was suggested in evidence to us—since we consider that the risks to capital involved in the tourist trade are such that they cannot with fairness be imposed upon the taxpayer and should be borne by private enterprise. The rewards, when success attends efforts to attract tourists, are considerable and, given a reasonable degree of encouragement by Governments, in the form of advertising, the provision of better roads (though not at the expense of agricultural needs) and the improvement of external communications, we see no reason why private capital should not become available for the development of this enterprise. Much will, however, depend on the state of public security.

Chapter XXIII. 388

Tourists will not visit, nor will investors risk their money in, territories which by repute are subject to disturbances such as those which have characterised West Indian life in recent years.

4. Praedial Larceny.

7. We have referred in Chapter XVI—and the question is discussed at greater length in paragraph 20 of Chapter II of the agricultural report—to the effect of praedial larceny on food production. The conclusion there reached was that the remedy lies in the hands of the West Indian peoples themselves, who must be aroused to the feeling that the theft of growing crops is an offence against the community. That will, as we fully realise, be no easy task. It is within the experience of British administration in Africa that action has been found necessary to prevent the infliction of barbarous penalties which native law and custom prescribed for the theft of agricultural produce. In the West Indies severe punishment has not proved so far to be an effective deterrent. We do not suggest that the penalties now normally imposed should be increased, but we do feel that the communities of the West Indies, now that they are demanding a standard of life nearer to that of western peoples, should recognise the corollary that a habit which would not be tolerated among those peoples must be checked by the force of public opinion.

5. Indebtedness.

8. The general problem of indebtedness among agriculturists has been considered in Chapters IV and XVI, where our major conclusion was that a completely satisfactory solution cannot be found in the present state of knowledge. In Chapter VI we discussed the question of the financial position of the several West Indian Governments, as disclosed by the size of their public debts in relation to resources and populations, and in the following Chapter we make recommendations for certain remission of debts which the Governments of British Guiana and British Honduras owe to Your Majesty's Government. Here we propose only to consider briefly how far the burden of the indebtedness of individuals can be relieved by official action.

9. The heavy weight of debt is often due to high rates of interest. Even more it is due in many cases to the hold which merchants, and producers who act as merchants for the crops of others, frequently have over agriculturists. Here the finding of any remedy presents much more difficulty, but some relief should follow from the adoption of our proposals in Chapter XVI that endeavours should be made to arrange for selected estates to act as central agents for their districts in such matters as the processing and sale of certain agricultural

produce at charges which, when the work is undertaken for peasants, should be fixed by the Government. The wise encouragement of co-operative associations, based on careful study and backed by the voluntary rationalisation or allocation of production between different areas, might also help to avoid the incurring of debt on the growing of crops which individuals cannot sell at remunerative prices. But even more important than any action which Governments can take is the need for the West Indian people to realise that forethought and the moral qualities of thrift and honesty are their greatest safeguards. Fondness for display and carelessness for the future are common causes of debt. Failure to repay small loans of capital or to meet other just obligations must prevent the proper development of holdings of land and, in both town and country, must ultimately result in distress. And nothing but harm can result from the lack of forethought which is shown when, as we have said in Chapter IV, the growing of a particular crop is unduly extended, under the stimulus of one favourable year, often with the aid of borrowed money.

6. Census and Other Statistics.

10. Many times in this report we have found it necessary to remark on the absence of the statistical information without which it is often impossible accurately to estimate the nature of important problems and to prescribe the most suitable remedies. In several West Indian Colonies the census, which ordinarily would have been made in or about 1931, was not taken. It is now generally recognised that this omission was a mistake and that both a census and other statistics are necessities.

11. We attach considerable importance to the collation and analysis of all forms of West Indian statistics by a qualified authority, capable of advising West Indian Governments and the Comptroller of the West Indian Welfare Fund on the deductions to be drawn from the information thus made available. Only through this means can plans for the future have a reliable basis. We have therefore suggested in Chapter XXI that the staff of the Comptroller should include a statistical officer, and we recommend that, at an early date after his appointment, he should consider, in consultation with the West Indian Governments, the question of establishing in the various Colonies adequate machinery for the collection of reliable statistical information as well for his use and that of the Comptroller and his staff as for the use of the Colonial Governments concerned.

12. At present, even when statistical information is available, the forms in which it is kept by the various West Indian Governments often differ so widely that comparison between the returns,

or the collection of data to cover the whole group, may be impossible. Clearly the figures thus lose much of their value. We suggest, therefore, that among the earliest duties of the statistical officer should be that of evolving, in concert with both the local Governments and the Colonial Office, methods whereby every important return emanating from these Colonies, whether it is rendered to him or to some other authority, is prepared on a common basis, which will facilitate both its use for comparative study and the compilation of statistics for the West Indies as a whole.

7. The Press.

13. We have indicated in Chapter V the influence which many organs of the Press in the West Indies now exercise on the relations between the public and the Civil Service, and on the important questions of colour prejudice and colour discrimination. On the wider issue of the general functions of the Press in these Colonies we wish to associate ourselves with the views expressed in the following quotation from the Report (Cmd. 5641) of the Commission of Inquiry into the disturbances which occurred in Trinidad in 1937:—

> "We feel that the Press can make an important contribution to the allaying of prejudice and mistrust. It is clear that the influence of the Press is an important potential factor for good or evil in any community, and that therefore a heavy responsibility falls upon the editors of various newspapers. It is in no spirit of criticism that we would urge upon editors in the Colony the necessity for proper moderation of expression with a view to the formation of a healthy public opinion."

14. It is not by any means only in Trinidad that these words need to be taken to heart. The influence of the Press is probably greatest among the smaller communities, for many members of which the reading of its columns provides the main occupation for their hours of leisure. But everywhere this influence must grow, as the reading public expands with the spread of education. It is all the more important, therefore, that the value of restraint and moderation should be fully appreciated by those responsible for the conduct and tone of the Press in all these territories, both large and small alike.

8. Fisheries.

15. We have touched on this subject in both Chapter II and Chapter XVI. In the former we said that while fish forms an important element in the diet of the people, this is mostly salt fish imported from Canada and Newfoundland; we also mentioned that few people in the West Indies appear to take any serious interest in fishing, and that in consequence we found it impossible to obtain any definite information that would enable us to judge how far future development might be

feasible. In Chapter XVI we suggested that an immediate expert inquiry should be made into the possibility of rapid expansion of the existing local fishery industries.

16. A successful outcome to this inquiry would have two important results. It would show that there is a West Indian industry capable of expansion; any development which will provide more occupation to relieve the pressure of population in these islands is clearly to be welcomed. Secondly, if an abundant supply of cheap fresh fish can be secured, and adequate arrangements are made for its marketing and distribution, a partial remedy will have been found for the deficiency in diet which contributes so largely to the malnutrition now greatly evident, particularly among young children, old people and the mothers of large families, and funds will be released for the purchase abroad of necessaries which cannot be produced in the West Indies.

17. If, as may well prove to be the case, the cost of financing a full investigation by a competent authority on fishery is beyond the resources of the Government of any Colony, and there is presumptive evidence that such an inquiry might be expected to have a successful outcome, we consider that there would be a strong claim for assistance from the Colonial Development Fund, or by a direct grant from Imperial funds.

CHAPTER XXIV.

LOCAL AND SECTIONAL QUESTIONS.

1. In this Chapter we shall deal with certain problems affecting individual territories or sections of the community, such as the East Indian populations of British Guiana and Trinidad, and also the aspects peculiar to certain Colonies of problems elsewhere dealt with in a more general way. We shall consider first the special problems affecting certain territories, taking them in alphabetical order.

1. Barbados.

2. Those of our number who had been conducting their investigations in the Windward Islands arrived in Barbados on the 14th January, 1939, and were joined by the remaining members on the 19th January. Making our headquarters in Bridgetown, we took evidence in public and private throughout our stay, hearing 22 witnesses or groups of witnesses. We also severally and jointly visited all parts of the island, acquainting ourselves with conditions in the estates and factories, in schools and public institutions and as regards the housing of the working people. Half of our number left Barbados for British Guiana on the 25th January, the remainder following on the 4th February.

3. The special problems of Barbados are in a sense an intensification of those affecting the West Indian group as a whole, and, having been dealt with fully in other Chapters, require little elaboration here. They are, in brief, a very heavy and increasing pressure of population (1,210 per square mile) on territory almost wholly dependent for its livelihood on the proceeds of a single export crop, sugar, of which the export has been limited by treaty and the disposal rendered barely profitable by depressed prices. The opportunities of employment abroad of which Barbadians have traditionally availed themselves in large numbers, have been drastically reduced, with the double result of an increased demand for work at home and a falling off in the former steady inflow of remittances from Barbadians abroad. No further land is available for development in Barbados, and while some little good may be done by the development of fisheries and the diversification of agricultural practice to enhance the local production of foodstuffs, some outlet on a fairly large scale for some of Barbados's surplus thousands is of pressing urgency. The settlement at Vieuxfort, in St. Lucia, can at best only accommodate a few hundreds, and is in any case bound up with the difficult problem of the sugar export quota for that island. Barbados is

notable for having a comparatively large white population of approximately 10,000 and it should not be forgotten that the need for emigration applies also to some extent to this section of the community. Given satisfactory arrangements with the authorities of the Dominions, we consider that some small emigration may prove to be a feasible step; not having had the opportunity of going into this particular matter in detail, we can only say that it seems to us worthy of careful investigation. For the bulk of potential emigrants, however, suitable homes can only be found in adjacent territories such as British Guiana and British Honduras. There are already a number of Barbadians in employment in British Guiana, especially in the bauxite works at Mackenzie on the Demerara River, and there is no doubt that with their habits of industry and aptitude for agricultural pursuits they would make successful and welcome settlers under any well-considered scheme. Opportunities also offer in British Honduras, where agricultural development for the production of foodstuffs is necessary both on economic and on health grounds, and where the local creole population tends to neglect agriculture in favour of the forestry work which has long been the mainstay of the Colony. Such developments depend on the solution of difficult problems of communication and, in British Guiana, of drainage and irrigation, and it is unlikely that even with the most rapid progress it will be possible to transfer any large number of West Indians for some time to come. When the time comes, however, the utmost importance must be attached to the claims of Barbados, which ranks as easily the most congested area in a group of territories of which a fundamental problem is that of a great and growing pressure of population. (See also Chapter XVI, paragraph 49.)

4. Mention has been made in Chapter V of the constitutional position in Barbados: some further comment is required on the extraordinary degree to which the functions of government are decentralised and distributed among 11 parishes in a territory measuring but 21 miles by 14. Your Majesty's Government may exercise the minimum of control over the activities of the Barbados Legislature: the Barbados Government exercise hardly more over the parochial authorities in vitally important matters of education, public works and public health. As we have stated in Chapter XXII, we consider that social improvement can be fostered by, and indeed may depend for its success upon, co-operation between Government and people through the medium of properly constituted local authorities. There is, however, a point beyond which flexibility and local participation in public work degenerate into chaotic discrepancies and lack of co-ordination, and that point seems to us to have been passed in Barbados. To take an obvious example, certain health measures require to be planned for the

island as a whole, and it is most unsatisfactory that the loyal co-operation of one parish with the central authority may be rendered completely nugatory by inaction on the part of its neighbour. The officers corresponding to the heads of technical departments elsewhere, such as Directors of Education and of Medical Services, are confined in Barbados to purely inspectorial, advisory and reporting functions, and have no means of controlling or enforcing the execution of measures which may have behind them the sanction of the Legislature of the Colony. Nor can the parochial authorities be described as in any way representative of the mass of the population. The local government franchise is very limited, and the whole system is closely bound up with the Church of England organisation of the island, an arrangement which involves the Church in a certain amount of obloquy from time to time, and of which more than one clergyman may wish himself well rid. As the constitution of the island stands at present, this is a matter which Barbadians must settle for themselves. We may content ourselves with observing that in the allocation of money from the British West Indian Welfare Fund, the Comptroller of that fund may well be influenced by the extent to which the Barbados system of government provides for the efficient and controlled execution of schemes financed by him.

2. British Guiana.

5. Those of our number who left Barbados on the 25th January arrived in Georgetown, British Guiana, on the 27th January, the remainder arriving on the 5th February. During our stay in British Guiana we heard 43 witnesses or groups of witnesses in public and in private. Individual members and parties visited various parts of the coastal area, including the Canals Polder area, the Essequibo Coast, New Amsterdam (where a public session was held) and many villages and estates. Four of our number travelled by a flying boat operated by the British Guiana Aviation Company to Bon Success on the Brazilian border, there having an opportunity of meeting and receiving representations from spokesmen of the aboriginal tribes inhabiting the hinterland, and we also flew to the Kaieteur Falls, 250 miles inland, and visited Mackenzie on the Demerara River, the scene of operations of the bauxite industry. Part of our number left for Trinidad by sea on the 18th February the remainder following by Pan-American flying-boat on the 20th February. One of our number, Mr. Morgan Jones, M.P. was obliged to return to England owing to serious ill-health and left on the 19th February.

6. Here again the facts governing the special situation hav been dealt with elsewhere. A population of 338,000, of whic the majority are East Indians, ex-indentured labourers or the

descendants, inhabit a territory consisting in part of a huge area of forest and savannah, very sparsely populated and of debatable economic value apart from its resources of greenheart timber, bauxite and some gold and diamonds, and in part of a coastal strip of alluvial mud, subject to inundation by river and rain and encroachment by the sea, which is kept out by an elaborate and costly system of sea-walls and defences. It is on this strip that the bulk of the population make their living and, in practice, the problems of British Guiana are the problems of this area, the consideration of which is constantly confused by red herrings in the shape of grandiose schemes for tapping the problematic wealth of the interior.

7. The main economic and social problems of British Guiana have been discussed in the Chapters on sugar policy and agriculture and in Part II of this Report, and the special problems of drainage and irrigation and the rice industry are dealt with in paragraphs 50-61 of Chapter XVI. We shall deal here with certain others.

(a) PUBLIC DEBT.

8. As shown in Chapter VI, paragraph 1, the total indebtedness of British Guiana on 31st December, 1938, at £4,394,914, represented £13 0s. 9d. per head of the estimated population and the proportion of debt charges to total expenditure, at 21·1 per cent., was, with the comparable figure for British Honduras, easily the highest in the West Indies. Of this debt, approximately one-third was incurred on account of sea-defence works and about £360,000 on account of drainage-works, the repayment of which sum it now appears will be beyond the resources of the local authorities to whom it was advanced. In British Guiana we were met with numerous representations that these charges, especially in so far as they related to drainage and sea defences, were beyond the power of the Colony to bear without serious impairment of necessary services. It was argued further that expenditure of this nature was so exceptional as to justify a claim that it should be met, either in whole or in part, by the Imperial Treasury; that the Colony was committed by history to living in circumstances requiring large and constant expenditure on sea-defences, drainage and irrigation, and that the Imperial Government should in equity assume some part of the burden of maintaining these defences and so free local funds for the more usual objects of governmental expenditure.

9. It is difficult not to have some sympathy with this view, and it is abundantly true that, whatever assistance may be afforded to British Guiana from the West Indian Welfare Fund, the claims of social and economic development will amply suffice to absorb any local funds available. It would also appear that, quite apart from the weight of the debt burden, an

appreciable proportion of the money has been spent on ill-planned and ill-executed schemes, owing to the lack of personnel of adequate knowledge and experience to cope with the extremely difficult technical questions presented by British Guiana's problems of sea-defence, drainage and irrigation. Although British Guiana now possesses in the Director of Public Works and Sea Defences an officer of experience in sea-defence work, it is not to be expected that a really adequate staff can be maintained from local resources to deal with these problems—which, it should be remembered, are continuous, and cannot be settled once and for all.

10. In addition to the debt to private persons, British Guiana is under a contingent liability to repay to the Imperial Exchequer the assistance granted during recent years by way of " loans-in-aid " to the amount of £549,500, and also about £453,000 on other counts. It is agreed that the honouring of these obligations would absorb any available funds for a long time to come, and that the virtual impossibility of looking forward to a time when British Guiana will be able to devote funds to local constructive purposes without large deductions on account of old debt, in the words of the Colonial Treasurer, " engenders a spirit of indifference and of dependence in the people of the Colony which is highly injurious to their morale and hinders efforts towards recovery ".

11. It must not be thought that the question of alleviating the debt burden of British Guiana has not received careful consideration by Your Majesty's Government. Since 1936 the matter has been under review in connexion with the general problem of colonial indebtedness, and it was then decided that further grant-in-aid should take the form of free grant instead of loan. More recently, the general question has again been under discussion between the Departments concerned, but we do not understand that this related to public debt other than to the Exchequer.

12. While understanding the difficulty of the Treasury in taking action in the case of British Guiana in advance of a decision on policy as regards Colonial indebtedness in general, we consider that there should be no further delay in the case of British Guiana, even at the cost of some discrepancy between steps taken in that case and such general decisions as may later be reached.

We recommend, therefore, that outstanding loans-in-aid should be converted into free grants, that the outstanding obligations on account of the work of the Boundary Commission and on account of loans from the Colonial Development Fund should be remitted; and that in future loans-in-aid should be avoided.

13. We do not find ourselves able to recommend the assumption by Your Majesty's Government of direct financial responsibility for the sea defence works of the Colony. As against the arguments set out above in favour of such a course, we feel that it would be impracticable for work so closely interwoven with the life and the administration of the Colony to be directly controlled by any other authority than the Government. On the other hand, we are of the opinion that Your Majesty's Government should recognise the vital importance for the Colony of the maintenance of adequate sea-defences and irrigation works, and the provision of adequate staff for these purposes, and the impossibility of adequate attention being paid to these matters without substantial assistance from the Imperial Exchequer. It will be necessary to face the fact that adequate expenditure on these lines will entail continued heavy deficits and consequent subventions from the Imperial Exchequer, the repayment of which would be very difficult if not impossible.

(b) AIR SERVICES.

14. The external air communications of British Guiana have been dealt with in Chapter XIX and no further comment is required here. There remains the question of internal services.

15. For communication with the hinterland and particularly those parts nearest the Brazilian border, air transport is and is likely to remain the only means of obviating lengthy and laborious surface travel. There is in existence an air transport concern named (since 1st January, 1939), the British Guiana Aviation Co., Ltd., operated and largely owned by Mr. A. J. Williams. This company is very well run, and Mr. Williams has accumulated experience and knowledge of flying conditions in the hinterland which could not easily be replaced. The value to Government of his services on such undertakings as the Boundary Commission has been considerable, and he has done much good work in bringing to Georgetown for medical treatment cases which could not have hoped to survive a land journey.

16. We found ourselves in agreement with the recommendations in this respect of Mr. Banks, of the Air Ministry who, in agreement with the Governor, proposed that Mr. Williams' aircraft be locally registered and his pilot's licence issued by the Governor, and that his company should be encouraged to develop by the grant of a five-year agreement, including the operation, if practicable, of regular mail services. We understand that such an agreement has now been made.

(c) Aboriginal Indians.

17. Apart from a few who inhabit the coastal area and have come into some contact with western civilisation, the bulk of the aboriginal tribes live in the remote interior under primitive tribal conditions. Accurate statistics are not available but we fear that there is no doubt that their numbers are rapidly diminishing with the growth of contacts with other races.

18. If these simple and peaceful peoples are to avoid extermination, early action is necessary to secure them in the use of adequate tracts of land where they may follow their traditional nomadic way of life. The Commissioner of Lands informed us that the Karasabai and Kanuku reservations were still only under consideration: we consider that this matter should be expedited, and that in addition the Indians should have rights of way and grazing rights on the ranchers' cattle-trails.

19. The grant of permission for ranchers, traders, etc., to operate on the Savannahs is a matter requiring much more care than has hitherto been given to it. The remoteness of these regions, the helplessness of the aborigines and the difficulty of administering justice there make it necessary to ensure as far as possible that such permits are only granted to persons of the best character. Where complaints against the conduct of any such person are substantiated, he should at once be deprived of his licence. We understand that at present the District Commissioner at Kurupukari, the nearest point, is empowered only to deal with cases of cattle-stealing involving sums up to $100 (£20 16s. 8d.). He should be granted wider powers in order to reduce the necessity for reference to Georgetown which in practice renders nugatory much of whatever protection the law affords to the aborigines.

20. Medical services are non-existent for these remote tribes, and health conditions among them are not so good as to render medical services superfluous. Such services would be welcomed, as they figured prominently among the requests put to those of us who travelled to the hinterland to meet some of the tribesmen. We recommend, therefore, that the District Commissioner who is stationed at Kurupukari should be supplemented by an Assistant Commissioner, who should be a medical man with a knowledge of tropical diseases and of practical anthropological training.

(d) Local Government.

21. It might be expected that in a colony such as British Guiana where highly important functions, such as the charge of drainage and irrigation, have in part been delegated to local

bodies, there would be a close control and oversight of local government. This is not the case, and in certain parts of the coastal areas control of the villages seems to be inadequate as regards drainage, the use of common pastures, and sanitation.

22. The system of local government dates from the first post-emancipation years, when ex-slaves formed themselves into companies and bought estates from planters, several of whom left the colony owing to labour shortage. The communities thus formed received some Government assistance, and after various modifications the oversight of their affairs was in 1907 put in the hands of a nominated Local Government Board. These communities were then grouped into two categories, " village districts ", administered by Village Councils now elected to the extent of two-thirds, and " country districts ", administered by wholly nominated Country Authorities. There are at present 25 village districts and 64 country districts. This system is not however all-inclusive. Areas are not declared to be village or country districts except at the request of the persons concerned. Communities in undeclared districts are understood to be under the supervision of the Local Government Board, but the Board levies rates and carries out works of a communal nature only as the result of representations by the proprietors. There appears to be no record of the number of village communities which have made no such representations. The advice and assistance of the District Commissioners and their officers are always available for such districts; but there seems to be little initiative on the part of any branch of the central government in dealing with them, and some communities are known to organise themselves somewhat primitively for communal effort without any advice or assistance from outside.

23. Where so much depends on the efficient maintenance of complicated drainage and irrigation works, such a state of affairs is obviously thoroughly undesirable, and some initiative is required of Government to ensure the proper organisation and administration of all communities, wherever situated, and whether or no they have happened to express a desire to be brought within the scope of the Local Government Board.

3. British Honduras.

24. Half of our members arrived in Belize on the 28th November, the remainder staying on to complete our investigations in Jamaica and proceeding thence, via Cuba, to Puerto Rico, where the Commission reunited. In British Honduras we heard 21 witnesses or groups of witnesses, and undertook such travels in the Colony as time and communications permitted. Members of the party visited Stann Creek by sea and Cayo, near the Guatemalan boundary, and Corozal by air;

at all three centres evidence was heard and at Corozal a deputation attended from Orange Walk, in the north of the Colony, which we were unable to visit. In addition, shorter excursions were made in the neighbourhood of Belize and every opportunity taken to obtain first-hand impression of conditions in the Colony.

25. The Colony has traditionally been associated with one industry, namely, the extraction and export of timber, mainly mahogany, from the extensive forests which cover a large part of its area. Seasonal employment is thus afforded to numbers of workers, most of whom spend the rest of the year in and around Belize and are averse from adopting the life of an ordinary agriculturist. This chief industry is not at present in the best circumstances, partly because of the decline in the world demand for mahogany, and partly because of the thriftless methods of many (but not all) of the contractors, who pay little or no attention to the regeneration of economic trees. Logging thus becomes more difficult and more expensive at a time when the market for the product is unpromising. At the same time, the population of British Honduras is steadily increasing (figures are given in Chapter II), and here, as elsewhere, there is a need for development on lines other than the traditional staple of the Colony, if the present and the additional population are to be supported. As stated elsewhere, we do not recommend the extension to British Honduras of banana-growing, as the land is not for the most part suited for this crop, and there is the practical certainty of serious disease. The citrus industry of British Honduras is valuable; but here too the prospects of expansion are limited, and the prospect of greatly enhanced production in Palestine renders the whole future of citrus most unpromising.

26. The need in British Honduras, as we indicate elsewhere, is for greater diversification of the economic life of the Colony, the local production of as many as possible of the necessities, notably foodstuffs, with the object of conserving and applying only to the purchase of articles incapable of local production the proceeds of a foreign trade which will tend to diminish in relation to population. In so far as these matters are of general application they have been dealt with elsewhere, and we make certain comments on the agricultural needs of the Colony in paragraph 46 of Chapter XVI. We shall here confine ourselves to a few outstanding points.

(a) LABOUR CONDITIONS FOR FOREST WORKERS.

27. Conditions among these workers are very different from those of most other workers in the West Indies. They involve several months' camp life in remote areas, virtually complete dependence on the employer or contractor for foodstuffs and

other necessities, and for housing, and remuneration largely in the form of an " advance " system which has worked its way into the habits of life of practically every inhabitant of Belize. There is a certain value in this system in that it enables a worker to make some provision for his dependants during his absence; but it also lays him open to the temptation, to which he all too often yields, to throw it away on a final spree before leaving town for the woods. We recommend that cash advances be limited to 5 per cent. of the total wage to be earned and to a credit at the Camp Commissary of a further 10 per cent. Prices charged by these Commissaries should be controlled on a cost + transport + 10 per cent. basis and, like all other aspects of camp life, should be the subject of frequent inspection and enforcement. Housing (see also paragraph 29 of Chapter IX) should be adequate and free, as well as health services and prophylactic drugs.

28. Apart from the mahogany cutters, there are also a number of persons engaged in tapping the Sapodilla tree for chicle, the basis of chewing-gum. We have reason to suppose that they are frequently very badly treated by those to whom they must sell their chicle, and we recommend that their accounts be liquidated monthly in cash or negotiable drafts, and that payment by means of credits at particular stores be made illegal.

29. In general, we recommend the adoption of the strongest measures to stamp out any traces of the truck system and its attendant evils of chronic indebtedness and fraud, which we found to be more widepread in British Honduras than in any other part of the West Indies.

(b) EDUCATION.

30. In addition to the more general recommendations in Chapter VII, we recommend:—

(1) that arrangements should be made for the training of teachers in Jamaica, as the size of the Colony does not warrant, and would render disproportionately expensive, the maintenance of a training college for the small numbers involved.

(2) that the present secondary scholarship system should be replaced by one whereby scholarships would be distributive in strict accordance with merit and without consideration of the denominations by which the schools are managed.

(3) that any funds released to the denomination by adoption of our recommendations at (d) below should be expended on the maintenance and improvement of existing schools, Government undertaking the direct provision of new schools.

(c) COMMUNICATIONS.

31. If the economic basis of the Colony is to be broadened, it is essential that access shall be provided to some of the more suitable agricultural areas hitherto practically untapped. Of these, the most important are the El Cayo district, and the Middlesex Valley. When part of our number were in British Honduras, there were hopes that assistance for the construction of a road from Belize to Cayo would be forthcoming from the Colonial Development Fund, but this hope, much to our regret, has been disappointed. We recommend that this proposal be reconsidered by the Colonial Deveolpment Advisory Committee when opportunity offers, as we consider it to be of great importance for the future of the Colony. If this road is constructed, as we trust it will be, we also consider that a further road be made from a suitable point on the Belize-Cayo road to connect it with the Middlesex Valley. Apart from the value of these roads to the inhabitants of the Colony (to whom their construction will incidentally afford much needed employment) it should not be overlooked that it is in the areas thus opened up that there is the best hope of an outlet for Barbadian agriculturist families.

(d) DEBT REMISSION.

32. Like British Guiana, the finances of British Honduras are heavily burdened with debt charges, which amount at present to about 20 per cent. of the Colony's revenues. Our attention was drawn to the fact that these charges are roughly equivalent to the annual grant-in-aid from the Imperial Exchequer. If, therefore, responsibility for these debts were assumed by Your Majesty's Government, there would be no loss to the Imperial Exchequer and British Honduras would be able to balance its own budget and be freed from its present unhealthy sense of dependence on external aid.

33. These debts were incurred partly for hurricane relief (as to which see below) and partly on account of the railway which is now being dismantled. They do not therefore represent any assets contributing to the economic welfare of the Colony and therefore indirectly to the ability of Government to repay them.

34. The Hurricane Loan was raised in order to enable advances to be made to individuals whose property was destroyed, and in particular to the denominations for the reconstruction of damaged school buildings. For reasons explained in Chapter VI, the interest and redemption charges have proved most onerous, and have seriously prejudiced the power of the denominations adequately to maintain their schools. If our recommedation above regarding the assumption by Your

Majesty's Government of liability for the public debt of British Honduras is accepted, we propose further in regard to the Hurricane Loan:—

(1) that the rate of interest to *individual* debtors should be substantially reduced, but the liability to repay the capital should remain;

(2) that the *denominations* should be relieved of all capital liability, but be required to pay interest at the reduced rate of ten years.

(e) THE NON-NEGRO POPULATION.

35. Of a total population of 57,000, Negroes account for some 27,000. Of the remainder, the bulk are the indigenous Mayas (14,000) and Caribs (5,000). Of the Mayas not much is known and little is done for them apart from the activities of certain Roman Catholic missions. They are a retiring, unaggressive race inhabiting the remoter parts of the Colony and practising a system of agriculture of great antiquity. Within its limits this system can be said to be efficient and does provide for all the simple wants of the tribes. In particular, the Mayas actually grow more maize than is imported into the Colony.

36. Like the indigenous peoples in British Guiana and Dominica, the Mayas are ill-equipped to resist the evil effects of unregulated contact with civilisation as it exists in parts of British Honduras. This is particularly true of the effects of the methods adopted in the chicle industry, where it can be said that the Mayan workers are being seriously exploited. We agree with the recommendation in the Agricultural Report (Chapter XXI, paragraph 9) that there is a case for the appointment of a special Commissioner for Mayas, who should work closely with the Agricultural and Forestry Departments, and should make use of the experience and knowledge of Mayan life and agriculture accumulated by the latter. The size of the Mayan population and the distinctiveness of their problems fully justify such a step.

37. The Carib population live and work in less remote areas and as a rule on better land. Their standard of cultivation is higher. They have intermarried to some extent with Negroes, and are better equipped than the Mayas to withstand the more deleterious effects of civilisation. The Caribs are often good boatmen, and could play an important part in the development of fisheries.

38. For both Caribs and Mayas, improvement in elementary education and in health instruction would be of great benefit.

Chapter XXIV.

4. Jamaica.

39. With the exception of the Chairman who arrived separately, we reached Kingston on 1st November, 1938, making our headquarters there for the duration of our stay. We heard 42 witnesses or groups of witnesses in public and in private, and conducted numerous visits and tours throughout the island, including Savannah-la-Mar, Lucea, Montego Bay (where evidence was taken), Ocho Rios, Port Antonio on the coast, and many townships, villages, estates, factories and agricultural areas in the interior. We visited public institutions, schools, hospitals, prisons, etc., and inspected the worst slum areas in Kingston itself. We availed ourselves of many opportunities apart from those of formal evidence of making ourselves acquainted with all shades of opinion in the island.

40. A party headed by the Chairman left by sea for British Honduras on 25th November, the remaining members left by air on 6th and 7th December.

41. Our Chairman was able to visit the Cayman Islands. Unfortunately it was not possible for any of us to visit the other Jamaican dependency of the Turks and Caicos Islands, but we had the opportunity of discussing the affairs of the Turks and Caicos Islands with the Commissioner who came to Jamaica for that purpose.

42. Although Jamaica is in some ways one of the more prosperous of the West Indian Colones, both actually and potentially, it is here that the problem of unemployment and the more widespread one of under-employment, complicated by the drift to the towns, is most acute. Large-scale agricultural development, though both feasible and desirable, will take time and cannot meet the immediate problem, which has recently been much accentuated by the threat to the banana industry (and not least to the small growers) of the rapid spread of leaf-spot disease. This matter is discussed in paragraphs 41-45 of Chapter XVI.

43. On the other hand, the industrial outlook is better in Jamaica than elsewhere. The Government is not without resources, and there is constructive work to be done which should provide a fair amount of employment and add to the economic resources of the island. There is a need for more and better communications to prepare the way for the agricultural developments discussed elsewhere, and those under consideration by the Jamaican Government, and scope exists for, e.g., irrigation and drainage works on a substantial scale. Many of these possible projects would have the advantage of drawing workers away from the overcrowded towns. The moral advantage of well-considered, constructive public works over hasty relief-works would be considerable and would, we feel, infuse a new spirit into workers, many of whom are in serious danger of irremediable casualisation and pauperisation.

44. As regards the dependencies of Jamaica, we have no recommendations to make on the Cayman Islands. We understand them to be, not wealthy, but socially homogeneous and self-sufficient and without the industrial problems which beset other parts of the West Indies.

45. The Turks and Caicos Islands, on the other hand, merit more attention than they have hitherto received from the Government of Jamaica under whose charge they are. Arid and infertile, they depend for the most part on the production of salt, a proportion of which returns to the West Indies by way of the curing-sheds of Canada and Newfoundland to be consumed as a component of the imported salt fish so popular there. We understand that many of the workers are chronically in debt to the merchant-middlemen, who in turn are largely in the hands of American firms. We should welcome any steps that may be taken to mitigate this dependence, although so far as the workers are concerned the ill effects of this indebtedness are lessened by the smallness and consanguinity of the population.

46. Geographically, these islands form part of the Bahamas group and they, especially the Caicos, would seem to have more in common with that group than with Jamaica. We suggest that Your Majesty's Government should consider whether it would not be desirable that they should be amalgamated with, or at least administered from, the Bahamas.

5. Leeward Islands.

47. After a short visit to Puerto Rico and the American Virgin Islands, the Chairman's party reached Tortola, in the British Virgin Islands group, on 19th December. Evidence was heard there and, on the following day, in Anguilla, a small island dependent on St. Kitts-Nevis. The party then proceeded to St. Kitts, and their visit to the Leeward Islands extended until their departure for Barbados, via the Windward Islands, on the 14th January, 1939. They remained in St. Kitts until 24th December, visited Nevis from 24th to 28th December, Antigua from 29th December to 2nd January, Montserrat from 2nd to 5th January, and Dominica from 6th to 14th January, a visit to Guadeloupe being made on 12th and 13th January. Evidence was heard from witnesses or groups of witnesses in the larger islands as follows:—

St. Kitts	7
Nevis	6
Antigua	13
Montserrat	10
Dominica	16

48. In the Leeward Islands, as elsewhere, members availed themselves of all possible opportunities of travelling and seeing for themselves conditions of life and of work, and of acquainting themselves at first hand with the views of all sections of the community.

49. The problems of the Leeward Islands, like those of the Windwards, are greatly complicated by the smallness of the constituent communities, their distribution over an area large enough to make speedy communication a fairly expensive matter, and the small scale of most of their economic activities. The most important industry is sugar, as carried on in Antigua and St. Kitts-Nevis; the other islands have depended in the past on a variety of products, notably coconuts and coconut products, some cotton and, in Dominica and Montserrat, limes, lime juice and lime oils. The production of sugar has been limited under the International Agreement. The future for citrus and coconuts is gloomy, and the market for the high grade sea island cotton is limited and fully supplied from St. Vincent and elsewhere. The diminution of opportunities for employment overseas has hit the Leewards more than the larger Colonies except Barbados, and there is a great need for the absorption at home of the growing population. Conditions of employment vary from the predominantly peasant agriculture of Anguilla, Nevis and Dominica to the estate cultivations of St. Kitts, and in several of the islands there lingers on the thoroughly undesirable system of share cropping, generally the sign of a rural economy in decay. Our proposals regarding the rehabilitation and possible extension of peasant agriculture are given in Chapters XVI and XVII, and the Nevis sugar industry is also discussed in paragraphs 47-8 of Chapter XVI. There remain certain points not touched on elsewhere:—

(a) ANGUILLA.

50. Like other small islands with no very pronounced eminence to bring about the precipitation of rain, Anguilla suffers from a scanty and irregular water-supply. The problem of improving supplies is far from simple, and in order to avoid delay, and waste of money and effort, we recommend that expert advice be sought at an early date. If, as we hope, Anguilla is to share in the advantages of mixed farming including stock-raising, an adequate water-supply is of prime necessity. In view of the poverty of the people and the cost of collecting land tax, we suggest that the question of abolishing this tax in the peculiar circumstances of this island should be seriously considered by the Government.

(b) ANTIGUA.

51. There is scope for much good work in the draining of marsh lands, not only for health reasons but for the reclamation of land suitable for agriculture. It is desirable that in any extension of peasant cultivation made possible thus or otherwise stress should be laid on the production of foodstuffs and livestock rather than on concentration on a single export crop as at present. There is also need for much improvement to the roads in the remoter parts, and more particularly to the " streets " if they may be so called in some of the villages. Many of these untended earthen pathways, worn by weather and traffic, are uneven and dangerous in dry weather, and practically quagmires in wet. In bad weather, moreover, refuse is often carried into the houses by flood water from the " streets ", neither the public authorities nor the residents being apparently concerned to prevent this.

(c) DOMINICA.

52. Of all the British West Indian Islands, Dominica presents the most striking contrast between the great poverty of a large proportion of the population, particularly in Roseau, the capital, and the beauty and fertility of the island. The land of Dominica is capable of providing sufficient and satisfactory food for its inhabitants, who are not over numerous in relation to the resources of the island—given better communications, the settlement of a greater proportion of the population as peasants on the land and the spread of knowledge of improved agricultural methods and of the elements of hygiene and nutrition.

53. At present there is no adequate land communication between the north and the south of the island, although there are roads at either end. The question of constructing a link between the Imperial Road and the Portsmouth road should be considered with a view to ascertaining whether this could be done at a reasonable cost and whether the economic advantages would be commensurate with the outlay involved.

54. There is in Dominica an area entitled the Carib Reserve, intended, as its name implies, for the occupation of one of the few remaining groups of the aboriginal inhabitants of these islands. The ownership of land within the declared reserve is surprisingly, not confined to Caribs and little control appears to be exercised over the type of person permitted to enter and take up land there. This position should be changed, steps should be taken to prove the title of existing occupiers and also to prevent the entry of undesirables.

55. It was represented to us that use could be found for Dominica's abundant water-power to operate hydro-electric generators, and the power used, among other things, for the operation of cold storage plant and in substitution for the present Government-operated diesel generator. We are unable in the absence of concrete proposals and estimates of cost to make a definite recommendation on this matter; but we consider that it is one worthy of expert examination.

56. There are malarial swamps in various areas, notably near Roseau (the capital), Portsmouth (the second town in the island) and in the Grand Bay neighbourhood, where about 12,000 people live. We recommend that speedy steps be taken to clear these swamps, which constitute a menace to the health of the nearby population. As they result partly from silting of river mouths, provision for regular silt-clearing will be required.

6. Trinidad.

57. We arrived in Trinidad on 20th February from British Guiana and made our headquarters at Port-of-Spain, the capital. We heard 43 witnesses or groups of witnesses in public and in private, and visited numerous sugar and cocoa estates, the oilfields and the pitch lake, scene of the asphalt industry. We also visited various land settlement areas and took all opportunities of inspecting the various experiments in workers' housing which are being carried on both by private concerns and by Government. We inspected also hospitals, prisons, the leper settlement on the island of Chacachacare, many schools and other public institutions, and the existing housing of the poorer classes alike in town and in country. We were able to visit Tobago and take evidence there, and also to travel about that island and inspect conditions.

58. Our Chairman was obliged to leave Trinidad for England on the 10th of March, 1939, and one other member on the 17th of March. Our Vice-Chairman left on the 21st of March, and the remainder on the 24th of March, reaching England via New York on the 7th of April.

59. There is little that we need say about problems peculiar to Trinidad. Owing largely to the direct and indirect effects of the prosperous asphalt and oil industries, and to a sugar industry well up to the standard of management which we found in the West Indies, the Colony is the most prosperous of those which we visited. The tenor of the memoranda and evidence submitted to us indicated that it is also in many ways politically and socially one of the most advanced, and the standard of life and range of interests of the ordinary inhabitant are certainly well ahead of what may

be found in the smaller islands. Owing largely again to the oil and asphalt industries and their contribution to public funds, the Government is in a sounder financial position than any other in the West Indies, and is well placed to finance schemes of development even beyond that already being put into operation.

60. The one serious exception to the comparative prosperity of Trinidad is the cocoa industry. Over-expanded and over-financed in times of prosperity, it is now suffering the full weight of low prices, low yields and heavy debt charges, to which have been added in recent years the depredations of witch-broom disease. For the last few years a complicated subsidy system has been in operation which, as explained in Chapter XXI of the agricultural report and in paragraph 62 of Chapter XVI of this, we consider to be palliative merely, and not conducive to the thorough rehabilitation which the industry requires. Whatever reforms may be effected in accordance with our proposals, we do not consider that the industry will again involve so large an acreage or afford a livelihood to so many workers. Indeed, the abandonment of unsuitable soil is, in our opinion, a necessary part of such reforms. It will be necessary, therefore, for careful attention to be paid to the adoption of alternative types of agriculture for the workers and areas which are certain to be thrown out of cocoa.

7. Windward Islands.

(a) St. Lucia.

61. Half of our number arrived in Castries from Martinique on the 17th December, 1938. Evidence was heard from 15 witnesses or groups of witnesses, and visits were made to schools, the Victoria Hospital, the housing in and about Castries, and to the scene of the disastrous landslide of November, 1938, when many lives were lost. The sugar estates and factories at Roseau and Cul-de-Sac were visited, and the new workers' housing which is being developed there. The landslide having swept away the only possible road across the island, it was not possible in the time to visit Dennery on the Windward coast; but the party travelled to Vieuxfort in the south of the island, and to meet a representative delegation at Soufriere, on the Leeward (Western) coast. The party left St. Lucia on the 27th December for St. Vincent.

62. One of the loveliest of the West Indian islands, St. Lucia is at present one of the most hard-hit, and we find difficulty in framing any recommendation that will provide immediate and effective relief on constructive lines. The past prosperity of the island was based mainly on coconuts and limes, but large areas,

now infertile, in the north of the island are pointed out as having once supported prosperous sugar estates. The loss of fertility points to the long continuance of soil erosion and bad cultivation which continues increasingly to be a menace to the productivity of the island. Some sugar is grown at Roseau and Cul-de-Sac, but the scale is small. We were met by demands for an increased quota from two sources: those connected with the Vieuxfort Settlement scheme in the south of the island which depends entirely for its success on permission to grow sugar, and the Soufriere deputation, who pleaded that the population in that neighbourhood were urgently in need of an opportunity of supplementing their subsistence-agriculture by wage-labour which could only be provided in this way.

63. Of the smaller islands, St. Lucia is the only one to have a serious urban problem like that of Kingston, Jamaica. Once an important coaling station, the port of Castries has sunk into insignificance, and the diminution of trade has left an unemployed population with no knowledge of or inclination for work on the land. Not only this, but on the rumour of work at the docks, workers come pouring into Castries from comparatively remote parts of the island, with the result that no one could earn a decent livelihood by dock labour, even were wages much higher than they are. The problem here is one of affording the peasantry a better livelihood by inculcating better methods of farming, and of reconditioning a large proportion of the urban workers to a life on the land, since the town no longer offers them anything.

64. The attention of the visitor to St. Lucia is at once caught by the existence round Castries of a number of large, well-constructed buildings on good sites. They prove to be for the most part disused barracks and other military buildings, the property of the War Department, who exercise complete control over them. At the present time, where not standing empty, they are leased at low rentals to clubs and private persons who could in our opinion well afford other accommodation and free this valuable public property for public purposes. There is a great dearth in the West Indies, and particularly in the smaller islands, of suitable buildings for such purposes as reformatories, industrial schools, pauper asylums, etc., and here are some admirably suitable and soundly-constructed buildings ready to hand. The adoption of our recommendations elsewhere in the report will create a demand for accommodation for such institutions which these buildings are admirably fitted to supply, not only for St. Lucia alone but perhaps for neighbouring territories as well. We consider that the departmental precautions and safeguards which at present hedge around the disposal of these buildings for such purposes should not be allowed to stand in the way of their ready availability should need arise.

(b) St. Vincent.

65. The Windward Islands party arrived at Kingstown on the 27th December from St. Lucia, and left on the 5th January, 1939. During their stay, 17 witnesses or groups of witnesses were heard, and visits undertaken, in addition to those to public institutions, schools, etc., near Kingstown, to Barrouaillie on the Leeward coast, and to estates and arrowroot factories on the Windward coast as far as Orange Hill. In the course of the journey to Grenada on the 5th January, a visit was made to Bequia, one of the Grenadines administered from St. Vincent, and, on the 12th January from Grenada, to Union, another dependency of St. Vincent. In both of these islands evidence was heard from officials and members of the public and such inspection of conditions carried out as time allowed.

66. St. Vincent is comparatively fortunate among the smaller islands in that it possesses two important export crops both of which enjoy at present a good market—arrowroot starch, of the finest quality of which St. Vincent enjoys a practical monopoly, and Sea Island cotton, an extremely high quality product in fairly good demand for certain specialised purposes. A moderately satisfactory proportion of both these crops is grown by peasant proprietors, although the greater proportion is produced on estates. There is a need for further settlement of peasant cultivators, in addition to the schemes already in operation and in contemplation. The extent of available land is not accurately known as, surprising though it may seem at this date, there are appreciable areas in the northern interior parts of the island which have scarcely been explored, and about the agricultural possibilities of which there is practically no information. During the visit of the Commission it was understood that some preliminary survey and soil investigation was to be set on foot: should this show encouraging results the improvement of communication on a fairly considerable scale will have to be undertaken.

67. The question of water supply is of some difficulty on the Leeward coast. By means of free grants from the Colonial Development Fund, adequate supplies have been furnished to some eight villages and districts, but more are needed; and a scheme is under consideration for Georgetown on the Windward coast, the second town of St. Vincent. The improvement of water supplies on the Leeward coast is an important element in the regeneration of that somewhat distressed area.

68. A final minor recommendation is that the long-considered project of erecting a beacon light near Brigton Point should be proceeded with. St. Vincent is at present the only important island in the Windwards and Leewards which fails to provide

Chapter XXIV.   412

lights for mariners, and navigation by night in the neighbourhood is consequently rendered needlessly dangerous. If our recommendations regarding the improvement of sea communications are carried out, such a facility is an obvious need, and the cost involved, estimated at £1,000, is comparatively trifling.

(c) GRENADA.

69. The Windwards party of the Commission arrived in St. George's from St. Vincent on the 5th January, 1939, and during their stay heard 16 witnesses or groups of witnesses, and conducted several tours of investigation throughout the island. They also visited the island of Carriacou in the Grenadines, which is administered from Grenada, on the 12th January, and there heard representations from several sections of the public.

70. The seat of government of the Windward Islands, Grenada is also the most thickly populated of the three islands, the density at over 600 per square mile, being second only in the British West Indies to that of Barbados. The staple crops are cocoa and spices, the latter now being somewhat more important than cocoa. A large proportion of the cultivable land of Grenada is in the hands of peasant cultivators, although a number of plantations remain which, in normal times, would afford wage-employment to a large number of workers and to others a useful means of supplementing the livelihood which they make from their holdings. But of late years the cacao industry has suffered in much the same way as that of Trinidad, being even more heavily cumbered by excessive debt improvidently incurred in years of artificial prosperity, though not as yet assailed by witch-broom disease. It may be noted that the adverse effect of the slump in cocoa on the ordinary worker is somewhat mitigated by the prevalence of peasant proprietorship and the consequent opportunity for a large proportion of the population to supplement their cash earnings by homegrown foodstuffs.

71. This forms the present economic background of Grenada, our general recommendations regarding which are given elsewhere.* One point not elsewhere covered requires attention in Grenada: that of water supply. Grenada itself has an adequate rainfall and streams, and the question is principally one of collecting and bringing the water to the villages where it is most required. As is usual in these islands, water scarcity is chiefly felt on the western or leeward coast. As the success of any further land settlement or rural regeneration schemes depends to a considerable extent on adequate and hygienic water-supplies

---

* For recommendations regarding the cacao industry of Grenada see Chapter XVI, paragraph 63.

we consider that improvements outside the financial powers of Grenada would be a worthy object for assistance from the Colonial Development Fund or in some other manner from Imperial funds.

72. The water supply problems of Carriacou and the other smaller islands in the Grenadines are more difficult. Like Anguilla, these islands have no hilly regions to cause precipitation on the scale of the mountainous larger islands, and droughts are common. A contributory factor is deforestation, steps to meet which are being taken in Carriacou. The difficulties are great, for a population of 10,000 is compelled to live on an area of 13 square miles, and cultivable land can ill be spared for forest. Further, during the droughts which are in part intensified by deforestation such young plants as do grow are liable to be devoured by livestock, notably goats, which abound. It would not be easy to prohibit the keeping of goats, which provide a useful source of milk, and can be relied on to pick up a living for themselves at little immediate cost to their owners, whatever may be the ultimate cost to the community at large. Partly because little attempt is made to practice skilled animal husbandry, these animals are not kept under proper control, and the provision-grounds of those who have the energy and enterprise to embark on this form of agriculture suffer seriously in consequence. The problems of increasing local food-supplies, improving animal husbandry and thus making mixed farming possible, and some measure of reafforestation are consequently closely bound up together. Agricultural advance must thus proceed on a broad front, and one factor which must not be neglected is a realisation among the people of Carriacou themselves that if they are to make up by a better use of the resources of their own island for the restricted opportunities of employment abroad, more care must be taken than at present to ensure that harm does not come through wandering and voracious animals to the growing produce of others. Water supply is here the key to agricultural advance, and external funds should if necessary be forthcoming to finance the necessary investigations and works.

8. The Smaller Islands.

73. Throughout the British West Indian Colonies there are numerous very small communities existing on small, remote islands, administered more or less from some larger Colony but for the most part living a simple and somewhat primitive existence. We have dealt above with the problems of certain of them, but feel it useful here to include some description of

these little communities which, taken together, comprise an appreciable population. The following table gives some information as to their extent and population:—

Islands	Administered by	Population	Area (sq. miles)
Turks & Caicos	Jamaica	5,612 (1921)	166
Cayman Is.	Jamaica	6,000 (1921)	89
Anguilla	St. Kitts-Nevis	4,230 (1921)	35
Barbuda	Antigua	902 (1921)	62
Virgin Islands (32 islands which apart from the following are normally uninhabited)	Are a Presidency of the Leeward Islands	5,061 (1921)	67
Tortola		3,987 (1921)	20
Virgin Gorda		381 (1921)	13
Anegada		358 (1921)	11
Jost Van Dykes		266 (1921)	7
Salt Island		37 (1921)	2½
Peter Island		32 (1921)	5
Carriacou (Lesser Grenadines of Grenada)	Grenada	9,500 (est. 1939)	13
Lesser Grenadines of St Vincent (including Bequia and Union)	St. Vincent	3,683 (1931)	17

74. It is apparent that, while all are small, the population per square mile varies widely. This is also true of the mode of life of the various islands: the Turks and Caicos Islands live mainly on the proceeds of the salt industry, the Caymans by turtling and boat-building, the British Virgin Islands by stock-breeding, and the Grenadines by growing Marie Galante cotton, a less fine grade than the Sea Island cotton of St. Vincent. In addition, subsistence agriculture is practised and much of the land is in the hands of peasant proprietors. Some fishing is indulged in, but not nearly as much as might be expected considering the aptitude displayed by many of the islanders for seamanship. The inhabitants of many of the islands, notably Carriacou, have depended to a large extent on obtaining employment abroad, and the practical cessation of opportunities for such employment, together with the prevailing low prices for such export crops as they produce, have added to the difficulties of these communities. The peoples of these remote islands are not in a position to press their claims for assistance as strongly as those near the seat of Government, especially those in or about the capital towns of the various colonies. Their needs should therefore be carefully borne in mind by the Governments responsible for their administration.

75. Primitive though conditions are in many of these islands, the inhabitants of them show a most praiseworthy and attractive spirit of enterprise, independence and resource—a spirit not

everywhere present in larger and comparatively more prosperous territories. They therefore deserve generous assistance and advice in dealing with problems outside the scope of their own resources such as water-supply, communications, education, sanitation, medical facilities and agriculture. We should, however, deplore any steps which would rob them of these characteristics and breed a spirit of undue dependence on the Government for all assistance.

9. East Indian Problems.

76. Having concluded a survey of some of the special problems of individual Colonies, we come to those of an important though not a dominant section of the population—the East Indians. In Jamaica they number approximately 18,000 and form a small proportion of the total population; in British Guiana they number 131,000 (42 per cent. of the total) and outnumber the negro population; in Trinidad they number 151,000 and form 34 per cent. of the total. Individual East Indians are encountered in other parts of the West Indies, but nowhere in such large numbers as to give rise to special problems. As we have said in earlier chapters, the introduction of East Indian labourers on a considerable scale was practised as a means of meeting the labour shortage which followed emancipation. These labourers were brought over on contract, with the right of repatriation at the end of their period of service, a right of which many availed themselves up to and after the ending of the indenture system in 1916-7. These persons did not represent a true cross-section of any Indian community, for all came to these colonies solely as labourers on the land, and to this fact are attributable many of their special grievances. Until the end of the period of immigration, their position was to some extent safeguarded by the existence of Immigration Officers whose function it was to ensure the observance of the terms of the contracts under which the immigrants were brought, and of the conditions attached to the system by the Government of India, including such matters as housing. These powers and functions have virtually lapsed, and the position in law of the East Indian labourer is now in no way different from that of the Creole, except in so far as certain rights to repatriation are still in force.

77. We heard evidence from representatives of the East Indian community in Jamaica, British Guiana and Trinidad, where varying degrees of co-operation had been achieved between the Hindus (who vastly preponderate in numbers) and the Moslems, on the one hand, and between the various Hindu sects on the other. Mr. J. D. Tyson, of the Indian Civil Service, was sent by his Government to visit these three Colonies,

and in British Guiana and Trinidad he assisted the Indian deputations in the preparation and submission of their evidence. We also had a discussion in Trinidad with Mr. Tyson himself, who had submitted a memorandum of evidence* in his capacity as representative of the Government of India.

78. The complaints made by the East Indian communities were manifold, and several of them related to general conditions and matters affecting the community as a whole. In so far as such representations fall within our terms of reference, they are dealt with in other Chapters: we restrict ourselves here to matters specifically affecting the East Indian community as distinct from any other.

79. In the first place, there was a widespread demand for the re-establishment of the post of Protector of Immigrants, and a connected but not identical demand for the appointment of an Agent-General for Indian affairs, who would be paid for by and be responsible to the Government of India.

80. Secondly, complaints were made that the number of Indians who have posts in the Government service, or who enjoy appointments made by Government, such as Justiceships of the Peace, membership of Executive Council, etc., was in no way proportionate to the number of the Indian population.

81. Thirdly, a similar complaint was made regarding education, in that the denominational system operated to the disadvantage of the vast bulk of the Indian population who, being non-Christian, were not adequately represented among the teaching staff. It was also pointed out that illiteracy was more prevalent among Indians than among other sections of the community, and that the school enrolment and attendance figures were also lower.

82. Fourthly, there were complaints regarding the registration and legitimisation of marriages according to Hindu and Moslem law, the position being that such marriages depended in law for their validation on subsequent registration, whereas other marriages did not so depend, even although registration is obligatory under penalty.

83. Fifthly, there were complaints that, whatever the exact position in law, difficulties were put in the way of the disposal of the Hindu dead by means of the cremation enjoined by their religion.

---

* Mr. Tyson's memorandum was subsequently published by the Government of India under the title "Memorandum of Evidence for the Royal Commission to the West Indies. Presented by J. D. Tyson, C.B.E., I.C.S., on behalf of the Government of India."

84. Sixthly, there was a general demand for an *ad hoc* Government inquiry into the general condition of East Indians as such, and for special measures to meet them.

85. While we have much sympathy with many of these complaints, and are satisfied that there is some foundation for them, we feel it necessary to emphasise at the outset that there are grave objections to treating the East Indian community separately from all others, objections which concern the interests of the East Indians themselves as well as of the other inhabitants of the West Indies. As Mr. Tyson pointed out, by far the majority of the East Indians of British Guiana and Trinidad, probably about 90 per cent., are now "Colonial born", and there is no question but that only an insignificant proportion of the remainder intend to, or can, return to India. The future of this population is bound up with the West Indies. This fact was admitted by most East Indian witnesses. In the circumstances, any measures which cause the East Indians to look upon themselves, or to be looked upon, as a people apart will at once pave the way for inter-racial rivalries and jealousies, and at the same time prejudice the proper handling of the many problems involving all the peoples of the West Indies. The major problems of these Colonies, as we have made clear in preceding chapters, are economic, social and agricultural. Their solution will be hampered if they are not treated and considered as such, but as problems peculiar to certain sections of the community.

86. This does not mean that, in our view, all sections of the community must be treated exactly alike. To do so would be to overlook certain real differences which must be taken into account to ensure the substantial equality of treatment which we desire. These differences are as follows. Although many East Indian families have now been established in the West Indies for upwards of a century, the tradition of indenture has kept alive the feeling that they are not permanent residents. Further, the conditions of their employment have kept them in compact groups, preventing as much mingling and assimilation with the remainder of the population as might have been expected. They have been until recently the least articulate section of the population: a number of the older Indians can speak only some Indian dialect and among the remainder the knowledge of English is even more imperfect than among the general population. While the post of Protector of Immigrants was in effective being, this difficulty of communication was not so urgent: its virtual disappearance has put the mass of the East Indian population at a definite relative disadvantage. Finally, the great majority of them are non-Christians (with Hindus in large majority) and are thus at some disadvantage as regards education owing to the prevalence of the dual or denominational educational system.

87. The demand for the re-establishment of the post of Protector must be judged in the light of these considerations. If we do not recommend the adoption of that proposal, it is not because we do not consider that there is real hardship but because in our judgment such a step would perpetuate and intensify a distinction between the East Indian and other communities which the more thoughtful East Indians recognise to be against the general interest. We consider that the machinery of government should be adapted to meet this difficulty as part of its ordinary organisation, and to this end we recommend that some officer or officers, preferably members of the Labour Departments, should specialise in East Indian questions and, if suitable candidates are forthcoming, be East Indians. These officers should have other functions in the Labour Departments in addition to this advisory work.

88. We noticed that few East Indians held appointments to Government posts in relation to the numbers of the East Indian community. We strongly recommend that the possibility of the appointment of suitable East Indians to such posts should be carefully borne in mind by Colonial Governments. At the same time, we would avoid any system of sectional quotas, which would lead to the deplorable system of " government by arithmetic ", the adoption of which in Palestine was considered by the Palestine Royal Commission to have if anything exacerbated communal feeling instead of allaying it. The same consideration applies to the question of the proportion of East Indians among the teaching staffs of the primary schools.

89. The educational facilities for East Indian children are not noticeably worse than those provided for the labouring population at large. It is true that attendance figures for these children are sometimes worse than for the general population; but this is due at least in part to the Indian practice of withdrawing girls from school long before the normal leaving age. The position in this respect should improve with the general improvements which we recommend in Chapter VII.

90. We find ourselves in full sympathy with the complaints regarding the arrangements for legitimisation and validation of East Indian marriages, and recommend that these marriages should, so far as the law is concerned, be put on exactly the same footing as other marriages. That is to say, the onus of registration should be placed, under penalty, on the priest or other religious functionary performing the ceremony; failure on his part to register the marriage should not, as at present, result in its invalidation at law. The selection of priests etc., to act as marriage officers should not present undue difficulty, especially if carried out in conjunction with responsible representatives of the Indian community. There was a further complaint in

British Guiana that the local law does not provide for the recognition of divorces according to Moslem usage. This recognition has been accorded in Trinidad and, we were assured, works satisfactorily. We recommend legislation where necessary on the Trinidad model to meet this grievance. The question does not arise for Hindus, whose religion does not permit divorce.

91. Numerous complaints were made to us that Hindus were unable to dispose of their dead in accordance with their religious custom, by cremation. Witnesses were unable to point to any enactment limiting their freedom of action in this matter; and Government officials assured us that there was no intention to prohibit cremations, subject to certain reasonable sanitary and other conditions. It seems to us that these complaints are largely based on misunderstanding, and we recommend that Governments take steps to make the legal position plain and to ensure that, subject to necessary safeguards, no obstacle should be placed in the way of the practice.

92. Finally, with regard to the proposal that there should be a special inquiry into the general conditions of East Indians, we can only re-emphasise our view that such an inquiry, or any similar step taken to deal, in respect of one section of the community, with problems affecting the population as a whole, could only encourage East Indians to continue their habit, unfortunately on the increase, of regarding themselves as a separate group. In order to avoid misconstruction, we repeat that we must not be taken to assume that East Indians do not suffer from bad conditions in many respects, but that problems affecting the community as a whole must be tackled for the community as a whole, and not differentially for certain sections of it.

PART V

CONCLUSIONS AND RECOMMENDATIONS

CHAPTER XXV.
CONCLUSIONS AND RECOMMENDATIONS.

1. In this concluding Chapter it is our object to present in a concise form the problem of the West Indies, followed by a summary of our main conclusions thereon. We do not propose to enter in any detail into the reasons which led us to these conclusions, for which we invite reference to the relevant parts of the foregoing Chapters. We shall then conclude by a summary statement of the more important of our recommendations, giving where necessary brief explanatory notes

1. The Problem.

2. The problem of the West Indies is essentially agrarian. Their populations came, or were brought, to establish and carry on the cultivation of tropical produce which for long periods (though not without interruption) brought great wealth to the proprietors (Chapter I, paragraph 5). At the time of our appointment, West Indian industries with few and local exceptions were suffering from a severe depression, which made itself chiefly felt to the bulk of the population through a disastrous reduction in the amount of employment available in rural as in urban areas (Chapter III, paragraphs 9 and 10). In time of peace there would be little prospect that any great change could of itself take place in this respect, and experience indicates that any war-time boom would not long outlast the cessation of hostilities. Public finances have suffered for the same reasons, and the power of governments to take action to mitigate the evils of depression has been progressively weakened as the need increased. In accordance with the declared policy of Your Majesty's Government, each administrative unit, however small, is expected financially to stand on its own feet. Apart from assistance for specified objects from the Colonial Development Fund, grants from the Imperial Exchequer are only made when essential requirements cannot be met from local resources, and conditionally on rigorous financial control (Chapter VI, paragraph 20).

3. At the same time, the cumulative effect of education, the press, wireless, the spectacle of the standards of living of white people, and the reports of West Indians who have lived and worked abroad, particularly in the United States of America, has been to create a demand for better conditions of work and life. This demand has found expression from time to time in disorders and bloodshed, but it is also strongly in evidence where there has been no resort to violence, and is different in kind from the blinder discontents which in the nineteenth century also led occasionally to disorder (Chapter I, paragraph 17).

4. Furthermore, the population of the West Indies shows a steady and rapid rise: in particular, the high birth-rate and decrease in infantile mortality are being and will increasingly be reflected in a proportionately still greater increase in the population of working age (Chapter II, paragraphs 1-10).

5. The crux of the West Indian problem is, then, that a demand for better living conditions is becoming increasingly insistent among an expanding population at a time when (apart from war conditions) world economic trends seriously endanger even the maintenance of present standards (Chapter I, paragraph 17).

2. Conclusions.

(*a*) SOCIAL CONDITIONS.

6. The prolonged economic depression of recent years found in the West Indies communities ill-equipped to withstand it. Many of the larger producers were severely handicapped as a result of ligh-hearted over-expansion during the brief period of prosperity which followed the war of 1914-1918, and through this weakness many an otherwise satisfactory concern has been forced out of business, thereby increasing unemployment. The labouring population have never had more than the slightest opportunity to save or establish themselves as economically independent, and for many of them the depression brought complete or partial unemployment, while rates of wages though varying greatly from one colony to another remained at a level meagre enough even were employment continuous (Chapter X, paragraphs 12-16). The case of the peasant proprietor is a little better; but he too has generally relied on the cultivation of an export crop and/or on the opportunity to supplement his income by seasonal employment on the estates. Inexperience, distrust on the part of the more prosperous sections of the community, and defective legislation have prevented a healthy development of trade unionism which might have helped to mitigate the most severe effects of the depression (Chapter X, paragraphs 21-33). The position of the workers was in no way safeguarded by the existing industrial and social legislation which was generally defective and imperfectly enforced (Chapter X, paragraphs 47-59).

7. Even before the depression, social standards and services were at a low level (Chapter XI, paragraphs 3-9). The institution of marriage was for historical reasons never the rule in the West Indies and the illegitimate birth-rate was always very high, standing to-day between 60 per cent. and 70 per cent. The traditional substitute, " faithful concubinage," which has many of the social advantages of legal marriage, is also losing ground in favour of casual and temporary unions. These facts are of

great economic as well as social importance, for the policy of land settlement to which some West Indian Governments are heavily committed depends for its success on the existence of a cohesive family unit. A connected evil is the low status accorded to women (Chapter III, paragraph 5; Chapter XI, paragraphs 10-26).

8. The social services in the West Indies are all far from adequate for the needs of the population, partly as a result of defects of policy, and largely through the paucity of the funds at the disposal of the Colonial Governments which are in the main necessarily responsible for these services. In education there is a great need for more teachers, better-trained teachers, more and better school accommodation and equipment, and curricula more closely related to the life and experience of residents in the West Indies (Chapter VII, paragraphs 1-29). Health conditions, though better than in some other British Colonies, are unsatisfactory, and much of the ill-health arises from poverty and ignorance (Chapter VIII, paragraph 57). Medical departments are handicapped by lack of funds, and far more attention has generally been devoted to the cure of disease than to its prevention (Chapter VIII, paragraph 17). The diets of the poorer people are often insufficient and usually ill-balanced, although nutritious foods of all kinds necessary for health can be produced without much difficulty in almost every West Indian Colony (Chapter VIII, paragraph 111). The reason for this appears to lie fundamentally in the divorce of the people from the land without the provision of compensatory arrangements which would help to ensure adequate food supplies for the displaced population (Chapter VIII, paragraph 117). Housing is generally deplorable, and sanitation primitive in the extreme, although sporadic improvements are being effected as well by Government as by private interests (Chapter IX, paragraphs 1-6). Such efforts, praiseworthy in themselves and of great value for future development, can never meet the problem, which demands vigorous co-operative action by all concerned—governments, local authorities, proprietors and, not least, the people themselves (Chapter IX. paragraph 7).

9. In the political sphere we found widely canvassed the idea of some form of federation of the West Indian Colonies into a single political unit, although the exact means by which it was proposed to achieve this end varied widely. Some advocated federation as a step towards a much greater degree of independence than exists at present, and associated with a great enlargement of the power of elected legislatures. It is impossible to arrive at agreement on detail between the views of the various protagonists of federation; and behind the very real sentiment of unity which is perceptible in the West Indies lies a great diversity of interest, particularly as between large and small

colonies. Several proposals for the unification of services or other co-operative efforts have come to nought owing to the unwillingness of the larger, and comparatively richer, territories to participate in them (Chapter XVIII, paragraphs 8-9). If the West Indies are to work towards a federation which has more than a nominal significance and if, as in the long run will be essential, conditions are to be effectively improved and the improvement maintained by local co-operation and mutual assistance, these prejudices must be overcome. While the United Kingdom must play an important part in the improvement of conditions by providing financial assistance for social services and markets to foster West Indian economy, it is equally important that an emergence of a spirit of self-help, thrift and independence should come about among the West Indian peoples themselves. Without some such change of outlook it would be difficult, for example, to arrange for better care of children and old people and take steps to curb the rapid increase more especially of the illegitimate children. The Churches too have an important part to play in the pursuance of more active campaigns for the improvement of family life and in social work generally.

(b) Economic Position and Outlook.

10. Apart from the depression which has afflicted West Indian export industries for several years, there remains the fundamental fact that the relation between population trends in the West Indies (as in other tropical producing countries) and in the great consuming countries has undergone a vitally important change. Up to the end of the nineteenth century, and despite periodical occurrences of low prices and consequent depression, the West Indies were producing for a market which, for a long time, was expanding quite as quickly as the production itself. This is no longer the case. Quite apart from the effect of such developments as the heavily-subsidised beet-sugar industries of Europe and the United States, the populations of Western Europe, the United States and Canada are now increasing far less rapidly and may be expected in a very few years actually to enter upon a period of decline, which will necessarily affect the growth of their consuming-power. But the population of the West Indies, owing largely to advances in public health and to the consequent growing margin of the birth-rate over the rate of mortality, is increasing faster than ever; and in addition technical advances continue to increase the output per head, thus limiting still further the available employment. Further, the proportion of children and young persons in the population in the West Indies is so high that, whatever means of family limitation may be adopted, the number of persons of working age will rise, and rise rapidly, for many years to come (Chapter XII).

11. Among long-term remedies for this situation must be included spread in knowledge of means by which population can be limited, and for this an awakening of public opinion is an indispensable condition. Every body and organisation which seeks to guide and influence opinion should recognise the responsibility which rests on it to assist and not obstruct the processes of public enlightenment (Chapter XII).

12. The traditional export industries of the West Indies cannot be expected to afford employment for the rapidly growing population, and indeed, in the absence of improvement in market prospects, it is probable that there would be a steady reduction in the numbers of those so engaged. It is essential, therefore, to seek means whereby the West Indian population of working age may otherwise be absorbed in useful activity. Some small increase of industrial employment may be afforded by the development of secondary industries; but these can at best only be of relatively unimportant proportions, and would be dependent for their prosperity on that of the main industry of the whole area, namely agriculture (Chapter XIII).

13. A new economic policy for the West Indies must therefore be an agricultural policy, and development must be away from reliance on production for export. The main use to which the proceeds of exports are put is the purchase of foodstuffs, particularly flour, salt fish, butter, etc. With a progressive decline in the amount of foreign purchasing-power per head of the population, it is not only possible, but necessary, to turn to a greater production of foodstuffs at home. There are many foreign commodities, impossible to manufacture in the West Indies, to the purchase of which the proceeds of export may usefully be devoted.

14. But it will be many years before a new policy, directed towards the elimination of the import of goods (notably food) which can be produced at home, can become effective, and in the meantime the wellbeing of the present increasing population requires to be safeguarded. Steps are necessary to foster such local industries as will not take away by raising the cost of living for the people what they give by increasing employment. An adequate, and reasonably steady, price is needed for the exports which will always remain, and arrangements must be perfected for the marketing of those export crops (such as citrus fruits) which are not at present the subject of such thorough organisation as the sugar industry (Chapter XIII, paragraphs 22-31).

(c) AGRICULTURAL POSITION AND OUTLOOK.

15. The present system is not adapted to effect unassisted a turnover from export to food crops (Chapter XVI, paragraph 1). Planter and peasant alike concentrate on production for

export when they can. Too little rotation is practised. There is, in general, no balanced farming system capable of maintaining soil fertility at a high level and of ensuring proper interplay of crops and stock (Chapter IV, paragraph 2). Especially on peasant holdings the soil tends to be exhausted and rendered liable to irreparable damage by erosion. This is particularly true of the careless cultivation of bananas on steep land (Chapter IV, paragraph 25). Really efficient agriculture is almost entirely confined to estate cultivation of sugar, where careful and thorough methods have enabled yields to be maintained and enhanced even without rotation or resting of the land. The cultivation of food crops does not stand high in the estimation of the West Indian farmer, and yields are low. Conditions of land tenure militate against good husbandry by peasants. Rents are high in relation to yields, tenure is uncertain, and is sometimes on the basis of share-cropping (Chapter IV, paragraphs 19-20). For an improvement it will be necessary to decide by investigation new and balanced systems of farming, to advance agricultural knowledge widely among all classes on the land and to provide better economic inducement (such as marketing facilities, security of tenure and equitable rents) for the smaller holders and peasants (Chapter XVI, paragraphs 13-16).

16. The main reliance for food production must be on peasant agriculture, although the possibility should be explored of developing mixed farming in estate cultivation hitherto concentrating on export crops alone (Chapter XVI, paragraph 5). So deeply entrenched in West Indian agricultural practice is production for export, and consequent concentration on a single crop, even among peasant proprietors, that the necessary development towards food production on the basis of mixed farming constitutes practically an agricultural revolution. Such a fundamental change will have to be based on a far greater mass of detailed information than yet exists on the nature of soils, land tenure, rural economy, the suitability of crops, plant diseases, farming systems, etc., etc., and an amount and quality of research will be required which can only be carried out under the aegis of the Imperial College of Tropical Agriculture. The College, suitably expanded to meet these new needs, is consequently the keystone of agricultural development in the West Indies (Chapter XVI, paragraphs 34-39).

3. Recommendations.

(a) WEST INDIAN WELFARE FUND AND COMPTROLLER.

(Chapters XX and XXI).

17. There is a pressing need for large expenditure on social services and development which not even the least poor of the West Indian Colonies can hope to undertake from their own

Chapter XXV. 428

resources. We therefore recommend the establishment for this purpose of a West Indian Welfare Fund to be financed by an annual grant of £1,000,000 from the Imperial Exchequer for a period of 20 years, and of a special organisation to administer this fund under the charge of a Comptroller. The objects of the Fund should be to finance schemes for the general improvement of education, the health services, housing and slum clearance, the creation of labour departments, the provision of social welfare facilities, and land settlement, apart from the cost of purchase of land. This proposal is so novel as to justify a brief restatement of the reasons which led us to adopt it (Chapter XX, paragraphs 12-15; Chapter XXI, paragraphs 5-9).

18. Most of the main social and economic defects of the West Indies have, in broad outline, been known and deplored for many years. They have been the subject of numerous enquiries, both by local committees and by investigators or commissioners sent out from Great Britain. It is only in regard to the more recent developments of social welfare, public health policy and labour organisation and legislation that we have found it necessary to add substantially to the large body of detailed proposals for reform which already existed. Nevertheless, the problems have remained, and the efforts of Your Majesty's Government and of the Colonial Governments concerned have failed to make for radical reform. We therefore conclude that the means do not exist for effecting improvement on an adequate scale. The West Indian Governments themselves and the Colonial Office do not have at their disposal adequate funds to undertake the necessary reforms (Chapter XX, paragraphs 8-9). Not even those West Indian Colonies whose finances permit of further borrowing can do more than touch the fringe of the many problems requiring comprehensive treatment; and Your Majesty's Government grants direct assistance only through the agency of the Colonial Development Fund (which is strictly limited both as to amount and as to purpose) and through grants-in-aid, conditional on rigorous financial control, to Colonial Governments where essential requirements cannot be met from local resources. The need is not for the immediate grant of large lump sums, but for a programme of development over a period of years, according to well-thought-out policies and administered by an organisation in a position constantly to control and review the execution of such a policy. Neither the Colonial Office nor the Colonial Governments are in a position to exercise such a continuous control; the Colonial Office because it is by its nature too remote (Chapter XXI, paragraph 6), the Colonial Governments because they cannot afford the large staffs of highly-qualified persons required for the wise execution of the necessary radical reforms (Chapter XXI, paragraphs 2-4). This is particularly the case in the smaller islands, which cannot possibly afford sufficient specialised staff,

and for which specialised guidance from outside is not at present adequately provided. In addition, the units of government in the West Indies are not large enough, and conditions do not vary sufficiently from one colony to another, to render necessary widely differing policies and methods of approach in the different territories. We recommend elsewhere the unification and reorganisation of certain of the social services; but without some central co-ordinating and directing authority any such measures would lose much of their value. Such co-ordination cannot, we consider, be provided by any feasible form of political federation, as the necessary knowledge will not become available by means of the pooling of inadequate resources.

19. We have been encouraged in putting forward the recommendation for the creation of a Welfare Fund by increasing evidence of a readiness on the part of Parliament and of the people of the United Kingdom to undertake greater responsibilities for the well-being of colonial peoples. Instances are the reception accorded to those parts of Lord Hailey's " African Survey " in which emphasis was laid on the need for the adoption in Africa of a policy designed to raise the standard of living and to improve social services, and the tone of the debate in the House of Commons on the 7th of June last on the Colonial Office Vote. It will be for others to consider what are the appropriate steps to be taken in other parts of the Colonial Empire: we content ourselves here with setting out the reasons which in our opinion justify the grant to the West Indies of a full share of assistance on the lines which we propose:—

(a) the extreme specialisation in the production of tropical crops for export, encouraged by this country, has exposed the West Indies to the full force of long-continued depression, and the consequent deterioration of the standard of living already perceptible may be expected to spread rapidly unless special measures are taken;

(b) the wide dispersal over a large area, and the smallness of many of the units of population make administration more difficult and more expensive than in any other large section of the Colonial Empire;

(c) the bulk of the population of the West Indies have lost their original cultures, and constructive efforts to provide a satisfactory alternative are long overdue;

(d) contact with white peoples, and the example of the United States of America and neighbouring territories, set for the West Indian a social standard to which he naturally aspires (Chapter XX, paragraph 10).

20. We consider it essential that the new organisation should be set up within the West Indies but be independent of the local Governments. Its head, the Comptroller of the West

Indian Welfare Fund, should constantly review the social problems of the West Indies, be available to advise the colonial administrations on their problems, and submit an annual report which would help to focus public attention in this country on progress in the West Indies (Chapter XXI, paragraph 11). The Comptroller should be responsible to the Secretary of State for the Colonies, and have the right of direct access to him. His principal duties would be:—

(1) to work out, with the aid of experts to be attached to him and in consultation with the local Governments concerned, long-term programmes of social reform for submission to the Secretary of State;

(2) to consider similar schemes submitted by local Governments whether on their own initiative or after consultation with his experts;

(3) to control the West Indian Welfare Fund and to approve grants from it for expenditure by West Indian Governments on schemes which he has accepted as conforming to the general programme approved by the Secretary of State;

(4) to supervise, through his staff, the administration of these grants; and

(5) to submit annually to the Secretary of State a report, in form suitable for presentation to Parliament, on the work carried out under his supervision during the preceding year (Chapter XXI, paragraph 9).

21. It will be seen that, subject to conformity with schemes approved by the Secretary of State, the Comptroller will have wide discretion in the allocation of funds from the West Indian Welfare Fund, and his operations will not be subject to such detailed scrutiny by the Treasury as are the estimates of colonies which are in receipt of grants-in-aid. This we regard as of great importance, and we consider that the aims of effective social development and in the long run of true economy will best be served by choosing a capable and experienced administrator for the post of Comptroller and giving him wide power to settle points of detail without reference. Any steps should in general be taken which would obviate delay without impairing a proper system of financial control (Chapter XX, paragraph 15).

22. The Comptroller should be paid a salary of not less than £3,000 per annum in addition to adequate travelling allowances. Although the exact composition of his staff will vary from time to time according to the nature of the schemes on which it is decided to embark, we should expect them to include from the outset experts on education, finance, health, housing, income tax, labour and social welfare, a civil engineer and a statistician. We assume that in the consideration of appropriate schemes

full use would be made of the services of the Inspector-General of Agriculture, whose appointment we recommend elsewhere (Chapter XXI, paragraphs 11-13).

23. The expenses of the new organisation, which may, when the scheme is fully developed, amount to £100,000 per annum, should not be borne by the West Indian Welfare Fund itself but by the Imperial Exchequer. At the same time, we consider it reasonable that, in view of the great disparity between the rates of direct taxation in the West Indies and in this country, the West Indian Colonies should make their contribution by bringing their rates of income tax more into line with the pre-war rates payable here. We do not recommend that further burdens should be laid on the payer of indirect taxation (Chapter XXI, paragraph 16 and Chapter VI, paragraphs 27 and 42).

24. To summarise, we recommend—

(1) That a fund should be established, to be known as the West Indian Welfare Fund, and to be financed by an annual grant of £1,000,000 from the Imperial Exchequer. This sum should be assured for a period of not less than 20 years. The object of the Fund should be to finance schemes for the general improvement of social conditions.

(2) That the administration of the West Indian Welfare Fund should be in the hands of an officer to be entitled the Comptroller of the West Indian Welfare Fund, who should be responsible only to the Secretary of State for the Colonies and have the right of direct access to him, and who should have wide discretion in the expenditure of moneys on schemes approved by the Secretary of State.

(3) That the Comptroller should have a staff of experts whose advice would also be available to the local administrations.

(4) That the cost of salaries and administrative expenses in connection with the Comptroller's organisation should not be a charge on the West Indian Welfare Fund but be defrayed separately from Imperial funds.

25. This in our view is a fundamental recommendation, and we consider that the effective implementation of many of those more detailed recommendations which follow will depend for its success on the establishment of some such machinery. In the following sections only the more important recommendations are set out in detail; for others reference is invited to the appropriate sections of the foregoing Chapters.

(b) SOCIAL SERVICES.

(i) *Education.* (*Chapter VII.*)

26. West Indian education falls far short of any satisfactory standard; if in some instances teaching and equipment are good, the provision of such facilities is totally inadequate for the population of school age. The most obvious and glaring deficiency is that of school buildings sufficient in numbers and suitable in design and equipment; the most serious, in our view, is the lack of trained teachers and of arrangements for training them, particularly in the smaller and poorer islands.

27. Our principal recommendations (Chapter VII, paragraphs 77-113) are as follows:—

(a) Steps should be taken to ensure that all teachers have had an adequate training at some properly organised training college. This will involve the provision of facilities at the training colleges in the larger Colonies for students from those Colonies (the Leeward Islands, the Windward Islands and British Honduras) for which separate training colleges on an adequate scale are not a practical proposition. In consequence, steps should be taken to eliminate the pupil-teacher system and, to cover the period until all teachers have been trained, supervisory teachers should be employed to superintend and advise the untrained teachers already in employment (Chapter VII, paragraphs 78-80).

(b) The provision of sufficient school accommodation should be actively proceeded with, special attention being paid to questions of design, the preservation of a balance between the needs of urban and rural areas, the use of local materials where possible, the provision of playground space and of water-supply and adequate sanitary equipment (Chapter VII, paragraphs 81-82).

(c) Additional equipment should be provided for many schools, and in some places the complete replacement of badly-designed equipment is necessary. The supply of equipment for physical training should not be overlooked. Text-books and school stationery should at once be provided free, costs being reduced by Education Departments dealing direct with the publishers (Chapter VII, paragraphs 83-84).

(d) The literary curriculum in the primary schools requires to be simplified and brought more into relation with the environment of the children. Stress should be laid on the formation of habits of clear and connected speech. The primary curriculum should in its later stages include practical and agricultural subjects for boys, and domestic training and child welfare instruction for girls. More junior secondary schools should be established giving training in practical subjects: these schools to be treated on an equal footing with the more academic secondary schools as regards accommodation, equipment and teaching staff (Chapter VII, paragraphs 85-86).

(*e*) The use and production of educational films should be investigated. Consideration should be given to the formation of a library of suitable films in, say, Trinidad, for use throughout the West Indies, and to the employment for a period of an expert on the production of documentary films who could visit the West Indies and instruct local personnel on the production of simple films of local subjects (Chapter VII, paragraphs 87-88).

(*f*) In order to enhance the value of the West Indian wireless transmitter or transmitters recommended elsewhere, school receivers should be provided, which could also play an important part in adult education (Chapter VII, paragraph 89).

(*g*) In countries so lacking in social amenities and organisations, the schools should play an important part as the centres for adult education in the ordinary sense, for instruction in agriculture and hygiene and for lending library services (Chapter VII, paragraphs 90-96).

(*h*) Educational policy as a whole should be under the supervision of some one officer in each Colony, and should be an important charge of the standing official social Welfare Committee of which the establishment is recommended elsewhere. In addition, education boards, which should be advisory only, and including a strong unofficial element, should be formed for the mutual enlightenment of Government and public opinion (Chapter VII, paragraphs 97-100).

(*i*) The primary school age should be restricted to 6-12, but only conditionally on, and side by side with, the establishment of junior secondary schools for ages 12-15 and of play centres or, in certain cases, of nursery schools for children under 6 (Chapter VII, paragraphs 101-102).

(*j*) The literary curriculum should remain the same for girls as for boys, but girls' vocational training (domestic science, child welfare, etc.) should begin at a somewhat earlier stage. In secondary education, provision should be made to enable girls to compete for scholarships on equal terms with boys. Facilities should generally be provided for post-primary vocational training for girls on the lines of the Carnegie Trade School in Georgetown, British Guiana (Chapter VII, paragraphs 103-108).

(*k*) There should be general provision of school meals, free where the economic circumstances of the children warrant it, and it should be possible to supply clothes for poor children. Some of these might be made at the schools (Chapter VII, paragraphs 109-110).

(*l*) In schools at present managed by the Denominations, if salaries are paid by the Government, complete control in staff matters should be assumed by Government; and new schools provided wholly from public funds should be in all respects administered by Government. The existing adequate facilities for religious instruction in Government schools should be maintained (Chapter VII, paragraphs 111-112).

(*m*) The staff of the Comptroller of the West Indian Welfare Fund should include an educational expert (Chapter VII, paragraph 113).

While some of these recommendations should be put into effect at an early date we recognise that many of them can only be applied gradually and may require drastic modification in the light of new experience (Chapter VII, paragraph 114 (3)).

(ii) *Public Health.* (*Chapter VIII.*)

28. The possibility of leading a healthy life is greater throughout most parts of the West Indies than in many other tropical areas, and this is reflected in the somewhat better health conditions which prevail there as compared with some other British Colonies. Nevertheless, health conditions remain unsatisfactory, and the two most disquieting aspects of the situation are the high infant mortality and the prevalence of chronic sickness. Much of the disease is of a social character, springing from poverty and ignorance. The poorer people are too often unable to afford adequate housing and satisfactory food and clothing, and their lack of knowledge of the elements of nutrition and hygiene prevents them from making the best use of what meagre resources they have. Medical departments are handicapped by lack of funds, and have in the past tended to concentrate too much on the cure of disease instead of on its prevention. There is also a tendency to neglect rural in favour of urban areas. The training of all classes of medical personnel is inadequate, and the small proportion of auxiliary medical staff to fully qualified doctors renders inevitable an uneconomic use of the latter. Research suffers from neglect, and there is too great a dispersion of inadequately-equipped medical institutions.

29. We recommend,

(*a*) the appointment of a Medical Adviser to the Comptroller of the West Indian Welfare Fund, who should have the duty of formulating a health programme for the West

Indies, stressing preventive medicine, and one of whose duties should be organising the unification of medical services and the co-ordination of other health activities as recommended below (Chapter VIII, paragraph 60);

(b) the unification of the medical services of the British West Indies, with the object of affording a better career to members of that service, rendering possible the employment of specialists, and fostering a comprehensive view of the health problems of the entire area (Chapter VIII, paragraphs 61-65).

(c) the centralisation of medical institutions, not only within each colony but as between neighbouring groups of Colonies, should be undertaken, both to secure greater efficiency and economy in the treatment of the sick and to render possible much better training facilities for all classes of medical personnel in curative medicine. This reform would involve the organisation of the outlying hospitals as collecting stations, and the provision of adequate ambulance and stretcher services (Chapter VIII, paragraphs 66-76);

(d) the creation of at least one School of Hygiene in the West Indies, for research and teaching in preventive medicine, and for the thorough training of auxiliary medical personnel (Chapter VIII, paragraphs 77-79);

(e) the formulation of long-term health policies, which should form part of the wider social welfare programmes of the various Colonies, and should be framed not by the Medical Departments in isolation, but in consultation with other Departments, particularly of Labour, Agriculture and Education, and with Social Welfare officers (Chapter VIII, paragraphs 80-83);

(f) the reorganisation of the medical services to secure the development of the preventive outlook, the provision of a relative increase in well-trained auxiliary staff such as sanitary inspectors, health visitors, district nurses and dispensers, the centralisation of medical institutions (see (c) above) and the provision of better facilities for medical treatment in the rural areas and for certain sections of the urban population. In this connexion the possibility of an extension of contributory health insurance schemes on the basis of a carefully selected membership should be studied by the Medical Adviser (*see* (a) above) in consultation with Governments, although we do not consider the wide or rapid application of this principle to be practicable (Chapter VIII, paragraphs 84-96);

(g) immediate progress with certain definite preventive measures, including housing, general sanitation (e.g., the introduction of the bore-hole latrine) both in dwellings and schools, the control of malarial areas, maternity and child welfare work, venereal disease clinics, school medical services, the employment of more women doctors and the better education of the public in health matters, both in and out of school (Chapter VIII, paragraphs 97-109).

(iii) *Housing (Chapter IX).*

30. The standard of the housing of most of the poorer people is deplorably low. The maintenance of housing is generally completely neglected by the landlords, some of whom in the towns at any rate are not in a position to effect improvements. Laudable efforts are being made by some Governments and employers within the limits of their finances, and some of the new building sets an altogether new standard for working-class housing in the West Indies; but the problem in general is of such magnitude that its solution will require the co-operation of all the agencies concerned, including Government, local authorities, private enterprise and, not least, the people themselves. Rehousing cannot in the West Indies be an economic proposition, in that economic rents for houses of a minimum standard are beyond the resources of those for whom they are required. The cost involved is very substantial—on the basis of certain assumptions it would amount to more than £16,000,000 —and most of it would have to be met by the United Kingdom through the medium of the West Indian Welfare Fund. With set-offs the total capital expenditure from public funds could not be below £10,000,000 and might well substantially exceed it.

31. We recommend—

(*a*) generally, that, where they do not exist, powers should be taken to control the siting of new housing and that this control should be exercised with regard to considerations of health, sanitation and water-supply; and that great care should be taken to maintain a balance between rural and urban housing (Chapter IX, paragraphs 10, 21 and 22);

(*b*) for urban housing, that powers should be taken, where they do not already exist, to condemn and clear bad slum housing, no compensation being paid except in cases of proved and extreme hardship and then only under rigid safeguards; that legislation and procedure should follow that of the United Kingdom unless it is certain that United Kingdom provisions are inappropriate; that West Indian Governments should have easily-applied powers for the compulsory acquisition of land for housing (Chapter IX, paragraphs 15, 17 and 19);

(*c*) for rural housing, that a distinction must be drawn between housing of estate labour and that of tenant and other peasants; in the case of estate housing, estates should provide the land including vegetable plots and give reasonable security of tenure, and the houses should be built under approved schemes financed by Government at low rates of interest, rent being charged against a corresponding increase in wages (Chapter IX, paragraph 26). As between ranges and separate cottages, while on general grounds we prefer cottages, reformed ranges are suitable for unmarried men and small ranges limited to four dwellings might be permitted for families where there are strong health or other reasons for this course (Chapter IX, paragraph 28). Peasant housing should where possible be included in a survey of estate housing; and demolition not ordered unless either the peasant can afford to replace or Government is prepared to help with rebuilding (Chapter IX, paragraph 32);

(d) that, since the large programme recommended will require supervision by persons with qualifications not available in the West Indies, the following appointments should be made to the staff of the Comptroller of the West Indian Welfare Fund:—

(1) (temporary) an expert to organise enquiry into methods of building and types of houses;

(2) a permanent advisory officer with wide knowledge of town planning;

(3) an officer in charge of the actual building having initiative, drive, and experience of large-scale building in the United Kingdom (Chapter IX, paragraph 35).

(iv) *Labour and Trade Unions (Chapter X).*

32. In spite of the development towards land settlement, there is a tendency in the West Indies for an increasing proportion of the adult population to become dependent on work for wages. Task work, i.e., payment by results, is the characteristic, though not the universal, mode of employment. Rates, though varying from one colony to another, are extremely low, but even more important for the standard of living of the West Indian worker is the fact that employment is increasingly difficult to obtain. While agricultural employers have effective organisations, the workers are either completely unorganised or at best only partly organised. Collective bargaining has thus been virtually impossible and wage rates have in effect followed standards laid down by the employers alone. Until recently there have been no Governmental organisations for the supervision of labour matters, and industrial legislation remains for the most part defective. Workmen's Compensation provisions, where they exist, do not cover agricultural workers, who comprise the vast majority of the workers in all these Colonies.

33. We recommend:—

(*a*) as regards Trade Unionism, the enactment of laws to protect Unions from actions for damages consequent on strikes, the legalisation of peaceful picketing (pickets being given access in reasonable numbers to workers both at the gates of the factories and at their homes), the compulsory registration of Trade Unions and audit of their funds (the latter duty could reasonably be undertaken free of charge by Governments) (Chapter X, paragraphs 21-33);

(*b*) to cover the period before Trade Unions are developed to the point at which they can play a decisive part in the regulation of wages and conditions of employment, action by Governments in this direction through the medium of Labour Departments or Officers, the appointment of whom is of great and immediate importance. These organisations should be assisted by Advisory Boards representative of employers and employed with an impartial Chairman (Chapter X, paragraphs 34-46);

(*c*) that the staff of the Comptroller of the West Indian Welfare Fund should include a Labour Adviser who should maintain close liaison with the Labour Officers and Departments in all the West Indian Colonies (Chapter X, paragraph 39);

(*d*) that a Labour Department should be established within the Colonial Office, and a Labour Advisory Committee appointed composed of persons with expert knowledge of labour and colonial questions (Chapter X, paragraphs 45-46);

(*e*) that Wages Boards should be created in each colony as a means of fixing wages preferable to legislation. The enactment of satisfactory legislation providing for the establishment of such Boards should be a condition of the participation of any colony in the arrangements proposed in paragraphs 41 and 42 below for the assistance of the sugar industry, and the payment of shares in these benefits to individual concerns should depend on the full execution of the decisions of the Wages Boards. Differences arising in industries not covered by Wages Boards should be handled by the staff of the Labour Departments or by arbitration panels. An Industrial Court should be established for the West Indies as a whole (Chapter X, paragraphs 52-55);

(*f*) that West Indian Governments should set an example in labour matters by forming Whitley Councils for civil services, and the principle should be extended to subordinate staff and to teachers (Chapter X, paragraphs 32 and 54);

(*g*) that the Governments of the larger colonies should examine carefully the possibility of establishing some arrangement for unemployment insurance in the case of those undertakings which are organised on a system of regular employment and with exemptions for those industries where, owing to the intermittent character of employment, a scheme based on that obtaining in Great Britain would be impracticable (Chapter X, paragraph 16);

(*h*) That adequate factory inspection should be undertaken and factory legislation should be closely co-ordinated with the laws and regulations relating to public health. In the larger territories a Medical Inspector should be seconded to the Labour Department and everywhere the closest co-operation should be maintained between the medical and social welfare authorities and that Department (Chapter X, paragraphs 47-51);

(*i*) that West Indian Governments should consider carefully the possibility of adopting the scheme of Workmen's Compensation based on Canadian practice described in Chapter X, paragraphs 60-65;

(*j*) that the Government of each Colony concerned should be invited to take early steps, in consultation with the sugar producers, with a view to the imposition of welfare levies at the rate of 2s. per ton of sugar produced, to finance welfare schemes similar in their main principles to those organised in Great Britain by the Miners' Welfare Committee (Chapter X, paragraphs 66-70).

(v) *Other Social Needs and Services.* (*Chapter XI.*)

34. Here we set out our recommendations on certain social matters not strictly coming within the scope of the four preceding sections. The chief matters here provided for are the need for improving the status of women in the West Indies, and for the establishment of an organ of Government especially charged with the function of formulating and carrying out social welfare policies.

35. Our recommendations are:—

(*a*) That women should be eligible for appointment to all Boards and local authorities and that, where the representation of women's interests has not been secured through election, the desirability of nominating a woman or women for membership (if the power exists and if well-qualified persons can be found) should be borne carefully in mind; that women should be equally eligible with men for appointment as magistrates and for service as jurors; that the same procedure should be followed in appointments to the civil service for women as for men; and that more hostels should be provided for women workers (Chapter XI, paragraphs 10-12).

(b) That each Government should appoint a Social Welfare Officer and form a Social Welfare Committee of representatives of each Department concerned, however indirectly, in the evolution of a programme of social welfare; that a social welfare expert should be a member of the staff of the Comptroller of the West Indian Welfare Fund, and that the appropriate members of the staff of the Comptroller should form themselves into a Social Welfare Committee which would be the central counterpart of the local Committees (Chapter XI, paragraphs 30-31).

(c) That provision should be made for the training of social welfare workers for service in the West Indies, their duties being as set out in Chapter XI, paragraph 48 (e). Care must be taken to supplement and support, and not replace, the valuable work now being done by voluntary organisations (Chapter XI, paragraphs 32-48).

(d) That certain improvements should be introduced into the penal system. These include the increased use of probation, the introduction of modern methods of dealing with young offenders, the abolition of ticket of leave, the establishment throughout of Prisoners' Aid Societies and Boards of Visitors and the improvement of conditions for women prisoners (Chapter XI, paragraphs 49-68).

(e) That an organised campaign should be undertaken against the social, moral and economic evils of promiscuity; the success of this will mainly depend on the extent to which the combined authority of the Churches is behind it (Chapter XI, paragraph 26).

(c) Economic Problems.

36. Behind the various economic and social defects in the West Indies, the question of the growth of numbers is to be found as a factor of extreme and fundamental importance, sometimes as a major cause of difficulty and distress and almost always as an aggravating factor. Our recommendations include many which will, we hope, help materially to increase the volume of employment, to raise the standard of living and to promote the development of the social services. But if the present growth of numbers continues unabated, these proposals will prove only to have been a palliative. In one sense, therefore, the most pressing need of the West Indies is a reduction of the birth-rate. The problem is far too complex to be the subject of concrete recommendations; and its solution can in the long run only take place through an awakening of public opinion. It is of the first importance, therefore, that West Indian public opinion should recognise the vital importance of the population problem; and every body that seeks, in whatever

sphere, to guide or influence opinion should recognise the responsibilities that rest upon it to assist and not to obstruct the process of public enlightenment (Chapter XII).

37. In order to provide the means of absorbing this growth of numbers it is essential on the one hand to secure a re-orientation of the agricultural system in the direction of a far greater home production of essential foodstuffs on a basis of mixed farming, and on the other to take whatever steps are practicable to improve the position of the agricultural exporting industries. We have examined various proposals made to us for achieving the latter purpose by increased preferential assistance. It is, however, only in respect of sugar that we are able to make any definite recommendations at this juncture for increased assistance in this particular form (Chapters XIV and XV).

38. The problems of the sugar industry fall under two main heads (1) the volume of production, (2) the level of prices. There was a very large expansion in the production of sugar in the West Indies between 1932 and 1937. But this expansion has been checked by the operation of the International Sugar Agreement which came into force in 1937, and which limits the amount of sugar that can be exported from the Colonial Empire to an assigned quota. In view of the need of the West Indies for expanding employment outlets and the unfavourable outlook for most branches of export agriculture, this restriction is, or at any rate would have been but for the outbreak of war, a most serious matter for the West Indian Colonies. We regard it, therefore, as of vital importance to secure an increase in the basic export quota assigned to the Colonial Empire (Chapter XV, paragraph 31).

39. The support given by Great Britain to the International Sugar Agreement was, however, based on solid grounds; and it must be recognised that a large expansion of Colonial sugar production would carry with it, under peace-time conditions, serious dangers and disadvantages, particularly if this were to entail a breakdown of the International Agreement. In view of the large excess of world capacity for sugar production, the world price of sugar might fall again to a very low level. If this should happen, it would not be easy in practice to maintain the price received by Colonial producers by adjustments of the preference. The scope which the British market provides for absorbing increased Colonial production is both limited and uncertain. Owing to differences in the seasons of shipment from different producing areas, there are periods when very little foreign sugar is available in London. If Colonial sugar were to displace foreign sugar to a materially increased extent, there might often be periods when the supply of Colonial sugar alone

would exceed the demands of the British market, and force down its price. In such circumstances, there would be a danger that a world price for sugar might disappear, and that the British export trade in refined sugar might be endangered. The British Exchequer, moreover, loses heavily in so far as Colonial sugar displaces foreign sugar in the British market (Chapter XV, paragraphs 13-24).

40. For the time being, however, the perspective of the problem is transformed by war conditions; for exchange reasons it becomes important to concentrate our purchases of imported goods as far as possible on countries that form an effective part of the sterling area. It is reasonable to assume therefore that no artificial restrictions will be retained during the war period upon the output of Colonial sugar, though the problem of world over-production will be aggravated when peace is restored by the increase of production that takes place in the meantime (Chapter XV, paragraphs 25 and 26).

41. After surveying the needs of the various Colonies in the light of the difficulties that have been indicated, we had reached the conclusion before the outbreak of war that the basic export quotas allocated to the West Indian Colonies should be increased by about 120,000 tons. An increase of this magnitude would be mainly required to avert the under-employment of plant and labour in districts where sugar is already grown. This increase is equivalent to about 20 per cent. of the combined export quotas of these Colonies. If the other sugar Colonies were treated on an equal footing, it would be necessary to secure an increase in the basic export quota of the Colonial Empire of fully 200,000 tons. The war may affect the problem in ways that it is not easy to foresee; but in the light of the knowledge at present available, this represents in our judgment a reasonable objective of policy, provided that the increase in sugar production goes hand in hand with an increase of the production of foodstuffs for local consumption (Chapter XV, paragraphs 27-32).

42. All Empire sugar, Dominion as well as Colonial, receives in the British market the benefit of a preference of £3 15s. per ton of 96° sugar. In addition a supplementary preference is given to Colonial as distinct from Dominion producers upon a limited quantity of " certificated " sugar. We propose certain changes in the arrangements regarding this supplementary preference with a view to improving and stabilising the price received by Colonial producers. These proposals may be summarised as follows:—

> (1) The amount of certificated sugar eligible for the supplementary Colonial preference shall be calculated in future for each Colony in any year so as to represent one-half of the total exports from that Colony in that year.

(2) The certificates shall be distributed among the different factories in each Colony on the basis of their permitted production or exports for that year, whichever may be most appropriate.

(3) The amount of the supplementary preference payable on " certificated " sugar shall be 3s. per cwt. as at present, but shall be reduced or increased in any year by 4d. per cwt. for each complete 3d. per cwt. by which the world price of sugar, for the average of the first six months of the year, exceeds or falls short of 7s. per cwt. (Chapter XV, paragraphs 33-44).

43. These proposals have been framed in the light of pre-war conditions, and on the basis of the pre-war purchasing-power of sterling. We leave open the questions how far they can be applied under war-time conditions and how far they may need modification when the war is over.

44. These proposals would effect an improvement in the position of the Colonial sugar producers which we are agreed in regarding as the minimum that is required. They should enable efficient sugar estates to earn satisfactory, though not exorbitant profits, to make some improvement in wages, and afford opportunities for a modest expenditure on purposes designed to improve the social conditions of their labourers. The majority of us would like to go further and establish a price for Colonial sugar which would render more immediately practicable a substantial improvement in the wage-rates of the sugar workers. We have to recognise on the other side that these proposals would impose a heavy burden on the British Exchequer. It seems probable that the total cost of our various proposals with regard to sugar would amount to over £1,500,000, though only two-thirds of this sum would be attributable to the West Indies. This represents as large an expenditure as it seems to some of us reasonable to propose for the benefit of a particular branch of export agriculture (Chapter XV, paragraphs 45-47).

45. Orderly marketing methods are a condition of the successful development of many of the minor agricultural products of the West Indies. They are important in connection not only with export trade but also with the development of food production for the local market. The experiments in orderly marketing now being undertaken in Jamaica deserve encouragement. So far as the export trade is concerned, however, it is important that close contact should be maintained between marketing organisations in the West Indies and the Colonial Empire Marketing Board, when reconstituted (Chapter XIII, paragraphs 26-31).

46. As regards non-agricultural industries, we do not recommend that West Indian Governments should conduct or finance speculative industrial enterprises. There are, however, certain

possible projects which Governments might do well to foster: e.g., the establishment of a cement works in Jamaica, possibly in co-operation with British manufacturers, and the development of the local manufacture of coconut products in Jamaica and elsewhere. The system of quantitative restriction of imports, coupled with safeguards for the consumer against an undue increase of price, may prove a satisfactory method of fostering local industries, and schemes based on this method ought not to be disallowed because they run counter to a general principle of British commercial policy, nor should any dislike of this method be permitted to prejudice the fair consideration of such schemes on their merits (Chapter XIII, paragraphs 3-17).

(d) AGRICULTURE. (CHAPTER XVI).

47. The technical needs of West Indian agriculture may be summed up as more intelligent use of natural resources, and the adoption of systems of land tenure for the smaller cultivators which are conducive to the development of habits of careful husbandry. These needs would exist at any time; they are doubly necessary when the trend of world trade makes it necessary for the West Indies to grow as much as possible of their own foodstuffs. This section is confined to our recommendations for the improvement of agricultural technique on the basis of the present distribution of land; the next section contains our recommendations to meet the special requirements of land settlement.

48. Our recommendations are:—

(a) Administrative reforms (Chapter XVI, paragraph 29) including—

(i) the appointment of an Inspector-General of Agriculture for the British West Indies, who should not be a member of the staff of the Comptroller of the West Indian Welfare Fund, but should be readily available for consultation regarding any schemes under consideration by the Comptroller which have an agricultural bearing;

(ii) the reduction of the specialist staffs of Agricultural Departments in conformity with the proposals in (b) below;

(iii) the assumption by the Director of Agriculture in Barbados of responsibility for the Leeward and Windward Islands; and by the Director of Agriculture in Jamaica for British Honduras;

(iv) provision for holding Agricultural Conferences every two or three years;

(b) The centralisation of all major research and investigation at the Imperial College of Tropical Agriculture which would thus add to its present functions the duty of serving as a research station for the West Indies. The money required for this extension of the functions of the Imperial College of Tropical Agriculture should be provided by Parliament, which should be invited to ensure the continuance of the scheme for a definite term (Chapter XVI, paragraphs 36-39);

(c) The provision at the Hope Agricultural School, Jamaica, of facilities for all the West Indian Colonies for agricultural education at the stage immediately preceding that of the Diploma courses at the Imperial College which should continue to serve all its present educational purposes (Chapter XVI, paragraphs 31-32);

(d) The institution of the following enquiries (Chapter XVI, paragraphs 37 and 38):—

(i) a comprehensive soil survey;

(ii) topographical survey to settle questions of land ownership;

(iii) survey of peasant agriculture, and investigations for the purpose of devising better peasant farming systems based on mixed farming and the complementary use of livestock and crops;

(iv) experimental investigation into the introduction of mixed farming methods into estate cultivation;

(v) a survey of, and investigation of preventive methods against, soil erosion;

(vi) investigations on methods of maintaining soil fertility;

(vii) investigation of the marketing of estate and peasant produce;

(viii) joint effort on veterinary research and veterinary advisory work;

(ix) expert investigation of the arrangements for promoting soundness and continuity of forest policy in British Guiana, British Honduras and Trinidad, and for assisting the Governments of those Colonies to find local and overseas markets for their forest products;

(e) Certain special measures for special territories as follows:—

(i) if the campaign against banana diseases in Jamaica cannot be financed locally, further assistance should be afforded by Your Majesty's Government (Chapter XVI, paragraphs 41-45);

(ii) the displacement of share-cropping by land settlement in Nevis on the basis of mixed farming with sugar as the chief crop; a sugar quota gradually increasing to at least 3,500 tons per annum; and the erection by means of assistance from Imperial funds of a small sugar factory, failing which special assistance would be required, e.g. by the provision of transport at uneconomical rates (Chapter XVI, paragraphs 47 and 48);

(iii) both capital works and maintenance of drainage in British Guiana should be the charge of a central Board; in order to secure effective co-operation with the existing Sea Defence Board, the Director of Public Works and Sea Defences should be Chairman of both Boards. The initial cost of drainage in British Guiana may have to be treated as an irrecoverable charge (Chapter XVI, paragraphs 50-58);

(iv) the adoption of the proposal to establish on the Essequibo Coast of British Guiana a central rice mill to be financed by Government (Chapter XVI, paragraphs 59-61);

(v) the Trinidad cocoa subsidy should be put on a new basis under which its objective would be the rehabilitation of the industry (Chapter XVI, paragraph 62);

(vi) subject to full consideration of recommendations made as a result of the recent survey of the cocoa industry in Grenada, assistance should be granted to it by Your Majesty's Government on the basis proposed for Trinidad (Chapter XVI, paragraph 63).

(*e*) LAND SETTLEMENT. (CHAPTER XVII).

49. This is no more than an orderly plan for settling considerable numbers of people on the land as small-holders and providing them with certain forms of assistance. It is only one of several ways by which the number and yield of peasant holdings may be increased, and is in the West Indies expensive in relation to the number of persons settled. Mixed farming and not specialisation on export crops must be the basis of land settlement; this involves a change in outlook and methods, and in the habits and tastes of the consuming public and in commercial organisation. At least equal attention must be paid to improving the husbandry of existing small-holders and to providing additional lands for their sons.

50. We recommend:—

(*a*) that the order of procedure should be, first, the improvement of the husbandry of existing small-holders, in the light of the results of some of the enquiries recommended in paragraph 48 (*d*) above; then, the improvement of existing land settlements and the establishment of new settlements (Chapter XVII, paragraphs 32-33);

(*b*) that Governments should not regard themselves as committed to the grant of freehold tenures, but should experiment with both freehold and leasehold tenures. The grant of freehold rights should be subject to appropriate conditions to prevent fragmentation of the land and to suitable safeguards of good husbandry including the prevention of erosion and the maintenance of soil fertility (Chapter XVII, paragraph 8);

(*c*) that Governments should take powers for the compulsory acquisition of agricultural land needed for land settlement and similar purposes (Chapter XVII, paragraph 12);

(*d*) that it should be firmly impressed on settlers and others that, while credit facilities will generally be required in the early stages of any scheme of land settlement, their success depends in the last resort on their own exertions and that Government cannot continue to provide financial support indefinitely (Chapter XVII, paragraph 7).

(*f*) COMMUNICATIONS. (CHAPTER XIX.)

51. In broad outline, the facilities for external communication are better between any point in the West Indies and the outside world than between the West Indies as a group. This is a serious obstacle to the development of economic and other interchange which will have to come about if the West Indies are to develop towards a greater degree of political and administrative co-operation. Improvements in such communications are also essential if the machinery proposed for the administration of the West Indian Welfare Fund is to be worked effectively. Internal communications vary widely in adequacy and efficiency, from the good road network of Barbados to the discontinuous and uneconomic system of Dominica. The existing railways have on the whole (like railways throughout the world) fallen on evil days as self-balancing services; to this unwise planning and capitalisation have contributed. They nevertheless perform an essential function in the economic life of Trinidad, Jamaica and British Guiana, and their maintenance even on the basis of chronic paper deficits is a social necessity. Internal telephone services, although showing improvement here and there, are for the most part startling in their chaotic disorganisation, and inter-island telephony is only now the subject of experiment. The West Indies are too dependent for wireless services on broadcasts from the outside world. Excellent though these services are in many ways, there is a need for a distinctive

Chapter XXV.

West Indian system which can play an important part in the education both of the child and of the adult, and for public enlightenment generally.

52. We recommend:—

(a) That on a return to normal conditions Your Majesty's Government should consider whether they should not offer a subsidy for the maintenance of a regular British passenger service to some of the West Indian Colonies, since British shipping is handicapped by the competition of subsidised foreign shipping (Chapter XIX, paragraph 14);

(b) That two small sea-going ships of the type described in Chapter XIX, paragraph 16, should be provided at the cost of Your Majesty's Government for trade between the smaller islands. Whether such a service should be operated by Government or be entrusted to private enterprise in return for a subsidy is a matter for further consideration;

(c) That effect be given to the proposals made by Mr. Banks for the provision of a regular air service from St. Kitts to Trinidad and covering Barbados and all the principal Leeward and Windward Islands (Chapter XIX, paragraph 18);

(d) That the Jamaica Government should consider whether a concession in respect of the island telephone service should not be granted to Telephone and General Trust Limited, subject to the inclusion of satisfactory safeguards, and on acceptance by the Company of an undertaking to assume responsibility for the telephone services in the smaller islands under a definite obligation to expand and improve these services (Chapter XIX, paragraph 34);

(e) That a wireless telephone service within the West Indies should be provided as soon as posible for the furtherance of economic development and administrative convenience (Chapter XIX, paragraphs 35-36);

(f) That the Empire services of the British Broadcasting Corporation should be supplemented, particularly as regards educational broadcasts, by the establishment of a wireless transmitter or transmitters in the Caribbean area, the initial cost being met by Your Majesty's Government and the maintenance costs by the Colonial Governments jointly, in proportion to their average annual revenue. The incidence of the cost of school receivers, etc., would have to be decided after requirements are known; where Colonial Governments cannot, from their own resources, provide adequately for these needs, the cost might be defrayed from the Colonial Development Fund or from the West Indian Welfare Fund (Chapter XIX, paragraphs 37-42).

(g) Constitutional and Closer Union.

(Chapters XVIII and XXII.)

53. We do not support either of the extreme proposals put before us for the grant of immediate and complete self-government based on universal suffrage, or for a wide increase of the authority of Governors which would convert the existing system into a virtual autocracy; the one because it would render impossible the financial control necessary if, as we consider to be inevitable, substantial assistance is to be afforded by Your Majesty's Government through the West Indian Welfare Fund and otherwise; the other because it would be politically a retrograde step. More, and not less, participation by the people in the work of government is a real necessity for lasting social advancement. At the present stage, we attach more importance to the truly representative character of Legislative Councils than to any drastic change in their functions.

54. As stated in paragraph 18 of this Chapter, political federation is not of itself an appropriate means of meeting the pressing needs of the West Indies. Nevertheless, it is the end to which policy should be directed.

55. There is no doubt that the representation of West Indian as of Colonial interests generally at Westminster is inadequate. The pressure of business on Parliament makes it impracticable to provide for this within the framework of present Parliamentary procedure, e.g., by the appointment of colonial representatives to the House of Commons, even if, as is desirable, more Parliamentary time were to be devoted to colonial business. A more hopeful plan would be the association of colonial delegates with the work of any standing Parliamentary Committee which may be created to consider colonial affairs.

56. We recommend:—

(a) That care should be taken to ensure that all important sections and interests of the community receive adequate representation in the Executive Councils (Chapter XXII, paragraph 8);

(b) That consideration should be given to the adoption of a Committee System on an advisory basis to give elected representatives an insight into the practical details of government (Chapter XXII, paragraphs 4-6);

(c) That official representation in Legislative Councils should be confined to the Colonial Secretary, the Treasurer and the Attorney-General, and the resulting vacancies filled by nominations in the spirit recommended in (a) above (Chapter XXII, paragraph 7);

(d) That in order to secure that the elected element in Legislative Councils shall be as truly representative as possible, the object of policy should be the introduction of universal adult suffrage. Some of us hold that this should be introduced forthwith; others that it should be reached by gradual stages and to this end recommend the appointment of local committees to consider the extension of the franchise, both for local and for central government. Such committees should keep in close touch with their counterparts in other West Indian Colonies, and should consider carefully whether, as is strongly desirable, their recommendations would assure substantial equality as between the sexes (Chapter XXII, paragraphs 12-17);

(e) That in all West Indian Colonies a careful examination should be made at an early date of the possibility of reducing substantially the margin between the qualifications for registration as a voter and those for membership of the Legislative Council, the latter being in many cases unnecessarily high (Chapter XXII, paragraphs 18 and 19);

(f) That a practical test of the advantages of federation should be made by combining the Leeward and Windward Islands in one federation on the lines of that existing in the former group (Chapter XVIII, paragraph 12);

(g) That means be found for devoting more Parliamentary time to the discussion of colonial affairs and, if it is decided to proceed with the establishment of a Standing Parliamentary Committee to consider colonial affairs, to devise means for the association of delegates from the Colonies concerned with the work of that Committee (Chapter XXII, paragraph 20).

(h) LOCAL UNIFICATION OF SERVICES. (CHAPTER XVIII.)

57. Officers of the public services in the West Indies are divided into those who, being members of unified services common to the whole Colonial Empire, are appointed by the Secretary of State for the Colonies, frequently from outside the West Indies, and those recruited locally. Although the latter greatly preponderate in numbers, the former include a high proportion of occupants of the higher and more responsible posts. The time is still distant when it will be possible to fill all posts, particularly those requiring technical and professional qualifications, by local appointments. This is the natural course of development and it might be hastened by the creation of unified services covering the Caribbean area, of which the less senior officers of the Government service would be members, thus affording a wider range of selection, the possibility of standardising methods of entry and qualifications, and of increased efficiency through the greater possibility of employing

officers in posts best suited to their talents. For the officers themselves the advantages of unification include better prospects of advancement, more opportunity for acquiring varied experience and a better prospect of congenial work. The difficulties consist chiefly in the diversity of salaries and conditions of service as between the different Colonies; and these will have to be faced and overcome if acceptance of the principle of unification is to be translated into reality.

58. We recommend:—

that West Indian Governments should be invited to accept the principle of local unified services and, if that is generally accepted, should address themselves to the task of giving practical effect to it at the earliest possible date. It should not be difficult to make a start by establishing a Unified Medical Service for the West Indies (Chapter XVIII, paras. 18-22).

(*i*) ADMINISTRATION AND PUBLIC OPINION. (CHAPTER V.)

59. The chief weakness of the Crown Colony system of government, widespread in the West Indies, is that the unofficial element, precluded from the exercise of complete administrative control, tends to adopt a consistently hostile attitude towards Government and Government officials. Associated with this problem is the regrettable fact that colour prejudice, although universally deprecated, is generally on the increase. This is a serious obstacle to the harmonious political development which is necessary as a preliminary to the eventual grant of wider powers to the elected representatives of the peoples of the West Indies. Our recommendations above regarding the institution of advisory committees with a strong unofficial element should do something to destroy the atmosphere of mistrust, suspicion and often misdirected criticism which is a feature of much West Indian politics, but more is needed. In moulding the attitude of the public towards Government policy, much power for good or ill is in the hands of the Press. This power is not always used wisely, and it is not unknown for certain organs to pursue campaigns of personal abuse and wilful misrepresentation for which there is no excuse. The public service is therefore rendered unattractive to officers of the ability which the islands sorely need, and this unattractiveness is enhanced by the prevailing ungenerous terms as regards pay and passages. Officers from outside with special qualifications are and will for long be needed in the West Indies, and the day of their departure will not be brought nearer by the creation of difficulties and a hostile attitude toward them. An improvement in the conditions of service of officers appointed to the West Indies, and an approximation of

Chapter XXV.

their emoluments, etc., to those prevailing elsewhere in the Colonial Empire are desirable on general grounds, and in the interests of the West Indies themselves; the case for such reforms becomes much stronger if, as we recommend, considerable assistance is to be granted to the West Indies through the agency of the West Indian Welfare Fund.

60. We received many complaints that senior officers in the West Indies were frequently transferred without adequate regard to the extent of the resultant loss of efficiency caused to the public service of the Colonies concerned, especially when a number of such transfers happened to coincide. We are satisfied that there is some justice in this complaint.

61. We recommend:—

(a) As regards the attitude of public opinion, that Governments should adopt a much more positive policy of bringing their point of view before the mass of the people, and of explaining in sufficiently simple terms the reasons which lie behind their decisions of major problems; and that the active assistance of all persons of standing, and of all available means of publicity, such as broadcasting, should be enlisted in an organised attempt to prevent any further extension of colour prejudice.

(b) As regards conditions of service for officers appointed from outside the West Indies,

(i) that West Indian Governments should reconsider their attitude on the question of the grant of passages to such officers both on first appointment and when proceeding on leave (Chapter XXI, para. 18);

(ii) that West Indian Governments, particularly those of the larger Colonies, should review the salaries of their senior officers (Chapter XXI, para. 19).

In the review of these questions it must be borne in mind that, unless salaries and other conditions of service conform more closely to the general Colonial level, it must become increasingly difficult to fill the higher administrative and professional appointments with men whose training, experience, and ability will fit them to co-operate effectively with the Comptroller of the West Indian Welfare Fund and his staff in schemes for the social betterment of the West Indies (Chapter XXI, para. 19).

(c) That the Comptroller of the West Indian Welfare Fund should be empowered, subject to the consent in each case of the employing Government, to grant a certain number of scholarships each year to serving officers for the purpose of study leave and to meet other costs of that leave where these cannot be borne by local funds (Chapter XXI, para. 18).

(*d*) That the Colonial Office should, where possible, avoid the dislocation of public business caused by too frequent changes in the holders of higher appointments (Chapter V, paras. 19-27).

(*j*) MISCELLANEOUS, LOCAL AND SECTIONAL QUESTIONS.

(CHAPTERS XXIII AND XXIV.)

62. In this section we recapitulate some of the more important recommendations set out in Chapters XXIII and XXIV of our Report.

(*a*) *Individual Indebtedness*: increase of co-operative effort, e.g., by arranging for selected estates to act as central agents for the processing and sale of certain products, and the encouragement of voluntary co-operation (Chapter XXIII, paragraphs 8-9);

(*b*) *Census and Other Statistics*: one of the earliest duties of the statistician who we propose should be attached to the staff of the Comptroller of the West Indian Welfare Fund should be that of evolving, in concert with both the local Governments and the Colonial Office, methods whereby every important return emanating from these Colonies, whether rendered to him or to some other authority, is prepared on a common basis. It should also be recognised that the omission of a census, as in several colonies in 1931, is a false economy and deprives Government of knowledge essential for the satisfactory formulation of policy (Chapter XXIII, paragraphs 10-12);

(*c*) *Fisheries*: if the cost of a full investigation as proposed in Chapter XVI, paragraph 4, is beyond the resources of any Colony, and there is presumptive evidence that such an enquiry might meet with success, there is a strong claim for assistance from the Colonial Development Fund or by a direct grant from Imperial Funds (Chapter XXIII, paragraphs 15-17);

(*d*) *Barbados*: the claims of this overcrowded colony must rank high for favourable consideration in connexion with any project for the transfer of populations within the West Indies (Chapter XXIV, paragraph 3).

(*e*) *British Guiana*: outstanding loans-in-aid from the Imperial Exchequer should be converted into free grants, outstanding obligations on account of the work of the Boundary Commission and of loans from the Colonial

Development Fund should be remitted, and in future loans-in-aid should be avoided. Certain special measures should be taken to protect the Amerindian peoples of the remote hinterland from exploitation (Chapter XXIV, paragraphs 8-13 and 17-20).

(f) *British Honduras*: (i) special measures are necessary to ensure sanitary living quarters for forest workers, and also steps to regulate the method of payment of wages and to ensure the disappearance of any traces of the truck system (Chapter XXIV, paragraphs 27-29);

(ii) with regard to the Hurricane Loan, there should be substantial alleviations, distinguishing between individual debtors and the denominations (Chapter XXIV, paragraphs 32-34).

(iii) Steps similar to those recommended for British Guiana are necessary in the interests of the aboriginal Mayan and Carib inhabitants (Chapter XXIV, paragraphs 35-38).

(g) *Jamaica*: the evolution of a systematic public works programme, to replace the present ill co-ordinated system of relief works, and to be correlated with future agricultural and land settlement developments (Chapter XXIV, paragraph 43).

(h) *Leeward Islands*: provision of water-supply in Anguilla, drainage in Antigua and roads and drainage in Dominica (Chapter XXIV, paragraphs 49-56).

(i) *Windward Islands*: steps should be taken to secure the use of the military buildings in St. Lucia, should such accommodation become required as a result of certain of our other recommendations. In St. Vincent improved water-supply is very necessary on the Leeward Coast. The better organisation of water-supply is also required in Grenada and the Grenadines (Chapter XXIV, paragraphs 61-72).

(j) *East Indian Questions*: East Indians should not in their own interests or those of the Colonies where they have now permanently taken up their residence be treated as a separate community. Nevertheless, certain measures are necessary, including specialisation in East Indian questions by some members of Labour Departments, the appointment of East Indians to government posts and teaching staffs where suitable candidates are available, reform on the lines suggested in Chapter XXIV of the law regarding the legitimisation and validation of East Indian marriages, and clarification of the position as regards cremation (Chapter XXIV, paragraphs 76-92).

ACKNOWLEDGEMENTS.

We have expressed in our preface our great appreciation of the arrangements made by the Governments of the Colonies which we visited for our accommodation, for our transport, and for the ready and speedy preparation of replies to our requests for information.

We wish also to record our gratitude to the many private persons throughout the West Indies who did everything in their power to facilitate our inquiry by the welcome which they gave us when we were making personal visits of inspection. Everywhere we were received with the greatest kindness and the most friendly hospitality was extended to us.

We cannot mention all of those to whom we are under a debt of gratitude for other courtesies and assistance. But we wish to place on record our sincere appreciation of the many ways in which the Governors, Acting Governors and Administrators of the several territories facilitated our mission and strove to assist us. We are also greatly indebted to many officers of Government Departments and in particular we would mention those who were attached to us as liaison officers and in that capacity contributed greatly to the arrangement of our programme and to its completion.

Our thanks are also due in no small measure to the many other members of local staffs who were seconded by the various West Indian Governments to assist our Secretariat in its work.

We wish to take this opportunity of thanking Mr. S. A. Hammond, Education Commissioner for the Leewards and Windwards, for permission to reproduce certain photographs, and the West India Committee and George Philip and Son Limited, for permission to use the West India Committee's Map of the West Indies as the basis for that appended to our Report.

Our continual travel threw exceptionally arduous work on our clerical and reporting staff, and we wish to make special mention of the devotion and efficiency with which Mr. G. Hurford, Miss E. L. Brown and Miss L. M. E. Parker of the Colonial Office, and the verbatim reporters, Miss H. Craig-Kelly and Miss F. M. Hayward, carried out their duties under most difficult conditions.

We wish to record our high appreciation of the ability and energy with which our Secretary, Mr. T. I. K. Lloyd, carried out the exacting task of organising the business of such an extensive and laborious inquiry. His wide grasp of the **details** of our subject and his skill in drafting were invaluable in connection with the preparation of our Report.

We are also much indebted to our Assistant Secretary, **Mr. C. Y. Carstairs**, who besides ably assisting Mr. Lloyd in all his duties, served as Secretary to that section of the Commission which took evidence in the Windward Islands.

ALL OF WHICH WE HUMBLY SUBMIT FOR YOUR MAJESTY'S GRACIOUS CONSIDERATION.

       MOYNE.

       R. E. STUBBS.

       RACHEL E. CROWDY.

       WALTER CITRINE.

       PERCY G. MACKINNON.

       MARY G. BLACKLOCK.

       F. L. ENGLEDOW.

       H. D. HENDERSON.

T. I. K. LLOYD,
  Secretary.

C. Y. CARSTAIRS,
  Assistant Secretary.

21st *December*, 1939.

APPENDIX A.
LIST OF WITNESSES WHO APPEARED BEFORE THE COMMISSION

London.

Date of hearing.
1938.

20th September	OLIVIER, The Right Hon. Lord, K.C.M.G., C.B.
20th September	BAILEY, Miss Amy.
20th September	O'BRIEN, Dr. A. J. R., C.M.G., M.C., Chief Medical Adviser to the Secretary of State for the Colonies.
21st September	STOCKDALE, Sir Frank, K.C.M.G., C.B.E., Agricultural Adviser to the Secretary of State for the Colonies.
22nd September	ELY, P. E.
22nd September	COX, Miss Peggy.
22nd September	HOLE, Major Hugh.
22nd September	JONES, G. A., C.M.G., ex-Commissioner of Agriculture for the Leeward and Windward Islands.
28th September	LETHEM, Sir Gordon, K.C.M.G., Governor of the Leeward Islands.
28th September	FLETCHER, Sir Murchison, K.C.M.G., C.B.E., ex-Governor of Trinidad.
28th September	EVANS, Sir Geoffrey, C.I.E., ex-Principal Imperial College of Tropical Agriculture.
28th September	DU BUISSON, J. M.
29th September	WEST INDIA COMMITTEE. Lt.-Col. Ivan DAVSON, O.B.E., T.D., and Mr. J. Gordon MILLER.
29th September	SHERLOCK, Sir Alfred.
29th September	LEAGUE OF COLOURED PEOPLES, INTERNATIONAL AFRICAN SERVICE BUREAU AND THE NEGRO WELFARE ASSOCIATION. Dr. Harold A. MOODY and Mr. BLACKMAN.
30th September	BRIANT, Miss B.
30th September	MOORE, Sir Henry, K.C.M.G., Assistant Under-Secretary of State, Colonial Office.
30th September	MARSON, Miss Una.
30th September	MAYHEW, A. I., C.M.G., C.I.E., Joint Secretary to the Advisory Committee on Education in the Colonies.
4th October	CLAUSON, G. L. M., C.M.G., O.B.E., Assistant Secretary, Economic Department, Colonial Office.

(For the list of witnesses who appeared before the Commission after their return from the West Indies, see page 474).

Jamaica.

KINGSTON.

3rd November	BARNES, A. C., C.M.G., ex-Director of Agriculture.
3rd November	WAINWRIGHT, G. C., O.B.E., Chairman, Banana Industry Aid Board.
7th November	GRANTHAM, A. W. G. H., Colonial Secretary; BROWN, F. L., O.B.E., M.C., Assistant Colonial Secretary; SHILLINGFORD, W., Director of Prisons.
8th November	EASTER, B. H., C.B.E., Director of Education.
8th November	JAMAICA UNION OF TEACHERS. Mr. C. A. LITTLE, Mr. H. A. JONES, Mr. J. J. MILLS, Mr. A. J. NEWMAN, M.C., Mr. A. A. ROBINSON, Mr. R. A. THOMPSON and Mrs. E. D. JAMES.

Date of hearing.	
1938.	
10th November	CHRISTIAN BODIES.
	The Right Rev. Edmund W. SARA, Assistant Bishop of Jamaica, Rev. W. L. BROWN, Rev. H. WARD, Rev. Father FRANCIS J. KELLY, S.J., Rev. E. Armon JONES, Rev. M. E. W. SAWYERS, Rev. J. Henerie ALLEN, Rev. W. A. KALTREIDER, Colonel H. S. HODGSON and Mr. LEWIS.
10th November	CLARKE, Miss Edith, Secretary, Board of Supervision.
11th November	COOPER, H. Austin, Registrar General.
11th November	HAWKES, Captain M. H., Collector General.
12th November	HODGES, A. H., Treasurer and Chairman of the Board of Conciliation.
14th November	JAMAICA WELFARE LIMITED.
	Mr. N. W. MANLEY, K.C., Mr. P. M. SHERLOCK, Mr. G. G. R. SHARP, Mr. L. ASHENHEIM, Mr. G. HAWKINS Mr. C. N. HEMING, Dr. W. E. McCULLOCH, Mr. N. N. NETHERSOLE, Mr. H. P. JACOBS and Miss EDITH CLARKE.
14th November	SCOTT, G. H., Unemployment Registration Bureau.
15th November	HALLINAN, Dr. T. J., C.B.E., Director of Medical Services.
15th November	BRITISH MEDICAL ASSOCIATION, JAMAICA BRANCH.
	Dr. A. G. CURPHEY, Dr. F. R. RITCHIE, Dr. G. P. ALLEN and Dr. W. E. McCULLOCH.
15th November	TOURIST TRADE DEVELOPMENT BOARD.
	Mr. F. H. ROBERTSON.
16th November	BUSTAMANTE INDUSTRIAL UNIONS.
	Mr. Alexander BUSTAMENTE, Mr. J. A. G. EDWARDS, Mr. Ross LIVINGSTON, Mr. S. GRANT, Mr. Ken HILL and Miss G. LONGBRIDGE.
17th November	JAMAICA PROGRESSIVE LEAGUE.
	Rev. Ethelred BROWN, Mr. C. T. SAUNDERS, Mr. C. A. McPHERSON, Mr. E. R. Dudley EVANS, Mrs. M. L. KNIBB and Dr. O. E. ANDERSON.
17th November	THE CUSTODES.
	Lt.-Col. L. G. HARRISON, Mr. G. W. MUIRHEAD, Mr. N. B. LIVINGSTON, Mr. S. E. MORRIS, Mr. F. M. KERR-JARRETT, Mr. S. R. CARGILL, Mr. T. ANDERSON, Mr. H. E. CRUM-EWING, Mr. A. C. WESTMORLAND, Mr. J. T. CALDER, Brigadier-General H. S. SEWELL, C.M.G., D.S.O., Sir Thomas ROXBURGH, C.M.G., and Mr. H. BUCKLEY.
18th November	JAMAICA IMPERIAL ASSOCIATION.
	Sir Charlton HARRISON, Mr. R. F. WILLIAMS and Mr. O. K. HENRIQUES.
21st November	JAMAICA COCONUT PRODUCERS' ASSOCIATION.
	Mr. R. T. HARRISON, Mr. S. G. FLETCHER, Mr. E. A. BARHAM AND Major BARKER-HAHLO.
21st November	JAMAICA AGRICULTURAL SOCIETY.
	Mr. G. Seymour SEYMOUR, O.B.E., Rev. W. J. THOMPSON, Mr. U. T. McKAY, Mr. J. J. CAWLEY, Mr. J. P. V. McDANIEL and Mr. A. F. THELWELL.
21st November	JAMAICA CITRUS PRODUCERS' ASSOCIATION.
	Mr. W. Chevalier SYER, Mr. C. A. REID, Mr. J. Hutton JEFFERSON, Mr. H. BRAHAM, Mr. H. G. DUNKLEY and Mr. A. G. SQUIRE.
21st November	SUGAR MANUFACTURERS' ASSOCIATION.
	Mr. F. M. KERR-JARRETT, Mr. A. E. MUSCHETT, Mr. J. B. CUTHILL and Mr. D. J. VERITY.

Date of hearing. 1938.	
22nd November	GORE, J. F.
22nd November	HILL, H. C. N., M.C., Commissioner of the Turks and Caicos Islands.
22nd November	JAMAICA CHAMBER OF COMMERCE. Mr. N. A. POLACK, Mr. F. V. LUMB, Mr. C. DE CORDOVA, Mr. L. ASHENHEIM, Mr. L. MORDECAI and Mr. E R. HANNA.
24th November	ASSOCIATION OF ELECTED MEMBERS OF LEGISLATIVE COUNCIL. Mr. G. Seymour SEYMOUR, O.B.E., Mr. A. B. LOWE, Mr. C. A. REID, Mr. R. EHRENSTEIN and Mr. H. E. ALLAN.
28th November	BOOTH TRANSPORT LIMITED AND COMMUNITY TRANSPORT LIMITED. Mr. A. E. BOOTH, Mr. C. P. MCDONALD and Mr. G. B. O'BRIEN.
28th November	CHINESE RESIDENTS. Mr. A. CHANG, Mr. H. C. TIE TEN QUEE and Mr. A. TIE TEN QUEE.
28th November	INDEPENDENT DRY GOODS RETAILERS. Mr. P. HICKSON, MR. S. MAHFOOD, Mr. D. STEWART and Mr. S. SETTON.
29th November	KIRKWOOD, R. L. M., West Indies Sugar Company, Limited.
29th November	JAMAICA UNITED CLERKS' ASSOCIATION. Mr. E. E. A. CAMPBELL and Mr. E. A. RAE.
30th November	EX-BRITISH WEST INDIES REGIMENT. Mr. A. G. BURKLEY, Mr. R. E. SANG, Mr. C. D. JOHNSON, Mr. R. LENARD and Mr. C. N. GOULDBOURNE.
30th November	EAST INDIAN NATIONAL UNION. Mr. MERHAI, Mr. H. M. H. COX, Mr. E. RAOUT, Mr. P. J. ARMS, Mr. G. P. MARAGH, Mr. SOMAN JHANGAI and Mr. W. J. THOMPSON.
30th November	DILLON, Rev. J. T.

MONTEGO BAY.

2nd December	JAMAICA WORKERS' AND TRADESMEN'S UNION. Mr. A. G. S. COOMBS, Mr. R. G. MURRAY and Mr. S. E. BUCHANAN.
2nd December	DEPUTATION FROM LUCEA. Mr. W. M. DICKSON, Mr. O. L. RICKORD, Mr. W. BETHUNE, Mr. C. A. TOMLINSON and Mr. W. N. BYLES.

KINGSTON.

5th December	JAMAICA BANANA PRODUCERS' ASSOCIATION. Mr. C. E. JOHNSTON and Mr. R. F. WILLIAMS.
5th December	SMITH, F. E. V., Development and Marketing Officer.
5th December	BUILDERS' AND ALLIED TRADES UNION. Mr. C. S. MAXWELL and Mr. P. A. AIKEN.
6th December	AGRICULTURAL LOAN SOCIETIES BOARD. Mr. H. V. ALEXANDER, Mr. P. W. SANGSTER and Mr. E. L. JACK.
6th December	ELECTRICAL CONTRACTORS' ASSOCIATION. Mr. C. H. STEPHENS, Mr. P. A. AIKEN and Mr. H. A. STANTON.

British Honduras.

BELIZE.

Date of hearing. 1938.	
28th November	STEVENSON, N. S., Conservator of Forests.
28th November	WARD, J. F., Agricultural Officer; KITCHING, R. A., Assistant Agricultural Officer.
29th November	BROWN, E., Assistant Superintendent of Education.
29th November	CHEVERTON, Dr. R. L., Senior Medical Officer.
30th November	JOHNSTON, W., Colonial Secretary.
30th November	BETSON, C. E., Ex-Service Men's Association.
30th November	METHODIST CHURCH AND METHODIST MEN'S LEAGUE. Rev. W. J. SMITH, Mr. E. A. LAING and Rev. F. T. LOVELOCK.
1st December	BRITISH HONDURAS TEACHERS' ASSOCIATION. Mr. M. S. N. CAMPBELL, Miss I. USHER, M.B.E., and Miss E. ALEXANDER.
1st December	THE SCHOOL MANAGERS. Canon KNOX, Rev. R. CLEGHORN, O.B.E., Adjutant MUFFETT, Father KAMMERER, S.J., and Rev. W. J. SMITH.
1st December	CHURCH SECONDARY COLLEGES. The Most Rev. His Grace the LORD ARCHBISHOP OF THE WEST INDIES, Canon KNOX, Rev. M. O'CONNOR, S.J., and Rev. W. J. SMITH.

CAYO.

2nd December	CAYO PRODUCERS' ASSOCIATION. Mr. ENRIGHT and Mr. P. A. MIDDLETON.

BELIZE.

3rd December	AGRICULTURAL SOCIETY. Mr. F. R. DRAGTEN, O.B.E., K.C., Mr. H. GABB, Mr. P. GOLDSON, Mr. H. S. CARMICHAEL, Mr. R. A. LAING and Mr. C. W. VERNON.

STANN CREEK.

3rd December	STANN CREEK DISTRICT IMPROVEMENT ASSOCIATION. Mr. S. G. BERESFORD, Mr. W. A. J. BOWMAN, O.B.E., Mr. R. T. MEIGHAN and Mr. C. J. BENGUCHI.

BELIZE.

5th December	LABOUR AND UNEMPLOYED ASSOCIATION. Mr. A. SOBERANIS, Mr. W. CADLE and Mrs. E. TRAPP.
5th December	ADDERLEY, G. H., International African Service Bureau.
5th December	WORKING PEOPLE OF BELIZE. Mr. L. D. KEMP, Mr. M. STAINE, Mr. C. L. FAIRWEATHER, Mr. E. A. FRANKLIN, Mr. J. MIDDLETON and Mr. R. EDWARDS.
5th December	WOLFFSOHN, A.
6th December	MELHADO, B. A.
6th December	BALDERAMOS, A.

COROZAL.

7th December	COROZAL PRODUCERS' ASSOCIATION. Captain H. C. MILLIGAN.
7th December	ORANGE WALK ECONOMIC COMMITTEE. Rev. FAIRWEATHER.

Date of hearing. 1938.	
7th December	NORTHERN DISTRICT COMMITTEE. Mr. W. SCHOFIELD.
7th December	HEDMAN, W. A., and FORD, H.
7th December	CITIZENS COMMITTEE OF COROZAL. Mr. A. BARNETT and Mr. A. V. ROMERO.

BELIZE.

8th December	CITIZENS' COMMITTEE OF BELIZE. Mr. R. T. MEIGHAN, Mr. C. M. STAINE, Mr. H. H. CAIN, Mr. E. TAYLOR and Mrs. SEAY, M.B.E.
8th December	BELIZE ESTATE AND PRODUCE COMPANY. Mr. C. A. GIBBS AND Mr. FELIX.

Leeward Islands.

TORTOLA, BRITISH VIRGIN ISLANDS.

19th December	TEACHERS' ASSOCIATION OF THE BRITISH VIRGIN ISLANDS. Mr. N. HARRIGAN, Mr. O. FLAX and Mr. C. S. ELMES.
19th December	VIRGIN ISLANDS CIVIC LEAGUE. Mr. ABBOTT, Mr. O'NEILL and Mr. PENN.
19th December	OWEN, G. G.
19th December	WAILLING, Dr. D.P., Doctor Commissioner.

ANGUILLA.

20th December	REY, Carter ; OWEN, J. B. ; LAKE, G. E.
20th December	ANGUILLA TEACHERS' UNION. Mr. U. A. GUMBS, Mr. M. A. EDWARDS, Mr. G. R. A. WENHAM, Mr. P. E. ADAMS and Mr. H. V. RICHARDSON.

BASSETERRE, ST. KITTS.

21st December	SUGAR CANE INVESTIGATION COMMITTEE. Mr. J. R. YEARWOOD, Mr. C. M. DAVIS, Mr. W. A. WALWYN and Mr. B. B. DAVIS.
21st December	UNOFFICIAL MEMBERS OF THE LEGISLATIVE COUNCIL OF ST. CHRISTOPHER AND NEVIS. Mr. C. MALONE, Mr. B. B. DAVIS, Mr. G. P. BOON, Mr. T. MANCHESTER and Mr. A. E. OWEN.
22nd December	ST. KITTS CHAMBER OF COMMERCE. Mr. P. E. RYAN, Mr. P. CHALLENGER and Mr. SMITH.
22nd December	ST. KITTS WORKERS' LEAGUE. Mr. T. MANCHESTER, Mr. E. O. CHALLENGER, Mr. J. N. FRANCE and Mr. J. M. SEBASTIAN.
23rd December	ST. KITTS SERVICE LEAGUE. Miss V. HORSFORD, Rev. W. SUNTER and Miss A. E. BERRIDGE.
23rd December	THOMSON, Dr. J. W., Senior Medical Officer.
23rd December	MINISTERS OF RELIGION. The Ven. Archdeacon H. T. JULLION, Rev. E. M. HILLIER, Rev. W. SUNTER and Rev. W. M. WILLIAMS.

CHARLESTOWN, NEVIS.

27th December	NEVIS AGRICULTURAL AND COMMERCIAL SOCIETY. Mr. F. HENVILLE, Mr. W. B. DE GRASSE, M.B.E., Mr. J. E. C. CHADERTON, Mr. A. L. EVELYN, Mr. C. LAURENCE and Rev. R. W. BEAVEN.

Date of hearing.	
1938.	
27th December	NEVIS CANE GROWERS' CO-OPERATIVE ASSOCIATION, LIMITED.
	Mr. R. J. GORDON and Mr. S. M. TYSON.
27th December	NEVIS (CANE GARDEN) CO-OPERATIVE SUGAR FACTORY, LIMITED.
	Mr. T. M. W. DEANE.
27th December	COMMITTEE OF SUGAR CANE GROWERS OF GINGERLAND.
	Mr. J. BRAZIER and Mr. R. WILLIAMS.
28th December	AGRICULTURAL OFFICERS.
	Mr. R. E. KELSICK, Agricultural Superintendent, St. Kitts-Nevis, and Mr. W. I. HOWELL, Agricultural Instructor, Nevis.
28th December	NEVIS TEACHERS' ASSOCIATION.
	Mr. J. M. COLE, Mr. WILLIAMS, Mr. J. M. ST. C. CROSSE and Mr. E. R. WHITE.

ST. JOHN'S, ANTIGUA.

29th December	ANTIGUA AGRICULTURAL AND COMMERCIAL SOCIETY.
	Mr. R. S. D. GOODWIN, O.B.E., Mr. A. K. PETRIE-HAY, Mr. A. MOODY STUART, M.C., Mr. L. I. HENZELL, O.B.E., and Mr. F. S. H. WARNEFORD.
29th December	ANTIGUA TEACHERS' ASSOCIATION.
	Mr. J. H. CARROTT, Mr. HILL, Miss PIGOTT and Mr. AMBROSE.
30th December	MOODY STUART, A., M.C.
30th December	ANTIGUA MERCHANTS' ASSOCIATION.
	Mr. A. E. MERCER, Mr. PIGOTT, Mr. JEFFERY and Mr. CHRISTIAN.
30th December	THE RIGHT REV. THE LORD BISHOP OF ANTIGUA.
31st December	BARNES, W. S. G., District Officer.
31st December	WRIGHT, Dr. J. E., Senior Medical Officer; WYNTER, Dr. L. R.
31st December	THOMAS, I. W., Acting Treasurer.
1939.	
2nd January	GOVERNMENT MEDICAL OFFICERS.
	Dr. J. E. WRIGHT, Dr. L. R. WYNTER and Dr. J. P. O'MAHONY.
2nd January	PICCADILLY AND SOUTH EASTERN PEASANTS' ASSOCIATION.
	Mr. M. D. L. BENJAMIN and Mr. T. QUINLAND.
2nd January	POTTERS VILLAGE COMMITTEE.
	Mr. A. W. WILLIAMS.
2nd January	JAMES, J. E., M.B.E.; HARNEY, J. A.
2nd January	ANTIGUA COTTON GROWERS' ASSOCIATION.
	Mr. F. H. S. WARNEFORD, Mr. R. S. D. GOODWIN, O.B.E., Mr. F. J. GOODWIN, Captain SCOTT-JOHNSTON and Mr. A. K. PETRIE-HAY.

PLYMOUTH, MONTSERRAT.

3rd January	MONTSERRAT TAXPAYERS' ASSOCIATION.
	Mr. H. F. SHAND, Mr. A. H. ALLEN, Mr. J. H. A. MEADE, Mr. T. M. PETERS, Mr. J. C. L. WALL and Mr. J. H. JEFFERS.
3rd January	SHAND, H. F.
3rd January	WALL, J. C. L.
4th January	TEACHERS' ASSOCIATION.
	Mr. R. A. BARTON, Mr. F. E. PETERS, Mr. R. MASON and Mr. C. EDWARDS.

Date of hearing. 1939.	
4th January	DAVIES, Rev. T. E.; LAWRENCE, Rev. G. E.; MORRIS, Rev. A.
5th January	HOWES, H. R., O.B.E.; GRIFFIN, A. W.
5th January	WADE, Miss E.; MASON, Mrs. A.; DYETT, Mrs. F.; TUITT, Miss M.
5th January	KELSICK, O. R.; PETERS, T. M.; MEADE, C. H.; KELSICK, T. H.
5th January	ROCK, H. G.; OSBORNE, R. E. D.
5th January	MARGETSON, Dr. N. J. L., Senior Medical Officer; OGILVIE, Dr. D. C.

ROSEAU, DOMINICA.

6th January	UNOFFICIAL MEMBERS OF THE LEGISLATIVE COUNCIL OF DOMINICA. Mr. R. E. A. NICHOLLS, Mr. H. D. SHILLINGFORD, Mr. F. E. DEGAZON, Captain W. J. R. STEBBINGS, O.B.E., Mr. J. B. CHARLES, Mr. A. S. BURLEIGH, Mr. S. L. V. GREEN and Mr. P. A. ROLLE.
7th January	MARIGOT VILLAGE BOARD. Captain G. F. ASHPITEL, M.C.; Mr. W. S. STEVENS and Rev. L. T. BYRON.
7th January	NORTHERN DISTRICT PLANTERS. Captain W. J. R. STEBBINGS, O.B.E.; Captain G. F. ASHPITEL, M.C.; Mr. H. D. SHILLINGFORD; Mr. A. S. BURLEIGH.
7th January	ASHPITEL, Captain G. F., M.C.
7th January	FEDERAL LEGISLATIVE COUNCIL REPRESENTATIVES. Mr. R. E. A. NICHOLLS and Mr. H. D. SHILLINGFORD.
9th January	MERCHANTS, PLANTERS AND PEASANT PROPRIETORS OF DOMINICA. Mr. I. N. SHILLINGFORD, Mr. P. K. AGAR, Mr. L. A. PIVETEAU and Mr. T. G. ANDREWS.
9th January	PEASANT PROPRIETORS OF VIELLE CASE. Mr. L. E. JOHNSON and Mr. L. PATRICK.
9th January	DOMINICA BANANA ASSOCIATION. Mr. W. F. HARRISON and Mr. J. H. C. GRELL.
9th January	PEASANT PROPRIETORS OF ST. JOSEPH AND ST. PETER. Mr. R. A. ROSSI and Mr. E. E. WILLIAMS.
9th January	HENDERSON, J. C.
10th January	HAWEIS, S.
10th January	GRIFFIN, Dr. C. N., Senior Medical Officer, Dominica.
10th January	HARNEY, E. E., Treasurer, Dominica.
10th January	ASSISTANT CLERKS OF THE DOMINICA CIVIL SERVICE. Mr. L. A. PINARD, Mr. J. BULLY, Mr. O. ST. C. ALLEYNE and Mr. L. A. ROBERTS.
10th January	LABOUR DEPUTATION. Mr. R. E. A. NICHOLLS, Mr. M. RYAN, Mr. G. KNIBBS, Mr. A. DARTEN, Mr. T. GUISTE, Mr. C. LOBLACK and Mrs. T. RAYMOND.

PORTSMOUTH, DOMINICA.

12th January	DOMINICA PEASANT PROPRIETORS' UNION. Mr. A. A. BARON, Mr. E. A. CAINES, Mr. N. E. B. WATTY, Mr. T. M. BERTRAND and Mr. J. C. BERNEY.

Windward Islands.

CASTRIES, ST. LUCIA.

Date of hearing. 1938.	
19th December	PALMER, G. H. W., Labour Commissioner.
19th December	WRIGHT-NOOTH, R. G., M.C., Colonial Engineer.
19th December	UNOFFICIAL MEMBERS OF THE LEGISLATIVE COUNCIL. Mr. G. WILLIAMS, O.B.E., Mr. G. McG. PETER, O.B.E., Mr. H. G. M. DEVAUX, Mr. A. E. AUGUSTIN, Mr. G. H. GORDON and Mr. R. G. H. CLARKE.
19th December	PILGRIM, J. H.
20th December	WARD, E. T., Agricultural Superintendent.
20th Dceember	CASTRIES TOWN BOARD. Mr. G. H. W. PALMER, Mr. H. G. BELMAR, Mr. E. D. CADET, Mr. J. F. LE GRAND, Mr. G. S. E. GORDON, Mr. T. A. HOWELL, Mr. F. J. CARASCO and Mr. J. DEVAUX.
20th December	BYER, Rev. G. B., Acting Inspector of Schools.
20th December	YOUTH DELEGATION. Mr. A. M. LEWIS, Mr. J. H. BELIZAIRE, Mr. L. JAUNAI, Mr. E. G. EUDOXIE and Mr. F. G. YORKE.
22nd December	BRITISH MEDICAL ASSOCIATION, ST. LUCIA BRANCH. Dr. L. A. P. SLINGER and Dr. H. P. S. GILLETTE.
22nd December	WEATHERHEAD, Dr. H. D., Senior Medical Officer.
22nd December	LAMBERT, Major W., Chief of Police and Central Relieving Officer.
22nd December	NON-PARTY COMMITTEE. Mr. G. S. E. GORDON, Mr. J. H. PILGRIM, Mr. R. G. H. CLARKE, Mr. E. D. CADET, Mr. J. M. ARTHUR, Mr. J. R. CHARLES and Mr. F. J. CARASCO.
23rd December	FRITH, G. H., Colonial Treasurer.
23rd December	CHASE, L. A., General Manager of the Barbados Land Settlement, Vieuxfort.
23rd December	BEAUBRUN, C. A.

SOUFRIÈRE, ST. LUCIA.

27th December	PLANTERS AND PEASANT PROPRIETORS OF SOUFRIERE. Mr. H. E. BELMAR, Mr. G. H. GORDON, Mr. André DU BOULAY and Mr. C. JONGUE.

KINGSTOWN, ST. VINCENT.

29th December	WORKINGMEN CO-OPERATIVE ASSOCIATION. Mr. G. A. McINTOSH, Mr. J. L. CATO, Mr. St. C. F. BONADIE, Mr. H. A. DAVIS, Mr. A. C. ALLEN and Mr. P. STEPHENS.
29th December	AGRICULTURAL CREDIT AND LOAN BANK, LIMITED. Mr. R. T. SAMUEL, Mr. G. A. McINTOSH, Mr. St. C. F. BONADIE and Mr. R. BONADIE.
29th December	CLERGYMAN'S FELLOWSHIP. Rev. H. H. COLE, Rev. Father Dom Carlos VERBEKE, O.S.B., and Canon A. W. JOHNSON.
30th December	SPENCE, L. P., Colonial Treasurer.
30th December	KINGSTOWN TOWN BOARD. Mr. L. P. SPENCE, Mr. H. A. DAVIS, Mr. G. A. McINTOSH, Mr. St. C. F. BONADIE, Mr. A. G. HAZELL, Mr. R. T. SAMUEL, Mr. R. G. CROPPER and Mr. H. A. BONADIE.
30th December	CHAMBER OF AGRICULTURE AND COMMERCE. Mr. A. G. HAZELL, Mr. O. W. FORDE, Mr. S. DE FREITAS, Mr. F. CHILDS, Mr. St. C. McCONNIE and Mr. W. GRANT.

Date of hearing.
1939.

2nd January	CO-OPERATIVE ARROWROOT ASSOCIATION. Mr. C. B. ISAACS and Mr. W. HADLEY.
2nd January	FRASER, A. M., O.B.E.; PUNNETT, A. M.
2nd January	BARNARD, C. de B.
2nd January	BARNARD, C. de B.; HAZELL, A. G.
2nd January	ROBINSON, C. K., Agricultural Superintendent.
2nd January	HADLEY, W.
3rd January	TEACHERS' ASSOCIATION. Mr. C. W. FRASER, Mr. J. P. COMPTON, Mr. H. DAISLEY, Mr. J. L. EUSTACE, Miss L. HAYWOOD, Miss N. JOHN, Mr. W. H. LEWIS, Mr. S. F. PETERS and Mr. G. THOMAS.
3rd January	EDWARDS, G. E., Labour Commissioner.
3rd January	GRIST, Major H. G., Chief of Police and Chief Relieving Officer.
4th January	HENDERSON, Dr. J. A., Senior Medical Officer.
4th January	PALMER, A. C. G., Inspector of Schools.

BEQUIA.

5th January	MACMILLAN, Dr. K. J. E., Medical District Officer, MITCHELL, C. M., Town Warden, McINTOSH, C. D., FARRELL, E., and others.

ST. GEORGE'S, GRENADA.

6th January	AGRICULTURAL ASSOCIATION. Sir Joseph DE LA MOTHE, Mr. W. Parry OKEDEN, Mr. W. C. DE GALE, Mr. R. RAPIER and Mr. C. A. O. PHILLIPS.
6th January	CHAMBER OF COMMERCE. Mr. G. S. W. SMITH, Mr. E. P. MCCARTNEY, Mr. S. SMITH, Mr. O. M. BAIN, Mr. E. Earle HUGHES, Mr. E. D. B. THOMAS, Mr. Ira BAIN and Mr. P. G. HOSTEN.
7th January	LANG, D., Labour and Land Settlement Officer.
7th January	GRENADA TRADES UNION. Mr. E. Maresse DONOVAN and Mr. G. B. W. OTWAY.
9th January	BOWRING, Rev. Father A. W.
9th January	PEASANTS' IMPROVEMENT ASSOCIATION. Mr. R. RAPIER, Mr. C. S. L. PITT, Mr. D. A. McDONALD and Mr. W. HUMPHREY.
9th January	RENWICK, J. B.
10th January	HEAPE, W. L., Colonial Secretary; BEAUBRUN, I. C., O.B.E., Colonial Treasurer; LANG, D., Labour and Land Settlement Officer; DONOVAN, W. O'Brien, Agricultural Superintendent.
11th January	BRITISH MEDICAL ASSOCIATION, GRENADA BRANCH. Dr. L. S. Morgan.
11th January	COCHRANE, Dr. E., Senior Medical Officer.
11th January	UNION OF TEACHERS. Mr. W. H. JACOBS, Mr. C. S. L. PITT, Mrs. W. H. JACOBS and Mr. S. H. GRAHAM.
11th January	UNOFFICIAL MEMBERS OF THE LEGISLATIVE COUNCIL OF GRENADA. Mr. J. E. MUNRO, O.B.E., Mr. F. B. PATERSON, Mr. C. F. P. RENWICK, O.B.E., Mr. T. E. N. SMITH, Mr. T. A. MARRYSHOW, Mr. J. F. FLEMING, Mr. H. F. PANTIN, Mr. G. A. REDHEAD, Mr. J. B. RENWICK and Mr. A. E. WILLIAMSON.
11th January	PILGRIM, H. H., Inspector of Schools.

Date of hearing.	
1939.	CARRIACOU.
12th January	PATERSON, F. B.; GEORGE, W. E.; HAYDOCK, Mr.; SIMMONDS, F. A., Agricultural Officer; THOMPSON, Father; SYLVESTER, Mr.; ALVES, R.; JOSEPH, N.
	UNION.
12th January	MACMILLAN, Dr. K. J. E. and others.
	ST. GEORGE'S, GRENADA.
13th January	THE AGRICULTURAL BOARD AND THE AGRICULTURAL ASSOCIATION JOINT COMMITTEE ON THE COCOA INDUSTRY. Mr. C. F. P. RENWICK, O.B.E.
13th January	STREAT, A.
13th January	ALEXIS, R. L. B.
13th January	DISTRICT BOARDS' JOINT COMMITTEE. Mr. J. H. V. REDHEAD, Mr. C. S. L. PITT, Mr. R. J. L. PITT, Mr. J. R. PHILLIP and Mr. D. M. B. CROMWELL.

Barbados.

BRIDGETOWN.

17th January	COMMITTEE OF CLERGY. The Right Rev. D. W. BENTLEY, C.B.E., The Lord Bishop of BARBADOS, Rev. W. A. BECKLES, Rev. E. S. M. PILGRIM, Rev. T. E. NEWLIN, Rev. W. M. WORRELL, Rev. A. B. HUTTON, Rev. A. C. PILGRIM and Major O. D. DADD.
17th January	PEEBLES, Major H. W., C.M.G., D.S.O., O.B.E.
17th January	COMMUNICATIONS AND TRANSPORT AUTHORITIES (including representatives of the Central Road Board and the Parochial Authorities). Mr. G. F. SHARP, Colonial Postmaster, Commander W. R. M. WYNNE, R.N. (Retd.), Harbour and Shipping Master, Mr. W. U. GOODING, Mr. S. C. C. GREENIDGE, Mr. J. A. HAYNES, Mr. J. H. WILKINSON, Mr. L. T. YEARWOOD, M.B.E., Mr. G. B. EVELYN, Dr. T. A. HERBERT and Mr. J. J. SEAL.
18th January	ALLEYNE, Dr. J. D., M.B.E., Chief Medical Officer; GRANNUM, Dr. F. N., Sanitation Officer.
18th January	HUTSON, Dr. J., O.B.E., V.D.
18th January	BAYLEY, Dr. H. H.
18th January	BRITISH MEDICAL ASSOCIATION, BARBADOS BRANCH. Dr. H. G. MASSIAH, Dr. H. E. SKEETE and Dr. A. P. MUIR.
19th January	SAINT, Dr. S. J., Director of Agriculture; McINTOSH, Dr. A. E. S., Assistant Director of Agriculture; PHILLIPS, Mr. T. O., Agricultural Instructor; WYNNE, Commander W. R. M., R.N. (Retd.), Harbour and Shipping Master.
20th January	SUGAR PRODUCERS' ASSOCIATION. Mr. G. D. L. PILE, Mr. J. D. CHANDLER, Mr. H. A. CUKE, Mr. G. C. MAHON, Mr. H. C. WATSON and Mr. D. G. LEACOCK.

Date of hearing. 1939.	
21st January	BENTLEY, The Right Rev. D. W., C.B.E., The Lord Bishop of Barbados, President of the Education Board; MAHON, M. T. G., Secretary, Education Board; GREENHALGH, N., Inspector of Schools.
23rd January	SOCIAL WELFARE WORKERS. Mr. E. K. WALCOTT, K.C., Attorney General, Mrs. BENTLEY, Mrs. A. J. HANSCHELL, M.B.E., Mr. A. D. V. CHASE, Mrs. BALLOU and Captain A. G. KINCH.
24th January	BARBADOS PROGRESSIVE LEAGUE. Mr. C. A. BRAITHWAITE, Mr. G. H. ADAMS, Dr. H. G. CUMMINS and Mr. W. H. SEALE.
25th January	FLINN, W. H., O.B.E., Colonial Secretary; GITTENS, D. E. W., Colonial Treasurer; JEMMOTT, H. S., Acting Auditor General; REED, C. A., O.B.E., V.D., Comptroller of Customs; WYNNE, Commander W. R. M., R.N. (Retd.), Harbour and Shipping Master; STOUTE, C. E., Manager, Government Savings Bank; CLAIRMONTE, F. A. C., Income Tax Commissioner; LEWIS, M. C., Officer-in-Charge, Employment Agency; CHASE, A. D. V.
26th January	YEARWOOD, L. T., M.B.E., Member of St. Michael's Vestry; THORNE, E. E. H., O.B.E., Chairman, Sanitary Commissioners and Highway Commissioners; BANCROFT, Dr. A. G., Parochial Medical Officer of St. Michael.
27th January	ELEMENTARY TEACHERS' ASSOCIATION. Mr. C. F. BROOME, Mr. T. A. D. CLARKE, Mr. R. TAYLOR, Mr. C. B. JACKMAN, Mr. L. B. WAITHE and Mr. A. G. JORDAN.
27th January	GREENHALGH, N., Inspector of Schools.
31st January	DAIRYING INDUSTRY. Mr. R. C. MURPHY, Mr. E. Carlton HILL, Mr. L. DAVIS and Dr. C. P. STOUTE.
31st January	EX-SERVICE MEN. Mr. H. WORRELL, Mr. D. BARROW, Mr. J. GARNER, Mr. W. GRANT and Mr. D. TROTMAN.
31st January	CRAWFORD, W. A.
1st February	TRADE UNIONS. Mr. V. BARKER, Mr. S. SKINNER, Mr. A. GIFFORD, Mr. R. CLARKE, Mr. R. HAREWOOD, Mr. E. HURDLE, Mr. M. E. COX and Mr. R. WHITE.
1st February	VAUGHAN, H. A.; GITTENS, A. G.; BRANCKER, J. E. T.; SEBRO, L.; PERKINS, W. I.
1st February	LEE-WARD WORKERS' ASSOCIATION. Mr. C. Van Roland EDWARDS.

British Guiana.

GEORGETOWN.

30th January	RELIGIOUS BODIES. The Right Rev. A. J. KNIGHT, The Lord Bishop of Guiana, Major AUSTEN, Rev. DINGWALL, Father MORRISON, Rev. W. H. BRYANT, Rev. E. GRIFFIN, Rev. R. MACKINNON, Rev. G. H. NICOL and Rev. J. DUNN.
30th January	DELEGATES TO THE INTER-COLONIAL CONFERENCE OF WOMEN SOCIAL WORKERS. Miss M. T. MANSFIELD and Miss G. L. WOOD.

Date of hearing.
1939.

31st January	CRANE, A. V.
31st January	CHRISTIANI, H. P., M.B.E., Commissioner of Lands and Mines and Protector of Aboriginal Indians; The Right Rev. A. J. KNIGHT, The Lord Bishop of Guiana.
31st January	SEYMOUR, S. H.
1st February	EX-SERVICE MEN'S ASSOCIATION OF BRITISH GUIANA. Mr. J. JACK, Mr. A. R. DAVIS, Mr. J. A. THOMPSON and Mr. C. H. BERRIDGE.
1st February	BRITISH GUIANA RETURNED EX-SOLDIERS' ASSOCIATION. Mr. C. H. CYRUS and Mr. C. BERNARD.
1st February	CANAL NO. 1 FARMERS' ASSOCIATION, LIMITED. Mr. Hira LALL, Mr. JAIKARANSINGH and Mr. Harri PERSAUD.
1st February	CANAL NO. 2 FARMERS' ASSOCIATION, LIMITED. Mr. N. R. LAM, Mr. C. MAGGA, Mr. M. YUSSUF and Mr. A. KARIM.
1st February	NO. 1 UNITED FARMERS' ASSOCIATION. Mr. S. EASTMAN and Mr. S. ANDERSON.
1st February	EVAN WONG, R. V.
2nd February	DASH, Professor J. S., Director of Agriculture.
2nd February	EAST COAST CANE FARMERS' CENTRAL COMMITTEE. Mr. J. R. STRAUGHN, Mr. D. A. BACCHUS, Mr. G. G. SEMPLE and Mr. J. E. WILLS.
6th February	BOARD OF COMMISSIONERS OF THE TRANSPORT AND HARBOURS DEPARTMENT. Mr. G. D. OWEN, C.M.G., Colonial Secretary, Mr. J. GONSALVES, O.B.E., Mr. P. C. WIGHT, O.B.E., Mr. W. A. D'ANDRADE, Mr. E. G. WOOLFORD, K.C., Mr. H. G. SEAFORD, O.B.E., Mr. R. V. EVAN WONG, Mr. A. MACDOUGALL and Mr. H. V. ABRAHAM.
6th February	MCDAVID, E. F., M.B.E., Colonial Treasurer; D'ANDRADE, W. A., Comptroller of Customs; CROAL, G. H., Clerk to the Comptroller.
6th February	CHAMBER OF COMMERCE OF GEORGETOWN. Mr. H. G. SEAFORD, O.B.E., Mr. T. R. COWELL, Mr. H. CHATTERTON, Mr. G. H. SMELLIE, Mr. J. I. DE AGUIAR, Mr. R. G. HUMPHREY, Mr. F. H. MARTIN-SPERRY, Mr. H. B. GAJRAJ, Mr. E. M. WALCOTT and Mr. W. S. JONES.
6th February	JORGE, J.
7th February	BRITISH GUIANA TEACHERS' ASSOCIATION. Mr. G. H. A. BUNYAN, Mr. H. D. DURANT, Mr. E. F. ARCHER, Mr. F. H. POLLARD, Miss I. WILSON, Mr. H. S. JACKSON and Mr. R. N. A. WALLACE.
7th February	UNIVERSITY OF LONDON ASSOCIATION OF BRITISH GUIANA. Captain H. NOBBS and Mr. G. P. DARTFORD.
7th February	NEGRO PROGRESS CONVENTION. Rev. A. E. DYETT, Dr. T. T. NICHOLS, Mr. S. D. MORRISON and Mr. W. G. HOLDER.
7th February	CREASE, L. G., Director of Education.
8th February	SOCIETY FOR THE PREVENTION AND TREATMENT OF TUBERCULOSIS. Mr. J. GONSALVES, O.B.E., Mrs. BAYLEY, Dr. MILLER and Mr. V. C. JOHNSON.
8th February	BRITISH MEDICAL ASSOCIATION, BRITISH GUIANA BRANCH. Dr. Q. B. DE FREITAS, M.B E., Dr. R. T. BAYLEY and Dr. O. M. FRANCIS.

Date of hearing.
1939.

8th February	TOWN COUNCIL OF GEORGETOWN. His Worship the Mayor, Mr. P. C. WIGHT, O.B.E., Mr. J. GONSALVES, O.B.E., Mr. C. V. WIGHT, Mr. R. E. BRASSINGTON, Mr. H. G. SEAFORD, O.B.E., Mr. M. P. CAMACHO, Mr. A. A. THORNE, Mr. J. L. WILLS, Mr H. B. GAJRAJ, Mr. C. SHANKLAND, Mr. A. E. PESTANO, Mr. G. RODDAM, Mr. G. D. BAYLEY, C.B.E., Mr. W. DE RYCK and Mr. M. RATTRAY.
8th February	MACLELLAN, Dr. N. M., Director of Medical Services; SNEATH, Dr. P. A. T.; ROSE, Dr.; FRANCIS, Dr. O. M.; GRIERSON, Dr. J. D.
9th February	BRITISH GUIANA SUGAR PRODUCERS' ASSOCIATION. Mr. F. J. SEAFORD, O.B.E., Lt.-Col. Ivan DAVSON, O.B.E., T.D., Dr. G. GIGLIOLI, Mr. G. M. ECCLES, Mr. W. H. RICHARDS, Mr. R. R. FOLLETT-SMITH and Mr. T. H. NAYLOR.
9th February	WOOD, B. R., Conservator of Forests.
10th February	VILLAGE CHAIRMEN'S CONFERENCE, WEST DEMERARA CHAIRMEN'S UNION AND UNIONS OF LOCAL AUTHORITIES OF EAST DEMERARA AND WEST BERBICE. Mr. R. P. CARRYL, Mr. T. P. JAUNDOO, Mr. T. T. THOMPSON, Mr. O. S. MCGARRELL, Mr. J. R. STRAUGHN, Mr. E. A. BORMAN, Mr. H. L. PALMER, Mr. B. N. RUSSELL and Mr. J. W. JACKSON.
10th February	BRITISH GUIANA DENTAL ASSOCIATION. Mr. H. WHYTE CAMERON, Mr. J. H. BRADFORD, Mr. J. C. FOX and Mr. E. E. WRAY.
10th February	EAST COAST DEMERARA COCONUT GROWERS' AND CRUDE OIL MANUFACTURERS' ASSOCIATION. Mr. J. L. GRIFFITH, Mr. D. A. BACCHUS, Mr. O. S. MCGARRELL, Mr. G. BRISTOL, Mr. A. FERNANDES, Mr. A. N. G. RAMOTAR and Mr. J. P. DUBLIN.
10th February	BOOKHAM, M., M.B.E., Superintendent of Prisons.

NEW AMSTERDAM.

11th February	TOWN COUNCIL OF NEW AMSTERDAM. His Worship the Mayor, Mr. J. ELEAZAR, Mr. BROUGHTON, Mr. LUCKHOO, Mr. ROHLEHR, Mr. FARRAR, Mr. CHAPMAN, Mr. FERREIRA and Mr. BRISTOL.
11th February	BERBICE CHAMBER OF COMMERCE. Mr. C. FARRAR, Mr. ELEAZAR, Mr. T. W. COOPER, Mr. FERREIRA, Mr. ROSS, Mr. BROUGHTON, Mr. LUCKHOO, Rev. A. E. DYETT and Mr. RODRIGUEZ.
11th February	YOUTH MOVEMENT OF BERBICE. Mr. R. NELSON, Mr. W. O. R. KENDALL, Mr. TAYLOR, Mr. LANCASTER, Mr. PATERSON, Mr. CODDETT, Mr. MORIAH, Mr. THOMPSON, Mr. RAWLINS and Mr. BENNETT.

GEORGETOWN.

13th February	EAST INDIAN ASSOCIATION.* Mr. C. R. JACOB, Mr. J. RAMLOGAN, Mr. M. M. BERAMSINGH, Dr. J. BISSESSAR, Mr. F. KAWALL, Mr. D. P. DEBIDIN and Mr. SEECHARAN.

---

* Mr. J. D. TYSON, C.B.E., I.C.S., Government of India Observer, accompanied the East Indian delegations.

Date of hearing. 1939.	
13th February	BOODHOO, Mr.
13th February	THE MAHA SABHA.* Pundit LALMAN and Mr. Parsram TARACHAND.
13th February	GAJRAJ, H. B.; RAYMAN, Abdool; MCDOOM, C. A.; LUCKHOO, J. A., K.C.; ADAMS, E. A.; RAMPHAL, J.; and GAJRAJ, R. B.*
13th February	ISLAMIC ASSOCIATION.* Mr. C. A. MCDOOM, Mr. Abdool RAYMAN and Mr. Kamideem ALI.
14th February	SUBORDINATE GOVERNMENT EMPLOYEES' ASSOCIATION. Mr. J. H. ADAMS and Mr. E. F. PONTON.
14th February	BRITISH GUIANA POST OFFICE WORKERS' UNION. Mr. A. L. JACKSON and Mr. G. E. DAVSON.
14th February	BRITISH GUIANA SEAMEN'S UNION. Mr. C. W. MCKENZIE and Mr. J. W. DANIELS.
14th February	TRANSPORT WORKERS' UNION OF BRITISH GUIANA. Mr. F. O. VAN SERTIMA and Mr. D. M. HARPER.
14th February	SUBORDINATE MEDICAL EMPLOYERS' UNION. Mr. W. MATTHEWS, Mr. COLLINS, Mr. A. A. THORNE and Nurse M. GREENIDGE.
14th February	BRITISH GUIANA CIVIL SERVICE ASSOCIATION. Mr. P. W. KING, Mr. J. A. M. OSBORN, Mr. C. W. B. DEANE, Mr. H. V. ABRAHAM and Mr. E. G. D. HINDS.
14th February	GOVERNMENT DISPENSERS. Mr. G. I. MARSHALL, Mr. M. Z. KHAN and Mr. B. C. TROTMAN.
14th February	COLONIAL CO-OPERATIVE SOCIETY, LIMITED. Mr. S. N. COLLINS, Mr. S. MOORE, Mr. J. A. BARBOUR-JAMES, Mr. J. A. E. PATTERSON, Mr. S. F. COLLYMORE and Mr. C. W. SLEEPER.
15th February	BRITISH GUIANA WORKERS' LEAGUE. Miss Hildred BRITTON and Mr. A. A. THORNE.
15th February	BRITISH GUIANA LABOUR UNION. Mrs. J. HARRIS, Mr. H. CRITCHLOW, Mr. T. LEE, Mr. J. L. WILLS, Mr. J. L. GRIFFITH, Mr. E. L. BASCH and Mr. H. O. PROCTOR.
15th February	BRITISH GUIANA CONGRESS OF GENERAL WORKERS. Mr. C. C. GLEN, Mr. H. H. W. LAWRENCE, Mr. A. T. GIBSON and Mr. G. S. GAINER.
15th February	MAN-POWER CITIZENS' ASSOCIATION. Mr. A. M. EDUN, Mr. C. R. JACOB, Miss E. SEWDIN, Mr. J. N. LONDON, Mr. F. P. WOOLFORD, Mr. A. A. COLE, Mr. H. BARRON, Mr. E. PILE and Mr. B. B. CUMMINGS.
15th February	BRITISH GUIANA MINERS' ASSOCIATION. Mr. J. L. GRIFFITH, Mr. WESTMORLAND, Mr. C. P. LASHLEY, Mr. CLEMENT, Mr. SOLOMON, Mr. LAMPKIN, Mr. J. B. LASHLEY, Mr. PATTERSON and Mr. PILE.
16th February	ELECTED MEMBERS OF THE LEGISLATIVE COUNCIL. Mr. E. G. WOOLFORD, K.C., Mr. A. G. KING, Mr. P. C. WIGHT, O.B.E., Mr. E. A. LUCKHOO, O.B.E., Mr. F. J. SEAFORD, O.B.E., Mr. J. I. DE AGUIAR, Mr. H. C. HUMPHRYS, K.C., Mr. Peer BACCHUS, Mr. J. ELEAZAR, Mr. C. R. JACOB, Mr. T. LEE and Mr. C. V. WIGHT.

* Mr. J. D. TYSON, C.B.E., I.C.S., Government of India Observer, accompanied the East Indian delegations.

Date *of hearing*
1939.

16th February	LAING, M. B., Commissioner of Labour and Local Government.
17th February	McDAVID, E. F., M.B.E., Colonial Treasurer.

Trinidad.
PORT OF SPAIN.

22nd February	NICOLL, J. F., Acting Colonial Secretary; dos SANTOS, E. L., C.B.E., Treasurer; WORTLEY, E. J., C.M.G., O.B.E., Director of Agriculture; CUTTERIDGE, Captain J. O., M.B.E., Director of Education; TYLER SMITH, H. A., Director of Works and Transport; RANKINE, Dr. A., M.C., Director of Medical Services; LINDON, A. G. V., Industrial Adviser; WALKER, R. B., Town Planner.
23rd February	ASSOCIATION OF COCOA GROWERS OF TRINIDAD AND TOBAGO. Mr. J. de VERTEUIL, Mr. H. E. ROBINSON, Mr. D. MCBRIDE, Mrs. M. GORDON, Mr. CHINNIA, Mr BARTHOLOMEW, Mr. A. A. SOBRIAN and Mr. Sankar NANAN.
23rd February	COCOA PLANTERS' ASSOCIATION OF TRINIDAD LIMITED. Mr. J. de VERTEUIL, Mr. A. V. STOLLMEYER and Hon. J. FORBES.
24th February	TRINIDAD CHAMBER OF COMMERCE. Mr. S. H. BANNING, Sir George F. HUGGINS, O.B.E., Mr. J. FORBES, Mr. A. EMLYN, Mr. S. W. FITT, Mr. G. W. ROCHFORD, Mr. M. V. LLOYD, Mr. A. KERR, Mr. A. P. BLAIR and Mr. W. C. RENNIE.
24th February	PORT-OF-SPAIN CITY COUNCIL. Captain A. A. Cipriani, Mr. L. A. PUJADAS, Dr. T. P. ACHONG, Mr. T. H. SCOTT, O.B.E., Mr. H. W. FARRELL and Dr. R. MARCANO.
24th February	CHINESE COMMERCIAL ASSOCIATION. Mr. J. R. HING KING and Mr. A. TSOI.
25th February	NICOLL, J. F., Acting Colonial Secretary; CUTTERIDGE, Captain J. O., M.B.E., Inspector of Orphanages and Industrial Schools.
25th February	PUCKERING, M. A., Superintendent of Prisons; COSTELLOE, Captain M., O.B.E., Secretary, Central Poor Relief Board.
25th February	COTERIE OF SOCIAL WORKERS. Miss Audrey JEFFERS, M.B.E., Miss L. VICTOR, Mrs. B. GREIG, Miss V. NURSE, SISTER GERTRUDE JOHNSTON (representing the Carmelite Sisters), Mrs. V. M. METIVIER and Captain H. F. JONES (Church Army).
25th February	ANGLICAN COMMUNITY. The Right Rev. A. H. ANSTEY, The Lord Bishop of Trinidad and Tobago, Rev. J. D. RAMKEESSOON and Rev. M. E. FARQUHAR.
25th February	PRESBYTERIAN CHURCH. Rev. C. D. LALLA and Rev. Dr. H. F. KEMP.
25th February	PORT-OF-SPAIN MINISTERIAL ASSOCIATION. Rev. A. E. ADAMSON, Rev. W. H. MAYHEW and Rev. R. W. CHARLESWORTH.

Date of hearing. 1939.	
27th February	SUGAR MANUFACTURERS' ASSOCIATION. Captain W. F. WATSON, O.B.E., Mr. E. A. ROBINSON Mr. H. E. ROBINSON, Mr. J. Gordon MILLER, Mr. G. B. WESTWOOD, Mr. J. du BUISSON, Mr. C. S. BUSH, Mr. F. G. GRANT, Mr. J. REID, Mr. J. H. TAYLOR and Mr. L. H. PALMER.
27th February	SOUTH TRINIDAD CANE FARMERS' ASSOCIATION. Mr. G. C. WYATT, Mr. Ramsamooj PERSAD, Mr. C. T. BOWEN, Mr. J. Bridglal SINGH, Mr. Rampergas MARAJH, Mr. Brijbookan MARAJ, Mr. E. J. WORTLEY, C.M.G., O.B.E., (Director of Agriculture) and Mr. E. L. dos SANTOS, C.B.E. (Treasurer).
27th February	WORTLEY, E. J., C.M.G., O.B.E., Director of Agriculture.
28th February	PETROLEUM ASSOCIATION OF TRINIDAD. Mr. H. D. FLETCHER, Mr. F. E. HUNTER, Mr. H. V. LAVINGTON, Mr. F. L. MELVILL, Mr. D. Ian FARQUHARSON.
2nd March	ELECTED MEMBERS OF LEGISLATIVE COUNCIL. Captain A. A. CIPRIANI, Mr. Timothy ROODAL, Mr. M. Aldwin MAILLARD, Mr. E. Vernon WHARTON, Mr. George de NOBRIGA and Mr. A. C. RIENZI.
3rd March	JOINT DEPUTATION OF THE BRITISH WEST INDIES AND BRITISH GUIANA TEACHERS' ASSOCIATION, AND THE TRINIDAD AND TOBAGO TEACHERS' UNION. Mr. H. A. MACNISH, Mr. J. H. PARTAP, Miss L. VICTOR, Miss A. CARRINGTON, Mr. D. W. ROGERS, Mr. A. T. FRASER, Mr. P. AKAL, Mr. L. EDWARDS, Mr. F. A. CAESAR, Mr. W. H. DOLLY, Mr. E. QUINLAN, Mr. C. F. WORM, Mr. H. M. JOSEPH and Mr. F. A. PATRICK.
3rd March	CUTTERIDGE, Captain J. O., M.B.E., Director of Education.

TOBAGO.

4th March	TOBAGO CHAMBER OF COMMERCE. Mr. K. REID, Mr. W. SHAW, Lieutenant-Commander L. M. ROBINSON, R.N. (Retd.), Mr. L. H. SHORT, Mr. H. R. HAMILTON and Mr. BRINKLEY.
4th March	EDWARDS, Mr. Laurence.

PORT OF SPAIN.

6th March	TRINIDAD LAKE ASPHALT OPERATING COMPANY, LIMITED. Mr. C. L. VANDEBURGH and Mr. W. M. ROSS.
6th March	DOS SANTOS, E. L., C.B.E., Treasurer; MACKILLIGIN, R. S., O.B.E., M.C., Inspector of Mines.
6th March	HAMMOND, S. A., Senior Education Commissioner in the West Indies.
7th March	LINDON, A. G. V., Industrial Adviser.
7th March	CIVIL SERVICE ASSOCIATION. Mr. J. Lyon SMITH, Mr. E. M. PATIENCE, Mr. A. A. THOMPSON, Mr. N. McLEAN and Miss D. CARR.
7th March	SANITARY INSPECTORS' ASSOCIATION. Mr. G. A. ATHERTON, Mr. V. CHARLES, Mr. H. LUCAS, Mr. I. WILSON, Mr. WAITHIE, Mr. SAMPSON and Mr. C. F. CARRINGTON.
7th March	PORT-OF-SPAIN NURSES' AND MIDWIVES' ASSOCIATION. Mrs. I. WATERMAN, Nurse ROBINSON and Nurse MITCHELL.

Date of hearing. 1939.	
7th March	TRINIDAD AND TOBAGO NURSES' ASSOCIATION. Rev. V. B. WALLS, Mrs. WALLS, Mrs. GRANT and Nurse CRITCHLOW.
7th March	ATTENDANTS AND NURSES OF ST. ANN'S MENTAL HOSPITAL. Mr. E. WRIGHT, Mr. H. J. SANDY, Nurse E. HOLDER and Nurse M. CONNOR.
7th March	ORDE-BROWNE, Major G. St. J., O.B.E., Labour Adviser to the Secretary of State for the Colonies.
8th March	COCONUT GROWERS' ASSOCIATION, LIMITED. Mr. E. V. WHARTON and Mr. L. H. S. SCOTT.
8th March	AGRICULTURAL SOCIETY OF TRINIDAD AND TOBAGO. Mr. E. V. WHARTON, Mr. W. S. E. BARNADO, Mr. C. W. FLEMING, Mr. J. S. LOVELL, Mr. R. JOHNSTONE, Mr. H. E. ROBINSON, Mr. J. de VERTEUIL, Mr. R. WHARTON and Mr. T. I. POTTER, O.B.E.
9th March	TRINIDAD LABOUR PARTY. Captain A. A. CIPRIANI, Mr. V. HENRY, Mr. T. ROODAL, Mr. A. GOODING, and Mr. A. F. CHARLES.
9th March	GUIANESE AND WEST INDIES LABOUR CONGRESS. Captain A. A. CIPRIANI, Mr. A. GOODING, Mr. A. C. RIENZI and Mr. R. MENTOR.
9th March	COMMITTEE OF INDUSTRIAL ORGANIZATION. Mr. A. C. RIENZI, Mr. R. MENTOR, Mr. E R BLADES, Mr McDonald MOSES, Mr R JOSEPH, Mr. C. C. ABIDH, Mr. J. F. ROJAS, Mr. A. N. WARNER and Mr. F. D. ALLEN.
9th March	TRADES UNIONS. Mr. A. C. RIENZI. Mr. R. GITTENS and Mr. G. GRANGER (Public Works and Public Service Workers' Union). Mr. G. CRICHLOW and Mr. L. SIMPSON (Printers' Industrial Union). Mr. E. ALLEYNE and Mr. C. HARPER (Seamen and Waterfront Workers' Trade Union). Mr. D. DOWNES, Mr. A. F. ANDREWS and Mr. A. L. MOORE (Railway Workers' Trade Union). Mr. SMART and Mr. C. ATKINSON (Amalgamated Building and Woodworkers' Union). Mr. Q. O'CONNOR and Mr. H. DUPRES (Trinidad and Tobago Union of Shop Assistants and Clerks). Mr. E. M. MITCHELL, Mr. J. L. GILL and Mr. S. L. PATRICK (Federated Workers' Trade Union).
10th March	FAULKNER, O. T., C.M.G., Principal, Imperial College of Tropical Agriculture.

TOBAGO.

11th March	ROBINSON, Lieutenant-Commander L. M., R.N. (Retd.), Director of the Tobago Development Company.
11th March	TOBAGO BRANCH OF TRINIDAD LABOUR PARTY. Mr. A. F. CHARLES.

PORT-OF-SPAIN.

13th March	EAST INDIAN ADVISORY BOARD.* Mr. H. MEADEN, M.B.E., Mr. O. Gobardhan PANDIT, Mr. Syed Mohammed HOSEIN and Moulvi Ameer ALI.

---

* Mr. J. D. TYSON, C.B.E., I.C.S., Government of India Observer, accompanied the East Indian delegations.

Date of hearing. 1939.	
13th March	EAST INDIAN EVIDENCE COMMITTEE.* Mr. S. TEELUCKSINGH, Mr. R. B. RAMKEESOON, Barrister-at-Law, Mr. A. OGEERALLY, Pundit PIARILAL, Mr. C. J. PILLAI and Pundit Ganesh DUTT.
13th March	SANATANA DHARMA BOARD OF CONTROL.* Pundit D. TIWARI, Mr. C. H. BUDDHU, Mr. H. R. MEAH, Mr. A. HOSEIN, Mr. J. HARRACKSINGH.
14th March	BRITISH MEDICAL ASSOCIATION (TRINIDAD AND TOBAGO BRANCH). Dr. P. A. ROSTANT, Dr. K. U. INNISS, Dr. J. E. BOUCAUD, Dr. E. de VERTEUIL, Dr. C. G. DEANE, M.C., Dr. G. R. MARCANO, DR. G. CAMPBELL, Dr. L. E. MURRAY, Dr. J. R. DICKSON, O.B.E.
14th March	MEDICAL BOARD. Dr. A. H. McSHINE, O.B.E., Dr. S. M. LAURENCE and Dr. J. R. DICKSON, O.B.E.
14th March	Dr. V. M. METIVIER and Mrs. METIVIER, Dr. S. M. LAURENCE and Dr. M. A. FORRESTER.
15th March	ANGLO-WEST INDIES CHIROPRACTIC ASSOCIATION. Dr. G. FERREIRA, Dr. J. R. FERREIRA, Dr. J. LOVELL and Mrs. D. BUSHE.
15th March	RANKINE, Dr. A., M.C., Director of Medical Services.
16th March	BOARD OF INDUSTRIAL TRAINING. Mr. T. H. SCOTT, O.B.E., and Mr. I. M. HOPKINS.
16th March	FRIENDLY SOCIETIES. Mrs. J. GODDARD, Mr. F. GRAVES, Mr. E. C. POLLONAIS and Mr. J. DAVID.
16th March	TYSON, J.D., C.B.E., I.C.S., Government of India Observer.

London.

28th April	ASSOCIATED PORTLAND CEMENT MANUFACTURERS LIMITED. Mr. W. G. CHAPMAN and Mr. G. H. E. VIVIAN.
28th April	SCOTT, FARNELL & PARTNERS, Trinidad, Mr. R. G. W. FARNELL.
28th April	BANKS, M., Air Ministry.
4th May	TELEPHONE AND GENERAL TRUST, LIMITED, Sir Alexander ROGER.
4th May	CLAUSON, G. L. M., C.M.G., O.B.E., Assistant Secretary, Economic Department, Colonial Office.
4th May	CASE, G. O., Director of Public Works, British Guiana.
4th May	HARRISON LINE. Mr. T. Harrison HUGHES.
5th May	DAISH, T., M.C., General Post Office
5th May	WAKELY, C. H., Board of Inland Revenue.
5th May	KING, B. L.
11th May	GEORGE, H. H., Ministry of Health.
11th May	COLONIAL FOREST RESOURCES DEVELOPMENT DEPARTMENT. Major F. M. OLIPHANT and Major J. R. COSGROVE.
12th May	BRITISH MEDICAL ASSOCIATION. Dr. J. L. GILKS and Dr. G. C. ANDERSON.

* Mr. J. D. TYSON, C.B.E., I.C.S., Government of India Observer, accompanied the East Indian delegations.

Date of hearing. 1939.	
12th May	DAVIES, T. W., Economic Department, Colonial Office; WILLIS, J. R., M.C., Board of Trade.
25th May	BUILDING INDUSTRIES NATIONAL COUNCIL. Mr. H. J. C. JOHNSTON, Mr. George HICKS, M.P., and Mr. H. B. BRYANT.
25th May	COLONIAL EMPIRE MARKETING BOARD. Mr. H. C. H. BULL.
25th May	JAMAICA MARKETING ASSOCIATION. Mr. E. C. JOYSEY, Mr. O. H. KEELING and Mr. J. M. PRINGLE.
1st June	KROYER-KEILBERG, F. M.
1st June	HEDLEY, J., I.S.O., late General Post Office.
1st June	ROOK, W.
2nd June	PARKINSON, Sir Cosmo, K.C.B., K.C.M.G., O.B.E., Permanent Under-Secretary of State, Colonial Office; JEFFRIES, C. J., C.M.G., O.B.E., Assistant Secretary, Colonial Service Department, Colonial Office.
2nd June	BECKETT, H., Assistant Secretary, West Indian Department, Colonial Office.
8th June	BRITISH BROADCASTING CORPORATION. Mr. C. A. L. CLIFFE and Mr. J. C. S. MACGREGOR.

APPENDIX B.

INDIVIDUALS AND ASSOCIATIONS, OTHER THAN THOSE WHO GAVE ORAL EVIDENCE, FROM WHOM MEMORANDA WERE RECEIVED.

England.

Aitkenhead, Miss C. E.
Baptist Missionary Society.
Barbour-James, Mr. J. A.
Campbell, Mr. E. R.
Carter, Mr. H. C.
Deverell, Mr. F.
Grier, Sir Selwyn, K.C.M.G.
Hodgson, Mr. D. K.
Hyman, Mr. C. A. S.
Ind Coope and Allsopp Limited.
Jeffery, Mr. A. E.
Jonas Browne and Son Limited.
Leacock, Mr. D. G.
Lewis, Mr. W. A.
MacDonald, Mrs. H.
Malcolm, Major M.
Methodist Missionary Society.
Murad, Mr. L. L.
Nankivell, Mrs. F.
National Union of Teachers.
Pease, Mr. G. B.
Previté (Trinidad Lake Asphalt) Continental Limited.
Randall, Mr. R.
Rhys Pryce, Mr. M. A.
Roberts, Mr. A. H.
Stannard, Mr. H.
Tengely, Mr. P. L.
Thompson, Rev. E. W.
Trinidad Oil Companies' London Committee.
Universal Negro Improvement Association and African Communities' League, August, 1929.
Warner, Mr. R.
Willoughby, Miss E. M.

Jamaica.

Accompong Maroons.
Alberga, Mr. L. O.
Allan, Mr. H. E.
Allen, Mr. E. L.
Allen, Mr. E. V.
Anderson, Dr. O. E.
Armon Jones, Rev. E., and Gibson, Rev. F. W.
Association of Parochial Boards of Jamaica.
Bailey, Mr. M. G.
Baker, Mr. P. N.
Banana Industry Aid Board.
Bernard, Mr. V. C.
Bethel Town Citizens' Association.
Bethune, Mr. W.
Blake, Mr. M.
Board of Education.
Bowman, Mr. G. A. H.
Boyd, Mr. B. W.
Brissett, Mr. S. S.
Brown, Mr. J. A.
Brown, Mr. L.
Buchanan, Mr. D. T.
Burke, Mr. S. H.
Cadogan, Mr. A. R., and McMahon, Mr. M.
Campbell, Mr. C. L.
Cawley, Mr. L.
Caws, Major B. F.
Centenary Patriotic Association of Jamaica.
Chaitao, Mr. J. J.
Chapman, Miss E.
Cigar Makers' Committee.
Citizens' Association of Newport.
Citrus Company of Jamaica Limited.
Clark, Mr. E. V.
Coconut Products Limited.
Constable, Mr. I. S.
Content and Lincoln Citizens.
Custos of St. Catherine.
Dickin, Rev. H. D.
Dickson, Mr. W. M.
Dillon, Mr. S. J. S.
Dodds, Mr. J.
Dowden, Mr. A.
Duncan, Mr. R. A.
Durham, Mr. V.
Edwards, Rev. E. A.
Employees of the Locomotive Workshops and Sheds, Jamaica Government Railway.
Evans, Mr. E. R. D.
Evans, Mr. F. L. B.
Ex-Constables Relief Association.
Ex-West India Regiment Association.
Farquharson, Sir Arthur.

Farquharson, Miss M.
Federation of St. Mary Citizens' Associations.
Finzi, Mr. J. A.
Fishers Brotherhood Union.
Francis, Mr. E.
Francis, Mr. E. I. and others.
Franklin, Mr. E. F.
Gallimore, Mr. H. L.
Gardiner, Mr. E. A.
Gauntlett, Mr. H. G.
Goodin, Mr. B. T.
Gordon, Mr. G. S. and others.
Graham, Rev. W. I.
Griffith, Mr. H. W.
Gunter, Mr. G. G.
Hamilton, Mr. B. C. S.
Harris, Mr. J.
Harvey, Mrs. A. M.
Heath, Mr. D. G.
Hodelin, Mr. B. L.
Institute of Jamaica.
Jacobs Commercial and Shipping Agency Limited.
Jamaica Apiarists Limited.
Jamaica Artisans' Federated Union.
Jamaica Association of Sanitary Inspectors.
Jamaica Canning Company Limited.
Jamaica Cordage Company Limited.
Jamaica Ex-Service Men's Labour Union.
Jamaica General Contractors' and Builders' Association.
Jamaica Independent Schools Association.
Jamaica Industrial Institute.
Jamaica Mental Hospital Sub-Staff.
Jamaica Progressive League of New York.
Jamaica Society for the Prevention of Cruelty to Animals.
Jamaica Utilities Limited and the Magnet Omnibus Company Limited.
Kavanagh, Mr. L. W.
Kennedy, Mr. A. W.
Kingston and St. Andrew Corporation.
Kingston and St. Andrew Federation of Citizens' Association.
Lewis, Mr. B. A.
Lindo, Mr. H. V.
Little, Mr. C. A.
Llewellyn, Mr. J. V.
Lockett, Mr. J.

Loutan, Mr. R.
Lowe, Mr. A. B.
Lower St. Andrews Citizens' Association.
Lynch, Mr. H. W.
Lyons, Mr. C. M.
MacDonald, Mr. D.
Malcolm, Mr. S.
McDaniel, Mr. T. P. V.
McLarty, Rev. R. W.
McLaughlin, Rev. E. E.
Melbourne, Mr. E. L.
Mendes, Mr. A. A.
Monteith, Mr. E. B.
Morris, Mr. E.
Native Industries Protection Committee.
Ocho Rios Citizens' Association.
Papine and Adjacent Districts Citizens' Association.
Parker, Mr. N. A.
Parkin, Mr. A. W.
Parrolds, Miss M.
Past Students of Stony Hill Industrial School.
Pilotage Service.
Police Delegation Committee.
Presbyterian Church of Jamaica.
Pryce, Mr. E. E.
Ramsay, Mr. J. and others.
Randall, Mr. C. E.
Reid, Mr. N. and others. (Public Works Department Asphalting Gang.)
Retired Teachers. (Mr. C. L. Forrest and others.)
Richards, Miss M.
Richards, Mr. R. W. V.
Robinson, Mr. R. C.
Rowe, Mr. G.
Rushie Grey, Mr. G. O.
Russell, Mr. J. A.
Rutty, Mr. F. S.
Samuel, Miss C.
Sangster, Mr. D. B.
Sherlock, Mr. P. M.
Small Farmers of Northern St. Elizabeth.
Smith, Mr. E. A.
Smith, Mr. E. E.
Smith, Mr. J. H. and others.
Smith Village Citizens' and Industrial Association.
Social Reconstruction League.
Soulette, Mr. J. A.
Southern St. Mary's Citizens' Association.
Spencer, Mr. J. B.

St. Ann's Bay, Lime Hall and Bamboo Citizens' Association.
St. George's Citizens' Association.
Supernumerary Outdoor Officers of H.M. Customs.
Surveyors' Association of Jamaica.
Thomas, Mr. A. A.
Thomas, Mr. J.
Tyler, Mr. W. F.
Upper Clarendon Parish Tenants.
Vernon, Mr. S. H.
Wainwright, Mr. C. G.
Westend Cane Farmers' Association.
White, Mr. A.
Williams, Mr. J. D.
Williams, Mr. R. F.
Wood, Mr. W. H.
Wortley, Mr. G. W.
Wright, Mr. W. and others.
Young, Mr. S. N.

British Honduras.

Arnold, Mr. W. H.
Black Cross Nurses Unit.
Bomb-Boat Engineers.
Bowen, Mr. E. W. M. and Nord, Mr. G. N. R.
British Honduras Citrus Association Limited.
Butchers and Traders.
Church Secondary Colleges.
Felix, Mr. A. N.
Felix, Mr. R. L.
Foote, Mr. R. E.
Francis, Mr. G. W. E.
Gillett, Mr. S. McL.
Grand Order of Free Labourers.
Jex, Mr. A. W.
Locke, Mr. C. H.
Martini, Mr. H.
Minty, Mr. J. R.
Native Shop-Keepers.
Newell, Rev. J. T.
Richardson, Mr. L.
Saldana, Mr. S. H.
Salt Creek Settlers.
Smith, Mr. C. L.
Stann Creek Caribs.
Turton, Mr. R. S.

Leeward Islands.

Brown, Mr. S. and others, Antigua.
Davis, Mr. W. R., St. Kitts.
James, Mr. O. V., Dominica.
Jullion, Mr. S. E. T. (Headmaster of Dominica Grammar School.)
Maynard, Mr. C. E., Nevis.
Maynard, Mr. G. E., Nevis.
Mutual Improvement Society, St. Kitts.
Nicholas, Mr. J., Antigua.
Peasants of Coulibistre, Dominica.
Stewart-Boyd, Mr. J. A., Dominica.
Wilson, Mr. H. F., Antigua.

Windward Islands.

Alves, Mr. J., and others, Petit Martinique.
Artisans of Georgetown, St. Vincent.
Caesar, Mr. J. V., and others, Union Island.
Child, Mr. F., St. Vincent.
de Bique, Mr. A. C., St. Vincent.
Employers' and Employees' Association, St. Vincent.
Ex-Service Men of British West Indies Regiment in St. Vincent.
Frew, Mr. J., St. Lucia.
General Welfare Committee, St. Vincent.
Harris, Mr. C. H., Grenada.
Harris, Mr. T. A. G., St. Lucia.
Inhabitants of Byera Village, St. Vincent.
Jack, Mr. S. O., St. Vincent.
James, Mr. B. R., St. Vincent.
Jasper, Mr. S., Grenada.
Logie, Mr. P. G., Grenada.
MacDonald, Mr. T. M., St. Vincent.
Moffett, Mr. A. J., St. Vincent.
St. Paul's Citizens' Association, Grenada.
Shaw, Venerable Archdeacon T., Grenada.
Slinger, Mr. D. M., Grenada.
Superioress, St. Joseph's Convent, Castries, St. Lucia.
Unofficial Members of Executive Council, St. Vincent.

Barbados.

Archer Mackenzie, Mr. R.
Barbados Co-operative Cotton Factory Limited.
Cox, Mr. M. E.
Godson, Rev. F.
Grant, Mr. O. McD.
Hutchinson, Mr. H. G.
King, Mrs. M.
Lovell, Mr. I.
Scott, Mr. D'A.
Sealy, Mr. J.
Thorpe, Mr. D. D. M.
Wippell, Rev. J. C. (Rawle Training Institute.)
Young Men's Progressive Club.

British Guiana.

Adams, Mr. J. A. and Boody, Mr. B. E.
Adman, Mr. H. and others.
Afro-American Association and League of Coloured Races.
Ajit, Mr. C.
Beterverwagting and Triumph Farmers' Union.
Bishop, Mr. J. E.
Bishopp, Mr. D. W.
British Guiana Chemists' and Druggists' Association.
British Guiana Militia Board.
British Guiana Sicknurses' and Dispensers' Association.
British Guiana West Indian Federation.
British Guiana Farmers' Federation.
Chan-A-Shing, Mr. S. B.
Chinese Association of British Guiana.
Croal, Mr. J. P.
Cummings, Mr. F. A.
Dyer, Mr. J. McF. and Patterson, Mr. J. H. E.
East Indian Intelligentsia.
Evelyn-Moe, Mr. L.
Ex-Members of the British Guiana Police Force.
Forbes, Mr. R.
Gomes, Mr. C.
Griffith, Mr. D. and others.
Harewood, Mr. H. R.
Inhabitants of Western Berbice.
Inhabitants of certain areas of East Coast, Demerara.
Jones, Mr. S.
Kampta, Mr. C. B.
La Grange Village Council.
Lucas, Mr. O. A.
Luther, Mr. S. M.
Mahraj, Mr. D.
Mansfield, Mr. E.
McLean Ogle, Mr. A.
Ministerial Fraternal of Berbice.
Narayan, Mr. S.
Osborne, Mrs. L.
Patients of the Leprosy Hospital, Mahaica.
Pestano, Mr. A. and de Freitas, Mr. J.
Pollydore, Mr. P. N.
Presbytery of the Church of Scotland, British Guiana.
Sadiq, Mr. M.
Semple, Mr. E. A.
Shankland, Mr. C.
Smith, Mr. C. N. and Klein, Mr. J. N. (Church Wayside Army Inc. etc.)
Ting-A-Kee, Mr. B. P. A.
United Domestic Servants Improvement Association.
Village Overseers of British Guiana.

Trinidad.

Achong, Dr. T. P.
Aide, Mr. A. R.
Armoogum, Mr. J. A.
Baddeley, Mr. A. W.
Basso, Mr. L. J. (Old Tenants of Trinidad Co-operative Bank Lands.)
Belgrave, Mr. J.
Calder-Marshall, Mr. A.
Clement, Mr. J. and others. (Plum Mitan, Mitan and Biche.)
Coronation Omnibus Association.
Courtland Estates (Coconuts) Limited, Tobago.
Cumana Improvement Association, Toco Unity and others.
Cuthbert, Mr. A. A.
Diego Martin Ward Ratepayers' Association.

Donawa, Mr. A. H.
Doyle, Mr. H.
Garcia, Mr. R.
Gordon Plantations Limited.
Henderson, Mr. A. S.
Hinds-Howell, Lt. Col., G.Ll.
Hovell, Mr. C. E.
Hudson, Mr. F. W.
Jawahir, Mr. E.
Laventille, San Juan and Santa Cruz Residents.
Melizan, Mr. H.
Naturopathic Association of the British West Indies.
New Reform Committee.
Parents' Union of Trinidad and Tobago.
People's Royal Commission Evidence Committee.
Sam, Mr. G. W. and others.
Samuel, Mr. G. F.
Singh, Mr. H. P.
Sladden, Mr. P. S.
Solis, Mr. F.
St. Patrick Indian Producers' Committee.
Student-Druggists.
Supersad, Mr. S. S.
Tayman, Mr. W.
" The West Indian Pilot."
Trinidad Cane Farmers' Association.
Trinidad Landowners' Association.
United Traders' Association.
Watch Tower Bible and Tract Society.
Williams, Mr. A.
Young Nationalists' Party.

www.ingramcontent.com/pod-product-compliance
Ingram Content Group UK Ltd.
Pitfield, Milton Keynes, MK11 3LW, UK
UKHW022229230426
12048UKWH00016BA/1148